Digital Performer
Power!

By Steve Thomas

THOMSON
COURSE TECHNOLOGY
Professional ■ Trade ■ Reference

DIGITAL PERFORMER
P O W E R !

SVP, Thomson Course Technology PTR: Andy Shafran
Publisher: Stacy L. Hiquet
Senior Marketing Manager: Sarah O'Donnell
Marketing Manager: Heather Hurley
Manager of Editorial Services: Heather Talbot
Senior Acquisitions Editor: Todd Jensen
Senior Editor: Mark Garvey
Associate Marketing Manager: Kristin Eisenzopf
Marketing Coordinator: Jordan Casey
Project Editor/Copy Editor: Estelle Manticas
Technical Reviewer: David Das
PTR Editorial Services Coordinator: Elizabeth Furbish
Interior Layout Tech: Marian Hartsough
Cover Designer: Mike Tanamachi
Indexer: Kevin Broccoli
Proofreader: Laura Gabler

Digital Performer is a registered trademark of Mark of the Unicorn. All other trademarks are the property of their respective owners.

Important: Thomson Course Technology PTR cannot provide software support. Please contact the appropriate software manufacturer's technical support line or Web site for assistance.

Thomson Course Technology PTR and the author have attempted throughout this book to distinguish proprietary trademarks from descriptive terms by following the capitalization style used by the manufacturer.

Information contained in this book has been obtained by Thomson Course Technology PTR from sources believed to be reliable. However, because of the possibility of human or mechanical error by our sources, Thomson Course Technology PTR, or others, the Publisher does not guarantee the accuracy, adequacy, or completeness of any information and is not responsible for any errors or omissions or the results obtained from use of such information. Readers should be particularly aware of the fact that the Internet is an ever-changing entity. Some facts may have changed since this book went to press.

Educational facilities, companies, and organizations interested in multiple copies or licensing of this book should contact the publisher for quantity discount information. Training manuals, CD-ROMs, and portions of this book are also available individually or can be tailored for specific needs.

ISBN: 1-59200-066-5
Library of Congress Catalog Card Number: 2003104191
Printed in the United States of America
05 06 07 08 09 BH 10 9 8 7 6 5 4 3 2 1

©2005 by Thomson Course Technology PTR. All rights reserved. No part of this book may be reproduced or transmitted in any form or by any means, electronic or mechanical, including photocopying, recording, or by any information storage or retrieval system without written permission from Thomson Course Technology PTR, except for the inclusion of brief quotations in a review.

The Muska & Lipman and Thomson Course Technology PTR logo and related trade dress are trademarks of Thomson Course Technology PTR and may not be used without written permission.

THOMSON
COURSE TECHNOLOGY
Professional ■ Trade ■ Reference

Thomson Course Technology PTR, a division of Thomson Course Technology
25 Thomson Place
Boston, MA 02210

http://www.courseptr.com

Dedication

I would like to dedicate this book to all my friends and family. Your unwavering sacrifices have helped me make it this far.

Acknowledgments

Steve Albanese, Estelle Manticas, David Das, Todd Jensen, Mark Garvey, MOTU, "Magic" Dave, Les Quindipan, DP beta testers, Chad Loughrige, Colin MacQueen, Matt Curry, Phil Castillo and DPusers.com, Angus F. Hewlett and Fxpansion, Mathew Nelson at Metric Halo, Arjen at AudioEase, Micheal Logue at Antares Audio Technologies, Jack Kellogg at Mezzo Technologies, Universal Audio, the Unicornation and OSXaudio DP forums, the Recording Workshop, Jim Rosebrook, Dan and Kristy Teckenbrock, Chuck Wheeler, Jeff Ling, Brian Muth, Brian Stritenberger, Rob Brumfiel, Greg Jennings, Dena Brookover, Mary Roberts, and Jennifer Conley-Keywise, my mom and dad, and Robert Metzger.

About the Author

STEVE THOMAS is a musician, composer, arranger, audio engineer, and all-around media producer based out of Columbus, Ohio. As a freelance technical writer, he has created and edited content for the *Cool School Interactus* series of educational CDs. Steve also served as an audio engineer and instructor at the Recording Workshop, teaching topics ranging from basic recording-engineering concepts to more advanced applications of Pro Tools and Digital Performer within music and post-production environments.

Thomas has been involved in the music industry for many years outside of his educational endeavors. He has worked as a session vocalist for Toshiba/EMI Records, a composer for Pass Music Japan, a VJ for BMJ Music Japan, and has accompanied various Japanese artists as a pianist/keyboardist. He is now currently hard at work promoting his media production company, Carrot and Celery Productions (www.carrotandcelery.com).

Contents at a Glance

Introduction xvii

Chapter 1 About Digital Performer and Your Mac 1

Chapter 2 Setting Up Digital Performer 9

Chapter 3 Navigating Digital Performer 33

Chapter 4 Setting Up a New Project 63

Chapter 5 Project Management: Part 1 89

Chapter 6 Project Management: Part 2 137

Chapter 7 Recording Audio 163

Chapter 8 Recording MIDI 185

Contents at a Glance

Chapter 9 Recording MIDI: Region Menu, Plug-ins, and Virtual Instruments.................................... 201

Chapter 10 Editing.................................... 219

Chapter 11 Arranging 253

Chapter 12 Mixing.................................... 301

Chapter 13 Processing and Mastering.................................... 331

Chapter 14 Notation and Scoring.................................... 369

Index.................................... 419

TABLE OF Contents

Introduction xvii

Chapter 1 About Digital Performer and Your Mac 1
   What Is a D.A.W.? 1
      Non-Linear Editing 2
      Host- and Non-Host-Based Systems 2
      Expansion Cards 2
      MIDI Interfaces 3
      Audio Interfaces 3
   Digital Performer Requirements 3
   The Mac and Your DP System 4
      Hard Drives 4
      Disk Maintenance 5
      SuperDrives 6
   Summary 7

Chapter 2 Setting Up Digital Performer 9
   Installing Digital Performer 9
      Installing Audio Hardware Drivers 9
      Installing Core MIDI Drivers 11
      Installing Digital Performer 11
      Installing Third-Party Plug-ins 13
   Launching Digital Performer for the First Time 15
   Audio Configuration 16
      Audio System: Choosing MAS, DAE, or MIDI Only 17
      The Configure Hardware Driver Window 17
      The Configure Studio Settings Window 21
      The Input Monitoring Mode Window 23
      The Audio Bundles Window 24

		MIDI Configuration. 26

- MIDI Configuration..26
    - The Audio MIDI Setup (AMS) Utility........................27
- Synchronization..30
    - Syncing DP...30
- Summary..32

Chapter 3   Navigating Digital Performer 33

- The Consolidated Window..................................33
- Control Panel..35
    - Transport and Counter....................................36
    - Tempo, Meter, and Metronome.............................38
    - Status Strip...38
    - Memory and Auto-Record Bar..............................39
    - DP's Drawers..40
- Tracks Window...42
    - Title Bar and Mini-Menu...................................42
    - Tracks List..45
    - The Tracks Overview Section...............................47
- The Sequence Editor......................................49
    - The Sequence Editor Title Bar..............................50
    - Mini-Menu..50
    - Track Information Panel...................................51
    - Graphic Editing..52
    - Time Rulers, Grids, and Zooming...........................52
- The Mixing Board...53
    - Title Bar and Mini-Menu...................................54
    - Track Strips...55
- Soundbites Window.......................................57
    - The Soundbites Title Bar and Mini-Menu.....................57
    - List...59
    - The Information Pane.....................................61
    - Edit...62
- Summary..62

Chapter 4   Setting Up a New Project............................63

- Project Basics..64
- The Default Workspace....................................66
- Setting the Sampling Rate and Bit Depth.....................67

Contents

Tracks in Digital Performer..68
  Deleting Tracks..68
  Adding Tracks..68
  Renaming Tracks..70
  Moving Tracks..70
Track Voices and Internal Busses...71
Input and Output Assignments...74
  Audio and Aux Track I/O..74
  MIDI Track I/O...76
  Monitoring External MIDI Devices...79
  Monitoring MAS/AU Instruments..80
  Monitoring Rewire Instruments..81
Tempo and Meter..82
  Setting the Tempo..83
  Setting the Meter..84
Setting Up a Click...85
Summary..87

Chapter 5 Project Management: Part 1 89

The Digital Performer Project..90
  Creating a New Project...90
  Opening an Existing Project..91
  Opening Other File Types...93
Saving Your Project..93
  The Save Command...93
  The Save As Command..93
  Save As Template...96
  Standard MIDI Files...100
  OMFI Files..103
Customizing Your Workspace..103
  The Consolidated Window...103
  The Preferences and Settings Command....................................111
  Window Sets...126
  Track Colors..128
  The Commands Window..133
Summary...136

Chapter 6 Project Management: Part 2 137
The Undo History 137
The Project Undo History 138
Branching. 139
Managing the Undo History Windows 144
Audio File Undo History Windows. 147
Polar Undo History Window 148
Managing Audio Files and Soundbites 149
Changing the Location of Audio Files and Soundbites 149
Organizing Audio Files and Soundbites into Folders 151
Renaming Existing Audio Files or Soundbites 151
Deleting Audio Files and Soundbites 152
Removing Audio Files and Soundbites 153
Locating Missing Audio Files or Soundbites. 154
Compacting an Audio File 156
Compacting a Project. 157
Backup and Project Archival 158
Backups. 158
Archiving 159
External Hard Drives 159
CD-R versus DVD-R 160
Rewritable Media 160
Software Solutions 161
Summary 162

Chapter 7 Recording Audio 163
Input Assignments and the Audio Assignments Window 163
Setting Input Levels 165
Arming a Track. 165
Audio Monitor Window 167
Monitoring Input Signals 169
Audio Patch Thru. 169
Monitoring with External Mixers 170
Direct Hardware Playthrough 170
Recording Audio 171
Recording and Managing Alternate Takes. 172
Punching In and Out 173
Overdub Record Mode. 175

Contents

    Cycle Record Mode...176
    Recording with Effects..177
Importing Audio...179
    Sound File Locations...179
    Automatic Conversions Preferences...............................180
    The Import Audio Command versus Drag and Drop...................181
Summary...184

Chapter 8   Recording MIDI...185
MIDI-Related Windows and Commands.......................................185
    The MIDI Monitor Window..186
    The Set Input Filter Command.....................................186
    The Input Quantize Command.......................................187
    MIDI Device Groups...188
    MIDI Patch Lists...191
Recording MIDI Data...192
    Setting Up to Record a MIDI Track................................193
    Setting Up an Instrument Track...................................194
    Overdub Recording..196
Summary...199

Chapter 9   Recording MIDI: Region Menu, Plug-ins, and Virtual Instruments..201
Region Menu Commands..201
    The Mini-Menu..202
    The Transpose Command..204
    The Quantize Command...206
    The Change Velocity Command......................................208
    The Split Notes Command..210
MIDI Effects Plug-ins...211
    Processing with the Region Menu's MIDI Effects Plug-ins..........212
    Inserting Real-time MIDI Plug-ins................................212
Virtual Instrument Plug-ins...212
    Assigned Instrument Tracks.......................................213
    Unassigned Instrument Tracks.....................................214
    Instrument Inserts and the Mixing Board..........................214
The Freeze Selected Tracks Command......................................216
Summary...217

Chapter 10 Editing.. 219
The Tools Palette.. 220
The Time Format Window, Time Ruler, and Edit Grid................ 221
The Time Format Window....................................... 221
The Time Ruler... 223
The Edit Grid.. 225
The View Filter.. 228
Zooming.. 228
Selecting and Moving... 229
Selecting and Moving Audio................................... 230
Selecting and Moving MIDI Notes.............................. 233
Basic Edit Commands.. 234
The Erase Command... 234
The Copy, Cut, Paste, Repeat, and Merge Commands............. 234
Editing Audio in the Sequence Editor........................... 237
Edge-Editing Soundbites...................................... 238
Soundbite Editing Shortcuts.................................. 239
Fades and Crossfades... 240
MIDI Editing in the Graphic Editor............................. 242
Inserting, Removing, and Modifying Notes in the Note Grid..... 243
The Median Strip and Continuous Data Grid................... 244
The Event List.. 250
Event List Basics.. 250
Editing the Parameter of an Event............................ 250
Summary.. 251

Chapter 11 Arranging... 253
The Conductor Track... 253
Modify Conductor Track Menu................................ 254
Editing Conductor Track Data................................ 255
Tempo.. 260
Tempo Sources and the Tempo Control Drawer................. 260
Adjusting Tempo.. 260
Audio Menu Tempo Commands................................ 268
Meter.. 271
The Change Meter Command................................. 272
Applying and Editing Meter Changes.......................... 273
Partial Measures... 273

Key	273
The Change Key Command	274
Transposing Audio and MIDI Data	276
Chunks	276
Sequences	277
The Chunks Window	280
Controlling Chunks	282
Songs	283
Looping	287
Region Menu Commands	288
Event List	288
The Loop Tool	289
Clipping Windows	291
Clipping Data Icons	291
Creating, Opening, and Managing Clippings	292
Where Clippings Are Stored	293
Adding Audio and MIDI Data	293
Saving Plug-in Settings	294
Documents, Folders, and URLs	294
Markers	294
Marker Basics	295
Creating Markers on the Fly	296
Quantizing Markers	297
Recalling Markers	297
Snapping and Shifting Data to a Marker Location	298
Selecting with Markers	298
Markers in Post-Production Work	299
Summary	299
Chapter 12 Mixing	**301**
Mixing Board Setup	302
Showing and Hiding Track Strip Sections	302
The Board Layout Feature	303
Track Groups	305
Alternate Mixes with Mix Mode	308
Inserts and Plug-ins	309
Signal Flow	310
Pre/Post Fader Divider	310
Dynamic versus Time-Based Effects	311

    Aux Tracks and Sends..312
        Sends and Returns..312
        Submixing...318
        Automation..319
    Summary...330

Chapter 13 Processing and Mastering............................331
    Audio Processing...332
        Automatic Delay Compensation...............................332
        Real-Time Effects..333
        File-Based Processing......................................335
        The Background Processing Window...........................339
        The Audio Performance Window...............................343
        Plug-in Formats..343
        The Effects Window...345
        Bypassing an Effect..346
        Saving and Recalling Effect Presets.........................346
        Time-Stretching Audio......................................352
    Mastering...355
        The Master Fader...355
        Bouncing to Disk...356
        Exporting Audio..359
        Exporting and Bouncing to the MP3 Format....................360
        Mastering in DP..360
        Processing Your Final Mix..................................361
        Compression versus Limiting................................364
    Summary...368

Chapter 14 Notation and Scoring................................369
    The Notation Editor..370
        The QuickScribe Editor.....................................373
        Customizing the Appearance of a Score......................375
        The Different QuickScribe Views............................375
        The Title Page...375
        Customizing the Appearance of an Individual Track...........381
        Linear versus Arranged Score...............................383
        Working with Markers.......................................383
        Working with Rests...385

Working with Text 387
Working with Measures 390
Inserting Key, Meter, and Tempo Changes. 396
Inserting Dynamic Symbols. 398
Arranging a Score. 399
Printing 408
Scoring for Picture 409
Movie Window. 410
Cue Sheets 415
Viewing Film Cues. 415
Hit Points 417
Using Hit Points to Find Tempos. 417
Summary 418

Index. 419

Introduction

Mark of the Unicorn's Digital Performer began as a MIDI-only application (Performer) back in the mid-1980s. It was a great program that gave the Mac user an intuitive way to record, edit, and play back MIDI performances. During the mid-1990s, MOTU added digital audio capabilities to this already successful MIDI software application and took the music software industry by storm. Since then, DP has undergone incredible upgrades and enhancements, allowing the end user to manipulate MIDI and digital audio to a degree never before imagined.

This book offers a comprehensive overview of DP 4's features, system setup, and configurations within the OS X environment, while also supplying useful engineering tips and shortcuts to help you get the most out of Digital Performer.

How to Use This Book

In this book, I have tried to address the many different proficiency levels of the Digital Performer user; I've attempted to jump-start the newbie, take the intermediate user to the next level, and show the power user an interesting trick or two.

I've organized the chapters and sections as they would appear within the context of the music production process. Reading straight through from start to finish will provide the user who is new to the program or unfamiliar with the audio production process with a solid grasp of how Digital Performer integrates within the studio environment. Users with an understanding of audio recording and mixing concepts may want to just skip to specific chapters.

Appendices covering the Beat Detection Engine introduced in Version 4.5, Polar, the Drum Editor, how Digital Performer handles multi-channel surround projects, and additional resources for DP and Mac OS X can be found on the Web at http://www.courseptr.com/downloads. For those users who also appreciate a more visual learning approach, check out the CD that's included in the back of the book. It contains movie tutorials on various features of Digital Performer 4.

For those who are already familiar with Digital Performer and are making the jump to OS X, Chapter 1 provides useful information on setting up and optimizing your Mac, while Chapter 2 walks you step-by-step through the DP4 setup and configuration process. If you're new to the world of digital audio and MIDI or multitrack recording in general, I suggest starting with Chapter 1.

How This Book Is Organized

Digital Performer Power! is divided into 14 chapters. As discussed earlier, you can find additional appendices on the Web, at http://www.courseptr.com/downloads.

- Chapter 1, "About Digital Performer and Your Mac," overviews the basic concepts of linear and non-linear editing, digital audio workstations, hardware requirements and recommendations for Digital Performer, and Mac OS X configuration and optimization.
- Chapter 2, "Setting Up Digital Performer," covers software installation, audio and MIDI configurations, and synchronization.
- Chapter 3, "Navigating Digital Performer," covers Digital Performer's main windows: the Consolidated window, Control Panel, Tracks window, Sequence Editor, Mixing Board, and Soundbites window.
- Chapter 4, "Setting Up a New Project," provides a detailed step-by-step guide to creating and preparing a project for recording.
- Chapter 5, "Project Management: Part 1," and Chapter 6, "Project Management: Part 2," cover the management of your project and media assets in order to help you streamline your production workflow.
- Chapter 7, "Recording Audio," focuses on getting the most out of your audio recordings, from proper gain staging and monitoring to working with alternate takes during the overdubbing process.
- Chapter 8, "Recording MIDI," focuses on the procedures involved with the recording and monitoring of your MIDI tracks.
- Chapter 9, "Recording MIDI: Region Menu, Plug-ins, and Virtual Instruments," overviews the Region Menu commands, MIDI plug-ins, and virtual instrument tracks.
- Chapter 10, "Editing," overviews the tools and procedures involved with editing digital audio, MIDI, and automation data within DP4.
- Chapter 11, "Arranging," covers the use of Chunks and Songs, as well as the detailed use of markers and clippings within the recording and mixing process.

* Chapter 12, "Mixing," discusses the fundamentals of mixing within Digital Performer, from setting up inserts and sends to creating submixes and using mix automation.
* Chapter 13, "Processing and Mastering," will cover the use of audio effects processing, the concepts of file-based and real-time processing, destructive Waveform Editor processing, as well as the basics of the mastering process. Procedures for bouncing to disk and exporting your mixes are also explained.

    This chapter will also familiarize you with the basic concepts and technical procedures involved with mastering music within the DP environment.
* Chapter 14, "Notation and Scoring," shows you how to transcribe MIDI notes into printable music, from individual parts to full blown orchestral scores. You can take an existing MIDI track or use the QuickScribe tools to "step-record" parts with the mouse. This chapter will take you through the process of transferring the music you hear within your tracks from computer screen to paper.

    Because of its flexible architecture, Digital Performer is also a popular scoring environment among sound designers and composers. This chapter will take you through the basic setup process for music scoring within DP.

What's Not in This Book

This book covers a lot of ground, but it doesn't cover everything—I have assumed some basic knowledge on your part, and have had to leave out certain topics due to space constraints.

Computer Basics. In this book, I assume that you already know how to get around on your Mac: how to make a new folder, empty the trash, install a program, or change the monitor resolution. If you're uncertain about some of these common procedures, seek out one of the numerous learning resources for the Mac, available in both print and online forms. Check out Appendix E for a list of books and Websites related to the Mac platform. Keep in mind that the Mac is the heart of your Digital Performer system, and being able to properly navigate and maintain it is essential to the health of your studio environment.

Older Versions of DP. Even though this book doesn't dive into the specifics relating to DP and OS 9, many of its features have remained unchanged in the transition to OS X, so users of previous DP versions should still find *Digital Performer Power!* a useful resource.

Other Programs. If you're like me, you probably have a number of other software applications that you incorporate into the production process. There isn't enough space in this book to include detailed explanations of all these other programs, but I will discuss some key applications that I feel are important to the DP user, such as CD burning software and virtual instruments.

Keeping It Current

The D.A.W.-related software and hardware industry is in constant state of change, ever evolving with the addition of faster computers, improved operating systems, and enhanced feature sets. Production cycles tend to run on a six-month schedule, so keeping the content of a book like this current is a challenge in itself. Everyone involved with the creation of *Digital Performer Power!* has made a concerted effort to include the most up-to-date information concerning Digital Performer, OS X, and the other applications mentioned within this book.

What's on the CD?

Included in the back of this book is a CD called Digital Performer CSi LE. This product utilizes the CSi AutoPlay interface and includes tutorials from the *Digital Performer 4 CSi STARTER* and *Digital Performer 4 CSi MASTER* products. Digital Performer CSi LE will include over one hour of tutorials that you can scroll through—or just sit back and watch them play one after another.

About Digital Performer and Your Mac

What is Digital Performer? Digital Performer is essentially a music studio in a box. Its comprehensive tools allow you to record, edit, mix, and master music. Of course, this is a simplification of a very deep program, but if you can keep yourself grounded in these basic processes, it will help you from getting overwhelmed by DP's many complex feature sets.

This chapter will discuss the basics of digital audio workstations, the requirements for DP, and suggestions for working with Mac OSX.

What Is a D.A.W.?

In case you're wondering, D.A.W. stands for *digital audio workstation*, which is usually composed of compositional and recording tools centered on a computer configured specifically for music production. The benefits of having all the necessary recording and mixing tools integrated into one place and right at your finger tips are great, but I would argue that the most incredible feature of any D.A.W.—which many users often take for granted—is its non-linearity.

Before the advent of programs like MOTU's Digital Performer and Digidesign's Pro Tools, modern audio was recorded in a linear fashion directly to tape. Yes, even digital audio can be recorded to tape. I won't get into the age-old argument of digital versus analog here, but suffice it to say that tape has many disadvantages when it comes to the world of editing. With tape, audio (and video) is recorded in a linear fashion. When tape travels across the head stack of a multitrack recorder, the audio is magnetically transferred in a continuous fashion until recording is stopped. If I wanted to "fix" a part within the recording, I'd have to physically rewind the tape machine and punch in, permanently erasing the previous material. If I blew the punch, or the musician's performance wasn't on, there

CHAPTER 1 } About Digital Performer and Your Mac

would be no way to get back (or undo!) the lost audio. Also, if I wanted to rearrange the order of the recorded material (maybe I need the chorus to happen two times instead of one, for example), I would have to cut and splice the different sections together, which would involve making two physical copies of the tape in real time (one for each chorus), then manually slicing it together with a razor blade!

Non-Linear Editing

What NLEs (or Non-Linear Editors) offer is the ability to change the order of recorded data in a non-destructive way. The recorded audio is stored on the hard drive of the workstation's computer, and can be instantaneously accessed (or read) from the hard drive in any specified order. It is a simple matter of building a playlist within the particular music program. Going back to my earlier example of creating two choruses for a song, if I'm working in a non-linear editor such as Digital Performer, I can just tell it to play the chorus twice instead of once—it's as easy as that.

Sounds simple—if we are thinking in terms of one audio file. However, multitrack sessions normally consist of many tracks with multiple audio files—sometimes as many as 100-plus tracks (a definite mixing challenge!). Audio recording and mixing can be a very taxing job for our Macs.

Host- and Non-Host-Based Systems

Digital Performer is a *host-based* application, meaning that it relies on the CPU of the computer for all of its audio needs. On top of crunching all those numbers for DP, the CPU also has to worry about running the Mac OS. This is why the quality and speed of your D.A.W. components is so important. Faster hard drives, for example, will be able to access audio faster, resulting in higher track counts and the ability to handle sessions that contain heavy edits. The amount of RAM available to Digital Performer impacts the number of voices you can record and playback simultaneously. A high-performance video card will provide faster screen redraws, taking strain off the host processor (it takes a lot of power to display all of those bouncing level meters and various windows in Digital Performer). The processor speed and amount of RAM in your computer also directly impacts the performance of virtual instruments and other processor-intensive tasks, such as real-time effects plug-ins.

Expansion Cards

Hardware peripherals dedicated to running plug-ins or software-based synthesizers can also be integrated into a host-based system for additional horsepower—and some D.A.W.s come preconfigured with these devices. Digidesign's top-of-the-line Pro Tools systems fall into the latter category. Instead of relying on the host processor to do all the work, PCI cards that contain dedicated processor chips are installed in your computer and supply the muscle for any audio processing. The computer's CPU only has to worry about running the program and the Mac OS, and the dedicated PCI card handles all of the audio tasks.

Multiple cards can be used simultaneously, allowing you to create a very powerful and stable workstation. The drawback for many is the high cost and proprietary nature of Pro Tools and similar systems. Luckily, there are a few companies out there that offer expansion cards or units that work with host-based audio applications such as Digital Performer. TC Electronic (http://www.tcelectronic.com) and Universal Audio (http://www.uaudio.com) are two such companies. These expansion peripherals are fairly inexpensive (around $1000) when compared to other integrated workstations, which can run into the tens or hundreds of thousands of dollars.

MIDI Interfaces

MIDI stands for Musical Instrument Digital Interface. MIDI is a language (or protocol) that allows electronic devices to communicate with each other. You need a MIDI interface to record MIDI data. The type of interface you choose usually depends on the number of external MIDI devices you need to control. The most basic setup will have a keyboard MIDI controller and a MIDI interface to get the data into your Mac. More elaborate setups may have multiple interfaces to send data to stacks of keyboards or outboard sound modules. These interfaces come in a variety of flavors, from the simple 1×2 configuration consisting of one MIDI input and two MIDI outputs, to the more feature-packed interfaces with multiple MIDI I/O and sophisticated synchronization capabilities.

Audio Interfaces

One of the most important aspects of a D.A.W. is the audio interface. Though you can rely on the Mac's built-in audio, you'll need a more "professional" device if you want to get the most out of your recording and mixing. A dedicated audio interface(s) that can handle multiple inputs of balanced audio should be used. The audio interface is in charge of getting audio in and out of your Mac. This process is done with analog to digital (A/D) and digital to analog (D/A) converters. The analog signal is converted to digital on the way in, then converted back to analog on the way out to your studio monitors. The quality of the converter has a direct impact on the sound of your digital audio, as well as on the price of the interface.

Digital Performer Requirements

To run MOTU's Digital Performer 4, a PowerMac (G3, G4, or G5) with 128MB of RAM running Mac OS 10.2 or higher is required. These are just the minimum requirements, however, and real-world experiences from Digital Performer users suggest a more powerful system is needed. If you plan on running a lot of tracks with effects processing, along with virtual instruments, you'll want at least 768MB of RAM—though 1GB+ of RAM will definitely provide you with better system performance. A dual processor G4 or G5 (single or dual processor) is also recommended.

CHAPTER 1 } About Digital Performer and Your Mac

> **ARE 128MB OF RAM ENOUGH FOR MY SYSTEM?**
> Even though some Mac's only ship with 128MB of RAM, don't think that this will be sufficient for running media based applications like Digital Performer. In reality, even Mac OSX will find it difficult to operate with such a small amount of memory. At a minimum, you really should have 512MB of RAM when working with DP.

The Mac and Your DP System

The Mac, the OS, and its connected peripherals form the foundation for your Digital Performer studio. Proper care and feeding of your Mac is critical to maintaining a healthy Digital Performer system. The ins and outs of Mac maintenance are beyond the scope of the book, so investing in a Mac OSX-specific book is highly recommended. You can find out more about the Mac on the Web by visiting the support section of Apple's Web site (http://www.apple.com). In addition to the official Apple Web site, there are also various third-party sites that serve up a wealth of information on all things Mac-related (refer to Appendix E for more information on these Mac resources).

Hard Drives

The hard drive is the container for your OS, applications, and associated media files. When you play back or record audio in Digital Performer, the OS must physically access the drive to retrieve or write the file. The faster the drive, the faster it will read or write a file. If DP were only reading or writing one file at a time, drive speed would not be a factor. But in actual use, the drive is very busy simultaneously playing back and recording multiple tracks, accessing OS-related files, streaming your large audio sample library, checking your e-mail, and so on.

In order to maximize your DP system's resources, you may want to consider using two hard drives: one drive for the Mac OS, and another for your DP projects. Keep in mind that your DP system must constantly access your hard drive when playing back and recording audio—the faster your hard drive, the more tracks you will be able to play back and record. If your project resides on the same drive as the Mac OS, the drive will have to split up its time between accessing OS-related data and playing back/recording audio. In addition to the performance boost, keeping the Mac OS on its own drive makes routine maintenance tasks much easier (I'll explain this more later in the chapter).

> **CAN I START WORKING IN DP WITH ONLY ONE HARD DRIVE?**
> Of course you can run your projects off your internal (or "boot") drive, and it's fine to get started that way. As your projects begin to increase in size and complexity, you'll start realizing the benefits of using additional drives.
>
> If the idea of installing multiple internal hard drives is overwhelming, you may want to consider connecting an external Firewire drive(s) instead.

Before you begin installing DP on your Mac, you should think about how you plan on using Digital Performer in your music production workflow. Will you be running virtual instruments that contain large sample libraries? Will you be working on large projects that contain a lot of audio tracks with effects processing? Or will your DP sessions be fairly small and consist of a few tracks of audio and MIDI?

If you plan on using large audio sample libraries within Digital Performer, you should also consider installing a separate hard drive dedicated to this purpose. Installing your audio sample libraries on a separate drive(s) will help alleviate the bottlenecks that can occur when DP is simultaneously playing back (or recording) multiple tracks of audio, triggering audio sample libraries, and so on.

> **MULTIPLE HARD DRIVES**
> An ideal system might contain four separate hard drives: one for the Mac OS, one for your Digital Performer audio files, another hard drive to which to back up your DP projects, and a fourth drive that contains your audio sample libraries.
>
> Of course, you can take this setup even further with multiple hard drives for your DP audio files and sample libraries. You could even install the Mac OS on another drive and use it specifically for your music applications (this means no Web surfing, word processing, or game playing on your DP related system drive). Having a duplicate "boot" drive is also a life-saver for when disaster strikes.

> **BACK UP YOUR DATA!**
> Keep in mind that you may need to also reinstall the Mac OS when reconfiguring or installing hard drives in your DP system. Make sure you back up any important data to another hard drive or optical media (such as CD+R and DVD+R) before beginning any system reconstruction.

Disk Maintenance

Disk maintenance is also another critical piece of the Mac OS maintenance puzzle. The two main maintenance procedures you need to worry about for Mac OSX are the repairing of disk permissions and the disk directory, if needed.

Repair Disk

The Repair Disk option, shown in Figure 1.1, in the Disk Utility window (OS Hard Drive > Applications > Utilities > Disk Utility) repairs (or corrects) the directory of any disks or disk partitions within your system when needed. A disk directory is like the table of contents for a book—it tells the OS where

Figure 1.1
The Disk Utility window allows you to repair a disk and its permissions.

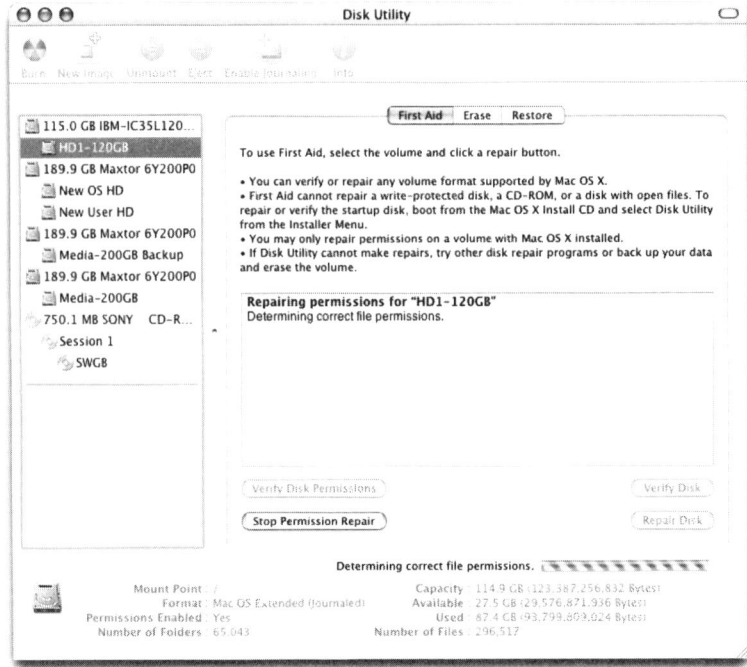

data is located on your hard drive(s). System crashes, hard restarts, or loss of power can lead to the corruption of a disk directory. Use the Repair Disk option to correct this kind of problem.

Repair Disk Permissions
The Repair Disk Permissions option (OS Hard Drive > Applications > Utilities > Disk Utility) repairs the permissions for a system related folder or file. When a file or folder is installed on the system, a file called a "receipt" is installed in the Receipts folder (OS Hard Drive > Library > Receipts). When the current permissions for a file/folder do not match the permissions described in its associated OS X receipt file, the Repair Disk Permissions option will reset (or correct) the disk permissions for that file or folder. Problems with disk permissions generally occur after the installation of new applications on your Mac, so be sure to repair disk permissions after the installation of any software.

SuperDrives
With the continuous fall in the price of DVD burners, you owe it to yourself to make the small investment and add a DVD burner to your Mac if you don't have one already. Your DP projects can increase in size very quickly, so you'll need a convenient and inexpensive solution for your larger archiving needs; the DVD fills this function nicely. Standard DVD+/-Rs will hold approx 4GB worth of

data, while dual layer discs (though more expensive) can hold double that amount. In addition, most DVD burners will also burn CDs—so you'll be able to put your mixes on CD, also.

Many users underestimate the importance of backing up their material. Having a DVD burner connected to your system can really take the stress out of backups and archivals, helping to ensure you don't lose any important work. Refer to Chapter 6 for a discussion of the backup and archival process.

Summary

Configuring your Mac to work with DP can be as involved as you want it to be. Some users will want to jump right in, install the program, and begin working in DP. Other users may want to take a more planned approach to the configuration process. Exactly how you confront the installation and configuration process is up to you; just remember to perform the basic maintenance procedures, such as repairing disk permissions. If you do decide, however, to reconfigure your Mac with additional hard drives, RAM, and so on, be sure to back up any important files and follow the proper procedures for installing each new device.

Setting Up Digital Performer

This chapter will focus on the setup procedures involved with Digital Performer, starting with the installation process and moving to the audio and MIDI configuration processes. I'll also discuss how you can use DP's Receive Sync and Transmit Sync commands to synchronize DP with other devices and applications.

The following topics will be discussed in this chapter:

- The installation process.
- How to configure your audio hardware to work with DP.
- How to enable "voices" and I/O routing assignments within a project.
- How to use the Audio MIDI Setup window to configure your MIDI devices.
- How to work with DP's synchronization features.

Installing Digital Performer

Once you have your Mac configured for your DP workflow (discussed in the previous chapter), you're ready to begin the installation process.

Installing Audio Hardware Drivers

Before installing the Digital Performer application, you should proceed with installing the necessary hardware driver(s) for your audio interfaces(s). These Core Audio drivers (explained later in the chapter) allow your audio interface to communicate with Digital Performer and other Mac OSX Core Audio-compatible applications. If you're working with MOTU audio interfaces, you can find the appropriate Firewire or PCI audio drivers in the MOTU Hardware Drivers folder located on the DP Installer disc. You can also visit the Download section of MOTU's Web site (http://www.motu.com). If you plan on using the Mac's built-in audio (not recommended), you can skip this process.

CHAPTER 2 } Setting Up Digital Performer

✻ UPDATING YOUR HARDWARE DRIVERS

Be aware that some manufacturers will update their hardware drivers on a regular basis, some more often than others. Before you install the drivers that are bundled with your installer disc, you should take a trip to the manufacturer's website and check that you have the most current drivers available.

✻ TESTING YOUR AUDIO INTERFACE

Once you have installed the necessary Core Audio driver for your specific audio interface, you should test that it is working properly. As DP isn't installed yet, you can use Mac OSX's iTunes music player instead. First, you'll need to open the Audio MIDI Setup Utility from the System Hard Drive > Application > Utilities folder. Select the Audio Devices tab and choose your audio interface from the Default Output pop-up menu, as shown in Figure 2.1. Your audio interface will appear in the list as long as its Core Audio driver is successfully installed. Make sure your audio interface is connected to a set of speakers (or headphones) so that you can verify playback. Open iTunes, play a song within your iTunes library, and you should hear the song play through your audio interface.

Figure 2.1

The audio section of the Audio MIDI Setup window.

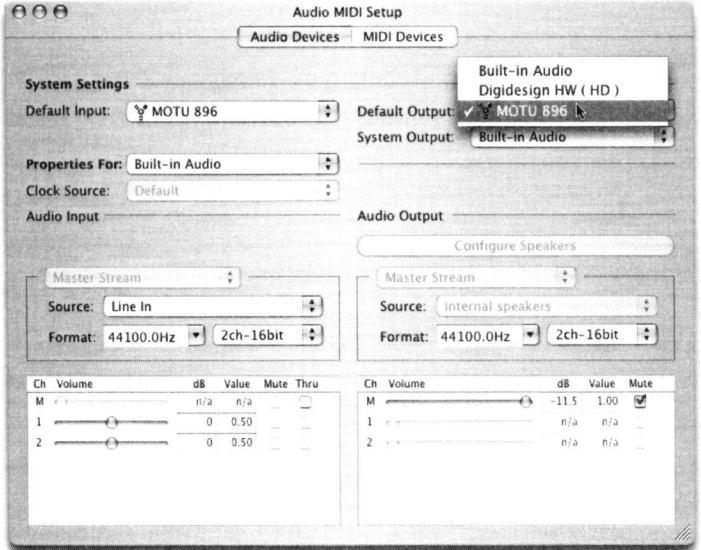

Installing Core MIDI Drivers

If you plan on connecting any MIDI devices to your DP system, you'll need to install the Core MIDI drivers (or additional software) for your particular MIDI interface. Be sure to follow the manufacturer's installation guidelines to ensure that you install your MIDI drivers properly.

Use the Audio MIDI Setup Utility (System Hard Drive > Application > Utilities folder) to connect any additional MIDI devices to your MIDI controller; these will automatically appear in Digital Performer when they are configured. Refer to the "MIDI Configuration" section of this chapter for an explanation of the MIDI device setup process.

Installing Digital Performer

Once you have confirmed that your audio interface(s) is working properly, begin installing DP onto your system's hard drive. Simply open up the installer disc and double-click the Install DP icon, as shown in Figure 2.2, and then follow the installation process as directed. After the DP items have been installed, the installer will need to run an optimization, as shown in Figure 2.3; click OK to proceed with the process. Once the OSX optimization process is complete, click the Quit button to exit the installer.

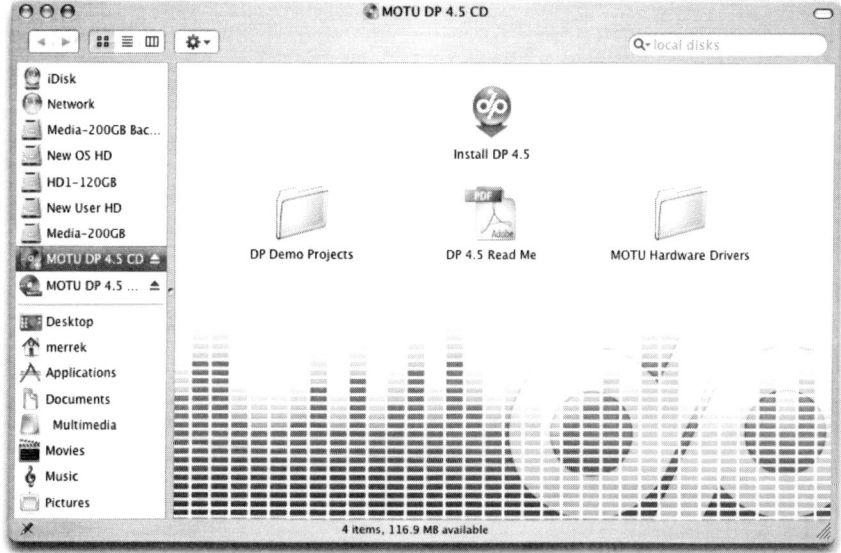

Figure 2.2

Click the DP installer icon to install Digital Performer on your Mac.

CHAPTER 2 } Setting Up Digital Performer

Figure 2.3

Click OK to begin the optimization process.

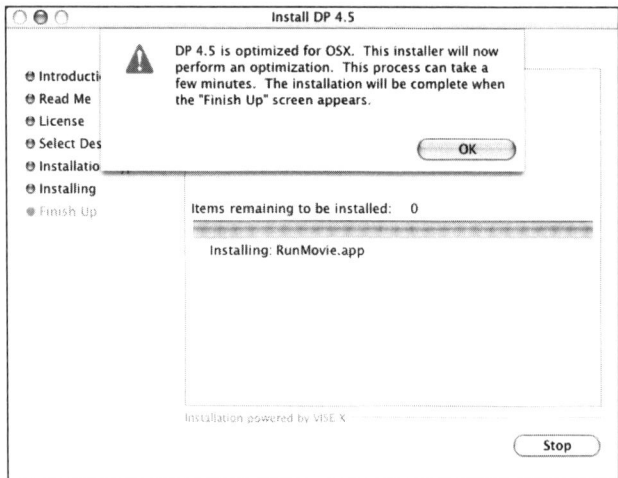

> ### THE CONSOLIDATED WINDOW MOVIE
> When you're working with the DP 4.5 installer, a QuickTime movie providing an overview of the Consolidated Window feature will automatically launch during the optimization process. If you want to skip the movie, simply press the Escape key on your computer keyboard to stop playback of the movie.

Once the installation process has been successfully completed, the MOTU DP folder containing the Digital Performer application (along with the Extras and Grooves folders) will automatically open, as shown in Figure 2.4.

Figure 2.4

The MOTU DP folder. The Consolidated Window QuickTime movie is also included in the DP 4.5 installation process.

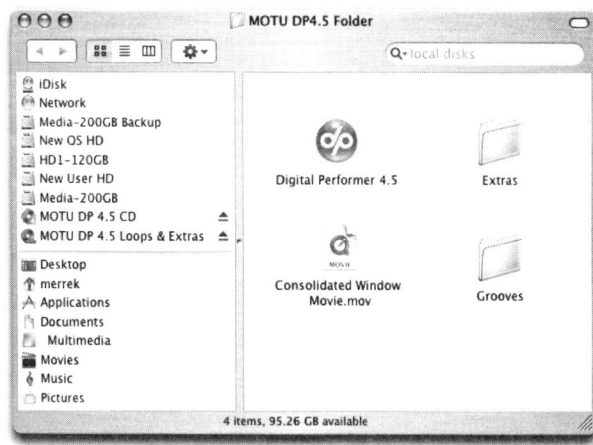

12

ADDING DP TO THE DOCK

For quick and easy access, try placing the DP application icon in the Dock. The Dock is the small strip that's located at the bottom of the screen. Think of the Dock as a container for your shortcuts that allows you to click on an application icon to launch the program without using the Mac's Finder. Simply drag the icon into the Dock and release the mouse, as shown in Figure 2.5. Once it is placed in the Dock, you can launch Digital Performer by clicking on DP's Dock icon.

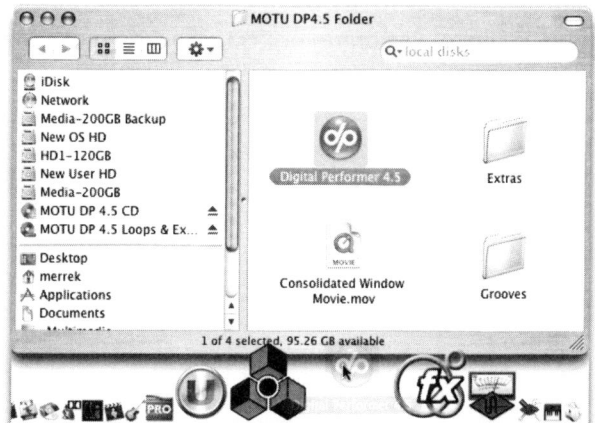

Figure 2.5

Drag the Digital Performer application icon into the Dock for easy access to DP.

DIGITAL PERFORMER EXTRAS DISC

Don't forget to take a look at the Digital Performer Extras disc that comes bundled with DP; it is packed with over 600MBs of royalty-free audio loops and REX files.

Installing Third-Party Plug-ins

In addition to audio hardware drivers, you may also have third-party plug-ins or virtual instruments to install for use with DP. Before installing them, however, you may want to launch DP first, to check that the installation process was successful and that DP is functioning properly. Once you're satisfied that DP is working correctly, quit the application and proceed with the installation of your third-party applications.

Audio plug-ins should be placed in the Library > Audio > Plug-ins folder. You can install them in either the System Hard Drive > Library folder, which will give all users on your Mac access to these plug-ins, or the User > Library folder, which will provide plug-in access only to that specific user. If you're the only person working on your system, it doesn't really matter which location you choose. Most

CHAPTER 2 } Setting Up Digital Performer

third party plug-in installers will automatically place the plug-in in the necessary folder(s), so you don't have to worry about manually placing them in the correct location(s). MAS plug-ins (DP's native audio plug-ins), for example, are automatically placed in the Audio Plug-ins > MAS folder when DP4 is first installed. There will be times, however, when you will need to manually place plug-ins in their correct location.

If you take a look at the Library > Audio Plug-ins folder, shown in Figure 2.6, you can see that there are sub-folders for each different plug-in type supported by Mac OSX (such as MAS, VST, and Audio Units). You'll also notice that there is no Audio Units plug-in folder. This is because AU plug-ins are actually stored in the Components folder (don't ask me why). If you run into a situation in which a plug-in isn't showing up in your Digital Performer project, check to make sure that it's in the proper plug-in folder.

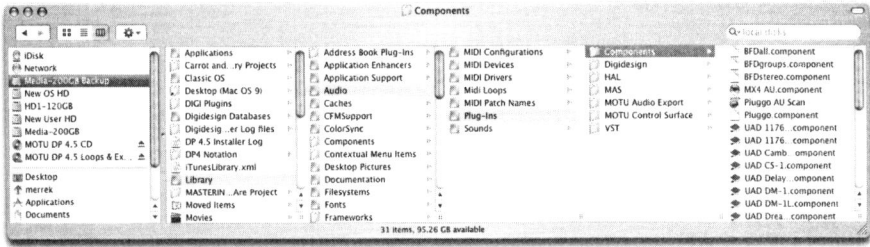

Figure 2.6

Audio plug-ins are located in the Library > Audio > Plug-ins folder. Audio Unit plug-ins can be found in the Components folder.

TRIAL VERSIONS

If you install trial versions of plug-ins, be aware that most will expire after a set period of time (typically 14 days). Once a plug-in has expired, DP will present you with the Expired Plug-in dialog, as shown in Figure 2.7. If you want to continue using the plug-in, you can purchase it using the Buy button on the dialog. If you don't want to purchase the plug-in, simply click the Quit button and DP will not load it.

Keep in mind that this window will open every time you launch Digital Performer, which can get very annoying. To stop this window from appearing, simply remove the plug-in from the appropriate plug-in folder.

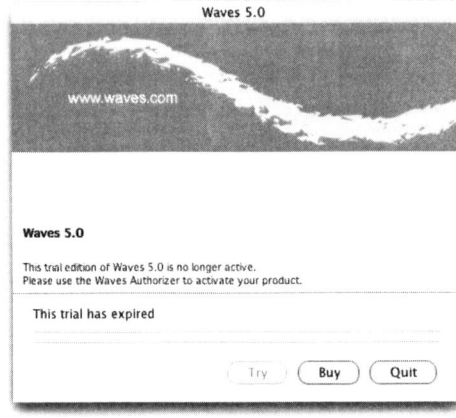

Figure 2.7

In this example, the trial versions of the Waves 5.0 plug-ins have expired.

Launching Digital Performer for the First Time

The first time you launch DP after installation, you will be presented with a Key Code dialog, as shown in Figure 2.8. Enter your name and the key code located on the inside cover of the DP user's manual. Click OK to continue loading the DP application; you should see DP loading available plug-ins, as shown in Figure 2.9. In addition, the first time DP is opened, it will examine the Audio Plug-in > Components folder for any Audio Unit plug-ins. Each AU plug-in is examined once. If DP finds a problem with an AU plug-in, the plug-in will not be loaded and will not be available in any of DP's plug-in menus. The results of the AU examination process are saved in a text file and placed on your hard drive.

DP will launch the Open project dialog by default, allowing you to open an existing project or create a new one, as shown in Figure 2.10. If you do not want to create or open a project, simply click the Cancel button. Keep in mind that you do not have to have a project open in order to configure DP's audio and MIDI settings. As long as Digital Performer is open, you will have access to the necessary audio configuration windows and menus (explained in the next section). MIDI device configurations are handled directly by OSX, so you don't need DP to be open at all when setting up your MIDI connections.

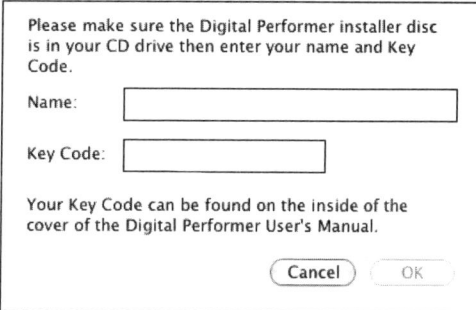

Figure 2.8
Your key code for DP is located on the inside cover of the user's manual.

Figure 2.9
When Digital Performer is launched, it will load available plug-ins for use in your DP projects.

CHAPTER 2 } Setting Up Digital Performer

Figure 2.10
By default, the Open project dialog will automatically open when you launch DP.

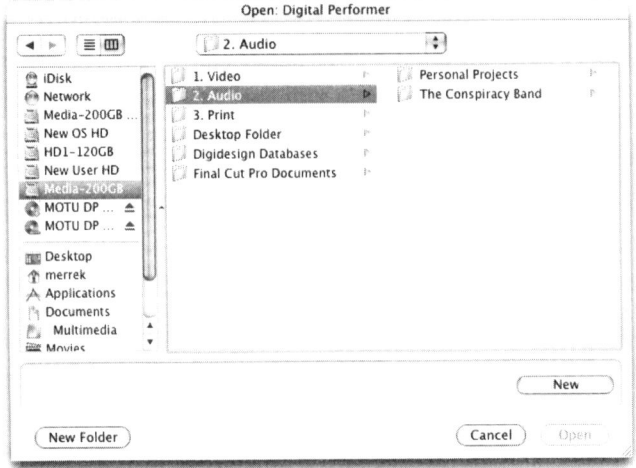

> ### CREATING AND OPENING A PROJECT
> Procedures for creating, opening, and setting up a Digital Performer project are discussed in Chapter 4, "Setting Up a New Project." Be sure to configure your audio and MIDI devices (explained in the next section) before proceeding with the audio and MIDI recording processes.

Audio Configuration

Before you jump into the audio playback and recording side of Digital Performer, you will need to configure any connected audio devices and their settings for your DP project. In addition, you must determine the specific audio system (MAS, DAE, or MIDI only), track voices and internal buses, available inputs and outputs, input recording mode, and sample rate/format for your project.

> ### CONFIGURING AUDIO SETTINGS WHEN A PROJECT IS CLOSED
> Remember that it is not required that you have a project open to configure many of DP's audio settings. In fact, Digital Performer seems happier when you make audio configuration changes in an empty DP workspace (or when a project isn't open).

Audio System: Choosing MAS, DAE, or MIDI Only

The Audio System submenu (Setup menu > Audio System), as shown in Figure 2.11, provides three audio system options: DAE, MOTU Audio System, and MIDI Only. These options determine how audio operations, if any, are handled within Digital Performer—or which audio engine will perform DP's audio-related tacks.

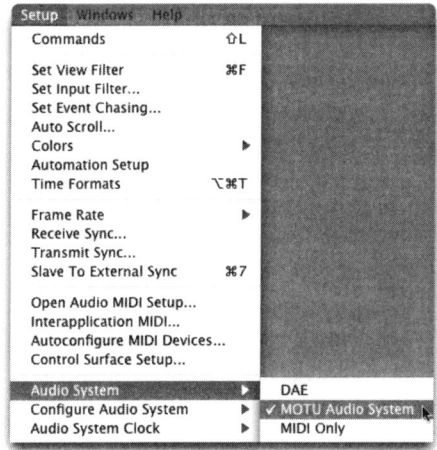

Figure 2.11

The Audio System submenu.

An audio engine basically provides or handles all of the audio-related processes (such as audio playback, recording, internal bussing, effects processing, and so on) for an application. For example, Mac OSX's built-in applications (such as iTunes) rely on Mac OSX's Core Audio engine to playback audio. Digital Performer has its own built-in audio engine called the MOTU Audio System, or MAS. In addition to MAS, DP can also run under the Digidesign audio engine or DAE. Selecting DAE will allow you to use Digital Performer as a front-end for Pro Tools MIX and TDM systems. MIDI Only, however, will turn off DP's audio playback and recording capabilities altogether—tremendously reducing the CPU consumption of your DP project.

- **DAE**. Choose this option if you wish to run DP under Digidesign's audio engine, providing a front-end for your Pro Tools TDM or MIX system. Keep in mind that, even though you will have access to TDM/HTDM and RTAS/AudioSuite plug-ins, you will not be able to use any of DP's native (built-in) plug-ins when operating under DAE.
- **MOTU Audio System**. Enabled by default, the MOTU audio engine (or MAS) is DP's built-in audio engine. When MAS is selected, you will have access to all of DP's native effects, along with any other third-party AU and MAS plug-ins installed within your system.
- **MIDI Only**. This option will turn off DP's audio playback and recording capabilities altogether.

The rest of this section will assume that you are running DP under the MOTU Audio Engine. For more information on DAE and using DP as a front end for Pro Tools TDM and MIX systems, consult the "Using Digital Performer with Pro Tools" chapter of the *Digital Performer User's Manual*.

The Configure Hardware Driver Window

As discussed earlier, you will need to install the necessary Core Audio driver for your audio hardware interface before DP will be able to start communicating with it. Consult the manual (or installer disc) of your particular audio interface if you're not sure how to complete this process.

CHAPTER 2 } Setting Up Digital Performer

> **CORE AUDIO**
>
> Core Audio is a built-in technology that provides OSX with its comprehensive audio capabilities. Mac OSX's Audio MIDI Setup utility (System Hard Drive > Applications > Utilities > Audio MIDI Setup) provides controls for managing Core Audio (and Core MIDI) devices. In order for an audio interface to work with DP, it must be Core Audio compatible and have its Core Audio driver installed within your Mac.

The Configure Hardware Driver window (Setup menu > Audio System > Configure Hardware Driver) allows you to control any Core Audio-compatible audio interfaces that are connected to your computer, including the Mac's built-in audio, as shown in Figure 2.12. Options for controlling the master device clock, sample rate, and audio clock mode for a selected hardware device are provided. In addition, global project settings for the buffer size, host buffer multiplier, and work priority are also displayed.

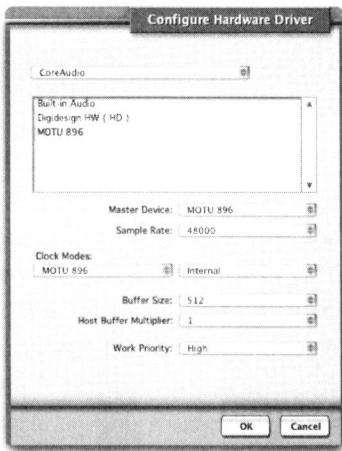

Figure 2.12

The Configure Hardware Driver window.

The Hardware Driver List

The Configure Hardware Driver window (Setup menu > Audio System > Configure Hardware Driver) allows you to control any Core Audio-compatible audio interfaces that are connected to your computer, including the Mac's built-in audio. Installed hardware drivers will appear in the hardware driver list.

To enable an audio device(s) for use with DP:

1. Open the Configure Hardware Driver by choosing Setup menu > Audio System > Configure Hardware Driver.
2. Click on a hardware driver within the list to enable it. Once enabled, it will be highlighted blue.
3. DP allows you to simultaneously use multiple audio devices. Simply Shift-click on another driver to enable multiple audio devices in DP. Be aware that you will need to resolve the audio clocks of each device when working with multiple drivers (explained later).

Master Device

The Master Device setting only comes into play when you have multiple hardware drivers enabled (explained in the previous section). Enabled digital devices will operate at the sample rate that is designated in the Sample Rate drop-down menu (explained in the next section). To keep their digital signals locked together, you must designate one of the devices as the master clock source. Once a master clock is specified, the other digital devices in your system should be set to listen to it.

In order for the other devices to "listen" to the master clock, you must output the audio clock of the master device to the other digital devices via a Word Clock, AES/EBU, or ADAT (9 pin) cable. The type of sync you choose will be determined by the specific devices you're working with. Resolving the audio clocks of multiple digital sources is essential when working with multiple digital devices. Audio clocks that are not resolved can cause digital distortion, as well as introduce digital "pops" and "clicks" in your audio signal.

Sample Rate

Choose the sample rate for the project from the Sample Rate drop-down menu. Only sample rates supported by the selected hardware driver will appear in the list. Keep in mind that the chosen setting will apply to all audio devices that are enabled in the hardware driver list.

> **SAMPLING RATE AND THE NYQUIST THEORY**
>
> The number of samples or "pictures" that are taken of an audio signal over a one second period of time is called the *sampling rate*. The sampling rate determines the number of frequencies that can be reproduced by your audio device every second. For example, with a 1Hz sine wave, the audio device needs to take two pictures during one period of the sound—one picture to describe the sine wave's positive 180° arc, and another to describe the negative. A frequency of 10,000Hz would need a sampling rate of 20kHz to accurately describe it. The sampling rate must be double the frequency of the original signal in order to reproduce it. This is called the *Nyquist Theory*.

Clock Modes

The Clock Modes section contains two drop-down menus—the device list (left) and the clock source (right). Only audio devices enabled in the hardware list will appear in the device list. Once a device is selected, its clock source will appear in the clock source menu. By default, the clock source for a device is set to Internal, which means the selected device will listen to its own internal audio clock. Digital Performer will also use this clock as its master clock source when playing back and recording audio. If you have only one device enabled in the list, be sure to set its clock source to Internal—once it's set, you'll never have to worry about it again.

CHAPTER 2 } Setting Up Digital Performer

When using multiple devices, however, you will need to resolve the audio clocks of each device. Set the Master device to Internal, then choose the appropriate audio clock for the "slaved" devices, as shown in Figure 2.13. As discussed earlier, the type of clock source you choose will be determined by how each device is being synced (or slaved) to the master device.

Figure 2.13

The Clock Source menu.

Buffer Size

A *buffer* is basically a small chunk of memory. When working with digital audio, the buffer temporarily holds onto the audio that is traveling between your Mac and audio device. The longer the buffer holds the audio, the more *monitoring latency*, or audible delay of the live signal, that is introduced. Lower buffer settings reduce monitoring latency but put additional strain on your Mac. The lower the buffer setting, the harder your computer must work to play back and record audio; this forces your Mac to allocate more CPU processing power for playback and recording functions, essentially reducing the number of effects plug-ins and processing that can be used in a project. Higher buffer settings have the opposite effect—monitoring latency is increased, freeing up your Mac's CPU for other tasks, such as effects processing.

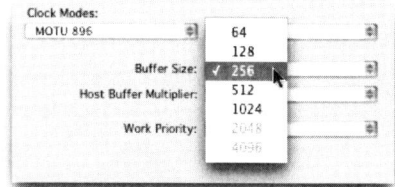

Figure 2.14

The Buffer Size menu. The actual settings listed will be dictated by the selected hardware device.

Buffer sizes are measured in samples, and can be changed by clicking on the Buffer Size menu, as shown in Figure 2.14.

> ### WHEN TO CHANGE THE BUFFER SIZE
>
> The general rule when working with buffer settings is: lower settings for recording (256 samples or lower), and higher settings for mixing (512 or 1024+ samples). If you're triggering virtual instruments within a project, however, you'll need to find a middle-ground—lowering the buffer enough to reduce monitoring latency, but not lowering it so much that you run out of CPU power for effects.
>
> Keep in mind that the buffer setting can be changed at any point in your project, and will be dictated by the specific task at hand. Be sure to use the Audio Performance window (explained in Chapter 13, "Processing and Mastering") to monitor buffer activity.

Host Buffer Multiplier

The Host Buffer Multiplier, shown in Figure 2.15, helps to improve the performance of Digital Performer. MOTU recommends the following Host Buffer Multiplier settings:

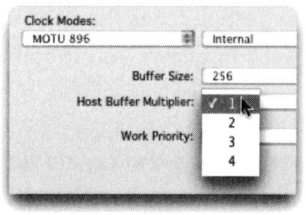

Figure 2.15
The Host Buffer Multiplier setting.

1. Use this setting if you only have one audio device enabled in the hardware driver list.
2. Choose 2 if you have two or more devices enabled.
3-4. Choose 3 or 4 if you are experiencing audio performance problems.

Work Priority

The Work Priority setting, shown in Figure 2.16, determines the priority the MAS engine receives from Mac OSX, so try to keep this setting as high as possible. MOTU audio devices can be set to High, while other devices may require Medium or Low settings. If you are working with third-party audio devices, you may need to experiment with this setting if you are experiencing performance problems.

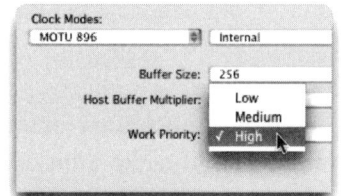

Figure 2.16
The Work Priority setting.

Once you have enabled the necessary audio devices and properly configured its settings, click OK to confirm the audio settings. Remember that you can change these settings at any time during the music production process, allowing you to tailor the responsiveness of Digital Performer to work with your specific project needs.

> **WORK PRIORITY AND POWERBOOKS**
> Many users have suggested that a Work Priority setting of Medium provides the best performance with single processor Powerbooks.

The Configure Studio Settings Window

The Configure Studio Settings window, shown in Figure 2.17, allows you to control the number of audio voices and stereo buses, along with the disk read/write and voice buffer sizes, in your project. In addition, you can turn on or off automatic delay compensation for plug-ins, and set the Quick Start pre-fill buffers. The Easy Configuration section provides presets of

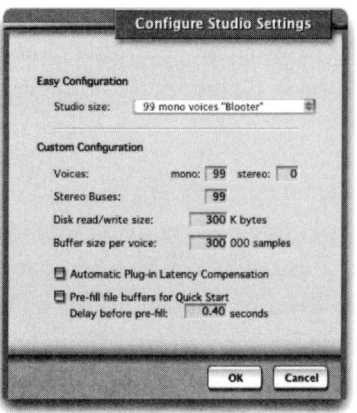

Figure 2.17
The Configure Studio Settings window.

different studio sizes (which takes the hassle out of the studio configuration process), while the Custom Configuration section allows you to tailor the studio size for your specific project needs.

Voices and Stereo Buses
Voices basically determine how many audio tracks will be available for simultaneous playback. Stereo buses are internal buses that allow you to internally route audio from one place to another within Digital Performer. Refer to the "Track Voices and Internal Buses" section of Chapter 4 for a detailed explanation of voices, buses, and the Easy Configuration section.

To set the number of available voices or buses:

* Click and enter the desired value in the corresponding input fields from your computer keyboard's numeric keypad. You can also click and drag to change the values.
* Choose a preset studio size from the Easy Configuration section.

Disk Read/Write Sizes
Audio is recorded and played back from your computer's hard drive(s) in blocks. This setting determines how large these blocks of audio data are. Smaller sizes will increase disk activity (while putting stress on the hard drive), but will improve the responsiveness of Digital Performer when playing back and recording audio. Larger sizes will allow the hard drive to not work as hard, but they degrade the responsiveness of DP.

Like the buffer size setting I discussed earlier, the setting you choose will be dictated by your specific project needs, as well as the overall speed of your hard drive(s). Faster drives will allow you to lower this setting, making DP snappier when executing audio related tasks. If you are working with a slower hard drive, however, you may be forced to raise this setting.

Buffer Size Per Voice
Voices require RAM. The amount of RAM that is used by each voice is determined by the Buffer Size Per Voice setting. This value determines the maximum number of samples per voice that can be readied for playback and/or recording. Smaller values will allow you to use more voices within your project, but will put a lot of strain on your Mac. If lower settings are too much for DP to handle, you'll be presented with a warning dialog. If this happens, you'll need to raise this setting or lower the number of available voices.

Automatic Plug-in Latency Compensation
This option will compensate for any delay that is introduced to an audio track when you're using real-time audio plug-ins. This option will also compensate for virtual instruments being triggered by prerecorded MIDI tracks. Refer to Chapter 13 for an explanation of the Automatic Plug-in Latency Compensation feature.

Pre-fill File Buffers for Quick Start
This setting tells DP to pre-fill the play buffers before playback is initiat[ed.]
the responsiveness of DP when you hit the Play button. DP fills this buff[er]
back wiper or perform any action that is playback-related.

The Input Monitoring Mode Window

The Input Monitoring Mode window, shown in Figure 2.18, determines how live audio signals are monitored in Digital Performer. The settings you choose here will affect overall monitoring latency and your ability to perform successful audio punches.

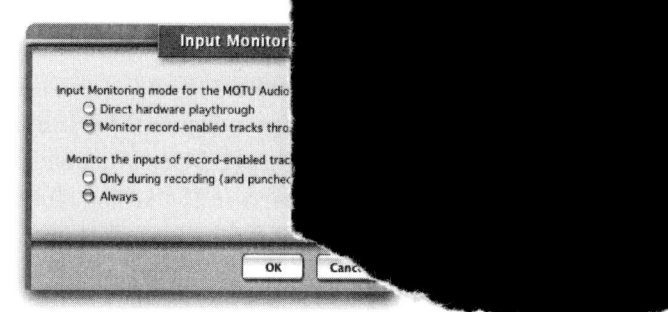

Monitoring Thru Effects versus Direct Hardware Playthrough
When the Input Monitoring Mode is set to the Monitor record-enabled tracks through effects option, live audio signals are routed through Digital Performer before going out to your audio interface. This allows you to listen to the live signal through any effects plug-ins inserted in DP. The trade-off is increased monitoring latency, as the audio signal must travel through Digital Performer and any plug-ins before you hear them.

> **RECORDING IN SYNC**
> Regardless of which Input Monitoring Mode setting you choose, live audio will always be recorded in the proper location, without any latency and in perfect sync with other tracks.

Direct Hardware Playthrough, however, introduces little (if any) delay to the live signal because it bypasses Digital Performer altogether. The disadvantage to this method is the inability to process the input signal with DP's cool effects plug-ins.

Monitor the Inputs of Record Enabled Tracks
The two settings provided here are like the Auto Input and All Input modes of a standard multitrack recorder. The setting you choose here will determine when you will hear live audio on record enabled tracks.

- **Only During Recording (and punched in).** This setting is like Auto Input. Live audio is only heard when you are recording or punching in on an armed track. In addition, the live signal will also be heard on a record-enabled track when the transport is stopped (and not playing back). Use this setting to successfully perform punch-in recording.

live audio will be heard on an armed track, regardless of whether playing back, or recording. This option is typically used when adjusting a tracking session, and during the first record pass. If you have this you are attempting to perform a punch-in (recording), you will not be the previously recorded performance—making punch-in recording impossible.

shown in Figure 2.19, is a one-stop location for enabling (or disabling) audio inputs, outputs, and internal buses. Unlike the other audio concerned so far, settings for the Audio Bundles window are project-specific DP project open before this window will be available.

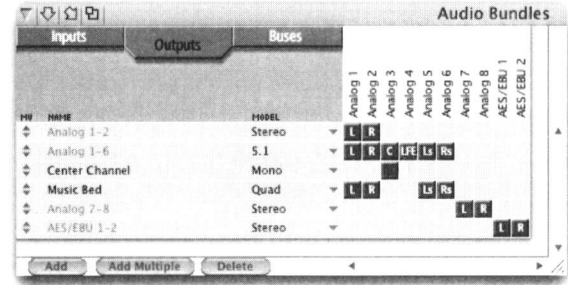

The Audio Bundles window.

The Audio Bundles window is divided into three tabbed sections, labeled Inputs, Outputs, and Buses. Each section displays the name, channel format (or model), and routing assignment for the bundle. Buttons for adding and deleting audio bundles are located at the bottom of the window.

What are Audio Bundles?

An audio bundle is basically a set of inputs, outputs, and internal buses. While it's possible to create audio bundles on the fly from DP's I/O assignment menus, the Audio Bundles window provides you with a graphic interface that allows the creation, removal, renaming, and rerouting of I/O assignments between Digital Performer and your connected audio interfaces (and third-party virtual instruments such as Reason or Ableton Live).

To create an audio bundle in the Audio Bundles window:

1. Select the desired Inputs, Outputs, or Buses tab and click the Add button.
2. Specify the channel format for the audio bundle by clicking on the Model menu, shown in Figure 2.20.

Launching Digital Performer for the First Time

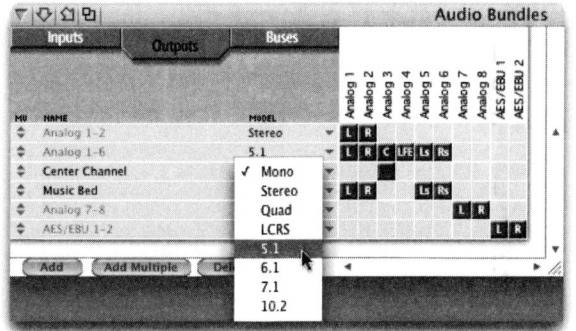

Figure 2.20
Set an audio bundle's channel format from the Model menu. Notice that you can also choose surround configurations.

To remove or delete an audio bundle:

1. Click on an audio bundle to select it. Drag to select multiple audio bundles.
2. Click the Delete button. You can also press the Delete key on your computer keyboard.

> **RENAMING AUDIO BUNDLES**
> Another benefit to using the Audio Bundles window versus DP's I/O assignment menus is the ability to rename a specific input, output, or bus. You could, for example, call bus 1-2 "Reverb" if you were using it as an effects send or customize the input/output bundle names to correspond to any studio gear that's physically connected to your audio interface. Customizing your audio bundle names can help to personalize and possibly speed up your Digital Performer workflow.
>
> To rename an audio bundle: Option-click the name of the bundle. Enter the new name and press the Return key on your Mac's keyboard to confirm the change.

Rerouting Input, Output, and Bussing Assignments

The Tile Grid of the Audio Bundles window is where you can change the routing assignment for a specific audio bundle. The selected audio hardware driver and third-party virtual instrument(s) you have installed determine the audio devices and virtual instrument I/O that appear above the assignment grid in each tabbed section. The location of the each tile determines the routing assignment of an audio bundle. Each bundle tile basically connects a specific Digital Performer input, output, or bus to a specific input or output (or bus) on your connected audio device or virtual instrument.

* To make a new I/O routing assignment, click and drag a bundle tile to a new assignment, as shown in Figure 2.21.

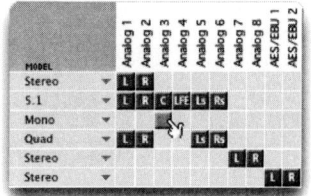

Figure 2.21
Click and drag a bundle tile to change the routing assignment for an audio bundle.

CHAPTER 2 } Setting Up Digital Performer

* To swap the left and right channels of a stereo bundle, drag the left or right bundle to the opposite channel

> **SHARING I/O ASSIGNMENTS**
> DP allows you to create bundles that share the same assignments as other bundles. This is especially handy when working with surround bundles, as you can create dedicated bundles for panning to specific speakers in a surround setup. This would allow you, for example, to pan specific "stems" to specific combinations of speakers (such as dialog in the center, the music score in the front left/right and rear left/right channels, FX stems in 5.1, and so on). Refer to Appendix D, "Surround and Digital Performer," for an explanation of surround bundles in Digital Performer

MIDI Configuration

MIDI device configuration has been greatly simplified in Mac OSX—you no longer have to rely on third-party applications (such as FreeMIDI or OMS) to connect Digital Performer with your studio's MIDI devices. Similar to how OSX handles audio (with Core Audio), Apple's Core MIDI technology connects your MIDI studio together at the system level, offering improved speed and performance. In addition, once your MIDI devices have been configured, other Core MIDI compatible applications you may have installed on your Mac (such as Pro Tools, Ableton Live, GarageBand, and so on) will also have access to this global MIDI setup.

The Audio MIDI Setup window, shown in Figure 2.22, provides a virtual representation of your MIDI studio's physical setup. Use this window to connect your MIDI interface and MIDI devices to DP (and other Core MIDI applications).

Figure 2.22
The MIDI tab of the Audio MIDI Setup window shows your system's MIDI routing assignments.

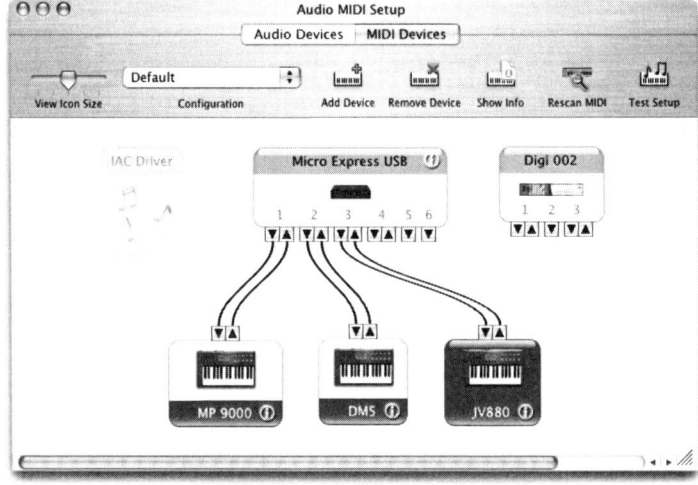

The Audio MIDI Setup (AMS) Utility

The (AMS) window allows you to configure the routing assignments for all of your connected MIDI devices. Once you install the Core MIDI drivers for your particular MIDI interface, the drivers will automatically appear in the AMS window, as shown in Figure 2.23. You can access this window directly in Digital Performer by choosing Setup menu > Open Audio MIDI Setup, or with Mac OSX's Finder.

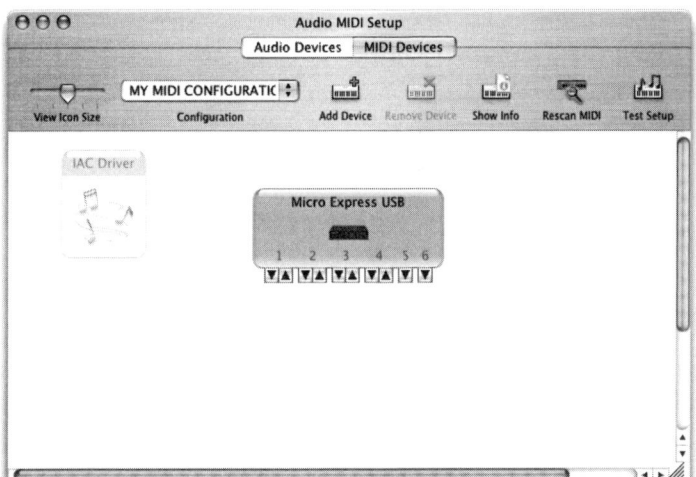

Figure 2.23

Once you have installed the Core MIDI driver for your particular MIDI interface, it will automatically appear in the AMS window.

Configuring your MIDI devices

Once your MIDI interface is visible in the MIDI tab of the AMS window, it's very easy to add, configure, and connect your MIDI devices.

To add a new MIDI device:

1. Open the AMS window by choosing System Hard Drive > Applications > Utilities > AMS. You can also open the window from DP by choosing Setup menu > Open Audio MIDI Setup.
2. Once AMS is opened, click the MIDI tab to display your MIDI configuration.
3. Click the Add Device button to add a new external MIDI device. You can also use the default keyboard shortcut Command+D. Once you've created the new device, a device called "new external device" will appear in the AMS window, as shown in Figure 2.24.

The new external device that is created will be a generic MIDI device. You can specify the manufacturer, model, and MIDI properties of the device from the Properties window. This allows DP to recognize a particular device's patch lists, and so on.

Figure 2.24

Click the Add Device button to add a new external MIDI device.

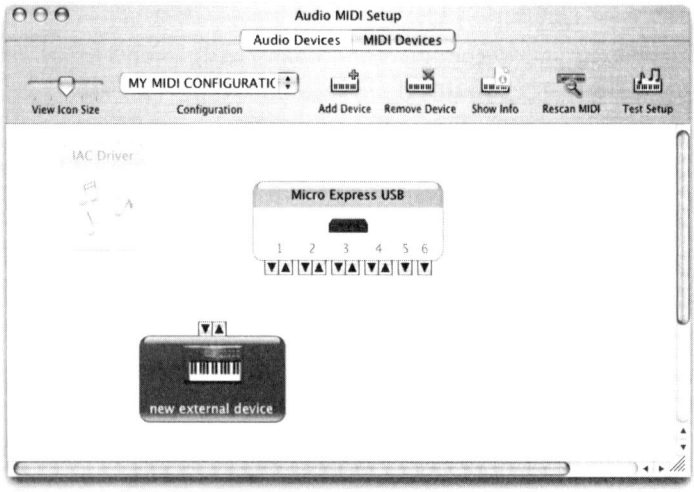

To configure the new MIDI device:

1. Double-click the new external device you created in the previous section. The Properties window will open, allowing you to change the generic device's MIDI properties.
2. Specify the manufacturer and model name from the appropriate menus, as shown in Figure 2.25.

Figure 2.25

Click the Add Device button to add a new external MIDI device.

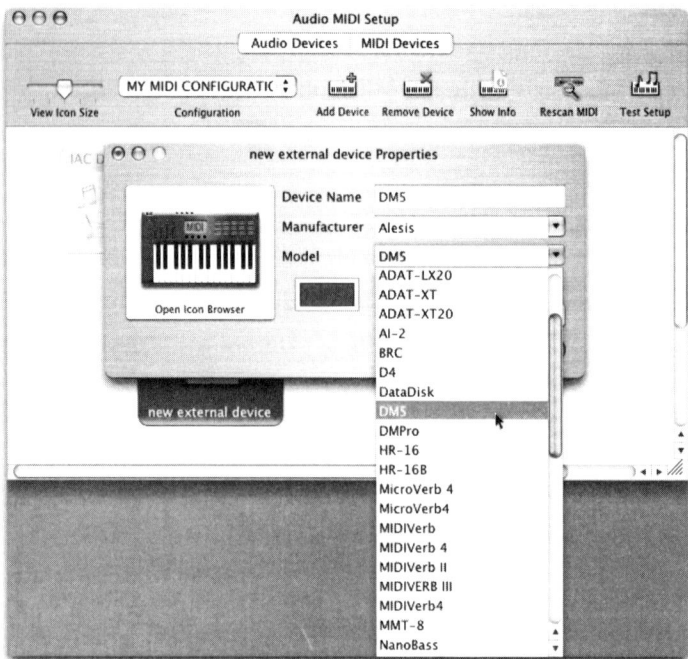

3. Once defined, the device's properties will automatically be configured for the specific device. To view the actual properties for the MIDI device, click the More/Less Information button, as shown in Figure 2.26.

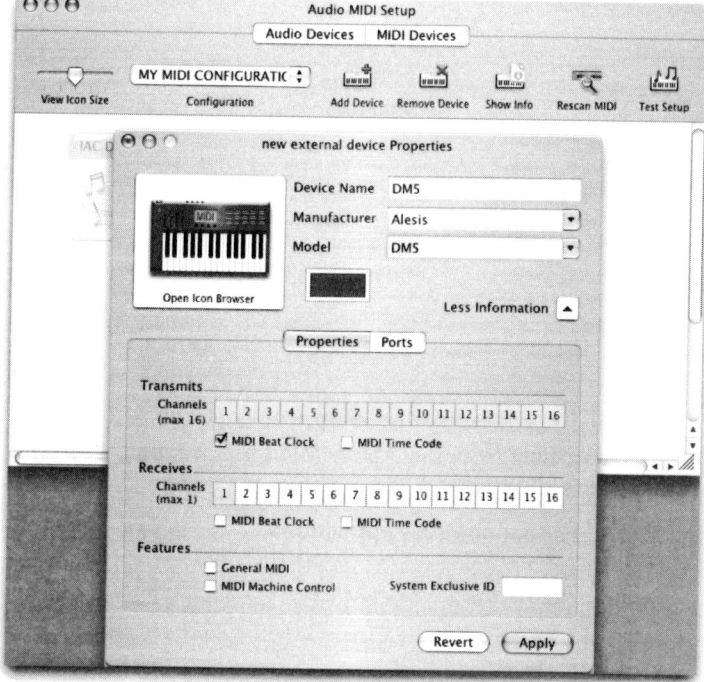

Figure 2.26

The Properties tab of the AMS window.

4. Make any necessary changes, and then click the Apply button to confirm them.
5. Close the Properties window by clicking on the window's red Close button (located at the top-right corner of the window).

Once you have configured the properties for your new MIDI device, it will appear with the model name you specified in the previous section (such as DM5).

Next, you need to connect the device to your MIDI interface. Make sure the virtual connections you are making in the AMS window match the physical connections of your MIDI studio.

To connect your MIDI device:

* Click and drag the device's output/input arrows to the MIDI interface's input/output arrows, as shown in Figure 2.27.

Figure 2.27
Drag the input/output arrows to connect devices in the AMS window.

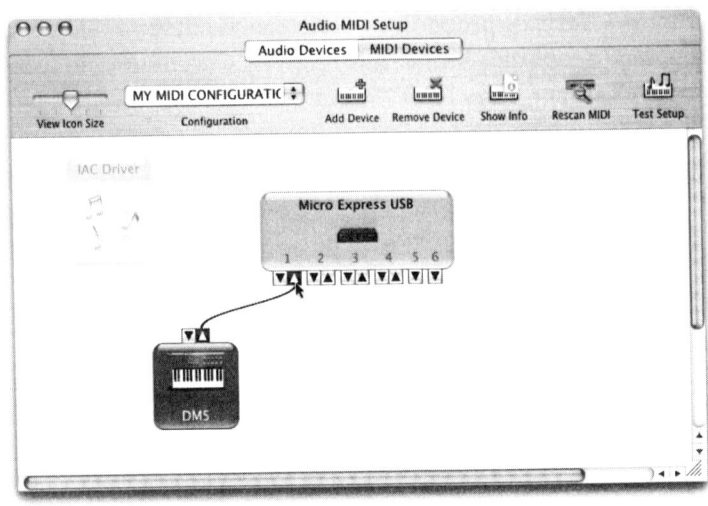

Once you have configured your MIDI devices, made the appropriate connections, and so on, quit the Audio MIDI Setup Utility by choosing Quit from the Audio MIDI Setup menu. You can also use the default keyboard shortcut Command+Q. Devices configured in AMS will automatically appear in Digital Performer and any other Core MIDI compatible application.

Synchronization

Digital Performer can be synchronized with other devices and applications. Digital Performer supports all standard synchronization modes, including SMPTE, standard MIDI beat clocks, and tap tempo sync. When receiving SMPTE timecode, you can choose MIDI Time Code, Direct Time Lock, and Indirect Time Lock for the SMPTE to MIDI conversion that is required for SMPTE. Refer to the "Synchronization" chapter of the *Digital Performer User's Manual* for an explanation of DP's different sync modes.

Syncing DP

You can synchronize DP with other devices (and applications) with the Receive Sync and Transmit Sync commands. Even though Digital Performer can receive sync from a wide variety of synchronization modes, DP can only transmit sync as MIDI beat clocks or MIDI timecode.

To slave DP to another device or application:

1. Open the Receive Sync command by choosing Setup menu > Receive Sync.
2. Click the Sync to Port menu and choose the sync source, as shown in Figure 2.28. Selecting Any will tell DP to sync to any timecode it receives.

※ Synchronization

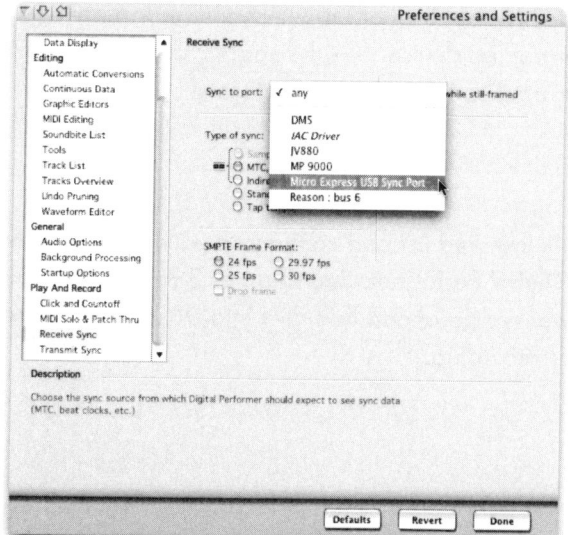

Figure 2.28

The Sync to Port menu allows you to set the sync source.

3. Choose the desired sync mode from the Type of Sync section.
4. Once you've specified the sync settings, click the Done button.
5. Next, select Slave to External Sync from the Setup menu. You can also use the default keyboard shortcut Command+7. Once enabled, the Control Panel's Slave to External Sync button will become highlighted, as shown in Figure 2.29.
6. Press the Control Panel's Play or Record buttons. The Play button will flash, indicating that DP is "waiting" to receive sync from the device specified in Step 2.

The External Sync button

Figure 2.29

The Slave to External Sync button. In addition to the methods provided in Step 5, you can also click on the Slave to External Sync button to toggle the Slave to External Sync feature on and off.

To slave another device or application to Digital Performer:

1. Open the Transmit Sync command by choosing Setup menu > Transmit Sync.
2. Decide which type of sync you wish to transmit (either MIDI beat clocks or MIDI time code [MTC]), and then specify the sync destination from the appropriate Transmit menu. Keep in mind that you can transmit both types of sync simultaneously to multiple destinations, simply by making the desired assignments.
3. Once you have made chosen the desired settings, click the Done button.

CHAPTER 2 } Setting Up Digital Performer

Keep in mind that the device (or application) to which you're transmitting sync must be set to receive sync in order for DP to control the device. See the specific device's user manual for instructions on how to slave the device or application to Digital Performer.

Summary

Once you have successfully installed DP and configured your audio and MIDI devices, you will be ready to start working in Digital Performer. See Chapter 3 for an overview of the major windows in Digital Performer. If you want to go ahead and dive into DP, refer to Chapter 4 for an explanation of how to set up a project for recording.

3 Navigating Digital Performer

DP's interface comprises various windows that allow you to access its numerous tools and features sets. This chapter will provide an overview of the most important windows, which serve as the backbone for Digital Performer (see Figure 3.1). For information on DP's other windows and important features, check the Table of Contents of this book to find its related chapter or appendix.

Following is a list of the windows discussed in this chapter:

- Consolidated Window
- Control Panel
- Tracks window
- Sequence Editor
- Mixing Board
- Soundbites window

The Consolidated Window

The Consolidated Window feature introduced in Version 4.5 allows you to view DP's various windows in a single, consolidated window, as shown in Figure 3.2. The Consolidated Window is broken up into different sections that can be added, subtracted, or resized to fit your specific production needs. If you want to jump right into using this feature, you can access the provided default Consolidated Window sets from the Window Sets menu (Window menu > Window Sets).

CHAPTER 3 } Navigating Digital Performer

Figure 3.1

Digital Performer's main windows: Control Panel, Tracks, Sequence, Mixing Board, and Soundbites.

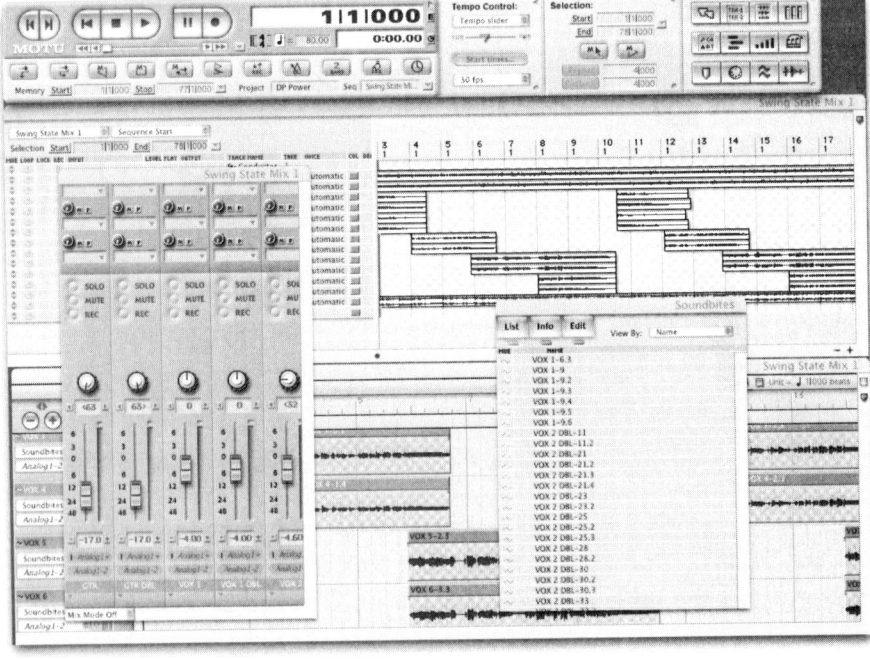

Figure 3.2

The Consolidated Window feature introduced in Version 4.5 allows you to display DP's various windows in a single, consolidated window. In this example, the default Tracking window set is displayed.

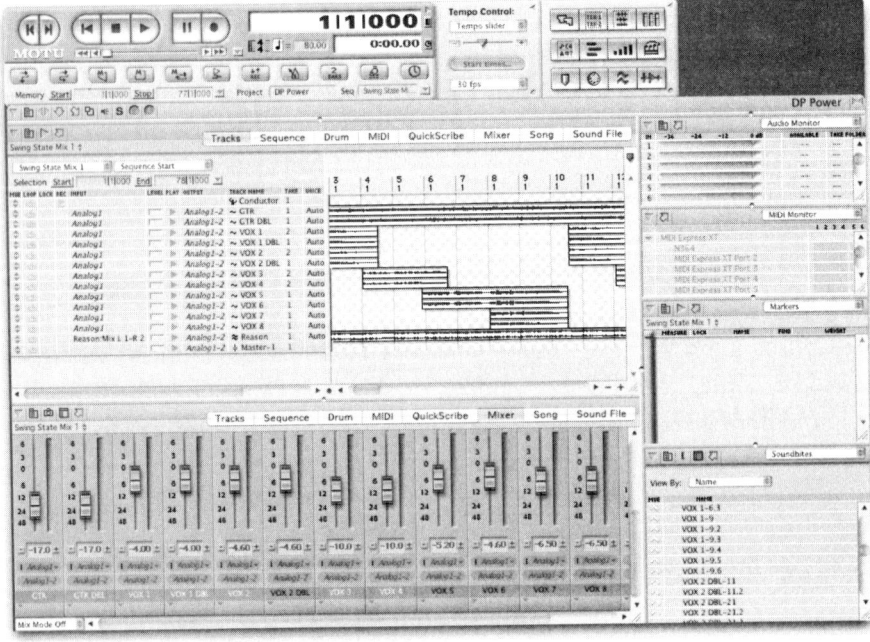

The Consolidated Window preferences (Digital Performer menu > Preferences > Display > Consolidated Window) control the functionality of the Consolidated Window, as shown in Figure 3.3. From here, you can decide which windows will automatically open in the Consolidated Window, and how many rows will initially appear, how projects created in older versions of DP are affected, and how the Mixing Board behaves when the Consolidated Window is turned on; you can also select options for enabling or disabling the Consolidated Window altogether.

See the "Customizing Your Workspace" section of Chapter 5 for an explanation of the Consolidated Window and the Consolidated Window preference settings. In addition, be sure to review The New Consolidated Window quick-reference card that MOTU has included with the DP 4.5 installer disc and manual.

Control Panel

The Control Panel in Digital Performer is the central location from which you can access the Transport, Control Tempo, and Metronome options; enable enhanced selection features; and open other important windows (see Figure 3.4). Unlike other DP windows, the Control Panel cannot be closed and will automatically open anytime a new session is created or opened.

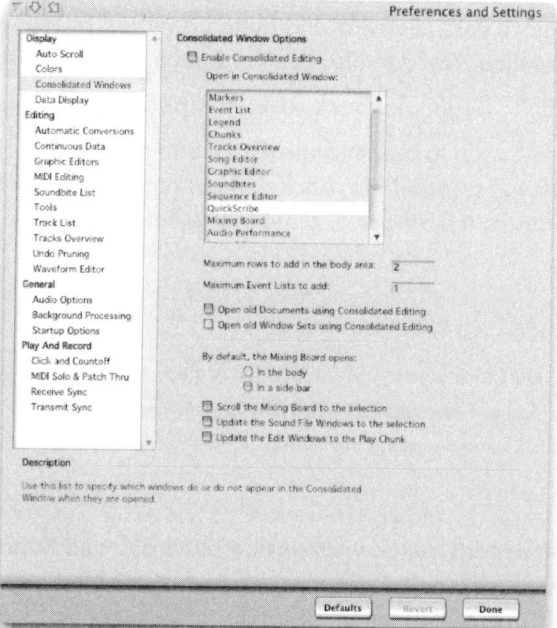

Figure 3.3

The Consolidated Window preferences control the functionality of the Consolidated Window.

Figure 3.4

The Control Panel with expanded Quick Access Drawers.

Transport and Counter

The Control Panel's Transport controls operate like any standard multi-track recorder, allowing you to perform the following functions (from left to right):

- **Skip Forward.** Skips to the next sequence, or Chunk (if you have multiple Chunks in your project).
- **Skip Backward.** Skips to the previous Chunk (see note above).
- **Rewind.** Click this button to go to the beginning of the current sequence. If you have the Memory Bar options enabled, the Transport will rewind to the Memory Start location. If pressed during playback, there will be a momentary pause before DP resumes playback at the proper location. Pressing this button during the record process will stop the recording and begin the rewind normally. You can also press the number 1 key on the numeric keypad to instantly locate to the beginning of your project or memory start location.
- **Stop.** This button will halt playback and recording, and will also turn off the Pause button, if it is engaged. If the Memory Bar's Auto-Rewind button is turned on, DP will automatically rewind to the Memory Start location. You can also use the Space bar to stop or start playback.
- **Play.** Press this button to begin playback. Use the Space bar to start or stop playback.
- **Pause.** Use the Pause button to suspend playback and put the Transport in standby. If pressed during playback, DP will suspend playback without turning off any sounding MIDI notes. If pressed while the Transport is stopped, playback will be suspended until the Transport is "unpaused."

> **CHUNKS**
> Digital Performer refers to sequences as *Chunks*. DP projects can contain an unlimited number of Chunks and are managed from the Chunks window (Project menu > Chunks). See Chapter 11 for a full explanation of Chunks.

- **Record.** Clicking the Record button will engage playback and begin recording from the playback cursor's current location. A track must be record-enabled in order for recording to begin. If you attempt to start recording when no tracks are armed, you will be presented with a warning dialog box (see Figure 3.5).

※ Control Panel

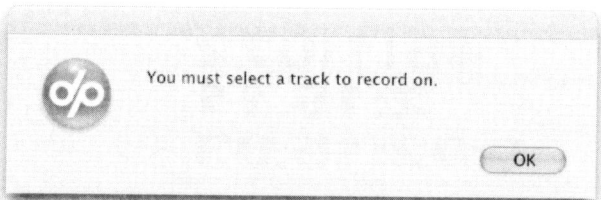

Figure 3.5
Tracks must be record-enabled before you can begin recording.

※ **Position Bar.** The Position Bar is located below the Transport's main Stop and Play buttons (see Figure 3.6). Use these buttons to rewind and fast-forward during playback. You can also drag the position slider to move to different points within the current sequence. Located to the right is the Marker menu. Click and select a marker to instantly jump to that Transport location.

Figure 3.6
The Control Panel's Position Bar

※ **Counter.** The counter windows display the current playback location for the enabled sequence. The Main and Auxiliary Counter can display four different formats: measures, real-time, SMPTE frames, and samples. Click on the time format buttons located to the right of each counter to change the display. Be aware that you cannot display the same time format in both counters (see Figure 3.7).

Figure 3.7
The Control Panel's Counter. In this example, the Main Counter is configured to display samples, while the Auxiliary Counter displays real-time.

※ **THE LARGER COUNTER WINDOW**

In addition to the Counter within the Control Panel, DP also has a "large" Counter window (see Figure 3.8) that can be accessed from the Studio menu (the default keyboard shortcut is Shift+J).

The large Counter consists of a Main Counter and 1-3 Auxiliary Counters, depending if you enable all four time formats from the Set Display command located in the mini-menu. This command also lets you specify the time format that will be displayed in the Main Counter.

The mini-menu (see Figure 3.9) also provides commands for setting the frame rate (see Chapter 14, "Notation and Scoring") and the Chunk Start Time (see Chapter 11, "Arranging," and Chapter 14).

CHAPTER 3 } Navigating Digital Performer

Figure 3.8
The large Counter window

Figure 3.9
The Counter window mini-menu

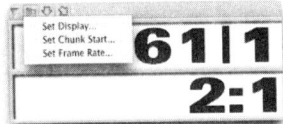

Tempo, Meter, and Metronome

Located below the Control Panel's Main Counter (see Figure 3.10) is the current Meter, Beat Value, and Tempo displays (from left to right).

Figure 3.10
The Control Panel's current Meter, Beat Value, and Tempo controls

- **Current Meter.** Displays the current time signature of the enabled sequence. This value can only be changed by selecting Project > Modify Conductor track > Change Meter. You could also insert a meter event directly into the Conductor track (see Chapter 4, "Setting Up a New Project" and Chapter 11 for details on working with meter within DP).
- **Current Beat Value.** This value determines which note gets the "beat," or subdivision, for the current tempo, displayed in beats-per-minute, or BPM (see Chapters 4 and 11 for details on working with tempo within DP).
- **Current Tempo.** Displays the current tempo, or BPM, of the enabled sequence. You can click and drag directly into the field controls to change the tempo, as long as the tempo is set to Tempo Slider within the Control Panel's Tempo Control Drawer (explained later).

Status Strip

The Status Strip is located at the very bottom of the Control Panel (see Figure 3.11), and offers two sections: a field to enter memory start and end times (on the left), and another section (on the right) that displays the name of the project and Chunk that is currently play-enabled. When Auto-Record mode is enabled, the project name and current Chunk fields will disappear and be replaced by the Punch-in and Punch-out fields, wherein you can specify the exact locations for punch-in and out recording.

Figure 3.11

Located at the very bottom of the Control Panel is the Status Strip.

Memory and Auto-Record Bar

Located directly above the Status Strip are (from left to right) the Chunks, Memory, Auto-Record, Metronome, Wait, and Slave to Sync buttons. Many of these options, such as Auto-Rewind, are there to help you automate routine Transport procedures. Used in combination, these buttons can help significantly streamline your workflow and allow you to concentrate more on the creative process.

- **Cue Chunks.** When multiple Chunks exist within a project, this option will automatically play-enable the next Chunk that appears in the Chunks window when playback reaches the end of a sequence. The Chunk will not auto-play, so you will need to manually initiate playback from the Control Panel or the keyboard (see Chapter 11 for an explanation of Chunks).

- **Chain Chunks.** This option will automatically begin playback of the next Chunk in the Chunks window when playback reaches the end of the current Chunk (see Chapter 11).

- **Auto-Rewind.** Use this feature to immediately rewind to the Memory Start Time when playback is stopped.

- **Auto Stop.** This option causes playback and recording to stop at the Memory Stop Time.

- **Memory Cycle.** This button will force playback and recording to loop infinitely between the designated Memory Start and End Times, located in the Memory Bar (below the Memory buttons).

- **Overdub record.** When engaged, this option will merge recorded MIDI data with any data that already exists within a MIDI track. When Overdub mode is turned off, previously recorded MIDI data will be replaced when recording starts.

  Audio tracks operate differently—with Overdub mode enabled, newly recorded material will not be merged, but will be layered over existing soundbites. When Overdub mode is off, previously recorded soundbites in that track are erased.

- **Marker menu.** Use this menu to go to a marker and other important locations, such as Memory and Auto Record Start/End Times.

- **Auto-Record.** Use this button to automate punches within DP (see Figure 3.12). Once enabled, the Punch Start and End times will become visible in the Status Strip (see Chapter 7, "Recording Audio").

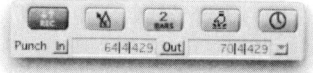

Figure 3.12

The Auto-Record section of the Control Panel.

CHAPTER 3 } Navigating Digital Performer

- **Metronome click.** This option will turn on DP's Metronome. Double-clicking on this button will open the Click and Countoff preferences. See the "Setting Up a Click" section of Chapter 4 for an explanation of Digital Performer's click.
- **Countoff.** This button enables the countoff for the MIDI metronome. The number of countoff measures can be set in the Click and Countoff preferences, which can be quickly accessed by double-clicking with the mouse.
- **Wait.** Click this button to place the Transport in standby. When playback or recording is initiated, DP will "wait" for a MIDI message before beginning playback or recording (see Chapter 8, "Recording MIDI").
- **Slave to External Sync.** This button will turn on external sync. Double-clicking will open the Receive Sync, where you can set specific sync options. Use this option when you wish to synchronize your Digital Performer system with another playback or recording device/application. See Chapter 2, "Setting Up Digital Performer," for an explanation of synchronization.

DP's Drawers

The Control Panel also provides four drawers, shown in Figure 3.13—the Quick Access, Audio, Selection, and Tempo Control drawers—that contain various controls or provide access to DP's main windows.

Figure 3.13
The Control Panel drawers

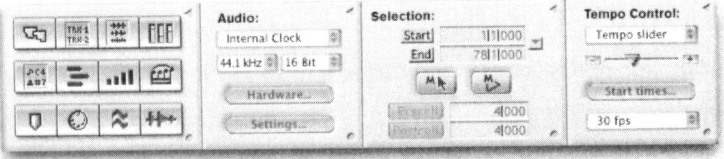

Besides offering you quick access to important features, these drawers can be hidden and their orders rearranged to further customize the Control Panel.

- Click on the Drawer button (the triangle icon) located to the right of the Main Counter to show and hide the Control Panel drawers, as shown in Figure 3.14.

Figure 3.14
Click on the Drawer button (the triangle icon) to show the Control Panel drawers.

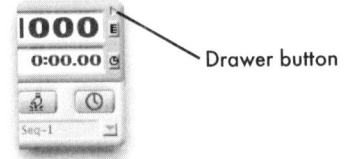

Drawer button

40

※ Control Panel

To change the order of the Control Panel drawers:

* Click on the dot located at the bottom-right corner of a drawer and drag the pane to the new position (see Figure 3.15).

Figure 3.15
Click on the dot and drag to change the drawer order.

The Quick Access Drawer
The buttons within the Quick Access drawer provide instant access to DP's main windows (see Figure 3.16).

Figure 3.16
The Control Panel's Quick Access drawer

The Audio Drawer
The Audio drawer (see Figure 3.17) allows you to specify audio clock sources, sampling rate, and bit depth without having to open their related windows. Clicking on the Hardware button will launch the Hardware Configurations window; clicking on the Settings button will launch the Studio Configuration window (see Chapters 2 and 4 for more information on these windows).

Figure 3.17
The Audio drawer

The Selection Drawer
The Selection drawer contains options for making time range selections within Digital Performer (see Figure 3.18).

Figure 3.18
The Selection Drawer

At the top of the window is the Start and End time selection options, which can be set by typing directly into the field controls or by clicking on the Selection menu (see Figure 3.19). This function is identical to the Tracks window's selection feature. Having the Selection Start and End time options located within the Control Panel allows you to access them when the Tracks window is closed. In addition, the Link Playback to Memory and Link Memory to Playback buttons, along with Pre and Post Roll buttons, offer further control of selections within DP.

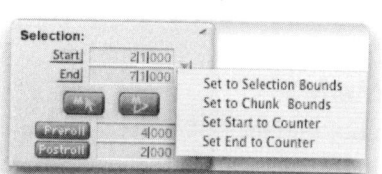

Figure 3.19
Link Playback to Memory and Link Memory to Playback buttons offer advanced selection features within Digital Performer. The Selection menu provides shortcuts for making selections within DP.

The Tempo Control Drawer

The Tempo Control drawer allows you to set the tempo source, Chunk start time, and frame rate (see Figure 3.20).

Figure 3.20

The Tempo Control drawer

- **Tempo Control Slider.** This button allows you to select either the Tempo Slider (manual), Conductor track, Tap Pad (tap tempo function), or Remote Control (MIDI source) as the current sequence's tempo source. See Chapters 4 and 11 for information on tempo in DP.
- **Start time.** Use this button to change the current sequence's (Chunk) start time. See Chapters 11 and 14 for information on Chunk start times.
- **Frame rate.** This menu allows you to change the current Chunk's frame rate. See Chapter 14, "Notation and Scoring" for related info on frame rates within DP.

Tracks Window

The Tracks window is the central window in Digital Performer (see Figure 3.21) and provides an overview of a project's tracks, track data, and available sequences. This window is really divided into three sections: the mini-menu and title bar, the Tracks List, and the Tracks Overview. Choose Project menu > Tracks, or use the default keyboard shortcut Shift+T to open the Tracks window.

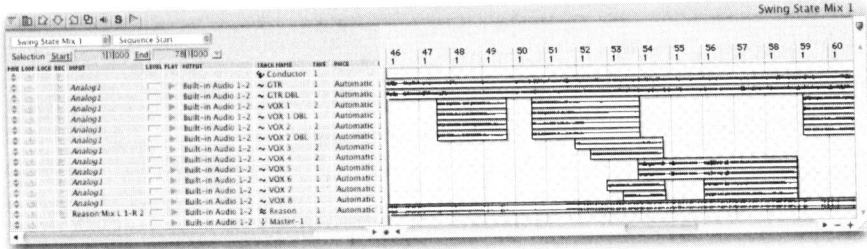

Figure 3.21

The Tracks window

Title Bar and Mini-Menu

The Tracks window's title bar and mini-menu (see Figure 3.22) provide options for managing, viewing, and monitoring tracks. Many of these features are very straightforward and do not need much explanation, while others will be explained in more detail in later chapters:

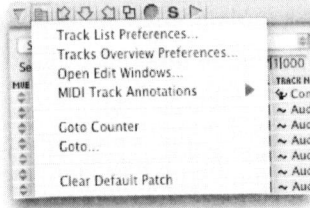

Figure 3.22

The title bar and mini-menu provide options for managing tracks within DP.

❋ **Mini-menu.** This menu provides preferences for controlling the Track List, Tracks Overview, the opening of Edit windows, and MIDI track annotations. Some of the mini-menu options that appeared in DP before Version 4.5 have been consolidated into the Preferences and Settings window. See Chapter 5 for an explanation of the Preferences and Settings window.

❋ **Minimize.** This button will send a window to the Dock. You can also double-click on the center of the title bar for the same effect. Once the window has been minimized, click on the window in the Dock to bring it back to the foreground.

❋ **Pushdown.** Clicking this button will send a window to the background. Use this option to hide the window onscreen without closing it.

❋ **Zoom.** Use this button to expand the window or shrink a window.

❋ **Audible Mode.** Click on the speaker icon to enable Audible mode, which will force MIDI data to play when you click on a note in the Tracks window. Dragging the playback wiper with Audible mode turned on will also allow you to "scrub" existing MIDI data.

❋ **Solo.** Click on the S icon to turn on Solo mode. By default, the Tracks window's Solo mode button will mute all tracks when enabled. See the side-note for a further explanation of the Tracks window's Solo mode button

❋ **Auto Scroll.** Enables auto-scrolling for the Tracks window. Option-click to open the Auto Scroll preferences (see Figure 3.23). The Auto Scroll preferences are explained in Chapter 5.

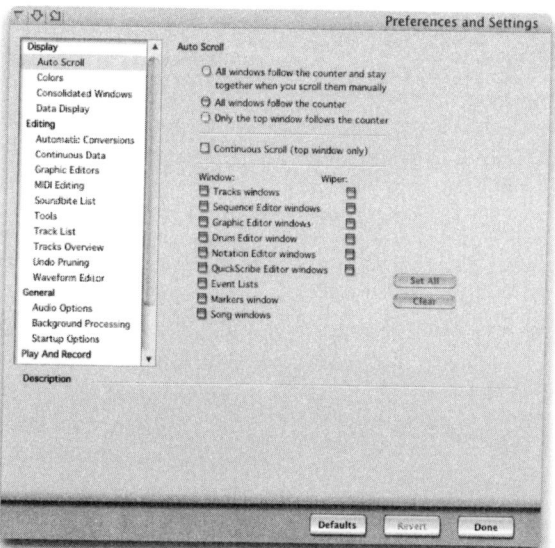

Figure 3.23
The Auto Scroll preferences allow you to determine how windows will automatically scroll in DP.

THE TITLE BAR'S SOLO BUTTON

When enabled, the Solo button (located in an editor's title bar) will temporarily mute all tracks. This can be confusing for users new to DP, as clicking on the Solo mode button does not necessarily solo a track. From here, you will need to click on an individual track's Play-Enable button (or dedicated track Solo button) to actually "solo" it. Unlike the Tracks window however, other editor windows (such as the Mixing Board or Sequence Editor) contain individual track solo buttons that allow you to solo a track with a single click.

The Solo mode button is global and affects all windows in a DP project. When working in the Consolidated Window (explained in Chapter 5), only one Solo mode button will be visible.

A track's Play-enable Button changes color depending on its current play back state. Orange indicates that the track is muted when in Solo mode, but will play back (and become blue) when Solo mode is turned off. Blue means that the track will always play back, whether it is soloed or not. When the play-enable button is grey, the track is muted and will not playback even if it is soloed.

Tracks can of course be soloed or muted at anytime during play back, and Digital Performer will remember a track's soloed and un-soloed play-enable state.

Preferences for further controlling how soloing functions in DP operate can be found in the MIDI Solo and Patch Thru section of the Preferences and Settings window, as shown in Figure 3.24. Option-clicking a title bar's Solo mode button will open the MIDI Solo Setup preferences directly from the Tracks window. See Chapter 5 for an explanation of the MIDI Solo Setup preferences.

Figure 3.24
The MIDI Solo Setup preferences allow you to determine how windows will scroll within DP.

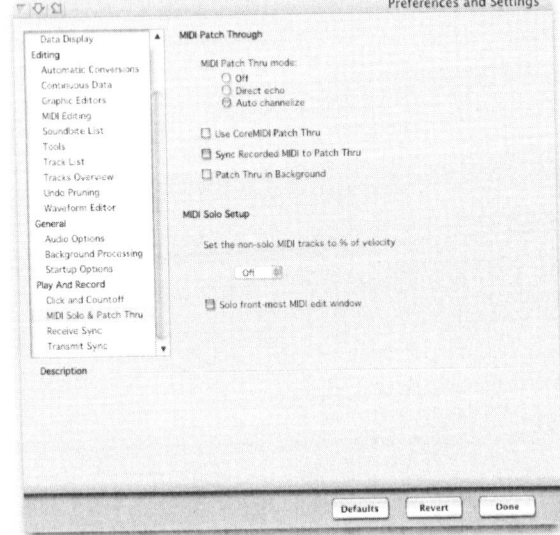

Tracks List

The Tracks List section, shown in Figure 3.25, displays various features that allow you to manage tracks within the Tracks window. The subsections below describe the features that you will find in the Tracks List section.

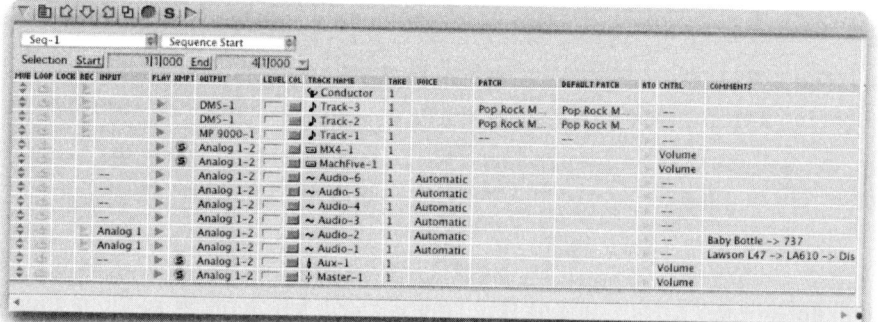

Figure 3.25

Columns within the Tracks List can be rearranged by dragging on the name of the column.

Sequence and Marker Menus

Located directly below the title bar buttons are the Sequence and Marker menus. Click on each menu to quickly navigate to another sequence (or Chunk) or to proceed to a marker location. The Marker menu also provides other important timeline locations such as the Sequence Start and End times.

Selection Bar

Below the Sequence and Marker menus are the Selection start and end times, which are used to define the in and out points of a selection. When clicked, the Start and End buttons will place the current counter location into the corresponding start or end field. You can also use the Sequence menu, shown in Figure 3.26.

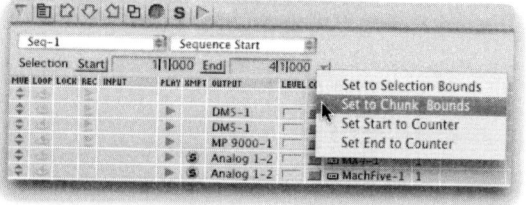

Figure 3.26

The Sequence menu provides options for making time range selections.

CHAPTER 3 } Navigating Digital Performer

The Track List's Sequence menu provides the following options for quickly making time-range selections.

- **Set to Selection Bounds.** This shortcut will automatically set the Selection start and end times to the current time range selections in and out points.
- **Set to Chunk Bounds.** This option will set the start and end times to the entire range of the current sequence.
- **Set Start to Counter.** This will set the selection start point to the time displayed within the Control Panel's Main Counter. You can also accomplish this by clicking the Sequence Start button.
- **Set End to Counter.** This will set the selection end time to the time displayed within the Control Panel's Main Counter. Clicking the Sequence End button will give the same results.

Track Columns

Located below the Selection Bar are the Track Columns (see Figure 3.27), which allow you to manage track I/O assignments, MIDI patches, takes, track order, comments, and so on. Choose Mini-menu > Track List Preferences to show and hide specific columns within this list. You can even double-click on a column heading to open the Track Columns Setup preferences without resorting to the mini-menu. To change the order of the columns within the list, click and drag on a column name. The various columns and their associated controls are as follows (from left to right):

- **Move.** Click on the Move Handle of a track and drag up or down to change the position of a track within the Track List.
- **Loop.** A track's loop icon will be highlighted when a track contains a loop. Keep in mind that you can't click directly on a track's loop icon to insert a loop. Use the Region menu's Set Loop command or the Loop tool to loop a track. See Chapter 11 for an explanation of looping in Digital Performer.
- **Lock.** Click the Lock button to "lock" a track. Once locked, all data within a track will be locked to its current SMPTE frame location. Be aware that this feature does not prevent or "lock" data from being edited within a track.

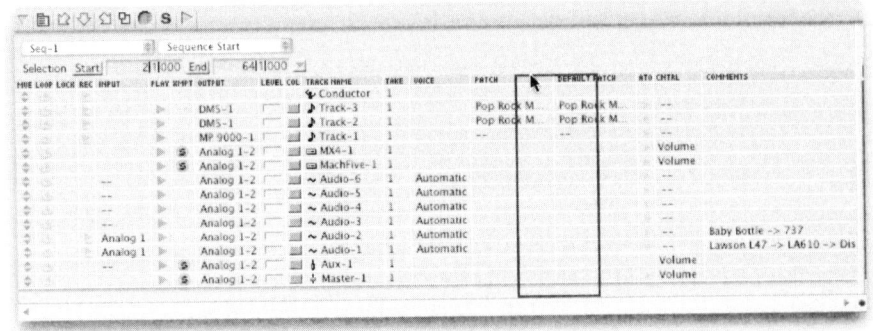

Figure 3.27
Track Columns display the settings for each track within a sequence. Click and drag the column heading to change the column order within the Track list.

Tracks Window

- **Record.** Click the record button to record-enable a track. Record-enabled tracks will be designated with a red record icon. An input and output assignment must be made before a track can be armed for recording.
- **Input.** This column provides the input assignment menu for each track.
- **Play.** Click the Play-Enable button to enable track playback. When the play icon is blue, tracks will play back. When it is dimmed, tracks will be muted. When in Solo mode, an orange state indicates the track is muted.
- **XMPT.** This is the Solo Exemption column. Enabling this feature will prevent a track from being muted when other tracks are soloed. This is especially handy for tracks that are usually never muted, like Aux and Master tracks.
- **Output.** This column provides the output assignment menu for each track.
- **Level.** These are activity meters that display the output level of a track.
- **Col.** Click on a track's Color column to change the color of a specific track. See Chapter 5, "Project Management: Part 1" for an explanation of Track colors.
- **Track Name.** This column displays the name of a track. Option-click the track name to rename a track.
- **Take.** Click on this column to access the Take menu for a track. See Chapter 7, "Recording Audio" for information on recording and managing alternate takes.
- **Voice.** The Voice column lets you manage the voicing assignments for a track (see Chapter 4 for new information).
- **Default Patch.** This MIDI-track-only feature determines what MIDI patch the track will always start with. This setting is saved with the project, allowing you to reopen a project and return to the correct sound or patch for a track.
- **Patch.** This is the "current" patch setting for the selected MIDI track. If a patch is not selected, the setting will be blank.
- **ATO.** This is the automation menu for each track. See Chapter 12, "Mixing" for an explanation of DP's track-automation features.
- **CNTRL.** This MIDI-track-only feature lets you choose controller data to overlay on top of existing data within a track.
- **Comments.** This column will display comments that have been entered within a track. To enter or change comments, simply click on a track's Comments column.

The Tracks Overview Section

The Tracks Overview section displays the audio and MIDI data for all available tracks, as shown in Figure 3.28. This is a global look at all the tracks within a sequence, including Conductor track data

Figure 3.28

The Track Overview section provides a global look at all audio and MIDI data within a sequence's tracks. Phrases of MIDI data are intuitively grouped into blocks. Data must first be selected before it can be edited.

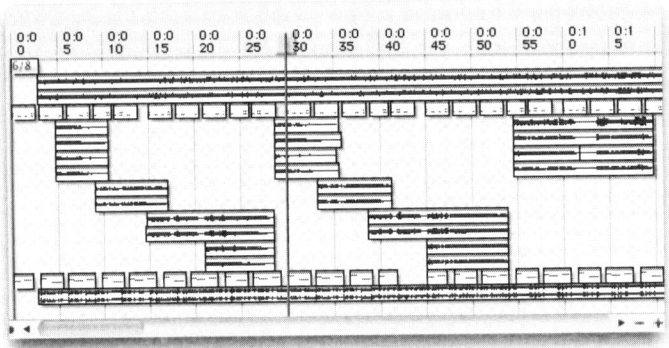

such as meter, tempo, and marker events. Within the Tracks Overview section of the Tracks window, you can view, select, make edits over entire sections of a sequence, or add and delete tracks from a project. Unlike other tracks however, the Conductor track cannot be deleted from a sequence. See Chapter 11 for an explanation of the Conductor track within Digital Performer.

MIDI and Audio Data

The Tracks Overview section displays MIDI and audio data in blocks. Phrases of MIDI data are intuitively grouped into blocks by Digital Performer's Dynamic Phrase Parsing feature. This feature looks at the amount of empty time between blocks, as well as density of the MIDI data. Within a MIDI block, notes are displayed as purple bars, while controller data appears as green bars. You can customize how MIDI data is phrased from the Tracks Overview section of the Preferences and Settings window (Digital Performer menu > Preferences and Settings) or by selecting the Tracks Overview Preferences in the Tracks window's mini-menu. See Chapter 5 for an explanation of the Tracks Overview preferences.

Audio soundbites appear as entire blocks that contain the waveform display of the audio data and are selected and edited as single objects. Although you can perform standard edits on audio tracks within the Tracks window, the edges of soundbites, however, cannot be trimmed in the Tracks Overview. Use the Sequence or Waveform Editor to trim the edges of soundbites in DP.

Time Rulers and Grids

The Time Ruler located directly above the Track Overview section is broken up into columns, or grids. By default, one grid column is equal to one measure of music. You can use the Zoom buttons (+ and –), located at the bottom right corner of the Tracks window, to change the resolution of the grid. If you wish to display other time formats within the Time Ruler, select Setup > Time Format and choose the appropriate options (see Figure 3.29). Unlike other editors within DP, the "grid" within the Tracks window cannot be disabled. It can be temporarily overridden by pressing the Command key.

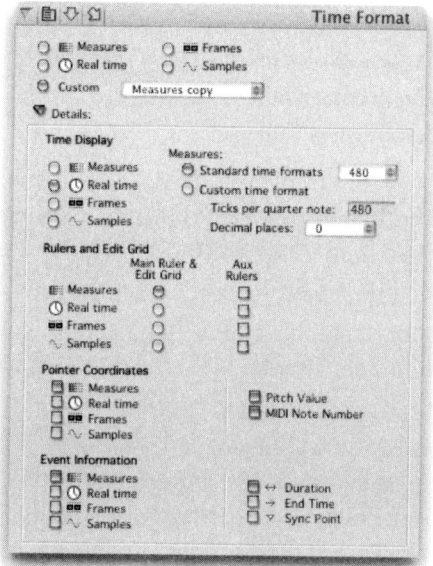

Figure 3.29
The Time Format window provides options for controlling the display of time formats within DP's various windows. Choose the Custom option to simultaneously show different time formats within a Time Ruler.

The Sequence Editor

The Sequence Editor is very similar to the Tracks window in that it displays audio and MIDI data, as well as Conductor track events (see Figure 3.30). Where it differs, however, is in its ability to display a project's QuickTime movie, show and hide specific tracks, display MIDI controller events, track automation data, and perform edits that are not constrained to a grid. This is a powerful, one-stop editing window for working with tracks in DP. Choose Project menu> Sequence Editor, or use the default keyboard shortcut Shift+S to open the Sequence Editor window.

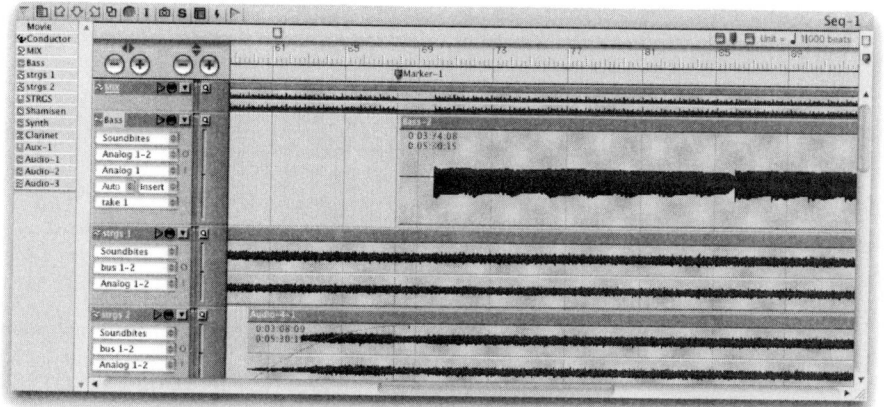

Figure 3.30
The Sequence Editor is a one-stop window for your track editing needs.

The Sequence Editor Title Bar

The Sequence Editor's title bar, shown in Figure 3.31, is similar to the Tracks window title bar, but with the following four additions:

Figure 3.31
The Sequence Editor title bar contains buttons for inserting soundbites, snapshot automation, showing and hiding tracks, and enabling automatic conversions.

* **Insert Soundbite**. This button (the I icon) inserts a selected soundbite at a specified location. See Chapter 10, "Editing," for an explanation of this feature.

* **Automation Snapshot**. Click this button (the camera icon) to take an automation snapshot. See Chapter 12, "Mixing," for an explanation of this process).

* **Track Selector**. This button will reveal or hide the Track Selector list (see Figure 3.32), from which you can choose to show or hide specific tracks within the Sequence Editor. Tracks that are showing will be highlighted in blue. You can click on a specific track or drag over multiple tracks to show and hide them. Option-clicking on the name of a track will hide all other tracks, while Command-clicking will reveal all tracks but the one you click on.

Figure 3.32
The Track Selector list allows you to show or hide specific tracks within an editor window.

* **Automatic Conversions**. This button (the lightning bolt icon) turns on/off automatic conversions with a project. See the "Importing Audio" section of Chapter 7 for an explanation of this feature.

Mini-Menu

The mini-menu provides various items and commands for controlling the Sequence Editor and accessing other important windows (see Figure 3.33). Some of these options have already been covered in the "Tracks Window" section of this chapter or are straightforward enough to not require an explanation. MIDI-related commands, such as the Continuous Data preferences, can be found in the "MIDI Editing" section of Chapter 10.

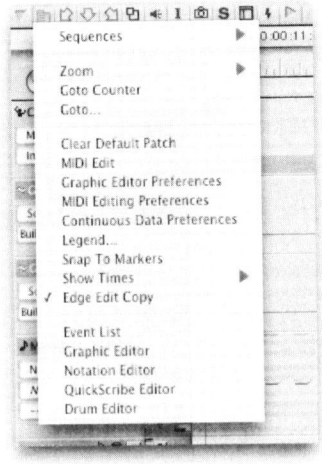

Figure 3.33
The Sequence Editor's mini-menu.

The items that are important or unique to the Sequence Editor are as follows:

* **Sequence.** This option is the same as the Tracks window's Sequence menu.
* **Snap to Markers.** Checking this option will force the edges of MIDI notes and audio soundbites to snap to a marker position when they are dragged near that marker.
* **Show Times.** This option will display the time stamp for soundbites within the Sequence Editor. Choose the appropriate format from the Show Times submenu.
* **Edge Edit Copy.** When enabled (checked), this feature will create a new soundbite when the edge of a soundbite is trimmed. This prevents the original soundbite from being modified, which is handy when you have multiple instances of the same soundbite within a track, but you only want to affect a single instance of that soundbite. Turning this feature off (unchecked) will cause the original soundbite (plus any instances of that soundbite) to be affected when trimmed. You can, however, Option-drag the edge of a soundbite to override the current Edge Edit Copy setting.

Track Information Panel

The Track information panel displays important information about a track, making it possible to complete the majority of your track management without having to return to the Tracks window. This panel varies slightly depending on whether you are working with an audio or MIDI track. The information panel for an audio track is shown in Figure 3.34.

Figure 3.34

The Sequence Editor's Audio Track Information panel

Many of these features—such as the Play/Mute and Record Enable buttons, the Take menu, automation settings, Lock, Solo Exempt, and Comments—are universal to other editors, and are covered in their respective chapters. The Track information panel's important and unique features are as follows (from top to bottom):

* **Track Type Icon/Color Selector.** This feature is located to the left of the track name. The track icon allows you to visually differentiate between track types. Clicking on this icon will also allow you to change the track color.
* **Track Name.** Click the name of a track to select it. Option-click to rename a track. Command+double-click to open the Mixing Board with only the selected track visible.
* **Track Settings menu.** This menu provides a list of all of a track's settings (see Figure 3.35). This is useful, as a track's

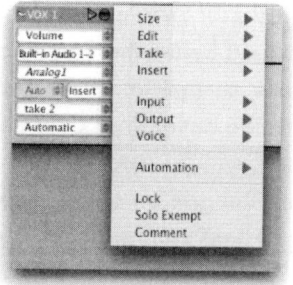

Figure 3.35

The Track Settings menu displays the track's various settings as a list.

size can be minimized to conceal all of the track settings contained within the Track information panel.

* **Waveform Vertical Zoom.** Located to the right of the Track Settings menu, this button (the magnifying glass icon) controls the vertical height of an audio track's waveform display, or a MIDI track's note data.

* **Active Layer.** This option allows you to choose the type of information or data that is displayed in the top layer of a track. Choosing Volume for an audio track, for example, will overlay volume automation data over the track's waveform display (which will be dimmed).

* **Insert menu.** This menu allows you to insert certain types of data into a track. See the "Automation" section of Chapter 11 for an explanation on inserting data within a track.

The track information panel for a MIDI track appears in Figure 3.36. Unique to a MIDI track's information panel are the following features:

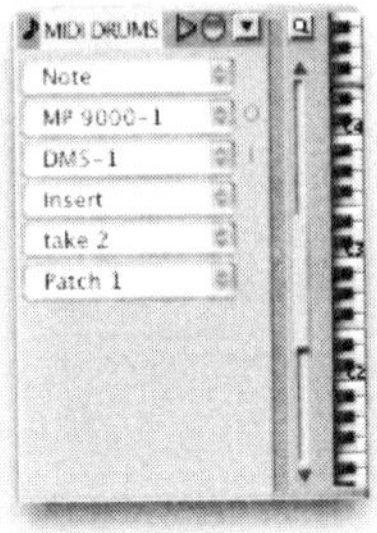

Figure 3.36
A MIDI track's information panel

* **Default Patch.** This button determines the MIDI patch that the track will always start with. You can clear this setting from the Tracks window's mini-menu.

* **Note Grid scroll bar.** Use this slider to scroll the Note grid up and down. The size of the slider is determined by the overall height of the MIDI track.

Graphic Editing

You can perform comprehensive graphic editing of audio and MIDI tracks in the area located to the right of each track's information panel. See Chapter 10 for a detailed look into the editing process.

Time Rulers, Grids, and Zooming

Like the Tracks window, the Sequence Editor can be configured to conform to a specific grid value. Any edits and selections made with the grid enabled will constrain the action(s) to the set grid resolution.

Event Information Bar and Edit Grid

The Information bar is located below the Sequence Editor's title bar. This strip displays information such as pointer coordinates, current selection, and edit grid resolutions. Located to the far right of the bar is the Edit Grid Resolution button and Grid Resolution setting. The current grid resolution is determined by the Unit indicator, which is represented by a note value. Click on the note icon to change the resolution grid. To turn the grid on or off, click the Edit Resolution button (to the right of the Unit indicator). In addition, grid lines can be enabled or disabled from the Sequence Editor's mini-menu.

Time Ruler
Below the Information bar is the Time Ruler, which consists of a "m[...]
of a sequence horizontally. The time formats that are displayed ar[...]
the Time Formats window (select Setup > Time Formats). Selecting [...]
to make time range selections across all visible tracks.

Zoom Buttons
Like the Tracks window, the Sequence Editor has zoom
controls built directly into the window. Located directly
above the Track information panel are four large zoom
buttons that control the vertical and horizontal zooming (see Figure 3.37). Click the plus and minus buttons

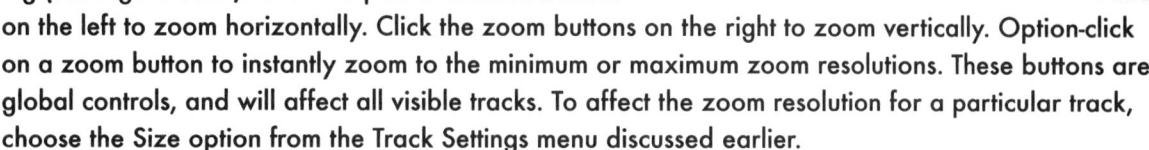
buttons.

on the left to zoom horizontally. Click the zoom buttons on the right to zoom vertically. Option-click
on a zoom button to instantly zoom to the minimum or maximum zoom resolutions. These buttons are
global controls, and will affect all visible tracks. To affect the zoom resolution for a particular track,
choose the Size option from the Track Settings menu discussed earlier.

The Mixing Board
The Mixing Board provides a comprehensive environment for mixing audio, MIDI, and virtual instrument tracks within Digital Performer. Modeled on traditional mixing consoles, the Mixing Board,
shown in Figure 3.38, also offers access to real-time plug-in inserts, sends, automation modes, and
helpful features for managing your mixes.

Figure 3.38

Digital Performer's Mixing Board offers a familiar environment for mixing audio and MIDI tracks.

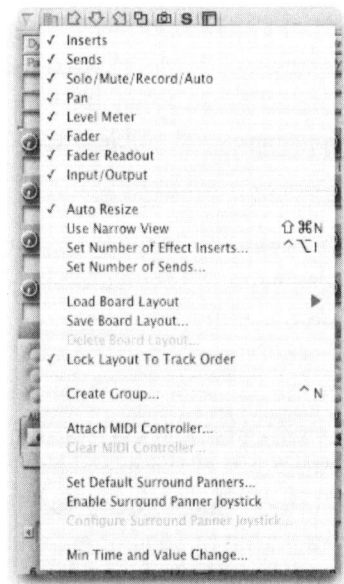

Figure 3.39

The Mixing Board's mini-menu provides options for managing track layouts, the number of effect inserts and sends, mix groups, and surround features within DP's mix window.

are
P.

chap-
ons.

mini-menu
re as fol-

...gs Show/Hide. The first section of the mini-menu (starting with Inserts and ending with the Input/Output settings) provides a list of mixer settings that can be shown (checked) or hidden (unchecked) from display within the Mixing Board. To show only one item while hiding all other items, Option-click with the mouse. Command-clicking an item will have the opposite effect, hiding one track and showing all the others. In order for this shortcut to work, be sure to press the Option or Command key before you access the mini-menu items.

- **Auto Resize.** When this option is checked, the Mixing Board will automatically resize itself when mix settings or tracks are shown or hidden.

- **Use Narrow View.** Turn this feature on to shrink tracks horizontally within the Mixing Board. This will allow you to display more tracks within the same amount of space.

- **Set Number of Effects Inserts.** Choose this option to set the number of inserts that will be displayed within the Mixing Board. The default number of effect inserts is five. A maximum number of 20 effect inserts per audio/aux track can be made available for mixing!

- **Set Number of Sends.** Choose this option to set the number of sends that will be displayed within the Mixing Board (see Figure 3.40). The default number of sends is four. A maximum number of 20 sends per audio/aux track are available in mono, stereo and surround formats.

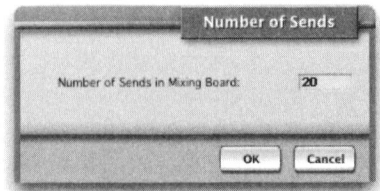

Figure 3.40

Use the Mixing Board mini-menu's Set Number of Sends option to specify the number of sends that will be available in a project.

- **Load/Save/Delete Board Layout.** These options are used to manage board layouts within the Mixing Board. See Chapter 12 for an explanation of these options.
- **Lock Layout to Board Order.** Checking this option will force the horizontal track order within the Mixing Board to adhere to the vertical track order within the Sequence Editor and Tracks window. Uncheck this option to make the track layout independent of these other windows.
- **Create Group.** This option will allow you to create track groups. See Chapter 12 for an explanation of track groups.
- **Attach/Clear MIDI Controller.** The attach feature lets you connect a fader or knob within the Mixing Board to a MIDI controller. Use the Clear option to remove the connection.
- **Set Default Surround Panners.** This option lets you set the surround panner plug-in that will be used when a surround track is first created. See Appendix D for information on surround mixing in Digital Performer.
- **Enable/Configure Surround Panner Joystick.** Use these features to enable and configure a standard USB joystick to control surround panner plug-ins within DP. See Appendix D for an explanation of these mini-menu options.
- **Min Time and Value Change.** This control sets the minimum amount of time between a volume or pan move that DP records when making changes with the volume faders and panners. You can use this to control the amount of data that is recorded when making automation moves for example. Using higher settings can reduce the amount of data, but may also introduce unwanted noise and artifacts.

Track Strips

The Track Strips within the Mixing Board, shown in Figure 3.41, are broken into sections that contain standard mixing options for inserting real-time plug-ins, controlling volume and panning, enabling automation, and so on. Audio and MIDI tracks differ in that MIDI tracks do not contain a Sends section. The various sections are as follows (from top to bottom):

- **Inserts.** Real-time audio and MIDI effects can be inserted by clicking on the Insert menus. Virtual Instrument plug-ins can also be inserted into Instrument tracks. See Chapter 12 and Chapter 9 for an explanation on this feature.

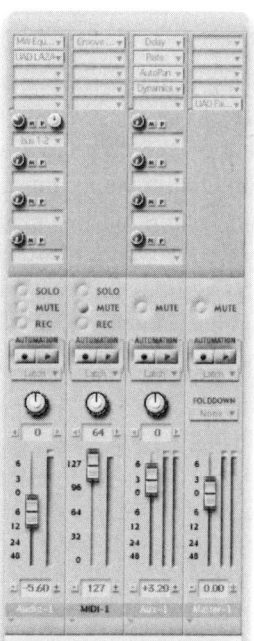

Figure 3.41
The Track Strips within the Mixing Board resemble traditional mixing console channel strips. MIDI and Master tracks do not contain a Sends section.

- **Sends.** Sends are used to "send," or route, signals from audio and aux tracks to additional sources within your system. See Chapter 12 for an explanation into this standard mixing feature.
- **Solo/Mute/Record.** Use these buttons to solo, mute, or record-enable a track. Instrument, aux, and master tracks only contain mute buttons.
- **Automation.** The Automation section provides buttons for turning on and record-enabling automation on a track. The different automation modes can be accessed from the automation menu. See Chapter 12 for an explanation into Digital Performer's automation features.
- **Pan Knob and Readout.** Click and drag a track's Pan knob to pan a track. You can also type a pan value directly into the Pan Readout field controls, or use the left and right arrow buttons, which will change the pan value by increments of 1 (see Chapter 12).
- **Volume and Metering.** The Volume slider controls the output (post hard disk) level of a signal, while the Level meters display the audio output level or MIDI velocities of a track. Like with the Pan Readout controls, you can use the Volume Readout section to make level adjustments to a track.
- **Input/Output menu.** These two menus display the current input and output assignments of a track. Click on each menu to access track I/O assignments without returning to the Tracks window or Sequence Editor. The I/O menu can be hidden from a channel strip altogether by unchecking it in the mini-menu.
- **Track Name.** Option-click to rename a track. You can change the track order within the Mix window by clicking and dragging on the name of a track. Double-clicking on a track name will launch an editor window for the track. This setting can be specified in DP's Preferences window (see Chapter 5).
- **Input/Output/Voicing Assignment menu.** Located directly below the track name, this menu can be accessed by clicking on the down arrow icon. Similar to the Input/Output menu, this menu lets you configure input, output, and voicing assignments without leaving the Mixing Board. Unlike the previous Input/Output menu, this menu cannot be hidden from the mini-menu, and it offers an additional option for solo exempting a track (see Figure 3.42).

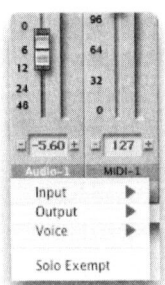

Figure 3.42

Hidden below the track name, the Input/Output/Voicing Assignment menu lets you configure I/O and voicing assignments without leaving the Mixing Board.

Soundbites Window

The Soundbites window allows you to view and manage soundbites within Digital Performer. This window is divided into three sections: List, Info, and Edit, as shown in Figure 3.43.

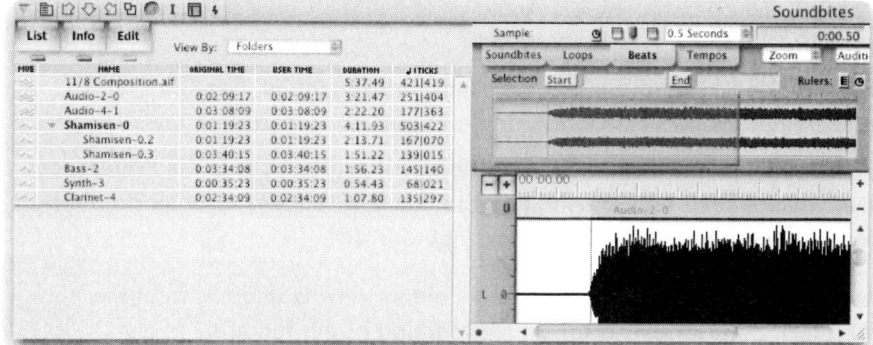

Figure 3.43
The Soundbites window.

The Soundbites Title Bar and Mini-Menu

The Soundbites title bar contains universal buttons for controlling viewing, auditioning, and conversion options (see the previous sections on the "Tracks Window" and "Sequence Editor").

The Soundbites window mini-menu's important options are explained below (starting from top to bottom). The mini-menu is shown in Figure 3.44.

* **New Soundfile.** This option creates a new empty audio file. Choose the file format (mono, stereo, and so on) from the New Soundfile submenu. Once created, the file will be 30 seconds long and will only contain silence. You can use this file for anything you like, from pasting audio data into it to using it like a "video slug."

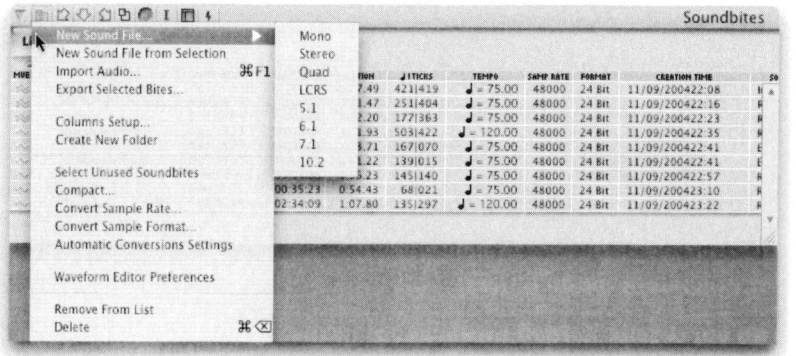

Figure 3.44
The Soundbites window mini-menu

CHAPTER 3 } Navigating Digital Performer

- **New Soundfile from Selection.** This option creates a new soundfile based on the audio selection within the Soundbites window Waveform Editor. Simply highlight a selection within the Waveform Editor and choose this command to create a new soundbite from the existing selection.
- **Import Audio.** This option will open the Import Audio window. See Chapter 7 for a detailed explanation of this feature.
- **Export Selected Bites.** Use this command to export a selected soundbite. See Chapter 13, "Processing and Mastering," for an explanation of the Export command.
- **Columns Setup.** Choose this option to open the Soundbite List preferences in the Preferences and Settings window, which allows you to configure the columns that are actually displayed within the List section of the Soundbites window (see Figure 3.45).
- **Create New Folder.** This option remains dimmed until Folders view is selected from the View By menu (explained later). See Chapter 6 for an explanation of this feature.
- **Select Unused Soundbites.** Use this command to select all the soundbites that are not being used in any tracks in any sequences within a project.
- **Compact.** This command will compact a selected audio file. See Chapter 6 for an explanation of the compacting process.
- **Convert Sample Rate and Sample Format.** Use these commands to convert a selected soundbite's sampling rate and bit depth. See Chapter 13 for more information on Sample Rate and Sample Format conversion. These options will remain dimmed until a soundbite is selected.

Figure 3.45
The Soundbite List preferences allow you to specify which columns to display in the List section of the Soundbites window.

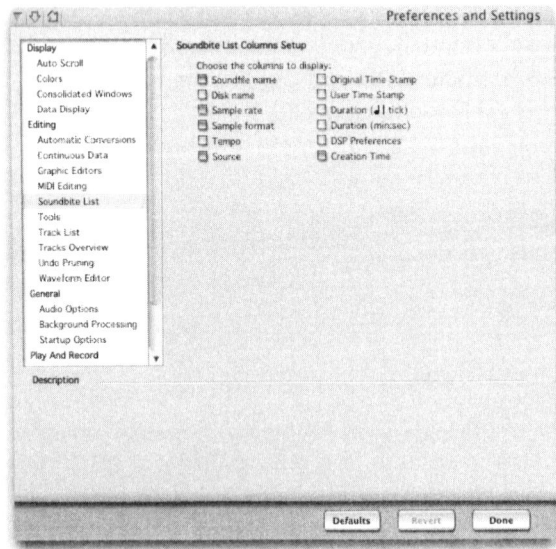

* **Automatic Conversions.** Select this option to open the Automatic Conversions window. See Chapter 7 for an explanation of the automatic conversions process.
* **Waveform Editor Preferences.** This option opens the Waveform Editor preferences, shown in Figure 3.46. The Waveform Editor preferences allow you to control the display of stereo audio waveforms, automatic crossfades, and stereo/mono conversion settings. See Chapter 13 for an explanation of the Waveform Editor and Waveform Editor preferences.

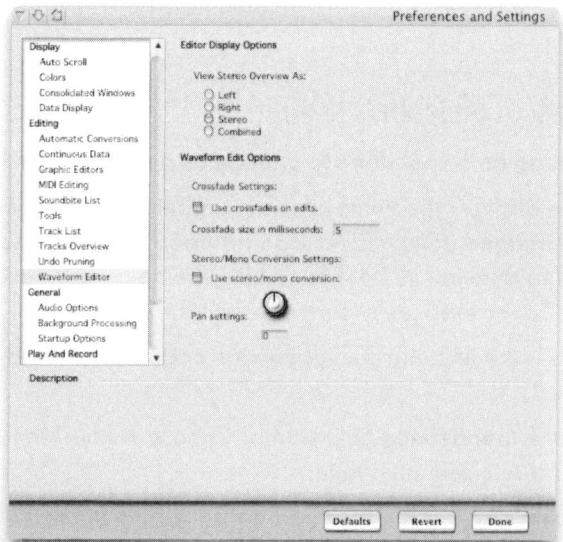

Figure 3.46
The Waveform Editor's preferences

* **Remove From List.** Use this option to remove selected soundbites from a project while leaving any corresponding regions intact (see the "Managing Audio Files and Soundbites" section of Chapter 6).
* **Delete.** This option removes selected soundbites from the Soundbites list, and also deletes any reference to its parent audio file. Parent audio files will not actually be deleted until the last referencing region is deleted (see the "Managing Audio Files and Soundbites" section of Chapter 6).

List

The Soundbites list displays a complete list of all soundbites that are in a project (see Figure 3.47). The List Columns provide detailed information on each soundbite and can be managed from the Soundbites window mini-menu (explained earlier), while the View By menu lets you sort the Soundbites list for easy viewing.

Figure 3.47
The Soundbites list displays detailed information of every soundbite contained within a project.

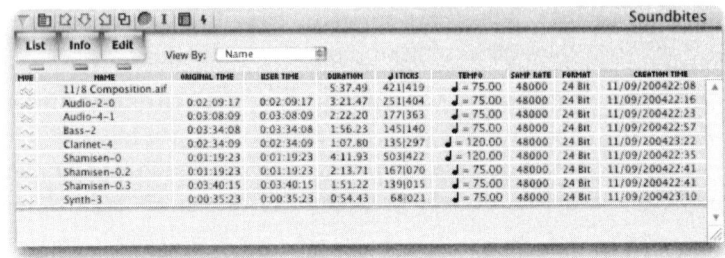

List Columns
The List columns are as follows (from left to right):

- **Move**. Click and drag on a soundbite to change its position in the list.
- **Name**. This column displays the name of the soundbite. Option-click to rename a soundbite. If Audible Mode is engaged (the speaker icon is turned on), then clicking on the name of soundbite will allow you to audition it. Double-clicking the name will open the soundbite in a separate Waveform Editor or third-party software editor.
- **Original Time**. This is the time the soundbite was originally created, often referred to as the *original time stamp*.
- **User Time**. This is the user-defined time stamp. Choose Audio Menu > Time Stamps to apply a user time stamp to a selected soundbite.
- **Duration**. This column displays the length of the soundbite in minutes, seconds, and milliseconds.
- **Ticks**. This column displays the length of a soundbite in quarter notes/ticks. The soundbite must have a defined tempo map or this column will be blank.
- **Tempo**. Shows the soundbite's tempo map. If the soundbite does not have a tempo map, then this column will be blank. To manually define the tempo map, choose Audio > Set Soundbite Tempo.
- **Sampling Rate**. Displays the soundbite's sampling rate.
- **Format**. Displays the sample format or bit depth of the soundbite.
- **Creation Time**. This column shows the date/time when the soundbite was created or imported into DP.
- **Source**. Offers a description of how the soundbite was created.
- **DSP**. This column shows how a soundbite's time scaling and transposing preferences are set (see Chapter 13 for an explanation of Pure DSP and transposition in Digital Performer).
- **File**. This is the audio file that the soundbite is referencing. Option-click to rename the audio file. Double-click on the file name to replace or relocate the soundbite.
- **Disk**. Displays the disk location of the soundbite.

※ Soundbites Window

View By Menu

The View By menu provides a menu that contains a list of sorting criteria (see Figure 3.48). Choose a specific criterion by which to sort the Soundbites List. Once sorted, the soundbites will be displayed with disclosure triangles that group soundbites into a specific hierarchy. Use this sorting feature to quickly find specific soundbites.

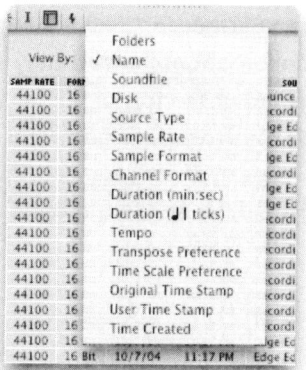

Figure 3.48
The View By menu allows you to sort the Soundbites List by specific criteria.

The Information Pane

The Information Pane, shown in Figure 3.49, displays important information about a selected soundbite. This pane is divided into three sections: the Sound File, Sound Bite, and Audio File panes.

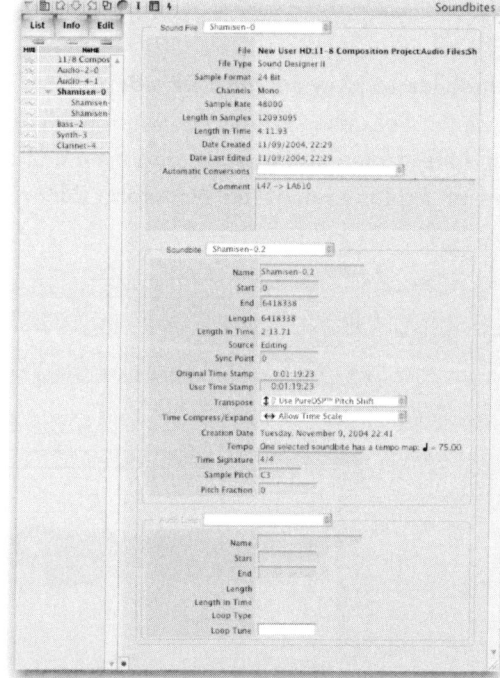

Figure 3.49
The Information Pane is divided into three sections that display important information on a selected soundbite.

The Sound File Information Pane

This first pane displays information on the soundbite's parent audio file. Click on the menu located at the top of this section to choose another parent audio file. You can use the Comments section to enter specific comments on the sound file. Comments are global, and will be important with the file when used in other Digital Performer projects.

CHAPTER 3 } Navigating Digital Performer

The Sound Bite Information Pane
This pane displays information about the currently selected soundbite. Like the Sound File Information pane, there is a menu located at the top of this section that will allow you to select other soundbites that exist within a project. The Transpose and Time Compression/Expansion menus allow you to set the preferences for their respective process (see Chapter 13 for information on Pure DSP and transposing a soundbite in DP) and the last two sample options are useful for exporting soundbites to a sampler.

The Audio Loop Information Pane
The Audio Loop Information pane allows you to view any loop points and settings that have been created by a sampler. If no settings exist, this section will be blank. These loop settings have no effect on the behavior of the file within DP.

Edit
The Edit section of the Soundbites window contains DP's destructive Waveform Editor, shown in Figure 3.50. As when editing in the Sequence Editor, this window allows you to zoom, make time range selections, create new soundbites from existing ones, and even edit out clicks and pops with the Pencil tool. See Chapter 13 for an explanation of the Waveform Editor.

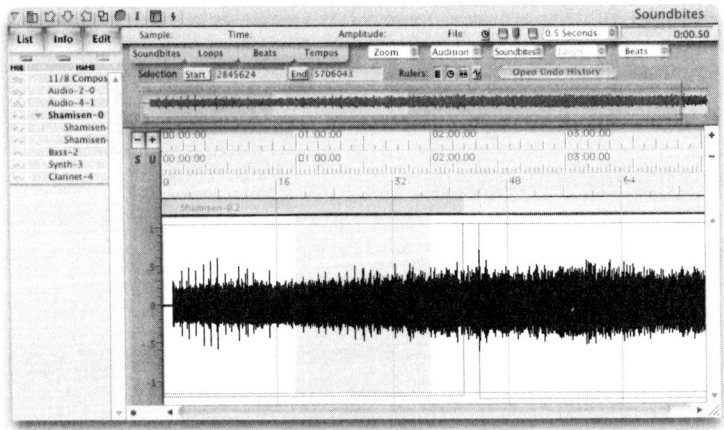

Figure 3.50

The Edit pane's Waveform Editor

Summary
This chapter has, I hope, provided you with a basic understanding of the way Digital Performer's main windows appear and function within DP. More detailed explanations of these and other DP features are covered throughout the various chapters and appendixes of this book.

# Setting Up a New Project

Now that we've discussed the optimization process for your Mac, installed Digital Performer, and connected and configured our audio and MIDI devices, we're ready to create a new project. Digital Performer offers a number of different ways to access its many comprehensive features: through the main application menus, various floating windows or consolidated window, and extensive keyboard shortcuts. Though this versatility allows you to really customize, it can be very overwhelming for the novice and even for the experienced DP user. Instead of bombarding you with every option and detailed function, this chapter will focus on helping you quickly and efficiently set up a project for recording.

The following topics are discussed in this chapter:

- How to create a new Digital Performer project.
- How to configure the project sampling rate and bit depth via the Control Panel.
- How to manage voices and busses with the Configure Studio Size window.
- How to add, delete, rename, and move audio and MIDI tracks.
- How to configure input and output routing assignments for audio and MIDI tracks.
- How to set up the tempo and meter for a project
- How to set up a click with internal and/or external MIDI sources.

CHAPTER 4 } Setting Up a New Project

Project Basics

Unlike some applications, Digital Performer will allow only one project to be open at a given time. A project must be closed before another one can be opened or created.

To create a new Digital Performer project:

1. Launch Digital Performer.
2. From the File menu, choose New. If you are prompted to open an existing project, click on the New button instead (see Figure 4.1). You can change the Startup options from the Preferences and Settings window (Digital Performer menu > Preferences). See Chapter 5 for an explanation of DP's Startup preferences.
3. In the Save As dialog, name your new project (see Figure 4.2).
4. Select the destination hard drive and folder for the new project file. If you wish to create a new folder for the project, click on the New Folder button. Name the folder and click OK.
5. Click on the Save button to save the new Digital Performer project.

Once saved, a new Digital Performer project folder will be created in the designated folder and hard drive. This project folder will contain your new project document and a folder called Audio Files (see Figure 4.3).

Figure 4.1

The Open Project dialog.

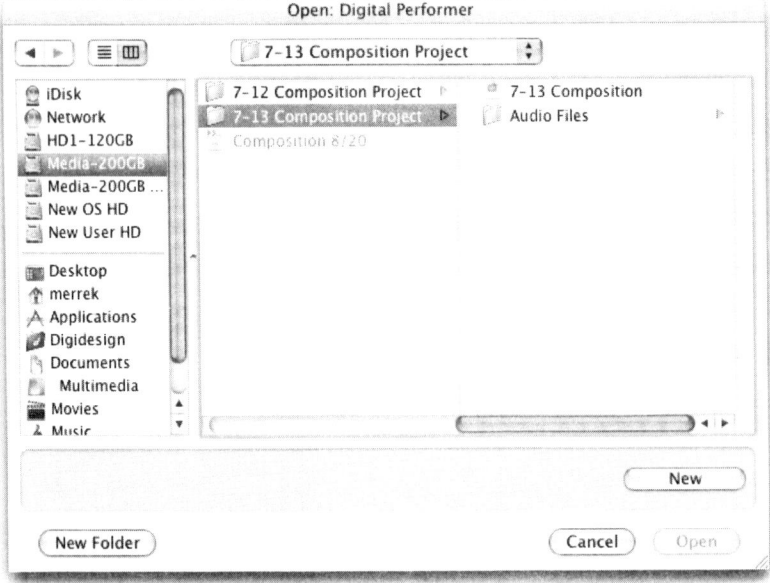

❋ Project Basics

Figure 4.2
The New Project dialog.

Figure 4.3
The Digital Performer Project folder.

> ❋ **PERIODICALLY SAVING YOUR PROJECT**
>
> Remember to periodically save your project (File > Save). How often you save really depends on your personal workflow habits. Keep in mind, however, when you experience a "crash" (the endless spinning beach-ball), any changes made to the project since your last save will be lost forever. If speed is a priority, try incorporating the default keyboard shortcut Command+S to save your project without the use of the mouse.

CHAPTER 4 } Setting Up a New Project

The Default Workspace

The default workspace within Digital Performer consists of two windows: the Control Panel and Tracks window. The Control Panel (see Figure 4.4) operates much like the standard transport of a multi-track recorder, with basic controls for playback, recording, and locating to specific points within your project. Buttons for customizing the project tempo and metronome, setting memory locate points, auto recording, and controlling sequences can also be found here. Positioned to the right of the main counter are the Control Panel drawers. Four individual drawers enable quick access to audio settings, tempo control, Pro Tools style-selection features, and shortcuts to frequently used windows. See Chapter 3 for a detailed look at Digital Performer's Control Panel.

Considered to be the "central" window by many DP users, the Tracks window (see Figure 4.5) is basically a container for viewing and editing all tracks within your project. Corresponding information, such as track name, I/O and voice assignments, playback level metering, Play and Record Enable buttons, as well as MIDI patch assignments, are located to the left of the window. Audio and MIDI data are stored to the right within the actual track. Any selections or edits made to audio or MIDI data in a track are conformed to a grid. The grid size is determined by the current viewing resolution of the Tracks window. Click on the plus or minus icons located at the bottom-right-hand corner of the Tracks window to change the grid resolution. See Chapter 3 for a detailed look into the Tracks window.

Figure 4.4
The Control Panel with visible drawers.

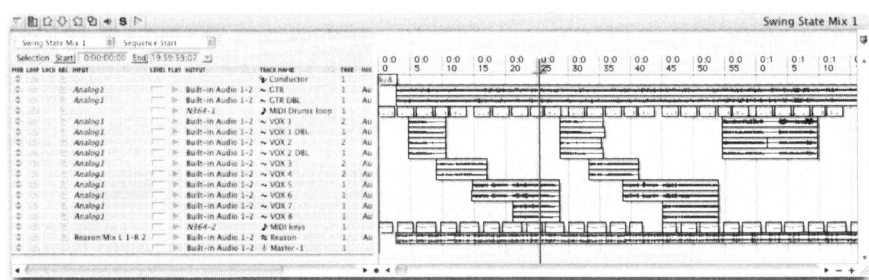

Figure 4.5
The Tracks window provides an overview of all tracks within a Digital Performer project.

> **CUSTOMIZING YOUR DP WORKSPACE**
> By default, Digital Performer adds blank MIDI and audio tracks to your new project. You can change this basic track configuration, along with any other default parameter, by creating and configuring a project to your liking, then saving the project as a template. Version 4.1 added support for multiple templates, allowing you to create templates for different project scenarios, which greatly reduced project setup time.

Setting the Sampling Rate and Bit Depth

Even though the sampling rate and bit depth were configured in Chapter 2, every new project you create will have its own specific setup needs and requirements. Just because you can record at 192kHz doesn't mean you should. Intended playback medium, the artist's budget, available hard drive space for the project, DAW performance issues—these are just some of the things you will need to take into consideration before your project begins. Careful planning in the early stages of a project will save you many headaches later in the production process.

To quickly change the sampling rate or bit depth of a project from the Control Panel:

1. Open the Audio drawer within the Control Panel. If the Audio drawer isn't visible, click on the small triangle located at the top right-hand corner of the Control Panel. Continue clicking on the triangle until the Audio drawer becomes visible (see Figure 4.6).
2. Click on the appropriate buttons to make the necessary changes.

Figure 4.6

The Control Panel's Audio drawer gives you quick access to the project's sampling rate, bit depth, audio clock, audio hardware, and Configure Studio Settings window.

> **CHANGING THE SAMPLING RATE OR BIT DEPTH WHEN AUDIO DATA ALREADY EXISTS WITHIN A PROJECT**
> The sampling rate and bit depth can be changed any time during a project, but be aware that audio files not matching the project's current sampling rate and bit depth will need to be converted before becoming available for playback. You can perform this procedure manually or configure DP to carry out the conversion automatically. Conversion options are located within the Soundbites and Preferences windows.

CHAPTER 4 } Setting Up a New Project

Tracks in Digital Performer

Tracks within Digital Performer (or any multi-track recorder or sequencer) are basically containers for storing audio and/or MIDI data. Different information is stored within different track types, and several methods can be employed to add audio and MIDI data to a DP project, including the following:

- Audio and MIDI data can be recorded directly to an audio or MIDI track.
- Audio and MIDI data can be loaded from another Digital Performer sequence.
- Audio can be imported from another source, such as a CD or hard drive.
- MIDI sequences can be opened from a standard MIDI file.
- MIDI data/events can be manually inserted within a track.

As tracks form the basic foundation of any multi-track recorder (digital or analog), familiarity with them will greatly enhance your music-production workflow, allowing you to move between various music applications and/or platforms with greater ease.

Deleting Tracks

As noted earlier, Digital Performer defaults to adding basic MIDI and audio tracks to newly created projects. If you would like to begin your project with a blank canvas, simply delete the existing tracks.

To delete an existing track or tracks:

1. Select the track you wish to delete by clicking on the name of the track within the Track window's Track Name column. To select multiple adjacent tracks, drag with the mouse. Shift-click to select multiple tracks that are not located next to each other.
2. Once your tracks are selected, choose Delete Tracks from the Project menu.

Adding Tracks

There are basically six types of tracks that can be created in Digital Performer (see Figure 4.7).

- MIDI tracks (see Chapter 8, "Recording MIDI," for more information).
- Instrument tracks (for use with virtual instrument plug-ins; see Chapter 9, "MIDI: Region Menu, Plug-ins and Virtual Instruments" for more information).
- Audio tracks (mono or stereo. See Chapter 7, "Recording Audio," for more information).
- Surround (multi-channel audio tracks; see Appendix D, "Surround and Digital Performer").
- Aux tracks (stereo-only auxiliary tracks; see Chapter 12, "Mixing").
- Master fader tracks (can be used to control a subgroup, or entire mix. See Chapter 13, "Processing and Mastering").

※ Tracks in Digital Performer

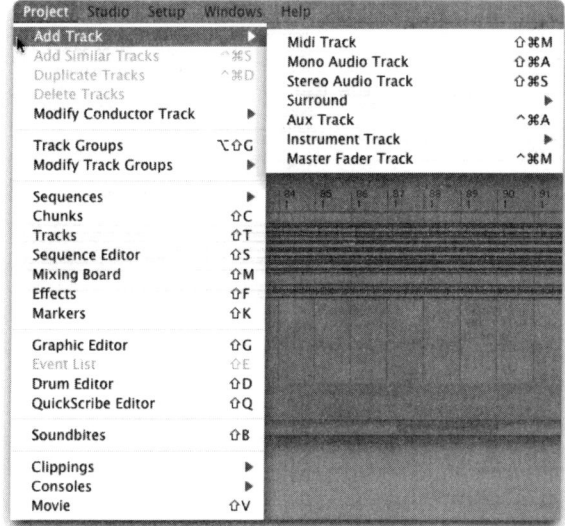

Figure 4.7
Tracks can be added from the Add Track submenu.

To add a track or tracks:

1. Select Project Menu > Add Track and choose the type of track you wish to create.
2. To add multiple tracks at once, press and hold the Option key before selecting Add Track from the Project menu. You'll notice the Add MIDI and Audio tracks commands now appear with the word *multiple* preceding them (such as Add Track > Multiple MIDI tracks). Once an Add Multiple Track command is selected, the Multiple Tracks options window will open.
3. Enter the number of tracks you wish to create in the pop-up window and click the OK button (see Figure 4.8).

Figure 4.8
The Multiple Tracks options window.

※ **ADDING MULTIPLE TRACKS**
Only multiple audio and MIDI tracks can be created with the Option key method. Surround, aux, instrument, and master fader tracks must be added individually.

69

CHAPTER 4 } Setting Up a New Project

Renaming Tracks

It's always a good idea to rename your tracks for easy identification. Audio files in particular benefit from this as, by default, their file names are based on their track names. Renaming your audio tracks before you begin recording can save you headaches and prevent your Soundbites window from filling up with files named Audio-1, Audio-2, Audio-3, and so on.

To rename a track:

1. Hold the Option key and click on the name of the track. The name will appear highlighted.
2. Type the desired name and press the Enter key to proceed to the next track.
3. Once all of your tracks are renamed, press the Return key to confirm the last change.

Moving Tracks

Once you have renamed your tracks, you may want to change their order within the Tracks window. Many engineers and producers like to categorize their tracks by specific groups or instruments. This is a matter of personal taste, of course, but keeping your tracks organized is another way to speed up your production workflow.

To move a track:

* By default, track move handles are located to the left of the Tracks window. They are represented by the up and down arrow icons within the MVE (Move) column.
* Click on the move handle icon and drag the track to a new location. A dotted outline will allow you to preview the new location for the track (see Figure 4.9).

Figure 4.9
Use the track move handles to change the track order.

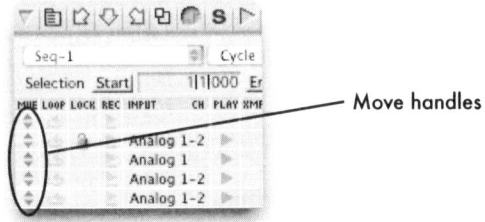

Move handles

> ❄ **TRACKS WINDOW COLUMNS**
>
> Tracks window columns can be shown or hidden from the Tracks List preferences by selecting Tracks window > Mini-menu > Track List Preferences, or by double-clicking directly on a Column heading. Unchecked items will not appear within the Tracks window (see Figure 4.10).
>
> To rearrange their order of appearance, click and drag the corresponding column heading to a new location. A dotted outline will allow you to preview the new location for the column.

Track Voices and Internal Busses

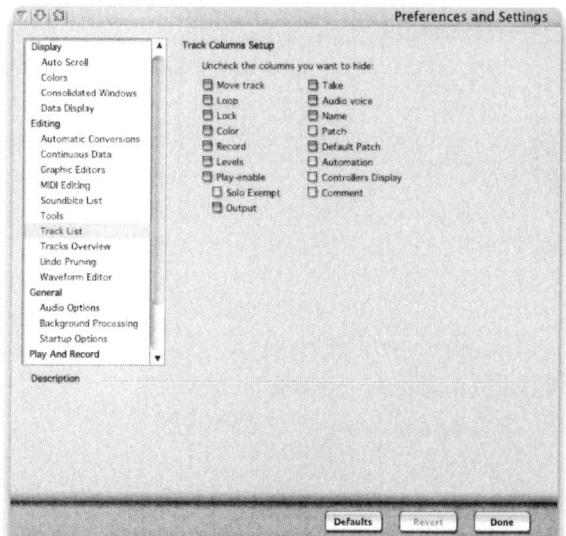

Figure 4.10
Use the Track List preferences to show or hide specific columns in the Tracks window.

Track Voices and Internal Busses

In Chapter 2, I explained how DP's built-in audio engine, the Motu Audio System (MAS), works to provide the digital audio capabilities (such as playback, recording, internal bussing, effects plug-ins, and so on) for Digital Performer. Similar to many other audio applications, DP uses audio engine resources called "voices." These voices are like channels that provide playback for your audio tracks. The number of available voices is determined by the speed of your computer, hard drive, and amount of available RAM. When DP is set to use MAS, a "voice" must be assigned to an audio track in order for it to play back from disk. By default, audio track voice assignments in a DP project are set to Automatic (explained later). Voices in Digital Performer determine the maximum number of audio tracks there are available for simultaneous playback. For example, if you wish to simultaneously play back four mono audio tracks, you will need to enable four mono or two stereo voices.

You can configure DP to support large numbers of voices, if your computer is fast enough to handle it, from the Configure Studio Size window (Setup menu > Configure Audio System > Configure Studio Size). Each audio track in a DP project must be manually assigned to a voice, or set to Automatic so they draw from a pool of available voices. First you need to enable the necessary mono or stereo voices in the Configure Studio Size window, shown in Figure 4.11. Keep in mind that tracks set to Automatic will ignore the separate mono and stereo voice settings, and simply pool the voices from the total number of available mono *and* stereo voices. Tracks manually assigned, however, will always adhere to individual mono and stereo voice settings.

Figure 4.11

The Studio Configuration window

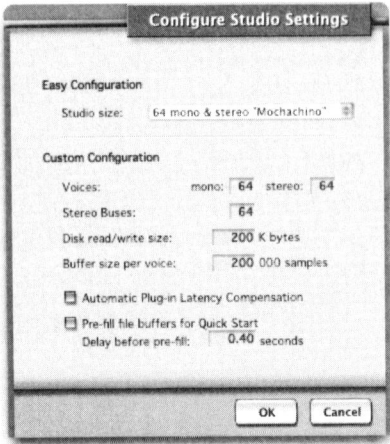

If you created an aux track(s) for your project, you must also make available the necessary number of internal busses. The Stereo Busses setting controls the total number of internal busses that are available within a project. Unlike audio tracks, aux tracks do not have voice assignments. See Chapter 2 for an in-depth look into the voicing and bussing options of the Configure Studio Size window. Be aware that MIDI tracks do not require voicing assignments, as they are only passing MIDI data.

To enable audio track voices or internal stereo busses:

1. Click on the Settings button within the Control Panel Audio drawer. You can also access the Configure Studio Settings window from the Setup Menu > Configure Audio System > Configure Studio Settings.
2. Within the Configure Studio Settings window, type in the desired number of stereo busses or voices. If a track's voice assignment is set to Automatic, then DP will ignore any distinctions between mono and stereo voices and draw from the total number of available voices. Be aware that DP will not present any warning messages when the number of tracks exceeds the number of available voices.
3. Once you have enabled the necessary voices and/or stereo busses, click the OK button.

> **EASY CONFIGURATION**
>
> The Easy Configuration section, shown in Figure 4.12, allows you to choose a preset number of voices and stereo busses from the Studio Size drop-down menu. Even though disk read/write and buffer sizes will be automatically calculated when a preset is selected, you still retain the ability to adjust their values manually. See Chapter 2 for details on optimizing the disk read/write settings for your specific Digital Performer system.

✤ Track Voices and Internal Busses

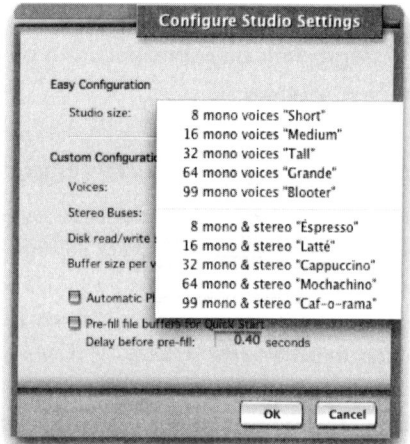

Figure 4.12

The Easy Configuration section of the Configure Studio Size window

To check the voice assignment for an audio track (from the Tracks window):

1. By default, audio tracks are given an assignment of Automatic. Voices set to Automatic will display a setting of *Automatic* in the Voice column of an audio track, as shown in Figure 4.13.

2. To manually change this assignment, click on the Voice column of the specific audio track. A pop-up menu will present you with three basic options.

    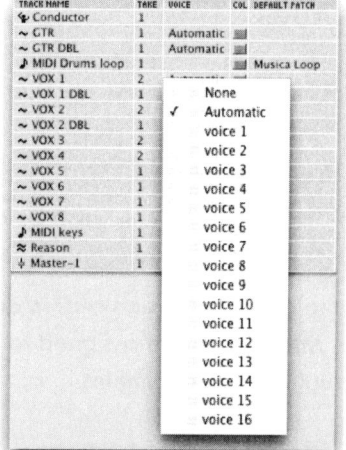

    Figure 4.13

    Click on an audio track's Voice menu to view or configure its current voice assignment.

    - **None.** Choose this option to unassign or "unregister" an audio track from a voice. Voices set to None will not play back and appear as a "—".

- **Voice 1, Voice 2, Voice 3…** Voices enabled in the Configure Studio Size window will appear in the Voice pop-up menu as individual voices. Click on a specific voice to make a manual voice assignment. When working with stereo audio tracks, individual stereo voices will appear with a letter "S" before the numeric value (Voice S1, Voice S2, Voice S3, and so on).

73

- **Automatic.** Voices set to Automatic will draw its voice assignment from the total number of enabled voices, disregarding any specific mono or stereo voice designations made in the Configure Studio Size window.

> **VOICE PRIORITY AND UNREGISTERED AUDIO TRACKS**
>
> When multiple audio tracks containing overlapping soundbites are assigned to the same voice, their voice priority is determined by their track position. Tracks that appear higher in the Tracks List take priority over lower tracks and will "steal" the voice assignments of these lower priority tracks. When you're working in the Mixing Board, tracks that appear to the leftmost of the window will have a higher voice priority. Tracks that become "unregistered," or temporarily lose their voice assignment, will not be available for playback or recording. In addition, Play-Enable buttons will disappear from unregistered tracks. Currently unregistered voice assignments will appear in italics, as shown in Figure 4.14.

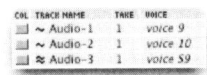

Figure 4.14
Voice assignments for unregistered tracks will appear in italics.

Input and Output Assignments

Besides being assigned to a voice, tracks must also be assigned or routed to the necessary inputs and outputs in order to record or play back audio and MIDI data.

Audio tracks are assigned to either the Mac's built-in audio or the inputs and outputs of a connected audio hardware interface. MIDI tracks are assigned to MIDI devices such as MIDI controllers, external sound modules, or virtual instrument plug-ins.

Audio and Aux Track I/O

Following are a few things to keep in mind when working with audio and aux tracks within Digital Performer:

- Audio and aux tracks cannot be assigned to multiple inputs or outputs.
- Aux tracks can be assigned only to internal busses.

To configure the I/O assignments for an audio or aux track:

1. Click on the track's Input or Output menu, located within the Input or Output columns of the Tracks window. Unassigned tracks will be designated with a dotted line, as shown in Figure 4.15.

※ Input and Output Assignments

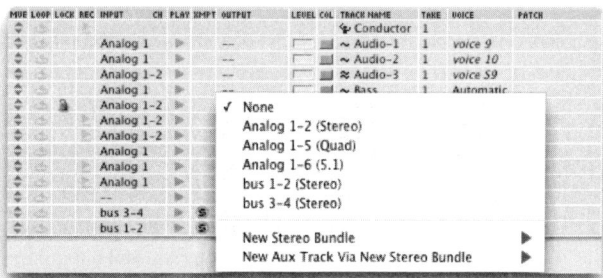

Figure 4.15

Tracks that are unassigned or set to None are designated with a dotted line. Enabled audio bundles will be listed directly below the None assignment.

2. Currently enabled inputs and outputs (also called audio bundles) will be listed below the None assignment. If the necessary audio bundles are not enabled, you will need to create a new bundle assignment from the New Mono or New Stereo Bundle drop-down menu. Here you will find a list of available hardware I/O and internal busses. (The default names for hardware I/O assignments are Analog 1, Analog 2, AES/EBU 1, AES/EBU 2, and so on.)
3. Make the necessary routing assignment by selecting the I/O destination with the mouse. Clicking again on the drop-down menu will reveal a check mark next to the track's current I/O assignment.
4. If you wish to change the current routing assignment of a track, simply click on the Input or Output menu and make a new selection.

> ※ **AUDIO BUNDLES**
>
> An audio bundle basically groups together a set of inputs, outputs, or internal busses. Bundles can be mono, stereo, or multi-channel I/O configurations. While you can create a bundle on the fly from within any assignment menu, the Audio Bundles window (Studio > Audio Bundles) provides you with a graphical interface that allows the creation, removal, and re-routing of I/O assignments between DP and any connected audio hardware interfaces (see Figure 4.16).
>
> When you're working with internal busses, only busses that have been made available from the Studio Configuration window (Setup > Configure Audio System > Configure Studio Size) will appear within the Audio Bundles window or in DP's various assignment menus. See Chapter 2 for a detailed look into the Audio Bundles window.

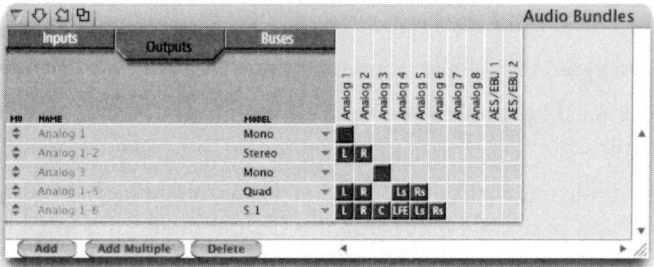

Figure 4.16

The Audio Bundles window with various audio bundle configurations

75

CHAPTER 4 } Setting Up a New Project

> **MAKING MULTIPLE I/O ASSIGNMENTS WITH THE AUDIO ASSIGNMENTS WINDOW**
>
> The Audio Assignments window (Studio > Audio Assignments) offers a convenient way to reassign the inputs, outputs, or voices for multiple tracks (see Figure 4.17).
>
> Begin by selecting the tracks you wish to affect by clicking on the name of the track, Shift-clicking to make multiple selections. Then open the Audio Assignments window (the default keyboard shortcut is Option+A). Make the appropriate reassignments and choose OK.
>
> Be aware that Audio Bundles must be enabled before they will become available within the appropriate Audio Assignment drop-down menus. See Chapter 7, "Recording Audio," for an in-depth look at the Audio Assignments window.

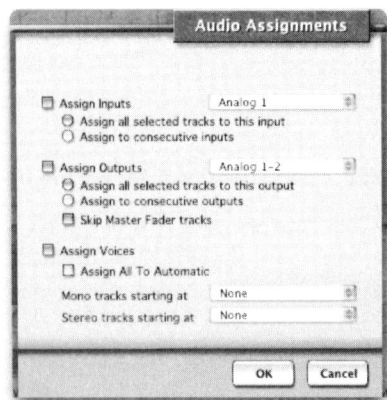

Figure 4.17
The Audio Assignments window lets you change the routing assignments of multiple tracks.

MIDI Track I/O

Following are a few things to keep in mind when working with MIDI tracks in Digital Performer:

- MIDI tracks can be assigned to either an external MIDI device or a virtual MIDI instrument.
- When you're working with MIDI tracks, only the output assignment needs to be configured if Multi Record mode is turned off. Turn Multi Record mode on from the Studio menu in order to specify input from a specific MIDI device.
- MIDI tracks can be assigned to multiple outputs through the use of MIDI device groups.
- An audio or aux track must be created to monitor external MIDI devices or Rewire synths within Digital Performer.
- Virtual AU or MAS instrument must be inserted in an instrument track before the virtual instrument plug-in's outputs will become available in the Output menu of a MIDI track.

※ Input and Output Assignments

※ Aux/audio tracks are not needed to monitor AU/MAS virtual instruments, as the audio output of the virtual instrument goes directly to the output of the associated instrument track.

※ By default (when Multi Record mode is turned off), DP will not allow you to change the input source of a MIDI track. When a MIDI track is record-enabled, it will receive MIDI data from any connected MIDI device and transmitting MIDI channel. If you do not need to record MIDI data from a specific source, you can skip this process.

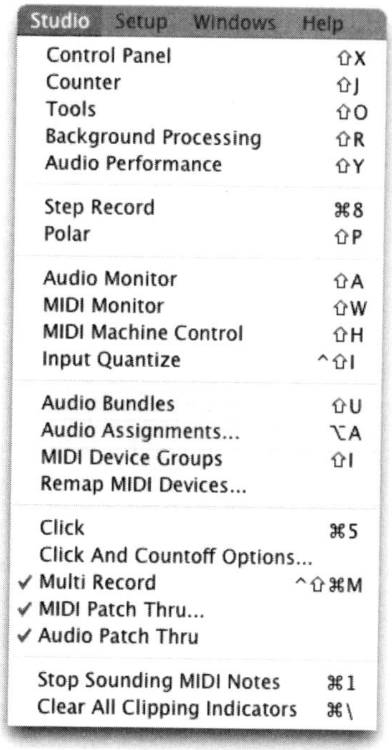

To set the input source for a MIDI track:

1. To record MIDI data from a specific MIDI device/channel, turn on Multi Record mode from the Studio menu. Once enabled, it will appear with a check mark, as shown in Figure 4.18.

2. Select the input source for the MIDI track. Only one MIDI device and MIDI channel can be specified for a track (see Figure 4.19).

Figure 4.18

Multi Record mode is enabled from the Studio menu and will appear with a check mark when enabled.

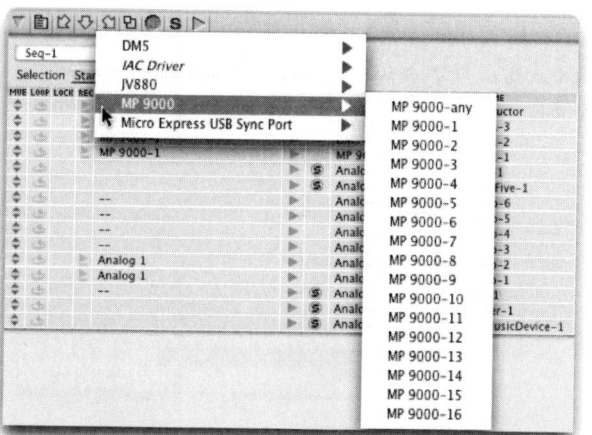

Figure 4.19

With Multi Record mode enabled, specific MIDI input sources can be assigned to a MIDI track.

To output MIDI data to an external MIDI device:

1. Click on the Output menu for the MIDI track in the Output column of the Tracks window. The default output for a MIDI track is MIDI channel 1 of your MIDI interface (see Figure 4.20).

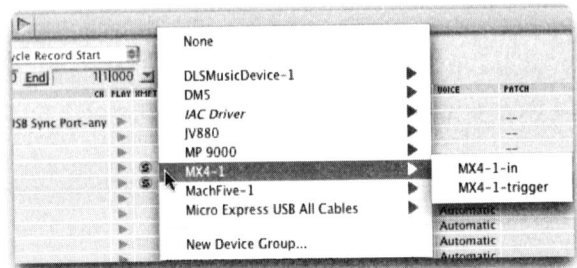

Figure 4.20
Configuring the output assignment for a MIDI track from the Output menu.

2. Connected external MIDI devices will be listed below the None assignment. Choose the appropriate device and MIDI channel. If the MIDI channel for a specific device is not listed, you will need to configure it from the Audio/MIDI Setup utility (Setup > Open Audio MIDI Setup). See Chapter 2 for a detailed look into this procedure.
3. If you wish to output your MIDI track to multiple MIDI devices, you will need to create a MIDI device group.

> **DEVICE GROUPS**
> MIDI device groups allow you to assign the output of a MIDI track to multiple MIDI channels and/or devices. A maximum of ten MIDI channels from any combination of devices can be used within a device group (see Figure 4.21).
>
> To output to a device group, select the device group from the MIDI track's Output menu. If you need to create a new device group, choose New Device Group and add the appropriate MIDI devices and/or MIDI channels. See Chapter 8 for a detailed look into the process of creating and editing MIDI device groups in Digital Performer.

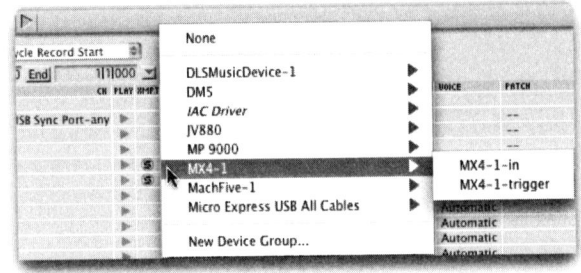

Figure 4.21
The Device Groups window lets you assign the output of a MIDI track to multiple MIDI channels/devices.

Monitoring External MIDI Devices

If you have the audio output of your MIDI instrument connected to an audio input of your audio hardware interface and you want to monitor the MIDI instrument in Digital Performer, you'll need to use an aux or audio track. The simplest setup, however, is through the use of aux tracks.

To monitor the audio output of an external MIDI device with an aux track:

1. Add an aux track (the default keyboard shortcut is Control + Command + A).
2. Assign the input of the aux track to the appropriate inputs of your connected audio hardware interface.
3. Confirm the output routing assignment of the track. The output should be assigned to the main outputs of your audio hardware interface in order for you to hear the audio through your studio monitors.

> **CONNECTING EXTERNAL MIDI DEVICES**
>
> For example, the physical outputs of my studio's MIDI piano are connected directly to analog inputs 1 and 2 of my MOTU 896 audio interface. In order to monitor this sound module, I would need to assign the input of the aux track to analog inputs 1 and 2.
>
> See Chapter 3 for additional info on the procedures for connecting external MIDI devices to your Digital Performer system.

> **MONITORING MIDI DEVICES WITH AN AUDIO TRACK**
>
> The setup procedures for monitoring an external MIDI device or virtual instrument with an audio track are similar to the procedures for monitoring with an aux track, but with a few exceptions.
>
> * Audio tracks must be record-enabled when monitoring.
> * The Input Monitoring mode (Setup > Configure Audio System > Input Monitoring Mode) must be set to Always Monitor the Inputs of Record Enabled Tracks or you will only be able to monitor the MIDI device/virtual instrument during the actual recording process (see Figure 4.22).

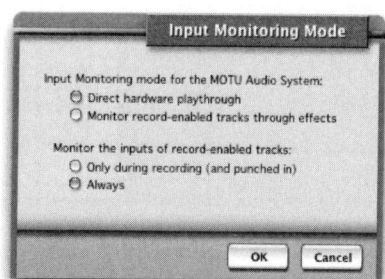

Figure 4.22

The Input Monitoring Mode window

CHAPTER 4 } Setting Up a New Project

> **THE PROS AND CONS OF MONITORING MIDI DEVICES AND INSTRUMENTS WITH AUDIO TRACKS**
>
> The advantage: When you are ready to record the output of the MIDI device or virtual instrument as audio, you simply start recording on the configured audio track.
>
> The disadvantage: You will not be able to record on another track while monitoring without actually recording the MIDI device in the process.

Monitoring MAS/AU Instruments

When working with AU or MAS virtual instruments, the new instrument track replaces the aux/audio track during the monitoring process. Keep in mind that you must first create an instrument track before the virtual instrument will become available within the Output menu of a MIDI track.

See Chapters 8 and 9 for an in-depth look into the process of working with virtual instruments and instrument tracks in Digital Performer.

To set up an AU or MAS virtual instrument track:

1. Begin by creating a new instrument track for the specific instrument. (Project menu > Add Track > Instrument Track > virtual instrument). Select Unassigned if you wish to create a blank instrument track.
2. Once the track is added, the virtual instrument will become available within the Output menu of any MIDI track (see Figure 4.23).
3. Assign the virtual instrument and its corresponding MIDI channel to the output of a MIDI track.

Figure 4.23
A MIDI track's Output menu with Motu's Mach-Five Universal Sampler plug-in

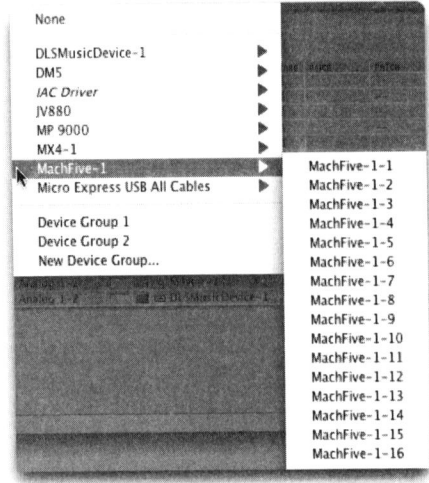

Input and Output Assignments

Monitoring Rewire Instruments

When working with Rewire virtual instruments, Digital Performer must be opened before launching the Rewire synth. Then you must create the necessary virtual instruments in the Rewire application before they will become published in the Output menu of DP's MIDI tracks. Once published, they will appear as a Reason bus. See Chapter 9 for a look into the process of working with Rewire virtual instruments within Digital Performer.

To set up a Rewire instrument within DP:

1. Start by launching Digital Performer.
2. Create an aux or audio track to monitor the Reason instrument and assign the audio input to any available Rewire output as shown in Figure 4.24. This is a crucial step since you must have at least one DP input assigned to a Rewire instrument output in order for the Rewire application to recognize DP as a valid audio output destination.
3. Launch the Rewire application and create the desired Rewire virtual instruments.
4. In Digital Performer, create a MIDI track and assign the MIDI output to the newly created Rewire instrument as shown in Figure 4.25. Once assigned, the MIDI track will send MIDI data from DP to the Rewire synth. Then the Rewire instrument will output its audio to the Digital Performer aux track we created and configured in step 2.

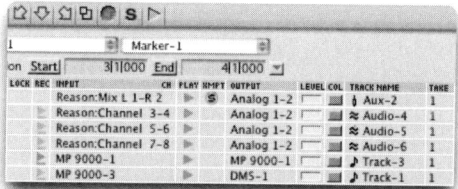

Figure 4.24

Digital Performer aux tracks that have been configured to monitor individual Rewire instruments.

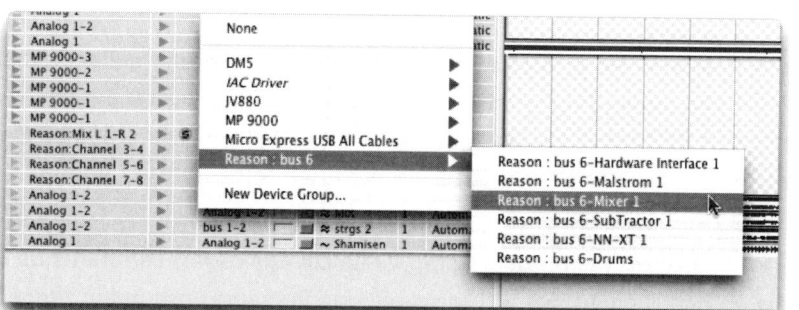

Figure 4.25

Propellerhead's Reason virtual instruments will appear as Reason busses within a MIDI track's Output menu.

CHAPTER 4 } Setting Up a New Project

> **INTERAPPLICATION MIDI**
>
> Many applications, such as Propellerhead's Reason, publish their own MIDI inputs and outputs that automatically appear within Digital Performer's assignment menus. There may be times, however, when you are working with programs (or older versions of programs) that do not have this capability. You can use Digital Performer's Interapplication MIDI feature to publish DP's MIDI inputs and outputs to these applications (see Figure 4.26). See Chapter 8 for an overview of the Interapplication MIDI window.

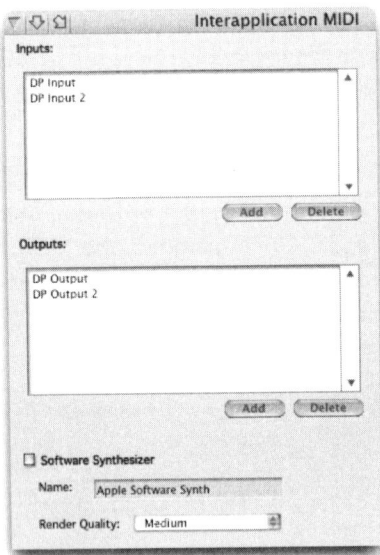

Figure 4.26
Digital Performer's Interapplication MIDI window

Tempo and Meter

Another integral part of any session is the proper setup of a project's tempo and meter. You can, of course, begin recording MIDI and audio data without worrying about this process. But you won't be able to take full of advantage of DP's non-linear editing capabilities, utilize the built-in metronome, make use of MIDI processes such as quantization, or properly output MIDI data within the QuickScribe Editor.

There are numerous ways of controlling tempo and meter within DP, but as this chapter is aimed at quickly getting your project up and running, we will focus only on the most basic setup procedures. See Chapter 11 for additional information on tempo and meter in Digital Performer.

✤ Tempo and Meter

Setting the Tempo

Digital Performer displays the currently enabled sequence's (Chunk's) tempo, tempo beat value, and meter within the metronome section of the Control Panel, shown in Figure 4.27. The Tempo Control drawer, shown in Figure 4.28, determines how tempo will be controlled, providing you with five different ways of controlling tempo, with the Tempo Slider being the most basic of these tempo sources.

To set the tempo with the Tempo slider:

1. Select the Tempo slider within the Control Panel's Tempo Control drawer. If the drawer isn't visible, open it by clicking on the Drawer button (the triangle icon) located at the top right corner of the Control Panel window as shown in Figure 4.29.
2. Adjust the tempo with the slider control. Dragging to the left will lower the tempo, while dragging to the right will increase it. You can also click on the + and - buttons to change the tempo in smaller increments, as shown in Figure 4.30.
3. If you need even further control over the actual beats per minute (BPM), you can type the desired tempo directly into the Control Panel's tempo box. Press the Return key to confirm the change.
4. Next you will need to set the beat value, which determines the note value the current tempo is based on. The default value is a quarter note. Click on the Beat Value pop-up menu to make a change (see Figure 4.31).

Figure 4.27

The Control Panel displays the tempo, tempo beat value, and meter for the currently enabled sequence.

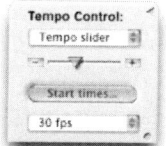

Figure 4.28

The Control Panel's Tempo Control drawer determines the tempo source and also provides quick access to the currently enabled Chunk's Start Time and frame rate.

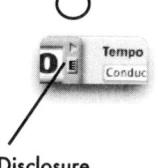

Disclosure triangle

Figure 4.29

Use the Drawer open button to show or hide the Control Panel drawers.

Figure 4.30

When the tempo control source is set to the Tempo Slider, you can use the slider, + or - buttons, as well as the Control Panel's tempo box to control tempo.

Figure 4.31

The Beat Value pop-up menu determines the note value on which the current tempo is based.

> ✤ **PROJECTS WITH A CONSTANT TEMPO**
>
> The Tempo slider can be used for sequences that have a constant tempo. As you are not working with a set tempo map, you are free to make changes to the tempo at anytime, even on the fly, without affecting playback. If your project requires tempo changes however, you will need to program the change and use another tempo source, such as the Conductor Track.

CHAPTER 4 } Setting Up a New Project

> ### THE CONDUCTOR TRACK
> The Conductor Track in Digital Performer, shown in Figure 4.32, is a container for tempo, meter, key change data, and markers. This information can be inserted directly into the Conductor Track and automated over time (this is how tempo ritards can be achieved within DP). See Chapter 11 for more information on the Conductor Track.

Figure 4.32
The Conductor Track contains tempo, meter, markers, and key change information.

Setting the Meter

Digital Performer sequences default to a meter of 4/4 (unless you are working with a Digital Performer template whose meter has been set to a different value). Like tempo, meter has a direct impact on event editing, click and countoff options, and the display of information within the QuickScribe Editor. Unlike the tempo slider, however, any meter changes made to a sequence must be programmed with the Change Meter command.

To set the meter of a sequence:

1. Open the Change Meter window by choosing Project Menu > Modify Conductor Track > Change Meter.

2. Enter the new meter by clicking and typing directly in the Change Meter To field (see Figure 4.33). You can also change the values by clicking and dragging up or down with the mouse.

3. Next, you will need to specify the measure start and end locations for the change. If you would like to change the meter for the entire project, enter a value of 1 in the From measure location box. In the To location section, click on the End of Sequence button.

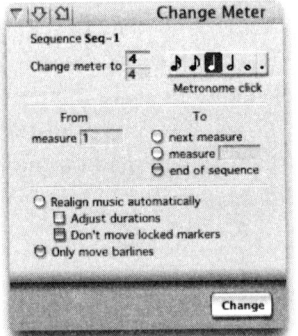

Figure 4.33
The Change Meter window

※ Setting Up a Click

4. In the Options section of the window, choose Only Move Barlines, which will leave any existing data within the sequence unaffected.
5. Once the meter parameters have been adjusted, click on the Change button to set the new meter for the sequence.
6. Close the window by clicking on the title bar's Close button.

Setting Up a Click

Recording audio and MIDI data to a click has many benefits. Besides giving the performer a stable timing reference, it also provides an easier recording and mixing environment for the audio engineer, allowing, for example, him or her to take advantage of bar/beat editing or quickly create time-based effects that are synced to a project's tempo, or achieve better results when working with Digital Performer's Beat Detection Engine (see Appendix A, "Beat Detection Engine").

Before you can successfully begin using a click within Digital Performer, you will need to configure it from the Click and Countoff preferences in the Preferences and Settings window.

To set up the click from the Click and Countoff preferences from the Preferences and Settings window:

1. Open the Click and Countoff preferences by double-clicking on the Metronome or Countoff buttons in the Control Panel as shown in Figure 4.34. You can also access the window by choosing Digital Performer menu > Preferences.

2. Select the Audition Click option to audition the current click settings. Once enabled, parameter changes made in this window will be updated in real time.

3. Choose the source of the click (see Figure 4.35).
   - The Internal Speaker option will generate a click sound from your computer's internal speaker.
   - The MIDI option will transmit a MIDI note (to a designated MIDI device/channel) for each click sound.
   - Selecting both options will produce click sounds from the Mac's internal speaker and designated MIDI device/channel.

Figure 4.34

Double-click on the Control Panel's Metronome or Countoff buttons to quickly open the Click and Countoff preferences located in the Preferences and Settings window.

CHAPTER 4 } Setting Up a New Project

Figure 4.35

Use the Click and Countoff preferences located in the Preferences and Settings window to configure Digital Performer's click.

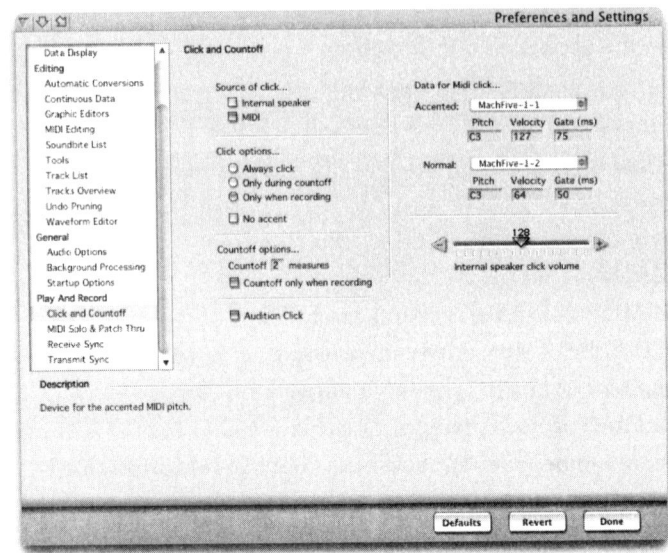

4. If you selected MIDI as the click source, you will need to specify the MIDI instrument that will be used to produce the Accented and Normal click sounds from the Data For MIDI Click section of the Click and Countoff preferences. If you selected Internal Speaker, you can proceed to Step 7.

   - The Accented click will be played on beat one of a measure.
   - The Normal click will be played on all other beats of a measure.

5. Choose the MIDI device and channel from the Accented and Normal pop-up menus. Devices within this list are determined by the Mac's Audio/MIDI Setup utility (AMS). See Chapter 2 for information on configuring MIDI devices with AMS.

6. Specify the Pitch, Velocity, and Gate values for the Accented and Normal click sounds.

   - **Pitch**. Determines the MIDI note that will be played when the click sounds. The "letter" represents the actual note within a scale, while the number represents the octave of the note. A pitch of C3 for example, represents middle C. Use the number sign (#) to designate a sharp, and the letter b to designate a flat.
   - **Velocity**. Sets the volume of the click sound. Values range from 0-127.
   - **Gate**. Determines the length of the note in milliseconds.

7. If you chose Internal Speaker, you can set the volume of the click with the Internal Speaker Click Volume slider (located below the Data For MIDI Click section). Keep in mind that the Mac's Sound Preference settings (Applications > System Preferences > Sound) will also affect the overall volume of Digital Performer's internal speaker click.
8. Next, specify when the click will sound with the Click options.
    - **Always click.** Forces the click to sound during countoff, recording, and playback.
    - **Only during countoff.** Forces the click to sound only during countoff measures. The click will stop once playback or recording actually begins.
    - **Only when recording.** Force the click to sound only during recording.
    - **No accent.** Eliminates the accent on beat one of a measure. This setting affects both the internal and MIDI click.
9. If you need a countoff for the click, specify the number of measures within the Countoff Options section by typing in the desired value. Selecting the Countoff Only During Recording option will force the click to countoff only before actual recording begins.
10. Save your project (File > Save)!
11. If you plan on reusing this specific project configuration, or want to base your future Digital Performer projects on the one you just created, then choose File > Save As Template. Name the project and click OK. (See Chapter 5 for details on creating Digital Performer templates).

Summary

Obviously, there may be other parameters or features specific to your project that you'll need to set up before recording or mixing. The steps and procedures provided in this chapter are meant to quickly get you up and running with Digital Performer. We'll dive into the details of DP's tools and enhanced feature sets within the other chapters of this book.

5 Project Management: Part 1

Project management is an extremely important, though sometimes overlooked, part of the music production process. Keeping audio files, multiple versions of a project, and your Digital Performer workspace organized requires careful planning and consideration, but it doesn't have to be an overwhelming task.

One of the common misconceptions about project management is that only serious professionals working on large projects need worry about it. On the contrary—even the smallest of projects and studio setups can benefit from some organization. Proper audio file management, for example, can provide a more stable operating environment for Digital Performer by preventing unneeded files from consuming precious disk space, which can negatively affect the performance of the Mac OS.

DP contains a number of features to help you manage the various aspects of your sessions, from customization of the Digital Performer workspace to the compacting and archiving of your projects. I've chosen to break up this complex topic into two chapters. Part 1 will discuss basic project management concepts, such as creating, saving, opening projects, and customizing your DP workspace. Part 2 (Chapter 6) will discuss the project Undo History window, audio file management, and backup solutions.

Here is a summary of topics discussed in this chapter:

- How to create, open, and save Digital Performer projects.
- The differences between Save and Save As.
- How to create and manage project templates.
- How to open and save Standard MIDI and OMFI files.
- How to customize the Digital Performer workspace.
- The Consolidated Window.

CHAPTER 5 } Project Management: Part 1

The Digital Performer Project

When you create a new Digital Performer project, a project file (document) is created and placed in the new project's folder. Within this document is contained all the information associated with the project, from track layout and window placement, to mix settings and recorded MIDI data. Everything that is needed to recreate the project is saved in this document, with the exception of audio files, audio file undo history information, fades, and analysis files. Soundbites (audio files/regions) in a DP project are only pointers that reference the actual audio files, which exist on a hard drive(s) within your system. This is why the project file is relatively small—the much larger audio files are not actually contained in the Digital Performer document.

As noted in Chapter 4, Digital Performer will allow only one project to be open at a given time (though an unlimited number of sequences, or Chunks can exist within a given project). You must close a project before you can open or create a new one. See Chapter 11 for a detailed look at Chunks within Digital Performer.

Creating a New Project

To create a new Digital Performer project:

1. Launch Digital Performer.
2. Choose File > New. If you are prompted to open an existing project, click on the New button instead.
3. In the Save As dialog, name your new project.
4. Select the destination hard drive and folder for the new project file. If you want to create a new folder for the project, click on the New Folder button. Name the folder and click OK.
5. Click on the Save button to save the new Digital Performer project.

When you save a new project, a new Digital Performer project folder will be created in the designated folder and hard drive. This project folder will contain your new project document and a folder called Audio Files. As your project progresses, separate folders for fades, undos, and analysis files will also be created (see Figure 5.1).

Figure 5.1
The Digital Performer Project folder

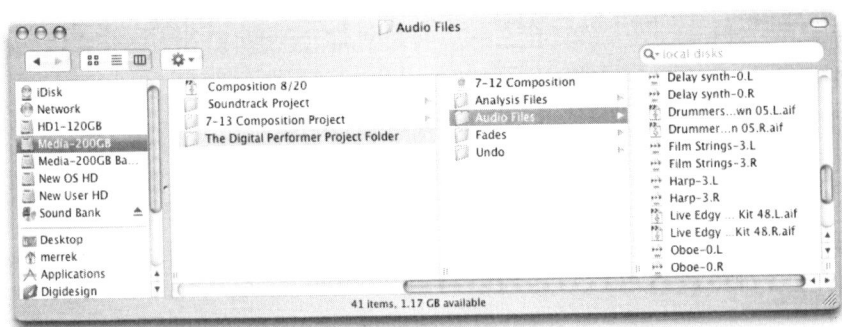

Opening an Existing Project

To open an existing Digital Performer Project from the File menu:

1. Launch Digital Performer.
2. Choose File > Open. The default keyboard shortcut is Command+O.
3. Choose the project file from the appropriate folder or hard drive and cl[ick]. [If an] unsaved project currently open, you will be prompted to save the file be[fore DP] opens the newly chosen one (see Figure 5.2). Choosing Don't Save will close the currently open project, discarding any changes made since your last save.

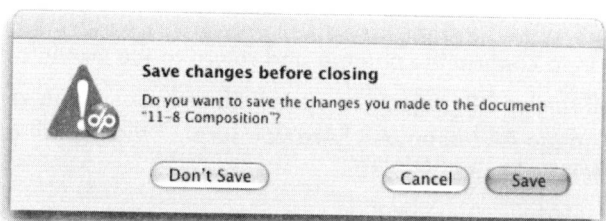

Figure 5.2

The Save changes before closing the dialog.

OTHER METHODS FOR OPENING A PROJECT

In addition to File > Open, there are two other methods for opening a Digital Performer project.

- **Drag and Drop.** Drag the Digital Performer project you wish to open directly onto the DP application icon. This method will also work when the application icon resides in the Dock.
- **Double-Clicking.** Double-click the Digital Performer document icon you wish to open. If DP is not currently running, this method will launch the program before opening the project file.

WORKING WITH MULTIPLE VERSIONS OF DP

If you have multiple versions of Digital Performer installed within your system (perhaps you are a developer), you may have experienced instances in which DP opened a project in the "wrong" version of the application when you used the double-click method. You can remedy this problem and force a file to open within a specific version of DP with the Finder's Get Info command (see Figure 5.3).

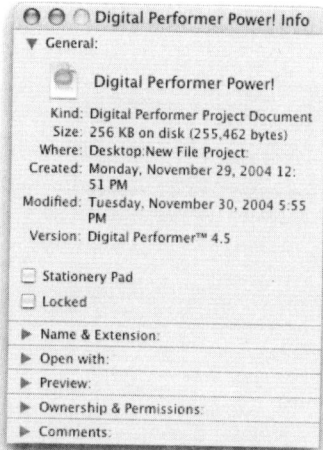

Figure 5.3

The Finder's Get Info command

a specific version of Digital Performer:

rmer project icon by clicking on it. Don't double-click or you will accidentally open the program and open the selected project.

From the File menu, choose Get Info. The default keyboard shortcut is Command+I.

Open the Open With section pane of the Get Info window.

Click on the With pop-up menu and choose Other. The Choose Other Application dialog will open (see Figure 5.4).

5. Select the specific version of the Digital Performer application in which you would like the file to open.
6. Click the Add button to confirm the change and return to the Get Info window.
7. If you would like all similar DP projects to open with the application version you just selected, then click on the Change All button. An "Are you sure..." dialog will open asking you to cancel or continue with the change.
8. Close the Get Info window.
9. Now, when you double-click on the project file, it will open in the designated version of DP.

Figure 5.4

The Choose Other Application dialog

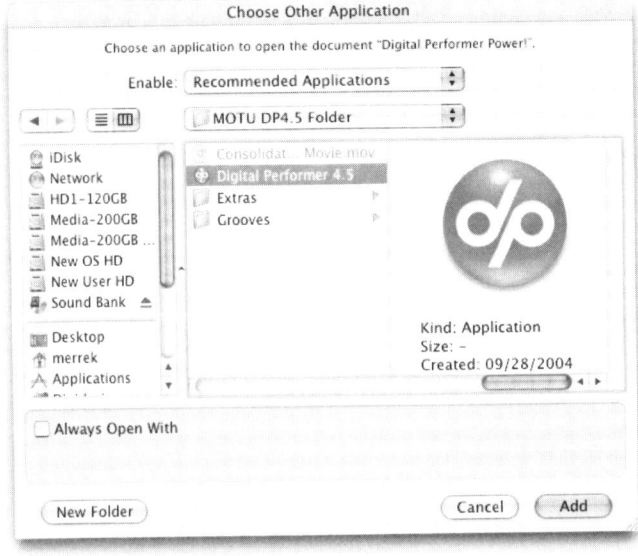

Opening Other File Types

Digital Performer can also open the following types of files created in earlier versions of DP, Performer, or other supported applications:

- Projects created in earlier versions of Digital Performer and Performer
- Projects created in Audio Desk
- Professional Composer files
- Standard MIDI files
- OMFI files

Once opened, the file will be converted to a Digital Performer file. Choose the Save As command to export a file back into its original format. Standard MIDI and OMF files are discussed in further detail later in this chapter.

Saving Your Project

Save! Save! Save! Why do we need to save? And why do we lose precious changes that haven't been saved, for example, when a program crashes? The answer is simple. When a project file is opened, it is loaded into RAM. So you are actually working on a copy of the project and not the original file, which is stored on your hard drive. Until you save, any modifications or changes you make to a file exist only in RAM and are not updated in the original document.

If you would like to save a different version of your project or export it into a different file format, you'll need to choose the Save As command.

The Save Command

To save a Digital Performer project:

1. From Digital Performer's File menu, choose Save. The universal keyboard shortcut for saving on a Mac is Command+S.
2. If you are saving a project for the first time, you will be prompted to name the file before saving.

The Save As Command

The Save As command (File > Save as) has multiple uses, including the following:

- Creating an alternate version of a project with a different file name.
- Exporting a project in a different file format.
- Saving to create a backup or duplicate copy of a project.

To save an alternate version of a project:

1. Choose Save As from Digital Performer's File menu.
2. Name the project. Try to choose a descriptive name, or devise a specific naming scheme to keep your alternate project files organized.
3. If you need to make duplicate copies of your project audio files to include with this alternate version, click the Duplicate Audio Files option.
4. Select the destination for the new version and click OK.
5. Once saved, DP will automatically save and close the original file, and you will be working on the new (alternate) version of the project.

> **SAVING A COPY AS...**
>
> If you would like to save an alternate version of a project but continue working on the current version, use the Save A Copy As command (File > Save A Copy As). Be aware that unlike the normal Save As command, Saving a Copy As will not automatically save the project you're currently working with. You will need to manually save to preserve any changes you have made since your last save.

> **BEWARE WHEN USING THE SAVE AS COMMAND**
>
> Many users find out the hard way: a new and separate Audio Files folder is not created when using the Save As command, unless you enable the Duplicate Audio Data option. When this option is left unchecked, any alternate versions of a project you create will still refer to the original Audio Files, Fades, Analysis, and Undo folders. If you delete an audio file in one version of a project, for example, it will disappear from any and all alternate versions that may have been created with the standard Save As command.
>
> If you like to keep the alternate versions of a project organized by removing unused audio files from the Soundbites window, be sure to use the Remove from list command (Soundbites Window > Mini-menu > Remove from list). This will remove the audio from the specific document's Soundbites window without actually deleting the regions (soundbites) associated with the original audio files.

✳ Saving Your Project

To export your project in a different file format:

1. Choose Save As from Digital Performer's File menu.
2. Name the project.
3. Choose the destination folder and/or hard drive for the file.
4. Select the new format from the Format pop-up menu shown in Figure 5.5.

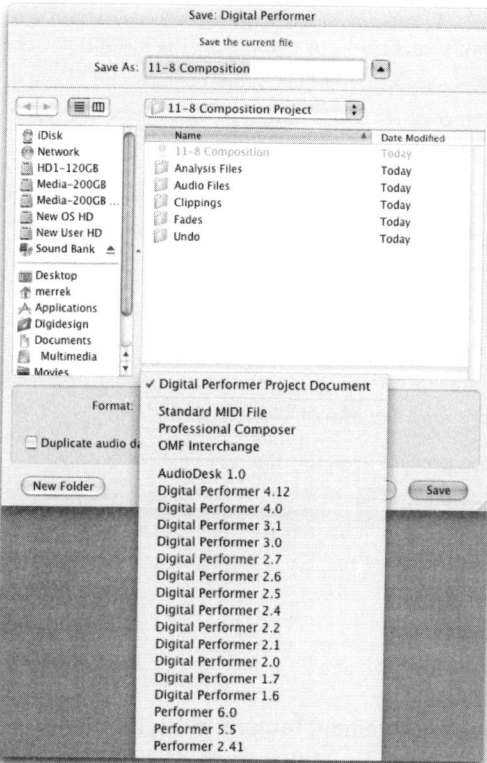

Figure 5.5

The Save As dialog with supported file format options.

> **WORKING WITH PREVIOUS VERSIONS OF DP**
>
> Digital Performer projects are not backwards-compatible with earlier versions. You cannot, for example, open a project created in DP 4.1 in Version 4.0. If you need to open a project in an earlier version of Digital Performer (perhaps you are collaborating with another musician who has an older version of DP), then use the Save As command to export to the appropriate format.

CHAPTER 5 } Project Management: Part 1

ENSURING COMPATIBILITY

Be aware that certain features, such as instrument tracks, may not be successfully exported to previous versions. For example, exporting a DP 4.1 project containing an instrument track to an older version will result in the instrument track appearing as an empty aux track.

Here are a few suggestions for ensuring compatibility with older versions of Digital Performer and/or differently configured systems:

- Print any existing instrument tracks as audio files. The method you choose (Freeze Tracks, Bounce to Disk, real-time audio bounce, and so on) will depend on your particular setup and workflow. Each feature is discussed in detail in upcoming chapters of this book.

- If you are supplying a project for another musician to perform overdubs (and not mix) for example, you may be able to get away with bouncing the entire project to disk as a stereo file.

- Find out what audio interface the other DP user is working with. Can his system handle your project's sampling rate, track, and plug-in count? If the answer is no, you may be forced to bounce to disk, remove effects plug-ins, or convert the project's sampling rate and/or bit-depth.

- Remember it's smart practice to supply the other user with only what he needs. Don't rely on him to "figure it out" when he receives your project! Besides being courteous, you'll be able to retain more control over how the project will return to you when the user's work is completed.

Save As Template

A much-overlooked project management feature in Digital Performer is the project template. If you constantly find yourself devoting a lot of time to setting up your projects, creating new tracks, renaming those tracks, making specific I/O assignments, arranging the workspace, and so on, you may want to incorporate templates into your production workflow. Though this handy feature has existed in previous versions of DP, Version 4.1 added the ability to save multiple project templates with the new and refined Save As Template command (File > Save As Template).

Saving a Template

You can create templates tailored to accommodate your specific recording, mixing, and/or composition needs. Prepare them ahead of time, or save them as your projects are created.

To create a project template with the Save As Template command:

1. Begin by setting up your Digital Performer project. This may entail adding and renaming specific tracks, configuring specific audio bundles, setting up the Mixing Board with effects plug-ins inserted on your tracks, and so on.
2. Once you have configured your project, choose Save As Template (File > Save As Template).
3. Name the template (see Figure 5.6). Try to choose a descriptive name to help you easily identify the nature of the template.
4. If you would like the template to become the default template, select the Use As Default New Template option.
5. Click OK to save the template.
6. Once saved, the template will appear in the File Menu > New submenu, as shown in Figure 5.7.

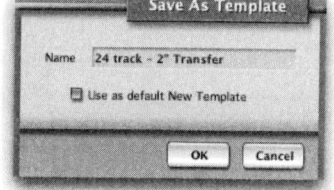

Figure 5.6

The Save As Template window.

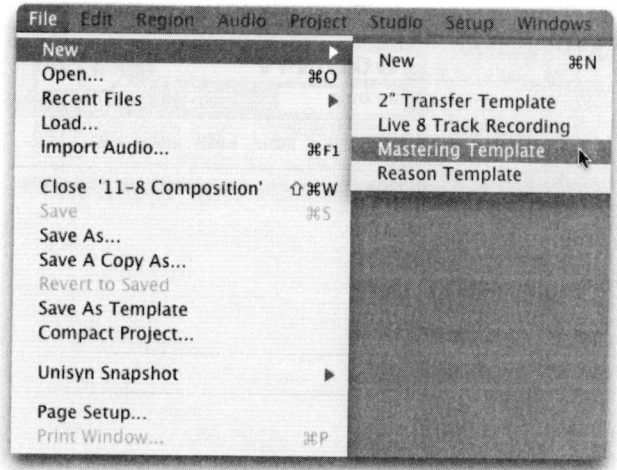

Figure 5.7

The New submenu. Descriptive naming schemes allow for easy identification of project templates.

CHAPTER 5 } Project Management: Part I

PREVENTING A TEMPLATE IN PREVIOUS VERSIONS FROM BEING OVERWRITTEN

The greatest benefit to DP's New Template submenu is that you cannot accidentally overwrite a project template. When you choose a template as the basis for a new project, you are not actually using the original project used to create the template; you are simply creating a new project based on the selected template.

When working with versions prior to DP 4.1, you are limited to the creation of one template with the Save As New Template command. To work around this restriction, you can use a normal DP project and choose Save As to create a pseudo template from which to build other projects on. In this scenario however, it is very easy to accidentally overwrite your makeshift template, or even worse, create "new" projects that share the same Audio Files folder!

Thankfully, there is an easy way to prevent a project from being overwritten, and believe it or not, it is a standard feature of the Mac OS—see the next set of steps.

To prevent a Digital Performer project from being overwritten:

1. Select the project's document icon by clicking on it. Be careful not to double-click on the document or you will accidentally open the project.
2. From the Finder's File menu, choose the Get Info command. The default keyboard shortcut is Command+I.
3. Click to show the General section pane of the Get Info window, shown in Figure 5.8.
4. Select the Stationery Pad option.
5. Close the Get Info window.

Figure 5.8

The General section pane of the Get Info window.

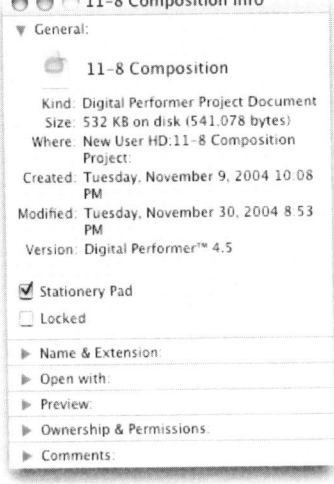

※ Saving Your Project

6. Now when you try to save this project, you will be forced to Save As, creating a new project (with its own audio files folder) that is entirely independent from the original "template" (see Figure 5.9).

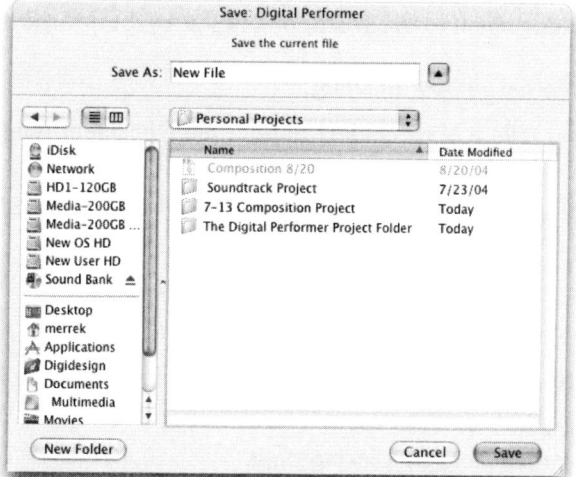

Figure 5.9
When attempting to save a project with the Stationery Pad feature enabled, you will be forced to Save As, ensuring the file is not overwritten.

DON'T DOUBLE-CLICK TO OPEN A PROJECT TEMPLATE
Be sure to use Digital Performer's Open command (File > Open) when opening a project (or pseudo template) protected with the Finder's Stationery Pad feature. If you use the double-click method, only a copy of the original file will be created and opened. This "copy" will be created in the project folder of the protected document, and more importantly, will share the Audio Files folder of the original project!

Deleting, Moving, and Renaming Templates
Digital Performer templates are stored in the User > Library > Preferences > Digital Performer > Document Templates folder (see Figure 5.10). Once a template is created in DP, it can be managed only from the Finder Menu. DP will automatically update to reflect any changes made to the Document Templates folder.

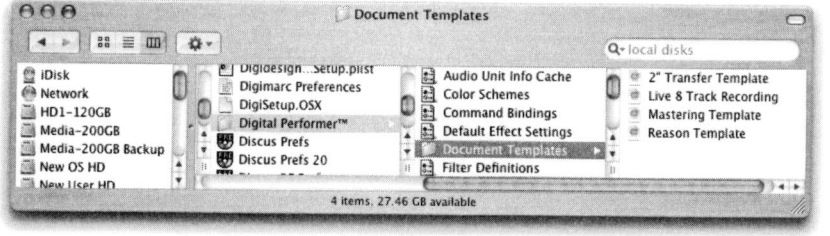

Figure 5.10
DP templates are stored in the Document templates folder.

99

CHAPTER 5 } Project Management: Part 1

To delete a project template:

1. Navigate to the User > Library > Preferences > Digital Performer > Document Templates folder.
2. Drag the template document to the Trash, or use the keyboard shortcut Command+Delete.

To remove the project template without deleting it:

1. Create a new folder (File > New Folder) outside the Document Templates folder in a location of your choosing.
2. Navigate to the User > Library > Preferences > Digital Performer > Document Templates folder.
3. Drag the template document to the folder you created in Step 1.

To rename a project template:

1. Navigate to the User > Library > Preferences > Digital Performer > Document Templates folder.
2. Select the document template by clicking on it.
3. Click again and the name will become highlighted.
4. Type the new name.
5. Press the Return key to confirm the change.

> **OPENING DOCUMENTS AND FOLDERS FROM WITHIN DP**
> Digital Performer's Clippings feature allows you to create shortcuts to documents and folders that reside outside of DP. This saves you the hassle of leaving the application and navigating with the Mac OS Finder. See Chapter 11 for details on using Clippings.

Standard MIDI Files

The standard MIDI file format (SMF) was created to facilitate the transfer of MIDI data across different applications and, most importantly, different computer platforms (see Figure 5.11). Almost every music software sequencer can open and save MIDI data in the SMF format. This allows a musician working in Digital Performer, for example, to save a MIDI sequence as an SMF and exchange it with a PC user without the loss of any data.

Figure 5.11
The Standard MIDI File icon created in Digital Performer

※ Saving Your Project

There are basically two types of standard MIDI files that DP can work with, Type 1 and Type 0. Digital Performer replaces the term *type* with *format*.

- **Format 1**. This setting preserves the layout of individual MIDI tracks and includes tempo and meter information.
- **Format 0**. This setting includes tempo and meter information, but merges all MIDI tracks into a single multi-channel track. DP also has the ability to save a format 0 SMF that only includes tempo and meter map information.

In addition to this information, track names and other descriptive data will be stored when opening and exporting standard MIDI files from Digital Performer.

Opening Standard MIDI Files
To open an SMF via the File menu:

1. In Digital Performer, choose File > Open. The default keyboard shortcut is Command+O.
2. Select the standard MIDI file and click the Open button.
3. If the MIDI assignments in the SMF do not match the MIDI configuration of Digital Performer, then the Device Remap window will appear and attempt to make the appropriate substitution (see Figure 5.12).
4. Click OK to confirm the recommended substitution. Choosing Cancel will ignore the substitutions and assign the MIDI inputs or outputs to NONE.

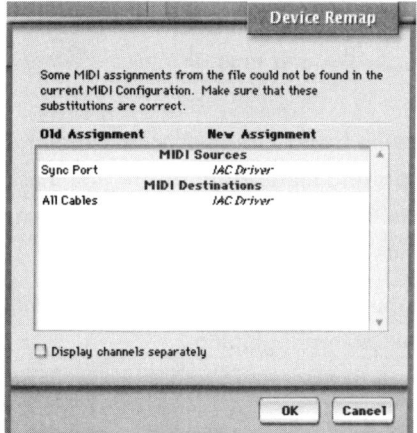

Figure 5.12
The Device Remap window.

To import an SMF into an existing project via the drag and drop method:

1. In Digital Performer, open the Chunks window (Project > Chunks). The default keyboard shortcut is Shift+C.
2. Within the Mac OS Finder, select the standard MIDI file and drag the SMF into DP's Chunks window. Once imported via drag and drop, the SMF will appear as a sequence in Digital Performer's Chunks window. MIDI assignments will not be substituted, but will default to an assignment of NONE. There is no need to Save As, as the SMF will be copied directly into the existing project.

CHAPTER 5 } Project Management: Part 1

Exporting Standard MIDI Files

To export a standard MIDI file with the Save As command:

1. In Digital Performer choose File > Save As.
2. Name the project and choose the destination folder and hard drive. Be aware that DP doesn't automatically add the standard .mid extension to the end of the file name. Be sure to include this extension (.mid) when naming the standard MIDI file to ensure that the destination program is able to read it correctly.
3. Select Standard MIDI File from the Format pop-up menu.
4. Click on the Save button.
5. Specify the SMF options in the MIDI File Options window, shown in Figure 5.13.
6. Select the options for the Standard MIDI File. Keep in mind that MIDI effects and MIDI loops cannot be exported with your SMF, you will need to enable the Expand Loops and Print Effects option, then use the End File At Time option to specify the end time of the printed loop.

Figure 5.13
The MIDI File Options window.

   - **Format 1—separate tracks**. This setting will maintain the separation of MIDI tracks and include the tempo and meter data as the first track. This standard exporting option is enabled by default. It's a good idea to use the Format 1 option if you're unsure of the standard MIDI file format you should be using.

   - **Format 0—one multi-channel track**. This option will create a multi-channel MIDI track with tempo and meter at the beginning.

   - **Format 0—tempo/meter map only**. This option will export only the Conductor Track with tempo and meter data.

   - **Save track names as plain text**. This option will only save plain text events like track names with the SMF. Track comments and other special text events will not be saved with the file. Use this option to ensure compatibility with programs that do not support special text.

   - **Expand loops and print effects**. Loops and real-time MIDI effects cannot be included in standard MIDI files. This option will print any real-time MIDI effects and convert any loops into a region of repeated MIDI data. Use the End File At Time option to specify the end time of the printed loop.

7. Once you have specified the MIDI file options, choose OK to export the Standard MIDI File.

OMFI Files

The OMFI format (*Open Media Framework Interchange* format) is an industry standard format for exchanging digital files between applications such as Digidesign's Pro Tools and Apple's Final Cut Pro. This format speeds up the production workflow by allowing media files and metadata created in one program to be made available in another.

Digital Performer supports both OMF 1.0 and 2.0 formats, and can also export OMF files that are compatible with Digidesign's DigiTranslator 2.0 (see Figure 5.14).

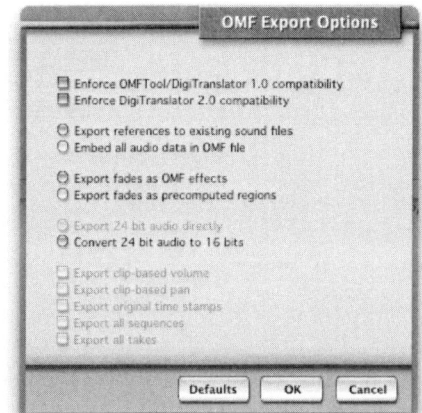

Figure 5.14

The OMF Export Options command.

Customizing Your Workspace

Organizing your Digital Performer workspace is much like organizing the desk in your office. When working in a physical space, it is important to keep files, documents, pens and pencils, and so on in logical locations that allow for easy access, storage, and management. These rules are just as applicable within the desktop environment. Digital Performer has many different windows that you will need to access within the course of the music production process. Like physical office space, screen real estate is limited—unless you are lucky enough to have a 30" Cinema display!

Digital Performer has a number of features that allow you to customize your DP workspace, from project-specific window configurations, track colors for easy track identification, to the customization of keyboard shortcut commands and preferences. Digital Performer's Consolidated Window feature introduced in Version 4.5 provides additional control for managing the numerous windows in DP.

The Consolidated Window

When enabled, the Consolidated Window feature allows you to view multiple windows in a single, consolidated environment. The Consolidated Window, shown in Figure 5.15, displays various tabs across the top of the window. These tabs provide quick access to many of DP's main windows — opening the desired window in the main body or center of the Consolidated Window when clicked. Sidebars are available for displaying other windows such as the Audio Monitor, Chunks, Markers, Event List, and the Undo History window.

CHAPTER 5 } Project Management: Part 1

Figure 5.15
Click on a tab to open the desired window in the main body of the Consolidated Window.

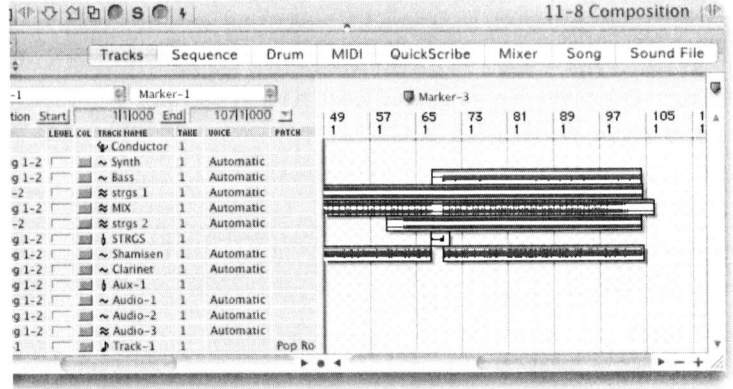

The Title Bar

The Consolidated Window's title bar closely resembles the title bars found in DP's editors, but adds extra buttons: the Show/Hide Left and Right Sidebar buttons. In addition, Popout buttons allow you to "pop-out," or remove, altogether a window from the Consolidated Window, as shown in Figure 5.16.

Figure 5.16
The Consolidated Window title bar contains buttons for toggling the visibility of the left and right sidebars. Click a window's Popout button to open the cell in a separate window that's independent of the Consolidated Window.

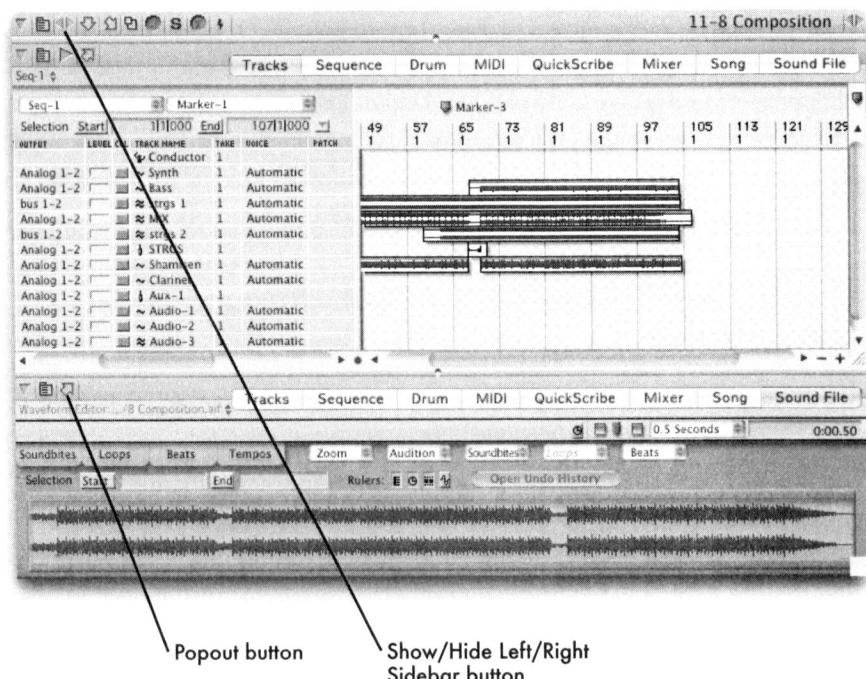

Windows (also called *cells*) that are popped-out will become independent of the Consolidated Window. Drag the dividers to show or hide multiple windows in the sidebars or main body of the Consolidated Window. Title bar features unique to the Consolidated Window are discussed below.

- **Show/Hide Left/Right Sidebar.** Click the show/hide sidebar buttons to toggle the visibility of the Consolidated Window sidebars. These additional sections (sidebars) allow you to display selected windows to the left or right of the main body (center section) of the Consolidated Window.
- **Sidebar Divider.** When a sidebar is visible, its sidebar divider will become available and allow you to resize the associated sidebar. Resizing a sidebar will cause the main body or center section of the Consolidated Window to be resized in the process.
- **Main Body.** The main body is the main section of the Consolidated Window. Tabs appearing across the top determine which windows or edit windows appear here. Only editor windows and other primary windows can appear in the main body.
- **Horizontal Divider.** Drag the horizontal divider to show or hide multiple windows within the main body or sidebars of the Consolidated Window.
- **Tabs.** Use the tabs located at the top of the Consolidated Window to switch the main body to the desired editor window.
- **Popout buttons.** Use the Popout buttons to pop-out a window from the Consolidated Window. Windows that are popped-out will become independent of the Consolidated Window, and will appear with a Pop-back-in button, as shown in Figure 5.17. Click the Pop-back-in button to force an independent window back into the Consolidated Window.

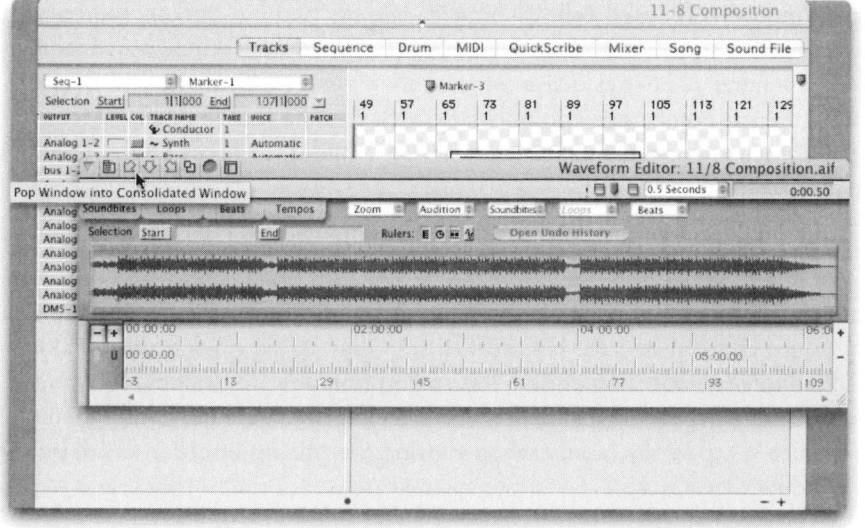

Figure 5.17

Use the Pop-back-in buttons to force an independent window back into the Consolidated Window.

CHAPTER 5 } Project Management: Part 1

* **Window Selector.** Use the sidebar window selectors to change the window that appears in a sidebar. Keep in mind that editor windows do not appear in this list and cannot be displayed in a sidebar.

Mini-Menu

The mini-menu, shown in Figure 5.18, provides commands for opening the Consolidated Window preferences, options for controlling the behavior of the Consolidated Window, along with window set commands and options for quick access to DP's default Consolidated Window sets. The mini-menu options are described below:

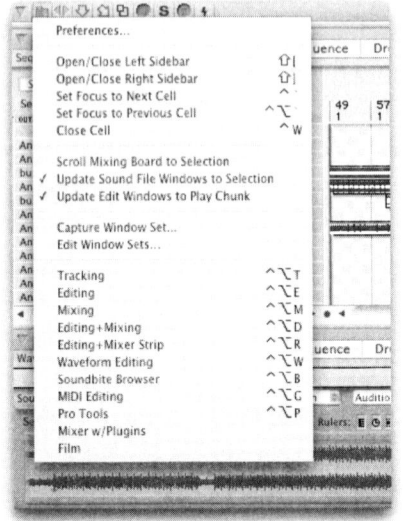

Figure 5.18

The Consolidated Window mini-menu.

* **Preferences.** Click this option to access the Consolidated Window preferences located in the Preferences and Settings window (explained later).
* **Open/Close Left/Right Sidebar.** Choose the desired option to toggle the visibility of the left or right sidebars. To toggle the left sidebar without the use of the mouse, press Shift+[. Press Shift+] to toggle the right sidebar.
* **Set Focus to Next/Previous Cell.** Use this option to quickly focus on the next or previous cell in the Consolidated Window. A focused cell will have its title bar shaded darker. The Focus feature allows you to make a specific cell (window) in the Consolidated Window active, much like how the front-most window is always active when working in a multiple window environment. Keep in mind that some commands can only be applied to the focused cell. To focus on the next cell, use the default keyboard shortcut Command+~ (tilde). To focus on the previous cell, press Command+Option+~.
* **Close Cell.** Use this option to remove or close a cell that has the current focus. The default keyboard shortcut is Control+W.
* **Scroll Mixing Board to Selection.** This option tells Digital Performer to automatically scroll and display the Mixing Board channel strip for a specific track when it (the track or its data) is selected within a DP editor. You can also enable this setting from the Consolidated Window preferences (Consolidated Window > mini-menu > Preferences, or Digital Performer menu > Preferences). This feature is especially handy when viewing the Mixing Board in a sidebar of the Consolidated Window.

※ **Update Sound File Windows to Selection.** Similar to the Scroll Mixing Board to Selection feature discussed above, this option causes a soundbite selected in a DP editor—such as the Sequence Editor or Track window—to always display in the Waveform Editor (when the Waveform Editor is visible in the Consolidated Window). You can also enable this setting from the Consolidated Window preferences.

※ **Update Edit Windows to Play Chunk.** Use this option if you want DP's various editor windows to always display tracks from the currently play-enabled Chunk. This setting is also located in the Consolidated Window preferences (explained later).

※ **Capture Window Set/Edit Window Sets.** Use these two commands to open the Capture Window Set and Edit Window Sets commands, explained later in the "Window Sets" section of this chapter.

※ **Window Set List.** Click a window set to load it. The default window sets contained in this list are the same window sets that appear in the Window Sets sub-menu (Windows menu > Window Sets).

Setting Up the Consolidated Window

The Consolidated Window feature can be enabled or disabled entirely from the Consolidated Window preferences, as shown in Figure 5.19. The preferences listed are global and will affect all Digital Performer projects.

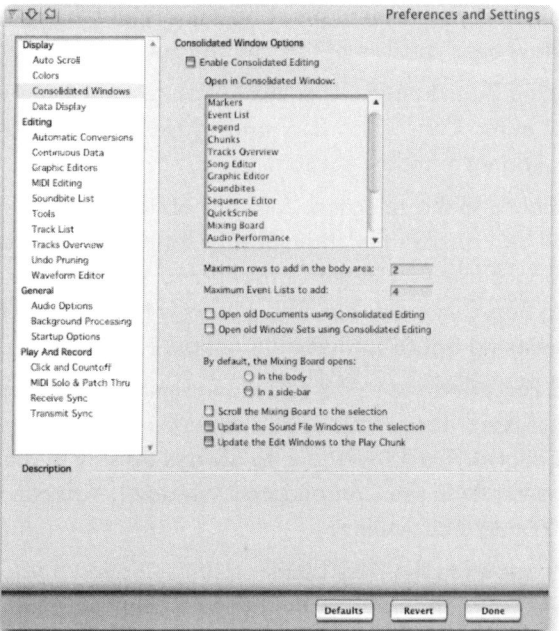

Figure 5.19
The Consolidated Window preferences allow you to enable or disable the Consolidated Window altogether.

The Consolidated Window preferences are as follows:

- **Enable Consolidated Editing**. This button toggles the Consolidated Window on and off.
- **Open in Consolidated Window**. This section contains a list of Digital Performer windows that can be included in the Consolidated Window. Windows highlighted in blue are included, while unhighlighted windows will open as separate windows.
- **Maximum rows to add in the body area**. This setting determines how many rows will be automatically added to the main body or center section of the Consolidated Window when opened. To add or remove rows manually, simply drag on the Consolidated Window's horizontal divider.
- **Maximum Event Lists to add**. This setting determines the maximum number of Event Lists you can open in the Consolidated Window. If you attempt to exceed the specified maximum number, DP will simply replace one of the Event Lists you have currently open with the new Event List. Keep in mind that this setting does not prevent you from manually opening an Event List from the Sidebar cell menus (explained later).
- **Open old documents using Consolidated Editing**. Enable this option if you want to have older DP projects (created in versions prior to 4.5) automatically open in the Consolidated Window layout. Turn this option off if you wish to work with these older documents in their original window layout. Keep in mind that you can always migrate these older documents into the Consolidated Window layout at your own pace.
- **Open old Window Sets using Consolidated Editing**. Enable this feature if you want Window Sets created in older versions of DP (prior to DP4.5) to open in a Consolidated Window layout. Disable this option if you want to preserve the original layout of the older Window Set. Refer to the "Window Sets" section of this chapter for an explanation of Window Sets.
- **By default, the Mixing Board opens**. Use this option to determine where the Mixing Board will automatically open in the Consolidated Window if you have the Mixing Board highlighted in the Open in Consolidated Window section.
- **Scroll the Mixing Board to the selection**. Turn this option on if you wish the Mixing Board to automatically scroll and display the channel strip for a selected track. This option only applies when the Mixing Board appears in the Consolidated Window and is especially handy when viewing the Mixing Board in a sidebar. This option is the same as the Consolidated Window mini-menu's Scroll Mixing Board to Selection option.
- **Update the Sound File Windows to the selection**. Similar to the Scroll the Mixing Board to selection option discussed above, this option causes a soundbite selected in a DP editor such as the Sequence Editor or Tracks window, to always display in the Waveform Editor (when the Waveform Editor is visible in the Consolidated Window). You can also enable this setting from the Consolidated Window mini-menu.
- **Update the Edit Windows to the Play Chunk**. Use this option if you want DP's various editor windows to always display tracks from the currently play-enabled Chunk. You can also enable this setting from the Consolidated Window mini-menu.

To enable or disable the Consolidated Window feature:

1. Open the Consolidated Window preferences by choosing Digital Performer menu > Preferences > Consolidated Window preferences.
2. Click the Enable Consolidated Editing button to toggle the Consolidated Window feature on or off.

Once you have decided to work in the Consolidated Window and enabled it from the Preferences and Settings window, you will need to decide which particular windows will open in the Consolidated Window. The Open in Consolidated Window section of the Consolidated Window preferences provides a list of windows that are to be included or excluded from the Consolidated Window. Windows highlighted in blue will be included, while un-highlighted windows will open independently. Keep in mind that you can use the Consolidated Windows Pop-out and Pop-in buttons (explained earlier) to manually separate a window or force it back into the Consolidated Window.

To determine which windows will open in the Consolidated Window:

1. Open the Consolidated Window preferences by choosing Digital Performer menu > Preferences > Consolidated Window preferences.
2. In the Open in Consolidated Window section, click to highlight the window or windows you want to have included. All the windows in the list should be highlighted (in blue) by default. Windows that are not highlighted will automatically open in a separate window.

The Main Body and Rows

The main body section is the center section of the Consolidated Window and is used to display the main windows in DP. Use the tabs located above the main body to display a particular window. Drag the main body section's horizontal divider to manually show or hide additional sections (or rows), as shown in Figure 5.20. New rows will appear with their own set of tabs, allowing you to display multiple windows in this center section of the Consolidated Window. Keep in mind that you can set the number of rows that are automatically opened in the main body section from the Consolidated Window preferences (explained earlier).

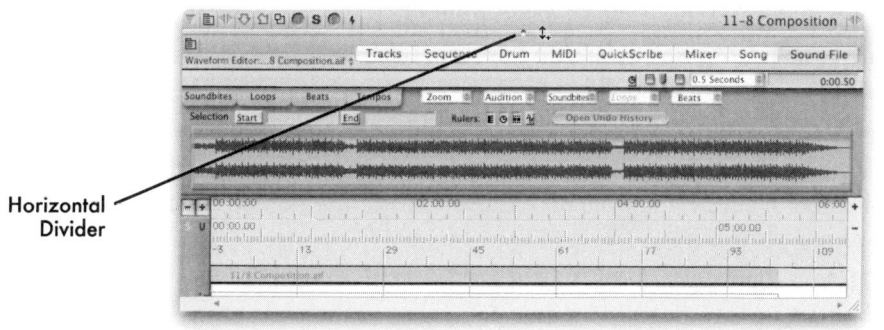

Figure 5.20

Drag on the main body section's horizontal divider to add or remove rows from the Consolidated Window.

CHAPTER 5 } Project Management: Part 1

The Sidebars and Cells

The left and right sidebars of the Consolidated Window are used to display DP's secondary windows, such as the list windows, and monitor windows (with the exception of the Mixing Board, which can be displayed in a sidebar or main body section). If a sidebar is hidden, drag vertically on its sidebar divider. Similar to the main body section, which contains rows, the sidebars are divided into individual cells. Drag on a sidebar's horizontal divider to create additional cells or horizontally resize a cell.

Unlike the main body section that contains tabs, each sidebar cell contains a window selector (or sidebar cell menu) that allows you to choose which window will be displayed in a particular cell (shown in Figure 5.21).

Figure 5.21
Use a cell's Window Selector to open a particular window in a sidebar's cell.

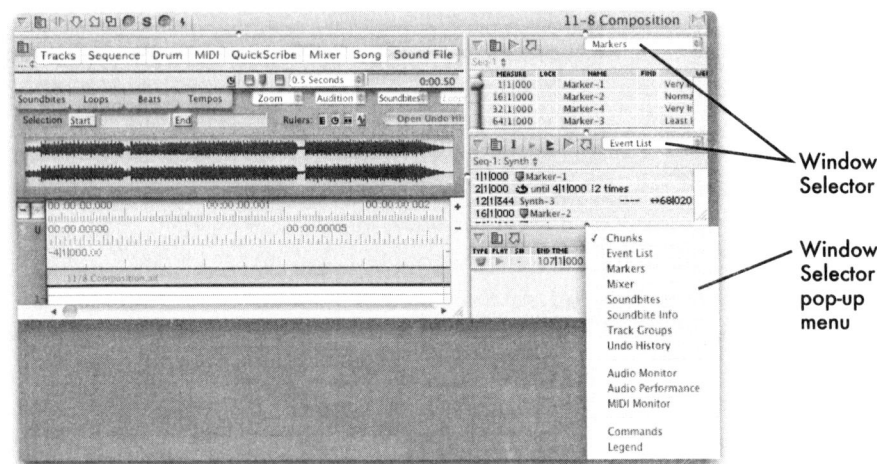

Working with Rows and Cells

Digital Performer provides various ways for controlling the Consolidated Window's rows and cells. Rows or cells that are currently selected (also called the *focus*) will appear with the title bar slightly darker, as shown in Figure 5.22. A row or cell that is in focus within the Consolidated Window is like the front-most active window when working with separate windows.

- **To open a new row or cell**: Drag downward on the main body section's or sidebar's horizontal divider to create a new row or cell.
- **To close an existing row or cell**: Click on the desired window's Close button, located to the left-most of the title bar. If the particular row/cell is in focus, you can also use the Close Cell command (Consolidated Window > mini-menu > Close Cell) or the default keyboard shortcut Command+W.
- **To open/close the left or right sidebar**: Click on the Consolidated Window title bar's Show/Hide Sidebar buttons.

※ **To vertically resize a sidebar**: Vertically drag on the sidebar's sidebar divider.

※ **To focus a row or cell**: Simply click on the title bar or any area within a particular row or cell. A window that is in focus will appear with its title bar shaded darker.

※ **To resize a row or cell**: To horizontally resize a row or cell, drag on its horizontal divider. To resize vertically, click and drag on the sidebar dividers.

※ **To pop-out a row or cell from the Consolidated Window**: Click on the row or cell's Pop-out button (located in the window's title bar) to open the desired window in a separate window that's independent of the Consolidated Window. Once popped-out, the title bar's Pop-out button will change to the Pop-back-in button. You can also use the default keyboard shortcut Control+1 to pop-out a focused row or cell.

※ **To force a separate window back into the Consolidated Window**: Click on the separated window's Pop-back-in button (located in the title bar). Once popped back into the Consolidated Window, the window's Pop-back-in button will change to a Pop-out button.

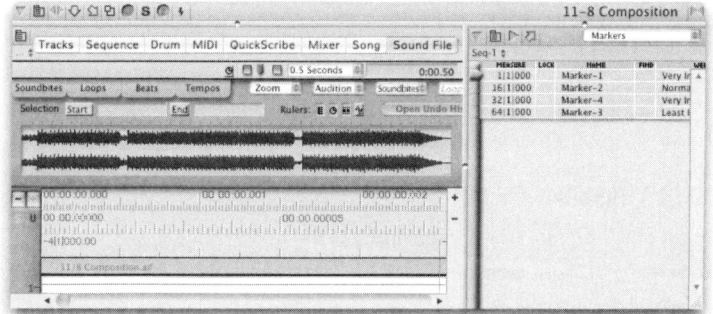

Figure 5.22

Cells or rows that are the "focus" will appear with the title bar colored slightly darker.

The Preferences and Settings Command

Digital Performer's Preferences and Settings command, shown in Figure 5.23, provides options for customizing DP. Choose Digital Performer menu > Preferences to open the Preferences and Settings window. The settings found here are global and affect all DP files.

Preferences are listed on the left side of the window with their descriptions appearing below the list. Place the cursor over a setting to see its description. Once a preference is selected from the list, its various settings will appear to the right.

If you have made changes to the current preferences and need to return to the previous settings, click the Revert button. Keep in mind that once you click the Done button and close the Preferences and Settings window, the Revert button will no longer remember the previous settings and will not be able to undo or revert to the last changes made before the window was closed. Use the Defaults button to restore the preferences to their factory default settings. Be aware this change is instantaneous and cannot be undone.

CHAPTER 5 } Project Management: Part 1

Figure 5.23

Digital Performer's Preferences and Settings window.

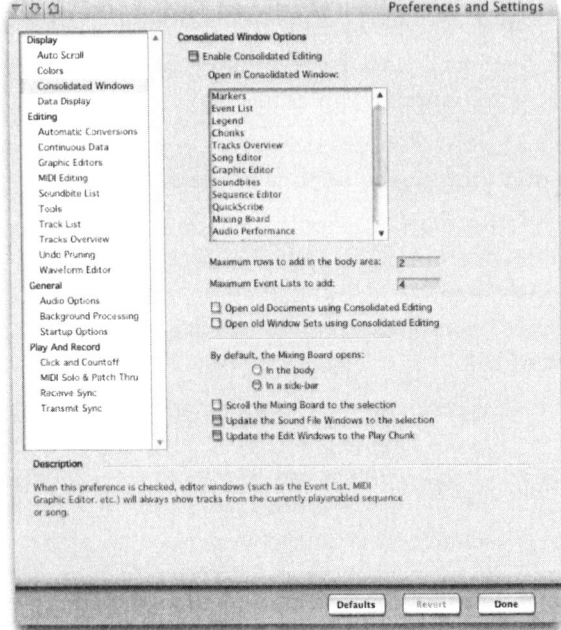

PREFERENCES IN OLDER VERSIONS OF DP

DP 4.5 has consolidated most of the preferences and settings into the new Preferences and Settings window, though many of these settings can still be accessed via DP's various menus. Users working with older versions of DP may find that many of the preferences discussed in this chapter do not apply to them, since they are new additions introduced in Version 4.5.

Display Preferences

The Display preferences provide options for controlling auto scrolling, colors, consolidated windows, and data display settings.

Auto Scroll

The Auto Scroll preferences shown in Figure 5.24 provide a centralized location for controlling how and if DP's various windows will scroll, whether a particular window's playback wiper will be visible, and what type of auto scrolling is used—paging or continuous scrolling.

✵ Customizing Your Workspace

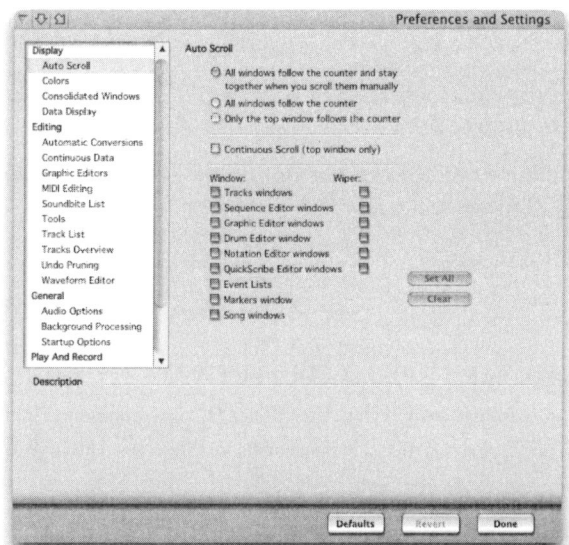

Figure 5.24
Digital Performer's Auto Scroll preferences.

Be aware that auto scrolling will only affect the windows that relate to the currently play-enabled sequence or Chunk.

- ✵ **All Windows Follow the Counter and Stay Together When You Scroll Them Manually.** This option basically forces all windows to scroll together during playback and recording, stopping, rewinding, fast-forwarding, or when performing any type of cueing function. Windows will also scroll together when dragging the playback wiper or horizontal scroll bar to manually scroll a window.

- ✵ **All Windows Follow the Counter.** This is the same as the first option, with the exception that the windows will not scroll together when scrolling a window manually.

- ✵ **Only the Top Window Follows the Counter.** This option will only scroll the top-most window within a sequence, providing the extra benefit of reducing the amount of processor load put on Digital Performer when scrolling. Depending on the speed of your computer, you may find this option improves the responsiveness of DP when scrolling is enabled.

- ✵ **Continuous Scroll.** With this option turned off, DP will scroll windows one "page" at a time. This feature is referred to as page scrolling or Paging. When the playback wiper reaches the last measure or event in a window, DP will automatically jump to the next measure or data event and update the window display—sort of like turning a page within a book.

    When the Continuous Scroll option is enabled, DP will continuously scroll the top-most window, smoothly from left to right, with the playback wiper centered in the window. If you want to move the playback wiper away from the center of the window when scrolling, you can press the Option key while dragging the playback wiper to the left or right.

CHAPTER 5 } Project Management: Part 1

- **Window.** Use the Window section to enable or disable auto scrolling for a specific window type.
- **Wiper.** This option determines whether or not the playback wiper is visible in a particular window.
- **Set All.** Click this button to enable all the options in both the Window and Wiper sections of the Preferences and Settings window.
- **Clear.** Click this button to quickly disable auto-scrolling and playback wiper visibility for all windows.

> **USING A WINDOW TITLE BAR'S AUTO SCROLL BUTTON**
> You can also click on the Auto Scroll button within a window's title bar, shown in Figure 5.25, to manually turn off/on auto scrolling for a specific window. This saves you the hassle of calling up the Preferences and Settings window if you need to temporarily enable or disable auto scrolling for the particular window you are working with.

Figure 5.25
Click a window title bar's Auto Scroll button to quickly enable or disable auto scrolling for that window.

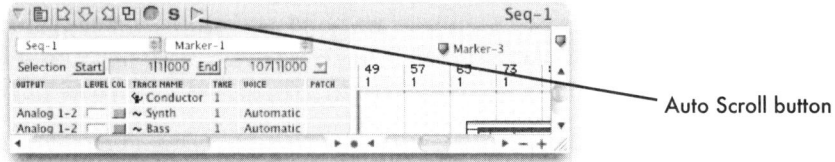

Colors
The Color preferences are explained later in the "Track Colors" section of this chapter.

Consolidated Windows
The Consolidated Windows preferences are explained earlier in "The Consolidated Window" section of this chapter.

Data Display
The Data Display preferences, shown in Figure 5.26, control how certain types of data are displayed within Digital Performer.

- **Pitch Display.** This option will allow you to determine how octaves are numbered and displayed in a project.
- **Tempo Display.** This option determines whether tempo is displayed as beats per minute (BPM) or frame clicks.

❉ Customizing Your Workspace

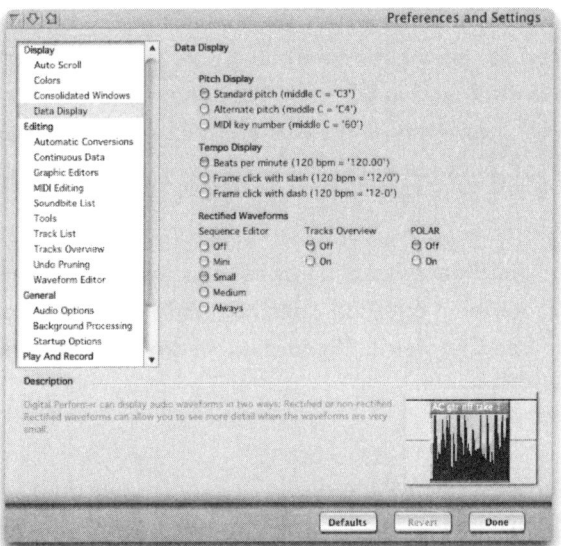

Figure 5.26
The Data Display preferences.

❉ **Rectified Waveforms.** This option will force DP to display only the positive arc of an audio waveform, allowing the information to be shown in half of the vertical space (see Figure 5.27). The Mini, Small, or Medium options will display waveforms rectified when a specific size of a track is selected. Checking the Medium option, for example, will display a track's waveforms rectified when a vertical track size of medium or smaller is selected. Separate options for displaying rectified waveforms within the Tracks and Polar window are also provided.

Figure 5.27
Rectified waveform display.

CHAPTER 5 } Project Management: Part 1

Editing Preferences
The Editing preferences provide options for controlling how the Automatic Conversions option behaves, how information is displayed in DP's various Editor windows, how the Tool palette functions, Undo Pruning settings, and so on. Many of these preferences used to have their own dedicated windows, but have now been consolidated in the Preferences and Settings window.

Automatic Conversions
The Automatic Conversions preferences provide options for controlling how and if audio is automatically converted when the material in question does not conform to the project's current tempo, sample rate, or sample format. See Chapter 7, "Recording Audio" for an explanation of the Automatic Conversions preferences in DP.

Continuous Data
The Continuous Data preferences control the display of continuous data within DP's various MIDI Graphic Editors. See the "MIDI Editing" section of Chapter 10 for an explanation of continuous MIDI data and the Continuous Data preferences.

Graphic Editors
The Graphic Editors preferences shown in Figure 5.28 control how DP handles partial measures, the display of grid lines within an edit window, and which specific Editor will open by default when working with specific types of data.

- **Fix Partial Measures Automatically**. *Partial measures* are bars that contain an incomplete number of beats. A partial measure is created when a meter change is inserted in the middle of a bar. This happens because meter changes will always create a new measure, essentially truncating the measure in the process.

  When the Fix Partial Measures Automatically option is checked, DP will automatically remove any partial measures by moving meter events as needed when a project is opened. You may need to check any MIDI data to make sure it aligns up with the readjusted meters the way you want it to. Be sure to uncheck this option if you want to have partial measures remain within a project.

- **Show Grid Lines.** Enable these options to turn on marker and edit grid lines within an edit window or beat grid lines within an audio track that has been analyzed with DP's Beat Detection Engine (BDE). Grid lines can be useful for making precise edits or moving around data that needs to conform to a specified grid. See Chapter 10 for an explanation of grid lines within DP.

- **Default Edit window.** This option determines which Editor window is opened when you double-click on a track.

❋ Customizing Your Workspace

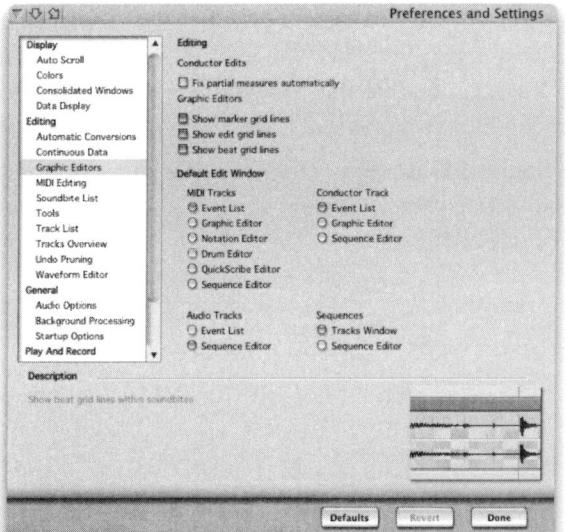

Figure 5.28
Digital Performer's Graphic Editors preferences.

MIDI Editing

The MIDI Editing preferences determine what happens when you double-click on a MIDI track for editing and also how MIDI notes are displayed in a track, as shown in Figure 5.29.

❋ **Open one Graphic Editor for each MIDI track.** This option will force a separate editor window to open for each MIDI track that only displays the data for that track.

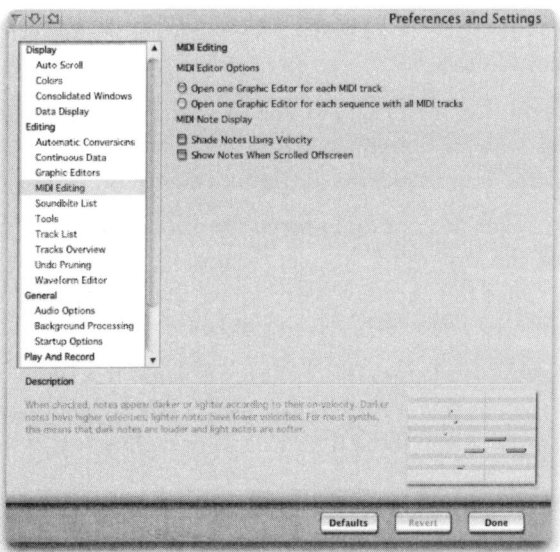

Figure 5.29
Digital Performer's MIDI Editing preferences.

117

CHAPTER 5 } Project Management: Part 1

- **Open one Graphic Editor for each sequence.** This option will open a global editor window capable of displaying multiple MIDI tracks.
- **Shade Notes Using Velocity.** Enable this option if you want MIDI notes to be shaded according to their velocity. The higher the velocity, the darker the color will be, and vice versa.
- **Show Notes When Scrolled Offscreen.** When a MIDI note appears outside the currently displayed pitch range of a MIDI track, DP will show a small bar at the top or bottom border of a track, as shown in Figure 5.30.

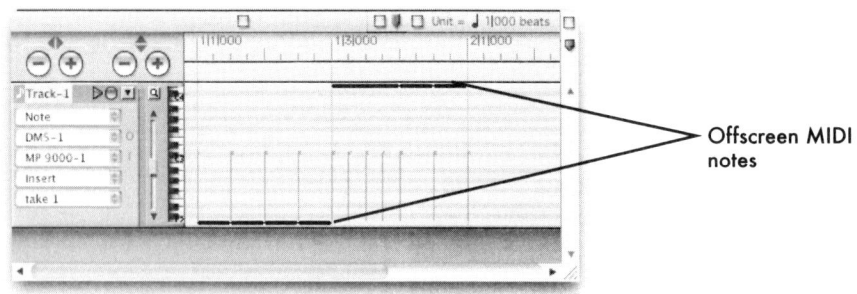

Figure 5.30
MIDI notes that appear outside the currently displayed pitch range of a MIDI track will appear as a small bar when the Show Notes Offscreen option is enabled in the MIDI Editing section of the Preferences and Settings window.

Soundbite List
The Soundbite List Columns Setup preferences determine what specific columns will appear in the Soundbites window. See Chapter 3 for an explanation of Digital Performer's Soundbites window.

Tools
The Tools preferences shown in Figure 5.31 determine how Pointer tool selections are executed, and how the Tool palette functions in DP.

- **Cursor Selection Mode.** This menu allows you to specify how Pointer tool selections function within the Tracks overview or Sequence Editor. See Chapter 10 for an explanation of the Pointer tool and Pointer Tool selections in Digital Performer.
- **Vertical Tool Palette.** Click this option to force the Tool Palette into a vertical position when opened. You can use the keyboard shortcut Control -~ (tilde) to toggle between a vertical and horizontal position. Once this shortcut is activated, the Tool Palette will automatically dock to the edge of the front-most edit window (see below).
- **Position Tool Palette Automatically.** This option will force the Tool Palette to automatically dock with the front-most edit window. When horizontal, it will snap to the bottom or top edge of the window. A vertical position will force it to the left or right edge of the window.

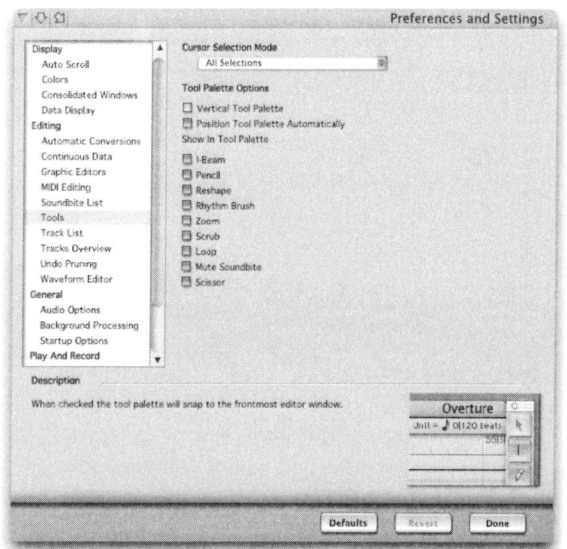

Figure 5.31
Digital Performer's Tool preferences.

- **Show in Tool Palette.** This option lets you choose which tools are displayed in the Tool palette. Keep in mind the keyboard shortcuts used to select a specific tool, will continue to function even when they are hidden from the Tool palette.

Tracks List
The Tracks List preferences are used to show or hide specific columns in the Tracks window. See Chapter 3 for an explanation of the Tracks window.

Tracks Overview
The Tracks Overview preferences provide options for controlling MIDI level meters and the phrasing of MIDI data, as shown in Figure 5.32. See Chapter 3 for an explanation of MIDI phrasing in the Tracks Overview section of the Tracks window.

- **Show MIDI Activity or Velocity.** MIDI level meters can display either MIDI data or note-on velocity. Choose MIDI Activity to trigger the MIDI level meter every time a MIDI event occurs. Choosing Velocity will trigger the MIDI level meter and display the note-on velocity of each MIDI note that is played back.
- **Level Decay Time.** This value (0-99) specifies how long it takes for a level meter to return to zero. The default setting is 5, but you may wish to experiment with other values if you have a situation where the metering does not occur fast or slow enough for the material you are working with. Generally speaking, use higher decay times for slower material or passages that do not contain many notes. Lower decay values work well with faster tempo material or passages with highly condensed notes.

CHAPTER 5 } Project Management: Part 1

Figure 5.32
Digital Performer's Tracks Overview preferences.

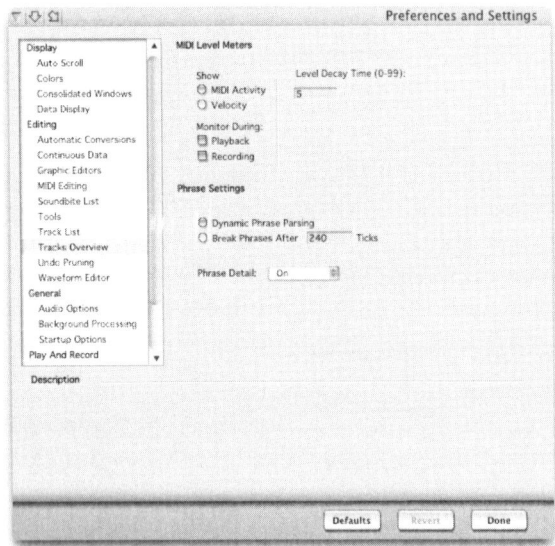

* **Monitor During Playback or Recording.** Use these two options to enable or disable MIDI level metering during the playback and/or recording process. If you are working on a slower Mac, you may find that disabling the MIDI level meters will make your DP system more responsive during playback and recording.
* **Dynamic Phrase Parsing.** Click this option to turn on DP's Dynamic Phrase Parsing feature, which will automatically control how MIDI data is phrased and placed into blocks in the Tracks window. See Chapter 3 for an explanation of the MIDI phrasing and MIDI blocks.
* **Break Phrases After__Ticks.** This option provides a simpler approach to MIDI phrasing by allowing you to specify the amount of empty space (specified in MIDI ticks) that must be present before a MIDI block ends and a new one begins.
* **Phrase Detail.** This option determines how much detail and priority is given to the data that is displayed in a MIDI block. Operations such as scrolling and zooming that cause DP to redraw data in the Tracks Overview are directly impacted by the Phrase Detail setting, and vice versa.
* **On.** This setting will give phrase detailing a high priority and will always be computed before any screen redrawing occurs. This option produces the best visual results, but also results in the slowest screen redraws.
* **On Demand.** This setting will cause DP to only display the outline of blocks when screen redraws are occurring. Once they are completed, DP will fill in the detail of the blocks. Though not as visually impressive, this option strikes a nice balance between high detail and responsiveness.
* **Off.** Select this option to completely turn off phrase detailing. Blocks are instead filled with a generic pattern. This setting provides the most responsiveness, though it sacrifices all the detail within a block.

Undo Pruning

The Undo Pruning preferences provide controls for determining how Digital Performer's Undo History windows manage overall disk space and RAM consumption, and the number of undoable actions that are remembered within a project. See Chapter 6, "Project Management: Part 2" for an explanation of the Undo History windows and their Undo Pruning preferences.

Waveform Editor

The Waveform Editor preferences allow you to control how stereo audio waveforms are displayed, if edits will be automatically crossfaded, and if Stereo/Mono Conversion settings will be applied when mono material is pasted into a stereo file, and vice versa.

General Preferences

The General preferences contain options for controlling audio recording, the locations of imported or processed audio files, background processing, and basic startup options.

Audio Options

These settings, as shown in Figure 5.33, affect how audio files are recorded and managed, and whether DP presents a warning when the processor overloads and playback is interrupted.

- **Show alert when playback overloads the processor**. Enabling this option will cause a warning dialog box to appear when a lack of system resources interrupts playback.
- **MultiRecord is always on for audio tracks**. When this option is checked, you can simultaneously record-enable two or more audio tracks. Disabling this option, however, will allow only one track to be armed for recording at a time.

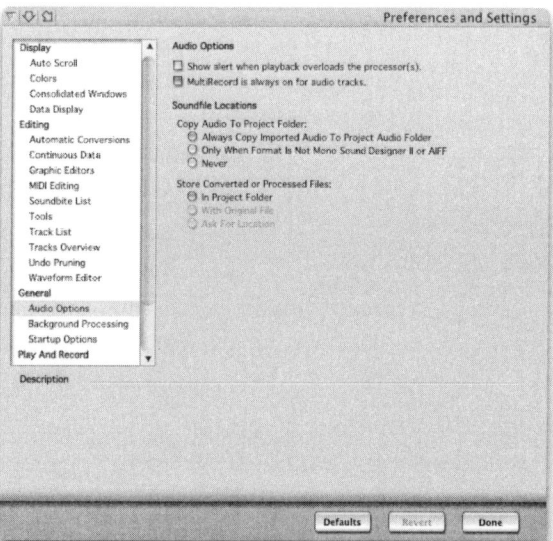

Figure 5.33

Digital Performer's Audio Options preferences.

- **Soundfile Locations**: These settings determine where imported, processed, and converted audio will be stored in a project. See the "Importing Audio" section of Chapter 7 for an explanation of the Soundfile Location preferences.

Background Processing

These settings affect how Background Processing occurs in Digital Performer. See Chapter 13 for an explanation of DP's Background Processing feature and the Background Processing preferences.

Startup Options

The Startup Options preferences control what happens after Digital Performer is launched, as shown in Figure 5.34.

- **None**. Once Digital Performer is launched, no window or dialog box will appear and prompt you to open or create a new project. Only DP's menu bar will be visible at the top of the screen. Choose Open or New from the File menu to begin working on a project.
- **New File**. The New Project dialog will automatically open when DP is launched, allowing you to create a new project.
- **"Open..." dialog**. This setting will launch the Open dialog, allowing you to choose a DP project to open.
- **Last File Opened**. This will automatically open the last DP project you had opened.
- **Upgrading Command Bindings**. This setting determines what happens to DP's command key bindings when upgrading to a newer version of Digital Performer.

Figure 5.34

Digital Performer's Startup Options preferences.

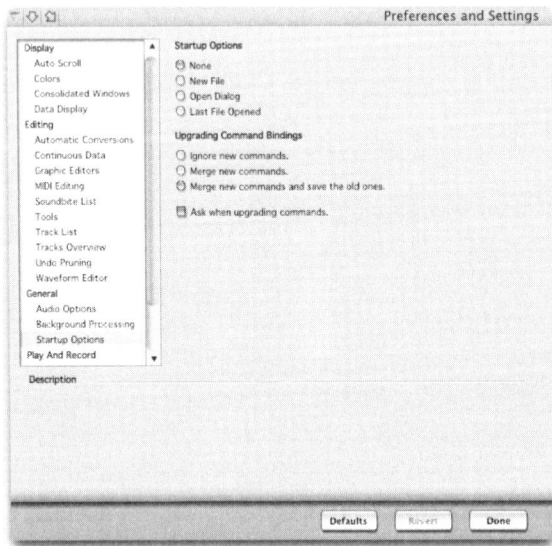

Play and Record Preferences

The Play and Record preferences provide settings for controlling DP's click and countoff options, how MIDI Patch Thru and track soloing behaves, and how DP's synchronization features operate.

Click and Countoff

Then Click and Countoff preferences allow you to configure Digital Performer's click. See the "Setting Up a Click" section of Chapter 4 for an explanation of DP's click and countoff options.

MIDI Solo and Patch Thru

MIDI Patch Thru allows Digital Performer to "patch" or route incoming MIDI data "thru" to any connected MIDI devices and/or virtual instruments. This feature basically lets you hear your MIDI devices or instrument plug-ins when you play a note on your MIDI controller. MIDI data will only be patched thru to MIDI tracks that have been record-enabled. The MIDI solo preferences shown in Figure 5.35 determine how soloed MIDI tracks function in DP.

* **MIDI Patch Thru mode—Off.** This setting turns off MIDI Patch thru altogether.
* **MIDI Patch Thru mode—Direct Echo.** Use this setting to echo incoming MIDI data on the same channel it was received. So if DP is receiving MIDI data from channel 16 of your MIDI controller for example, Digital Performer will echo or send that MIDI data out on MIDI channel 16. Data that is direct-echoed bypasses most of DP's MIDI processing and is unaffected by the Setup menu's Input Filter settings. See Chapter 8 for an explanation of the Input Filter window.

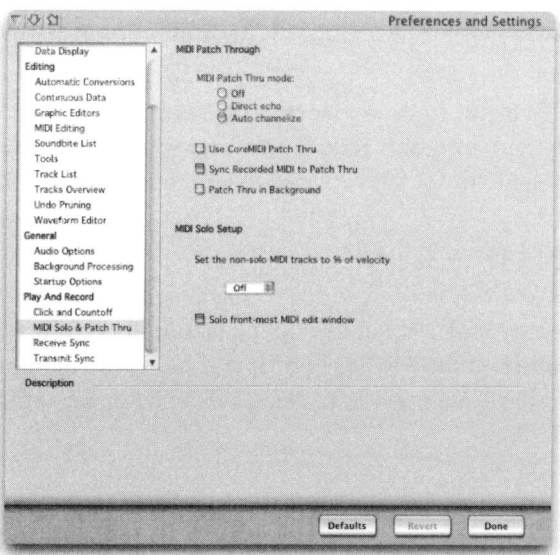

Figure 5.35
Digital Performer's MIDI Patch Thru and MIDI Solo preferences.

- **Auto channelize.** This option is enabled by default and will route MIDI data from your MIDI controller to the currently record-enabled track, regardless of the MIDI device or virtual instrument the MIDI track is assigned to. Simply arm a track, play a note on your MIDI controller, and the data will be routed to the MIDI device assigned to the output of the record-enabled MIDI track. If the MIDI output of a track is assigned to a device group, all devices in the group will sound.

    Unlike the Direct-Echo setting, auto channelizing is directly affected by the Setup menu's Input Filter settings. Any MIDI data options that are disabled in the Input Filter window will not be passed thru to connected MIDI devices, device groups, or virtual instruments.

- **Use CoreMIDI Patch Thru.** This option lets DP utilize the Mac's CoreMIDI enhancements introduced in Mac OS 10.3. MIDI tracks that contain MIDI effects plug-ins, however, will not utilize this feature, even if it is turned on. CoreMIDI functions much like DP's MIDI Patch Thru feature, except it operates at the OS level, which in some instances may provide you with improved MIDI Patch thru performance. Keep in mind that you must be using Mac OS 10.3 to have this option available. In versions earlier than OS 10.3, this option is dimmed.

- **Sync Recorded MIDI to Patch Thru.** This option compensates for the small millisecond delay that occurs when recording MIDI tracks via DP's MIDI Patch Thru option, ensuring what you hear when recording your MIDI tracks will be what is heard during playback. This option is unavailable if you have the Use Core MIDI Patch Thru option turned on.

- **Patch Thru in Background.** Turn this option on if you need to continue to patch thru MIDI data even when DP is in the background, and not the currently active application. When working with Rewire synths such as Propellerhead's Reason for example, this option allows you to play a note on your MIDI controller and trigger a Reason Instrument—even when DP is operating in the background.

- **Set the non-solo MIDI tracks to % of velocity.** Also called Partial Solo, this option lets muted MIDI tracks actually be heard at a reduced volume when other tracks are soloed. Click the Partial Solo pop-up menu to set the reduced percentage value, or to turn off partial soloing altogether.

- **Solo front-most MIDI Edit window.** This option determines what is soloed when soloing a track in an editor window such as the Sequence or Graphic Editors. When enabled, that track you are soloing is soloed by itself. When this option is turned off, the soloed tracks will be determined by what is soloed in the Mixing Board, and how Solo mode is configured in the Tracks Overview section of the Tracks window. See Chapter 3 for an explanation of the Tracks window's Solo Mode feature.

※ Customizing Your Workspace

Receive and Transmit Sync

The Receive Sync and Transmit Sync preferences, shown in Figure 5.36, control how DP's synchronization features operate—whether DP will be transmitting or receiving sync, and what type of source clock will be used in the synchronization process. See Chapter 2 for an explanation of DP's Receive Sync and Transmit Sync commands.

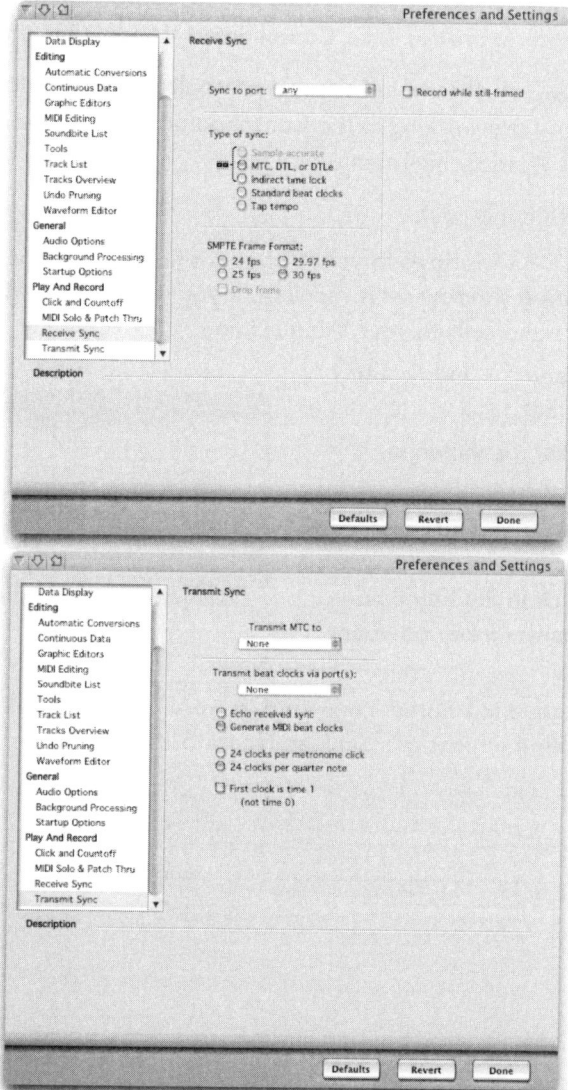

Figure 5.36
Digital Performer's Receive Sync and Transmit Sync preferences.

Window Sets

A much-overlooked feature of Digital Performer is the ability to create window sets. One of the most daunting and overwhelming obstacles for even the advanced DP user is management of its various windows. This becomes even more apparent if you are short on screen real estate. Creating window sets allows you to name, capture, and save window layouts, allowing you to instantly reconfigure your Digital Performer workspace to suit your specific music-production needs. Even though the default window sets provided with Digital Performer are all based on a Consolidated Window layout, the Window Sets feature can be used regardless if the Consolidated Window feature is turned on or off.

To recall an existing window set, choose the desired preset from the Window Sets submenu (Window menu > Window Sets). If you are working in the Consolidated Window, you can also access window sets from the Consolidated Window mini-menu.

To save a window configuration layout:

1. Begin by arranging DP's windows to your liking. Position them in the location that you want them to appear when a window set is recalled. If you are using the Consolidated Window feature, adjust the rows and cells to your liking instead.

2. Choose Window menu > Window Sets > Capture Window Set.

3. Name the window set, as shown in Figure 5.37.

4. If you would like to assign your new window set to a desired hot key or custom key binding, click in the Key Binding input field and press a key on your computer keyboard.

5. If the hotkey is assigned to another command, a warning dialog will open, asking whether you want to continue with the reassignment (see Figure 5.38).

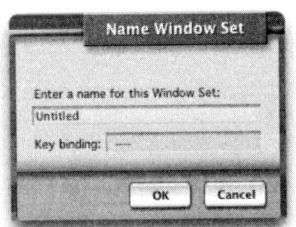

Figure 5.37

The Name Window Set command.

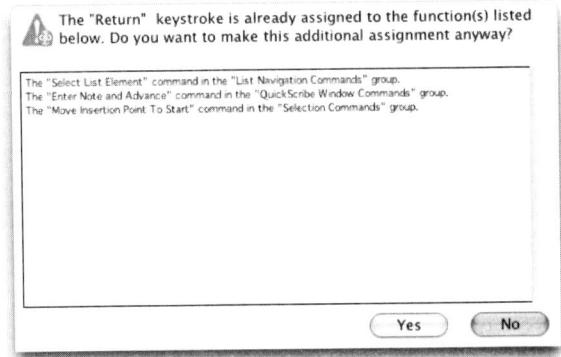

Figure 5.38

When attempting to assign a key binding that is already in use by another command, DP will present you with a warning dialog.

6. Once named, click the OK button and your window set will appear within the Window Sets submenu, as shown in Figure 5.39.

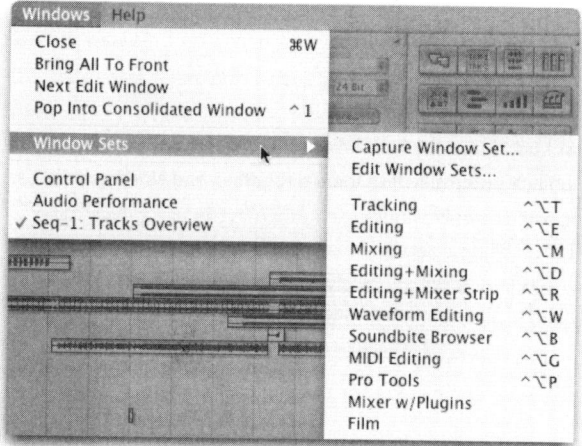

Figure 5.39

The Window Sets submenu.

To modify an existing window set:

1. Repeat the steps for creating a new window set.
2. When naming the set, however, choose the exact name as the window set you wish to modify.

To delete or rename an existing window set:

1. Choose Windows menu > Window Sets > Edit Window Sets.
2. Select the window set you wish to modify.
3. To rename the window set, click the Rename button and type the new name. Click OK to confirm the change.
4. To delete the window set, click the Delete button. A warning dialog will open, asking you to confirm the action. Click OK to delete the window set.

To change the order of window sets within the Window Sets menu:

1. Choose Windows menu > Window Sets > Edit Window Sets.
2. Click on the icon located to the left on the window set name and drag it up or down within the menu.

To assign a keyboard shortcut (key binding) to an existing window set:

1. Choose Windows menu > Window Sets > Edit Window Sets.
2. Associated key bindings are listed to the right of each window set. If the window set doesn't contain a key binding it will appear as a dash.

CHAPTER 5 } Project Management: Part 1

3. Click on the existing key binding or empty slot (indicated by a double-dash) and enter the desired hotkey (key combination).
4. If the hotkey is assigned to another command, a warning dialog will open, asking whether you want to continue with the assignment.

> **STREAMLINE THE WINDOW SETS MENU**
> If the default window sets that appear in the Window Sets menu don't fit your production needs, you may want to think about deleting them altogether and starting from scratch. Having a menu that contains only window sets you actually use will certainly be more helpful than a list full of window sets you never look at. Of course, you don't have to create your window sets in one sitting; simply create them during the normal course of production and you'll have a menu full of useful window sets within no time at all.

Track Colors

Another customization feature in DP is the ability to assign track colors. You can assign any color you wish to a single track, selected tracks, or tracks of the same type. This feature is just another way to quickly distinguish between different tracks or track types within the various editor windows. Colors within DP are grouped into color schemes (preset color groups), which can be edited to suit your specific needs. You can also create your own color schemes by duplicating and modifying existing ones.

Color Schemes

A color scheme is a set of colors that are displayed within Digital Performer's Color palette pop-up window. Stock color scheme presets are listed in the Colors submenu (in the Setup menu). Simply choose a preset to change the color scheme for a project. Schemes can also be edited by choosing Setup menu > Colors > Edit Color Schemes. The Edit Color Schemes window provides you with several options for customizing these presets (see Figure 5.40).

Figure 5.40
The Edit Color Schemes window provides several options for modifying color schemes. The currently selected scheme will be highlighted.

* **Edit.** Double-click on a color scheme, or select it and click the Edit button to modify an existing preset. This will open the Color palette for the selected color scheme (see Figure 5.41). Click to modify the color of a tile. This action will cause the Mac OS Color Picker to open, allowing you to choose a specific color for the tile (see Figure 5.42). Only the left- and right-most color tiles within the palette can be modified, however. You can also change the position of these "heavy bordered" tiles by dragging with the mouse. DP will automatically fill in the in-between tiles with a variable shade of the two colors.
* **Duplicate.** This option will duplicate the currently selected (highlighted) color scheme. Once you choose a color scheme, you will be prompted to enter a new name for the duplicated scheme (see Figure 5.43). Use this option when you want to create your own preset. Once the scheme is duplicated and given a new name, click the Edit button to customize the preset.
* **Delete.** Click this button to delete a color scheme. A warning dialog will open, asking you to confirm the action (see Figure 5.44).
* **Rename.** Click this button to rename a color scheme.
* **Done.** Click this button to close the Edit Color Schemes window.

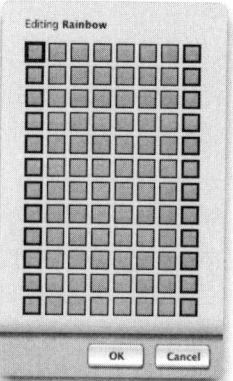

Figure 5.41

Click the Edit Color Schemes' Edit button to modify the selected color scheme. Only the left- and right-most color tiles (designated with a heavy border) can be modified.

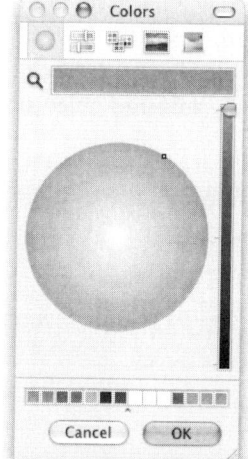

Figure 5.42

Double-clicking on the left or right (heavy bordered) color tiles within a color scheme will launch the Mac OS Color Picker.

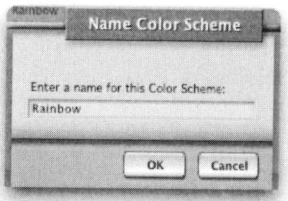

Figure 5.43

The Name Color Scheme window.

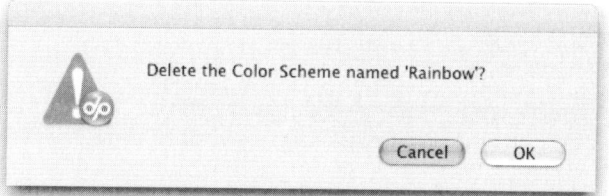

Figure 5.44

The Delete Color Scheme warning dialog

CHAPTER 5 } Project Management: Part 1

Color Preferences

The Color Preferences (Setup menu > Colors > Color Preferences or Digital Performer menu > Preferences and Settings) will affect how colors are used throughout DP's various edit windows (see Figure 5.45).

- **Use Custom Track Colors.** These options will allow you to specify whether custom colors are used within Digital Performer's various edit windows.
- **Assign New Tracks.** These options will determine how custom colors are assigned to new tracks. If you choose the To Different Shades of the Same Color or To the Same Color option, the Color preferences will update and display the Use Different Colors for Different Track Types option, shown in Figure 5.46.
- **Use Different Colors for Different Track Types.** When this option is unchecked, you can change the specific color that will be assigned to a track by clicking on the Pick a Color option. When this option is checked, however, DP will display multiple color swatches, allowing you to choose a different color for each track type (see Figure 5.47). Available colors will be determined by the currently selected color scheme.

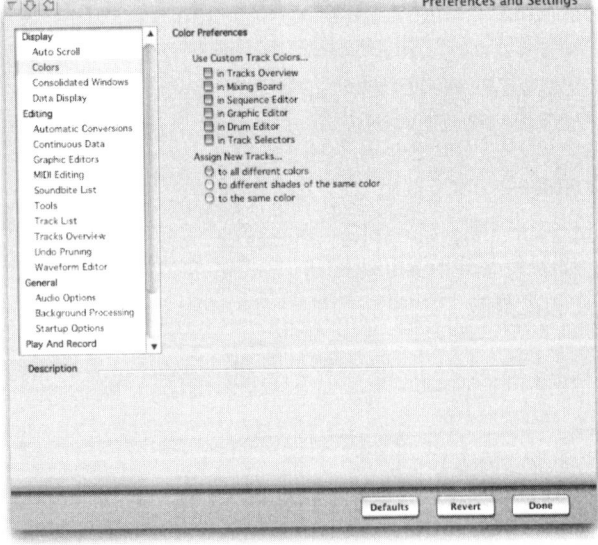

Figure 5.45
The Color preferences are located in the Preferences and Settings window.

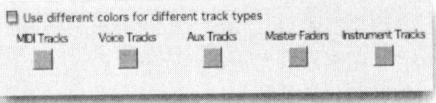

Figure 5.46
The Use Different Colors for Different Track Types option.

※ Customizing Your Workspace

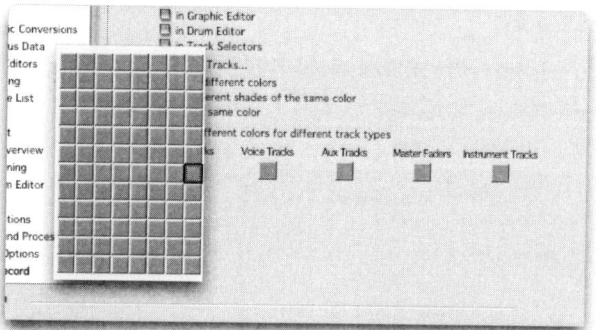

Figure 5.47
The Use Different Colors for Different Track Types option. Once enabled, color swatches for each track type will become available.

Changing the Colors of Tracks
To set the color for a track:

1. In the Tracks Window, click on the color swatch of the desired track within the Color column. A Color palette pop-up window will appear, as shown in Figure 5.48.
2. Click on a tile within the Color palette to assign the new color to the track.
3. If the Color Column isn't visible, choose Digital Performer > Preferences and Settings > Track List and enable the Color Column (see Figure 5.49).

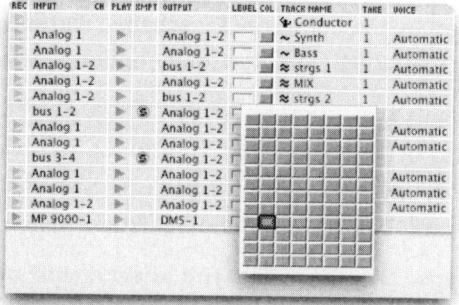

Figure 5.48
Click on a color swatch within the Tracks window's Color column to assign a color to a specific track.

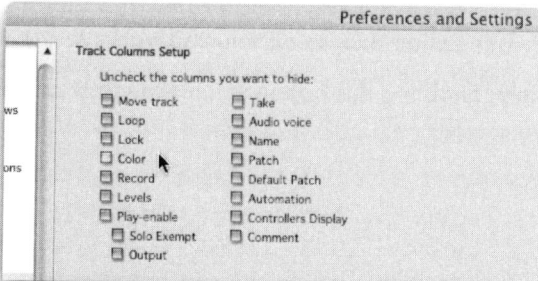

Figure 5.49
Click the Color option to make the Color column visible within the Tracks window.

CHAPTER 5 } Project Management: Part 1

To set the color for multiple tracks:

1. Select the tracks you wish to affect. Remember to Shift-click to make multiple selections.
2. Choose Setup menu > Colors > Assign Colors (see Figure 5.50).

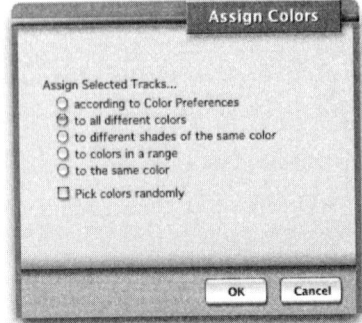

Figure 5.50
The Assign Colors command determines how colors are assigned to multiple tracks.

3. Choose the option you want from the following:
   - **According to Color Preferences.** This option will allow you to make color assignments according to the settings within the Colors preferences.
   - **To all different colors.** This option automatically assigns a color to the selected tracks. Colors are determined by the current color scheme, starting with the beginning color of the palette. Enabling the Pick Colors Randomly option will force colors to be assigned in a random order.
   - **To different shades of the same color.** This option will allow you to designate a specific color from the Color palette. Once a color is chosen for the first track, only colors from the same palette row will be used for the other tracks within the selection.
   - **To colors in a range.** This option lets you select a start and end color from the current color palette. Once start and end colors are chosen, DP will cycle through the in-between colors when making color assignments to the selected tracks.
   - **To the same color.** This option assigns all selected tracks to the same color.
   - **Pick colors randomly.** Enabling this option will make many of the above color assignments happen in a random order.

The Commands Window

The Commands window, shown in Figure 5.51, provides a central location for accessing and customizing Digital Performer's extensive keyboard shortcut commands. You can even assign specific MIDI events to functions within DP, which allows you to trigger commands from your MIDI controller in place of the computer keyboard. Keyboard shortcuts within DP are called key bindings.

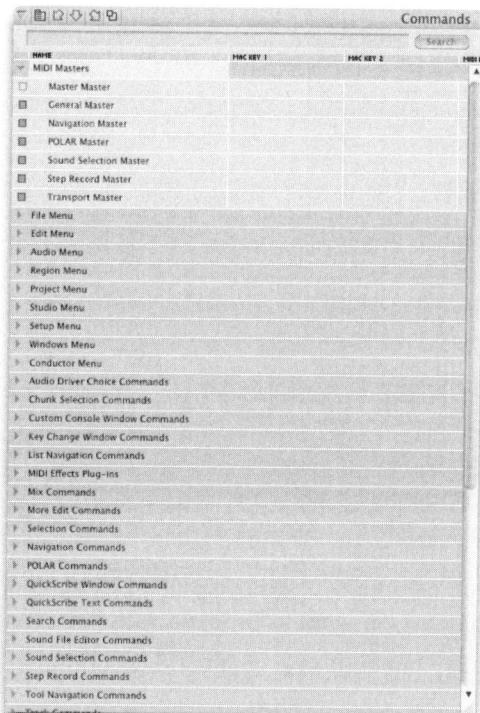

Figure 5.51
The Commands window provides a central location for accessing and customizing key bindings in Digital Performer.

Navigating the Commands Window

All commands within the Commands window are organized into logical groups. Click on the triangle located to the left of the group name to view the commands within that group. Option-click on a triangle icon to show or hide all command groups.

To search for a specific command:

1. Choose Setup menu > Commands, or use the default keyboard shortcut Shift+L.
2. In the search field located at the top of the window, type in the command (or text string) you wish to find.
3. Click the Search button, or press the Return key to begin searching.
4. DP will return the results by highlighting the appropriate command (see Figure 5.52).

To assign a keyboard shortcut (key binding) to a specific command:

1. Find the command you wish to modify.
2. Click in the Mac Key column.
3. Press the desired key combination; it will be entered into the Mac Key column.

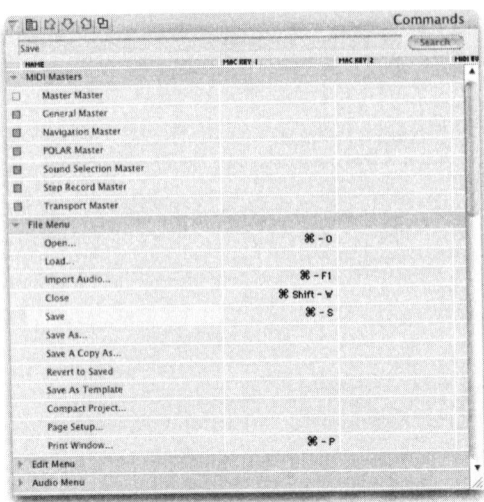

Figure 5.52
DP will return search results by highlighting the appropriate command within the commands list. In this example, the Save command has been searched for and found.

4. If the key binding you entered is already assigned to another command, a warning dialog will open asking whether you want to proceed with the assignment.
5. You can assign two key bindings to a command by using both the Mac Key 1 and Mac Key 2 columns.

To assign a MIDI event to a specific command:

1. Find the command you wish to modify.
2. Click with the mouse in the MIDI event column.
3. Enter the MIDI event by pressing the appropriate key on your MIDI controller.
4. For even further customization, specify the MIDI source by clicking in the Source column and choosing the specific MIDI device.

Numeric Base Note
When entering numeric values for certain commands (recalling Markers, for example), DP will allow you to use your MIDI controller in place of the numeric keypad on your keyboard. In order to properly take advantage of this feature, you must set the numeric MIDI base note by choosing Set Numeric MIDI Base Note from the Commands window's mini-menu. This option sets the value for the base MIDI note, or basically tells DP which MIDI note will correspond to the number 1 key on your computer keyboard. If you choose C4, for example, a value of 1 will be the C4 key on your MIDI controller. A value of 2 will be C#4, a value of 3 will be the pitch D4, and so on.

Customizing Your Workspace

To set the numeric base note value:

1. Choose Commands window > mini-menu > Set Numeric MIDI Base Note (see Figure 5.53).
2. Specify the base pitch by pressing the appropriate note on your MIDI controller.
3. Click OK to confirm the change.

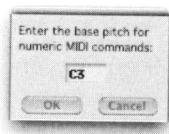

Figure 5.53

The Set Numeric MIDI Base Note command.

Key Bindings

Key commands in DP are called *key bindings*. A key binding can be a single key command or a set of commands that are contained in a project. Project key bindings are saved in the Command Bindings file located in the Digital Performer Preferences folder, as shown in Figure 5.54.

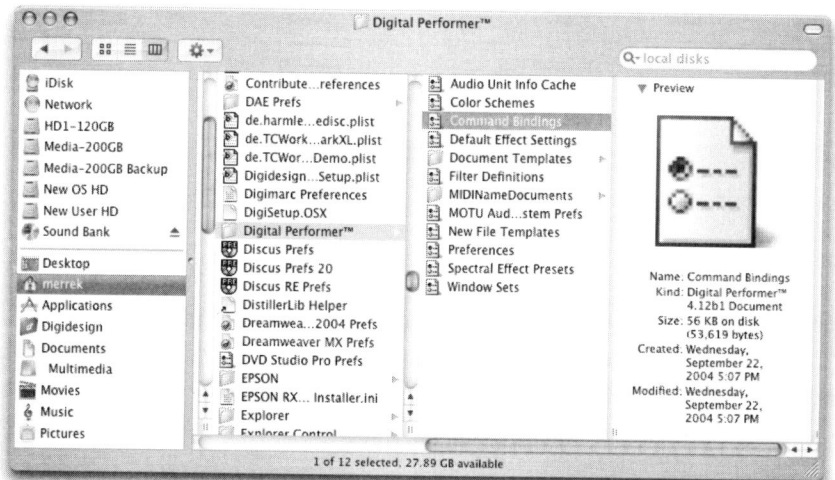

Figure 5.54

Project key bindings are stored within the User > Library > Preferences > Digital Performer > Command Bindings file.

Key bindings can be exported or imported into a Digital Performer project, allowing you to further customize the DP workspace. This allows you to create personalized key bindings that you can save and open in another Digital Performer system, back up your key bindings, or save them before importing a different set of commands.

To export a set of key bindings:

1. Choose Commands window > mini-menu > Export Key Bindings.
2. A standard Save dialog will open. Choose the destination for the new Key Bindings file.
3. Click the Save button to export the key binding.

CHAPTER 5 } Project Management: Part 1

To import a set of key bindings:

1. Choose Commands window > mini-menu > Import Key Bindings.
2. Choose the Key Bindings file you wish to open.
3. Click Open.
4. Next, DP will open a dialog, shown in Figure 5.55, asking you to either merge any new custom bindings that differ from the current set or to simply import the entire file and replace the current key bindings.
5. Click on the desired button to import or merge the new key bindings.

Figure 5.55
When importing key bindings, DP gives you the option of merging any bindings that differ from the current set or to simply import the entire key binding.

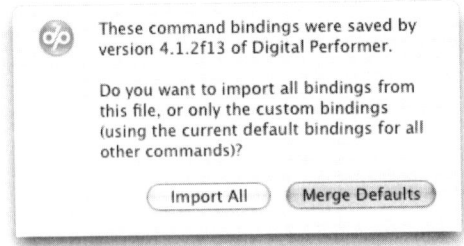

Summary

Digital Performer has a number of feature sets that allow you to organize and customize your DP projects. Each feature by itself may have only a limited impact on your workflow, but used in combination, these features offer a powerful solution for managing the music production process. The next chapter (Part 2 of project management) will focus on the more complex Undo History, audio management, and backup processes.

6 Project Management: Part 2

In this chapter, we will dive deeper into the topic of project management within Digital Performer. Here is a summary of topics discussed within this chapter:

- How to use DP's Undo History windows.
- How to efficiently manage audio files and hard drive space.
- Options and solutions for backup and archival of your DP projects, including third-party software.

The Undo History

Digital Performer supports unlimited undos and redos, which can be managed from the Undo History windows. There are basically three Undo History windows in DP—the main project Undo History, the Polar Undo History, and the audio files Undo History windows. The audio files Undo History windows are unique in that each individual audio file in DP has its own independent Undo history windows. Each Undo History window provides you with a complete list of actions, a timeline, and preferences for controlling undo behaviors. DP even supports unlimited branching, which I'll discuss later on in this section. Every action you take when working on a project is remembered, unless you configure the Undo History preferences (called the *Pruning Preferences*) to do otherwise.

Though the main project Undo History window is found in the Edit Menu, I've chosen to discuss this feature within the "Project Management: Part 2" chapter of this book because of its direct impact on the project management process. Many of the features that will be discussed in this chapter require an understanding of the Undo History, the Pruning Preferences, and their related terms.

Undo commands contained within the Edit Menu, however, will be covered in detail in Chapter 10.

CHAPTER 6 } Project Management: Part 2

The Project Undo History

The project Undo History window (Edit menu > Undo History) displays a complete list of actions taken within the project (see Figure 6.1). Besides the name of the action, other information, such as the time and the amount of memory and disk space required to remember the action, is listed. Although every action remembered will require a small amount of RAM, disk space is only needed for actions that require it in the first place, such as recording or disk-based processing.

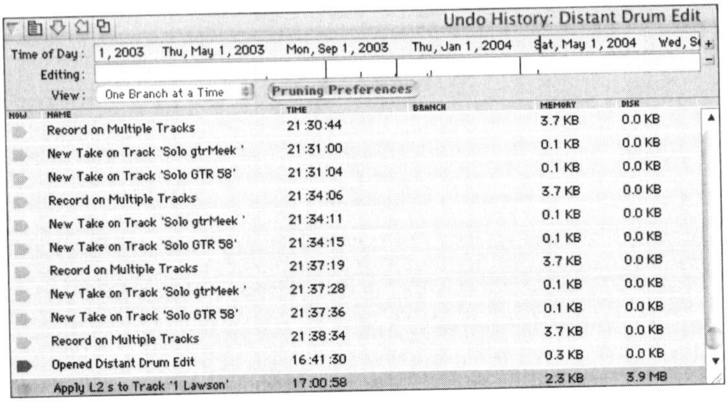

Figure 6.1
The Undo History window

The Undo History Timeline

At the top of the Undo History window is the timeline. The Time of Day strip provides a linear timeline that can be dragged to the left and right to move backward or forward in time. Zoom buttons (+/ -) located to the right of the strip let you magnify or shrink the timeline. The green line or current action marker indicates the timeline position of the current action.

Directly below the Time of Day strip is the Editing strip. The white area represents the life of the project, from the beginning to the most recent action. Actions are displayed as vertical lines. You can click and drag vertically in this white area to quickly zoom within the timeline. Clicking directly on a vertical action line will highlight it in blue and automatically locate the action within the History list for easy identification.

The Undo History List

The Undo History list is located below the timeline, in the main body of the Undo History window. There are six columns that provide important information about the listed actions.

* **Now**. A dot in this column represents the current action. Double-click in this column next to an action to jump to that point in your project's history. Actions that have been "undone" will be shaded in blue. This dot corresponds to the Time of Day strip's current action marker (the vertical green line).

- **Name.** This column offers a brief description of the action. Renaming your tracks, sequences, and soundfiles in your project can help you quickly identify an action.
- **Time.** This column shows the time the action occurred.
- **Branch.** This column indicates whether a branch has occurred within the Undo History timeline (I'll explain branches shortly). Branches are separated from other actions by heavy lines. A branch menu, which is indicated with an inverted triangle, will be displayed if One Branch at a Time is chosen in the View pop-up menu.
- **Memory.** This column displays the amount of RAM needed to remember the action.
- **Disk.** This column displays the amount of hard drive space required to remember the action. Only certain actions (such as recording and processing) will consume disk space.

> **TAKING ADVANTAGE OF THE NAME COLUMN**
>
> In order to speed up your navigation of the Undo History list, be sure to rename your tracks, audio files, soundbites, and sequences with appropriate, descriptive names. DP will add a brief description of the action within the Name column of the Undo History window, based on the name of the file in question.
>
> For example, if your tracks are called "Audio 1," "Audio 2," "Audio 3," and so on, then you may wind up with an action called "recorded on track Audio 4" or "edit fade in track Audio 5." If you are working on a larger project, you may not remember offhand what track "Audio 4" is. Renaming your tracks something specific, such as "Bass," may spare you the need to constantly double-check your work.

Branching

What sets Digital Performer's Undo History apart from that of other applications, such as Adobe's Photoshop or Illustrator, is its support for unlimited branching. You can think of branches as separate but dependent undo timelines. Here is how branching works: As Digital Performer remembers all of your actions within a project, you can jump backward within the timeline (undoing the current action) and begin a new set of actions (branch off), and DP will remember both sets of actions, or branches. The new actions are basically "branching off" in a new direction, so to speak, creating two branches in the process. The first branch is the set of undone actions, while the second branch is the new set of actions. DP will create a branch at the point where your new actions start. When working with branches, the currently active set of actions (the "not undone" actions) is always considered the main branch. Any branches that you are not working on will be undone.

CHAPTER 6 } Project Management: Part 2

Once you've created a branch, you can choose it by clicking on the Branch pop-up menu. When you select another branch, its actions will be displayed in a shade of blue, indicating that the branch is in an undone state. Double-click in the Now column next to the name of an undone action to make the branch active. This branch will become the main branch, and all other branches will be immediately undone.

The Undo History in Action

The concept of branching can be difficult to grasp when just reading about it, so to demonstrate better how it works, I'll walk you through a hypothetical session, complete with screen shots. It begins with the recording of a piano track.

1. First I create a session called "DP Power!" I record a few passes on the piano track. The track is processed with a UAD-1 Fairchild compressor, then a few more passes are recorded. At this point in time the Undo History would look like that in Figure 6.2.

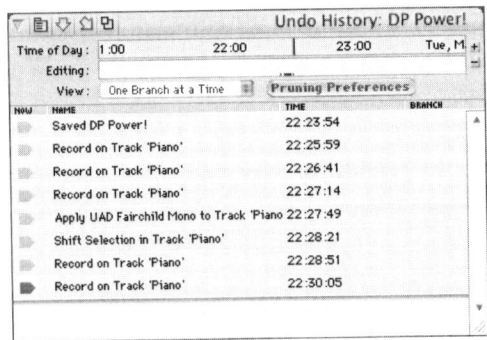

Figure 6.2
The Undo History window for our example.

2. I decide to undo the processing from the piano track, so I double-click in the Now column next to the Piano Track action, the one that immediately precedes the Apply UAD Fairchild Mono to Track Piano action (see Figure 6.3).

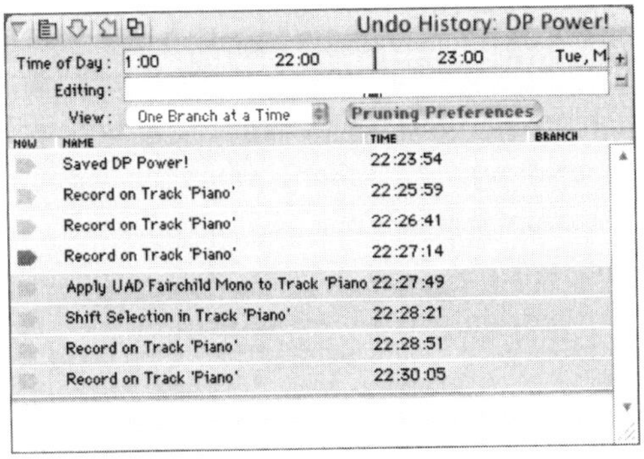

Figure 6.3
The UAD-1 processing has been undone. Undone actions are shaded in blue.

※ The Undo History

3. Next, I record a Cello track. This new action automatically creates a new branch, preserving the undone UAD processing actions (see Figure 6.4).

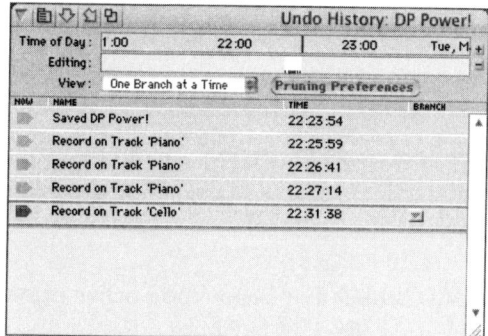

Figure 6.4

A cello track is recorded, automatically creating a new branch. Branch points are indicated with heavy lines.

4. Two more cello passes are recorded, as shown in Figure 6.5.

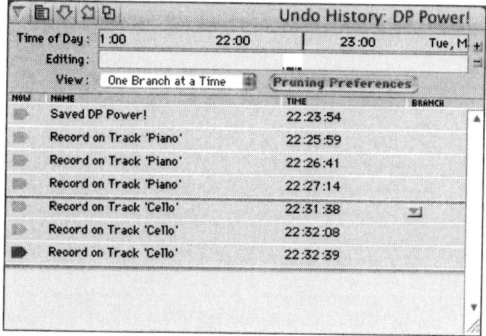

Figure 6.5

Two more cello passes are recorded.

5. Clicking on the Branch pop-up menu reveals the original undone UAD process, as shown in Figure 6.6. Selecting the UAD branch displays the undone actions, as shown in Figure 6.7.

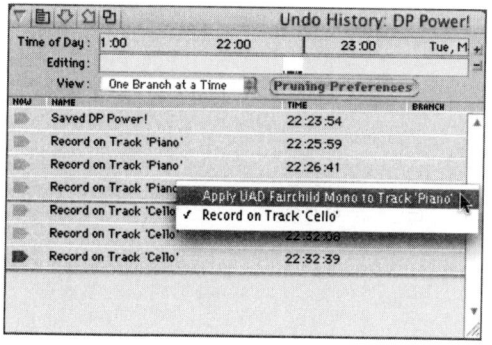

Figure 6.6

Clicking on the Branch menu reveals a check mark next to the currently selected main branch and the UAD processing branch that has been undone.

CHAPTER 6 } Project Management: Part 2

Figure 6.7

Selecting the UAD branch in the Branch menu displays the undone actions.

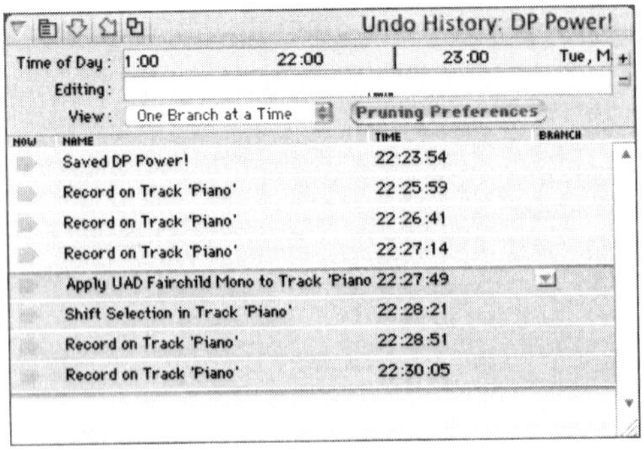

6. In Figure 6.8, the UAD branch has been made active again. If you were to view the undone cello branch, it would look like that in Figure 6.9.

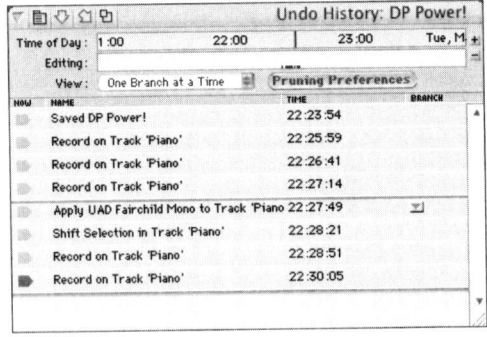

Figure 6.8

The UAD branch that was previously undone is made active again.

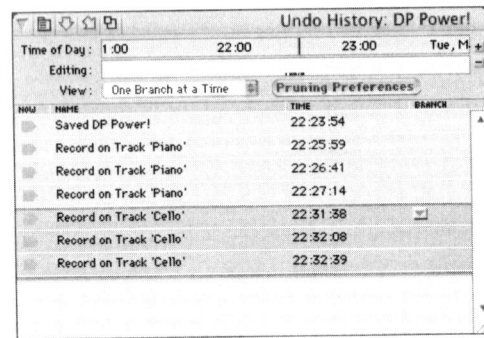

Figure 6.9

Selecting the cello branch reveals that it has been undone.

7. Next, I decide to undo both sets of actions, the original UAD branch and the newly created Cello recordings (see Figure 6.10), and I decide to record a vocal take (see Figure 6.11).

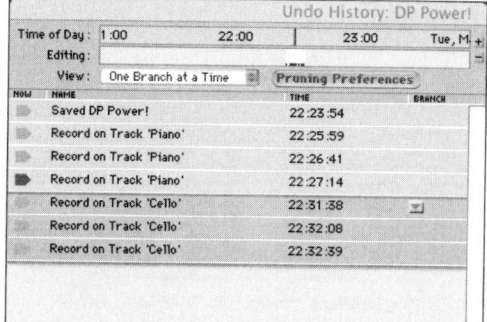

Figure 6.10

Both branches have been undone.

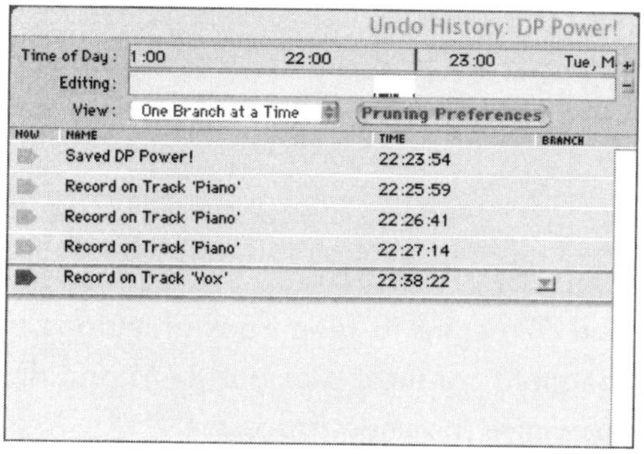

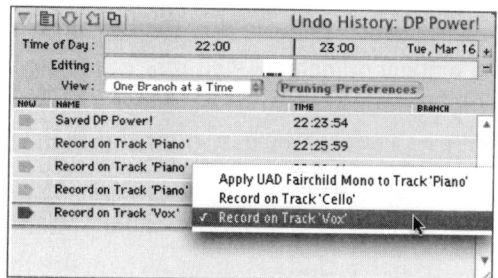

Figure 6.11

A new vocal (vox) track has been recorded, creating a third branch within the Undo History timeline.

8. If you click on the Branch pop-up menu, you can see all three branches, as shown in Figure 6.12. The check mark next to the vox branch tells us that it is the main branch, and that it is currently active.

Figure 6.12

The Branch menu displays all three branches. The main, or active, branch is designated with a check mark.

9. In Figure 6.13, you can see that I've recorded another vocal take. In the View pop-up menu, however, I've selected All Branches at Once. Notice that the branch menus are no longer visible and the non-active branches (which have been undone) are displayed shaded in blue and separated with heavy lines.

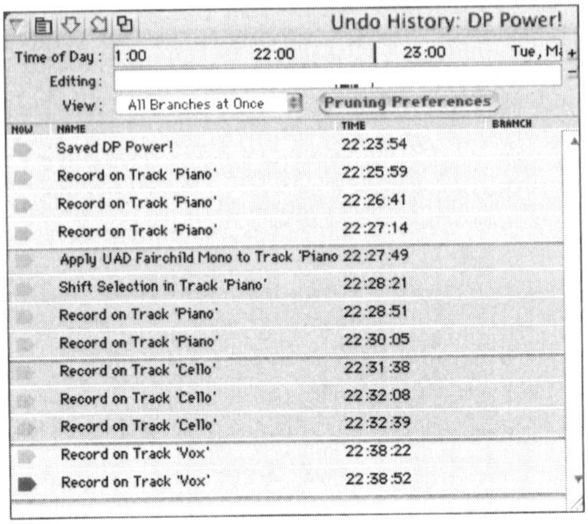

Figure 6.13

Selecting All Branches at Once will display all actions within all branches. Actions within a branch will appear grouped in chronological order.

Managing the Undo History Windows

As a project progresses and DP begins to keep track of undone actions, branches, and so on, the remembered actions will begin to consume precious RAM and disk space. Digital Performer provides a number of features to customize the undo process. DP's Undo History windows can be set up to automatically manage themselves through the Pruning Preferences, or you can control them manually with options contained in the Undo History window's mini-menu.

Pruning Preferences

Each Undo History window has its own independent preferences located in the Undo Pruning section of the Preferences and Settings window. These preferences allow you to establish a set of criteria to automatically manage the amount of memory and disk space that the Undo History windows can consume. The Undo Pruning preferences can be accessed from any one of DP's Undo History windows by clicking on the Pruning Preferences button, as shown in Figure 6.14. You can also choose Digital Performer menu > Preferences.

Unlike the three Undo History windows, the Undo Pruning preferences are centralized in the Preferences and Settings window. From the Undo Pruning section, use the Undo Pruning drop-down menu, shown in Figure 6.15, to set the Undo Pruning preferences for a specific Undo History window.

The Undo History

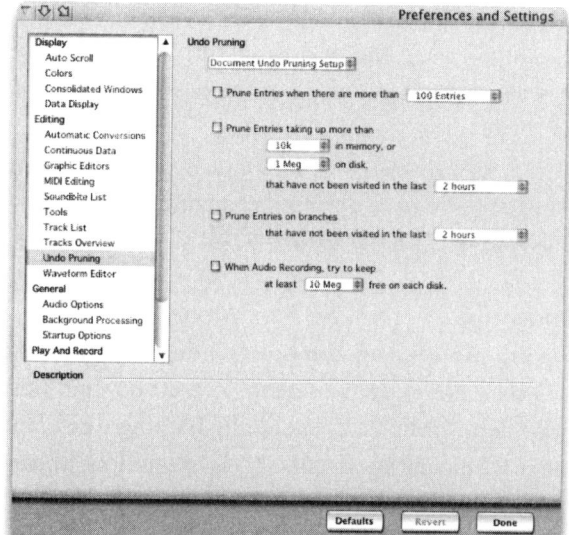

Figure 6.14
Click the Pruning Preferences button in any of DP's Undo History windows to open the Undo Pruning preferences, located in the Preferences and Settings window.

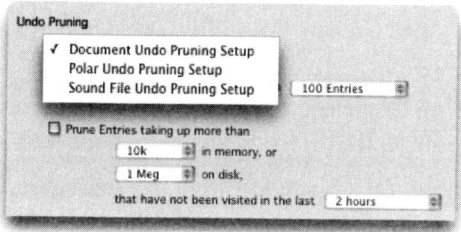

Figure 6.15
Click on the Undo Pruning drop-down menu to set the Pruning Preferences for a specific Undo History window.

This Undo Pruning drop-down menu is explained below.

- **Document Undo Pruning Setup.** Preferences for a project's main Undo History window.
- **Polar Undo Pruning Setup.** Preferences for Polar's Undo History window.
- **Sound File Undo Pruning Setup.** Preferences for audio file Undo History windows.

Within the Undo Pruning preferences, you have the following four options for controlling each Undo History window:

- **Prune Entries when there are more than.** This setting limits the total number of entries that will be remembered in an Undo History list.
- **Prune Entries taking up more than.** This option is used to automatically discard (or prune) any action that consumes a specific amount of memory and disk space and hasn't been visited within a set time. This option will affect actions within all branches.

145

CHAPTER 6 } Project Management: Part 2

- **Prune Entries on branches**. This option only affects actions that are on branches (that is, actions that have been undone). This option will discard actions within branches that have not been visited within a set amount of time. Actions on the main branch, or current actions, will not be affected.
- **When audio recording, try to keep**. This option will discard actions when available hard drive space falls below a specified value during the recording process. Actions that are furthest back within the Undo History list will be pruned first.

Manually Pruning the Undo History from the Mini-Menu

Even though the Undo Pruning preferences can be set independently for each Undo History list to automatically discard, or flush, actions. These settings are global and not project-specific. For even greater control, DP provides extra options for manually flushing each Undo History list. These options are contained within the mini-menus of each Undo History window, shown in Figure 6.16, and can also be accessed from the Commands window.

- **Flush Undo Entries Prior to Current Point**. This command will discard any entries, or actions, that occur before the current action (the action designated with a dot in the Now column).
- **Flush Undo Entries After Current Point**. This command will discard any entries that occur after the current action.
- **Flush Undo Entries on Branches**. This command will discard entries on all branches that are not part of the main branch. These are basically actions that have been undone.
- **Flush All Undo Entries**. This command will flush the entire Undo History list, so use it with caution!
- **Apply Pruning Prefs to All Undo Entries Now**. This command will immediately apply any settings you have within the Undo Pruning preferences (minus any time settings) to all actions within the Undo History window.

Figure 6.16

Contained in each Undo History window's mini-menu are controls for manually flushing the undo entries and branches.

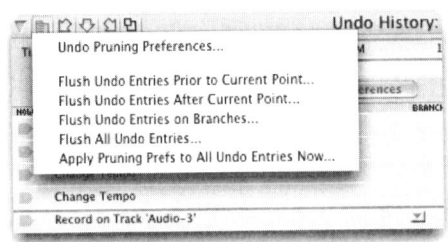

146

The Undo History

Following are a few points to keep in mind when working with DP's manual flush commands:

- Flush commands always apply to the front-most Undo History window. If no window is open, the commands will be applied to the project's main Undo History window.
- If the Polar Undo History window is in the foreground, then pruning commands will be applied to the open Polar session.
- If the Soundbites window is in the foreground, then pruning commands will be applied to any selected parent audio files. Only the Flush All Undo Entries and Apply Pruning Prefs to All Undo Entries Now commands can be applied in this manner, however. To use the other commands, open the Undo History window for the specific audio file.

Audio File Undo History Windows

Each audio file in DP has its own independent Undo History window, which can be accessed from an audio file's Waveform Editor (see Figure 6.17). This is one of the most overlooked components of the Undo History because many users have yet to discover its versatility. What sets this Undo History window apart from the main project and Polar Undo History windows is your ability to modify or remove an action without affecting the actions that come after it. Modifications can be made to plug-ins or to DSP processing that has been applied to an audio file.

In the following example, a Waves Ren EQ, UAD compressor, and fade have been applied to a soundbite called "cello". The file has been processed in the Waveform Editor, so the actions are stored within the audio file's independent Undo History window, shown in Figure 6.18. To modify the REQ 2 action, simply double-click on the name of the action. This will re-open the EQ plug-in window with the original settings used to EQ the cello soundbite. Make the necessary changes to the EQ setting and reapply the effect.

Figure 6.17
The Waveform Editor. Click on the Open Undo History button to open an audio file's Undo History window.

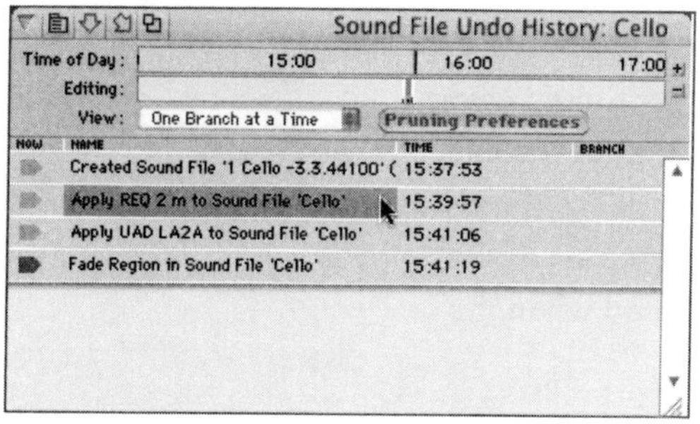

Figure 6.18
An audio file's Undo History window.

CHAPTER 6 } Project Management: Part 2

Keep in mind that modifications made to actions within an audio file's Undo History list are not undoable. To return to your original setting you will need to reapply the effect. If you would like to remove the action, click the name of the action and choose Edit > Delete, or use the Delete key. Deleting an action will not affect actions that occur after it, as shown in Figure 6.19! Once an action is removed, DP will essentially "fix" the audio file in order to reflect the change that has been made, as shown in Figure 6.20. Keep in mind the Fix Soundbites action is only displayed during the update process. In Figure 6.20, notice that there are two "dots" showing us that there are two current actions. The Fade Region action is the current action, while the Fix Soundbites action is temporary. Once the soundbite has been updated to reflect the change, this action will be removed from the list.

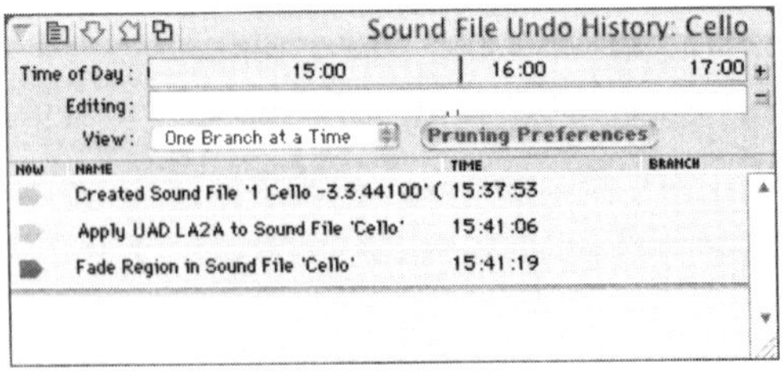

Figure 6.19
Deleted actions will not affect actions that come after it. Notice the UAD LA2A and Fade actions have been left intact even though the preceding REQ action has been removed.

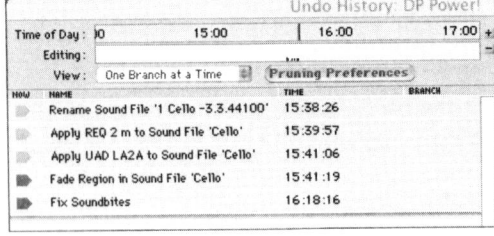

Figure 6.20
The main project Undo History window shows DP "fixing" or updating the audio file that has been modified within the audio file's Undo History list. The Fix Soundbites action is only displayed during the update process.

Polar Undo History Window

The Polar window also has its own independent Undo History window, as shown in Figure 6.21. The Polar Undo History works much like the project's main Undo History. The undo list applies to the currently open Polar session. Unlike the other Undo History windows, however, Polar Undo Histories are discarded when the Polar session is closed.

Figure 6.21
Click the History button to open Polar's Undo History window.

Managing Audio Files and Soundbites

By default, audio files in a new DP project are stored within the project's Audio Files folder, shown in Figure 6.22. This allows you to take a hands-off approach, relying on DP to automatically place newly created takefiles in the proper location.

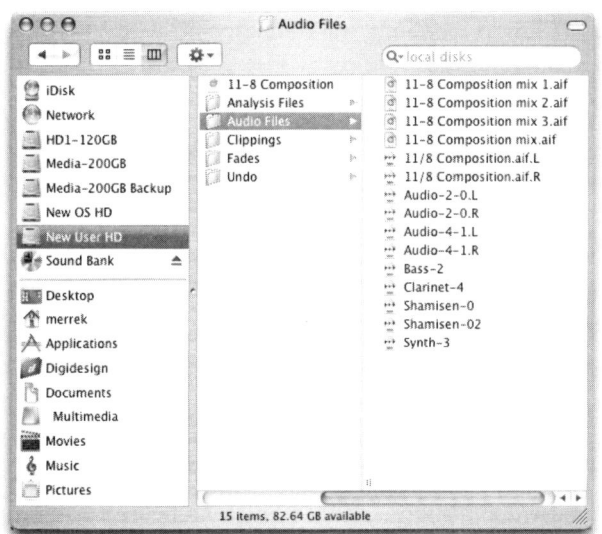

Figure 6.22

The project folder's Audio Files folder

Changing the Location of Audio Files and Soundbites

Audio files do not have to be placed in this folder, however. They can be located within different folders, or even across multiple hard drives. You can change the location of your audio files before the actual recording process or after audio has been placed within the Audio Files folder. Digital Performer will automatically keep track of the audio files regardless of which folder or hard drives they are moved to.

Though it may be easier to simply rely on DP to automatically manage your audio files, there are benefits to placing your audio within different folders or hard drives. For example, you could create subfolders within the project folder's main Audio Files folder to store files that relate to a specific instrument. Or you could use multiple hard drives, which would increase disk performance by distributing the workload across more than one disk, allowing for higher track counts and audio edits. As I said earlier, file locations can be designated before the actual recording process, or they can be changed even if they already exist within a project.

Keep in mind that Soundbites only reference a portion of audio within an audio file. This region information is stored within its associated sound file and therefore cannot be separated from its parent audio file.

CHAPTER 6 } Project Management: Part 2

To change the destination folder or hard drive before recording:

1. In Digital Performer, choose Studio > Audio Monitor. The Audio Monitor window provides information concerning the inputs of record-enabled tracks, including input level meters, location, and available hard drive space for that location.
2. Double-click on the location of the takefile in the Take Folder column to display the full path name for a file. Abbreviated locations will be indicated with a double colon separating the hard drive and project Audio files folder.
3. The destination for each armed audio input can be set independently or globally for all takefiles. To change the location for a specific takefile: double-click on the name of the takefile. The Choose a Folder dialog window will open, asking you to choose the location for the specific audio input (see Figure 6.23).
4. Navigate to the desired folder or hard drive. If you would like to create a new folder, click on the New Folder button. Rename the folder and click Open. To choose an existing folder, select the folder and click Choose.
5. If you would like to simultaneously change the destination folder for multiple/all takefiles, select the takefiles by clicking on the first takefile then shift-clicking the rest. To quickly select adjacent takefiles, drag over them with the mouse. To select all the files in the list, use the default keyboard shortcut Command+A.
6. From the Audio Monitor's mini-menu, choose Set Take Folder. A dialog asking you to select the destination folder or hard drive for the selected takefiles will open.
7. If you need to set the takefile locations for other takefiles, repeat Steps 4-6 as needed.

Figure 6.23
Double-clicking on the name of a takefile within the Audio Monitor window will allow you to specify the destination folder of audio files before recording.

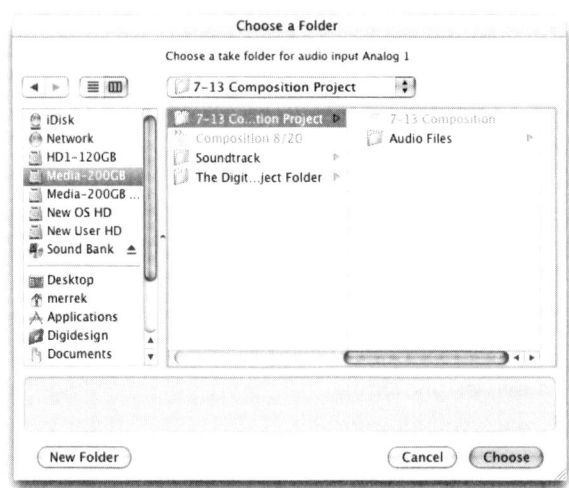

✺ Managing Audio Files and Soundbites

To change the location of existing audio files:
1. Within the Finder, simply move the audio file(s) to a new location by dragging with the mouse. DP will automatically keep track of the audio file's new location.
2. If, for some reason, DP loses track of a file, it will ask you to manually locate the file.

To find the location of an existing audio file:
- ✺ Select the audio file or soundbite within the Soundbites window and then click on the Info Pane button. The File column of the parent file will display the full path.
- ✺ You can also select the audio file or soundbite and use the keyboard shortcut Option+R. This method will launch the Finder and open up the actual folder the selected audio file is located in. Keep in mind that you can use this method to determine the location of an audio file or soundbite without opening the Soundbites window.

Organizing Audio Files and Soundbites into Folders

Within the Soundbites window, audio files and soundbites can be organized into folders. This much-overlooked feature allows you to clean up and organize the Soundbites window List section. Placing soundbites into folders will also keep any regions created by the editing process with its parent soundbite.

To create a folder within the Soundbites window:
1. Open the Soundbites window by choosing Project > Soundbites. You can also use the default keyboard shortcut Shift+B.
2. With the List section visible, click on the View By menu and choose Folders.
3. Choose Create New Folder from the Soundbites window mini-menu. Folders will be indicated with a dark-gray band.
4. To rename the new folder, Option-click on the folder name.
5. Drag the desired soundbite or soundbites into the folder.

Renaming Existing Audio Files or Soundbites

Audio file and soundbite names can be changed from any location in which they appear within DP, including the Mac OS Finder. Regardless of where you change the name, Digital Performer will automatically update the name wherever the file appears.

To change the name of an existing audio file or soundbite:
- ✺ To rename an audio file or soundbite within the Soundbites window (or any other editor that the file appears), Option-click the name with the mouse.
- ✺ To rename an audio file from within the Finder, click on the name of the file and type the new name.

Deleting Audio Files and Soundbites

One of the most frightening processes of project management is the deletion of media files. This is why you should make a backup copy of your project (including its audio files folder) before continuing with this process. Accidents do happen—seemingly unimportant files that you delete turn out to be the lead vocal tracks, or the band decides that they really *did* want that alternate track you just deleted to regain disk space. Chances are, you have been in some situation where you deleted something, only to discover that you shouldn't have. Making backups of your important files can prevent or at least minimize the damage of losing precious data.

You can delete a project's audio files from within the Finder by dragging them directly to the trash, but if you do so, DP will not know what happened to them. They will remain in the project's Soundbites window but will appear as lost soundfiles. More importantly, however, you won't be able to verify whether the audio file in question contains regions that are actually being used within a project.

The Delete command in the Soundbites window will delete an audio file and/or its associated soundbites. This command will also permanently delete a soundbite's region or reference points within its parent audio file. The actual audio file will not be deleted, however, until the last region referring to the audio file is also deleted. Keep in mind that this command will only delete the sound file from the project, not from disk. To permanently delete a file from disk you must utilize DP's Compact file command, or drag the files to the trash within the Finder.

If you would like to delete an audio file from a project without deleting its corresponding region information from the file, use the Soundbites window's Remove from List command. This is useful when you have a soundbite that is being used within the sequence of another project—a common situation if you have used the Save As command (without duplicating audio) to create an alternate version of a project.

To delete an audio file and/or region from a project:

1. In the Soundbites window, select Soundfile from the View By menu. This will ensure that any soundbites will be listed with their parent audio files. If you need to audition the soundbite, make sure Audible mode (the title bar's speaker icon) is turned on.
2. Select the soundbite you wish to delete. Shift-click to make multiple selections.
3. Choose Mini-menu > Delete to delete the audio. The keyboard shortcut is Command+Delete.
4. If the soundbite currently exists within a track, DP will display a warning dialog asking if you really want to delete the selection. Click OK to continue.

5. A dialog will open asking if you wish to delete the audio selection the next time the Undo History is flushed (see Figure 6.24).

    - Choose No to delete the audio file or region without flushing the Undo History. Since the action still resides within the Undo History list, you can use the keyboard shortcut Command+Z to undo the process.

    - Choose Yes to delete the audio file/soundbite. This will launch another dialog asking if you wish to immediately flush the Undo History.

6. Another dialog will open asking if you wish to immediately flush the Undo History (see Figure 6.25).

    - Choose Don't Flush to preserve the audio file or soundbite within the Undo History until it is manually flushed.

    - Choose Flush to immediately flush the Undo History, permanently deleting the selected audio file(s) and/or regions from the project.

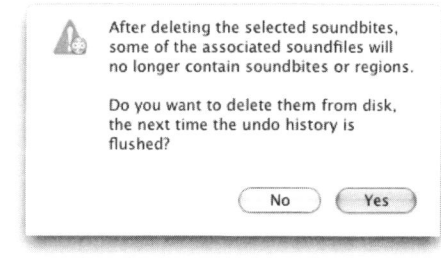

Figure 6.24

You can undo the deletion process, as long as the Undo History has not been flushed! To bypass this warning dialog, hold down the Option key before selecting Delete from the mini-menu.

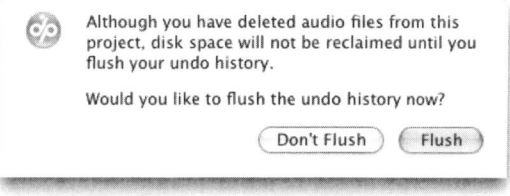

Figure 6.25

Immediately flushing the Undo History will permanently delete the selected audio files and/or regions from the project. Choosing Don't Flush will preserve the data within the Undo History until it is manually flushed.

Removing Audio Files and Soundbites

There will be times when you wish to simply remove an audio file or soundbite from a project without actually deleting the region information from its parent file—perha[...] another project, or you simply wish to preserve the soundfile's regi[...] future use. This can be accomplished with the Remove from List comr[...] window's mini-menu.

CHAPTER 6 } Project Management: Part 2

To remove a file or soundbite from a project:
1. In the Soundbites window, select Soundfile from the View By menu. This will ensure that any individual soundbites will be listed with their parent audio files.
2. Click with the mouse to select the soundbite you wish to remove. Shift-click to make multiple selections.
3. Choose Mini Menu > Remove from list. This will remove the soundbite from the project without deleting the region information from its parent audio file.
4. If the soundbite currently exists within a track, DP will display a warning asking if you really want to delete the selection. Click OK to continue. This action will remain in the Undo History list until it is manually flushed.

Locating Missing Audio Files or Soundbites

Occasionally, DP may lose track of or misplace a soundbite—perhaps you moved it to another location, or deleted it with the Finder. When this happens, you can correct the situation by simply pointing DP to the new location. Lost soundbites will be indicated with a question mark icon over the move handle of a soundbite within the Soundbites window, as shown in Figure 6.26.

Figure 6.26
The question mark icon indicates that the soundbite's location is unknown to Digital Performer.

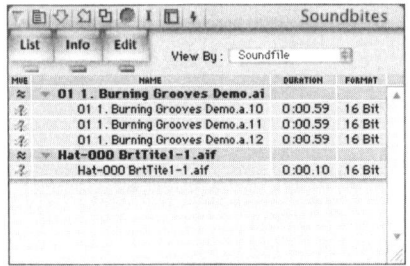

If you are opening a project that contains missing soundbites or soundfiles, DP will first launch the Missing Sound Files window, shown in Figure 6.27, which will allow you to locate the files before opening the project.

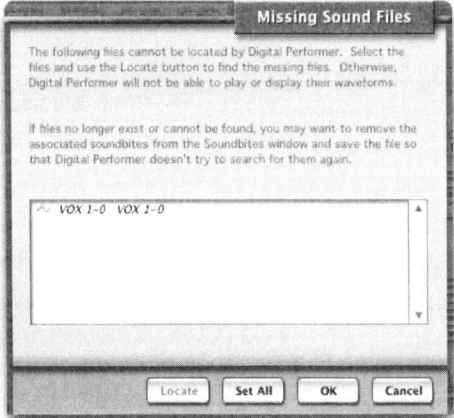

Figure 6.27
The Missing Sound Files window will appear when you attempt to open a project with missing soundbites.

✳ Managing Audio Files and Soundbites

To locate a missing file in an open project:

1. In the Soundbites window, select the soundbite you wish to find. Missing soundbites will be indicated with a question mark.
2. Choose Audio > Replace Soundbite.
3. Navigate to the missing soundbite and click Open (see Figure 6.28).

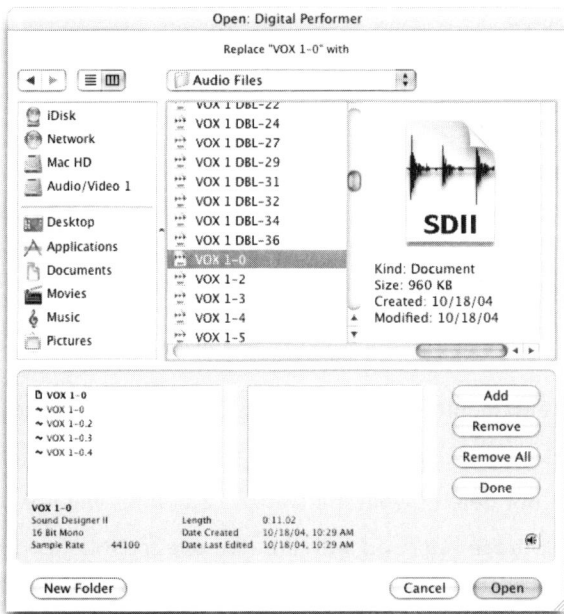

Figure 6.28
The Replace Soundbites command can be used to locate and replace missing soundbites.

To locate a missing file when you first open a project:

1. Open a project that contains missing soundbites. DP will launch the Missing Sound Files window prompting you to locate the files. Missing files will be displayed in *italics*. Once opened, you will be presented with three choices.
   - **Cancel**. Click this button to cancel the process and close the selected project.
   - **OK**. Click this button to skip the location process and open the project. Lost files will appear as missing soundbites within the Soundbites window. You can use the Replace Soundbite command to find the missing files.
   - **Set All**. Click this button to select all the missing files within this window. Once a file is selected, the Locate button will become available. You can also skip the Set All button and simply click on a file to begin the location process.

155

2. To locate a missing file, click the file and choose Locate. Click the Set All button to select all of the missing sound files.
3. In the Open dialog window, navigate to the location of the missing file.
4. Select the file and click Open.
5. If you have chosen the location for more than one sound file, repeat Steps 3-4.
6. Once found, the missing file will no longer appear in italics, indicating that DP is aware of its location in your system.
7. Once you have found the selected files, click OK. The Soundbites window will automatically update to reflect the changes.

Compacting an Audio File

Even though the Delete and Remove from List commands will delete soundfiles and regions from a project, the soundbites will still reside on your hard drive and consume valuable disk space. DP's compact commands, however, will permanently delete portions of unused audio files from disk. In this process, unused audio data within a soundfile is erased and the remaining portions are placed end to end. This is a destructive procedure and should be used with caution.

Here are a few points to keep in mind when using the Compact commands:

- Only data that does not belong to a region in the audio file is deleted.
- Soundbites that are not deleted with the Delete command will not be compacted.
- Soundbites that have been removed with the Remove from List command will not be deleted. If you wish to compact a soundbite that has been removed, import the soundbite again and use the Delete command to delete the region.
- The amount of time it takes to compact a file depends on the amount of data that is being removed.
- Once a file or project is compacted and the Undo History flushed, any deleted audio files will be permanently discarded.

To compact an audio file or files:

1. In the Soundbites window, begin by selecting the soundbites or regions you wish to discard from the project.
2. You can quickly select all of the unused soundbites in a project by choosing Mini-menu > Select Unused Soundbites. This will highlight all of the soundbites that are not in use within the current project.
3. Choose Mini Menu > Delete. This will remove the soundbite(s) from the project while deleting its region data from its parent audio file.
4. Select a soundbite from the audio file you wish to compact. Shift-click to make multiple soundbite selections.

5. Choose Mini-menu > Select All if you want to compact all of the audio files within the Soundbites window. The default keyboard shortcut is Command+A.
6. Choose Mini-menu > Compact File.
7. Within the Compact Soundfiles window, specify the amount of extra audio at the beginning and end of each soundbite that you wish to preserve. This is necessary if you have crossfades, wish to use crossfades, or make any edits to the edges of the soundbites (see Figure 6.29).
8. Another dialog box will open asking if you wish to immediately flush the Undo History. Click the Flush button to flush the Undo History and permanently discard the removed audio data.

Figure 6.29
The Compact Soundfiles window

Compacting a Project

The File menu's Compact Project command allows you to discard the unwanted portions of a project: from flushing the main undo history and audio undo histories, to deleting unused soundbites and soundfiles. The Compact Project window provides you with various options for managing the compact process (see Figure 6.30) and has the benefit of regaining significant portions of unused disk space. This command can be applied at any time during a project. Be aware, however, that this procedure is permanent and will flush the project's main undo history!

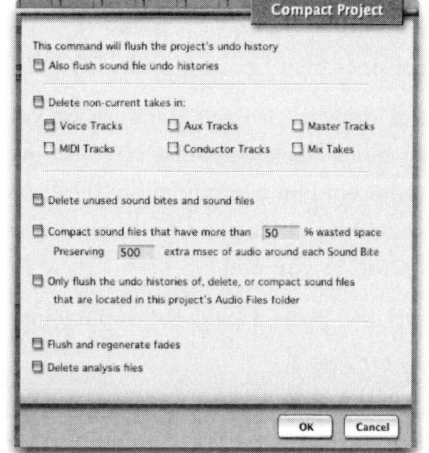

Figure 6.30
The Compact Project window

To compact an entire project:

1. Choose File > Compact Project.
2. In the Compact Project window, select the items you wish to discard.
3. Click OK. A warning dialog will launch, informing you that the procedure is not undoable.
4. Click OK to proceed. The data you selected will be immediately discarded.

CHAPTER 6 } Project Management: Part 2

Backup and Project Archival

Though seemingly similar, backing up a project and archiving it are very different procedures. A backup is more of a temporary procedure, while archiving is more long-term or permanent. Both are extremely important within the music production process (or any production process, for that matter), and can help prevent loss of valuable work or safeguard data that you may wish to access even after a project has been completed. This section will discuss different approaches and solutions for backing up and archiving your Digital Performer projects.

Backups

As stated earlier, backups can be thought of as temporary solutions or precautions for protecting work in progress. It is imperative that you back up regularly to prevent the accidental loss of data. Even the most stable of systems can fail; having a current back-up copy of your project can spare you the time and hassle (and even embarrassment) of recreating hours or days of lost work.

It's best to save your backups to a separate hard drive. It won't do you any good to back up to the same drive as your original copy if the drive fails or is damaged. Although it may seem like an unnecessary additional expense, having an extra hard drive is really the most convenient and cost effective solution for backing up your data. If a separate drive isn't available, then go ahead and back up to your main drive. Though not ideal, doing so is better than not backing up at all. As an extra precaution, though, you might consider also backing up to CD (CD-RW) or DVD (DVD-RW).

How often you should back up your projects depends on your personal workflow and setup. You might consider performing quick backups every 10 to 15 minutes, then perform a more substantial backup procedure later, wherein you actually make duplicate copies of the project's audio files. This more substantial backup could be performed at the end of the day, or perhaps every six hours. As a general rule, back up as often as you can.

To perform a quick backup of a project (without duplicating audio files):

1. Choose File > Save A Copy As.
2. Rename the project. You might try devising a naming system for these temporary backup copies—something as simple as adding a number after the project name might do. This will help you easily recognize which version is which when you're saving every 15 minutes.
3. Choose the destination for the backup copy. Consider creating a new folder called "temporary back ups," or something similar, for quick recognition. You might place this new folder within the main project folder; but if you *really* want to be safe, save the folder to a separate drive.
4. Click Save. Remember that the Save As Copy command will not save the current version you are working on. It only creates a backup copy (alternate version) of the current project.

To back up a project and its audio files:

1. First, choose File > Save to save the project.
2. Choose File > Save As Copy. If you choose Save As, DP will close the original project and you will be working on the new backup copy when you hit the Save button. To keep working on the original copy after creating your backup copy, choose the Save As Copy command.
3. Rename the project. You might also try devising a naming system for your more serious backup copies, or creating a backup folder.
4. Choose the destination. This copy should be placed on a separate drive (if possible). Creating a new folder called "Back Ups," for example, can help you easily locate the project when disaster strikes.
5. Click the Duplicate Audio Data option. This option will make a duplicate copy of every audio file contained within the current project, even if the audio is scattered across multiple hard drives. Analysis and fade files will also be duplicated.
6. Click Save to create your backup copy.

Archiving

The archival process can be thought of as a more permanent backup solution. Finished projects and files that are rarely used should be archived and stored in a safe location. This process will usually involve archiving to a separate storage medium in order to regain precious disk space within your system. DP's Compact Project command can be a handy feature for reducing the overall file size of a project by eliminating unused audio files that can take up huge amounts of disk space. Besides archiving to a separate drive or removable storage medium, you should also try to store your archived projects in a separate room or building. Investing in a fireproof safe for storage of important projects, software disks, serial numbers, and so on is just another way of protecting your studio assets against catastrophe.

There are many storage possibilities for your archived projects, from external Firewire/USB2 drives to various forms of removable media. The solution you choose will really depend on your personal workflow, budget, and overall size of your projects.

External Hard Drives

External drives are basically IDE drives (5400 RPM or 7200 RPM) housed in a Firewire or USB2 enclosure. Currently, these enclosures come in a variety of flavors supporting USB2, FW400 and/or FW800 formats. Some allow you to install your own IDE drive, some are preconfigured, while others allow you to hot-swap drives for easy removal and installation. Generally speaking, external kits do not provide a real price advantage over normal external drives, but they do allow you to take an internal drive from your computer, for example, and instantly turn it into an external unit. Hot-swappable drives are typically more expensive, but can provide you with greater flexibility.

Firewire and USB2 drives are becoming more and more common as the overall price of hard drives falls. The greatest benefits, however, come from the inherent nature of the storage medium. Large projects can be quickly backed up and easily moved between different systems. Some engineers are even using these external drives as their main recording drives.

CD-R versus DVD-R

CD-Rs are not the greatest backup or archival solution because of their limited storage capacity. 600–700 megabytes of data may seem like a lot of storage, but where audio (or video) files are concerned, it is very small. A four-minute/16-track project recorded at 24bit/48kHz would consume about 550MB of disk space. Start editing and processing the tracks, and the project will quickly grow larger than the 700MB capacity of the CD-R. You can, of course, spread the project files over multiple disks, but this can be an inconvenient as well as time-consuming endeavor.

The DVD-R/DVD+R format is quickly becoming the choice medium for archiving DAW projects. A typical 4.7GB DVD can actually hold about 4.2 gigabytes worth of data, which should be enough space to contain a typical DP project. DVD-R technology is steadily progressing, with read/write speeds becoming faster and faster. Double-sided DVD-R media sporting capacities of 9.4GB is also available.

> **TAKING ADVANTAGE OF THE NAME COLUMN**
> Keep in mind that even though you can archive your projects to both CD-R and DVD-R formats, you can't actually run a project off it due to the medium's slow read speeds. It's really only suitable for archiving, contrasted with external hard drives, which you can run a session from.

All of these recent advances in technology can be confusing for the end user. If you already have a DVD burner (perhaps a built-in Apple SuperDrive), be aware of its maximum burning speed (1x, 2x, 4x, 8x, 16x) when purchasing DVD-R media. Pricing is based on write speeds, so there is no need to purchase 16x DVDs if your burner only has 4x write capabilities.

Rewritable Media

Rewritable media is typically much more expensive than write once disks. For archival purposes, they are not very practical because you probably won't be rewriting data onto the disk on a regular basis, which defeats the purpose of using rewritable media. On top of this, many consumer CD players will not play audio that is burned to a CDRW.

On the DVD rewritable side of things, there are different formats to choose from, such as DVD-RAM and DVD+RW. The various manufacturers are constantly refining these formats, and the format wars are still ongoing, making it difficult for the consumer to choose one over the other. Keep this in mind when looking at DVD rewritable media as a backup or archival solution. Longevity of a format should be a key consideration when deciding which solution is best for you. You do not want to have to re-archive your projects two years from now because the format you chose has become obsolete.

Software Solutions

Roxio's Toast Titanium software, shown in Figure 6.31, is probably the most widely used CD/DVD burning software for the Mac. Its simple yet intuitive interface makes burning disks a no-brainer (of course, you cannot schedule a backup with a burning program like this; archival and backup must be performed manually). As of this writing, supported formats include CD-R, CD-RW, DVD-R, DVD+RW, and DVD-RAM. Be aware that the "lite" version bundled with many CD burners doesn't support DVD burning. You will need to upgrade to the Titanium version in order to burn DVDs and take advantage of the program's more advanced features.

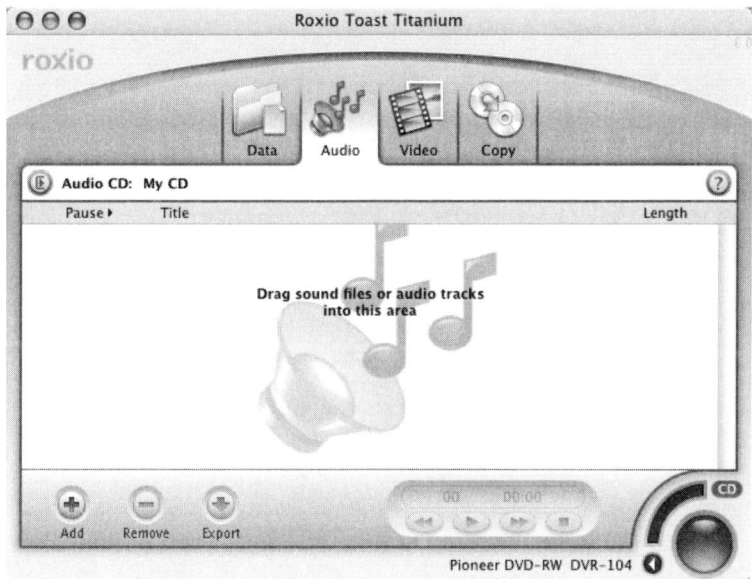

Figure 6.31
Roxio's Toast Titanium.

A more sophisticated approach is to utilize dedicated backup software, such as Retrospect by Dantz Development Corporation. This application is highly respected and widely used within the Mac and PC world. Various disk types and tape drive formats are supported. Data existing on multiple drives or networked computers can be backed up according to a user-specified schedule. Full or incremental backups can be performed. Keep in mind that programs like this are not tailored to understand the specific requirements of media applications like Digital Performer. If you have files that are scattered over multiple drives, you will need to tell the program exactly which files need to be backed up.

CHAPTER 6 } Project Management: Part 2

Mezzo by Mezzo Technologies' is a dedicated backup/archival program built specifically for media applications such as DP, Pro Tools, and Final Cut Pro (see Figure 6.32). Disk mirroring (simultaneous backups to multiple hard drives) CD, DVD, and various tape devices are supported. Full and incremental backups can be performed manually or automatically at specific times and intervals, even in the background. So far, this program sounds much like Retrospect. Where this program shines, however, is in its understanding of Digital Performer projects. Once you tell Mezzo that it is working with a DP project, you can simply drag the project document into Mezzo and it will search and back up all related project files! Restoring a project is just as easy, placing the files back to their original multiple disk locations. Mezzo also tracks changes in your DP projects, allowing you to back up only the data that has been changed. Mezzo is discussed in detail in Appendix F, "Third Party Expansion."

Figure 6.32
Dedicated backup and archival software such as Mezzo by Mezzo Technologies is specifically designed for media applications such as Digital Performer, Pro Tools, and Final Cut Pro.

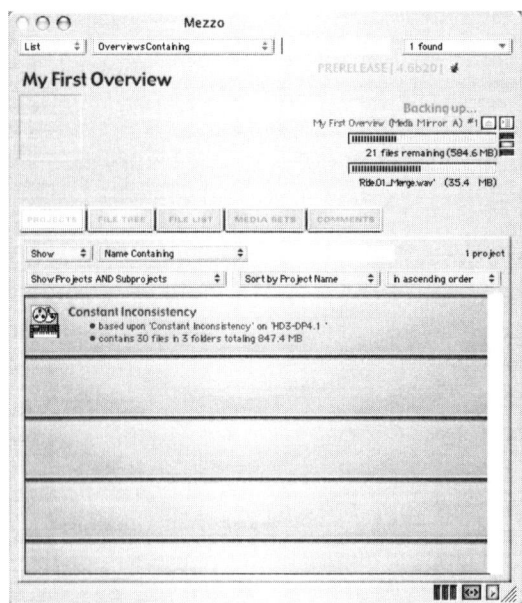

Summary

Project management is an integral part of the music production process. Besides speeding up routine functions such as project setup, backup and archival procedures can prevent the loss of important data when disaster strikes.

7 Recording Audio

Digital Performer offers a number of powerful tools and feature sets for recording audio. This chapter will focus on the steps necessary for getting audio into DP and for properly recording it. Besides audio recording basics, recording features such as the Audio Assignments window, alternate takes, cycle recording, and recording with effects will be discussed. Be sure to take a look at the "Overdub and Cycle Regions" QuickTime interactive movie tutorial contained on the included CD-ROM.

Following is a list of topics covered in this chapter:

- How to use the Audio Assignments window to configure multiple track I/O assignments.
- How to set input levels and monitor incoming audio.
- How to designate a specific location for recorded audio files.
- How to record, overdub, and import audio.
- How to work with alternate takes.
- How to record with audio with effects.

Input Assignments and the Audio Assignments Window

Before you can begin setting audio levels for recording, you will need to arm the necessary audio track(s). Before you can record-enable a track, however, you must assign the input to either the Mac's built-in audio or connected hardware interface (such as a MOTU 896). The specific steps for configuring the input assignment of a single audio track, as well as those for making multiple audio assignments with the Audio Assignments window are covered in Chapter 4. Here, I'll cover the Audio Assignments window in greater detail (see Figure 7.1).

CHAPTER 7 } Recording Audio

Figure 7.1

The Audio Assignments window allows you to make I/O and voice assignments for multiple tracks.

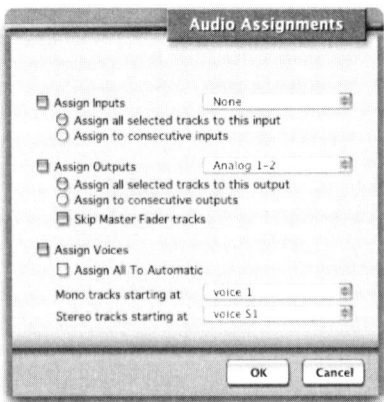

Two or more audio tracks must be selected before the Audio Assignments window will become available. Simply click on the name of a track to select it, and then Shift-click to make multiple track selections. Once you have selected the necessary tracks, open the Audio Assignments window from the Studio menu. The default keyboard shortcut is Option+A. Be aware that inputs and outputs must be enabled from the Audio Bundles window before they will appear in the Audio Assignments window.

To configure the input assignment for multiple tracks:

1. Make the necessary track selections.
2. Open the Audio Assignments window (Option+A).
3 Enable the Assign Inputs option.
4. Choose the desired input from the Input pop-up menu. Be aware that only inputs (audio bundles) that are already enabled will appear in this menu. If the input assignment you wish to use isn't listed, close the window and enable the desired inputs from the Audio Bundles window (refer to Chapter 2).
5. Next, choose the appropriate option from the Assign Inputs section.
    - **Assign all selected tracks to this input**. This option will assign the selected tracks to the input that is selected within the Input menu.
    - **Assign to consecutive inputs**. Enabling this option will assign the tracks to consecutive inputs starting with the input that is selected within the Input menu.
6. Click OK to confirm the input assignments. If you wish to continue with output and voice assignments, proceed to Step 1 of the next section before clicking the OK button.

To configure the output assignment for multiple tracks:

1. Enable the Assign Outputs option.

2. Choose the desired output from the Output menu. Again, be aware that only outputs (audio bundles) that are already enabled will appear in this menu. If the output assignment you wish to use isn't listed, close the window and enable the desired outputs from the Audio Bundles window (refer to Chapter 2).

3. Choose the appropriate option from the Assign Output section.
   - **Assign all selected tracks to this output.** This option will assign the selected tracks to the output that is selected within the Output menu.
   - **Assign to consecutive outputs.** Enabling this option will assign the tracks to consecutive outputs, starting with the output that is selected within the Output menu.
   - **Skip Master Fader tracks.** This option will ignore Master Fader tracks when making output assignments.

To configure the voice assignment for multiple tracks:

1. Enable the Assign Voices option.
2. Choose the appropriate option(s) from the Assign Voices section of the window.
   - **Assign All To Automatic.** This option will assign the selected tracks voicing assignments to automatic.
   - **Mono tracks starting at.** Enabling this option will assign selected mono tracks to consecutive voices, starting with the mono voice that is chosen in this option's pop-up menu.
   - **Stereo tracks starting at.** Enabling this option will assign selected stereo tracks to consecutive voices, starting with the stereo voice that is chosen in this option's pop-up menu.

Once you have chosen the desired settings, click OK to confirm the input, output, or voicing assignments.

Setting Input Levels

Before you begin recording, you'll need to set the level of any incoming audio. This is a crucial step in the recording process. Setting levels too low may result in a noisier track, and setting the levels too high may result in digital distortion. Before you can "see" the input levels within Digital Performer, however, you must first "arm" or record-enable a track.

Arming a Track

Remember that tracks are like containers for audio and MIDI data. Before you can bring an audio signal into Digital Performer, its input must be assigned to a track and the track must be armed. For information on making basic track I/O assignments, see Chapter 4.

CHAPTER 7 } Recording Audio

To record-enable an audio track(s):

1. First, make sure the audio track's input, output, and voicing assignments have been properly configured. If the output is not assigned, for example, the Record-enable buttons for the track will not be available.

> **THE RECORD COLUMN**
>
> If the I/O and voice assignments have been properly made but the Record-enable buttons are still not visible, check whether the Record column within the Tracks window is showing. If the Record column is hidden, choose the Tracks window > mini-menu > Columns Setup option. Once the window is open, enable the Record option to make the Record-enable buttons within the Tracks window visible. Be aware that when working in the Sequence Editor, however, the Columns Setup options will have no effect on the visibility of the Record-enable buttons, and will become available as soon as the proper track I/O assignments are made.

2. Click on the track's Record-Enable icon to arm the track.
3. To arm adjacent audio tracks, click and drag with the mouse. Remember that you must enable the Audio Options preferences "Multi record is always on..." feature (located in the Preferences and Settings window) in order to simultaneously arm multiple audio tracks.

> **SHORTCUTS FOR ARMING TRACKS**
>
> * **Shift-Control+R.** This key command will open the Track Record Enable window (see Figure 7.2). Enter the track you wish to record-enable and click OK. Tracks can also be chosen from your connected MIDI keyboard.
> * **Up/Down Arrow Keys.** If a track is record-enabled, you can use the keyboard's Up and Down Arrow keys to proceed to the next or previous record track.
> * **Command-clicking the Record-enable button.** This will arm all other tracks within a sequence that can be record-enabled while ignoring the track in question. If the selected track was already record-enabled, it will be unarmed in the process.
> * **Option-clicking the Record-enable button.** This shortcut will arm the track in question while simultaneously unarming all other tracks.

Figure 7.2

The Track Record Enable window can be accessed with the keyboard shortcut Shift-Control+R.

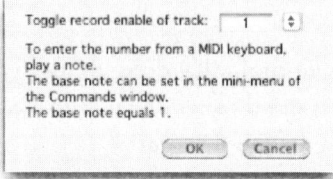

Setting Input Levels

ARMING TRACKS ON THE FLY
Tracks can be armed or unarmed on the fly during playback, but not during the actual recording process (when the Record button is red or flashing red). The ability to arm tracks on the fly may sound like a really useful feature, but doing so isn't actually such a smooth process—actual playback tends to be momentarily interrupted.

Audio Monitor Window

Once a track or set of tracks has been record-enabled, you will be able to view the incoming signal(s) in Digital Performer. In keeping with the DP standard of dedicated windows (insert laugh-track), input signals can only be viewed in the Audio Monitor window (see Figure 7.3). Besides displaying incoming signal levels, DP allows you to change the location of takefiles and control how these files are named.

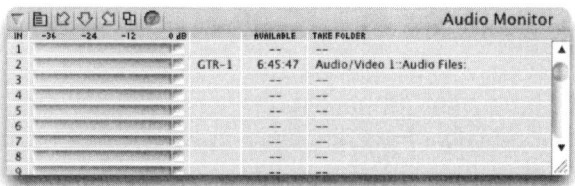

Figure 7.3
The Audio Monitor window.

To set input levels with the Audio Monitor window:

1. Once a track or set of tracks has been armed, its corresponding input row will be highlighted in red (see Figure 7.4). If you have the Scroll to Record Enabled Inputs option enabled from the mini-menu (which is turned on by default), the Audio Monitor window will automatically scroll to the record-enabled track.

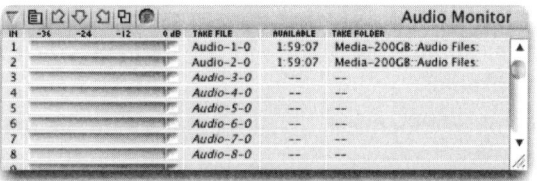

Figure 7.4
In this example, tracks 1 and 2 have been armed. Besides being highlighted in red, the takefile names will also change from italicized to standard text.

2. Click on the Audio Patch Thru button (the headphones icon) in order to hear the incoming audio.
3. Check your audio input level.

167

4. You can change the meter resolution by choosing Audio Monitor > Level Range. Remember that signals recorded at low levels may result in increased noise levels, while signals that are too hot can clip, causing unwanted digital distortion. When operating in the MOTU Audio System (MAS), the Retain Clip (Audio Monitor > mini-menu) option is enabled by default to help you see if a signal actually clips. If you notice that clips are not being retained, check to see if this option is actually turned on.

> **TIPS ON SETTING INPUT LEVELS**
>
> Even after your input levels are set, you'll probably want to keep the Audio Monitor open throughout the recording process. Input levels tend to change over the course of a recording session, so it's good to have constant visual feedback warning you when adjustments are necessary. Also keep in mind that performers tend to play louder and with more energy when you actually press the red button, so you should set your levels accordingly. If the incoming signals get too high and overload, you've now distorted the signal and may want to rerecord it. Remember that digital distortion can instantly render a great performance useless.

In addition to highlighting a track's corresponding row in red, DP will also display takefile names in standard text, along with the available hard disk space, when a track is armed. Checking these settings is an important part of the DP recording process.

To check the takefile location and amount of available hard disk space:

1. When a track is armed, the takefile location name changes from italicized to standard text. The default takefile location is the project's Audio File folder. The abbreviated takefile location will appear within the Take Folder column. Double-click on the folder name to display the full path. You can change this location by double-clicking on the takefile name in the Take File column.
2. This will open a dialog window asking you to choose a new take folder for the specific audio input (see Figure 7.5).
3. Choose the location for the takefile. Keep in mind that you can even designate separate hard drives for individual takefiles.
4. After confirming the takefile location, be sure to check on the amount of free hard disk space. Click to toggle the display between minutes and megabytes. It's always best to have extra disk space when recording audio, so you should plan accordingly.

Besides setting levels in DP, you must take care that the signal chain going into DP has been set properly in order to get the most out of your audio signal. Check the integrity of the audio at each point in the input chain to maximize levels and keep noise at a minimum.

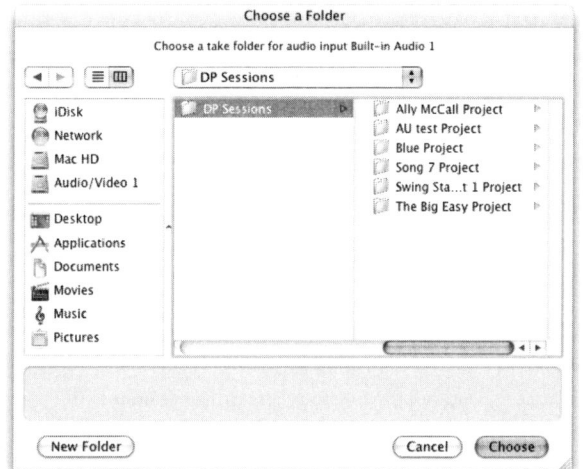

Figure 7.5
Double-clicking on the name of a takefile within the Take File column will open the Choose a Folder dialog window.

Monitoring Input Signals

An essential part of recording is the monitoring of your live input signal. You basically have three choices when working with Digital Performer (or any other D.A.W., for that matter).

- Monitor through the application with Audio Patch Thru (MOTU Audio System).
- Monitor through your hardware interface with Direct Hardware Playthrough (bypassing the MOTU Audio System).
- Connect your DP system to an external mixer.

Refer to Chapter 2 for an in-depth look into the different monitoring configurations within Digital Performer.

Audio Patch Thru

In order to monitor a live signal thru Digital Performer (MAS), Audio Patch Thru must be turned on from the Studio menu or by clicking on the headphones icon located within the Audio Monitor's title bar. Once enabled, Audio Patch Thru passes incoming audio from a track's designated input to its specified output assignment. Choose an output destination (such as the outputs of your hardware interface) that is connected to a set of speakers or a pair of headphones, and you'll be able to listen to the signal.

When monitoring audio with an audio track, the track must be record-enabled before you will be able to hear the incoming audio. You can also use an aux track to monitor audio signals. The setup procedure is the same as for audio tracks, except that it is always active (instead of only being active when record-enabled).

Monitoring with External Mixers

If your system is connected to an external mixer, then it is possible for you to monitor live signals directly through your console instead of through Digital Performer. Be sure to turn off Audio Patch Thru to avoid hearing the live signal twice. With this configuration, you will be listening to the audio signal before it actually reaches Digital Performer, or pre-multitrack. The advantage to this setup, of course, is the elimination of any monitoring latency.

> **WHAT IS MONITORING LATENCY?**
> Monitoring latency is the slight delay of a live input signal. When monitoring through Digital Performer, for example, the signal must first travel through your sound card, through DP, back to the soundcard, and out to your speakers or headphones. This monitoring setup introduces an audible delay in the live signal. How much delay is introduced is determined by the buffer settings of your sound card and Digital Performer. With monitoring latency, even though you will be hearing the signal "late," the audio will actually be recorded in time, precisely as it's being input into DP.

Direct Hardware Playthrough

As noted earlier, the best way of dealing with monitoring latency is to use an external mixer within your DP system. You can, of course, monitor without external equipment and get excellent results. Another option is to use your soundcard or connected audio interface to directly monitor the live signal (as long as your audio hardware device has this monitoring capability).

When using MOTU hardware, you can monitor the signal with DP's Direct Hardware Playthrough option, located in the Input Monitoring Mode window. With this configuration, monitoring latency is eliminated or dramatically reduced, the trade-off being the inability to listen to the signal through any DP effects (see Figure 7.6)

Figure 7.6
The Input Monitoring Mode window.

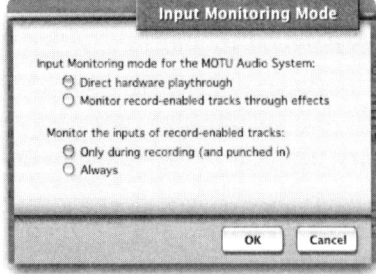

MOTU hardware users can utilize the supplied MOTU PCI Console application to lower the sample's per buffer settings. MOTU Firewire hardware users can also use the built-in CueMix feature to eliminate any monitoring latency.

Recording Audio

In previous chapters, I discussed the proper optimization and setup procedures for your Mac, connected audio hardware, and Digital Performer project. Now your Digital Performer system should be configured for recording audio, also. If you are still hesitant or unclear on the steps leading up to this point in the music production process, you might want to refer to Chapters 2 and 4 before proceeding.

Once you have armed your track(s) and checked the levels of the incoming audio signal, you will be ready to begin recording.

To record audio into DP:

1. Start by moving the counter location to the point where you wish to begin recording. You can type a location directly into the Control Panel's Counter window or you can click and drag the playback wiper to the desired location.
2. If you need to, turn on the built-in Click. Though not strictly necessary, it's always a good idea to record your audio and MIDI data to a click, preferably the click within Digital Performer. Doing so will ensure that your recorded tracks will be properly aligned with DP's grid, allowing you to take full advantage of the program's editing features. (Refer to the "Setting Up a Click" section of Chapter 4 for a detailed look into the setup procedures for DP's built-in metronome.)
3. To start recording, click on the Control Panel's Record button. (You can also begin recording by pressing the number 3 key on your computer keyboard's numeric keypad. If you have a MIDI keyboard controller attached to your system, you can also send a MIDI message to begin recording. For specific information on assigning a MIDI event to a specific command, see the "Command Window" section in Chapter 5.) Once recording begins, DP will display the audio as a red bar.
4. When you are finished, click the Control Panel's Stop button. (You can also use the keyboard's Space bar or the 0 key.)

    Once recording has stopped, Digital Performer will take a moment to process the audio data and convert the red bar to a normal waveform display. Only when recording has stopped and the waveform display has been fully updated will you be able to edit the soundbite. Newly recorded audio will appear in the Soundbites window.

CHAPTER 7 } Recording Audio

To undo recorded audio:

1. To undo a record pass, choose Edit > Undo. You must immediately choose this option before beginning another action. Once undone, the takefile will be placed in the trash. Only when another undoable action is performed will the discarded takefile be deleted from disk.
2. If you decide to undo a recording after you have taken other actions, you will need to use the Undo History list. Keep in mind that any actions that were taken after the undone action will also be undone in the process. Refer to Chapter 6 for details on the Undo History Window.

Recording and Managing Alternate Takes

Takes are basically alternate versions of any data that's stored within a Digital Performer track. By default, DP records data into Take 1 of a track (see Figure 7.7). A track can contain an unlimited number of takes.

Figure 7.7
The Take Column menu allows you to manage takes for individual tracks.

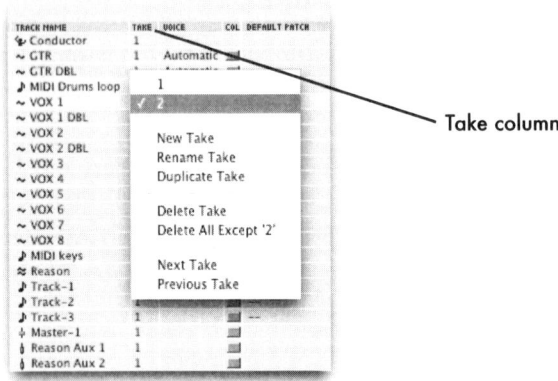

Takes are managed through DP's Take Column menu. The options are as follows:

- **New Take**. This option will create a new, blank take.
- **Rename Take**. This option will allow you to rename the currently selected take. Current takes are indicated with a check mark.
- **Duplicate Take**. Choose this option to create a duplicate of the current take.
- **Delete Take**. Deletes the currently selected take.
- **Delete All Except "current take."** This option will discard all of the takes except the current take.
- **Next Take**. This option will select and display the next available take.
- **Previous Take**. This option will select and display the previous available take.

To create a new take for recording:

1. Arm the appropriate audio tracks.
2. Click on the track's Take menu and choose New Take. This will create a new, blank take, while preserving the track's original data in the previous (original) take.
3. To rename the new take, simply Option-click on the name of the take within the track's Take column. You can also use the Take menu's Rename Take option.
4. To return to the original take, click on the track's Take menu column and select it with the mouse.

> **KEYBOARD SHORTCUTS FOR MANAGING TAKES**
>
> The appropriate track(s) must be armed and selected before you can use the keyboard shortcuts to manage takes. Remember that you can select a track by clicking on the name of the track. Shift-click to make multiple track selections.
>
> * To create a new take(s), press Control+Option+N.
> * To delete the current take(s), press Shift+Control+ Delete.
> * To erase the contents of the current take(s), press Option+Control+Delete.
> * To proceed to the next available take(s), press Option+Control+ the Up Arrow key.
> * To proceed to the previous available take(s), press Option+Control+ the Down Arrow key.

Punching In and Out

Punching in and *punching out* refers to the process of starting and stopping recording in the middle of a track. Instead of recording from the very beginning of your project, you can start and stop recording at any point in a track during playback, regardless of how many tracks are armed. Digital Performer allows you to perform both manual on the fly (punching in and out during playback) and automated punches. Automating a punch saves you the hassle of pressing the Record button on the transport and allows you to perform very precise punches. This a great feature for when you are recording yourself and need your hands free to play an instrument.

Punching can occur within an empty track or in the middle of recorded material. Punching in the middle of existing audio to replace what is currently there is called *overdubbing*.

CHAPTER 7 } Recording Audio

MONITORING DURING THE OVERDUB PROCESS

In order to properly overdub audio data, you need to be able to hear (monitor) what already exists on a track. Auto Input mode allows you to do this. Auto Input automatically switches between the "live" input signal and playback (preexisting audio) depending on the state of the transport. When playing back and not recording, you will hear playback of any existing audio material. As soon as recording is initiated (you've punched in), Digital Performer will automatically switch to the "live" signal, allowing you to hear what you are actually recording. Once you punch out, you will immediately hear playback of the material that already existed within the track.

The Input Monitoring Mode window (shown in Figure 7.8), located in the Setup menu, allows you to set DP to Auto Input by choosing the Only during recording and punched in option. Refer to Chapter 2 for more information on the Input Monitoring Mode window.

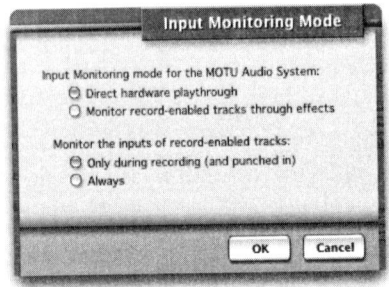

Figure 7.8
During the overdub process, set the Input Monitoring Mode window's Monitor the inputs of record-enabled tracks option to Only during recording (and punched in).

To punch in manually on the fly:

1. Arm the appropriate audio tracks.
2. Press the Space bar to begin playback.
3. Press the number 3 key on your computer keyboard's numeric keypad to punch in (begin recording). Or, press the Control Panel's Record button to begin recording.
4. Press the number 3 key again to punch out (stop recording).
5. Repeat Steps 3 and 4 as needed.
6. Press the Space bar when you are through recording to halt playback.

To automate a punch:

1. Arm the appropriate audio tracks.
2. Enable the Control Panel's Auto Record button (see Figure 7.9). A Punch In and Out field will appear within the status strip and the Auto Record button will be highlighted.

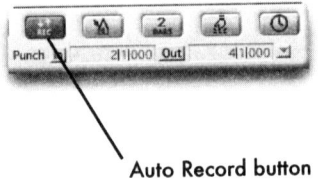

Auto Record button

Figure 7.9
The Control Panel's Auto Record button allows you to perform punches at precise locations within a track.

3. Enter the location for when recording is to start and stop. The punch in point is where recording will begin, and the punch out point is where recording will stop.
4. Position the playback cursor at a point before the punch in location. Remember to give yourself or the artist enough pre-roll so that you can properly prepare for the punch.
5. Press the number 3 key on your computer keyboard's numeric keypad to begin recording. Once recording is engaged, playback will begin with the Record button flashing. Actual recording will begin at the specified punch in point, and the Record button will be continuously highlighted. When the punch out location is reached, Digital Performer will go out of Record mode and the Record button will begin flashing again. Playback will continue until it is stopped.
6. Press the Space bar to stop playback.

> **TIPS ON PERFORMING SEAMLESS PUNCHES**
> Here are a few tips for getting the most out of your punches:
> * When possible, punch in and out on a downbeat, and avoid punching in the middle of a line or continuous note. Of course, you can always go back and "fix" your edit point if the punch is audible, but it's good practice to make your initial punches as seamless as possible, for when you are working on that "old school" analog recorder.
> * When recording other performers, remember to give them sufficient pre-roll. If you're trying to overdub on an existing track, ask the performers to start playing or singing along as soon as they know where they are at in the recording. This will help ensure that they are breathing properly and will give them time to match their own tones and nuances from their previous performance. Continuity is a key factor in executing seamless punches.
> * When recording vocalists, be conscious of their breathing and don't cut off the breaths.
> * Set up markers before beginning an overdub session. Being able to quickly jump to any important locations within a track will keep your session running smoothly and, most importantly, will keep your artists happy. There is nothing that will frustrate your performers more than having to wait while you try to locate that third chorus. See Chapter 11 for information on using markers within your projects.

Overdub Record Mode

Overdub Record mode is a handy feature that allows further control over the overdubbing process. Under normal recording circumstances (with Overdub Recording Mode off), existing audio (and/or MIDI data) is removed and replaced by new data when you punch in on a track. When the Overdub Record feature is enabled, however (see Figure 7.10), new data is placed on top of any existing soundbites.

Figure 7.10

The Overdub Record Mode button.

Deleting the new recording will reveal the original audio data, allowing you to quickly return to the previous performance.

Overdub Record mode can be combined with Cycle Recording to achieve a looping-style recording mode that automatically creates new takes during each record pass.

Cycle Record Mode

Cycle, or loop-style, recording can be achieved by enabling both the Memory Cycle and Overdub Record features (see Figure 7.11). This is handy for when you wish to record multiple passes of audio or MIDI data over a specific section of a project. When cycle-recording audio data, DP will automatically create a new take for each record pass, preventing the previous passes from being recorded over. You can also incorporate DP's Auto Punch feature to initiate recording in a designated section within the Memory Cycle in and out points, essentially providing you with pre-roll and post-roll roll when cycle recording.

Figure 7.11

Enable the Memory Cycle and Overdub Record mode buttons to cycle-record within Digital Performer. The Memory Bar's start and end times determine the length of the section that will be looped.

For even greater control over the cycle recording process, utilize Digital Performer's comprehensive Polar window, discussed in Appendix C, "Polar."

To enable cycle recording:

1. Engage the Memory Cycle and Overdub Record buttons within the Control panel.
2. In the Memory Bar, specify the start and end points for the section to loop. The end time should be the beginning of the next measure of where you wish the loop to end. For example, when setting an 8-bar loop that starts on measure 1/1/000, the end time would be measure 9/1/000.
3. Begin the recording process as discussed earlier in this chapter. Keep in mind that recording will be continuous, and will create a new record take for each record pass.
4. To allow yourself some pre-roll and post-roll time during the cycle-record process, incorporate DP's Auto Punch In and Out feature (Auto Record). Turn on Auto Record and set the punch in and punch out times (see the previous section on punching in and out for more information on this feature).

5. Readjust your original Memory Cycle start and end times to reflect the changes. Now when you begin recording, DP will cycle through the specified section but will only record in between the punch in and punch out points (see Figure 7.12).

Figure 7.12
In this example, the Auto Punch In and Out feature is being used together with Cycle Recording mode. The transport is set to loop between measures 1 and 8, but will only record audio between measures 4 and 6. Incorporate the Auto Record feature to provide pre-roll and post-roll during the cycle recording process.

Recording with Effects

When it comes to recording a signal with processing to disk (or tape), opinions vary widely. Some people will argue that you shouldn't risk screwing up your audio and that you can always add any processing in the mix, and others say that if you know what you want, then recording with effects will save you time from having to process later. Then there is the middle path, where engineers use effects like mild compression to get a hotter signal to disk (tape) or brick-wall limiters to prevent digital distortion. Regardless of your philosophy, just keep in mind that there aren't any rules. Better safe than sorry, though, so if you aren't confident about using effects during recording, save the processing for later. Once a signal is recorded with an effect, you can't remove it.

When you insert a plug-in or effect on a record-enabled audio track in Digital Performer, you won't actually be recording the effected signal to your hard drive. You will be only listening to the effected signal post-hard disk. This is like placing an effect in the "monitor section" of traditional signal flow. In order to record a signal that has a plug-in inserted in it, you need to send the effected signal to the hard disk to be recorded. How do you do this? By creating an "input" fader, then bussing the effected signal to an audio track (see Figure 7.13).

Figure 7.13
A basic example of recording an effected audio signal to disk. In this setup, the aux track receives the incoming signal and processes it with a compressor plug-in. The effected signal is then routed from the aux track, via bus 1, to Audio Track 1, where it is recorded to disk.

CHAPTER 7 } Recording Audio

To record an effected signal to disk:

1. First create an aux track. The default keyboard shortcut is Control+Command+A.
2. Rename this track Input Fader, or something else appropriate. It's always good practice to name your tracks as you create them. This will keep you organized and will save you many headaches later on down the line.
3. Assign the aux track's input as if you were recording on an audio track; be sure to choose the input for the signal you wish to record.
4. Assign the aux track's output to an available bus.
5. Now create an audio track. Assign its input to the same bus as the output of the aux track. The output assignment for the audio track should be whatever output you use to monitor with (analog 1 and 2, for example).
6. Arm the track and check your levels with the Audio Monitor window.
7. Now insert the desired effect on the aux track or Input Fader you created in Step 1.
8. Adjust the effects parameters to your liking.

> **AUDIO LEVELS AND PROPER GAIN STRUCTURE**
>
> Once you have set your plug-in parameters, you may notice that there is a rise or drop in input level because of the processing that is occurring. Be careful that you don't readjust the input level going into DP (your preamp, for example) to compensate! If you do, you will be increasing the signal level going into your audio interface, possibly distorting the audio and throwing off all your plug-in parameter settings in the process.
>
> Here is where proper gain structure is important. You need to adjust audio levels at the output stage of the plug-in. If you are inserting a compressor, for example, adjust the output level to boost or cut the signal level leaving the plug-in and going into the Audio track. If there is no available output level adjustment on the effect, then insert DP's Trim plug-in and adjust the output of the aux track there.
>
> Be sure to keep an eye on the Audio Monitor window!

9. If necessary, adjust the output level of the plug-in to compensate for the processing. Check the levels of the audio track in the Audio Monitor window while making any changes.
10. Begin recording, and the effected signal will be recorded to disk.

> **SIMULTANEOUSLY RECORDING THE DRY AND EFFECTED SIGNAL**
>
> If you would rather be safe than sorry, you can simultaneously record the dry and effected signals by creating another audio track and assigning its input to the same input as the aux track (input fader).

Importing Audio

In addition to recording audio directly to a track, you can import existing audio into Digital Performer as well. This audio can reside in DP's native Sound Designer II format, or can exist in other formats, such as AIFF, MP3, .WAV, Broadcast WAV, REX, and even AVI and QuickTime movie soundtracks. Imported AIFF files will remain unchanged, while all other formats will be converted to SDII files. Interleaved stereo files are not supported by DP, and will be broken up into two mono files. These separated files will appear as .L (left) and .R (right) mono Sound Designer II files.

Before you begin importing audio, there are a few settings that you should take a look at.

Sound File Locations

Located in the Preferences and Settings Command is the Audio Options. This global preference window determines where imported, converted, and processed audio is stored. The Soundfile Locations preferences are described below.

The settings contained in this section of the Audio Options preferences decides where imported audio will be stored within a project. By default, imported files will always be copied to the project folder.

- **Always Copy Imported Audio To Project Audio Folder.** This option tells DP to always copy any imported audio files to the project's Audio Files folder. This option is enabled by default, and is convenient if you wish to consolidate all of your project audio files into one central location.
- **Only When Format Is Not Mono Sound Designer II or AIFF.** This option will convert and import any non-native formatted audio files into the project's Audio Files folder.
- **Never.** This option will place any imported files—even if they need to be converted—in the same location as the original files.

Store Converted or Processed Files

This setting specifies where converted and processed audio will be stored. By default, all processed and converted files are saved to the project's Audio Files folder.

- **In Project Folder.** This option will place converted and processed files in the project's Audio Files folder.
- **With Original File.** This option will keep converted and processed files with the originals.
- **Ask For Location.** Choosing this option will force you to specify a location when importing converted audio files into DP.

CHAPTER 7 } Recording Audio

Automatic Conversions Preferences

Also located in the Soundbites window > mini-menu are the Automatic Conversions preferences. When audio that does not conform to a project's sampling rate, bit depth, or tempo is imported into Digital Performer, this command will automatically convert those files and force them to adhere to the project's current settings. Processing is done in the background, and can also be used to convert the files of an existing project to new sampling rate, bit depth, and/or tempo. The Automatic Conversion preferences are described below.

* Enable Automatic Conversions for this project: Check this option to turn on Automatic Conversions for the current project. You can also turn on Automatic Conversions by clicking on the lightning bolt icon located within the Soundbites window and Sequence Editor's title bar (see Figure 7.14).

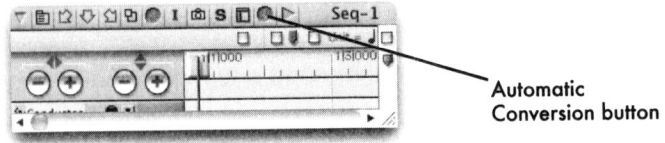

Figure 7.14
The "lightning bolt" icon allows you to toggle on or off Automatic Conversions for a project.

The Convert Sample Rate, Convert Sample Format, and Convert To Sequence Tempo options provide you with three setting choices, and are explained below.

* **On Import.** This option will force files that do not match the project to be converted on import. Files that do not match the project tempo will be converted when they are placed on a track.
* **Whenever File Doesn't Match.** This option does the same thing as the On Import option, but will also convert audio anytime there is a circumstance in which a file's settings differ from the project. For example, if you change the sample format in the middle of a project, DP will automatically convert existing soundbites to the new setting.
* **When Bite is Added to a Track.** Unique to the Convert to Sequence Tempo option, this setting will force a soundbite that contains embedded tempo data to conform to the sequence tempo when added to a track.
* **Never.** Choosing this option will turn off automatic conversions for the specific file setting. Remember that you can use the Enable Automatic Conversions for this project option to globally enable or disable automatic conversions for a project.

※ Importing Audio

> **CONVERT TO SEQUENCE TEMPO**
>
> Files that contain embedded tempo data, such as REX files and Apple Loops, for example, will automatically adjust to the sequence tempo if you have the Convert to Sequence Tempo preference set to either the When Bite is Added to a Track or Whenever File Doesn't Match settings.

The Import Audio Command versus Drag and Drop

There are several ways to import audio into Digital Performer, including using the Import Audio Command and dragging and dropping files directly into DP. The benefit of using the Import Audio command is that you can import specific regions that are associated with an audio file. With the drag and drop method (though it is more convenient at times) you are limited to the importation of entire files. The two methods of importing audio are further described below.

To import audio without leaving Digital Performer, first choose one of the following methods for importing:

* File > Import Audio.
* The Command+F1 default keyboard shortcut.
* From the Soundbites window, choose mini-menu > Import Audio or click on the Import Audio button (see Figure 7.15).

Figure 7.15
The Import Audio button.

Import Audio button

1. When you use one of the methods for importing audio, the Import Audio dialog window will open, allowing you to audition audio files before they are imported into DP. This window also lets you import soundbites, or individual *regions*. Regions associated with a soundfile will automatically appear underneath the parent file within the Add list.
2. Navigate to the desired folder/hard disk.
3. Select the file you wish to import. The file will appear in the bottom-left pane of the Import Audio window. The audio file will be indicated in bold type, with any individual regions listed below the parent audio file.
4. If you want to audition the file or regions before importing, click on the speaker icon, located below the Done button, to enable the Audition feature (see Figure 7.16). Once the Audition feature is enabled, simply click on an audio file or region to audition the selection.

CHAPTER 7 } Recording Audio

Figure 7.16

The Import Audio window. Click the speaker icon to enable the Audition feature and audition a selected soundbite or region.

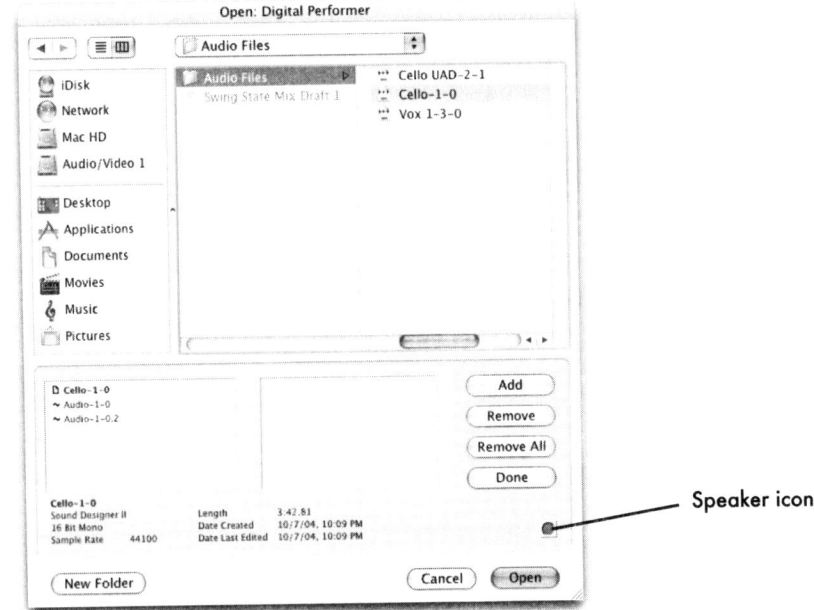

5. Press the Add button to place the file or region in the To be imported column (right pane).
6. If you decide that you do not want to import a file that has been placed in this column, select it and click the Remove button. Use the Remove All button to clear the list of any files or regions.
7. Once you have added your selections to the To be imported column, click OK. The files and/or regions will be imported into DP.

To import audio with the drag and drop method:

1 Before you import any files, decide if you want DP to automatically convert the files to the project's current settings.
2. Locate the file you wish to import from the Mac's Finder window. You can hold down the Command key and press the Tab key to quickly navigate to the Finder (or any open application) within Mac OS X Panther. Tab to the Finder application within the list and release the Command key.
3. With both the selected file and the target Digital Performer window visible, click and drag the file into DP.

4. If the Automatic Conversions feature is turned on, DP will automatically convert the file to the project's current settings and allow for immediate playback of the file(s). If you have Automatic Conversions disabled, the file will appear with an X icon next to the file name within the Move Column of the Soundbites window, as shown in Figure 7.17. In addition, if the soundbite resides on a track, it will appear dimmed within the Sequence Editor.

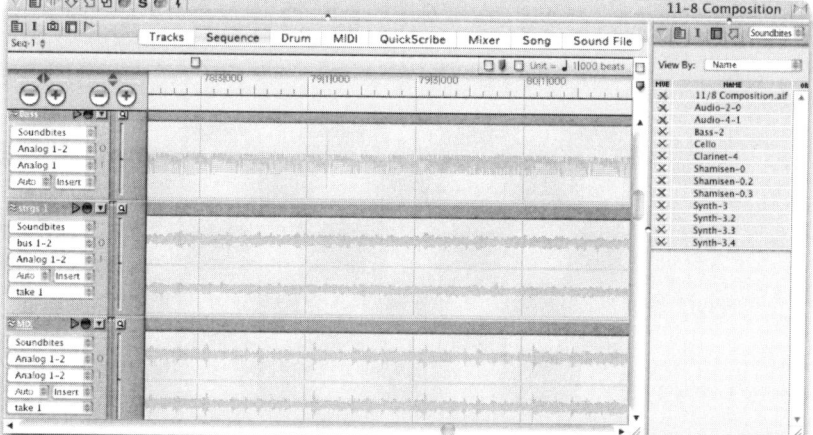

Figure 7.17

Files that do not match the project's current sample rate or bit depth will appear in the Soundbites window with an X icon and dimmed in the Sequence Editor.

DRAGGING FILES INTO DP

Files can be dragged to any windows that hold audio. Files can be dragged directly into an audio track as long as the channel format is the same. For example, you cannot drop a mono file onto a stereo track, and vice-versa. If you need to drag files of mixed channel formats, drag them into the Soundbites window instead.

EXPORTING AUDIO FILES VIA DRAG AND DROP

You can also export audio files by dragging them from DP and dropping them into a Finder window or desktop. Exported files will be in the Sound Designer II format. Keep in mind that stereo files will be exported as separate left (.L) and right (.R) mono. To export them as an Interleaved stereo file, use the Export command from the mini-menu of the Soundbites window.

CHAPTER 7 } Recording Audio

Summary

Digital Performer offers a powerful approach to digital audio with sophisticated audio recording and importing capabilities. Comprehensive features such as the Automatic Conversions preferences allow you to further customize how Digital Performer handles audio, while the dedicated Audio Monitor window provides visual feedback during the audio recording process. In addition to its standard recording capabilities, Digital Performer's Polar window provides a self-contained RAM based loop recording module.

8 } Recording MIDI

Digital Performer provides a number of powerful features for managing how MIDI is handled within a project. In this chapter I will discuss the basic process of recording data on your MIDI tracks, as well as how to overdub MIDI data, cycle record, step record, and record with MIDI quantizing. In addition to these MIDI recording-related operations, I'll discuss other MIDI features, such as the Input Filter, MIDI Patch Thru, Interapplication MIDI, and Device Groups.

Following is a list of topics covered in this chapter:

- How to use the MIDI Monitor window to verify incoming MIDI signals.
- How to alter recorded MIDI data with the Input Filter and Input Quantize commands.
- How to create multiple MIDI output destinations with MIDI device groups.
- How to select MIDI patches for specific MIDI channels.
- How to set up MIDI tracks for recording.
- How to output MIDI data to external MIDI devices and virtual instruments.
- How to record MIDI data.
- How to overdub, punch-in, cycle record, and step record MIDI data.

MIDI-Related Windows and Commands

In this section—before you dive into the actual MIDI recording process—I'll discuss a few of Digital Performer's MIDI-related windows and commands that can be used to affect how MIDI data is recorded within a project.

The MIDI Monitor Window

The MIDI Monitor window, shown in Figure 8.1, provides a visual display of any MIDI data, system controller information, or MIDI sync data (such as MIDI beat clocks, DTL, DTLe, and system reset commands) that is being received by Digital Performer. Use this window to verify that DP is actually receiving MIDI signals from a connected MIDI device. To open the MIDI monitor, choose Studio menu > MIDI Monitor, or use the default keyboard shortcut Shift+W.

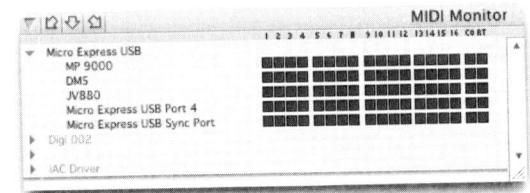

Figure 8.1

The MIDI Monitor window.

Each MIDI interface that is connected to DP in the current AMS configuration (explained in Chapter 2) will appear in the MIDI Monitor window. Click the MIDI interface's disclosure triangle to reveal MIDI devices that are connected to the interface. Each device row displays a green indicator box that will light up when a MIDI signal is being received on a specific MIDI channel (numbered from 1-16). The "Co" indicators, or *System Common* indicators, will display MIDI data that is non-channel specific, such as system exclusive data. The "RT" indicators, or *System Real-Time* indicators, display real-time sync data such as MIDI beat clocks.

Keep in mind that the Input Filter has no effect on the MIDI monitor window (explained in the next section).

The Set Input Filter Command

The Input Filter, shown in Figure 8.2, "filters" incoming MIDI data—it basically determines what type of MIDI data can be recorded in a MIDI track. Choose Setup menu > Set Input Filter to open this window. Be aware that these settings are global and will affect all MIDI data that is recorded.

To prevent a specific type of MIDI data from being recorded on a track:

1. Open the Input Filter window by choosing Setup menu > Set Input Filter.
2. Uncheck the box located to left of the data type, as shown in Figure 8.3.

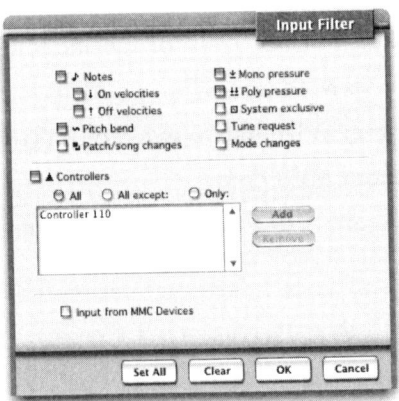

Figure 8.2

The Input Filter allows you to filter out MIDI data that you do not wish to record.

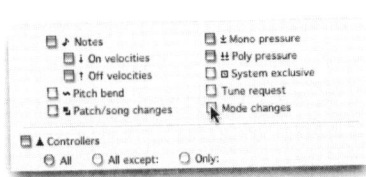

Figure 8.3

Simply uncheck an item to prevent it from being recorded.

MIDI-Related Windows and Commands

To determines the type(s) of MIDI controller data that is recorded:

1. Enable the Controllers section of the Input Filter window by clicking on its check box.
2. Use the buttons located above the Controllers list to quickly determine the type of data that will be affected, as shown in Figure 8.4.

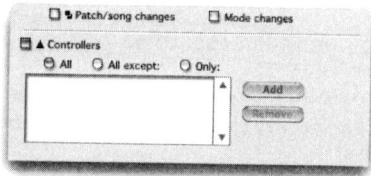

Figure 8.4

Use the buttons located below the Controllers check box to determine the type(s) of controller data that is recorded.

- **All**. Click this option to record all types of MIDI controller data.
- **All except**. Click this option to record all types of controller data except the specific controller number(s) added to the Controllers list (explained in the next section).
- **Only**. Click this option to record only the controller number(s) added to the Controllers list.

To add or remove a controller number from the Controllers list:

- To add a controller number, click the Add button and type the controller number in the pop-up window, as shown in Figure 8.5. Click OK to enter the controller number into the Controllers list.

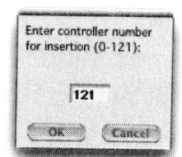

Figure 8.5

The Controllers section pop-up window.

- To remove a controller number, click on the specific number (which will become highlighted blue) and click the Remove button. To quickly select more than one controller number in the list, drag with your mouse.

THE SET VIEW FILTER COMMAND

Similar to the Input Filter I just discussed, the View Filters window determines the type of MIDI data (already contained in a project) that is displayed within a project or Event List. Soundbites, audio volume and panning, as well as automation data can also be affected. See Chapter 10 for more information on the View Filters window.

The Input Quantize Command

Use the Input Quantize command, shown in Figure 8.6, to quantize incoming MIDI data that is being recorded to a track. Choose Studio menu > Input Quantize to open this window. MIDI data being received is automatically quantized and then recorded to the specified MIDI track.

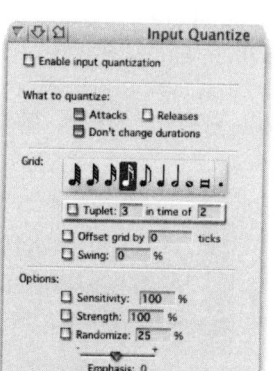

Figure 8.6

The Input Quantize command quantizes MIDI data as it is being recorded to a track.

CHAPTER 8 } Recording MIDI

If you're already familiar with the standard Quantize command (explained in Chapter 9), you'll find this command very straightforward.

To quantize MIDI data during the recording process:

1. Open the Input Quantize window by choosing Studio menu > Input Quantize. You can also use the default keyboard shortcut Shift+Control+I.
2. Click the Enable input quantize option to turn on Input Quantize, and then choose the desired quantize settings. Once Input Quantize is enabled, MIDI data being recorded to a track will automatically be quantized.

The quantize settings listed in the Input Quantize window are identical to the settings found in the Note section of the standard Quantize command. Refer to Chapter 9 for an explanation of the Region menu's Quantize command.

MIDI Device Groups

Digital Performer's MIDI Device Groups command, shown in Figure 8.7, allows you to send MIDI data to multiple MIDI output destinations. Choose Studio menu > MIDI Device Groups to open this window.

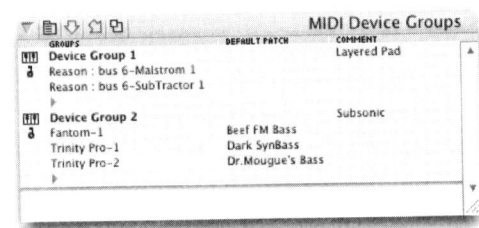

Figure 8.7

The MIDI Device Groups window.

MIDI device groups are especially useful when you are stacking multiple MIDI sound modules (or virtual instruments) to create a layered "patch" or sound. For example, you might have three external MIDI devices in your studio that you use to create a "layered" bass sound. Instead of creating separate MIDI tracks for each sound, you can create a MIDI device group containing the three devices you're using. Once created, the group will appear in the output assignment menus of all MIDI tracks, as shown in Figure 8.8.

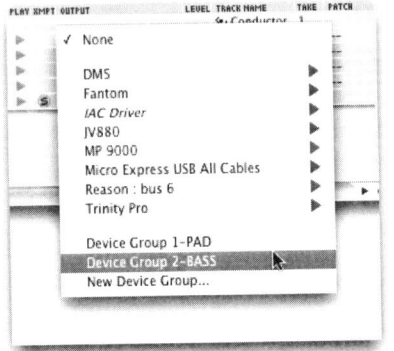

Figure 8.8

Once created, device groups will appear in the output assignment menus of a MIDI track.

> **THE MAX NUMBER OF MIDI CHANNELS IN A DEVICE GROUP**
> The maximum number of MIDI devices/channels that can be added to a MIDI device group is 10.

188

※ MIDI-Related Windows and Commands

To create a new MIDI device group:

1. Open the MIDI Device Groups window by choosing Studio menu > MIDI Device Groups, or by using the default keyboard shortcut Shift+I. If you want to create a new device group without going to the Studio menu, simply choose New Device Group from a MIDI track's output assignment menu. If you use this method, proceed to Step 3.

2. From the MIDI Device Group window's mini-menu, choose the Add Device Group option, as shown in Figure 8.9. An empty device group called Device Group 1 will appear in the window. Hold the Option key while creating a new device group to quickly add multiple device groups.

   Figure 8.9
   Choose Add Device Group to create a new device group.

3. You'll probably want to customize the new device group's name so that you can easily recognize it. To rename the device group, Option-click the device group name.

To add/remove a specific MIDI device/channel to your new device group:

1. Click the disclosure triangle located below the device group name. A list of connected MIDI devices and channels will open. Select the specific MIDI device and channel from the list, as shown in Figure 8.10. Once chosen, the MIDI device/channel will be added to the MIDI device group.

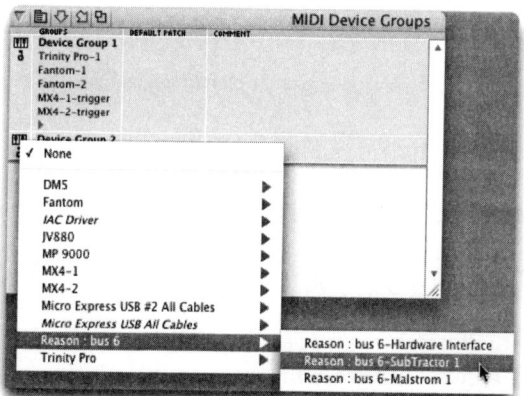

Figure 8.10
Add a MIDI device to the group from the MIDI device list.

2. To add additional devices to the group, repeat Step 1 (or see the side note on the Expand/Compress icon).

3. To remove a device from the group, select it and choose Delete from the mini-menu.

CHAPTER 8 } Recording MIDI

THE EXPAND/COMPRESS ICON

The Expand/Compress icon, shown in Figure 8.11, toggles the display of all MIDI devices that are connected to your MIDI interface. As in the MIDI Monitor window, each MIDI device channel is displayed as a box. Clicking a channel box will add that MIDI channel to the selected device group. MIDI channels assigned to the device group will appear highlighted green.

Use the expanded view to quickly add (or remove) MIDI channels to a device group without using the MIDI device list which only allows you to add one MIDI channel at a time.

Figure 8.11

Click the Expand/Compress icon to view all connected MIDI devices/channels within the MIDI Device Group window. MIDI channel boxes that are highlighted green indicate that they are part of the device group.

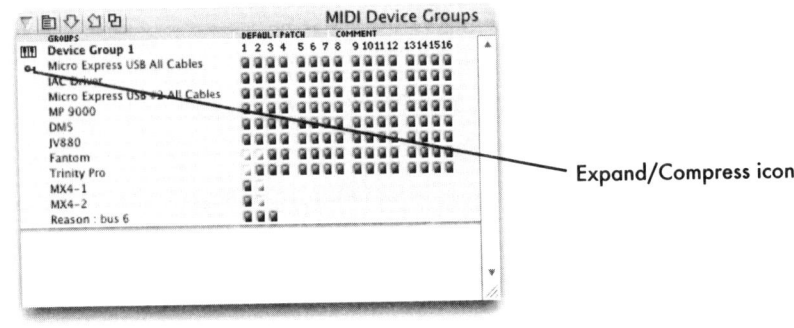

UNDOING ACTIONS TAKEN IN THE MIDI DEVICE GROUP WINDOW

Be aware that any actions (such as creating and deleting device groups) are instantaneous and cannot be undone.

To set or clear the default patch for a specific MIDI channel contained in your device group:

- To set the default patch, click in the Default Patch column directly to the right of the particular channel and choose the desired patch from the list.
- To clear the default patch for a specific MIDI channel, click the MIDI channel name and choose Clear Default Patch from the mini-menu.
- To clear the default patch lists for an entire device group, click the device group name and choose Clear Default Patch from the mini-menu.

THE DEFAULT PATCH

A MIDI channel's default patch is basically the first patch (or sound) that DP uses when you play a MIDI track. This patch is remembered and saved with the project, so the next time you open the session, DP will know what patch to select and play back. Be aware that when a MIDI channel is using a default patch, it will automatically override any manual patch changes you make on the specific MIDI device. To have a different patch play back, you will need to change the default patch, remove the default patch, or program a patch change.

Be sure not to confuse the standard Patch (or Current Patch) column with the Default Patch column. MIDI patches selected in the Patch column won't be remembered with a project, so be sure to use the Default Patch column if you want DP to recall the patch the next time you open your project. DP's MIDI patch lists are explained in the next section.

MIDI Patch Lists

A patch list contains the names of a MIDI device's (or virtual instrument's) sounds or patches, as shown in Figure 8.12.

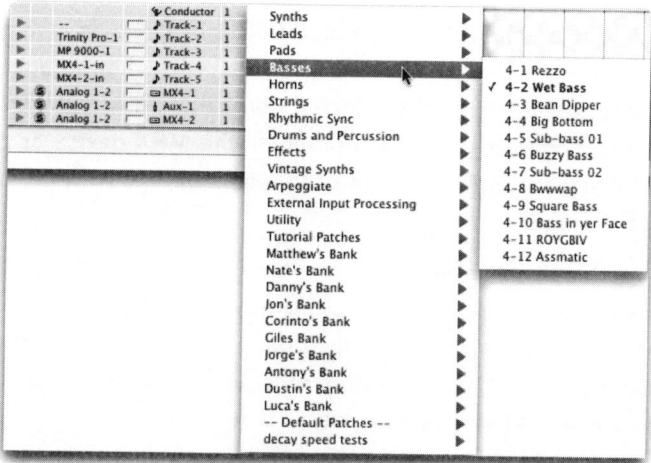

Figure 8.12
Patch names recognized by OSX will be displayed with their factory default names.

Digital Performer relies on Mac OSX to supply the default factory patch names of connected MIDI devices. The patch names for most of the popular MIDI devices and instruments in use today are recognized by OSX. Patch names that aren't recognized, however, will be listed with generic patch names, such as Patch-1, Patch-2, Patch-3, and so on (see Figure 8.13).

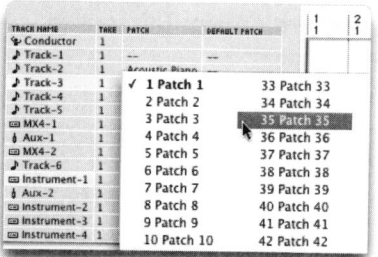

Figure 8.13
A patch list containing generic patch names.

CHAPTER 8 } Recording MIDI

> ### PATCH LIST EDITORS/LIBRARIANS
> If you're tired of seeing generic patch names in your patch lists, you can use a dedicated MIDI patch list editor/librarian application, such as MOTU's Unisyn, to supply DP with the correct patch names. These programs contain expanded lists of different MIDI devices and their patch names. MOTU's Unisyn will even allow you to edit a device's sounds and rename them.

The Current Patch versus the Default Patch

Digital Performer basically contains two different patch lists: the current patch and the default patch lists, as shown in Figure 8.14. The patches contained in each list are identical. Where they differ is in their function.

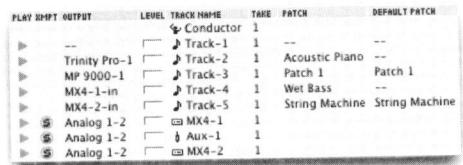

Figure 8.14

The (Current) Patch and Default Patch columns allow you to set the current or default patch assignment for a specific MIDI channel in the Tracks window.

As explained earlier, the default patch list tells DP which MIDI patch should always be played first on a specific MIDI track. As long as the patch change doesn't exist with a MIDI track (via controller data automation), the selected default patch will always play when playback is engaged—even if you manually change the patch on the MIDI device or virtual instrument. Use the default patch list if you want Digital Performer to remember the MIDI patches you are using even after you close your DP project.

The Current Patch list (or Patch column) always displays the currently selected MIDI patch and will even update on the fly when you have patch changes inserted on a MIDI track. As with the Default Patch list, MIDI channels can be assigned to a specific patch by choosing the desired patch from the list. If you don't want DP to automatically play certain patches (or the default patch), use the current patch list when you assign a MIDI channel to a specific patch.

Recording MIDI Data

Now that you've seen some of the various MIDI-related features that can affect the MIDI recording process, you're ready to begin recording. This section will cover the various ways of recording MIDI data on your MIDI tracks.

❄ Recording MIDI Data

> **SETTING UP YOUR MIDI TRACKS**
>
> Chapter 4, "Setting Up a New Project" demonstrates the proper setup procedures for creating MIDI and instrument tracks, setting the MIDI input and output assignments, and monitoring your MIDI devices and/or virtual instruments. If you're shaky on the ins and outs of this process, refer to Chapter 4 for an in-depth look at how to set up your MIDI tracks for recording.

Setting Up to Record a MIDI Track

As I have already explained the MIDI track setup process in detail in Chapter 4, I'll assume that you understand MIDI track configuration and I'll only provide a review of the track and I/O setup process here.

To set up a MIDI track for recording:

1. Create a MIDI track with the default keyboard shortcut Shift+Command+M. To create multiple MIDI tracks, press Shift+Option+Command+M. By default, the track will automatically be record-enabled.
2. Assign the MIDI track to the desired MIDI device (and channel) from the track's output menu. If you want to assign the track to a virtual instrument instead, you'll need to create the instrument before it will show up in the output menu.
3. Next, setup an aux track to monitor your MIDI device. Press Control+Command+A to add an aux track.
4. In the aux track's input menu, choose the audio hardware inputs that correspond to your MIDI device. For example, if the physical outputs of your MIDI device are connected to Analog 1 & 2 of your audio interface, choose Analog 1 & 2 for the aux track inputs.
5. If necessary, select the specific sound you want to use for your MIDI track from the Current or Default Patch list (explained earlier).
6. As the track is already record-enabled, press some notes on your MIDI controller to make sure you "have signal." If you aren't hearing anything, open up the MIDI monitor window (explained earlier) and verify that DP is receiving MIDI data from the specific MIDI device.

> **MIDI PATCH THRU**
>
> MIDI Patch Thru allows you to hear your MIDI devices or instrument plug-ins when you play a note on your MIDI controller. Be sure to enable MIDI Patch Thru or you won't hear anything when you press a note on your MIDI controller, regardless of whether DP is receiving MIDI data from your connected MIDI devices.

CHAPTER 8 } Recording MIDI

Setting Up an Instrument Track

When working with virtual instruments (VIs), you need to create the desired instrument track before it will become available in a MIDI track's output menu. There are a couple of different ways to create your Digital Performer instrument tracks. One way is to add a specific type of instrument track. The other way is to create an empty (or unassigned) instrument track and assign its instrument at a later time. Unassigned instrument tracks are especially useful when you are creating project templates.

> **WORKING WITH VIRTUAL INSTRUMENTS THAT EXIST IN ANOTHER APPLICATION**
>
> If you want to assign a MIDI track to a virtual instrument that exists in another application (outside DP), you need to create the VI before it will show up in DP. Some third-party applications have specific setup requirements that must be followed in order to publish its VI in a Digital Performer MIDI track. Consult the specific program's user manual for the proper setup instructions. If you're working with Propellerhead's Reason application, you can refer to Chapter 4 for an overview of the Reason setup process.

To add a Digital Performer instrument track that's assigned to a specific virtual instrument:

- Choose Project menu > Add Track > Instrument Track, and select the specific virtual instrument from the instrument track list.

To add an unassigned (empty) instrument track:

- Choose Project menu > Add Track > Instrument Track > Unassigned or press Shift+Command+I.
- To create multiple assigned tracks, choose Project menu > Add Track > Instrument Track > Add Multiple. You can also use the default keyboard shortcut Shift+Option+Command+I.

Basic Recording

Once you have configured your MIDI and/or instrument tracks, and have confirmed that you have signal, you're ready to begin recording.

To record on a MIDI track:

1. Record-enable (or arm) the MIDI track.
2. Test the signal by playing a few notes on your MIDI controller.
3. Click the Control Panel's Record button to begin recording. You can also press the number 3 key on the numeric keypad to start recording.
4. Press the number 3 key again to stop recording but continue playback (or punch out of record), or hit the Space bar to stop recording and playback at the same time.

5. If you don't like the recording and wish to try it again, press Command+Z to undo the record pass. You can also use the Undo History window to undo the performance (as explained in Chapter 6). Press the number 1 key on the numeric keypad to rewind to the beginning of the sequence.
6. Repeat Steps 3-5 as needed.

Punch Recording

Punch Recording (or punching in on a track) is the process of replacing existing material by recording over a specific portion of a track. For example, say you record a 16-bar MIDI performance, and upon listening to playback of the track, you decide you're very happy with the first half of the track but you're not satisfied with the second half (bars 8-16). Instead of rerecording the entire track and losing your great performance during bars 1-8, you could just rerecord bars 8-16; this is called *punching in* on a track. There are basically two ways to execute a punch within DP: manually and automatically.

To manually punch in on a MIDI track:

1. Arm the MIDI track you wish to punch in on.
2. Move the playback wiper close to where you want to start recording—anywhere from 5-20 seconds (or 4-16 bars) before the punch-in point. Exactly how much pre-roll you use is really up to you.
3. Press the Space bar to begin playback.
4. In order to make the punch-in as seamless as possible, make sure you (or the artist you're recording) start playing along with the track as soon as you know where you are within the song.
5. At the desired location, press the number 3 key on the numeric keypad to start recording and "punch-in" on the track.
6. Press the number 3 key again to punch out of record.
7. Repeat Steps 4-6 as needed. When you've completed your punches, press the Space bar to stop recording and playback.
8. Hit the number 1 key to return to the beginning of the sequence.

To automatically punch in on a MIDI track:

1. Arm the MIDI track you wish to record on.
2. Engage the Control Panel's Auto Record button, as shown in Figure 8.15.

Figure 8.15
Use the Control Panel's Auto Record button to perform an "auto-punch."

CHAPTER 8 } Recording MIDI

3. With the Auto Record button turned on, set the punch-in and punch-out times, as shown in Figure 8.16.

Figure 8.16
Use the Auto Record button's punch in and out times to set the duration of the punch in.

4. Move the playback wiper close to where you wish to start recording—anywhere from five to 20 seconds (or four to 16 bars) before the punch in point. How much pre-roll you use is really up to you.
5. Press the Space bar to begin playback.
6. In order to make the punch-in as seamless as possible, make sure you (or the artist you're recording) start playing along with the track as soon as you know where you are in the song.
7. When playback reaches the designated punch-in start time, DP will punch in on the track. At the specified punch out time, DP will punch out of record.
8. Press the Space bar to stop playback.
9. Press the number 1 key on the numeric keypad to locate to the beginning of the sequence.

Overdub Recording

After you get a satisfactory first MIDI record pass, you may wish to add (or layer) on additional passes of the same sound or MIDI channel (you might want to add another chord on top of the previous record pass, for example). This is called *overdub recording*, or *overdubbing*.

When you're working with audio tracks, you must use a new track to perform overdub recording, or overdubs. If you overdub in the same audio track, you will actually be erasing the existing material when you press the Record button. Digital Performer MIDI tracks, however, allow you the option of layering new MIDI record passes onto existing material without actually deleting the existing MIDI data—essentially you're merging the new data with the existing data.

To overdub record on a MIDI track:

1. Arm the track you want to overdub on.
2. Click the Overdub button on the Control Panel, shown in Figure 8.17.

Figure 8.17
The Overdub button, when engaged, will allow you to "layer," or overdub, new MIDI data onto existing data within a MIDI track.

3. Press the number 3 key on the numeric keypad to start playback and recording.
4. Begin playing your MIDI controller to layer your new performance onto the existing MIDI data.
5. When you are ready, press the number 3 key to punch out of record.
6. Press the Space bar to stop recording and playback altogether.
7. Press the number 1 key on the numeric keypad to return to the beginning of the sequence.

※ Recording MIDI Data

Cycle-Recording
When the Overdub record feature is combined with the Control Panel's Memory Cycle feature, DP allows you to cycle-record (or "loop-record") audio and MIDI data. Set the Transport to loop continuously, engage the overdub record feature, and you can overdub continuously over a specific time-range.

To engage cycle-record mode:

1. Click the Control Panel's Memory Cycle and set the Memory Start and End times, as shown in Figure 8.18. The start and end times will basically define the loop beginning and end.
2. Engage the Overdub button.
3. Press the number 3 key on the numeric keypad to start playback and recording.
4. Begin playing your MIDI controller to layer your new performance onto the existing MIDI data.
5. When DP reaches the end of the specified end time for the loop, it will jump back to the memory start time and continue overdub recording, merging the new material with the existing MIDI data.
6. When you are through recording, press the number 3 key to punch out of record.
7. Press the Space bar to stop recording and playback altogether.
8. Press the number 1 key on the numeric keypad to return to the beginning of the sequence.

Figure 8.18
Use the Control Panel's Memory Start and End times to specify the loop points for the cycle-record process.

> ※ **RECORDING ALTERNATIVE TAKES**
> The process of using takes with MIDI tracks is identical to that of audio tracks. Refer to the "Recording and Managing Alternate Takes" section of Chapter 7 for an explanation of takes within Digital Performer.

Step Recording
When you're step recording, MIDI data is not recorded in real-time, but is inserted one note at a time into a MIDI track. Digital Performer's Step Record command, shown in Figure 8.19, allows you to step record MIDI notes of a specific duration that are automatically quantized. This feature can be useful for entering especially difficult rhythmic passages that you cannot perform or to create a lead sheet for use in DP's QuickScribe Editor or other notation software applications, such as Finale.

CHAPTER 8 } Recording MIDI

Figure 8.19
The Step Record window.

The basic process of inserting a MIDI note with the Step Record command is very simple. Refer to Chapter 19 of the *Digital Performer User's Manual* for an in-depth discussion of the Step Record command.

To step record MIDI notes:

1. Open the Step Record window by pressing Command+8, or by choosing Studio menu > Step Record.
2. Select the MIDI track you want to step record on from the Current Record Track pop-up menu, as shown in Figure 8.20.
3. Choose the desired note duration with the Step Duration buttons, shown in Figure 8.21.
4. If you want to have the Step Record window linked to DP's main Transport controls, click the title bar's Transport Lock button, shown in Figure 8.22. Use this button to toggle the locked or unlocked state of the Step Record window.
5. If you want DP to automatically advance to the next step once you have inserted a MIDI note, make sure the Auto Step button (shown in Figure 8.23) is engaged.
6. To insert a note (or chord), press and hold the desired notes on your MIDI controller. Be sure to press the notes together, and cleanly, to ensure that the notes are inserted in the same location (or step).

Figure 8.20
The Current Record Track menu determines the track that will be step recorded into.

Figure 8.21
Use the Step Duration buttons to specify the note value to be entered.

Transport Lock button

Figure 8.22
The Transport Lock button.

Figure 8.23
The Auto Step button.

7. Release the note(s), and they will be automatically inserted in the selected MIDI track.
8. If you step record a wrong note(s), use the Backstep button.
9. Repeat Steps 3, 5, and 6 to continue step recording.

> **STEP-RECORDING VERSUS THE PENCIL TOOL**
> Don't confuse step recording with the basic process of inserting notes with the Pencil tool. Although they are technically similar in function, the Pencil tool provides more versatility when inserting notes directly into a MIDI track within the Graphic Editor or Sequence Editors. The process of inserting notes with the Pencil tool is discussed in the "Editing MIDI" section of Chapter 10.

Summary

In addition to the basic MIDI recording process, Digital Performer contains a number of powerful MIDI recording features. Features such as cycle, overdub, and step recording allow you to tailor the recording process to meet your specific MIDI production needs.

9 Recording MIDI: Region Menu, Plug-ins, and Virtual Instruments

Now that you've seen the MIDI recording process in Chapter 8, I'll discuss DP's related MIDI commands, plug-ins, and virtual instruments tracks.

Following is a list of topics covered in this chapter:

- The Region Menu command.
- How to use MIDI plug-ins.
- How DP handles virtual instruments and instrument tracks.
- How to use the Freeze Selected Tracks command.

Region Menu Commands

The majority of Digital Performer's MIDI commands are located in the Region Menu, shown in Figure 9.1. Region menu commands allow you to apply changes to selected MIDI data and tracks—similar to the way Audio menu plug-ins can be applied to audio tracks for file based processing. Region menu commands will alter the original MIDI data you're working with, so you may want to create a copy of the tracks you're modifying by duplicating the track take, or by duplicating the track altogether.

Many of the Region menu commands (including the MIDI Effects plug-ins) can be used non-destructively, and in real-time, by inserting the desired effect within the Mixing Board. Real-time effects have the benefit of not altering your MIDI track's original data. In addition, you can change the plug-in settings at any time if you aren't satisfied with its current settings.

CHAPTER 9 } Recording MIDI: Region Menu, Plug-ins, and Virtual Instruments

Figure 9.1

The Region menu.

This section will highlight some of the more frequently used Region commands and provide a basic overview of their processes. We'll also discuss how the Region command windows function compared to DP's other edit commands. Refer to the "Region Menu" chapter of the *Digital Performer User's Manual* for a comprehensive look at the Region menu commands.

The Mini-Menu

Unlike DP's standard edit command windows, which won't allow you to perform other operations until you apply or cancel the command, Region command windows can stay open while you perform other actions within a project—though you can only have one Region command open at a given time. Choosing another Region menu command will replace the current window with the new one.

The mini-menu options, shown in Figure 9.2, control what happens to a Region command window after a setting is applied. Keep in mind that the options listed are global, and will affect all Region command windows that contain a mini-menu.

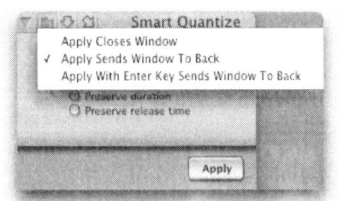

Figure 9.2

These mini-menu options control what happens to a window when a setting is applied.

* **Apply Closes Window.** This option will close the window when you hit the Apply button or press the Enter key on your Mac's keyboard.

Region Menu Commands

- **Apply Sends Window to Back.** This option will force the window into the background when you hit the Apply button or press the Enter key on your Mac's keyboard.
- **Apply With Enter Key Sends Window To Back.** This option will force the window into the background when you press the Enter key on your Mac's keyboard. Hitting the Apply button will apply the command but keep the window in the foreground.

Some of the Region menu commands allow you to audition or preview settings before applying them. Click the window's Preview button to turn on previewing, as shown in Figure 9.3.

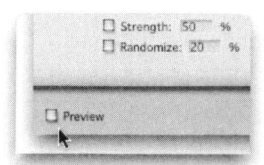

Figure 9.3
The Preview button.

If the window supports previewing, the mini-menu will also contain a previewing option that controls how the preview feature behaves when a window is not in the foreground, shown in Figure 9.4.

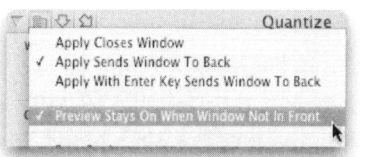

Figure 9.4
Use the mini-menu's Preview option to keep previewing turned on when a window is in the background.

Check the Preview Stays On When Window Not In Front option if you want the window to continue auditioning its settings, even when the window is forced to the background.

Similar to audio plug-in presets, some of the Region commands allow you to save the window's current settings for future use or to edit existing presets, as

Figure 9.5
The Save Settings and Edit Settings commands.

shown in Figure 9.5. If you have a particular setting that you wish to use again, use the Save Settings command in the window's mini-menu. To edit a preset choose mini-menu > Edit Settings.

- To save a preset, choose mini-menu > Save Settings. Enter the name for your new preset in the Name Effect Preset window. Click OK to name the new preset.
- If you wish to delete a preset, choose mini-menu > Edit Settings. Click the Delete button. When the warning dialog opens, click OK to proceed with the removal of the preset. Click the Done button to close the Edit Effect Presets window.
- To rename a preset, choose mini-menu Edit Settings. Select the preset you want to modify from the preset list and click the Rename button. In the Name Effect Preset pop-up window, enter the preset name. Click the Done button to close the Edit Effect Presets window.

CHAPTER 9 } Recording MIDI: Region Menu, Plug-ins, and Virtual Instruments

The Transpose Command

Use the Region menu's Transpose command, shown in Figure 9.6, to change the pitch of selected MIDI notes (and audio files). Choose Region menu > Transpose or use the default keyboard shortcut Command+9 to open the Transpose command. Once it is open, you can choose to transpose selected notes, modifying the original data in the process, or you can harmonize the selected notes, which will create a new harmonized version and merge it with the original material. Use the Transpose and Harmonize options to set the window to either transpose or harmonize.

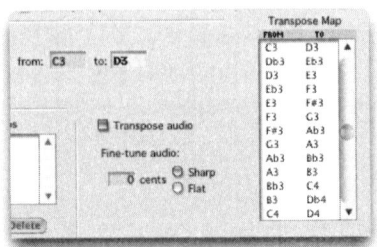

Figure 9.6

The Region menu's Transpose command.

The Transpose Map

The Transpose Map, shown in Figure 9.7, contains two columns: From and To. The From column is a list of all 128 MIDI pitches. The To column displays the note that the pitch in the From column will be changed to. The Transpose Map is like a "before and after" list, with the note on the left representing the "before" (or starting pitch), and the note on the right representing the "after" (or destination pitch).

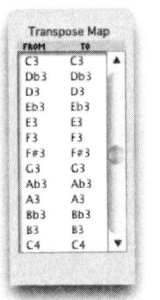

Figure 9.7

The Transpose Map.

The Interval, Diatonic, Key/Scale, and Custom Map Options

The Interval, Diatonic, Key/Scale, and Custom Map options (shown in Figure 9.8) determine what notes will actually be displayed in the To column of the Transpose Map. Use these different options to transpose pitches to a certain type of scale (chromatically, diatonically, and so on).

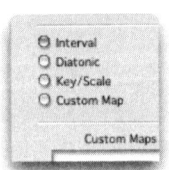

Figure 9.8

The Transpose command's different scale options.

* **Interval**. Select this option when you want to transpose or harmonize notes chromatically. All selected notes will be pitched up or down according to the interval that you set in the From and To input fields, as shown in Figure 9.9. The actual notes you enter do not matter—only the interval will be used when changing the notes. You can also use the Interval option to transpose audio data. Refer to Chapter 13, "Processing and Mastering," for an explanation of pitch-shifting audio. Click Apply to transpose the selected data.

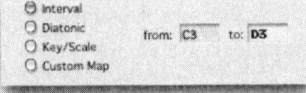

Figure 9.9

Use the To and From input fields to set the interval for the pitch change.

204

※ Region Menu Commands

※ **Diatonic.** The Diatonic option, shown in Figure 9.10, allows you to change the pitch of a note (up or down) by a specific number of scale steps within a designated key (or scale mode).

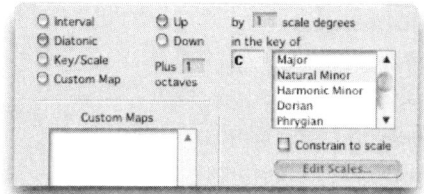

Figure 9.10
The Diatonic option and related settings.

Start by choosing the proper key and scale mode for the selected data. Type in the number of scale steps by which the selected data is to be transposed in the By___Scale Degrees input field. Set the direction for the pitch change with the Up and Down options. Use the Plus___Octaves setting to pitch-shift notes by more than one octave. Click the Apply button to diatonically transpose the selected data.

※ **Key/Scale.** Use the Key/Scale option, shown in Figure 9.11, to change a selection from one scale to another. Set the selection's current key in the From input field and set the scale mode from the list. Use the To input field and list to specify the destination key and scale mode. Set the direction of the pitch change with the Up or Down and Plus___Octaves options. Click Apply to pitch-shift the selection.

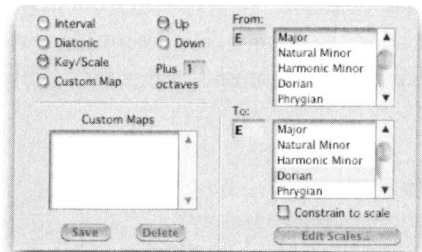

Figure 9.11
The Key/Scale option and related settings.

THE CONSTRAIN TO SCALE BUTTON

The Constrain To Scale option forces all notes that are not contained in the set scale to be shifted to the closest note within the destination scale. This option will only appear when the Diatonic and Key/Scale options are selected.

※ **Custom Map.** Use the Custom Map to create a custom scale of notes. Choose the transpose option (Interval, Diatonic, or Key/Scale) on which you wish to base your custom transpose map . In the To column of the Transpose map, pop-edit a note to edit the scale. Once a note is changed, the window will automatically change to the Custom Map. Continue modifying the new scale as needed.

To save the custom scale for later use, name the Custom Map and click the Save button, shown in Figure 9.12. Click the Apply button to apply your customized scale to the current MIDI selection.

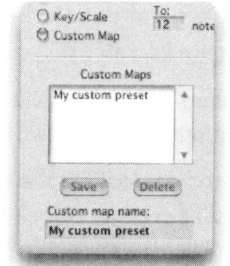

Figure 9.12
Saved Custom Map presets will appear in the Custom Map list.

205

The Quantize Command

The Quantize command, shown in Figure 9.13, is probably the most popular and widely used Region menu command. Choose Region menu > Quantize or use the default keyboard shortcut Command+0 to open the Quantize command. Use this option to constrain the locations of selected data to a set rhythmic grid.

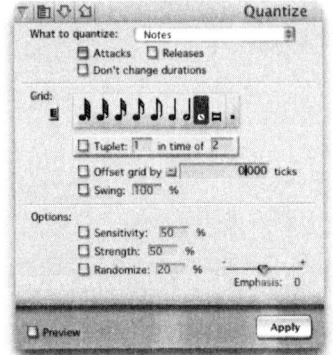

Figure 9.13

The Region menu's Quantize command.

Quantizing MIDI Notes

The most basic use of the Quantize command is to correct the rhythmic timing of a recorded MIDI performance. To quantize selected MIDI notes, select the notes you wish to quantize, open the Quantize window, and then choose the Note option from the What to Quantize menu. Set the Grid and Options settings as needed, and then click the Apply button. Remember that you can preview the selection before applying the Quantize settings by enabling the Preview option, located at the bottom of the window.

The What To Quantize Menu

The Quantize command can alter the attack/release times of MIDI data, change the start locations of soundbites and markers, and even change the locations of beats within a soundbite. The What to Quantize menu, shown in Figure 9.14, allows you to specify the type (or types) of data that will be quantized when you hit the window's Apply button.

Figure 9.14

Use the What to Quantize menu to select the type of data that will be quantized.

The Quantize options that appear in the window are dependent on the data type selected in the What to Quantize menu. Choose Notes to quantize a selection of MIDI notes.

Quantizing the Attacks, Releases, and/or Durations of Notes

Once you specify the type of data to be quantized in the What to Quantize menu, you'll need to decide whether the attacks, releases, and/or durations will be quantized.

* **Attacks**. Enabling this option will cause the attack (or start) of the note to be moved to the closest grid location.
* **Releases**. This option causes the release times of notes to be moved to the closest grid location, while preserving the attack times (or start times) of the selected MIDI notes.

※ **Enabling Both Attacks and Releases.** Choosing both options will cause both the attacks and releases of selected notes to be moved to their closest grid locations; this can change note durations in the process. When both the Attacks and Releases options are enabled, the Don't Change Durations option will be disabled, as note durations will be automatically changed when quantizing both the attacks and releases of a selection.

※ **Don't Change Durations.** Enable this option to preserve the durations of quantized MIDI notes. If this option is turned off, notes (or other types of data) may be truncated or lengthened when quantized—and this can significantly alter the performance of a selection. Be aware that this option is disabled when both the Attacks and Releases options are turned on.

Setting the Resolution for the Quantize Grid
The Grid section of the Quantize window determines the resolution of the Quantize Grid, or basically divides the quantize grid into the specified duration. By default, the Measures time format will be displayed in the grid section. This allows you to align your MIDI data to specific note values, as shown in Figure 9.15.

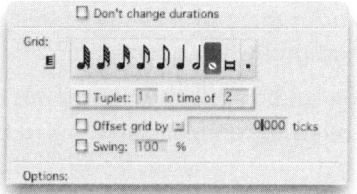

Figure 9.15
The Measures time format allows you to set the Quantize Grid to a specific note value.

To change the time format that's displayed in the Grid section, click the Time Format button, as shown in Figure 9.16. Continue clicking to cycle through the available time formats. Keep in mind that MIDI notes can be quantized to any time format grid and are not limited to just the Measures time format.

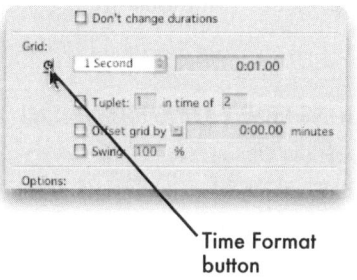

Time Format button

Figure 9.16
The Quantize window's Time Format button changes the time format of the Quantize Grid. In this example, the Minutes and Seconds time format has been selected.

Use the Grid section to choose the value for the Quantize Grid. You can even specify the tuplet and swing settings, and even offset the Quantize Grid by a certain number of ticks. Generally speaking, choosing the smallest note value that appears in your MIDI selection will allow you to "clean up" your performance without totally altering the performance (assuming that your original performance isn't too rhythmically inaccurate).

The Quantize Options
Of course, there will be many times when you do not wish to quantize (or realign) your MIDI selection to the Quantize Grid, as doing so can cause your performance to feel robotic and emotionless.

You can use the Options section, shown in Figure 9.17, to help maintain the rhythmic "feel" of a performance. When these options are disabled, however, data set to be quantized will be moved and aligned precisely to the chosen Grid value.

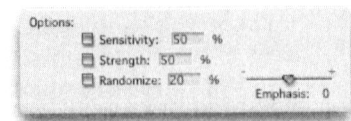

Figure 9.17
The Quantize Options section.

* **Sensitivity.** Use positive Sensitivity values to only affect the downbeats of a selection, and negative values to only affect notes that are rhythmically inaccurate. The lower the Sensitivity value, the less the MIDI selection will be precisely aligned to the Quantize Grid. A setting of 100% will be the same as not having the option turned on.
* **Strength.** Use settings lower than 100% to quantize a selection but still retain the overall "feel" of the performance. A setting of 50%, for example, will only move a selection halfway towards the specified grid when quantized.
* **Randomize.** Randomize basically has the opposite effect of quantizing. A setting of 100% will allow the attacks, releases, and/or durations to be placed in totally random locations within the specified grid.
* **Emphasis.** Use this setting to determine whether randomly placed notes will appear earlier or later within the designated randomize range. Positive values will place notes ahead of the beat, while negative values will place notes behind the beat, resulting in a more laid-back performance.

> **THE QUANTIZE OPTIONS QUICKTIME MOVIE TUTORIAL**
> Refer to the Quantize Command Options QuickTime movie tutorial on the Digital Performer 4 CSi LE CD included in the back of this book for an in-depth explanation of the Quantize Command's Sensitivity, Strength, and Randomize/Emphasis options.

The Change Velocity Command

The Change Velocity command, shown in Figure 9.18, is used to alter the velocities (or change the volume) of a selection of MIDI notes. You can choose to modify a note's on or off velocities with the On Velocities or Off Velocities options. Be aware that this command has no effect on audio data.

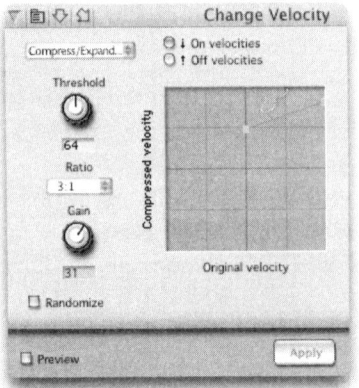

Figure 9.18
The region menu's Change Velocity command. In this example, the Compress/Expand option has been selected.

※ Region Menu Commands

The Velocity command allows you to change the velocity of notes in different ways, as shown in Figure 9.19.

* **Set**. Use this option to change (or set) selected notes to a specific velocity. For example, entering a value of 127 in the Set All Velocities To____ input field will change all selected notes to a velocity of 127, as shown in Figure 9.20.

* **Add**. This option, shown in Figure 9.21, will allow you to add a set number of velocity values to a MIDI note selection. Use the Add____To All Velocities input field to set the velocity value that will be added.

* **Scale**. This option scales a MIDI note selection by a percentage value. Use the Change to____% of Current Value input field to specify the percentage value, as shown in Figure 9.22.

* **Limit**. This option will limit the velocity values of a MIDI selection to a set velocity range, as shown in Figure 9.23.

* **Compress/Expand**. This option, shown in Figure 9.24, is similar to an audio compressor/expander plug-in. The Threshold knob determines when velocity compression/expansion will start and stop. How much compression/expansion that's applied is determined by the Ratio setting. Use the Gain knob to make up any gain that's lost in the process.

* **Smooth Velocity**. The Smooth option, shown in Figure 9.25, basically automates a smooth velocity change along a set curve. The ____% to ____% of Current Value option is similar to the previously

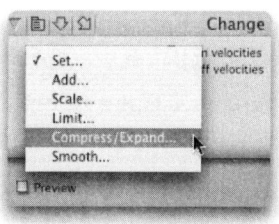

Figure 9.19
Select an option from this list to determine how velocities will be changed with the Change Velocity command.

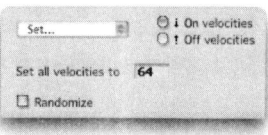

Figure 9.20
The Set velocity option.

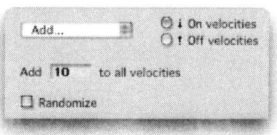

Figure 9.21
The Add velocity option.

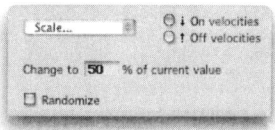

Figure 9.22
The Scale velocity option.

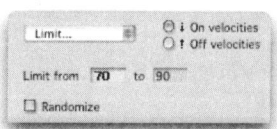

Figure 9.23
The Limit Velocity option.

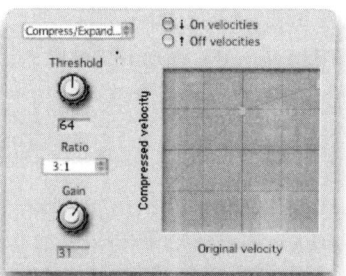

Figure 9.24
The Compress/Expand velocity option.

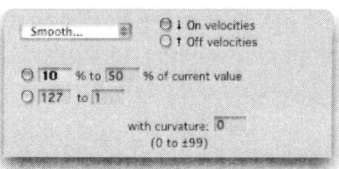

Figure 9.25
The Smooth velocity option.

CHAPTER 9 } Recording MIDI: Region Menu, Plug-ins, and Virtual Instruments

discussed scale command, except that the MIDI selection will be scaled between the first and second percentage values that you specify.

The ____ to ____ option sets the velocity of the first MIDI note within your selection to the first value, and the last note velocity in your MIDI selection to the last value. Once set, the in-between values will automatically be calculated to create a smooth velocity transition between the first and last note in your selection.

The With Curvature setting determines the type of curve that will be used. A setting of zero will create a linear curve. Positive values will apply the majority of the velocity changes towards the end of the curve, while negative values have the opposite effect.

The Split Notes Command

The Split Notes command, shown in Figure 9.26, is used to copy or cut specific notes from a MIDI track. Use this command to "explode" selected MIDI notes onto their own individual tracks.

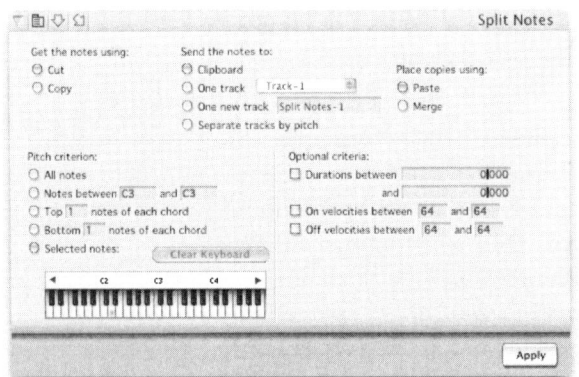

Figure 9.26

The Split Notes command.

At first glance, the Split Notes window may seem confusing, but actually it's fairly straightforward. Once you've selected a MIDI region to work with (or entire MIDI track), simply proceed to each section within the window and make the desired settings.

- **Get the notes using**. Select how DP will retrieve the specified notes from the MIDI selection by copying the notes (leaving the original MIDI data intact) or by cutting the notes (which will remove the selected notes altogether), as shown in Figure 9.27. If you are using the Cut option, you may want to duplicate the track or take before beginning this process.

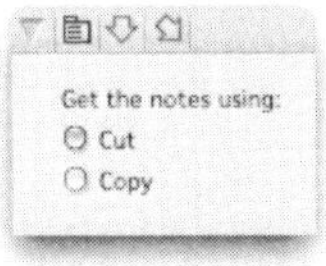

- **Send the notes to**. This section, shown in Figure 9.28, determines where the copied or cut material will be placed once you hit the Apply button. Notes can be placed in the Mac's clipboard, on an existing track, or on a new track. Choosing the Separate Tracks By Pitch option can be used to explode each different pitch onto its own new track.

Figure 9.27

The Get Notes Using section.

Figure 9.28

The Send the Notes To section.

210

❋ **Place Copies Using.** This section, shown in Figure 9.29, determines whether copied or cut notes will be pasted in the destination track (overwriting the existing material) or merged with any existing data.

Figure 9.29
The Place Copies Using section.

❋ **Pitch Criterion.** The Pitch Criterion section, shown in Figure 9.30, allows you to specify exactly which notes will be copied or cut with the Split Notes command. Choose the appropriate setting from the list. To choose specific notes, simply click on the note within the keyboard.

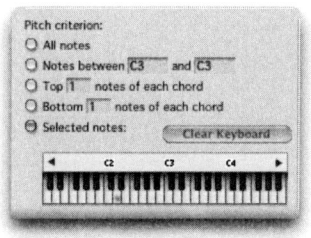

Figure 9.30
The Pitch Criterion section.

❋ **Optional Criteria.** The optional criteria section, shown in Figure 9.31, allows you to further specify the exact notes that will be split from the MIDI selection.

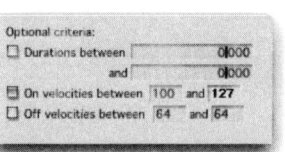

Figure 9.31
The Optional Criteria section.

Once you have specified how and where the specified notes will be split, click the Apply button to execute the Split Notes command.

MIDI Effects Plug-ins

Similar to audio plug-ins, MIDI effects plug-ins can be applied in real-time or as a file-based process. MIDI plug-ins located in the Region menu, shown in Figure 9.32, will permanently alter MIDI data that it processes; real-time MIDI plug-ins inserted in the Mixing Board, shown in Figure 9.33, will only affect the real-time playback of a MIDI track.

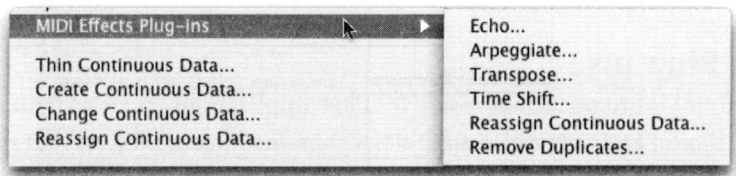

Figure 9.32
Region menu's MIDI effects plug-ins are destructive processes that permanently alter the original MIDI data in a track.

CHAPTER 9 } Recording MIDI: Region Menu, Plug-ins, and Virtual Instruments

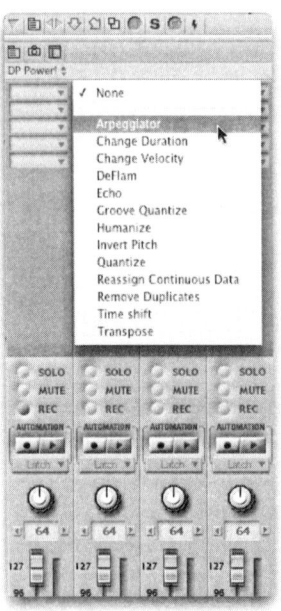

Figure 9.33
Real-time MIDI plug-ins affect the playback of MIDI tracks while keeping the original MIDI data intact. Notice that the Mixing Board's MIDI plug-ins menu even contains real-time versions of the Region menu's various commands.

Processing with the Region Menu's MIDI Effects Plug-ins

The procedures for processing selected MIDI data with the Region menu's MIDI effects plug-ins are identical to those of the Region menu commands. Simply select the MIDI data you wish to modify and choose the desired plug-in from the Region menu's MIDI Effects Plug-ins sub-menu. Once you have configured the plug-in and hit the Apply button, the selected data will be destructively processed with the specified settings—permanently altering the selected MIDI data.

Inserting Real-time MIDI Plug-ins

To insert a real-time MIDI plug-in, open the Mixing Board by pressing Shift+M. Navigate to the desired MIDI track, click on an available Insert slot, and then choose the MIDI plug-in from the list. Start playback to hear the inserted MIDI effect in real-time.

Virtual Instrument Plug-ins

In addition to supporting virtual instruments that reside in other applications (such as Propellerhead's Reason and Ableton Live), Digital Performer also supports virtual instrument plug-ins that reside within DP. In order for a virtual instrument plug-in to show up in Digital Performer, it must be in the MAS (MOTU Audio System) or AU (Audio Units) format (explained in Chapter 2). If you have a "wrapper" installed (explained in Chapter 13), you'll also be able to use virtual instrument plug-ins that are in the popular VST format.

✤ VIRTUAL INSTRUMENTS AND DAE
Keep in mind that when running Digital Performer under DAE (Digidesign Audio Engine) and not MAS, AU/MAS/VST plug-ins will not be available. You will, however, be able to open up plug-ins and virtual instruments that are in the TDM, RTAS, and AudioSuite formats.

✤ WORKING WITH REWIRE VIRTUAL INSTRUMENTS
Refer to Chapter 4, "Setting Up a New Project," for an explanation of the setup process involved with ReWire virtual instruments. You can also check out the "Integrating Reason" QuickTime movie tutorial on the Digital Performer 4 CSi LE CD included in the back of this book.

Once a supported virtual instrument plug-in has been installed, it will appear in the Instrument Track sub-menu, as shown in Figure 9.34.

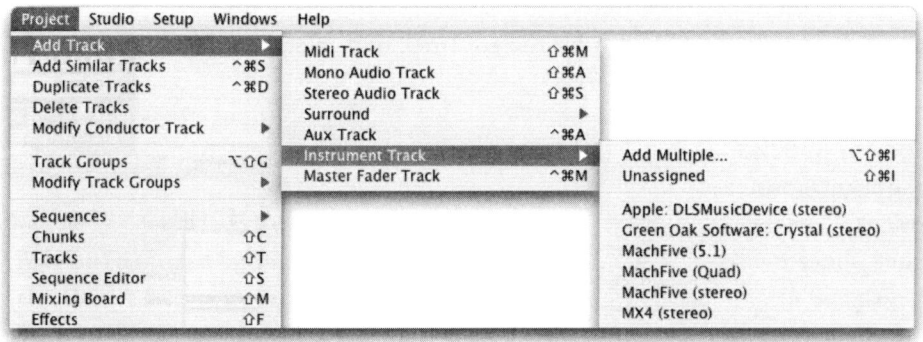

Figure 9.34
The Instrument Track sub-menu provides a list of installed MAS and AU virtual instrument plug-ins.

As explained in Chapter 8, "Recording MIDI," virtual instrument plug-ins must first be opened within an instrument track before they will appear in the output assignment menu of a MIDI track. Basically, you will not be able to send MIDI data to a virtual instrument plug-in until its instrument track has been created.

Assigned Instrument Tracks
Digital Performer allows you to create two basic types of instrument tracks: assigned and unassigned. Assigned instrument tracks are tracks that are created with a virtual instrument already assigned to them—simply choose the desired virtual instrument plug-in from the Instrument Track sub-menu. For example, to create an instrument track with MOTU's MX4 virtual instrument assigned to it, just choose MX4 in the instrument track list, as shown in Figure 9.35.

Figure 9.35

An MX4 virtual instrument is created by choosing MX4 from the Instrument Track sub-menu.

To create an instrument track, choose Add Track > Instrument Track and select the virtual instrument from the list.

Unassigned Instrument Tracks

Unassigned instrument tracks, shown in Figure 9.36, are basically "empty" tracks that do not currently have a virtual instrument plug-in assigned or inserted. Unassigned instrument tracks are handy for creating project templates—they allow you to make a virtual instrument plug-in assignment at a later time.

Figure 9.36

Unassigned instrument tracks will be created with the default name "Instrument." Notice that the "assigned" MX4 instrument tracks appear with the name MX4.

To create an unassigned instrument track, choose Add Track > Instrument Track > Unassigned. You can also use the default keyboard shortcut Shift+Command+I.

Instrument Inserts and the Mixing Board

Within the Mixing Board, an instrument track functions almost identical to an audio track. You are free to insert effects, utilize Sends, and so on. The difference, however, is that instrument tracks contain a special type of Insert called an *Instrument Insert* that appears shaded red within the track's

✤ Virtual Instrument Plug-ins

Insert section. Clicking on the Insert will reveal a list of available virtual instrument plug-ins. Use the Instrument Insert to assign an instrument to an unassigned track or to change the existing instrument to a new one.

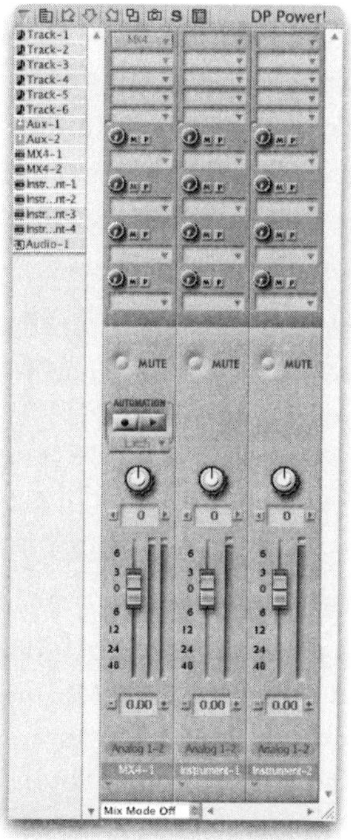

To assign a virtual instrument to an unassigned instrument track:

1. Open the Mixing Board by pressing Shift+M.
2. Navigate to the unassigned instrument track. At the top of the channel strip, you'll notice that the first Insert menu is shaded red, as shown in Figure 9.37. This is called the Instrument Insert.
3. Click on the Instrument Insert and choose the desired instrument plug-in from the list, as shown in Figure 9.38.

Figure 9.37
Within the Mixing Board, virtual instrument plug-ins have their own Instrument Inserts, which are shaded red. Unassigned Instrument Inserts will appear blank.

To insert a different virtual instrument in an assigned instrument track:

1. Open the Mixing Board by pressing Shift+M.
2. Navigate to the unassigned instrument track. The name of the existing virtual instrument plug-in will be displayed in the Instrument Insert that's shaded red.

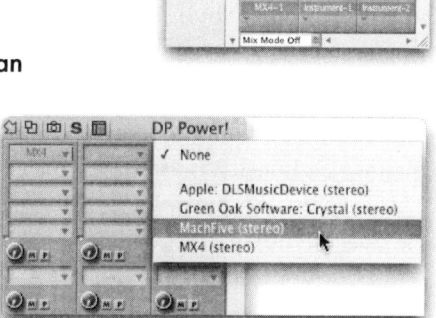

Figure 9.38
Click the Instrument Insert to choose an instrument plug-in.

3. Click on the Instrument Insert and choose another instrument from the list.

✤ **BOUNCING VIRTUAL INSTRUMENTS TO DISK**

Be aware that when bouncing a project that contains instrument tracks, you must either "freeze" the tracks with the Freeze Selected Tracks command or record the audio output of the instrument tracks to a separate audio track(s).

To record the audio output of an instrument track, create a new audio track and assign its input to an available bus, such as Bus 1-2. Change the instrument's output assignment to Bus 1-2. Arm the audio track and hit Record, and the audio from the instrument track will be recorded in real-time.

CHAPTER 9 } Recording MIDI: Region Menu, Plug-ins, and Virtual Instruments

The Freeze Selected Tracks Command

The Audio menu's Freeze Selected Tracks command allows you to automatically "print" or temporarily bounce selected tracks in real-time, allowing you to free up your system's resources for other CPU-intensive tasks. The Freeze Selected Tracks command is especially handy when you need to record the output of a virtual instrument plug-in so that you can bounce a project to disk or print an audio track that contains real-time effects plug-ins.

When you freeze a track, DP will automatically assign tracks that are to be frozen to a new bus, create a new audio track with its input assigned to the new bus, and begin recording the outputs of the frozen tracks to the new audio track.

To freeze an audio, aux, or instrument track:

1. Click the name of the instrument track in the Tracks Overview section of the Tracks window.
2. Select the data you wish to freeze.
3. If you're freezing an instrument track or aux/audio track being used to monitor a MIDI device, be sure to include the associated MIDI track in the selection. Remember that you can Shift-click the names of tracks within the Tracks window to select multiple tracks. This is an important step—if you don't include the corresponding MIDI track, DP will create a frozen track that contains silence.
4. Choose Audio menu > Freeze Selected Tracks.
5. DP will start the freeze process. In this example, DP automatically creates a new audio track with an input assignment on bus 1-2 and assigns the tracks selected in Steps 1-2 to the new bus, as shown in Figure 9.39. The progress bar that appears is identical to the Bounce To Disk commands progress bar, as shown in Figure 9.40.

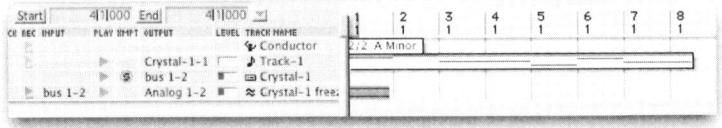

Figure 9.39
Tracks are automatically created and assigned during the freeze process.

Figure 9.40
The Freezing Selected Tracks progress bar.

6. Once the Freeze Selected Tracks process is completed, you'll need to mute the original MIDI track (shown in Figure 9.41) or assign the instrument track's voice to None so that you don't hear playback from the original tracks along with the newly created frozen track.

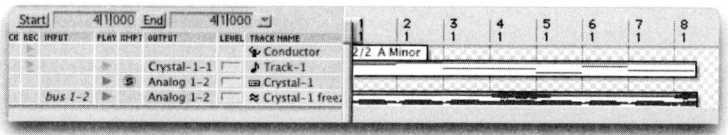

Figure 9.41

In this example, the Freeze Selected Tracks process has been completed and the MIDI track has been muted to prevent simultaneous playback of the original and frozen tracks.

To unfreeze a frozen track, press and hold the Shift key and choose Audio menu > Unfreeze Selected track. Use the Shift key to toggle between the Freeze and Unfreeze Selected Tracks commands.

Summary

DP's Region menu contains many powerful commands for altering MIDI data. In addition to these destructive MIDI operations, you can also use the Mixing Board's MIDI effects plug-ins to process MIDI tracks in real-time, allowing you to audition different settings or change plug-ins altogether without altering the original MIDI data within a track. Support for virtual instrument plug-ins, along with DP's instrument tracks, allows you to expand your library of sounds, while the Freeze Selected Tracks command helps to reallocate precious CPU resources when working with complex projects.

10 Editing

Arguably the greatest advantage of non-linear editors (such as Digital Performer, Pro Tools, Final Cut Pro, Photoshop, and so on) are their powerful features and tools for editing data. Every aspect of a track or project can be "refined"—wrong notes can be fixed, timing inaccuracies corrected, and so on. Non-linear editors provide you with powerful ways of enhancing and improving—or unknowingly destroying—your media projects. Just because you can tune the vocal to "harmonic perfection" doesn't mean you should. The Quantize command, for example, is a great tool for correcting rhythmic imperfections within a performance. Used (or abused) too aggressively, however, it can render a grooving track lifeless and robotic.

Digital Performer packs a powerful set of editing tools and feature sets. Various tools, editor windows, and keyboard shortcuts provide you with an arsenal of editing capabilities. DP is so comprehensive in its approach to selecting and editing data that explaining every possible method of editing is far beyond the scope of this book. In this section, I'll provide an overview of the basic (and most widely used) ways of editing audio and MIDI data. For an all-out explanation of the DP's selection capabilities, refer to the *Digital Performer User's Manual*.

Following is a list of topics covered in this chapter:

- The Tools palette.
- How to work with time formats, Time Rulers, and edit grids.
- How to use the View Filter.
- How to zoom.
- How to make select and move audio and MIDI data.
- How to use DP's standard Edit menu commands.
- How to edit audio in the Sequence Editor.

CHAPTER 10 } Editing

- How to create fades and crossfades.
- How to edit MIDI notes and controller events in the Graphic Editor.
- How to use the Event List.

The Tools Palette

The Tools palette is the container for Digital Performer's various editing tools. You can call up, or open, the Tools palette by pressing Shift+O. You can also choose Studio menu > Tools.

> **POSITIONING THE TOOLS PALETTE**
> The Tools palette can be positioned vertically or horizontally. You can even force it to automatically stay docked with the active edit window.

Each tool within the Tools palette allows you to perform a certain function. Simply click on a tool to select it. You can also use DP's many default keyboard shortcuts to quickly select a particular tool. To toggle (or temporarily select) a particular tool, press and hold its corresponding letter key. Double-tap the letter key to make the tool selection stick.

Following is a description of the various tools contained in the Tools palette, which is shown in Figure 10.1. The letter that comes after the tool name (in parentheses) is the tool's default keyboard shortcut. Keep in mind that Insert/Reshape Curve and Reshape Mode cannot be accessed from the Mac's keyboard.

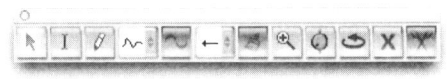

Figure 10.1
The Tools palette.

- **The Pointer tool (A).** Use the Pointer tool (also called the Arrow tool) to select and move audio and MIDI data.
- **The I-Beam tool (I).** Use the I-Beam tool (also called the Selector tool) to make time-range selections within an editor window, regardless of the type data you're working with.
- **The Pencil tool (P).** Use the Pencil tool to insert note and automation data. The Insert/Reshape Curve determines the shape or type of waveform that is drawn with the Pencil tool.
- **The Insert/Reshape Curve.** Use this menu to set the shape/curve of the Pencil tool.
- **The Reshape tool (R).** Use the Reshape tool to change the shape or curve of existing automation and controller data.
- **The Reshape Mode.** Use the Reshape Mode to determine how data is affected by the Reshape tool.

- **The Rhythm Brush (E).** The Rhythm Brush (also called the Pattern Brush) allows you to "paint" or draw notes within the Drum Editor. Refer to Appendix B for an explanation of the Drum Editor and the Rhythm Brush.
- **The Zoom tool (Z).** Use the Zoom tool (or Zoomer tool) to zoom in or out on a selection.
- **The Scrub tool (S).** Use the Scrub tool to "scrub" or audition the playback of data within an audio and MIDI track.
- **The Mute Soundbites tool (M).** Use this tool to quickly mute or un-mute a soundbite. Once muted, the soundbite will appear dimmed. Keep in mind that the Automation Setup window's Mute Frees System Resources setting has no effect on soundbites muted with the Mute tool.
- **The Scissors tool (C).** Use the Scissors tool to split a soundbite or MIDI note. You can repeatedly split a soundbite or note into sections that are constrained to a specific grid value by dragging with this tool (with the Edit Grid turned on).

The Time Format Window, Time Ruler, and Edit Grid

There are a few specific features that you should be familiar with in order to efficiently edit data within Digital Performer. Time formats and the Time Ruler directly affect how audio and MIDI data is selected, while the Edit Grid constrains edits and selections to a specified grid value.

The Time Format Window

Digital Performer provides four different time formats that can be displayed within a project—Measures, Real-time (minutes and seconds), Frames (SMPTE), and Samples (audio samples). Each time format can be displayed individually or simultaneously. The Time Format window, shown in Figure 10.2, allows you to set the time formats that will appear throughout a project—including the various counters, rulers, Event Lists, and so on.

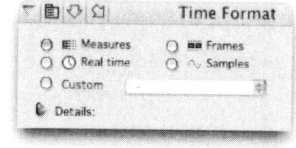

Figure 10.2

The Time Format window.

To set the time format for a project:

1. Choose Setup menu > Time Formats. The Time Format window will open.
2. Select the time format to be displayed. Changes are instantaneous and will be reflected anywhere time can be shown.

Multiple time formats can also be displayed. You can even specify different time formats for the Time Ruler, Edit Grid, pointer coordinates, and event information from the Details section of the Time Formats window, as shown in Figure 10.3. The Rulers and Edit Grid section uses aux rulers to display multiple time formats, as only one time format can be designated as the main ruler.

CHAPTER 10 } Editing

Figure 10.3
The Details section of the Time Format window is displayed by clicking the Details disclosure triangle, located below the Custom option.

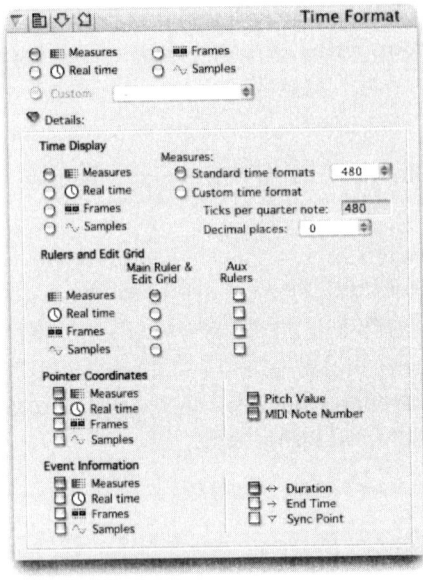

The Pointer Coordinates and Event Information sections, however, allow you to enable multiple time formats by simply clicking on each time format check box. Additional parameter setting information, such as Pitch Value, MIDI Note Number, Duration, End Time, and Sync Point, can also be displayed.

To enable multiple time formats for a project:

1. Open the Time Format window by pressing Option+Command+T.
2. Click the Details disclosure triangle to display the Custom options.
3. In the Time Display section, select the main Time Ruler that will be displayed throughout your project. If you select Measures, you can further customize the Measures time format from the Measures section of the window, as shown in Figure 10.4.

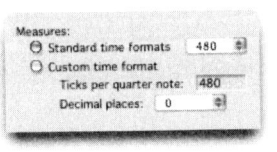

Figure 10.4
Use the Measures section to further customize how the Measures time format will be displayed in DP.

4. Next, choose the desired time format settings for the Rulers and Edit Grid section, Pointer Coordinates section, and Event Information section. Notice that the Rulers and Edit Grid section allows you to display multiple time formats with the use of aux rulers, as shown in Figure 10.5. Once an

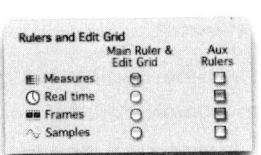

Figure 10.5
Enable an aux ruler to display multiple time formats within a Time Ruler.

❋ The Time Format Window, Time Ruler, and Edit Grid

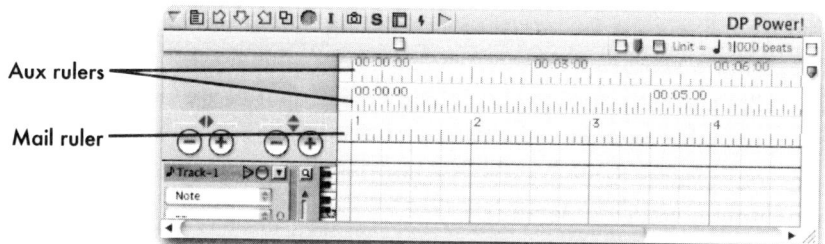

Figure 10.6
In this example, the Time Ruler's main ruler is set to Measures.

aux ruler (or secondary time format) is enabled, the particular time format will appear above a Time Ruler's main ruler, as shown in Figure 10.6.

5. Close the Time Format window. There is no need to apply the new settings, as any changes made to the Time Format window will be instantaneous.

The Time Ruler

Each editor window in DP (except the QuickScribe Editor) contains a Time Ruler that is located below the window's title and/or Information bars, as shown in Figures 10.7 and 10.8. A Time Ruler consists of a main ruler and/or secondary aux rulers. To designate a specific time format for the main and aux rulers, refer to the previous section.

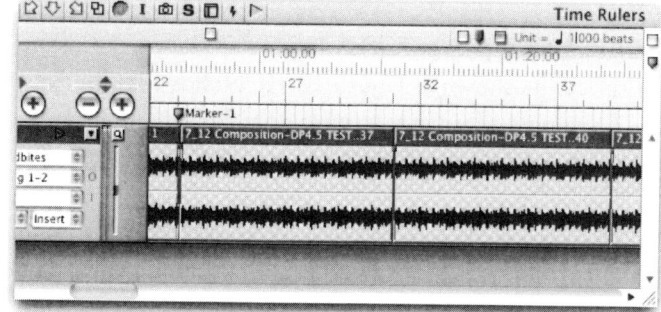

Figure 10.7
In this example, the Sequence Editor's main Time Ruler is shown as Measures. Notice that a secondary (aux) ruler displaying Real-time has been enabled. Vertical lines divide the window into sections or subdivisions.

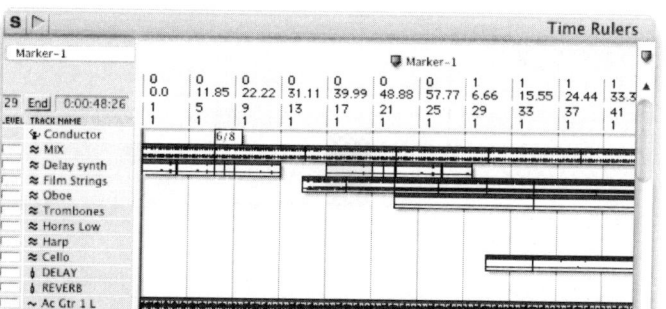

Figure 10.8
The Tracks window's Time Ruler appearance is simple, compared to the other editor windows.

The Time Ruler basically displays a linear measurement of time throughout an editor window, with vertical lines that extend and divide a window into equal segments (or subdivisions). The size of each subdivided section depends on the current zoom resolution and time format that's displayed in the main ruler. For example, if I zoom in far enough in the Sequence Editor, I can view each separate measure within a track, as shown in Figure 10.9. Notice that the Time Ruler's vertical lines extend from beat 1 of each measure through each visible track.

Figure 10.9

The Time Ruler displays vertical lines that extend through an editor's window. These lines divide a track (or window) into equal subdivisions.

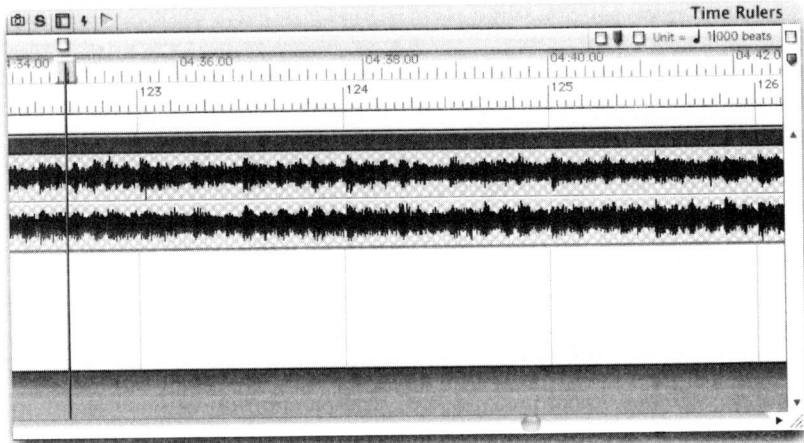

If I zoom out, the subdivisions will become larger, allowing me to view more of the track's data within the same amount of physical space, as shown in Figure 10.10. Notice that the Time Ruler's vertical lines no longer appear at the beginning of each measure; now they appear every eight measures—basically subdividing the tracks into eight-bar segments.

Figure 10.10

In this example, I have zoomed out on the tracks. Notice that the main Time Ruler now displays eight bar subdivisions.

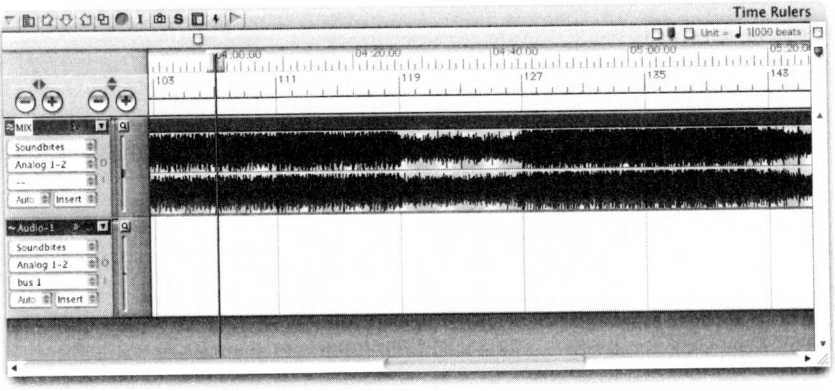

The Time Format Window, Time Ruler, and Edit Grid

The Time Ruler is a critical part of DP's editor windows that allows you to visually navigate to specific times or points within a sequence and view the relationship between a sequence's timeline and data within a track. You can even make time-range selections directly in the Time Ruler (this is explained later). In addition to the Time Ruler's vertical lines that subdivide an editor window, edit grid lines can be enabled to constrain edits to a specified grid. The Edit Grid is explained in the following section.

> **WHICH TIME FORMAT(S) SHOULD YOU DISPLAY IN THE TIME RULER?**
>
> Remember that the type of time measurement that is displayed in the Time Ruler's main and aux rulers is determined by the specific time format(s) selected in the Time Format window. Exactly which formats you choose to work with and display is entirely up to you, and will be dictated by the type of project and specific type of editing tasks you need to accomplish. Feel free to change the displayed time formats at any time within a project.

The Edit Grid

An edit grid is a staple of non-linear editing applications. Edit grids basically subdivide a window or track into equal segments (or grid). An edit grid's resolution setting (or value) determines the amount of time between each grid line. For example, if you enable the Edit Grid and set its resolution to a quarter note value, any edits that are made will be automatically constrained to quarter note divisions, as shown in Figure 10.11.

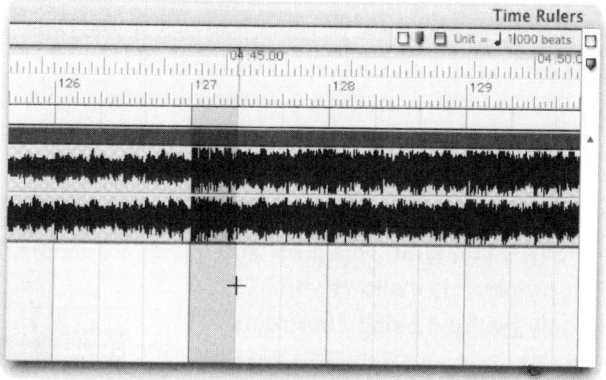

Figure 10.11
In this example, the Sequence Editor's Edit Grid has been enabled and set to a quarter note value.

With the Edit Grid set to a quarter note resolution, you could make a quarter note time range selection, a half note selection (two quarter notes), a whole note selection (four quarter notes), and so on. Any time range that can be divided by a quarter note is possible. An eighth note selection, however, would not be possible, as it is smaller than the specified quarter note grid.

CHAPTER 10 } Editing

Working with DP's Edit Grids
Some of DP's editor windows (such as the Tracks window, Notation Editor, and Drum Editor) automatically constrain edits and selections to an edit grid, and will not allow you to disable this grid. Other windows, such as the QuickScribe Editor and Event List, do not contain edit grids. The Sequence, Graphic, and Waveform Editors, however, give you an option for enabling and disabling the Edit Grid and setting its resolution—providing you increased flexibility when editing audio and MIDI data (see Figure 10.12).

The Tracks Window
The Tracks window, by its nature, automatically constrains edits and selections to a grid. The Time Ruler's main time format, along with the current zoom setting, determines the actual size of the grid. Zooming in within the Tracks window, for example, will reduce the size of the grid, allowing you to make smaller edits and selections, as shown in Figure 10.12.

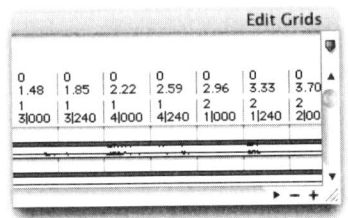

Figure 10.12
In this example, I've zoomed in enough within the Tracks window to allow quarter note edits.

> **OVERRIDING THE GRID IN THE TRACKS WINDOW**
> Digital Performer won't allow you to permanently turn off the Tracks window's grid, but you can temporarily override the feature. Simply press and hold the Command key to temporarily toggle the grid off.

The Sequence, Graphic, and Waveform Editors
The Sequence, Graphic, and Waveform Editors allow you to enable or disable the window's Edit Grid. This gives you more flexibility in the editing process, as it allows you to make edits and selections freely (without being constrained to a set grid value). The Edit Grid Box and Edit Grid Resolution settings can be found at the far-right corner of the Information bar, as shown in Figure 10.13.

Figure 10.13
The Edit Grid box and Edit Grid Resolution settings.

The Time Format Window, Time Ruler, and Edit Grid

To enable/disable the Edit Grid:

- Click on the Edit Grid box to turn the Edit Grid on or off. The box will be highlighted blue when the grid is on.
- Press the Command key to temporarily toggle the Edit Grid on or off. Keep in mind that this will not work in the Waveform Editor.

When you're working in the Measures time format, the Edit Resolution pop-up menu, shown in Figure 10.14, will display note values, along with dotted, double dotted, and triplet markings. When the main ruler is set to Real-time, Frames, or Samples, the Edit Resolution pop-up menu will change to display the corresponding values, as shown in Figure 10.15. An input field allows you to type in the exact value if you need to.

Figure 10.14

Note values will be displayed in the Grid Resolution pop-up menu when the main ruler is set to Measures.

To set the resolution for the Edit Grid:

1. Click the Grid Resolution pop-up menu. If you're working with Measures, note values will be displayed in the pop-up menu.
2. Choose the desired grid value from the pop-up menu. Changes to the Edit Grid are instantaneous.

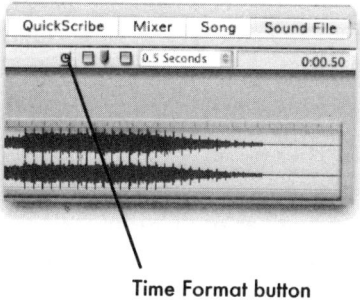

Figure 10.15

In this example, the Edit Grid Resolution is set to Real-time.

CHANGING THE TIME FORMAT IN THE WAVEFORM EDITOR

When you're working with the Waveform Editor's Edit Grid, an additional Time Format button is included in the Event Information bar, as shown in Figure 10.16. Click this button to choose the time format for the grid without calling up the Time Format window.

Time Format button

Figure 10.16

Click the Waveform Editor's Time Format button to cycle through and change the Edit Grid's time format.

CHAPTER 10 } Editing

The View Filter

In Chapter 8, I discussed the use and function of the Input Filter window and how it's used to determine what type of MIDI data will be recorded—as well as how the window basically filters out selected data during the MIDI input stage. The View Filter, shown in Figure 10.17, operates in a similar fashion, except that it determines what types of data will be visible in a track *after* it's been recorded or inserted. This allows you to decide what types of data can be edited within DP by filtering out the data you don't wish to work with. Keep in mind that this only affects the global appearance of data within a project—it doesn't actually remove or alter it.

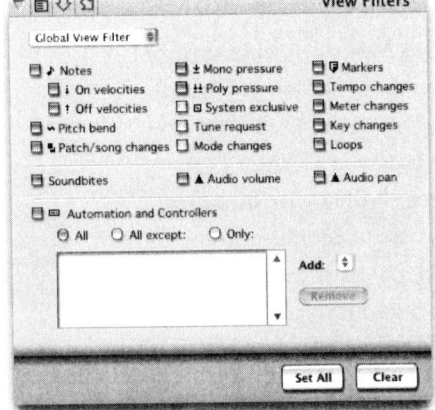

Figure 10.17
The View Filter.

You can open the View Filter window by choosing Setup Set View Filter or by using the default keyboard shortcut Command+F. Once the window is open, click to enable or disable the particular type or types of data you wish to view within your project. Data that is unchecked will not be visible. You can set the View Filter separately for the Event Lists by clicking on the pop-up menu, as shown in Figure 10.18

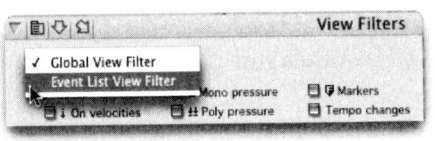

Figure 10.18
Select the Event List View Filter from the pop-up menu to configure the view settings for all Event Lists within a project.

Zooming

Digital Performer provides a number of different methods for zooming in and out within a window or data selection. In addition to an editor window's dedicated zoom buttons, the Zoomer tool allows you to zoom in and out and also provides more control for zooming in on specific data or parts of a track.

To zoom with the Zoomer tool:

1. Call up the Zoomer tool by double-tapping the Z key. You can temporarily invoke the tool by pressing and holding the Z key.

2. Click at the desired location to zoom.
3. To control exactly what you're zooming in on, click and drag over a selection of data instead. Release the mouse and DP will zoom into the section.
4. To zoom out, press and hold the Option key while zooming.

You can also zoom from the keyboard, even when the Zoomer tool is not enabled. Keep in mind, however, that this method will simply enlarge/shrink the current view of the window—you'll need to use the Zoomer tool to zoom in on specific selections.

To zoom from the keyboard:

- To zoom horizontally, press and hold the Command key while hitting the Left and Right Arrow keys to zoom in and out.
- To zoom vertically in the Sequence or Graphic Editors, press and hold the Command key while hitting the Up and Down Arrow keys to zoom vertically. This basically increases or decreases the height of visible tracks.

Selecting and Moving

Within Digital Performer, you can use the Pointer and I-Beam tools to select and move audio, MIDI, and breakpoint automation data—you can even change the duration of MIDI notes. This section will discuss the procedures for selecting and moving audio data and MIDI notes (selecting and moving MIDI data, such as continuous controller data and event flags, will be explained later).

Selecting is the most basic part of the editing process—data must be selected before it can be edited. There are basically two ways to select data within DP: by clicking on it or by dragging with a selected tool. Once data is selected, it will become highlighted.

To select the Pointer tool:

- Click on the Pointer tool in the Tools palette.
- Double-tap the letter A key.
- Press and hold the letter A key to temporarily invoke the Pointer tool.

To select the I-Beam tool:

- Click on the I-Beam tool in the Tools palette.
- Double-tap the letter I key.
- Press and hold the letter I key to temporarily invoke the I-Beam tool.

CHAPTER 10 } Editing

> ### SELECTING WITH THE EDIT GRID TURNED ON
> The Edit Grid, when enabled, will constrain any selections and confine them to the current grid resolution. If you want to select freely, be sure to turn the Edit Grid off. To temporarily disable the Edit Grid, press and hold the Command key.

> ### THE SELECT ALL/DESELECT ALL COMMANDS
> If you want to select all of the contents of a window, such as audio and MIDI data on all tracks within the Tracks window or an entire soundbite within the Waveform Editor, use the Edit menu's Select All command. (The default keyboard shortcut is Command+A.) Keep in mind that this command only works on visible data and affects the active window (the window in the foreground). To deselect everything, choose Edit menu > Deselect All, or press Command+D.

Selecting and Moving Audio

Audio data can be edited in the Tracks window, Sequence Editor, Event List, or Waveform Editor. When audio data is selected with the I-Beam tool or Cross-Hair cursor (explained later), it will appear highlighted blue. When an entire soundbite is selected, however, it will be highlighted yellow in the Tracks window and yellow with a blue band in the Sequence Editor.

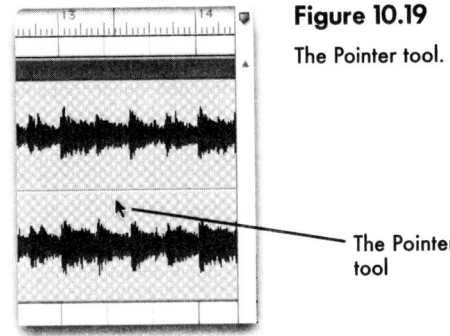

Figure 10.19
The Pointer tool.

The Pointer Tool

The Pointer tool is unique in that it will change states depending on where it's positioned. Position the Pointer over a soundbite, about a third of the way up the soundbite, and you will see the normal Pointer (or Arrow) tool, as shown in Figure 10.19. Move the Pointer below this area and it will change to the Cross-Hair cursor, as shown in Figure 10.20.

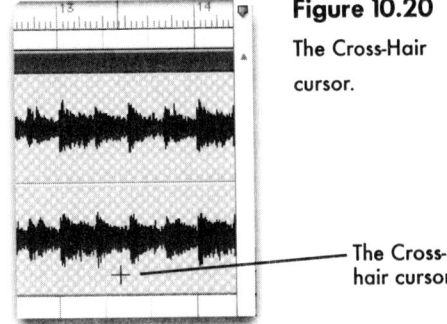

Figure 10.20
The Cross-Hair cursor.

※ Selecting and Moving

If you place the Pointer tool over a selected soundbite, however, it will change to the Finger cursor. The Finger cursor, shown in Figure 10.21, is identical to the normal Pointer tool and is used by DP to indicate that you have positioned the Pointer over a selected soundbite.

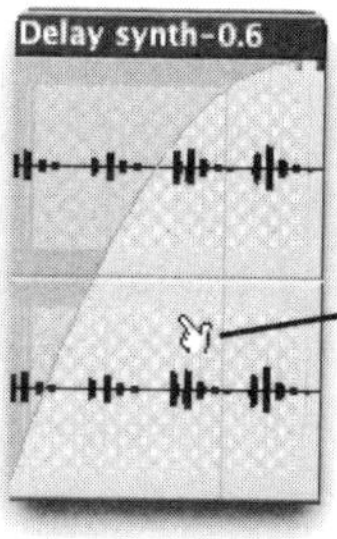

Figure 10.21
The Finger cursor.

Use the Pointer tool to do the following:

※ **Select a single soundbite.** Click on a soundbite to select it.

※ **Move a soundbite.** Click and drag a soundbite to move it. The soundbite will be placed where you release the mouse. This allows you to drag audio between different tracks and even different windows.

Use the Cross-Hair cursor to do the following:

※ **Select a single soundbite.** Click and drag across the entire soundbite.

※ **Select a portion of a soundbite.** Click and drag over the portion of audio you want to select.

※ **Shorten/extend/add to an existing selection.** After you have made an initial selection, press and hold the Shift key while making a new selection or adjusting the existing one, as shown in Figure 10.22. You can even make selections that aren't adjacent to one another.

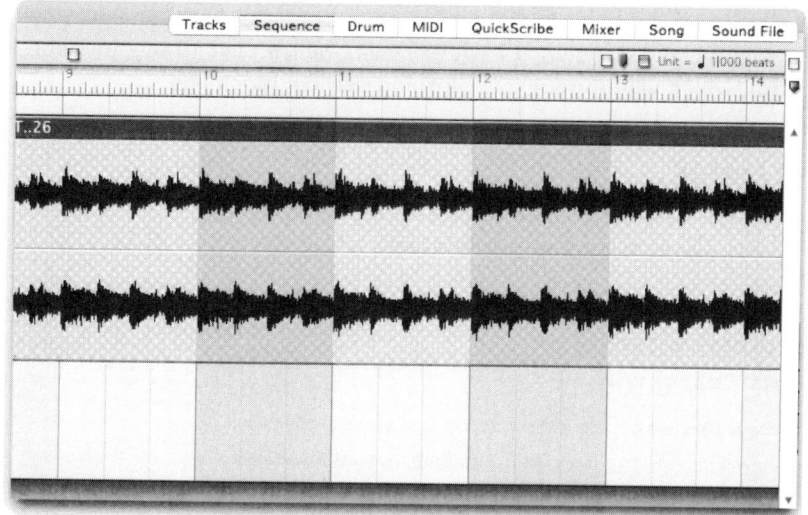

Figure 10.22
You can Shift and drag with the Cross-Hair cursor to make non-contiguous selections.

231

The I-Beam Tool

The I-Beam tool is used to make time-range selections. Selections can be made that contain audio data, or they can be made in an empty part of a track. When you're selecting audio with the I-Beam tool, the top soundbite will be selected along with any underlying automation data. Incorporate the Shift key to shorten or extend a selection. Unlike the Cross-Hair cursor, the I-Beam tool cannot be used to make non-contiguous selections.

> **THE I-BEAM TOOL VERSUS THE CROSS-HAIR CURSOR**
> The I-Beam tool and Cross-Hair cursor are nearly identical to one another in behavior and function. Both will make time range selections and both can select both audio and MIDI data. Unlike the I-Beam tool, however, the Cross-Hair cursor will not allow you to create insertion points or anchor points for selections (explained below).

Use the I-Beam to do the following:

- **Make an empty time-range selection.** Click and drag across an empty portion of a track. Press the Shift key while dragging to extend or shorten a selection.
- **Make a time-range selection of audio data.** Click and drag across a soundbite.
- **Select data across all tracks.** Click and drag in the Time Ruler.
- **Select an entire soundbite.** Double-click on a soundbite.
- **Create an insertion point for edit commands such as Paste.** Simply click at any location to insert the I-Beam cursor, which will appear as a flashing vertical black line.

> **THE FLASHING I-BEAM CURSOR**
> Once placed into a track, the I-Beam cursor becomes an anchor point for selections and edit commands such as Paste, Merge, Split, Splice, and Trim End.

> **SELECTING ONLY THE VISIBLE PORTION OF A SOUNDBITE WITH THE I-BEAM TOOL**
> When a portion of a soundbite is covered by another soundbite and you double-click on it with the I-Beam tool, you will be selecting the entire soundbite, not just the visible portion. To work around this, press and hold the Option key before double-clicking the soundbite with the I-Beam tool.

Selecting and Moving MIDI Notes

Digital Performer can edit MIDI data in every editor window except the Waveform Editor. Each editor window provides a different way of displaying MIDI data. The Tracks window shows MIDI data as phrases and blocks, the Notation and QuickScribe Editors show MIDI notes as standard notation, the Event List displays MIDI notes (and MIDI data) as event information within a list, and the Graphic and Sequence Editors show MIDI notes as horizontal bars within a "scrolling-piano"-style Note Grid.

MIDI note selection with the Pointer tool and Cross-Hair cursor is similar to audio data selection. Position the Pointer tool directly over a MIDI note to see the normal Pointer, as shown in Figure 10.23. Move the Pointer outside a note to see the Cross-Hair cursor, as shown in Figure 10.24. If you place the Pointer over a MIDI note that has been selected, you will see the Finger cursor, as shown in Figure 10.25. Selected notes will be shaded lighter (or brighter) than non-selected notes.

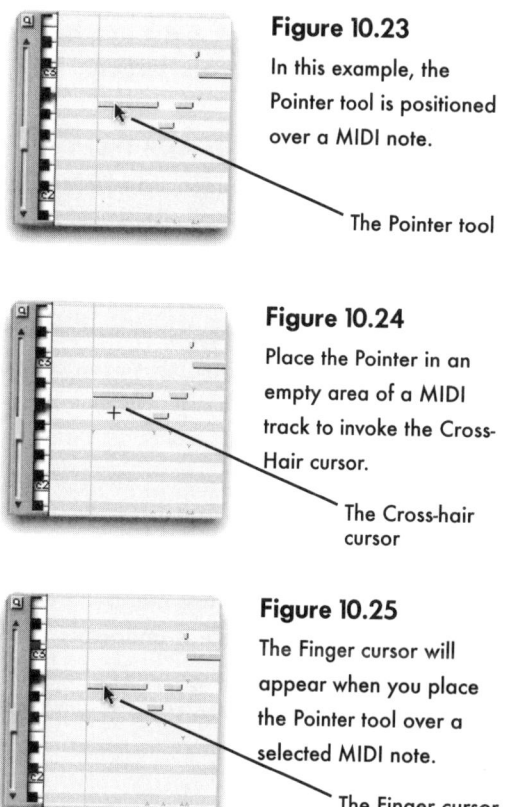

Figure 10.23
In this example, the Pointer tool is positioned over a MIDI note.

The Pointer tool

Figure 10.24
Place the Pointer in an empty area of a MIDI track to invoke the Cross-Hair cursor.

The Cross-hair cursor

Figure 10.25
The Finger cursor will appear when you place the Pointer tool over a selected MIDI note.

The Finger cursor

The Finger cursor is identical to the normal Pointer tool and is only used by DP to indicate that you have positioned the Pointer over a selected note. The Finger and Cross-Hair cursors will not be available when working in the Event List and QuickScribe Editor. Use the normal Pointer tool when working in these windows.

Use the Pointer tool to do the following:

- **Select a single note.** Click on a note to select it.
- **Move a note.** Click and drag a note to move it. The note will be placed where you release the mouse. This allows you to drag notes between different tracks. Move the note horizontally to change its location within the track.
- **Change the pitch of a note in the Graphic Editor.** Click and drag the note vertically. Drag the note up to raise the pitch. Drag the note down to lower the pitch.

CHAPTER 10 } Editing

Use the Cross-Hair cursor to do the following:

- **Select a single note.** Click and drag over the note.
- **Select multiple notes.** Click and drag over the notes.
- **Add notes to an existing MIDI note selection.** After you have made an initial selection of notes as described above, press and hold the Shift key while dragging to include (or exclude) notes from the current note selection.

> **NUDGING AUDIO AND MIDI DATA**
> Data that exists within a track can be moved, or nudged, in small increments. Simply press the keyboard's Left and Right Arrow keys to nudge data forward or backward in time. This feature is especially useful in post-production work, where you need to nudge a sound by single frame increments to match it to a specific cue or action on screen.
> You can set the nudge amount from the Edit menu's Set Nudge Amount command (Edit menu > Set Nudge Amount). This window only contains one drop-down menu. Select the time format from the menu to set the nudge amount.

Basic Edit Commands

In this section, I'll discuss some of the more common and useful edit commands contained in DP. Keep in mind that these commands can be used to affect audio and/or MIDI data. In addition, each command that's discussed here is undoable. Simply press Command+Z to undo an action. If you need more control over the undo operations in DP, refer to the "Undo History" section of Chapter 6 for an in-depth look into the Undo History windows.

The Erase Command

The Erase command (Edit menu > Erase) will basically delete or remove a selection from a track or window. The default keyboard shortcut is Command+B, though most users will simply use the Mac keyboard's Delete key instead. Be aware that some windows will not allow the use of the Erase command. When the Erase command is unavailable, it will appear dimmed within the Edit menu.

The Copy, Cut, Paste, Repeat, and Merge Commands

Probably the most fundamental part of the editing process (next to the selection process) in any software program—including non-music applications—are the basic Copy, Cut, and Paste commands. Like most applications on the Mac, these commands are located in DP's Edit menu.

The Copy and Cut Commands

The Copy command will copy a selection and place the contents within the Mac's virtual clipboard, leaving the original data in the selection intact. The copied data will remain stored in the clipboard until other data is copied with the Copy or Cut commands. The Cut command is similar to Copy, except that it erases (or removes) the original data once it has been copied to the clipboard.

To copy or cut a selection:

1. Start by selecting the data you wish to affect.
2. Choose the Copy or the Cut command from the Edit menu. You can also use the default keyboard shortcuts Command+C to copy a selection and Command+X to cut a selection.

The Paste Command

Once a selection has been copied or cut and stored in the clipboard, it can be placed or pasted into another track or window. Choose Edit menu > Paste or use the default keyboard shortcut Command+V.

In order to use the Paste command, you have to tell Digital Performer *where* the copied or cut material needs to be placed. There are a couple of different ways to do this.

To paste a copied or cut selection into a track:

- Enable the I-Beam tool with the letter I key and click at the desired location. The flashing I-Beam cursor will appear. Press Command+V to paste the copied/cut selection at the I-Beam cursor location.
- Make a time-range selection with the Cross-Hair cursor or I-Beam tool. Press Command+V and DP will paste the copied/cut material at the start of the time-range selection.
- Deselect everything and do not use the I-Beam cursor. This will tell DP to paste the copied/cut material at the current location of the Playback Wiper within the original track. Press Command+V to paste the data that's residing in the clipboard.

To paste a selection into the Event List:

- Enable the I-Beam tool with the letter I key and click on the white line that separates two events. The flashing I-Beam cursor will appear, as shown in Figure 10.26. Press Command+V to paste the copied/cut selection at the I-Beam cursor location.

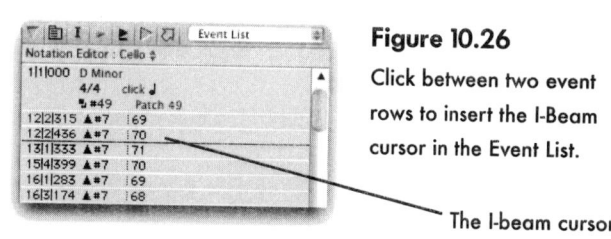

Figure 10.26

Click between two event rows to insert the I-Beam cursor in the Event List.

The I-beam cursor

The Repeat Command

The Repeat command (Edit menu > Repeat) basically takes a selection of data and repeats it a specified number of times. The repeated material can be pasted, merged, or spliced into the destination track. Once you have made a selection and selected Repeat from the Edit menu, the Repeat window

CHAPTER 10 } Editing

(shown in Figure 10.27) will open, presenting you with the following options:

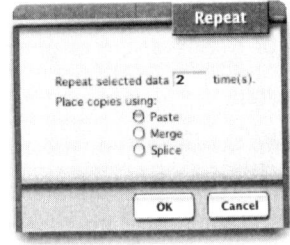

Figure 10.27
The Repeat window.

* **Repeat selected data ____ time(s)**. Use this option to set the number of times the selection will be repeated.
* **Paste**. Paste will copy and repeat the selection while overwriting any data that exists on the track.
* **Merge**. Merge will merge (or combine) the repeated material with the existing data on the track.
* **Splice**. Splice will move any existing data forward in time to make room for the repeated material.

To repeat a selection:

1. Start by making a data selection.
2. Press Command+R or choose Edit menu > Repeat.
3. The Repeat window will open. Set the number of times the selection is to be repeated.
4. Next, choose what happens to the repeated data from the Place Copies Using section of the window.
5. Hit the OK button to repeat the selected material

The Paste Repeat Command

The Paste Repeat command combines the standard Paste and Repeat commands. Use this command to fill a time-range selection with the copied or cut material that resides in the clipboard. DP will automatically paste and repeat the clipboard contents as needed to fill the time-range selection.

To paste repeat into a track:

1. Start by copying or cutting a selection of data.
2. Make a time-range selection.
3. Press Control+Command+V or choose Edit menu > Paste Repeat.

The Paste Multiple and Paste Multiple Repeat Commands

Another variation to the standard Paste command is the Paste Multiple command and the Paste Multiple Repeat command. The Paste Multiple command allows you to copy or cut a selection from one track and paste into multiple target tracks. The Paste Multiple command is only visible when you press and hold the Option key.

To paste into multiple tracks:

1. Start by copying or cutting a selection of data from a single track.
2. Select the target tracks by following the selection procedures for the standard Paste command. If you're using the I-Beam cursor, use the Shift key to place the cursor in multiple tracks.
3. Press Option+Command+V to paste the clipboard contents into multiple tracks. You can also press and hold the Option key and then choose Edit menu > Paste Multiple.

The Paste Multiple Repeat command takes the Paste command a step further by combining the Paste Multiple and the Paste Repeat commands. Like the Paste Multiple command, you must press and hold the Option key in order for this command to appear within the Edit menu.

To paste repeat into multiple tracks:

1. Start by copying or cutting a selection of data from a single track.
2. Make a time-range selection across the target tracks. Remember to Shift-click to include multiple tracks.
3. Press Control+Option+Command+V to paste repeat the clipboard contents into multiple tracks. You can also press and hold the Option key and then choose Edit menu > Paste Multiple Repeat.

The Merge Command

The Merge command (Edit menu > Merge) allows you to combine selected track data with the contents in the clipboard. New data is mixed (or merged) with the existing data on the track. When you're working with soundbites, however, data isn't merged together but is placed on top of any existing soundbite data instead. If you drag the new soundbite or remove it, you'll find that the old soundbite still exists in its original location.

To merge selected data:

1. Start by copying or cutting a selection of data from a single track.
2. Select the data in the track with which you want to have the clipboard contents merged.
3. Command+M or choose Edit menu > Merge to merge the data.

Editing Audio in the Sequence Editor

The Sequence Editor is by far the most versatile and comprehensive editor window for editing audio data. The Sequence Editor's graphic environment allows for standard editing commands such as Copy, Paste, and Repeat, and it also provides unique operational features that allow you to quickly trim (edge-edit), fade, crossfade, mute, and even time-stretch audio data.

CHAPTER 10 } Editing

Edge-Editing Soundbites

A soundbite, as you know, is a region of audio. Soundbites are not, however, audio files. They are only references, or pointers, to their parent audio file that resides on your hard drive. Soundbites can represent an entire audio file or only a portion of it.

Edge edits allow you to shorten or extend the duration of a soundbite, for example, if you have a one-minute long soundbite that references a much longer soundbite that's five minutes long (see Figure 10.28).

If you trimmed the edge of the soundbite to the right, you could drag to extend its duration until the entire five-minute soundbite was displayed, as shown in Figure 10.29. Keep in mind, however, that you cannot extend a soundbite beyond its original boundaries.

Figure 10.28

A one-minute long soundbite (Soundbite.6) and its related five-minute long soundbite (Soundbite.2).

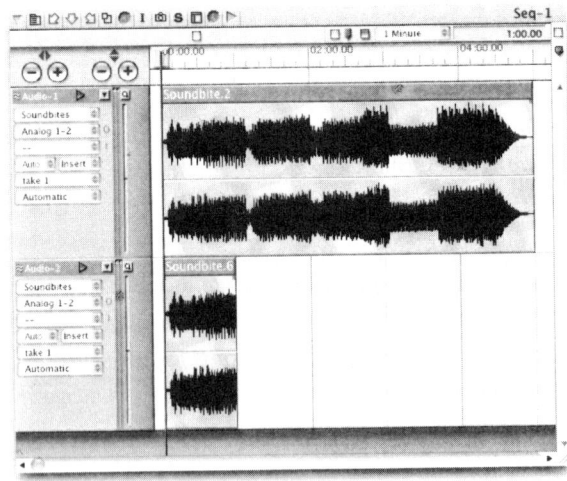

Figure 10.29

The shorter soundbite (Soundbite.6) has been edge-edited, displaying the entire length of the soundbite. Even though Soundbite.2 and Soundbite.6 are individual soundbites, they both reference the same parent audio file.

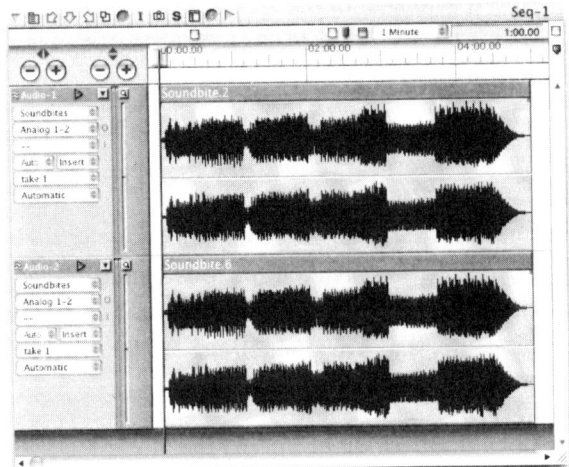

The Trim Cursor

The Trim cursor, shown in Figure 10.30, allows you to edge-edit or trim soundbites within the Sequence Editor. Like many other tools within DP, the Trim cursor must positioned in the correct place in order for it to be visible. Place the Pointer tool at the very edge of a soundbite, and below the colored title bar to invoke the Trim cursor.

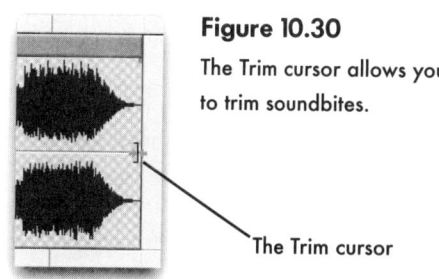

Figure 10.30
The Trim cursor allows you to trim soundbites.

The Edge-Edit Copy Option

When the Edge-Edit Copy feature is turned on, a new soundbite (or alternate version of the soundbite) will be created when you edge-edit a soundbite with the Trim cursor. This can be a helpful feature when you have multiple instances of the same soundbite within a project and you want to trim a single instance of that soundbite. Instead of affecting each instance of the soundbite, DP just creates a new, trimmed version of the soundbite

If Edge-Edit Copy is turned off, however, when you edit an instance of a soundbite, each and every other instance of that soundbite will also be edited. Sometimes this is just how you need the Edge-Edit feature to operate—it really depends on the type of editing you need to do and whether you want to affect all instances or just a single instance of a soundbite.

To temporarily disable the Edge-Edit Copy option, press and hold the Option key while edge-editing a soundbite. To turn off this option altogether, choose Sequence Editor > mini-menu > Edge Edit Copy and then uncheck the option.

Soundbite Editing Shortcuts

In addition to the standard Edit menu commands discussed earlier, Digital Performer provides a number of keyboard shortcuts that affect how audio is handled (or edited) in the Sequence Editor. This section will provide a list of various keyboard shortcuts and a brief description of how they are used.

* To constrain vertical and horizontal movements, press the Shift key while dragging.
* To quickly copy a soundbite, Option-drag a soundbite.
* To force a soundbite to snap to another soundbite when dragging, select the soundbite, and then Control-drag in the desired direction.
* To copy a soundbite and "shuffle" it end to end with an adjacent soundbite, press Control+Option, and then drag (or throw) the soundbite in the desired direction.
* To nudge a soundbite, press the Mac keyboard's Left and/or Right Arrow keys. Remember that you can set the nudge value from the Edit menu's Set Nudge Amount command, shown in Figure 10.31.

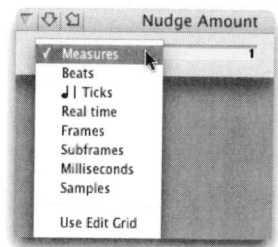

Figure 10.31
The Nudge Amount window.

CHAPTER 10 } Editing

- To trim the edge (or edge-edit) of a soundbite, position the cursor at the beginning or end of a soundbite. The cursor will change to the Trim cursor, as shown in Figure 10.32. Click and drag to trim (or change the boundary of) the soundbite.

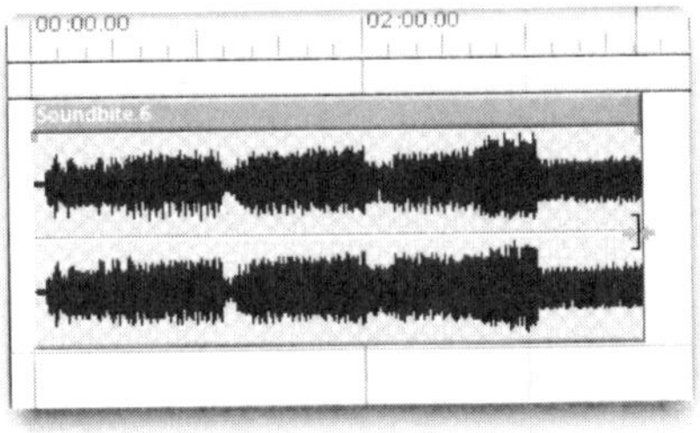

- To quickly mute a soundbite(s), invoke the Mute Soundbites tool by pressing and holding the letter M key and clicking on a soundbite to mute it. Drag with the Mute Soundbites tool to mute multiple adjacent soundbites.

- To quickly split a soundbite, invoke the Scissors tool by pressing and holding the letter C key, and then click on a soundbite to split it. Drag the Scissors tool across a soundbite (with the Edit Grid turned on) in order to split soundbites into sections that conform to the current grid resolution.

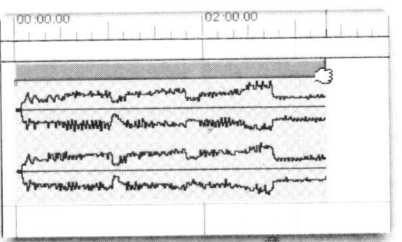

Figure 10.32
Use the Trim cursor to edge-edit soundbites.

Figure 10.33
Dragging to graphically time-stretch a soundbite.

- To graphically time-stretch audio, position the Pointer over the left or right edge of a soundbite's colored title bar (as shown in Figure 10.33) to display the Hand cursor. Click and drag to time-stretch the soundbite. See Chapter 13 for an explanation of time-stretching in DP.

Fades and Crossfades

Fades and crossfades are continuous gain or volume changes that are computed by Digital Performer. Fades can occur at the beginning (a fade-in) or end of a soundbite (a fade-out), while crossfades can only be placed at the boundary points (or splice points) of two adjacent soundbites.

There are two ways to insert fades within Digital Performer: with the Sequence Editor's Fade Handles and with the Audio menu's Fades command. Fades and crossfades within DP are non-destructive (unless they are created with the destructive Fade In and Fade Out commands). When a fade is created, DP calculates the volume change and then places this new audio over the original soundbite. Calculated Fade files are stored in the Fades folder within the main project folder.

Fade Handles

A soundbite's Fade Handles, shown in Figure 10.34, are located at the left and right edges of the soundbite, directly below the colored title bar. When you position the

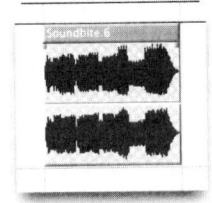

Figure 10.34
The Fade Handles.

※ Editing Audio in the Sequence Editor

Pointer tool over a Fade Handle, the Fade/Crossfade cursor will appear. Click and drag to insert a fade, as shown in Figure 10.35.

When the edges of two soundbites are touching (are adjacent), you can drag on either soundbite's Fade Handle to crossfade them together. Once a fade or crossfade is created, you can double-click on it to open the Create Fades window (explained in the next section), allowing you to edit the curve of the fade or change the fade type altogether.

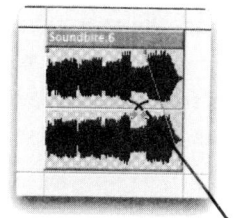

Figure 10.35
Drag the Fade Handles to insert a fade. Notice that the Fade/Crossfade cursor appears when you're creating or adjusting fades.

The Fade/Crossfade cursor

You can remove a fade or crossfade by dragging the Fade Handle again—until the fade is no longer visible—or you can select it and choose the Delete Fade command (explained in the next section). When you position the Pointer over an existing fade, the Select/Edit Fade/Crossfade cursor will appear, as shown in Figure 10.36

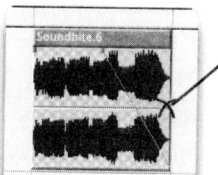

Figure 10.36
The Select/Edit Fade/Crossfade cursor.

The Fade and Delete Fade Commands

In addition to the Fade Handles, you can also use the Audio menu's Fade command. Start by making a time range selection at the beginning (to fade in) or end (to fade out) of a soundbite. The length of the selection will determine the length of the fade-in or fade-out. Next, choose Audio menu > Fade to open the Create Fades window. You can also use the default keyboard shortcut Control+F.

When the Create Fades window (shown in Figure 10.37) opens, DP will automatically select the fade type it thinks is most appropriate for your time-range selection. If you're satisfied with the type DP has chosen, simply click the OK button. If you want to edit or change the selected fade type, choose the fade you want from the various options before clicking OK.

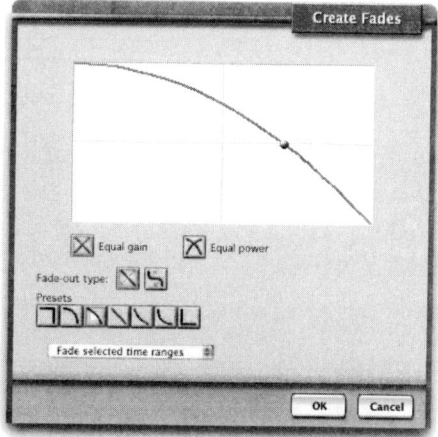

Figure 10.37
The Create Fades window.

241

CHAPTER 10 } Editing

The Delete Fades command allows you to permanently remove or delete a fade or crossfade. Click the fade or crossfade you wish to remove and press Shift+Control+F, or choose Audio menu > Delete Fades to delete the selected fade. To remove multiple fades, simply drag to select the fades before choosing the Delete Fades command.

DESTRUCTIVE FADES

Fades can be applied destructively from within the Waveform Editor by using the Audio menu's Fade In and Fade Out commands. See the "Processing" section of Chapter 13 for an explanation of destructive fades.

MIDI Editing in the Graphic Editor

Just as the Sequence Editor is the choice editor for soundbite editing, the Graphic Editor provides tremendous control over the MIDI editing process. Even though the Graphic Editor, shown in Figure 10.38, is a MIDI only editing window; it is nearly identical to the Sequence Editor in that it allows for standard editing commands such as Copy, Paste, and Repeat. Unlike the Sequence Editor, where MIDI controller data is layered below the notes of a MIDI track, the Graphic Editor provides two sections of the window that are dedicated to the editing of MIDI controller events. These sections are called the Continuous Data Grid and Median Strip. In addition, the Graphic Editor will not display MIDI data in separate tracks; it will overlay MIDI notes into the same Note Grid when multiple tracks are being shown with the window's Track selector. Unlike with the Sequence Editor, multiple Graphic Editors can be opened at the same time.

Figure 10.38

The Graphic Editor.

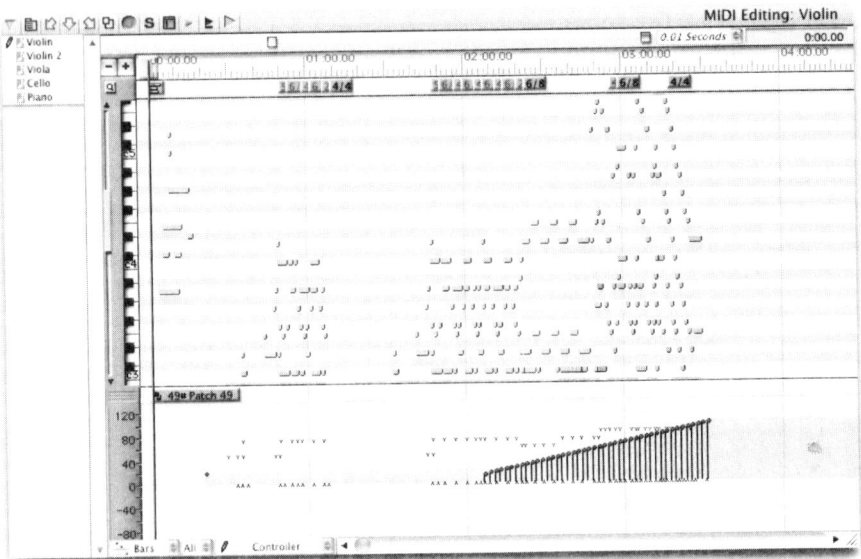

MIDI Editing in the Graphic Editor

> **THE MASTER TRACK SELECTOR**
>
> If you're displaying multiple tracks within a Graphic Editor (or Drum Editor), the Master Track Selector, shown in Figure 10.39, determines which track's Controller Data and Median Strip will be displayed. It also tells DP which track's MIDI notes will be affected when you're inserting and editing MIDI notes within the Note Grid.

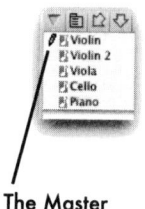

Figure 10.39

The Consolidated Window preferences control the functionality of the Consolidated Window.

The Master Track Selector

Inserting, Removing, and Modifying Notes in the Note Grid

The Note Grid allows you to insert, remove, or modify MIDI notes within a MIDI track. MIDI notes are displayed as solid lines or bars, as shown in Figure 10.40. As with all tracks within DP, horizontal positioning determines where in the sequence a MIDI note will appear, while the length of a note sets the duration for that note. Vertical positioning determines the pitch.

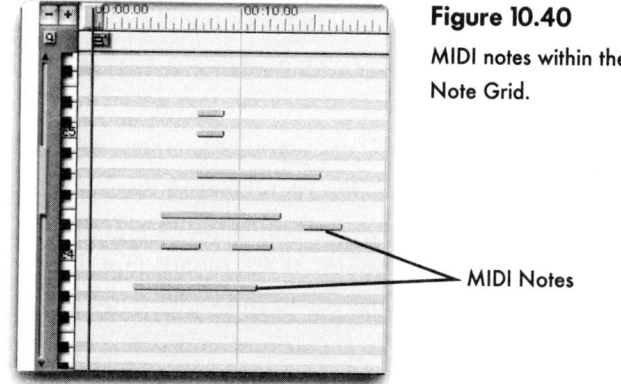

Figure 10.40

MIDI notes within the Note Grid.

To the left of the Note Grid is the Pitch Ruler (the piano keys) and the Pitch Ruler scroll bar (the vertical slider). Each line or row that extends out from a piano key determines a note's pitch within the Note Grid. Click and drag the Pitch Ruler scroll bar to scroll the Note Grid up or down; doing so will reveal hidden pitches. To display more pitches within the Note Grid, zoom vertically in the Graphic Editor.

To insert a note within the Note Grid of the Graphic Editor (or Sequence Editor):

1. Select the Pencil tool with the letter P key. Make sure you double-tap the P key to make the selection stick.
2. Specify the Master Track if you're working with multiple tracks.
3. If you need to, scroll the Pitch Ruler to display the appropriate pitches.
4. Click with the Pencil tool at the location you wish the note to start.

5. Drag horizontally to set the duration and vertically to set the pitch, as shown in Figure 10.41.

6. If you need to change the position or pitch of the note once it's been inserted, invoke the Pointer tool by pressing and holding the letter A key. Click and drag the note to the new location and pitch. Release the letter A key to revert back to the Pencil tool.

7. Repeat Steps 3-5 as needed.

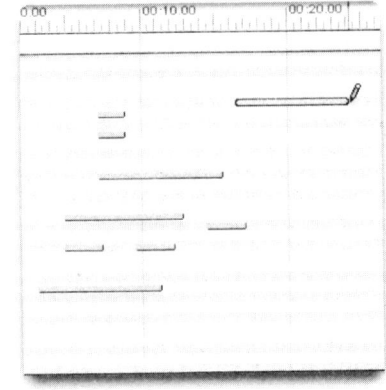

Figure 10.41

Inserting a MIDI note with the Pencil tool.

To change the duration of a note within the Note Grid of the Graphic Editor (or Sequence Editor):

1. Select the Pointer tool with the letter A key. Make sure you double-tap the A key to make the selection stick.

2. Specify the Master Track if you're working with multiple tracks.

3. If you need to, scroll the Pitch Ruler to display the appropriate note.

4. Position the Pointer at the beginning or end of a note, as shown in Figure 10.42. Notice that the tool changes to allow you to grasp the edge of the note.

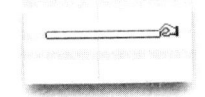

Figure 10.42

Changing the duration of a MIDI note with the Pointer tool.

5. Drag to the left or right to shorten or extend the duration of the note.

6. Repeat Steps 4 and 5 as needed.

> **THE EDIT GRID**
>
> The Edit Grid, when enabled, will constrain any edits and movements to the set grid resolution. If you want to work freely within the Note Grid, make sure you turn the Edit Grid off or press and hold the Command key to temporarily disable it.

The Median Strip and Continuous Data Grid

There are basically two types of MIDI controller data: events that are discrete (or do not have durations) and continuous controller data (events that occur over a period of time). Discrete events are displayed in the Graphic Editor's Median Strip, while continuous controller data will appear in the Continuous Data Grid (see Figure 10.43).

MIDI Editing in the Graphic Editor

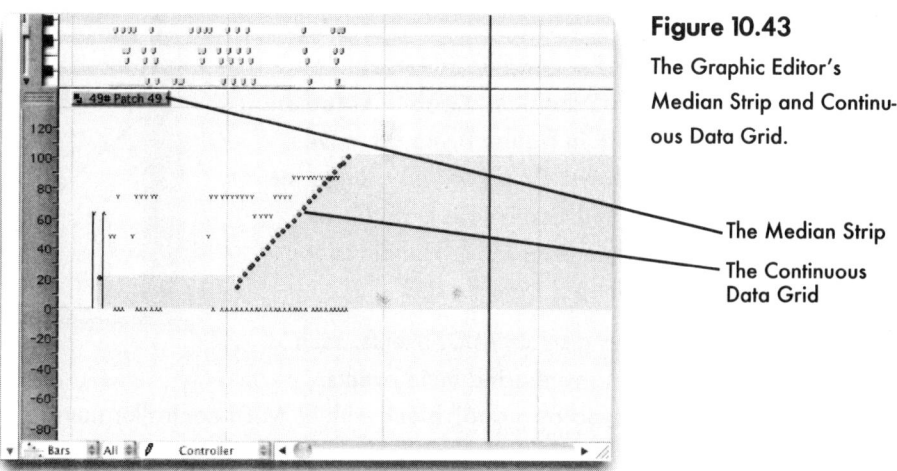

Figure 10.43
The Graphic Editor's Median Strip and Continuous Data Grid.

The Median Strip

The Continuous Data Grid

Each type of MIDI controller data within Digital Performer will be displayed with its own icon, indicating what type of MIDI event it is. To see a list of these icons and their MIDI event names, open the Legend window from the Graphic Editor, Sequence Editor, or Event List mini-menu. If you're working in the Consolidated Window, you can also open the Legend window from a sidebar's Window Selector.

> **THE LEGEND WINDOW**
> Use the Legend window, shown in Figure 10.44, to see the names of MIDI events and their associated icons. Learning these icons can help you speed up your MIDI controller editing tasks by allowing you to quickly determine what type of event you're working with.

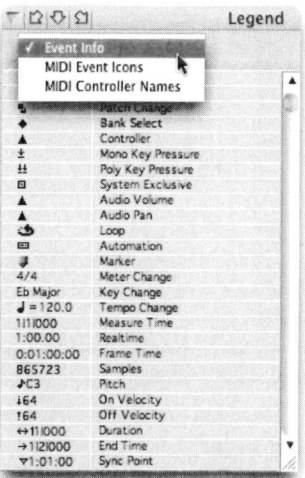

Figure 10.44
The Legend Window.

245

The Median Strip

The Median Strip divides the Graphic Editor's Note Grid from the Continuous Data Grid. Grab the Median Strip Move Handle, shown in Figure 10.45, to move the Median Strip up or down. Doing so will change the overall size of the Note and Continuous Data Grids. Double-click on the Median Strip Move Handle to toggle the view of the Continuous Data Grid.

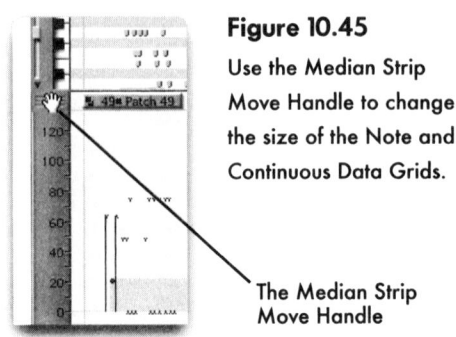

Figure 10.45

Use the Median Strip Move Handle to change the size of the Note and Continuous Data Grids.

The Median Strip Move Handle

The Median Strip displays discrete MIDI events, such as patch changes, sustain events, and mute events. Each event will be displayed as a small block with its MIDI controller number, event name, and corresponding icon.

The Continuous Data Grid

The Continuous Data Grid, shown in Figure 10.46, displays continuous controller data, such as volume and pan changes, modulation changes, and so on. If you're new to MIDI and find this topic confusing, just think of continuous controller data as automation for your MIDI tracks that can be created via a MIDI controller, with DP's various MIDI features (such as the Tracks window's Patch and Default Patch columns), or by directly inserting a controller event into a MIDI track.

Figure 10.46

The Graphic Editor's Continuous Data Grid.

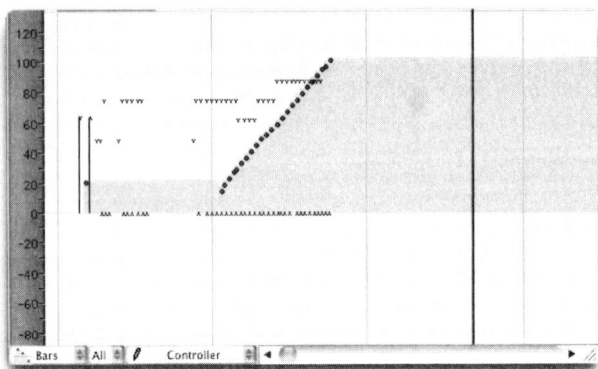

The Continuous Data Grid Ruler

On the left side of the Continuous Data Grid is the Continuous Data Grid Ruler, which displays a controller scale (from 0-127), a pitch bend scale (from -8192 to 8191) that starts at the middle of the Continuous Data Grid, and a third scale that displays a combination of the controller and pitch bend scales. Click on the Continuous Data Grid Ruler to toggle between the three different scales.

The Grid Display Mode

The Continuous Data Grid will display continuous MIDI data in three different ways: as points, bars, or lines. Use the Grid Display Mode pop-up menu to choose between the different view types. Points mode, shown in Figure 10.47, will display controller data as small points or dots within the grid. Controller data that's selected will appear with a small vertical line extending from the bottom of the window to the controller point.

Bars mode will display continuous controller data with small points that are connected by a colored bar, as shown in Figure 10.48. Use this view when you want to easily see the relationship between the current value of the event and its duration.

Lines mode, shown in Figure 10.49, will display continuous controller data as points connected by lines. These lines attempt to approximate the shape of the curve of the controller points. This view is similar to how breakpoint automation is displayed in non-MIDI tracks. Users more comfortable with breakpoint automation may find this view easier to work in, compared to the Points and Bars Grid Display modes.

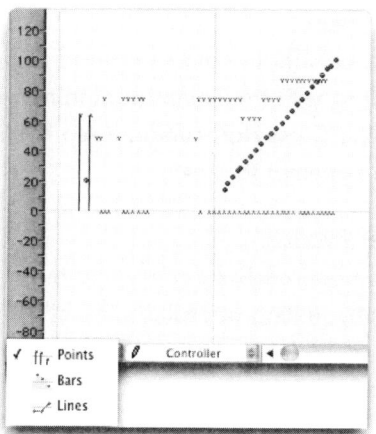

Figure 10.47

Points mode will display continuous controller data as small points. Selected data will also appear with small vertical lines.

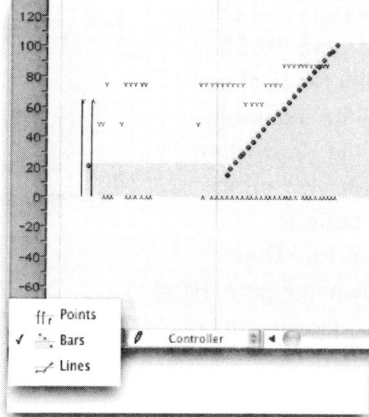

Figure 10.48

Bars mode connects each controller point with a colored bar.

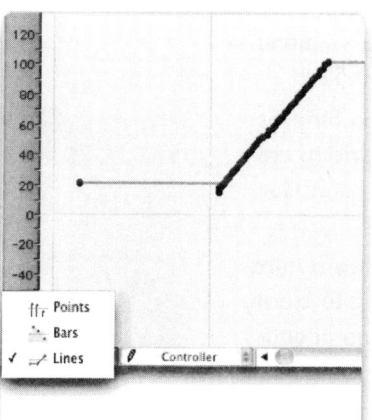

Figure 10.49

Lines mode connects each controller point with a line.

Moving MIDI Controller Events

Moving MIDI controller events (both continuous and non-continuous) is identical to moving MIDI notes. Simply click and drag with the Pointer tool to move the event. To select multiple events, drag over the MIDI data with the Cross-Hair cursor. Keep in mind that the Edit Grid, if enabled, will constrain any movements you attempt to make.

Inserting MIDI Controller Events

MIDI controller events can be inserted directly into the Median Strip and Continuous Data Grid. Remember that, as with any editing operation, the Edit Grid directly affects how data can be inserted, moved, and so on. If you want to constrain your edits to a specific grid resolution, be sure to turn on the Edit Grid and select the desired grid value.

To insert an event directly into the Median Strip or Continuous Data Grid:

1. Select the type of event you want to create from the Pencil Tool Data Selector, shown in Figure 10.50. Keep in mind that the types of controller data that will be available are determined by the View Filter. Data that has been turned off in the View Filter will appear dimmed in the Pencil Tool Data Selector list, as shown in Figure 10.51.

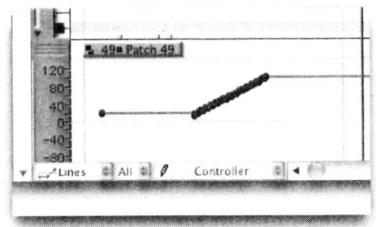

Figure 10.50
The Pencil Tool Data Selector.

2. Enable the Pencil tool by double-tapping the letter P key.

3. If you're going to be inserting continuous data, choose the shape of the curve to be inserted from the Tools palette's Insert/Reshape Curve menu, shown in Figure 10.52.

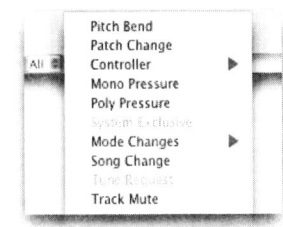

Figure 10.51
Controller data that appears dimmed has been disabled in the View Filter.

4. Click in the Median Strip or Continuous Data grid to create a single MIDI controller event.

5. If the MIDI event has a duration, click and drag to create a continuous stream of controller events.

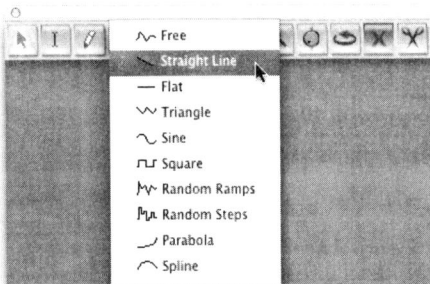

Figure 10.52
The Insert/Reshape Curve menu.

Editing Existing MIDI Controller Events

MIDI events in the Median Strip and Continuous Data Grids can be modified or changed altogether.

To edit a MIDI event within the Median Strip:

- To delete an event, select the event and press the Delete key.
- To change or modify the properties of the MIDI event, select the event and press Shift+E to open it in an Event List. Once the Event List opens, the selected MIDI event will become highlighted blue. Click on the desired property to pop-edit its value. The Event List is explained in the next section.
- To move the event within the Median Strip, click and drag with the Pointer tool.

To edit continuous controller data within the Continuous Data Grid:

- To delete MIDI controller data, select the MIDI event and press the Delete key. To delete a stream of continuous MIDI data, click and drag over the events with the Cross-Hair cursor, and then press the Delete key.
- To change the value of MIDI controller data, vertically drag the data within the grid.
- To move the data to a different location in the track, horizontally drag the data.
- To change the existing curve of a stream of continuous controller data, select the Reshape tool by double-tapping the letter R key. Select the shape for the new curve from the Insert/Reshape Curve menu. Click where you wish to start changing the curve, and then drag to reshape the existing stream of data, as shown in Figure 10.53.

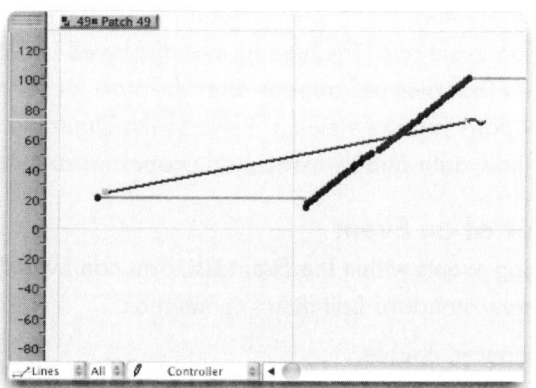

Figure 10.53

In this example, the Insert/Reshape Curve menu's Straight Line curve is being used to modify the existing stream of continuous MIDI controller data.

CHAPTER 10 } Editing

> **MIDI CONTROLLER DATA WITHIN THE SEQUENCE EDITOR**
> When you're working in the Sequence Editor, MIDI tracks do not have separate Continuous Data Grids and Median Strips. Instead, MIDI controller data will appear stacked within a MIDI track. Use the track's Active View Layer to bring notes and controller data into the foreground of the track. Only active layers can be edited.

The Event List

The Event List, shown in Figure 10.54, displays selected audio and MIDI data in rows that are chronologically organized from top to bottom. Multiple Event Lists can be opened for each track within a project. Simply select the track or any data contained in the track and press Shift+E. You can also choose Project menu > Event List.

The Event List may seem intimidating at first glance because the data listed is displayed only as text. Understanding all the symbols and positioning of the data takes time, but with a little patience and help from the Legend window (if you're working with MIDI controller data), you'll be editing away in the Event List like a seasoned pro.

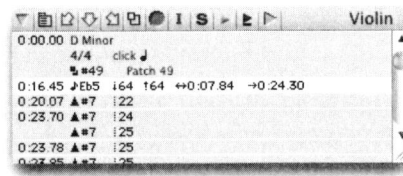

Figure 10.54

The Event List.

Event List Basics

The Event List displays event information in rows. If multiple events occur at the same time location, they will appear as a block of information. The location (or start time) of an event will be displayed all the way to the right of an event row. The time format displayed is determined by the Time Format window settings. The event properties will appear after the start location; which properties appear will depend on the type of data you are viewing. Refer to the *Digital Performer User's Manual* for a detailed explanation of how data and its associated properties are shown.

Editing the Parameter of an Event

It's very easy to edit existing events within the Event List. You can even insert MIDI controller data directly into the list and apply standard Edit menu commands.

* To edit an event property, double-click on its parameter field, as shown in Figure 10.55. A pop-up text box will allow you to change the current parameter setting.

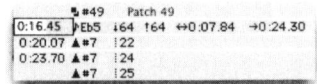

Figure 10.55

Double-click on an event property to modify its current parameter setting.

250

- To apply standard Edit menu commands, select the event and choose the desired command. To paste material that exists in the clipboard, insert the I-Beam cursor at the desired location before pressing Command+V.

- To insert MIDI controller data, click on the Event List title bar's Insert button (I) and choose the type of data you want to insert. A new event row will appear. Set the controller data's properties from the pop-up text boxes. Press the Return key to confirm the property settings.

> **DISPLAYING DURATION, END TIME, AND SYNC POINT PARAMETERS**
> If you want to display the Duration, End Time, and Sync Point parameters within the Event List, make sure you enable these options in the Event Information section of the Time Format window.

Summary

The audio and MIDI editing capabilities of Digital Performer are really amazing. Every parameter of a soundbite, MIDI note, and automation/controller point can be manipulated to your heart's desire—from trimming off unwanted silence within a soundbite to tweaking individual MIDI notes and associated controller data.

As I discussed very early on in this chapter, however, it's a fine line between fixing and improving a performance and editing the life out of one. Stay focused and look at the big picture (meaning the song itself, not necessarily the individual tracks or notes), and you'll be able to edit your projects with positive, satisfying results.

11 } Arranging

Arranging, as a musical term, sometimes refers to the act of creating the structure of a song or composition (for example, verse-chorus-bridge-chorus). It can also describe the selection of the instrumentation used within a composition (for example, piano-drums-bass). Digital Performer's arrangement tools allow you to manage the overall structure of a project, provide location points for easy navigation, or control compositional aspects such as meter and tempo.

Some of the features discussed in this chapter have been mentioned or briefly explained in other parts of this book and I could have discussed them in those chapters, but to maintain a degree of familiarity, I decided to follow MOTU's structuring scheme (as described in the official DP manual) and discuss certain features here in the "Arranging" chapter.

Following is a list of topics covered in this chapter:

- How to work with tempo, meter, key, and the Conductor Track
- How to manage sequences within Digital Performer
- How to use Chunks and songs
- How to set up loops within a track
- How to make your projects more efficient through the use of Clippings
- How to use markers

The Conductor Track

The job of a musical conductor is to literally "conduct" a musical piece or ensemble. The conductor controls the tempo of a composition, indicates meter, gives cues for musical entrances and dynamics, and so on. Digital Performer's Conductor Track takes on the role of conductor and provides a "track," in which tempo, meter, key change, and marker information is stored.

CHAPTER 11 } Arranging

The Conductor Track is similar to other tracks in that basic edit commands—such as copying, pasting, and deleting—can be executed, and alternate takes can be created. The Conductor Track can also be record-enabled to input tap tempo event information (explained later). Unlike other tracks, however, the Conductor Track cannot be moved, deleted, looped, or renamed. The Conductor Track can be edited in the Event List and other editor windows where the Conductor Track is visible. Here, we are going to discuss two windows specifically: the Event List (shown in Figure 11.1) and the Graphic Editor (shown in Figure 11.2). Conductor events can be edited in both windows, though the method for viewing and modifying event data in each window is very different.

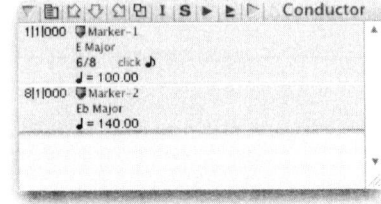

Figure 11.1
The Event List.

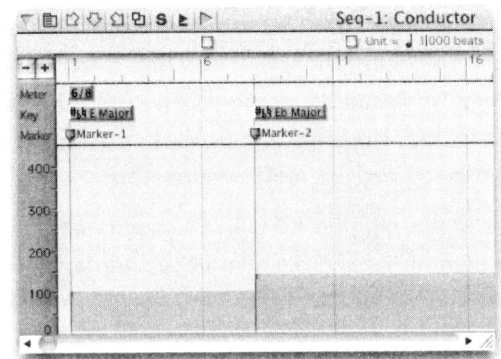

Figure 11.2
The Graphic Editor displays Conductor Track data in a linear fashion. Meter, key, and marker information appears below the Time Ruler at a fixed viewing resolution, while tempo data is shown as continuous controller data, represented by a colored bar.

Modify Conductor Track Menu

The Modify Conductor Track menu, located in the Project menu, contains separate commands for inserting key, meter, and tempo data, as shown in Figure 11.3. Additional commands for inserting measures (explained below), as well as for adjusting and recording beats, can also be found here.

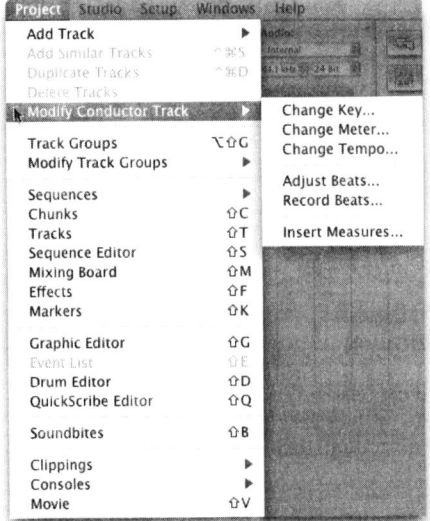

Figure 11.3
The Modify Conductor Track menu provides commands for inserting measures and changing the key, meter, and tempo of a sequence. Advanced options for adjusting and recording beats are also provided.

254

The Conductor Track

To insert a measure with the Insert Measure command:

1. Open the Insert Measure command by choosing Project menu > Modify Conductor Track > Insert Measures (see Figure 11.4).
2. Specify the number of measures you wish to insert in the Insert field.
3. In the start of the Measure field, enter the location (measure number) at which you wish to insert the measures.
4. If you want to preserve the SMPTE times of all events that occur after the insertion point, turn on the Maintain all times following the insertion point option.
5. Click OK to insert the measures.

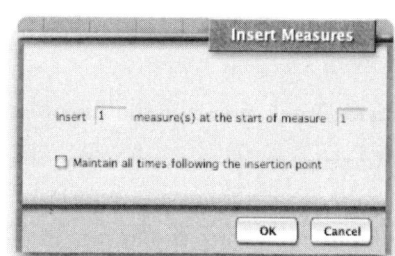

Figure 11.4
The Insert Measure command allows you to insert a blank measure at any location within a sequence.

> **INSERTING MEASURES**
> Be aware that audio data that resides at the insertion point will be split, while MIDI notes will not. If you would like MIDI to be split, use the Edit menu's Split command (Command+Y) before inserting any measures.

Editing Conductor Track Data

Conductor Track events can be edited directly in the Conductor Track of DP's various editors and in the Event List. The window(s) you choose will determine how and what type of editing can be executed. Standard edit commands such as Cut, Copy, and Paste, however, can be used regardless of the window you are editing in.

When working with markers, be aware that they behave differently, depending on the window you are working in. For example, markers within the Event List will react to standard edit commands such as Cut, Copy, Paste, and Delete, but their properties cannot be modified within the Event List window. The Graphic Editor, however, will allow you to rename a marker and also change its location.

The Event List

In the Event List, Conductor Track data will appear as a list, similar to the way in which MIDI data is presented and viewed (see Figure 11.1). You can open the Event List for the Conductor Track by selecting the Conductor Track within the Tracks window or Sequence Editor and pressing Shift+E on your keyboard. Remember that markers will only accept standard edit commands, such as Cut, Copy,

Paste, and Delete. Marker properties, such as location and name, must be edited in another window, such as the Marker window or Graphic Editor.

To modify existing Conductor Track events in the Event List:

1. Double-click on a Conductor Track event within the Event List. The specific event will become active, allowing you to modify the existing data.
2. Make the necessary modifications, then press the Return key to confirm the change.

To insert new Conductor Track data within the Event List:

1. Click on the Event List's Insert button. This is the I button located in the title bar.
2. Choose the type of event you wish to insert.
3. Enter the location (in measures) and press the Return key. Use the Tab key to quickly move to the next input field.
4. Double-click on the new event to make any changes, and then hit the Return key to confirm the modification.

The Graphic Editor

When editing the Conductor Track in the Graphic Editor, events such as key, meter, and markers are displayed within the window's Median Strip. Once an event is selected, its settings will be displayed in the Graphic Editor's Information bar. Located below the Median Strip are any tempo events that exist; these are displayed as continuous controller data and are represented by a colored bar (see Figure 11.2).

THE CONDUCTOR TRACK MEDIAN STRIP
Unlike median strips in normal MIDI tracks, the Conductor Track's Median Strip is larger, with a fixed width, and is positioned directly below the Time Ruler. In addition, there is no Note Grid, as the Conductor Track does not contain any notes.

To insert a key or meter event within the Conductor Track's Graphic Editor:

1. Enable the Pencil tool by double-tapping the letter P key on the Mac keyboard.
2. If you need to, enable the Edit Grid to constrain the event location to the current grid value.
3. Click on the Median Strip to insert a key or meter event. The vertical position will determine which type of event (key or meter) is inserted. The horizontal position will determine the location in time. Marker events cannot be inserted using this method.

To edit existing key or meter events in the Conductor Track's Graphic Editor:

1. Begin by clicking on a key or meter event. Once selected, the event will become visible in the Information bar, which is located directly below the title bar.
2. In the Information bar, click on the event data. It will immediately become active, allowing you to make any modifications (see Figure 11.5).
3. When you're finished, press the Return key to confirm the changes.

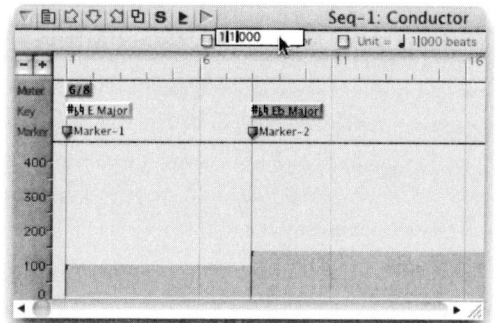

Figure 11.5

Click on an event within the Graphic Editor's Information bar to make changes to the selected key or meter event.

> ※ **DRAGGING IN THE MEDIAN STRIP**
> In addition to the procedures just described, you can also click and drag an event within the Median Strip to change its location.

Unlike in the Event List, marker properties such as location and name can be modified in the Graphic Editor:

※ To change the position of a marker, click on it within the Median Strip and drag with the mouse.

※ To rename a marker, double-click on it. Hit the Return key to confirm the change.

The Tempo Change Grid

Located below the Graphic Editor's Median Strip is the Tempo Change Grid, which shows tempo events as continuous controller data. The Tempo Ruler on the left side of the grid vertically displays tempo, with slower values appearing at the bottom and increasing towards the top. Placing the mouse over the Tempo Ruler changes the cursor to a magnifying glass icon that allows you to zoom in for greater accuracy when inserting and editing tempo events (see Figure 11.6). Clicking on the ruler will allow you to toggle between the normal zoom and magnified resolutions.

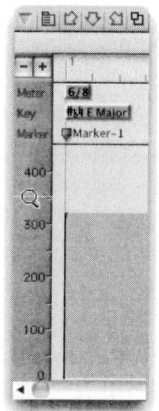

Figure 11.6

Click on the Tempo Ruler (indicated with the magnifying glass icon) to change the viewing resolution.

CHAPTER 11 } Arranging

Keep in mind that the tempo source must be set to Conductor Track in order for Digital Performer to follow any tempo changes that reside in the Conductor Track.

> **INSERTING TEMPO CHANGE EVENTS**
> Tempo events can be inserted directly into the Tempo Change Grid by enabling the Pencil tool and clicking with the mouse. Though this sounds like a simple procedure, getting your events exactly where you want them with one mouse click can be challenging, as DP does not constrain your mouse movements to the Edit Grid, even when it is enabled! The Information bar will prove helpful in this situation, as it will display the vertical (tempo) and horizontal (Time Ruler location) of the mouse. Once you insert the tempo event and discover that it isn't exactly where you want it, simply select it with the Arrow tool and edit it in the Information bar or Event List.

To insert a single tempo event within the Conductor Track's Graphic Editor:

1. Double-tap the letter P key on your computer keyboard to quickly enable the Pencil tool.
2. Click in the Tempo Change Grid to insert a tempo event. The vertical position will determine the tempo, while the horizontal position determines its location within the Time Ruler. Once the event is inserted, a colored bar will appear with a small icon located at the top-left corner. This small icon is the actual tempo event, while the bar represents the duration of the tempo change.
3. If the actual tempo and/or location isn't exactly where you want it, enable the Arrow tool and select the event by clicking on the small tempo event icon. Once the event is selected, its settings will appear in the Graphic Editor's Information bar.
4. Click on the setting you wish to change (either the location or actual tempo) and change it as needed. Hit the Return key to confirm the change.

In addition to single events, tempo events that change over time (such as accelerandos and ritards) can also be inserted in the Graphic Editor. The Change Tempo command also provides options for creating tempo changes that need to occur over a specific period of time (explained later).

To insert a tempo event that changes over time:

1. Enable the Pencil tool by double-tapping the letter P key on the Mac keyboard.

2. Choose the shape of the curve you wish to insert from the Tool palette's Insert/Reshape Curve button, shown in Figure 11.7. Choosing a straight line, for example, will allow you to insert a continuous and even tempo change.

3. Click in the Tempo Grid where you wish the tempo change to begin, and drag the mouse to the position where you wish the change to end. Dragging up or down will change the tempo, and dragging to the left or right will set the length of the tempo change.

4. Release the mouse to insert the tempo change (see Figure 11.8). Once the tempo change is inserted, multiple tempo events will be created between the start and end points of the tempo change.

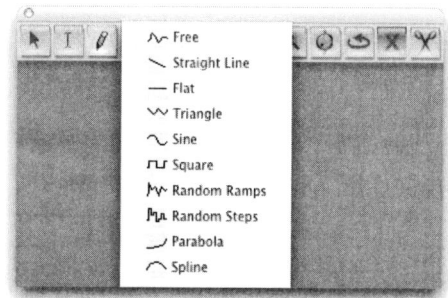

Figure 11.7
The Tool Palette's Insert/Reshape Curve button lets you choose the type of curve that will be used when creating tempo events that change over time.

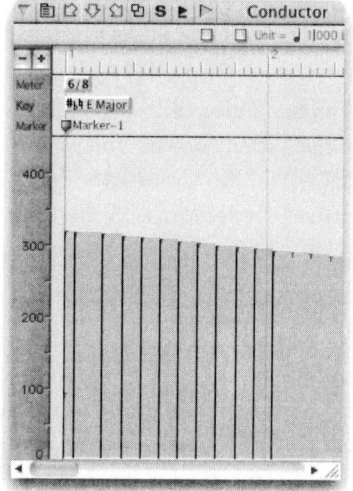

Figure 11.8
Tempo change events created with the Straight-Line tool. In this example, the newly created events are selected (indicated by vertical black lines).

To edit existing tempo events:

* To change the actual tempo or location of an event, enable the Arrow tool and drag the event with the mouse. Drag vertically to change the tempo or horizontally to change the event's location within the Time Ruler.

* You can also select the event and edit its properties within the Graphic Editor's Information bar. Click on an Information bar setting to activate it, and then enter the change and hit the Return key.

* To cut, copy, and/or delete, select the event(s) with the Arrow tool and apply the appropriate command from the Edit menu or keyboard.

* To paste a cut/copied event, place the cursor at the position you wish the event(s) to be pasted and choose Edit > Paste, or use the default keyboard shortcut Command+P.

Tempo

Now that you know how to create and edit tempo events within the Graphic Editor, I'll discuss how to set tempo sources within Digital Performer, the use of the more standard Change Tempo command window, and advanced Tap Tempo features. I'll also explain the various Audio menu tempo commands.

Tempo Sources and the Tempo Control Drawer

Tempo sources basically tell Digital Performer what tempo a sequence should follow. There are four tempo sources to choose from, though only one tempo source can be chosen at a time. The Control Panel's Tempo Control Drawer allows you to set the tempo source for a project (refer to Chapter 3 for a look at the Tempo Control Drawer). Simply click on a source within the Tempo Control Drawer to set DP's source tempo.

- **Tempo Slider**. The Tempo Slider allows you to change the tempo of a sequence at any time by simply dragging on the slider control. This is like a manual setting, and will ignore any tempo events that may exist within the Conductor Track. The Tempo Slider is the simplest way to set a project's tempo—just set the tempo with the slider and start recording.
- **Conductor Track**. Setting the control to Conductor Track will tell DP to follow the sequence's tempo map or tempo events that exist within the Conductor Track (this was explained earlier in the chapter).
- **Tap Pad**. Use this setting to force DP to listen to a "tap" from any designated MIDI source. Click on the Tap Pad button repeatedly to establish a tap tempo. The Tap Pad feature, however, does not function while playback is engaged, so you'll need to tap in your tempo while the transport is stopped. To have DP track your tapping during playback, you need to use the Receive Sync command's Tap Tempo feature (explained later).
- **Remote Control**. This setting will allow you to control DP's Tempo Slider from a MIDI controller's modulation wheel or any other source that can output continuous controller data (this is explained in detail later).

Adjusting Tempo

There are several ways to set the tempo of a sequence in Digital Performer. I've already discussed the use of the Conductor Track's Graphic Editor. This section will cover the creation of tempo events with the following methods:

- The Change Tempo command
- The Tap Tempo feature
- The Adjust and Record Beats commands

Change Tempo Command

The Change Tempo command is located within the Project menu's Modify Conductor Track submenu (Project > Modify Conductor Track > Change Tempo). The Change Tempo window provides options for creating and inserting tempo events within a sequence's Conductor Track (see Figure 11.9). Its various settings and options are explained below.

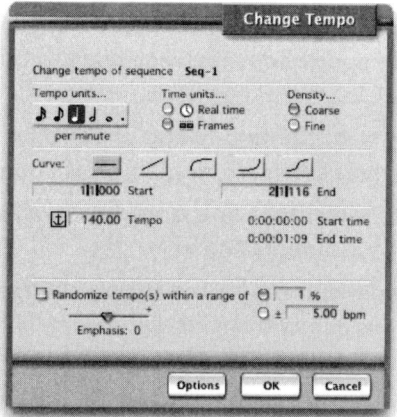

Figure 11.9
The Change Tempo window

- **Tempo Units**. This is the beat value of the tempo, or the note value that the tempo will be based on.
- **Time Units**. Click on this setting to set the tempo parameter display to real-time or frames.
- **Density**. This option will determine the number of tempo events that are created for every beat. The Fine setting will create 12 tempo events for every beat, while the Coarse setting will create fewer events. Use the Fine setting when you need more accuracy and control over tempo events.
- **Curve**. Use this setting to set the type of tempo change that will be created. Each setting has its own options that will be displayed directly below the Curve section of the window (this will be explained later in the chapter).
- **Randomize tempos**. You can use this setting to randomize the tempo changes by a percentage or bpm value. Use the Emphasis slider to force the randomization to occur at higher or lower tempo values. Positive settings will randomize higher tempos, while negative values will randomize lower ones.
- **Options button**. The Options button (located next to the OK button) will allow you to toggle between the different methods of setting curve parameters. The parameter settings that are displayed are dependent on the type of curve selected. You can use the End Time setting to have DP calculate the tempo for a specific duration, which is handy when you're working with film or video and you need tempo changes to occur at specific points in time.
- **Anchoring**. Located next to the Start and End tempos is an anchor icon, which enables the Anchoring feature. Anchoring allows you to use the current tempo that is at the sequence's current location. Use this feature to ensure that the tempos before and after the region match; doing so will prevent any sudden changes or jumps between tempo changes.

CHAPTER 11 } Arranging

To insert a static tempo change:

1. Open the Change Tempo window by choosing Project menu > Modify Conductor Track > Change Tempo.
2. Set the tempo unit. For a standard tempo of 120bpm, for example, choose a quarter-note value. This basically tells DP that a single beat is equal to one-quarter note.
3. Set the tempo curve to constant. This is the first button within the Curve section of the window and is represented by a straight-line icon.
4. Set the Start and End measures for the Tempo change. The Start time is where the tempo change will begin, and the End time is where the change will stop.
5. Type a value in the Tempo field. This value is in beats per minute, or bpm.
6. If needed, set the Randomize Tempo options, then click OK.

> **TEMPO CURVES**
>
> DP provides five different tempo curves that allow for greater control over tempo changes (see Figure 11.10). Instead of manually inserting multiple tempo changes, you can use the provided curves to automate much of the process. The various curves determine how a change will be implemented over a specified period of time. The first curve (Straight-line) will insert one tempo at the beginning of a region, while the remaining curves (Linear, Logarithmic, Exponential, and Polynomial) will create multiple tempo events to simulate the shape of the chosen curve.
>
> When working with the last three curves, you have an additional curve setting called Curvature. This setting controls the amount of tempo change that will occur at the "changing" point of the curve, allowing you to smooth out or over-exaggerate the shape of a chosen curve. Lower values will smooth out the tempo change and force it to more closely resemble the Linear curve setting. Higher values will force any tempo changes to happen closer to the beginning or end of a curve, depending on which one is selected. For example, when you're using the Logarithmic curve (the middle curve button), higher curvature values will cause the majority of the tempo change events to happen towards the beginning of the curve.
>
> When working with the Polynomial curve (the left-most curve button), you can also specify the Mid-beat parameter. This setting tells DP where the most rapid tempo changes will occur.

Figure 11.10

The Change Tempo command's five tempo curves are, from left to right: Straight-line, Linear, Logarithmic, Exponential, and Polynomial.

262

To insert a smooth tempo change that starts with one tempo and ends with another:
1. Repeat Steps 1 and 2 from the previous "How To" section.
2. Choose the curve you want (any curve except the Straight Line curve). Notice the settings update to provide additional options for setting the End tempo, Curvature, and/or Mid-beat settings.
3. Set the Start and End measure.
4. Enter the Start (beginning tempo) and End tempos for the change. Remember that you can toggle the Option button to activate the End Time setting, which will let DP automatically calculate the start or end tempos for you.
5. Set the Randomize, Curvature, and/or Mid-beat settings as needed and click OK.

Tap Tempo and the Receive Sync Command

The simplest form of DP's Tap Tempo commands is the Control Panel's Tap Pad feature. Simply click on the Tap Pad button to "tap" in a tempo. Unfortunately, you cannot use the Tap Pad function while playback is engaged. To have DP track a tempo during playback, or to record a tapped tempo into the Conductor Track, you'll need to use the Receive Sync command's Tap Tempo option (see Figure 11.11). Setting DP to receive sync from a tap tempo source will basically slave Digital Performer to an incoming tap tempo MIDI source, and can be used during any part of the music production process. Keep in mind that this setting will override any Conductor Track tempo settings!

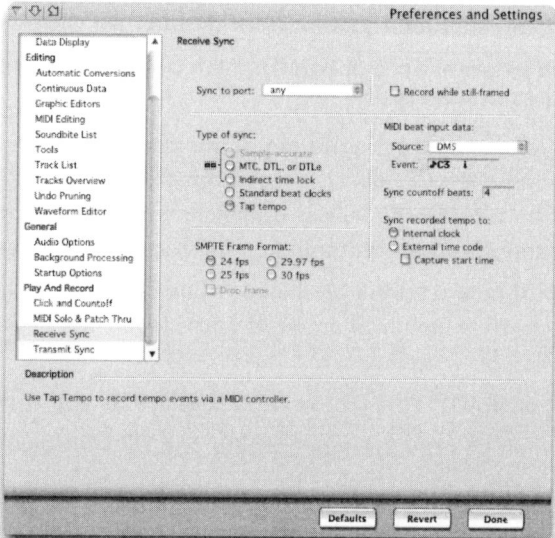

Figure 11.11
The Receive Sync preference Tap Tempo option allows you to slave DP to an external tap tempo source.

Once the Tap Tempo command is chosen, DP's Tap Tempo options become available. They are as follows:

- **MIDI beat input data**. This section controls the MIDI source and event number (note). Use the Source section to set the MIDI device you will be using to tap tempos. Once the device is chosen, press a note on your MIDI controller to set the MIDI Event or note that will be used to tap the tempo.
- **Sync countoff beats**. This setting is the number of taps that will be used as a countoff. You can set the number from 1-127.
- **Sync recorded tempo to**. The External setting will let you slave DP to an external clock source while in Tap Tempo mode. Enabling the Capture Start Time option will tell DP to remember the exact SMPTE frame of the first tap after the countoff. This will ensure that the sequence will always start at the correct time.

To record Tap Tempo events into the Conductor Track:

1. Begin by ensuring that DP is set to the correct meter(s) with the Change Meter command (Project menu > Modify Conductor Track > Change Meter).
2. Choose Receive Sync (Studio > Receive Sync). Set the MIDI source and Event. If you are planning to simultaneously record a MIDI performance into MIDI tracks, make sure you choose a MIDI event that will not be in use for this "performance." Also remember to have the Multi Record option enabled from the Studio menu.
3. Set the number of countoff taps in the Sync Countoff Beats section (as explained earlier).
4. Set the Sync options to either Internal or External, and then click OK.
5. Enable the Slave the External Sync option from the Setup menu; the default keyboard shortcut for this is Command+7.
6. Record-enable the Conductor Track (and any other tracks, if needed). Be aware that Overdub mode will not function on the Conductor Track during this process. Any tempo events that exist within the track will be erased, regardless of which recording mode is selected. To get around this, create an alternate take before beginning the recording process.
7. Start tapping the MIDI note or event on the specified MIDI controller. Digital Performer will wait to "hear" the specific number of countoff beats (specified in Step 3) before playback and recording begins.
8. Enter (tap) the tempo into DP. You can be as expressive as you wish.
9. Hit the Space bar when you are through tapping and DP will calculate the new tempo.
10. Unarm any record-enabled tracks, place the Control Panel's Tempo Source into Conductor Track mode, and hit Play to check your results.

Adjust Beats and Record Beats Commands

Digital Performer contains more advanced commands that allow you to adjust the tempo for a sequence: the Adjust Beats and Record Beats commands (Project menu > Modify Conductor Track > Adjust Beats or Record Beats). These commands allow you to realign DP's barlines to match the tempo of existing music. Both commands are extremely useful for situations in which you have an existing piece of music that was not recorded to a metronome click, and you would like to align DP's bar and beat lines to the music without changing the original performance.

The Record Beats Command

The Record Beats command lets you tap a new tempo while listening to playback of existing material. Once you have finished, DP will calculate the new tempo and automatically readjust barlines and beat markers to match the tempo you entered, while leaving the existing musical material intact. This feature is very similar to the Tap Tempo feature, but offers dedicated options for greater control in this specific type of situation (see Figure 11.12).

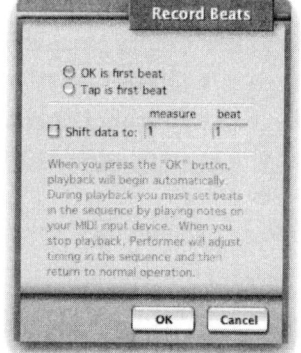

Figure 11.12
The Record Beats command window

- ❊ **OK is first Beat.** This option will make the first beat or tempo event occur at the counter's current location.
- ❊ **Tap is first beat.** Use this option to make your first tap the first beat of the realignment procedure. This is like a manual setting, allowing you to begin playback and wait before you begin tapping the new tempo.
- ❊ **Shift data to.** Use this setting to compensate for any pickup notes (notes that may occur before the actual beginning of a measure). For example, if you have material that starts on beat 1 of measure 3, but contains two quarter-note pickups, set the values to measure 2 beat 3.

To use the Record Beats feature:

1. First record new material (without concern for the click) or import an existing piece of music.
2. Place the playback cursor at the precise location at which the material starts. If the material is an audio region, you can zoom in and manually place the playback cursor at the proper location. If it is a MIDI track, open the Event List (Shift+E) and make note of the location of the first MIDI event.
3. Open the Record Beats command by choosing Project menu > Modify Conductor Track > Record Beats.

4. Choose the OK is first beat option. This will automatically place the first beat at the current location that you set in Step 2.
5. If the material contains pickup notes, use the Shift data to option to compensate.
6. Now you should get ready to start tapping any note on your MIDI controller. Once you hit the OK button, DP will automatically tap the first beat and you will need to begin tapping on the second beat.
7. Click OK and start tapping on the second beat.
8. When the song is finished, press the Space bar to stop playback. DP will automatically calculate the new tempo for the song and realign the bar/beat lines.
9. Unarm any record-enabled tracks, place the Control Panel's Tempo Source into Conductor Track mode, and hit Play to check your results.
10. If you wish to use the Tap is first beat option to manually place the first beat, start by placing the playback cursor at a location prior to where you wish the first tap to occur. In other words, give yourself some *pre-roll*.
11. Open the Record Beats command and select the Tap is first beat option.
12. Click OK to begin playback.
13. Start tapping at the desired location. DP will not begin recording beats until your first tap.
14. Repeat Steps 8-10 as needed.

The Adjust Beats Command

The Adjust Beats command (see Figure 11.13) allows you to manually realign DP's Time Ruler to match the tempo of existing material. Instead of tapping in a tempo as you listen back to an existing audio or MIDI track (as with the Record Beats command), you manually drag the bar and beat lines of the Time Ruler. As you might have guessed, this can be a time-consuming process depending on the length of the material you are working with; this option is really aimed at tempo-mapping rubato passages, or other material that the built-in Beat Detection Engine has trouble analyzing.

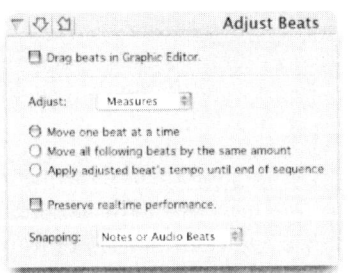

Figure 11.13
The Adjust Beats command window.

For simpler situations in which you need to realign a sequence to an existing soundbite with a constant tempo or clearly defined transients, use the Beat Detection Engine to analyze the soundbite, and then use the Adjust Sequence to Soundbites Tempo command to align the sequence to the soundbite in question (explained later in this chapter). See Appendix A for an in-depth look into Digital Performer's Beat Detection Engine.

The Adjust Beats command window provides options for controlling the adjustment process. They are, from top to bottom:

- **Drag Beats in Graphic Editor.** Click this option to turn on the Adjust Beats feature.
- **Adjust pop-up menu.** The Adjust option's pop-up menu, shown in Figure 11.13, allows you to adjust beats by entire measures, individual beats, or by a fixed note duration. When the Fixed Duration option is selected, a note value pop-up menu will appear and allow you to choose the specific note duration you wish to work with.
- **Move one beat at a time.** Choose this setting when you need to make individual beat adjustments in the Time Ruler.
- **Move all following beats by the same amount.** Select this option when you want to move one beat and have all the beats that appear after it move by the same amount.
- **Apply adjusted beat's tempo until end of sequence.** When this option is selected, the tempo change generated by moving a beat will be applied until the end of the sequence.
- **Preserve realtime performance.** This option tells DP to only adjust the Time Ruler and not the original audio or MIDI data.
- **Snapping.** This option will force realigned beats to snap to MIDI notes and audio beats (if they exist within the track you are dragging in), or markers. Choose None to turn off snapping altogether.

To use the Adjust Beats feature:

1. First record new material or import an existing piece of music.
2. Open the Adjust Beats command by choosing Project menu > Modify Conductor Track > Adjust Beats.
3. Click the Adjust Beats in Graphic Editor option to enable the Adjust Beats command. Keep in mind that the Adjust Beats window must be open in order for the Adjust Beats feature to work.
4. Start by adjusting the down beats of the first measure. Choose Measures from the Adjust pop-up menu.
5. Open the Sequence Editor for the track, zooming as needed so that you can see the individual measures within the Time Ruler. It also helps if the track you are working on is at the very top of the window, so use the Show/Hide list to hide all the other tracks, including the Conductor Track.
6. Position the cursor over the downbeat of the first measure within the Time Ruler.

    The actual data that you wish to align may start later within your sequence, let's say measure 8. If this is the case, simply start with that measure. You could also trim the soundbite or MIDI region so that it begins precisely on beat 1 of measure 1.

7. Drag the downbeat of the measure within the Time Ruler to the actual beginning of beat 1 in the track. As you drag, you should see a red bar line appear, indicating the new bar/beat position.
8. Release the mouse and DP will realign the Time Ruler.
9. Proceed with adjusting the individual beats. Change the Adjust pop-up menu to Beats.
10. Click and drag the Time Ruler's individual bar/beat markers and align them with the individual beats of the music.
11. If you are working with a rubato passage, make sure you enable the Move one beat at a time option, which will let you adjust each beat independently.
12. Repeat Steps 5-11 as needed.

Audio Menu Tempo Commands

Soundbites within DP may or may not contain a tempo map. Audio that is recorded within DP will take on the tempo of the sequence at the time of recording, while audio that is imported will contain a tempo map only if it is present in the original file (for example, an audio file from a "loop" sound library).

Digital Performer's Audio Menu contains a number of tempo commands, shown in Figure 11.14, that allow you to set or change the tempo map for an existing soundbite, force a soundbite to match the sequence tempo (time compressing or expanding it in the process), or changing the sequence tempo to match a soundbite's tempo. These commands give you tremendous control over how audio and your sequences interact with each other, providing you with the flexibility to work with many different audio sources without worrying about their original tempo maps.

Figure 11.14
The Audio menu's various tempo commands.

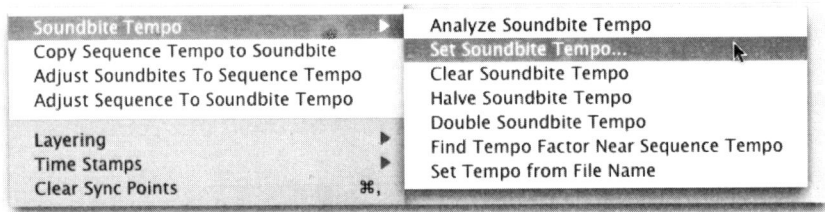

Soundbite Tempos

If a soundbite contains a tempo map, then it will be displayed throughout DP's various windows. The List section of the Soundbites window displays this information in the Tempo and Quarter note columns. If these columns are blank, then the soundbite does not contain a tempo map (see Chapter 3 for information on the columns within the Soundbites window). Within the Sequence Editor, soundbites with tempo maps are displayed with gray lines, as shown in Figure 11.15. If the tempo map matches the sequence's tempo, these gray lines will line up with the Sequence Editor's Time Ruler. If the tempo map is different, however, these lines will change from gray to red, and will not line up with the sequence's Time Ruler (see Figure 11.16).

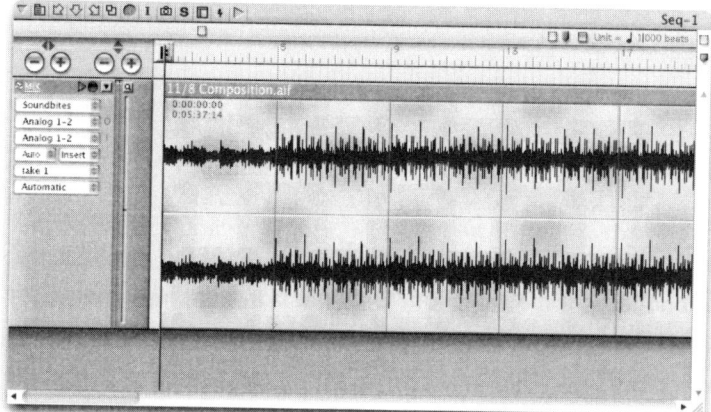

Figure 11.15

If a soundbite contains a tempo map that matches the sequence's tempo, it will be displayed with a gray line.

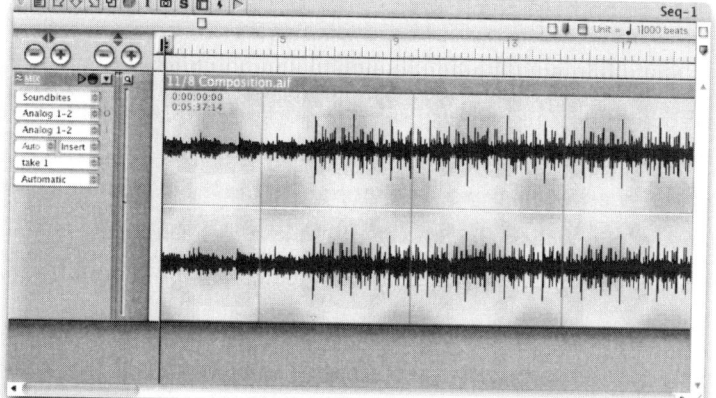

Figure 11.16

Soundbites that contain tempo maps that do not match the sequence tempo are displayed with red lines. Notice in this example how the lines no longer match the Time Ruler.

Tempo maps can be applied to a soundbite(s) by using the Set Soundbite Tempo or Copy Sequence Tempo to Soundbite commands. These commands will not change the actual audio of the soundbite; they only change the tempo maps associated with the files. Soundbites must contain a tempo map in order for you to take advantage of DP's more advanced time stretching and compression features, such as the Adjust Soundbites to Sequence and Adjust Sequence To Soundbite Tempo commands (these commands are explained later in this chapter).

Set Soundbite Tempo

Use the Set Soundbite Tempo command to define a constant tempo map for a soundbite or selected portion of a soundbite (see Figure 11.17). You must know the duration of the soundbite for this command to work properly. The options provided in the Set Soundbite Tempo command window are as follows:

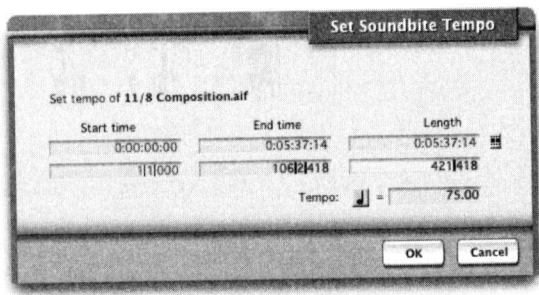

Figure 11.17
The Set Soundbite Tempo window.

- **Start time.** Displays the start time of the selection. This value cannot be edited.
- **End time.** Shows the end time of the selection. Only the bar/beat input fields can be modified.
- **Length.** The duration of the selection is displayed here. Like the End time values, only the bar/beat input fields can be modified.
- **Tempo.** The calculated tempo is displayed here. Once a value is entered in the End time or Length sections, the tempo is automatically calculated for the soundbite. You can also enter a tempo directly into the Tempo field if you wish.

To apply a tempo map to a soundbite with the Set Soundbite Tempo command:

1. Begin by selecting a soundbite. You can also select a portion of a soundbite. Be aware that this command will only work on one soundbite at a time.
2. Open the Set Soundbite Tempo command by choosing Audio > Set Soundbite Tempo.
3. Enter the value for the length of the selected soundbite in quarter notes.
4. Once the information is entered, DP will automatically calculate the tempo for the selection.
5. Click OK.

To remove a tempo map from a soundbite with the Clear Soundbite Tempo command:

1. Begin by selecting a soundbite. You can also select a portion of a soundbite. Be aware that this command will only work on one soundbite at a time.
2. Choose the Clear Soundbite Tempo command and the tempo map will be immediately removed from the soundbite.

Copy Sequence To Soundbite Tempo

Use this option to copy the tempo of a sequence to selected soundbites. This command will affect multiple soundbites, but will not function on portions of a soundbite. The entire soundbite must be selected before this command will function.

To copy the sequence tempo to a soundbite:

1. Begin by selecting a soundbite or soundbites. You must select an entire soundbite, as this command will not work on portions of a soundbite.
2. Choose the proper tempo control from the Control Panel. For example, if you have the Conductor Track selected, any tempo events or custom tempo maps will be copied.
3. Choose Audio menu > Copy Sequence Tempo to Soundbite to copy the sequence tempo to a soundbite.

Adjust Soundbites To Sequence Tempo

Once a soundbite contains a tempo map, you can take advantage of DP's more advanced tempo features. Unlike the previous Audio menu tempo commands, the Adjust Soundbites To Sequence Tempo command will automatically time stretch or compress a selected soundbite to match the sequence tempo. Keep in mind that this will only work on soundbites that contain a tempo map. If a soundbite doesn't have a tempo map, then use the Set Soundbite Tempo command to apply one. Also, set Time Compressing and Expanding option, in the Soundbites window's Info pane, to Allow Time Scale (see Chapter 3).

Adjust Sequence To Soundbite Tempo

This command has the opposite effect from the previous Adjust Soundbites to Sequence Tempo command. It copies the tempo map from a soundbite into the sequence. The new tempo will be copied into the current tempo source (for example, a Tempo Slider or Conductor Track).

Meter

Meter, along with tempo and key, serves as the foundation for modern music (*modern* being a relative term) and recording, determining how music is divided and counted within a song. Meter, displayed as a fraction (for example, 4/4 or 6/8), is made up of two parts, a numerator and denominator. The first (or top) number is the numerator, which tells the musician or writer how many beats will be contained in a measure of music. The second (or bottom) number is the denominator, which represents the beat value. A denominator of 4 is a quarter note, a value of 8 is an eighth note, a value of 2 would be a half note, and so on. So a standard meter of 4/4 tells us that there are four quarter notes within one measure of music; 6/8 would be six eighth notes to a measure, and 5/4 would be five quarter notes to a measure, and so on.

The intricacies of meter and its complex role within music and music theory is beyond the scope of this book, and this section will focus on the functionality of meter as it applies to your Digital Performer projects. Basic use of DP's Change Meter command was briefly discussed at the end of Chapter 4, "Setting Up a New Project"; this section will offer further explanations on the options available in this window, while also discussing more advanced concepts, such as partial measures.

CHAPTER 11 } Arranging

The Change Meter Command

Choose Project menu > Modify Conductor Track > Change Meter to open the Change Meter command window, shown in Figure 11.18. This window provides a number of options for modifying the meter of a sequence; they are as follows:

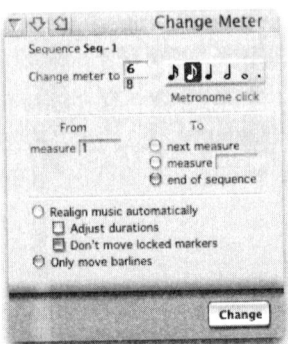

Figure 11.18

The Change Meter command window

- **Change meter to.** Click on the numerator and denominator values to change the meter.
- **Metronome click.** This is the number of clicks within a measure; it also determines how often the transport's Counter will be updated. For example, when a meter of 4/4 is chosen, a value of one quarter note will tell DP to click four times within a measure. Selecting an eighth note would force the metronome to click eight times, and so on.
- **From.** This is the start location for the meter change, indicated in measures.
- **To.** This is the end location for the meter change. The next measure option will tell DP to affect one measure at a time.

  The measure to option will force a meter change up to the measure number entered in this field. Keep in mind that this ending measure will not be included in the change. For example, a meter change starting at measure 1 and ending at measure 9 would change measures 1-8, leaving measure 9 unaffected.

  The end of sequence option will tell DP to apply the meter change from the start measure until the end of the sequence.
- **Realign music automatically.** When this option is enabled (and the Adjust durations option is turned off), DP will automatically delete notes or add rests as needed to force a sequence to adhere to applied meter changes.
- **Adjust durations.** This option can only be enabled when the Realign Music Automatically option is selected. Adjust durations will shorten or lengthen notes to force existing notes to conform to the new meter change. Only notes that fall on the beats affected by the meter change will be modified.
- **Only move barlines.** This option keeps existing music intact and only moves the Time Ruler's bar lines when a meter change is applied.

Applying and Editing Meter Changes

Applying meter changes with the Change Meter command is a fairly straightforward process. Simply open the Change Meter window by choosing Project menu > Modify Conductor Track > Change Meter. Set the new meter, enter the start and end locations, enable any extra options as needed, then choose OK.

Once applied, meter events can be edited within the Conductor Track. See the previous "Conductor Track" section of this chapter for an explanation into the process of editing Conductor Track events.

Partial Measures

Partial measures can occur when meter changes are applied within the middle of an existing measure. How does this happen? Well, meter events within DP will always start a new measure. This is the rule, so if you insert a meter change on beat 4 of a 4/4 measure, DP will insert the meter event and create a new measure at that location. Now you have a situation where the previous measure only contains 3 beats, but still retains a meter marking of 4/4.

Even though partial measures do not have an effect on the actual playback of music, they can be annoying when you're trying to make edits, or can be totally unacceptable when you're working with notation in the QuickScribe Editor. DP provides a few options for correcting partial measures or for preventing them from occurring in the first place.

The most basic way to fix a partial measure is to open up the Conductor Track's Event List and erase the change you previously applied and start over, or to insert a new meter change to "correct" the partial measure. Another way is to have DP automatically correct partial measures for you. Simply enable the Auto Fix-up Partial Measures option within the Preferences window (Setup menu > Preferences). When this option is turned on, DP will automatically move meter changes as needed to prevent partial measures from being created.

Key

Within music, the *key* represents the musical scale that is used in a composition, and is named after the dominant pitch of the scale called the *tonic* (for example, the key of C). So if you are working in the key of C (major or minor), all of the notes within this scale will relate to and gravitate towards the pitch of C. In music of the western hemisphere, key signatures are the combination of flat (b) and sharp (#) symbols that are used to represent a certain key. Musicians and writers who read music could look at a key signature and automatically know which pitches within a scale should be flat or sharp. Of course, this explanation is a simplification of this part of music theory; knowing the available scales and their various forms takes training and practice. Simply put, music notation, along with its key and time signatures, is a visual language that represents music.

Luckily, key signatures within DP only affect the visual representation of notes, so you don't need to know about key signatures and key unless you are working with notation or are preparing to transpose (pitch shift) MIDI and/or audio data.

Within Digital Performer, only one key change event can exist in a single location and will affect all tracks within a sequence (though you can have as many key changes as needed). If a sequence does not contain key change events, then a default key of C will be used. Key changes can only be edited in the Conductor Track (either in the Event List or the Graphic or Sequence Editors) and in the QuickScribe Editor.

The Change Key Command

Digital Performer's Change Key command window (see Figure 11.19) provides options for inserting key change events within a sequence. These options are as follows:

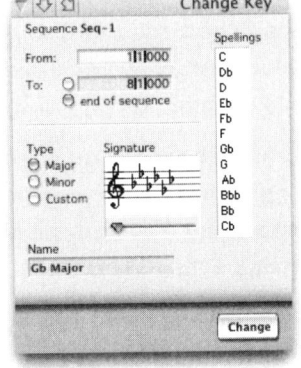

Figure 11.19

The Change Key command window

- **From.** This is the start location for the key change, indicated in bars and beats.
- **To.** This is the end location for the key change. The end of sequence option will tell DP to change the key from the start location to the end of the sequence.
- **Type.** Here you can specify whether the scale is major, minor, or whether you would like to use a custom (modal) scale.
- **Signature.** Use the slider to choose a key signature. The Spellings list will automatically update to reflect the selection.
- **Name.** Displays the default name for the selected key signature. You can type in a new name if you wish; this can be useful when creating custom key signatures (for example, modal keys such as Phrygian, Mixolydian, Dorian, and so on). Names are only used for your reference and will not appear within the key event display in the Conductor Track or Editor windows.
- **Spellings.** The Spellings list provides a table with the existing notes of a selected scale. Use this column to change how notes are "spelled" within a standard key signature (for example, spelling a C as B# or Dbb) or when you are creating custom key signatures.

To apply a key change with the Change Key command:

1. Start by choosing Project menu > Modify Conductor Track > Change Key to open the Change Key window.

2. Set the start and end locations for the key change.
3. Set the key type (Major, Minor, or Custom) and move the slider to select the appropriate key.
4. If necessary, modify the note spellings in the Spellings list and name of the key.
5. Click the Change button and the new key event will be inserted.

> **WHERE KEY CHANGES ARE INSERTED...**
> Be aware that key changes are inserted into the active sequence window/editor or highlighted Chunk window. If a Chunk isn't selected, the key event will be placed in the Play-enabled Chunk. Digital Performer helpfully displays the sequence you will be modifying in the top portion of the Change Key command window.

To edit the key signature of an existing key change event:

1. Navigate to the Conductor Track within the Tracks window and double-click on the key change event. This will open the Event list for the Conductor Track. If you are working in the Graphic Editor, clicking on the Conductor Track's key change event will display the event within the Information bar.
2. Within the Event List, double-click on the key change event. If you are in the Graphic Editor, click on the key signature that appears in the Information bar.
3. The Change Key dialog window will open. This window is identical to the Change Key window, minus the start and end location section (see Figure 11.20).
4. Choose a new key signature and click the OK button.

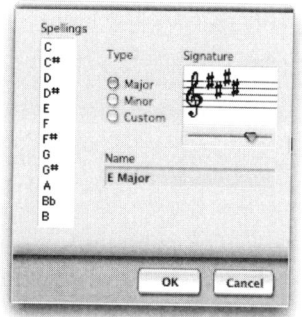

Figure 11.20
The Change Key dialog window is identical to the Change Key command window, minus the start and end location section.

To edit the location of an existing key change event:

1. In the Conductor Track's Event List, double-click on the location of the key change event. The location will become active, allowing you to type in a new value.
2. If you are working in the Conductor Track's Graphic Editor, select the event to display it in the Information bar. Click on the location and enter a new value. You could also horizontally drag the event within the Conductor Track and drop it in a new location. The drag and drop method also works in the Tracks window and Sequence Editor.

CHAPTER 11 } Arranging

Standard editing commands, such as Copy, Cut, and Paste can also be used with key change events. See the previous Conductor Track section of this chapter for related information.

Transposing Audio and MIDI Data

The difference between inserting a key change and transposing audio or MIDI data is huge. Key changes only affect the visual display of notes, while transposing data will change the actual pitch of MIDI and audio data. The Region menu's Transpose command window, shown in Figure 11.21, provides powerful options for controlling how selected MIDI data and soundbites are transposed. Refer to Chapters 9 and 13 for an exploration into the use of the Transpose command.

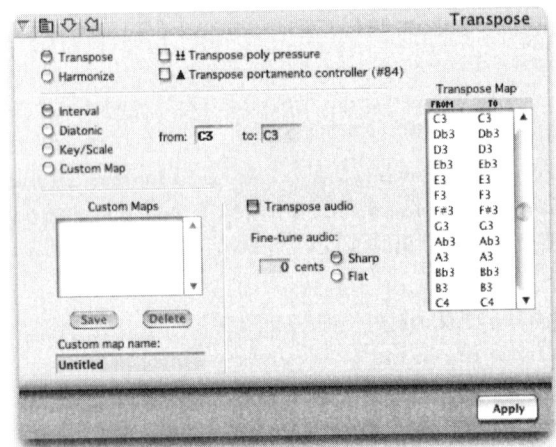

Figure 11.21
The Region menu's Transpose Command allows you to change the pitch of selected MIDI and audio data.

Chunks

Many DP users find the term *Chunk* confusing. What is a Chunk? Well, I'm glad you asked. A *Chunk* can be either a sequence (which is made up of multiple tracks) or a song (which is made up of multiple sequences or other songs). That's it. Sounds too simple, doesn't it? Well, it is, really, once you understand how sequences, Chunks, and songs interact with each other. Now, even though sequences and Chunks are the same thing, you may have noticed throughout the book that I tend to favor one word or the other depending on the situation and topic I'm discussing. Usually, when I'm referring to a single sequence, I use the word *sequence*, and when I'm referring to multiple sequences I will use the word *Chunk*. This is more of a nuance than anything, and some of you power users out there may have a different take on the subject. Regardless, a sequence is a Chunk and a Chunk is a sequence. I'll leave it up to you to decide if it's a "tomayto" or "tomahto."

This section will explain the procedures for managing individual sequences within the Tracks window, and will also discuss the Chunks window, which provides a dedicated location for managing multiple sequences (Chunks) and songs.

Sequences

A *sequence* is basically a container for your audio and MIDI tracks. By default, a new sequence is automatically created when you create a new project. This sequence is called Seq-1 and is displayed in the Control Panel's Sequence menu, shown in Figure 11.22.

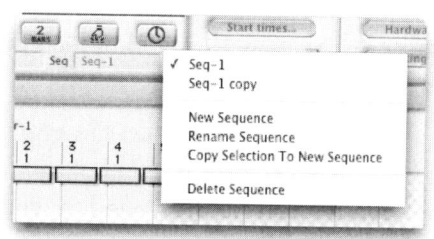

Figure 11.22

The Control Panel's Sequence menu provides options for creating, renaming, and play-enabling sequences.

The Sequence Menu

You can click on this pop-up menu to rename the sequence or create a new one. If multiple sequences already exist, they will be listed within this menu. Simply select a sequence to Play-enable it (that is, to make it the active sequence).

An unlimited number of sequences can exist within a project; the number is only limited by the amount of RAM you have installed within your system. Now read that last sentence again—the amount of RAM dictates the number of sequences you can efficiently have within a project. If you are going to be using multiple sequences (or Chunks) in a project, then make sure you have a ton of memory available to DP.

Incorporating Sequences into Your Workflow

If you look beyond the clear-cut definition of a sequence, you may begin to imagine the various ways you can incorporate the strength of sequences into your production workflow.

A really handy, though sometimes overlooked feature is the Sequence menu's Copy Selection to New Sequence option. This command will take any track selection (including all its current settings) and place it into a new sequence. Simple enough, so what's the big deal? Well, this powerful feature can really help you streamline your entire workflow. The subsections below present a few examples of how you can incorporate this command into the music production process.

> **COPY SELECTION TO NEW SEQUENCE**
>
> The music-production process is a very dynamic and fluid combination of events. In a perfect world, we would move from one stage to another (for example, recording, then editing, then mixing, then mastering). In the real world, however, we find that many of these processes overlap. For example, you may be mixing a tune while you are still performing those last-minute overdubs and edits at 2 AM! When it comes to your studio workflow, flexibility is the key and the Copy Selection To New Sequence command is just one of the many helpful features that DP provides to help you accomplish this goal; it allows you to easily move (arrange) tracks or portions of tracks into separate sequences.

CHAPTER 11 } Arranging

Recording

If you are working on a project that contains multiple songs, such as an album project, you could record each song into a separate sequence instead of recording them into separate projects. This, of course, has its advantages and disadvantages.

The advantages are that you have each song within this single project under one roof, so to speak. If you would like to use a soundbite from one song and place it in another, you can easily do so. You can quickly switch between sequences when you need to, and project management is simplified since all your work is consolidated into a single project.

The disadvantage is that there is a danger in keeping all of your eggs (sequences) in one basket—if the project is corrupted for some reason, you run the risk of losing every sequence contained in the project. However, if you are executing proper backups this shouldn't be a concern. There also is the RAM issue; you'll need plenty of it with this scenario.

Overdubbing

When you're overdubbing, preparing your project to be as responsive and efficient as possible—for example, using low buffer settings, freeing up RAM and CPU—should be a prime concern. How to provide a streamlined recording environment for your performer should be your main focus and priority. Now this can be a problem if you are also in the middle of mixing the material to which you will be overdubbing (with many plug-ins), or if you have a ton of tracks eating up precious CPU and RAM. The Copy Selection to New Sequence feature can be the solution to this problem; read on to find out how.

To use the Copy Selection to New Sequence command during the overdub process:

1. Create a stereo version of your mix by bouncing your tracks to disk or by recording the summed output to a stereo track (make sure you name the track before recording) in real-time.
2. If you're using the Bounce to Disk command, make sure to tell DP to import the bounced file into the current sequence. Name it something appropriate like "2Mix" or "Stereo Mix." At this point, you should have a new stereo track (or multiple tracks) that contains a stereo mix of your song.
3. If latency was introduced during Step 1 because of inserted plug-ins or high buffer settings, trim the beginning off the new file and use the Shift command to shift the track(s) earlier by the amount you want.
4. Select the new stereo file(s) along with the Conductor Track (this is important) and choose Copy Selection to New Sequence from the Sequence menu. The Create Chunk window will

open, allowing you to name the new Chunk. Name it something appropriate, such as Piano Overdubs or Vocal Overdubs. Set the End time to Auto and click OK.

You need the Conductor Track so that your new sequence will retain the same meter, tempo, and any other Conductor Track events.

If you're really organized, you should have already created markers at important song structure locations (for example, the intro, verse, chorus, bridge, outro, and so on). These location points will be copied over with the Conductor Track into the new sequence. Markers are discussed in detail later, in the "Markers" section of this chapter.

5. Now, from the same menu, select the new Overdub sequence and it will become active within the Tracks window. At this point, you should be viewing a streamlined sequence (with freed up RAM and CPU) that only contains the Conductor Track and bounced stereo mix of your song.

6. Next, lower your buffer settings if you need to reduce any monitoring latency. Create your headphone mix, and you're ready to begin recording.

Once you have overdubbed any necessary parts, you're ready to combine your new tracks with the main sequence. To combine your tracks using the "copy" method:

1. Start by selecting all of the new tracks you overdubbed by choosing Edit menu > Select All. The default keyboard shortcut is Command+A. Make a note of the number and type of tracks you are selecting. This is important because you will need to duplicate the track layout in the main sequence in order for the material to be copied over correctly. If you have a combination of different tracks (for example, mono, stereo, and MIDI), you might want to group them together by type by changing the track order. This might make it easier for you when creating the new tracks within the original sequence.

2. Next, press the Shift key and click on the name of the Conductor Track to exclude it from this procedure.

3. Once your tracks are selected, choose Edit menu > Copy (Command+C).

4. Next, choose the main sequence from the Sequence menu.

5. Create the same number of tracks (with the same format, for example, mono or stereo) within this main sequence. Make sure the order of the tracks is exactly like the order within the Overdub sequence.

6. Make sure your new tracks are selected by clicking on their track names.

7. Cue the main counter to the beginning of your sequence and choose Edit menu > Paste (Command+V) to paste the material into the main sequence.

8. Mute the bounced file you created in Step 1, then hit the Space bar to check your work.

CHAPTER 11 } Arranging

CHUNKS WINDOW
Another method for combining tracks from one sequence into another is by using the Chunks window's Song feature. See the "Chunks Window" section of this chapter for an explanation of this procedure.

Arranging
You could also use the steps outlined in the preceding section to split the different sections of your song (the verse, chorus, and so on) into separate parts. Once they are separated into individual sequences, you could use the Chunks window to place them into a song (explained later) to experiment with different versions or arrangements.

Mastering
This is always a very touchy and controversial subject, so I'll start by adding my disclaimer: Mastering should be left up to the professional mastering engineers! They *are* called "mastering" engineers for a reason. It takes many years of training, practice, and the right gear and studio environment to properly master a recording (see Chapter 13 for a continuation of this discussion).

Okay, with that said, the reality is that we DP users sometimes need to use Digital Performer for our mastering needs. As the application was built to function more like a multitrack recorder than a dedicated 2-track recorder, mastering can be a confusing task. How do you set up a DP project for mastering a collection of songs (such as for an album)? One way is through the use of Chunks. Start by placing each song in its own sequence (with its own plug-in chain), and open a separate Track window for each song. Then use the Chunks window (explained next) to quickly switch between them. This setup lets you instantly jump between each song, allowing you to easily check the sonic and dynamic relationships between them.

The Chunks Window

Now that I've covered a few different situations where you might use Chunks within a project, let's take a look at the Chunks window, shown in Figure 11.23.

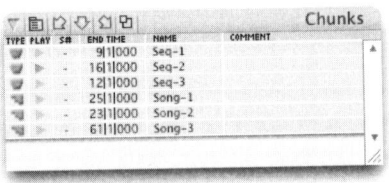

Figure 11.23
The Chunks window. In this example, the first three items are Chunks and the last three items are songs. Notice the different icons that are used to represent them. Only one song or Chunk can be Play-enabled at a time.

The Chunks window can be accessed by choosing Project menu > Chunks, or by using the default keyboard shortcut Shift+C. You can also click on the first button in the Control Panel's Quick Access Drawer (refer to Chapter 3). The main area of the Chunks window lets you specify the

※ Chunks

order of existing Chunks or songs, Play-enable a specific Chunk/song, enter comments, and set song select numbers for cueing Chunks from a MIDI controller.

The options included in the Chunks window are as follows:

- **Type**. This column displays the Chunk or song icon. Chunk icons are yellow and song icons are purple.
- **Play**. This column indicates which Chunk or song is currently Play-enabled. Only one item can be Play-enabled at a time.
- **S#**. This is the Song Select Number column, which is the number from 1-127 that can be assigned to a song or Chunk so that it can be cued from your MIDI controller. If the column contains a dash, then there is no song select number assignment. Playback order is also based on its placement within the list, so if a Chunk or song contains the same number, DP will play back the top-most item in the list first. Be aware that your MIDI controller must be able to send a Song Select message in order to take advantage of this feature.
- **End Time**. This is the end time of the Chunk. When this is set to Auto End Time, the measure after the last full measure of the Chunk is used and cannot be edited from this column. If it's set to manual (which can be done by selecting the Chunk and choosing the mini-menu's Auto/manual End Time option), the end time will be displayed in bold and can be edited directly in this column.
- **Name**. This column shows the name of the Chunk. Option-click to rename a Chunk.
- **Comment**. Click on the Comment column to enter comments for a specific Chunk.

The Chunks window's mini-menu options, shown in Figure 11.24, are as follows:

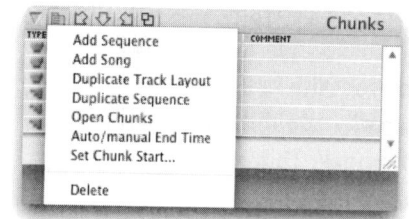

Figure 11.24

The Chunks window's mini-menu.

- **Add Sequence**. This option creates a new sequence. Holding down the Option key before opening up the mini-menu will allow you to create multiple sequences at once.
- **Add Song**. This option creates a new song. Holding down the Option key before opening up the mini-menu will allow you to create multiple songs at once.
- **Duplicate Track Layout**. Once a Chunk is selected, this command will become available. This option will create a blank sequence with the exact track layout as the selected Chunk.
- **Open Chunks**. This option will open separate Tracks windows for selected Chunks, and separate Song windows for selected songs.

281

CHAPTER 11 } Arranging

- **Auto/manual End Time**. Use this option to toggle a Chunk's end time to be either auto or manual. Only manual end times can be pop-edited in the main Chunks window.

- **Set Chunk Start**. This option will open the Set Chunk Start window, shown in Figure 11.25, where you can change the actual start time for the selected Chunk. This is the same window you see when clicking on the Start Times button in the Control Panel's Tempo Control Drawer.

- **Delete**. This option will delete selected Chunks.

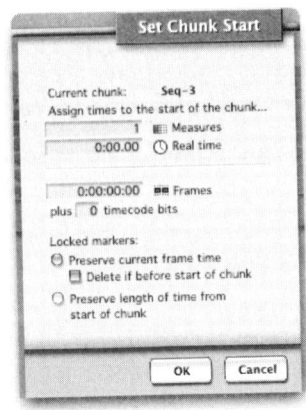

Figure 11.25
The Set Chunk Start Time window allows you to change the start time for a Chunk. This window allows you to even set negative start times, such as measure -1.

Controlling Chunks

The Control Panel contains a number of features that control the playback of Chunks within a DP project. (Refer to Chapter 3 for a detailed look at the Control Panel.) Keep in mind that all of these features cannot provide smooth playback transitions between each Chunk, but you can use DP's Song feature to accomplish this (I'll explain how to do that later).

Cueing and Chaining Chunks

The Control Panel's Memory bar provides buttons for controlling the playback of Chunks within DP (see Figure 11.26). The Cue Chunks button—the first button in the Memory Bar—will automatically cue the next Chunk within the Chunks window for playback. This is why the order of the Chunks within the Chunks list is so important. If you would like to use this feature, then make sure you have your Chunks in the correct playback order. You can rearrange the Chunks by simply grabbing the Chunks icon and dragging it to the desired location.

Figure 11.26
The first two buttons within the Control Panel's Memory Bar control the playback of Chunks within DP.

The second button, Chain Chunks, will cause the next Chunk to automatically play back when the end of the current Chunk is reached. If you require a pause between the playback of one Chunk into another, simply change the end time of the first Chunk by the amount you want. Remember you will need to set the end time to manual to accomplish this.

When using the Cue Chunks or Chain Chunks features, the Memory Bar's Start and End Time settings will update to show the start and end times for the current Chunk. In addition, the Time Ruler will display the start and end barline markers (see Figure 11.27), which offer a visual representation of where and when the Chunk will start and end playback. You can drag these barlines to new locations in order to quickly change when playback of the current Chunk will begin and end.

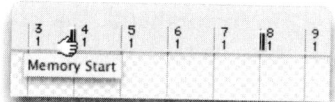

Figure 11.27
Drag the start and end barlines within the Time Ruler to quickly change when playback will begin and end for the current Chunk.

Selecting the Previous and Next Chunk
Use the Control Panel's Skip buttons to quickly move to the previous and next Chunk within the Chunks window. Once clicked, playback of the current Chunk will be interrupted and the next or previous Chunk will automatically begin playback.

Songs

The Songs window provides an environment for combining Chunks together. They can be daisy-chained for seamless playback, stacked for simultaneous playback, or a combination of both. Why would you need to do any of this? Well, let's go back to our previous "arranging" scenario. You could take an existing sequence and break the major sections (the intro, verse, chorus, and so on) into separate Chunks, then use the Song window to arrange them in different orders to audition multiple versions of your song. Maybe you find that verse-verse-chorus works better than verse-chorus-verse. You could also create smaller Chunks (say a four-bar pattern) of various instruments (drums, bass, keyboard riffs, and so on) and use the Song window to construct a song. Once your arrangement has been created, you can even merge your song (with its multiple Chunks) into a single Chunk. The possibilities are endless.

The Song Window
The Song window provides a flexible grid for arranging Chunks. Remember that a Chunk can also be a song, so it's entirely possible to have a song nested within another song (see Figure 11.28). Chunks will appear as a blue bar with the Chunk icon located in top middle portion of the Chunk. Songs will appear as dark green bars, also with the song icon as an identifier. Selected Chunks and songs will always be highlighted yellow.

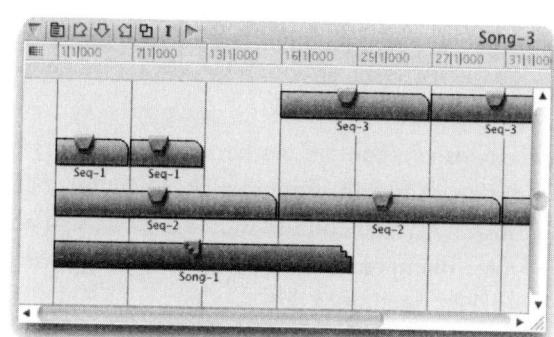

Figure 11.28
The Song window can contain sequence Chunks and song Chunks.

CHAPTER 11 } Arranging

The Chunk Grid is fairly easy to comprehend. The grid is divided into columns, or placement guides, that are represented by blue lines. When a song is created, a column is automatically placed at the beginning of the Song window. Columns must exist in order for a Chunk to be placed at a specific location. For example, if you want to place your first Chunk at measure 8, you will need to manually insert a column at measure 8, as the only column will exist at measure 1/1/000. Be aware that DP will automatically delete manually inserted columns if a Chunk does not exist in that location. Be sure to place a Chunk in that location before DP redraws the Chunk Grid.

To insert a column:

1. Click the Insert button in the Song window's title bar (located to the left of the Auto Scroll button, represented with a letter I). The Insert Column window, shown in Figure 11.29, will open.
2. Enter a value of **8** in the measure section. Click OK. Your new column will appear at measure 8.
3. Now you can drag and drop a Chunk at that location. Once placed on the grid, DP will automatically insert another column at the end of the new Chunk.

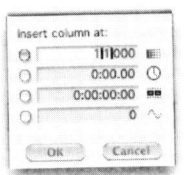

Figure 11.29

The Insert Column window. Four different time formats allow you to insert columns at precise locations.

To place a Chunk within the Chunk Grid:

1. Start by creating a grid column at the location you wish to place the Chunk. If you need to place the Chunk at the beginning, don't worry about this step. DP automatically places a grid column at the start of the Song window (measure 1/1/000).
2. Drag and drop a Chunk from the Chunks window into the Song window's Chunks Grid. Again, if there aren't any columns available, then the Chunk will be placed at the start of the song. Besides vertical grid columns, the Song window is also divided into Chunk rows. These rows are invisible, but allow you to horizontally stack Chunks so they can play back simultaneously depending on their vertical locations.
3. To change the location of this Chunk, simply drag it to a new location (remember to insert a column if one isn't present already).

Markers in the Song Window

Just like a normal sequence, songs can contain markers. Song markers appear beneath the Song window's Time Ruler. Markers not only provide organizational benefits, but they will also automatically create grid columns at their locations. You can use markers when you need to create multiple grid columns without the fear of them being removed by DP. For an explanation of Digital Performer's markers feature, see the "Markers" section of this chapter.

Chunks

To place a marker in the Song window:

1. With the Song window active and in the foreground, open the Marker window (Shift+K).
2. Click on the marker's mini-menu and choose ADD.
3. Once you've created the marker, type in the desired location in the marker's Measure column. Your marker will be placed in the correct location along with a blue grid column.
4. To delete these markers, select the marker within the Marker window and choose Delete.

When working with song and Chunk markers in DP, you can delete any markers that are duplicated between your song and a selected Chunk.

To delete duplicate markers:

1. Start by selecting a Chunk(s).
2. Open the Song window's mini-menu and choose Delete Markers. Any song markers that are identical to the selected Chunk's markers will be removed.

Markers can also be merged between selected Chunks and placed in the Song window.

To merge Chunk markers:

1. Start by selecting the Chunks that contain the markers you wish to merge.
2. Open the Song window's mini-menu and choose Merge Markers. The merged markers will be copied into the Song window.

Mini-menu

I've already covered some of the mini-menu's features, but the mini-menu includes some additional controls (see Figure 11.30) that can allow you to dive deeper into the Song window.

Figure 11.30
The Song window's mini-menu provides options for controlling songs and their related Chunks.

* **Copy Conductor Tracks.** This option copies the Conductor Track from a selected Chunk into the Song window. If multiple Chunks are selected, DP will use the top-most Chunk when copying.
* **Edit Conductor Track.** Opens the Event List or Graphic Editor for the Song's Conductor Track.
* **Record Enable Conductor Track.** Record-enables the Song window's Conductor Track so you can record tap tempo data. See the "Tempo" section of this chapter for an explanation of tap tempo.

- **Insert Column.** This option will open the Insert Column window. It is identical to the title bar's Insert button (I).
- **Set Record Sequence.** Toggles the Record-enable button for a selected Chunk. This feature allows you to record into a selected sequence while hearing playback of the entire song.
- **Merge Markers.** This option merges the markers of selected Chunks and places them into the Song window.
- **Delete Markers.** This option will delete Markers that are duplicated between a song and selected Chunk(s).
- **Merge Chunks to Sequence.** Use this command to combine selected Chunks into a single Chunk. When you choose this option, the Merge Chunks window will open and present you with two options (see Figure 11.31). The Copy all tracks option will copy all of the tracks of the selected Chunks and place them into a new sequence. The Merge Tracks with Identical Names option is identical to the previous Merge Chunks to Sequence option except that it merges tracks that have the same names. Both options will place the new sequence in the Chunks window.
- **Time ruler settings.** Here you can enable the listed time formats and they will appear in the Song window's Time Ruler.

Controlling Songs

Just as with a "normal" sequence or Chunk, DP allows you to playback, record into, and edit songs.

To playback a song:

1. Click on the song's Play-enable button in the Chunks window.
2. Press the Space bar.
3. You can also select the song within the Control Panel's Sequence menu.

To record audio or MIDI data into a song:

1. Double-click on the song in the Chunks window to open the Song window.
2. Double-click to select the Chunk you wish to record into. It will be opened in the Tracks window. Notice that there aren't any Record-enable buttons.
3. Choose Set Record Sequence from the Song window's mini-menu to record-enable the selected Chunk. You should see the Chunk icon display a red dot, indicating that the Chunk is record-enabled. The Record-Enable buttons for each track within the Chunk will also become visible.
4. Arm the necessary tracks and proceed with the normal recording procedure.
5. When you are through recording and have stopped the transport, return to the Song window's mini-menu and choose Set Record Sequence to toggle off or disable the Chunk's recording capabilities.

To record Tap Tempo data into a song's Conductor Track:

1. Double-click on the song in the Chunks window to open the Song window.
2. From the mini-menu choose Record Enable Conductor Track. This will arm the Song's Conductor Track and will be indicated by a check mark next to this option.
3. Double-click the Control Panel's Slave to External Sync button. The Slave to External Sync option will be enabled and the Receive Sync window will open.
4. In the Receive Sync window, select the Tap Tempo option. Choose the Tap Tempo options you want and click OK.
5. Click the Record button and start tapping (see the "Tap Tempo" section of this chapter for a detailed look into the procedure).
6. Click the Stop button when you are finished.
7. Return to the Song window's mini-menu and click the Record Enable Conductor Track option to toggle off this feature.

To edit Chunks in the Song window:

1. Double-click on the song in the Chunks window to open the Song window.
2. Select the Chunk you wish to modify and apply the necessary command from the Edit menu (Cut, Copy, Paste, Erase, Select All, or Undo). The results of each command are identical to DP's standard Editor windows.
3. When using the Paste command, you will need to click with the mouse to tell Digital Performer where you would like to paste the selected Chunk.

Looping

Digital Performer's looping feature allows you to loop or repeat selected regions in a track(s). Each track has its own independent loop capabilities, allowing you to set different loops for different tracks. Loops can even be nested within another loop. DP's looping capabilities provide a more efficient use of your Mac's resources than the more standard approach of copying and pasting the same region multiple times. In addition, you can quickly execute modifications to a loop, as you only have to change the loop points of the region. If you used the Copy-Paste method, you would have to edit multiple regions to make any changes.

There are three components that define a loop: the start point, the end point, and the number of repetitions. Loops within a track are indicated with a Loop icon, as shown in Figure 11.31. The length of the loop indicator (either

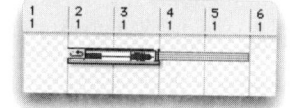

Figure 11.31

Regions within a track will appear with a Loop icon. These icons are only visual markers to indicate that a loop is present and cannot be edited directly within a track.

CHAPTER 11 } Arranging

a gray bar or a gray bar with solid lines) identifies the duration of the loop and points to where the region will begin repeating. Audio or MIDI data that appears below the loop indicator bar will not playback and will be ignored by DP.

Region Menu Commands

There are numerous ways to insert a loop: You can use the Region menu's Set Loop command, the Event List's Insert Button (I), or the Loop tool. The Set Loop command differs from the other methods in that it is global and will allow you to insert a loop regardless of the window you are working in.

To insert a loop with the Set Loop command:

1. Begin by selecting the region or regions you wish to loop. Keep in mind that the length of your selection will also define the amount of data that will be looped. For example, if a region is two bars long but you make a time range selection of four bars (which includes the two-bar region), DP will loop the entire four-bar selection. So you will essentially be looping the two bars of music along with two bars of silence. In addition, you can make selections across multiple tracks to set multiple track loops with one command.

2. Choose Region menu > Set Loop. The Set Loop window, shown in Figure 11.32, will open.

3. Set the start and end points for the loop. The initial values that appear will be based on the time range selection you made in Step 1, so depending on your needs, you may not have to change these values.

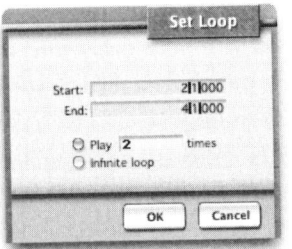

Figure 11.32

The Set Loop window

4. Set the number of repeats for the loop. The Play ___ Times option will let you enter a specific value. The Infinite loop option will force the selection to loop indefinitely.

5. Click OK. The selection will update and appear with the loop icon indicating that the region is looping.

To remove a loop with the Clear Loop command:

1. Select the region that contains the loop.
2. Choose Region menu > Clear Loop. The loop will be removed.

Event List

Loops can also be managed from the Event List. Unlike the Region menu commands, which will allow you to only create and delete loops, the Event List also lets you edit existing loop parameters and will display nested loops if any are present.

To insert or delete a loop in the Event List:

1. Select the region or regions you wish to loop.
2. Press Shift+E to open the Event List.
3. Click on the title bar's Insert button (the I icon) and choose Loop.
4. The Start point setting will appear, allowing you to enter a start value.
5. Tab to the End Point pop-up field and enter the loop's end point.
6. Tab to the Repeat pop-up field and enter the number of repetitions for the loop.
7. Press Return to confirm the settings. The Event List will display the location of the loop and the loop settings. The notes or soundbites being looped will be listed below the Loop event.
8. To remove the loop, select the Loop event within the Event List and press the Delete key.

To edit a loop in the Event List:

1. With the looped region selected and the Event List open, click on the parameter you wish to modify. The setting will appear, allowing you to make the necessary changes.
2. Once modified, press the Return key to confirm the change.

The Loop Tool

With the Loop tool, you can insert a loop directly into the Sequence, Graphic, or Drum Editor. The loop settings will appear in the Editor's Information bar and you can simply click on a setting to edit the values.

To insert or edit a loop in the Sequence Editor:

1. Activate the Loop tool by double-tapping the L key.
2. Click at the beginning of the desired region and drag to the right, stopping at the end of the region. Notice that a gray bar appears at the end of the selection (see Figure 11.33). This represents the duration of the loop—where the region will begin to repeat and where it will end.

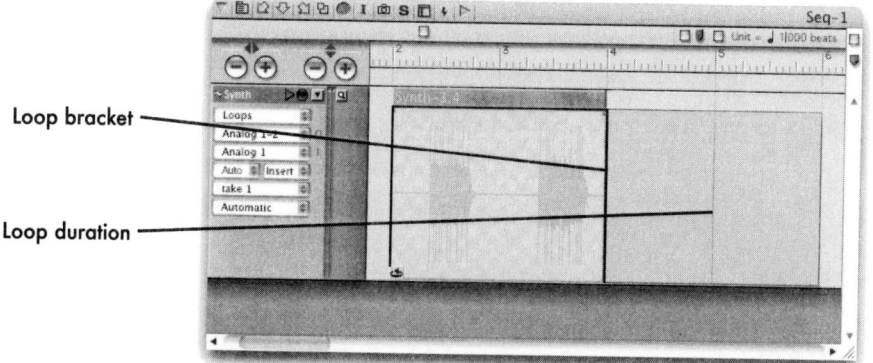

Figure 11.33

The Loop icon indicates the beginning of a loop, while a loop bracket designates the loop end point. The gray bar that appears after the loop bracket shows the duration of the loop.

3. The loop settings will also appear in the Editor's Information bar when the loop is selected. To change a value, simply click on the setting to edit it.
4. You can also change the loop start and end points directly in the track by dragging on the beginning loop icon or the ending loop bracket. The loop duration, however, can only be changed within the Information bar.

To insert or edit a loop in the Graphic Editor:
1. Activate the Loop tool by double-tapping the L key.
2. In the Marker Strip (located below the Time Ruler), click at the desired location and drag to the right, stopping where you wish the end loop point to be. Notice that a gray bar (with solid lines) appears at the end of the selection (see Figure 3.34). This bar represents the duration of the loop—where the region will begin to repeat and where it will end.

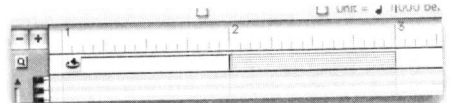

Figure 11.34
A loop within the Graphic Editor's Marker Strip.

3. The loop settings will also appear in the Editor's Information bar when the loop is selected. To change a value, simply click on the setting to edit it.
4. You can also change the loop start and end points directly in the Marker Strip by dragging on the beginning loop icon or the ending loop bracket. The loop duration, however, can only be changed within the Information bar.

To insert or edit a loop in the Drum Editor:
1. Open the Drum Editor (Shift+D) and activate the Loop tool by double-tapping the L key.
2. Drag with the Loop tool in the Note Grid row that appears with the track name (see Figure 3.35). All other edit procedures are identical to those concerning the Graphic Editor, described previously.

Figure 11.35
To insert a loop within the Drum Editor, drag with the Loop tool in the grid row that contains the track name.

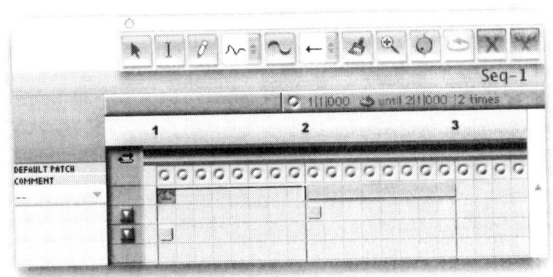

Clipping Windows

Clipping windows in Digital Performer (see Figure 11.36) are like containers for holding anything to which you would like to have quick access. A clipping can be an audio or MIDI file, an FX chain consisting of your favorite plug-ins, sequences, and even text documents, web links, or entire folders located on your Mac's hard drives.

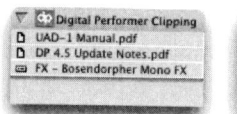  

Figure 11.36

The Digital Performer Clipping windows (from left to right): a Digital Performer Clipping window, a Project Clipping window, and a Startup Clipping window.

There are three types of clipping windows in Digital Performer: Digital Performer clippings, which are global and can be accessed from within a DP project, and project clippings, which are saved and closed with the specific project they were created in.

- **Digital Performer.** This Clipping window is global and can be accessed within any DP project.
- **Project.** This Clipping window is project specific and can only be opened in the project it was created in.
- **Startup.** Introduced in DP 4.5, this Clipping window is used to hold aliases of other documents that will automatically launch when a project is opened. Startup Clipping windows are project specific, allowing you to launch different documents or applications with specific DP projects. Keep in mind that the Startup Clipping windows, like the other Clipping windows, can also contain normal MIDI and audio data.

How can you use clippings in your everyday workflow? Well, let's say you're working on a film score and you have created a recurring theme that consists of four tracks of strings. You want to be able to get to this composition quickly without having to import audio or load a sequence every time you need it, so all you do is copy your string tracks into a Digital Performer clipping and it instantly becomes available in any DP project on your computer.

Clipping Data Icons

Items that are placed in a Clipping window are given their own icons, allowing you to quickly determine the type of data that is held in the window:

- **Audio.** Soundbites will appear with a single or double waveform icon, depending on their format (mono or stereo). If the audio is grouped as a sequence, however, it will appear with a note icon.
- **Track data.** Track data is represented by an eighth note icon and consists of MIDI data, Conductor Track information, and/or entire sequences (containing track data).

CHAPTER 11 } Arranging

- **Plug-ins.** Individual plug-ins and plug-in chains are indicated by a small bar with dotted lines.
- **Documents.** Page icons represent documents.
- **Folders.** Folders will appear with folder icons.

Creating, Opening, and Managing Clippings

The Project menu's Clippings submenu (Project menu > Clippings) allows you to create new Clipping windows or access existing ones. Once a Clipping window is open, commands for deleting and changing the viewing options for the active Clipping window will become available (see Figure 11.37).

Figure 11.37
The Project menu's Clippings submenu provides options for creating, deleting, opening, and managing the viewing options of clippings.

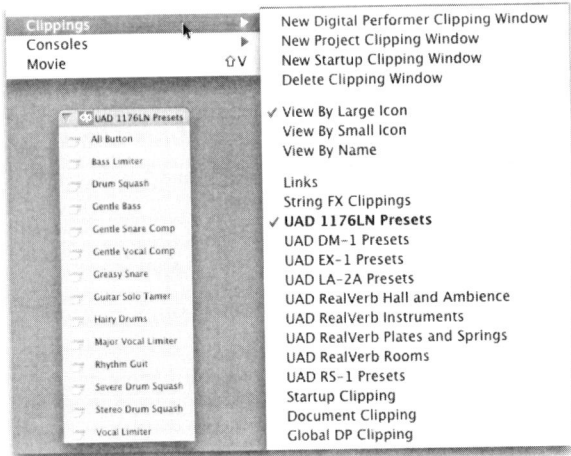

To create a new Clipping window:

1. Choose Project menu > Clippings, and select the type of clipping you wish to create (Project, Digital Performer, or Startup).
2. Name the clipping and press the Return key to confirm the change.

To open or delete an existing Clipping window:

1. Choose Project menu > Clippings, and select the Clipping window you wish to open from the list.
2. To delete an existing Clipping window, repeat Step 1. Click the Clipping window to make it active.
3. Choose Project menu > Clippings > Delete Clipping Window.

To change the order of clippings within a Clipping window:

1. Open the desired Clippings window.
2. Place the cursor over a clipping and a hand icon will appear. Click and drag the clipping to the desired position.

To delete a clipping:

1. Open the desired Clippings window.
2. Click on the desired clipping and press the Delete key.

Where Clippings Are Stored

Clipping windows are actually folders and are stored in the project's Clippings folder (Project folder > Clippings folder), or in the case of Digital Performer clippings, in the User Library Preferences folder (User > Library > Preferences > MOTU Clippings). Once you realize that clipping windows are actually folders on your hard drive, you can actually manage them directly within these locations. Creating a folder within the actual Clippings folder will create a new Clipping window that is accessible in Digital Performer. In addition, clipping folders are dynamic and will automatically update in DP if they are changed at the Project or Preference folder level.

> **ADDING FOLDERS TO THE PROJECT CLIPPINGS FOLDER**
> Adding a folder directly to the project Clippings folder will result in a standard Project Clipping window being created in that project. Startup Clipping windows can only be created by using the New Startup Clipping window command (Project menu > Clippings > New Startup Clipping window).

Adding Audio and MIDI Data

A soundbite and any data that is contained within a track (for example, audio, MIDI, and Conductor Track data) can be added to a Clipping window by dragging it from a track or Soundbites window into the Clipping window. An item that is dragged individually into the Clipping window will appear as its own clipping. If you make a selection of multiple track items and drag them into the Clippings window, however, they will appear grouped as a single sequence or clipping.

You can also select data and choose Edit menu > Copy to Clipping window or use the keyboard shortcut Command+Option+C, which will copy the selected data to the last Clipping window you copied data to.

CHAPTER 11 } Arranging

Saving Plug-in Settings

Plug-ins can also be placed within a Clippings window. This is an incredibly useful feature, as it allows you to take an FX chain, for example, copy it into a global Digital Performer Clipping window, and access it within other projects.

To save a plug-in chain as a clipping:

1. Start by creating or opening a Digital Performer Clipping window.
2. Open the Mixing Board and select the plug-in from the Inserts section. Shift-click to select multiple plug-ins.
3. Drag the plug-in chain into the Clipping window. DP will automatically name the new clipping according to the plug-ins that you added.
4. You can rename the clipping by Option-clicking.

Documents, Folders, and URLs

Documents, folders, and URLs can also be added to a Clippings window for quick access. Think of these clippings as shortcuts to your favorite items or Web sites. To add a document or folder, simply drag the item into the Clippings window, or add an alias of the item directly into the project Clippings folder or MOTU Clippings folder. Remember that you can place these items in any type of Clipping window. If you need certain documents or applications to automatically launch when you open a project, use the Startup Clipping feature.

URLs cannot be added by dragging them directly into a Clipping window. You will need to drag the address from your Web browser into the project's Clippings folder or the MOTU Clippings folder instead.

Markers

The Markers window offers you a quick way of navigating to specific points within your Digital Performer projects. Markers are also referred to as *memory location points* or simply *locate points*. Users working with standard multitrack recorders—whether they are digital or analog—are probably already familiar with this very common, yet indispensable feature. In addition to offering navigational benefits, markers can be given custom names in order to help identify various sections of a project, can be used to quickly make time range selections, and can be recorded in real-time, making the process of setting up cues for film and video scores a simpler process.

Marker Basics

Before we dive into the actual use of markers, let's take a look at the interface (see Figure 11.38). The Markers window can be accessed by

- choosing Project menu > Markers,
- using the default keyboard shortcut Shift+K, or
- clicking on the chevron button in the Control Panel's Quick Access Drawer.

Located in the Marker title bar are standard controls for collapsing, resizing, and auto-scrolling. Markers that have been created are listed in the main body of the window, with basic columns describing the marker's name and location as well as any comments about the marker. The interface also includes advanced features that allow you to configure markers to be included within the mini-menu's powerful Find Tempo Command (see Chapter 14, "Notation and Scoring").

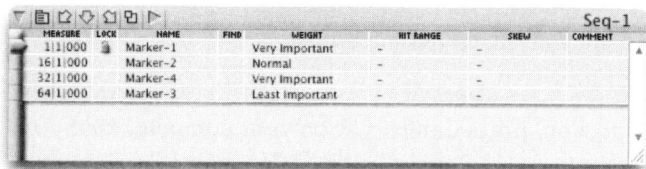

Figure 11.38

The Markers window

To create or add a marker:

1. Open the Markers window by pressing Shift+K.
2. Click on the mini-menu and choose Add. A marker will be created at the current counter position with a default name of Marker-1.
3. Click on the yellow position indicator (located to the left of the Measure column) to instantly locate to that marker position.

> **THE MARKER BIN**
> When working in the Tracks window, you can drag a track from the Marker Bin to quickly add a marker to the Time Ruler (see Figure 11.39).

Figure 11.39

Markers are indicated by a yellow chevron icon and will appear globally throughout DP's various Event and Editor windows. The Tracks window's Marker Bin (the chevron icon in the top right corner) allows you to drag markers into the Time Ruler.

Once a marker has been created, it will appear throughout DP's Track Event and Editor windows. A marker will be displayed with a yellow chevron icon along with its name (see Figure 11.39).

To change the name of an existing marker:

1. Option-click the name of a marker within the Tracks or Markers window to change its name.
2. Press the Return key to confirm the change.

To change the location an existing marker:

- Open the Markers window and click a value in the Measure column to edit the location.
- Within an Editor window, simply click and drag the marker to a new location.

Creating Markers on the Fly

Digital Performer also allows you to create markers while you listen to a track by pressing the default keyboard shortcut Control+M during playback, or by using the mini-menu's Record Hits feature. In order to take advantage of this latter feature, however, you must have a MIDI controller attached to your DP system.

To add markers on the fly from your computer keyboard:

1. Begin playback.
2. At the desired time location, press Control+M on your computer keyboard to insert a marker on the fly.

To add markers on the fly with the Record Hits feature:

1. Begin by cueing up the playback cursor to the location at which you want to begin playback.
2. Open the Marker window and choose Mini-menu > Record Hits. The Record Hits window (see Figure 11.40) will open.
3. Choose whether the markers will be locked or unlocked.

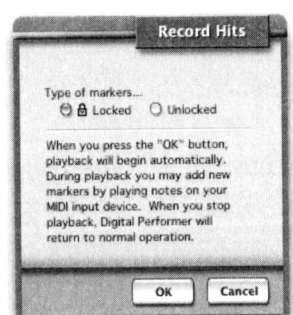

Figure 11.40

The Record Hits window.

LOCKED VERSUS UNLOCKED MARKERS

Markers that are *locked* will be anchored to an SMPTE frame location. This will force the marker to retain that SMPTE frame location even if the tempo is changed; this is handy for post-production work, where you may want markers to remain locked to a specific scene within a movie. An *unlocked* marker will be anchored to its Bar/Beat location. Click on a marker's Lock column in the Marker window to toggle its locked state.

4. Click OK and playback will automatically begin.
5. Press any note on your MIDI controller to add a marker at that location.
6. Press the Space bar to halt playback.

Quantizing Markers

When you use the Record Hits feature, your marker location may be a little off—some markers may be early, while others may be late. You could manually move each marker by dragging it with the mouse or by typing in a new value in the Markers window, but there is an easier way.

The Quantize window isn't just for quantizing MIDI data or soundbites. Hidden within the Quantize window's Custom menu is an option to also quantize markers, allowing you to precisely align markers to a specified bar/beat grid or absolute time location. Of course, this isn't a solution to all your marker-location problems—it may be only appropriate for situations in which you want selected markers to snap to specific beats, such as the downbeats of measures. See the "MIDI Editing" section in Chapter 10 for a detailed look at the Quantize window.

To quantize selected markers:

1. Click and drag in the Marker window to select the markers you wish to quantize.
2. Open the Quantize window by pressing Command+0.
3. Click on the What to Quantize button and choose Custom.
4. Make sure the Markers option is enabled.
5. Select the Grid value, specify any options, and click Apply. The selected markers will instantly snap to the specified Grid value.

Recalling Markers

Besides clicking on a marker's position indicator in the Markers window, there are different ways to navigate to a specific marker location.

* You can click on the Marker menu in the Tracks window (located to the right of the Sequence menu) and choose a marker.
* Click on the Marker menu in the Control Panel (located to the left of the Current Meter value) and choose a marker
* Use the Go-To-Marker window, as shown in Figure 11.41

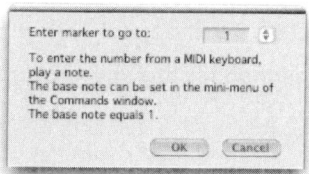

Figure 11.41
The Go-To-Marker window.

CHAPTER 11 } Arranging

To navigate to a marker with the Go-To-Marker window:

1. Use the default keyboard shortcut Shift+Control+M to open the Go-To-Marker window.
2. Click on the Marker menu (the Up and Down Arrow button) and choose a marker. (You can also type the marker number directly into the field control.) Click OK to navigate to the specified marker.
3. You can also use your MIDI controller to specify the marker number by simply pressing the corresponding note.

   You may need to confirm the Numeric Base Note value from the Commands window mini-menu. See the "Commands" section in Chapter 5. If the Numeric Base Note value were set to C3, then pressing C3 on your MIDI controller would recall Marker 1. Pressing C#3 would recall Marker 2, and so on.

Snapping and Shifting Data to a Marker Location

Slightly newer additions to DP4 are the Shift to Marker feature and Snap to Marker command.

To shift selected data to a marker location:

1. Select the data you wish to shift.
2. Open the Shift command window by pressing Command+L (see Figure 11.42).
3. Choose Shift to Time or Marker from the pop-up menu.
4. Select the marker you wish to shift to from the Marker pop-up menu.
5. Click OK. The selected material will be moved to the specified marker location.

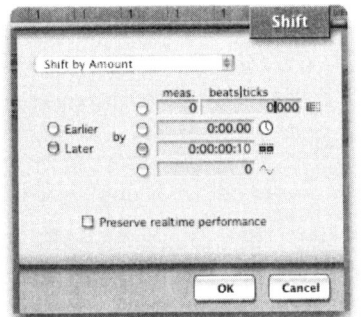

Figure 11.42

The Shift command window.

To snap data to a marker location:

1. Open the Sequence Editor's (or Graphic Editor's) mini-menu and turn on the Snap to Markers feature. Once enabled, it will appear with a check mark.
2. Now any notes or soundbites that are dragged near a marker will "snap" to the marker location.

Selecting with Markers

Markers can also be used to make time-range selections for editing and recording by simply clicking on a marker within a non-Conductor Track. Shift-click to select multiple markers and extend the time-range selection. Once you define a selection, you can use the Memory Bar's Set to Selection Bounds feature (refer to Chapter 3) to set the memory locate points and to define In and Out points for an automated punch (see Chapter 7).

Markers in Post-Production Work
Markers can also be used in more advanced post-production settings when you are working with film and video scores. See the "Scoring for Picture" section of Chapter 14 for a discussion of these complex features.

Summary
Digital Performer provides many powerful tools and feature sets for controlling how your project's sequences, Chunks, and songs behave. Some of these features (such as tempo and meter) form the foundation of your DP projects, while others are there to help streamline your production workflow.

12 } Mixing

Mixing in Digital Performer is mainly accomplished from the Mixing Board (see Figure 12.1). Similar to a traditional mixing console, the Mixing Board provides standard mixing features such as volume and panning, inserts and sends, solos and mutes, automation modes, alternate mixes, access to I/O assignments and mix groups, along with mini-menu features for controlling how the Mixing Board reacts to user commands.

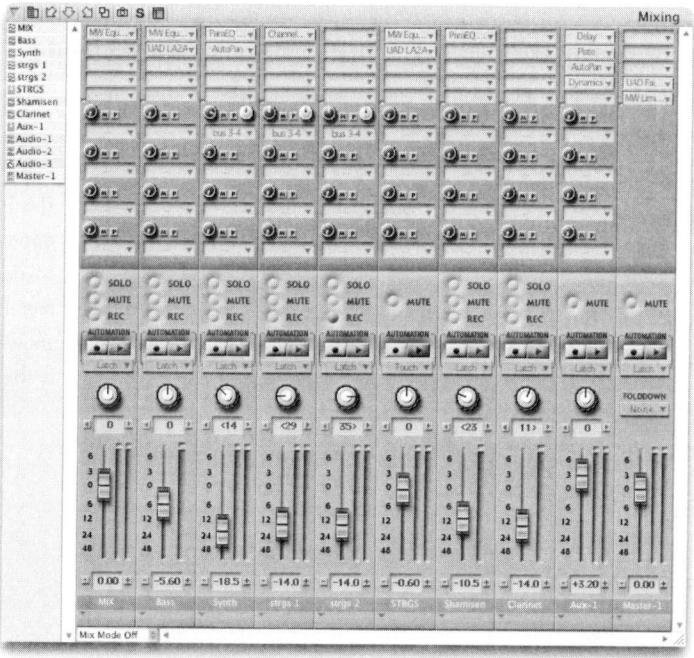

Figure 12.1

Digital Performer's Mixing Board resembles a traditional mixing console and can be customized for specific mixing needs.

CHAPTER 12 } Mixing

Here is a summary of what you'll learn in this chapter:

- How to customize the Mixing Board interface with Board Layouts.
- How to create and manage mix groups.
- How to create and manage alternate mixes.
- How to use Inserts and real-time plug-ins.
- How to use aux tracks for send/returns and submixing.
- How to use DP's mix automation features.

Mixing Board Setup

Digital Performer provides various features for controlling the look and feel of the Mixing Board, allowing you to show or hide the different sections (for example, Inserts, Sends, faders, meters, and so on) in the Track Strips. This allows you to get certain features out of the way when you're not using them. I discussed the actual Mixing Board interface (the mini-menu and Track Strip) in Chapter 3, so let's dive straight into the actual mixing processes. If you need a refresher on the mini-menu options or sections within the Track Strips, refer to Chapter 3 before reading further.

Showing and Hiding Track Strip Sections

A Track Strip's various sections can be shown or hidden from view. Showing or hiding sections affects the Mixing Board globally, meaning it will affect all tracks within the Mixing Board.

To show or hide a section within a Track Strip:

1. Open the Mixing Board by choosing Project menu > Mixing Board. You can also use the default keyboard shortcut Shift+M, or click on the Mixing Board icon in the Control Panel's Quick Access Drawer (see Chapter 3 for more on Quick Access Drawers).

2. Each Track Strip section is listed at the top of the Mixing Board's mini-menu (see Figure 12.2). Click on a section to toggle its visibility on and off. A check mark will indicate whether the section is showing.

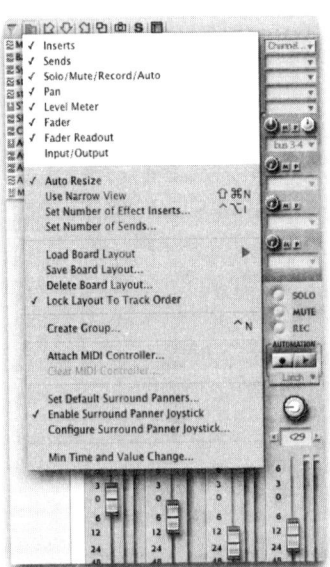

Figure 12.2

The Track Strip sections appear at the top of the Mixing Board's mini-menu. Sections that are showing will appear with a check mark.

3. To show all sections but the one you click on, press and hold the Command key before opening the mini-menu and clicking on the section you want to hide.

4. To hide all sections but the one you click on, press and hold the Option key before opening the mini-menu and clicking on the section you want to show.

The Board Layout Feature

The Board Layout feature is a much-overlooked feature of the Mixing Board; it gives you the ability to save and load different Mixing Board configurations. If you use the Board Layouts feature in conjunction with the previously discussed Show/Hide feature, you can really simplify the viewing process and tailor the Mixing Board to your specific needs. You could, for example, create a board layout that only shows your rhythm tracks, or a layout for using headphone mixes that only contains the Sends section for all of your tracks. The possible combinations are endless.

To save a board layout:

1. Start by configuring the Mixing Board to your liking. Show or hide specific sections from the mini-menu, and show or hide specific tracks within your mix.

2. Once your layout is set, choose the Mixing Board mini-menu > Save Board Layout.

3. Name the layout and click OK (see Figure 12.3).

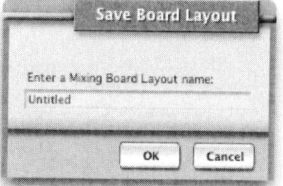

Figure 12.3
The Save Board Layout window.

WHAT'S IN A NAME?
No need to get fancy with your naming schemes. The idea here is to have instant access to different mix configurations so that you can speed up your workflow. Choose something that's direct and to the point (for example, "Headphones" or "Audio Tracks") so you know at a glance what items the layout contains.

To load or rename a board layout:

1. Choose the Load Board Layout submenu from the Mixing Board's mini-menu. You'll be presented with a list that contains your custom board layouts, as well as standard layout presets such as Showing All Tracks, Showing All Sections, and Showing Everything.

2. To rename an existing custom layout, choose the Rename Board Layout option. Select the layout you wish to modify, enter the new name, and click OK (see Figure 12.4).

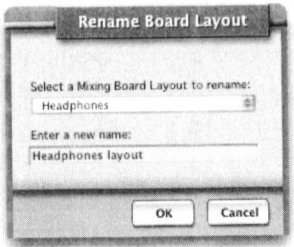

Figure 12.4
The Rename Board Layout window. Choose from the list and rename the configuration.

LOAD BOARD LAYOUT SHORTCUT

Many users tend to overlook the Board Layout feature because they think they must return to the mini-menu every time they need to recall a layout, which can be a tedious affair. I myself ignored the Board Layout feature until I discovered a shortcut: Simply Option-click the name of the sequence within the Mixing Board's title bar (the right-most part of the title bar) and you'll get a drop-down menu of your board layouts that is identical to the mini-menu's Load Board Layout command (see Figure 12.5).

Figure 12.5
Option-click the Mixing Board's title bar to load a board layout.

To delete a board layout:

1. Choose Delete Board Layout from the Mixing Board's mini-menu. The Delete Board Layout window (see Figure 12.6) will open.
2. Select the layout you want to delete and click OK.
3. A warning dialog will open, asking you to confirm the change (see Figure 12.7). Click OK.

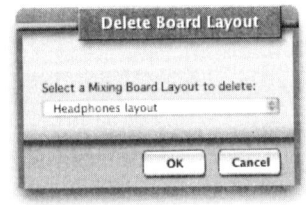

Figure 12.6
The Delete Board Layout window.

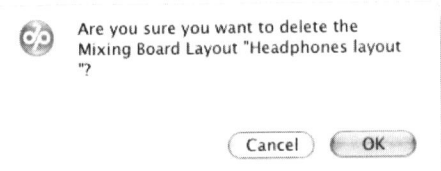

Figure 12.7
The Delete Board Layout warning dialog.

Track Groups

Track Groups (commonly referred to as "groups") are a standard feature of the music production process that let you link, or "group," together selected tracks so that they act as one. You can specify exactly which type of track parameters will be linked together (for example, volume and panning, solos and mutes, and so on). In DP, you can create an unlimited number of Track Groups that can be designated as Mix groups, Edit groups, or a combination of the two (the Edit & Mix option). You can also create specialized custom Track Groups.

Even though track grouping is also used in the editing and arranging processes, we'll discuss Digital Performer's Track Group feature here, as it's especially used during the mixing process.

To create a track group from the Mixing Board:

1. Choose the Mixing Board mini-menu > Create Group. You can also use the keyboard shortcut Control+N.
2. The cursor will change into a large + icon. Click on the faders or pan knobs of the tracks you wish to group together. Selected tracks will be highlighted with a flashing green box.
3. To remove a track from the group selection, Shift-click the track.
4. Once you have selected the tracks you wish to group together, press the Return or Enter key.
5. The New Track Group window will open (see Figure 12.8).
6. From the drop-down menu, choose the group type:
   - **Mix**. Mix groups will link volume, solos and mutes, solo exempt status (Solo Isolate), and automation controls (Automation Play Enable, Record Enable, and Automation modes).

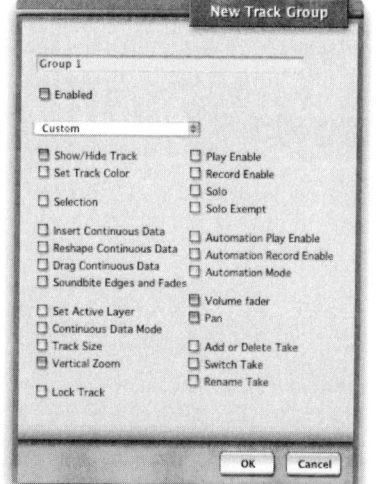

Figure 12.8
The Custom group setting in the New Track Group window lets you pick and choose the specific parameters to link.

   - **Edit**. Edit groups will link time-range selections; the inserting, reshaping, and dragging of continuous data; and Sequence Editor active layer, continuous data mode, track resize and vertical zoom characteristics.
   - **Edit & Mix**. This option will link both Mix and Edit group functions explained above.
   - **Custom**. The Custom option will allow you to choose specific parameters for grouping.

CHAPTER 12 } Mixing

7. Name the group and click OK.
8. Once a parameter is linked, adjusting it on one track will affect the same parameter on all tracks within the group.

> **SHOW AND HIDE TRACK**
> When tracks are grouped together as edit, mix, or edit/mix groups—their show/hide settings will become linked together. Clicking on a track in the Track Selector of a window will show or hide all the tracks within its associated group. To override this feature, create a custom group and disable the Show/Hide Track option.

> **TEMPORARLY OVERRIDING A GROUP**
> When working with tracks that are grouped, you will sometimes need to adjust a setting on only one track. You could delete the group entirely, but that's not a very productive solution to the problem. Instead, temporarily override the group by pressing the Option key before making a parameter adjustment.

> **MODIFY TRACK GROUPS SUBMENU**
> The Project menu's Modify Track Group submenu also allows you to group and ungroup tracks. This is handy for when you're not working in the Mixing Board. You can even temporarily suspend a group with the Suspend Track Grouping option.

The Track Groups Window
Once you create a track group, you can manage it from the Track Groups window (Project menu > Track Groups), shown in Figure 12.9. You can open this window using the default keyboard shortcut Shift+Option+G.

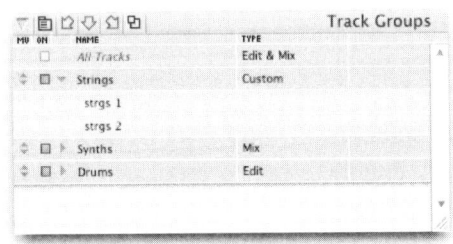

Figure 12.9
You can manage a track group from the Project menu's Track Groups window.

The main body of the Track Groups window displays the group name, group type, move handles (for changing the list order), and a button for turning the group on or off. The disclosure triangle, located to the left of the group name, will show the tracks that are contained within the group. At the very

※ Mixing Board Setup

top of the group list is a group called All Tracks—turned off by default (indicated by italics)—which lets you quickly group all tracks within a sequence. The mini-menu, shown in Figure 12.10, provides options for further managing your groups.

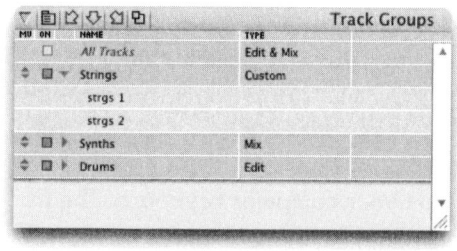

Figure 12.10
The Track Groups mini-menu contains options for managing existing track groups.

To add a track to an existing track group:

1. Select the desired track (or a part of the track) you wish to add to the Track group. Keep in mind that you can make this track selection from the Tracks window or other editor window by clicking on the name of the track.
2. Select the group to which you want to add the selected track(s) in the Track Group window.
3. Choose the Track Groups mini-menu > Add Selection to Group.

To remove or delete a track from an existing track group:

1. Click the track group's disclosure triangle and select the track(s).
2. Choose the Track Groups Mini-menu > Remove/Delete Tracks From Group.

To temporarily suspend an existing track group:

1. Click the track group's On/Off check box in the Track Groups window. Disabled groups will appear in italics. You can also press Command+Option+G and enter the number for the group you wish to disable (see Figure 12.11). The group number is listed in the order (from top to bottom) in which the group appears within the Track Groups window. Clicking #0 will choose the All Tracks group.

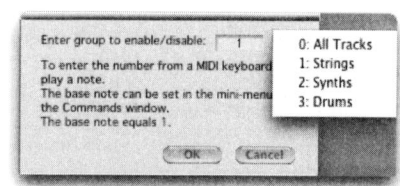

Figure 12.11
The Suspend Track Groups window

2. To globally suspend all track groups, choose Project menu > Modify Track Groups > Suspend All Track Grouping. You can also press and hold down the G key to temporarily disable all groups. Releasing the key will instantly re-enable all groups.

To change the type of an existing track group:

1. Open the Track Groups window (Shift+Option+G).
2. Click on the Type column of the desired group and select a new group type.

CHAPTER 12 } Mixing

Temporarily Track Groups
You can create a temporary track group of selected tracks that aren't already in a track group:

To create a temporary group:

1. Select the desired tracks.
2. Press the letter T key on your computer keyboard. The tracks will remain grouped until you tap the letter T key again.
3. If you are working in the Sequence Editor, you can temporarily group all visible tracks by pressing the letter W key. Tap the W key again to remove the group.

> **GROUPS VERSUS SUBGROUPS?**
>
> In addition to linking tracks together with the Track Group command, you can also place your tracks into subgroups or submixes. In this process, you basically bus desired tracks to an aux track (or Master Fader). This configuration is tremendously flexible; as the selected tracks are not "track grouped," you still have independent control of each track's parameters. The greatest benefit, however, is the ability to insert effects across your entire subgroup, which is a popular and effective mixing technique. This allows you, for example, to compress an entire drum kit or group of background vocals.

Alternate Mixes with Mix Mode

Another handy feature of the Mixing Board is the Mix Mode menu, shown in Figure 12.12, which allows you to create and manage new or alternate versions of a mix. By default, projects will start with Mix Mode turned off, so you can think of this setting as your default mix.

The New Mix command will create a new mix that contains the same volume, pan, and send positions. Duplicate Mix will create a copy of your current mix with all the previously mentioned data, including any automation and effect Inserts. To delete an alternate mix, select it from the Mix Mode menu and choose Delete Mix. To return to your original (default) mix, choose Turn Mix Mode Off.

Figure 12.12
The Mixing Board's Mix Mode menu provides options for creating and managing alternative versions of a mix.

> **IS IT REALLY A NEW MIX?**
> Be aware that when using Mix Mode, any volume, pan, and send positions will be linked between your alternate mixes! Changing these parameters in one mix will affect their positions globally throughout all of your mixes unless automation data already exists to lock their positions in place.

Inserts and Plug-ins

The Inserts section of the Mixing Board allows you to place, or "insert," real-time processing on an audio or MIDI track. You can also insert virtual instrument plug-ins (such as MOTU's MX4) on an Instrument track. Real-time effects are non-destructive—meaning they will not change or modify the original audio or MIDI data that exists within a track, allowing you to audition different parameter settings or even change the inserted plug-in entirely. The disadvantage is that real-time effects consume CPU resources—some more than others. Time-based effects, such as reverb in particular, can be hungry when it comes to CPU usage. If Digital Performer starts to act sluggish, try increasing the Buffer Size setting located in the Configure Hardware Driver window (Setup menu > Configure Audio System > Configure Hardware Setting. For more information on buffer size and audio configuration settings in general, refer to Chapter 2. Refer to Chapter 13 for a more in-depth look at effects plug-ins within Digital Performer.

> **MONITORING CPU USAGE**
> You can monitor DP's CPU consumption from the Audio Performance window (Studio Menu > Audio Performance).

By default, Digital Performer creates five blank insert menus on every track. To change the number of inserts, choose Mixing Board > mini-menu > Set Number of Effect Inserts (see Figure 12.13). You can have up to an incredible 20 inserts available on each track!

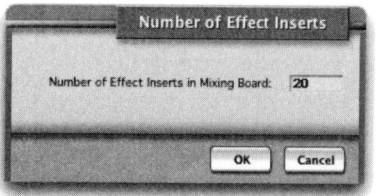

Figure 12.13
The Number of Effect Inserts window allows you to set a maximum number of 20 effect inserts!

CHAPTER 12 } Mixing

Signal Flow

Inserts are labeled A, B, C, D, and so on from top to bottom, and are set to pre-fader by default. This means that an audio signal, for example, will playback from your Mac's hard drive, travel through the Insert section (from top to bottom), continue through the Send section, and will then go through the fader (see Figure 12.14). Any adjustment you make to the level of the track will have no effect on the signal going into the Insert section.

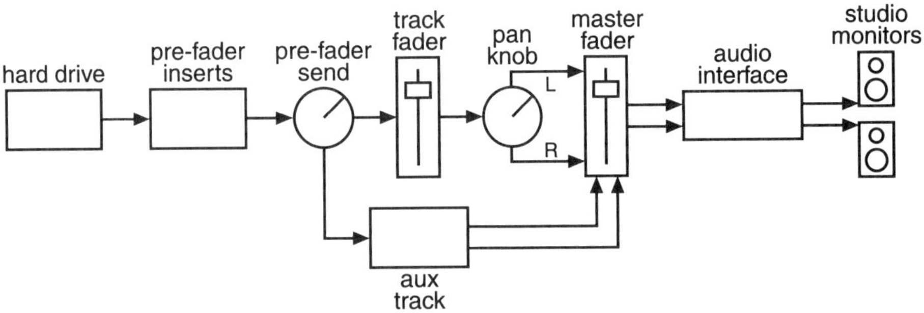

Figure 12.14
Pre-fader inserts are independent of the track fader.

Because the signal is traveling through the inserts (or plug-ins) from top to bottom, the order in which you apply your effects is extremely important. A will have an effect on B, which will have an affect on C, and so forth. To change the order of inserted plug-ins, simply click and drag them to a new location.

Pre/Post Fader Divider

If you would like to set the Insert section to post-fader (where an inserted plug-in will appear after the fader in signal flow), you will need to move the pre-post fader divider. By default, the divider is located at the bottom of the Inserts section. Place the cursor at this location and it will change to an up/down arrow icon (see Figure 12.15). Click and drag the divider up to the location where you wish the post fader section to begin.

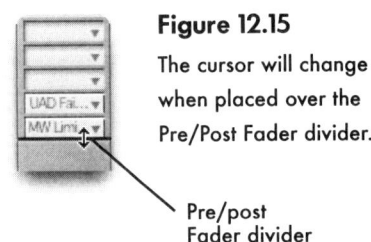

Figure 12.15
The cursor will change when placed over the Pre/Post Fader divider.

Pre/post Fader divider

Once an insert is designated as post-fader, the signal flow of the Mixing Board changes. Post-fader insert(s) will have a dependent relationship with the track fader (see Figure 12.16).

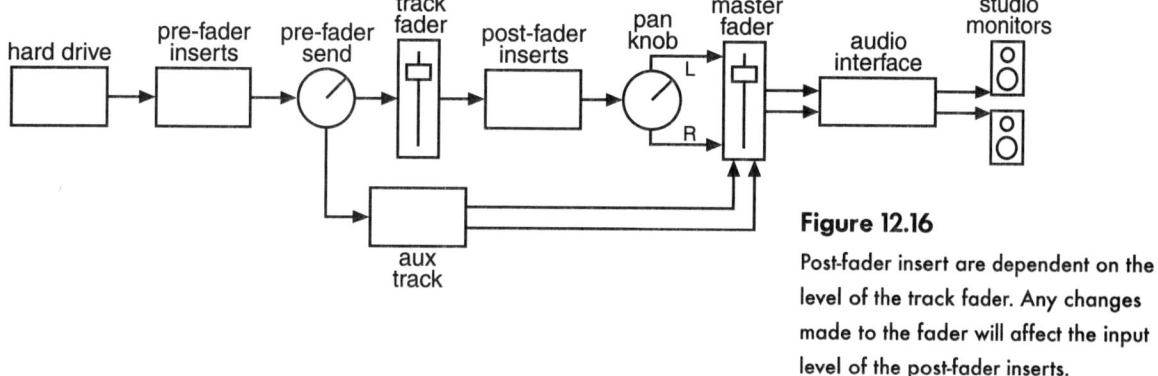

Figure 12.16
Post-fader insert are dependent on the level of the track fader. Any changes made to the fader will affect the input level of the post-fader inserts.

Dynamic versus Time-Based Effects

Generally speaking, *dynamic effects* are effects that are used to control gain. Compressors, limiters, expanders, gates, and EQ are all considered dynamic effects. Digital Performer's Trim plug-in also falls into this category. Examples of time-based effects are reverb, delay, and echo.

Knowing when and where to place dynamic and time-based plug-ins within your tracks is very important. For example, will you use an insert or a send?

Insert or Send?

The general rule is this: direct inserts are used for dynamic effects and sends are for *time-based* effects. Why? Well, the thinking is that dynamic effects, such as compression are usually meant to work on one signal. The vocal is loud, so you strap a compressor across it. The voice is thin, so you insert an EQ and boost 200Hz. In these scenarios, you want the entire signal to be affected. When the signal leaves the plug-ins you want it to be 100 percent wet. In other words, you only want to hear the compressed and EQ'd signal. If you used a send for this, you would have both a dry vocal and a compressed/EQ'd vocal being mixed together (though I know this is sometimes exactly what you want).

When working with time-based effects, you usually want to control the ratio between the dry (unaffected) and wet (affected) signals, so a send is just what the doctor ordered. You insert your reverb plug-in (such as AudioEase's Altiverb plug-in) on an aux track (100 percent wet), send to the aux track from your audio track, and blend the two together. The fader level on your aux track determines how much reverb is heard on the track.

There's also another benefit to using sends; if you decide you want that reverb on another track, you simply turn up the Send Level for that track and it also goes to the Altiverb plug-in. If you inserted your Altiverb plug-in directly on an audio track, however, you could only use it for that specific track.

To have reverb on another track, you would be forced to insert a new instance of the plug-in. Conceptually, this scenario works, but it is hardly efficient. Besides having to open up the plug-in every time you need to adjust the wet/dry ratios, you would also be wasting valuable CPU resources. If you transplant this situation to the analog world, you would need a separate reverb unit for every track you wanted to include reverb—a very costly and wasteful endeavor!

Special FX
Special effects, such as flange, chorus, tremolo, and phasers, can be inserted or sent depending on your needs. If you would like to use the same effect across multiple tracks (with the same parameters) you can employ a send. If you need the effect to be unique to a specific track, you could use an insert. Just realize that you must control the wet/dry ratio from the plug-in when using a direct insert.

Aux Tracks and Sends

Aux tracks are similar to audio tracks, except they cannot contain audio data and have no voicing assignments. Digital Performer aux tracks are similar to empty channels on a traditional analog console—like a miscellaneous track or channel. Aux tracks can be used as effects returns, to sum together a set of tracks (submix), or to shuffle audio from one place to another. Inserts and sends, as well as solo, mute, volume, panning, and automation controls, are identical in nature to those for audio tracks. The channel format of an aux track is determined by its input assignment. For example, a Mono input assignment will force the aux track to be mono.

Sends allow you to "split" off a signal and send it to another destination. This destination can be a virtual bus or a physical hardware out, which could, for example, be connected to a headphone amp or external reverb device. A Send has no effect on the original signal from which it branches off, but it has a direct relationship to the original track depending on its pre- or post-fader setting.

Sends and Returns

There are several ways to utilize aux tracks within the music production process. The main use for an aux track would be as a container for time-based effects such as reverb. I have already discussed the benefits of using Sends in the mixing process, and aux tracks are an integral part of the send "equation." Once you create an aux track, you insert a reverb plug-in; next, you assign the track's input to a bus, then you send from a track to that corresponding bus. The "sent" signal travels through the reverb plug-in and the 100 percent wet reverb signal continues to the Master fader, where it is mixed in (or *returned*) with the original dry signal. To change the amount of reverb on the original track, you simply adjust the aux track's fader. The term *send and return* originates from the process of sending a signal to another destination—which could be a plug-in or external FX unit—and returning it through an auxiliary track (or Master Fader) back into the mix.

※ Aux Tracks and Sends

Pre- versus Post-Fader Sends

You designate a send to be either pre- or post- with the Pre/post Fader Switch. This button (switch) is located to the right of the Send Level knob (the letter P button), adjacent to the Send Mute button (the letter M button). As I discussed earlier, in the "Inserts and Plug-ins" section of this chapter, a pre-fader setting allows a send (or an Insert) to be independent of the track fader. Because of its location, turning up or down the track fader will have no effect on the level of the signal sent to the headphone amplifier (Figure 12.17).

Soloing or muting the track will have no effect on the send. A post-fader reverb send, however, is located after the track fader in signal flow (see Figure 12.18).

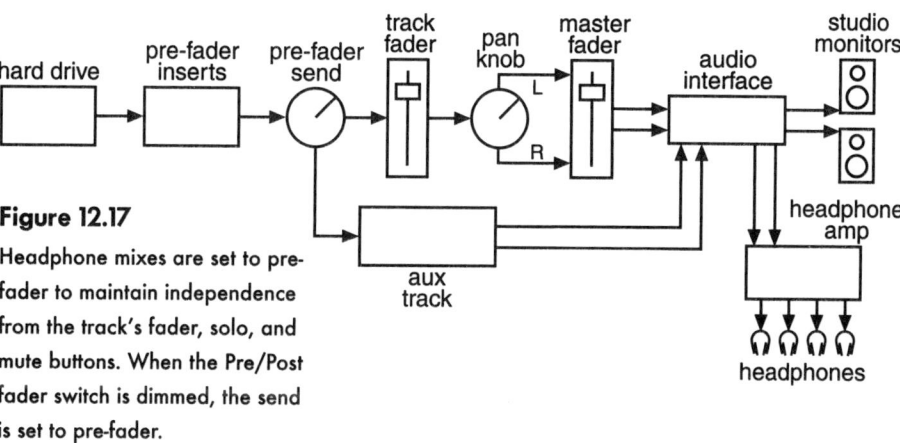

Figure 12.17
Headphone mixes are set to pre-fader to maintain independence from the track's fader, solo, and mute buttons. When the Pre/Post fader switch is dimmed, the send is set to pre-fader.

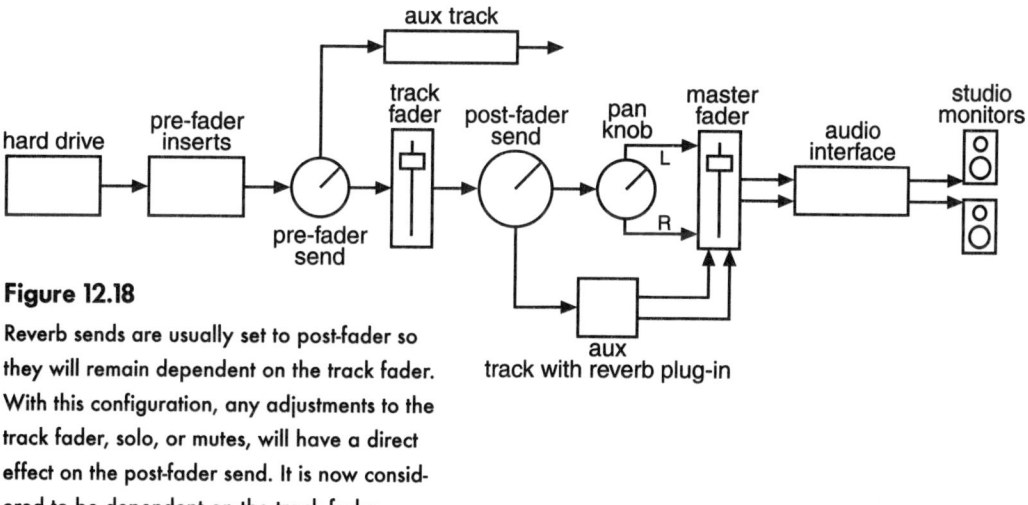

Figure 12.18
Reverb sends are usually set to post-fader so they will remain dependent on the track fader. With this configuration, any adjustments to the track fader, solo, or mutes, will have a direct effect on the post-fader send. It is now considered to be dependent on the track fader.

So when should you use a pre-fader send and when should you use a post-fader send? Here is the general rule: Pre- is for headphone mixes and post- is for effects. Why are headphone mixes pre-fader? You need a headphone send to be pre-fader so that it's independent of your mix. When you adjust a fader in the studio or when you solo a track, you don't want the artist to hear your adjustments. If the artists' headphone mix were dependent on yours, you wouldn't be able to multitask (for example, mix while you record or solo a track for troubleshooting purposes).

Effects, however, are typically post-fader because you usually want the relationship between the dry and wet signals to stay the same. So if you turn the level down on your original track, the reverb gets turned down with it. In this scenario, your reverb would be dependent on your original track fader. Of course, there will be times when you may want your effects to be pre-fader, allowing you to turn down the original track and have the reverb signal remain in the mix. Pre-fader effects are not an uncommon part of the mixing process.

The Send Level Knobs

In previous versions of Digital Performer (versions prior to DP 4.5), Sends were visually grouped into pairs of two, for a total of four sends. Sends in DP 4.5, however, have been greatly enhanced, providing a total of 20 sends per audio track, as shown in Figure 12.19. Each send can be assigned to a mono, stereo, or multi-channel output destination.

Pre/post Fader switch

Figure 12.19

The Pre/post Fader Switch toggles the send's pre/post fader settings. When the Mixing Board is set to Narrow View, the pre/post fader settings will be listed in the Send menu.

Each Send Level knob allows you to adjust the level of the send, and by default are set to Infinity (turned off). The small blue dot next to the knob (located at the 2 o'clock position) is called the Unity Gain Dot, and designates the unity gain or zero position of the Send Level knob. Double-click (or Control-click) the knob to force it to unity gain. When a Send Level knob is adjusted, the dB value is displayed in a pop-up box, as shown in Figure 12.20. The M buttons designate mutes; simply click on a button to mute a send.

Figure 12.20

When adjusting a Send Level knob, the dB value of the send is displayed in a pop-up box.

To set the number of available sends:

1. Choose Mixing Board mini-menu > Set Number of Sends to open the Number of Sends window, as shown in Figure 12.21.
2. Enter the desired number of sends (up to a total of 20).
3. Click OK to confirm the change.

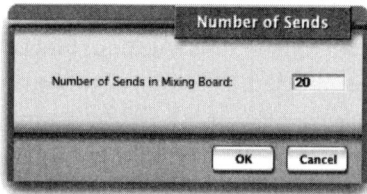

Figure 12.21

Use the Number of Sends window to set the number of sends that are available in the Mixing Board.

The Send Menu

The Send menu allows you to choose the desired routing assignment for a send and determine the channel source (L, R, or Stereo) for the specific send. When the Mixing Board is set to Narrow View, the pre/post fader options will also be listed here. In addition to any currently enabled audio bundles, the Send assignment submenus located at the bottom of the list (shown in Figure 12.22) allow you to create new audio bundles and aux tracks directly from the Send menu. The assignment submenus are described below.

Figure 12.22

Use the Send menu to route the send to an existing audio or bus output destination. New audio bundles, as well as new aux tracks, can be created directly in the Send menu.

* **New Mono/Stereo Bundle.** Choose an output assignment from the desired submenu to create a new audio bundle. The number of busses appearing in the list is determined by the Stereo Bus setting in the Configure Studio Settings window (Setup > Configure Audio Settings > Configure Studio Settings).

* **New Aux Track Via New Mono/Stereo Bundle.** These two submenu options allow you to create a new aux track when you create a new mono or stereo audio bundle. The new audio bundle will then feed the newly created aux track. Think of these two options as shortcuts that allow you to quickly create an aux track while you're configuring a Send assignment.

CHAPTER 12 } Mixing

To set up a send and return (aux track):

1. Click the Send menu (located below the Send Level knob) on the desired audio track.
2. Choose the New Aux Track via New Mono/Stereo Bundle option and select a bus from the drop-down list. Once selected, DP will assign the send to the chosen bus and create a new aux track. The input of the new aux track will be assigned to the send output in the process.

If you already have an aux track (effects return) configured, you can simply assign the send to a new or existing audio bundle.

To set up a Send (without setting up a new aux track):

1. Click the Send menu (located below the Send Level knob) on the desired audio track.
2. Assign the send to an available bus or audio hardware output. If you need to create a new audio bundle, choose the New Mono Bundle or New Stereo Bundle option and the appropriate audio bundle from the drop-down list.

Effects Returns

As I discussed earlier, effects returns (or returns) are used for returning a signal that has been sent from a track back into your mix. Within Digital Performer, aux tracks are used as returns. Aux tracks can be automatically created via the aux track shortcuts, or you can configure them manually as needed. The following How To Section describes the procedures for setting up a reverb return. If you wish to create a different type of effects return, such as an effects return for a delay plug-in, simply substitute the example reverb plug-in with a different plug-in.

To manually configure an aux track as a reverb return:

1. Create an aux track by choosing Project > Add Track > Aux track. You can also use the default keyboard shortcut Control+Command+A.
2. Assign the input of the track to an available bus (for example, bus 1). Keep in mind that the channel format of the aux track is determined by the input assignment.
3. Assign the aux track's output to your main outs (for example, analog 1-2).
4. Insert a plug-in on the aux track, making sure to set the plug-in's Mix parameter to 100%.
5. Now you can send a signal to bus 1 and it will be bussed to the reverb plug-in and returned to your main mix (analog 1-2) via the configured aux track.
6. Your aux track's fader level sets the amount of reverb being mixed with the audio track's dry signal, so adjust it accordingly (for example, for less reverb in the mix, simply turn down the aux fader).

Aux Tracks and Sends

> **SENDING PLUG-INS INTO OTHER PLUG-INS?**
>
> Here is a great way to add depth to any reverb effect: Create another aux track and insert a Stereo Delay plug-in, basically repeating the steps for setting up a reverb return (that is, instead of inserting a reverb plug-in, insert the Stereo Delay plug-in). Assign this new aux track to an available stereo bus (for example, bus 3-4). Now go to your existing reverb return and assign an empty send to bus 3-4 (the Stereo Delay aux track). Turn up the Send Level knob for bus 3/4 and your reverb will be sent to the Stereo Delay plug-in. Adjust the delay parameters to taste (longer delay times can be used to create a luscious reverb effect, which is great for vocal ballads).

Setting Up a Headphone Mix

Headphone mixes are different from typical reverb configurations, in that they don't require an effects return. Once the signal is sent off to a headphone amp (and to each pair of your artist's headphones), the journey ends. The setup process is almost identical to that of the reverb send and return configuration. The aux track, however, is utilized as a group fader and not a return. Of course, you don't have to employ an aux fader in a headphone mix; you could send directly to the outputs of your audio interface (which is connected to your headphone amp). This setup configuration doesn't allow you much flexibility, but using an aux fader as a headphone-group master between your individual track Sends and your headphone amp will let you control the overall level going to the amplifier with relative ease. In addition, you'll have the ability to insert plug-ins if needed, allowing you, for example, to EQ or compress your entire headphone mix.

To set up a headphone mix (with a headphone-group master):

1. Make sure your headphone amp is directly connected to the outputs of your audio hardware interface (such as Analog 7-8).
2. Follow the procedures for setting up a send and assign the send to an available stereo bus, such as bus 3-4. Be sure to use the Send menu's New Aux Track Via Stereo Bundle option to create a new aux track in the process.
3. Set the output for the new aux track to Analog 7-8.
4. Rename the aux track to something appropriate, like "Phones Mix."
5. Turn up the Send Level fader you configured in Step 2 to send the track's audio signal to the headphone amp via the Phones Mix aux track.
6. To send from another track: assign a send on the desired track to bus 3-4 and turn up the Send Level knob.
7. To adjust the overall output level of the headphone mix, simply turn up or down the "Phones Mix" aux track fader.

CHAPTER 12 } Mixing

> **PRE-FADER HEADPHONE SENDS**
> Sends are set to pre-fader by default, so you do not have to worry about manually configuring each headphone level send to pre-.

Submixing

Submixing is the act of combining multiple signals and sending them through either an internal or external bus. Submixing allows you to work around I/O limitations, efficiently apply effects across multiple tracks, establish send and returns, and can greatly simply complex mixes. Submixing is an especially common practice in the film and video post-production process, where multiple submixes (or stems) are used to group common elements such as dialog, music, and sound effects. Submixing works especially well with instruments that are normally treated as one unit, such as string sections, or for instruments that are recorded with multiple microphones, such as drums and piano.

Submixing differs from track grouping in that it allows individual tracks within a subgroup to remain independent. For example, you can still make track-specific volume adjustments and insert individual plug-ins while controlling the overall volume of the entire group from the group master fader.

Within Digital Performer, subgroups are very easy to set up.

To set up a subgroup:

1. Create an aux track by choosing Project > Add Track > Aux track. You can also use the default keyboard shortcut Control+Command+A.
2. Assign the input of the track to an available stereo bus (for example, bus 5-6).
3. Assign the aux track's output to your main outs (for example, analog 1-2).
4. Remember it's always a good idea to rename your tracks for easy identification. To rename the new aux track, Option-click on the name of the track.
5. Change the output for the audio tracks you wish to put in this subgroup to bus 5-6. Remember that you can use the Assignments window to quickly assign multiple tracks to the same output channel (see Chapter 7). Now the desired audio tracks will be bussed through your aux track (group master fader) allowing you to easily control the overall volume or insert effects across the entire group.

Aux Tracks and Sends

> **AUX TRACK SHORTCUTS**
>
> Remember you can use the aux track shortcuts introduced in Version 4.5 to create a new aux track while assigning an audio track to a bus, as shown in Figure 12.23. Once created, the bus will route the audio signal to the new aux track. Aux track shortcuts are available in DP's assignment menus.

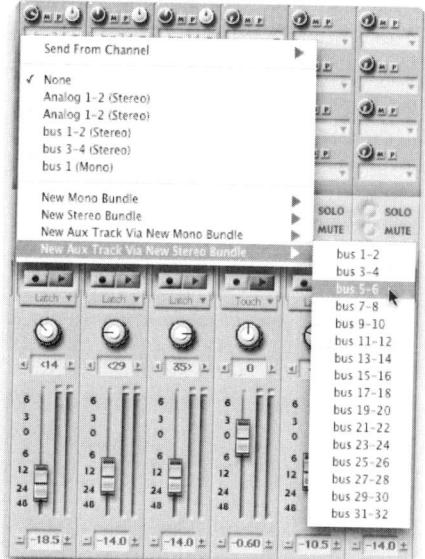

Figure 12.23
Aux track shortcuts that appear in an assignment menu allow you to create a new aux track while making a bus assignment.

Automation

Automation is the process of automating various aspects of the mixing process, from simple fader moves (or volume changes) to more complex actions like plug-in morphing. Automation allows the mix engineer to fine-tune his mixes and perform real-time changes to multiple audio and MIDI events. Such changes would be nearly impossible without the automation process.

Track automation within Digital Performer is recorded as MIDI controller data. Automation events can be inserted with DP's various tools or recorded in real-time by adjusting track/plug-in parameters with the mouse. Automation modes determine how real-time automation is handled within a track, allowing you to write new data or update existing events. The Automation Setup window allows you to set track-specific and global automation parameters that affect how this data is recorded.

Automation Setup Window

Digital Performer's automation features are so easy to use that you may never need to pay a visit to the Automation Setup window (I'm sure there are plenty of users out there who never have). You owe it to yourself to get familiar with this window, however; besides providing a complete list of parameters that can be automated within DP, the Automation Setup window also allows you to turn off specific automation settings, control how automation modes react within a track, and free up system resources. The Automation Setup window can be accessed by choosing Setup > Automation Setup (see Figure 12.24).

CHAPTER 12 } Mixing

Figure 12.24
The Automation Setup window provides global and track specific automation preferences.

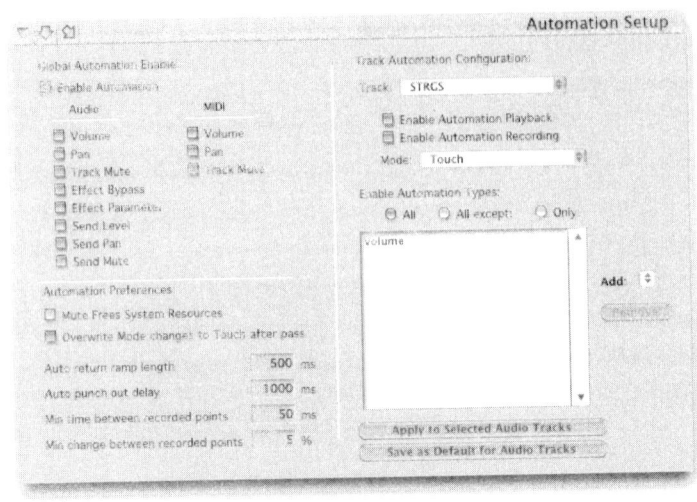

Global Automation Enable
This section determines the type of data that can be automated within DP. Notice that only the Volume, Pan, and Track Mute settings can be automated within a MIDI track; audio tracks provide more extensive automation capabilities. Click on a specific parameter button to globally enable/disable an automation parameter (buttons will appear blue when enabled). Click the Enable Automation button to globally turn on or off automation within a project.

Track Automation Configuration
This section lets you control automation for a specific track. The Track list is a drop-down menu of all tracks within the current sequence. Choose a track to set its automation preferences. Below this list are buttons for enabling/disabling automation playback or recording for the track. The Mode menu sets the automation mode for the selected track (explained later in this chapter). These settings are identical to the automation play-enable and mode buttons in the Mixing Board's individual Track Lists.

The Enable Automation Types section is where you can decide which parameters will or will not be turned on or off.

To enable/disable specific automation parameters:

1. Select the desired track from the Track list.
2. Click the Add drop-down menu to select a setting and place it in the Track list.
3. Next, use the radial buttons at the top of the Track list to decide whether the listed parameters will be turned on or off. All except will exclude the parameters in the list, while Only will turn

on automation only for the listed parameters. All, of course, will enable all parameters for automation, regardless of the items that appear in the list.

4. To remove a parameter from the list, select it and click the Remove button.
5. If you would like to use the same settings on other tracks, select the tracks you wish to affect and click the Apply to Selected Audio Tracks button.
6. To make the current list parameters the default settings for all audio tracks, click the Save as Default for Audio Tracks button.

Automation Preferences

The Automation Preferences section provides several different preferences:

- **Mute Frees System Resources.** When this option is enabled, muting a track will automatically free up any system resources (for example, CPU) that the track may be consuming. Keep in mind that mutes cannot be automated when this preference is turned on and you may experience a couple seconds of silence as DP frees up/adds the system resources demanded by the track(s).
- **Overwrite Mode changes to Touch after pass.** This option will force a track's automation mode to Touch mode (explained later) when an overwrite pass has been completed.
- **Auto Return Ramp Length.** When automation recording is stopped, DP automatically inserts a "return ramp," which creates a smooth transition between the new automation and previous parameter setting. This option determines the length of the transition.
- **Auto punch out delay.** This is the amount of time that DP waits before stopping the recording of automation after it receives the last automation event from an external controller.
- **Min. time/Change between recorded points.** The last two options set the number of control points that are recorded when making any automation moves. Higher numbers and lower percentages provide finer tracking of automation moves.

Automation Modes

Digital Performer's five automation modes determine how automation data is recorded within a track. The mode for a specific track can be set from either the Automation Setup window or directly with a track's Automation Mode menu (see Figure 12.25).

- **Overwrite.** This mode writes new automation from when playback starts until it is stopped. Any existing automation data will be overwritten in the process. This mode will automatically switch to Touch if the Overwrite Mode changes to Touch after the pass option is turned on from the Automation Setup window. When you begin your first automation pass or wish to erase any existing automation, use this mode.

Figure 12.25

A track's Automation Mode menu provides a list of automation modes and access to the Automation Setup window (Setup...).

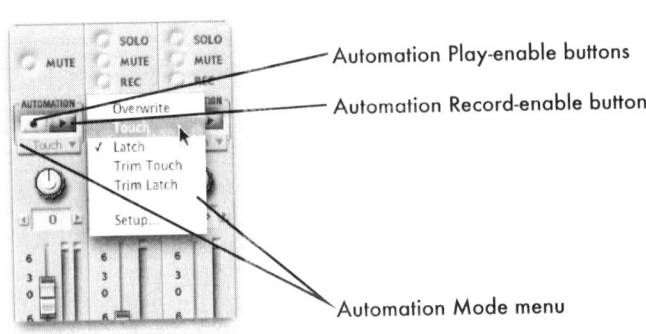

- **Touch.** Touch mode will begin to write new automation data as soon as a fader or knob is touched, and will continue to write data until it is released. The Automation Setup window's Auto Ramp Length option determines how long it takes for DP to return to the original automation data once recording is stopped. Use this mode when you need to update only a portion of existing automation, and you want DP to return to the existing automation when you release the fader or knob.
- **Latch.** When Latch mode is engaged, automation will begin as soon as you grab a fader or knob, but unlike in Touch mode, automation data will continue to be written until recording is stopped.
- **Trim Touch/Latch.** This setting is identical to both normal Touch and Latch modes, except that the fader will change to display 0 (unity gain) as the current volume in the track. These two modes can only be used to update volume and pan data. All other automation events will be overwritten. This mode is handy when you need to raise or lower the overall automation values, while preserving the existing automation curves.

Enabling and Disabling Automation

Automation in DP can be enabled or disabled from two locations: the Automation Setup window (explained earlier) and a track's Automation menu (see Figure 12.26).

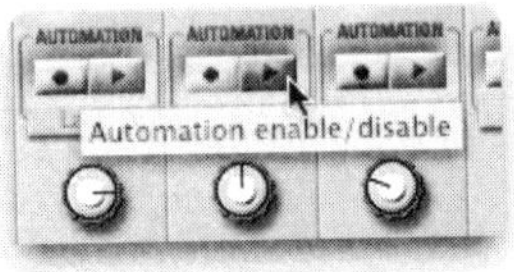

Figure 12.26

You can enable or disable a track's automation by clicking on the Automation Play-enable or Record-enable buttons.

To enable the playback of recorded track automation, click the automation Play-enable button; it will be highlighted green. Click again to disable automation playback for the track; the button will return to a normal state. To record automation, click on the automation Record-enable button and it will be highlighted red. Click again to turn off this feature.

Automation that is enabled will appear in bold, while disabled automation will appear as a dashed line (- - -) within the Sequence Editor (see Figure 12.27).

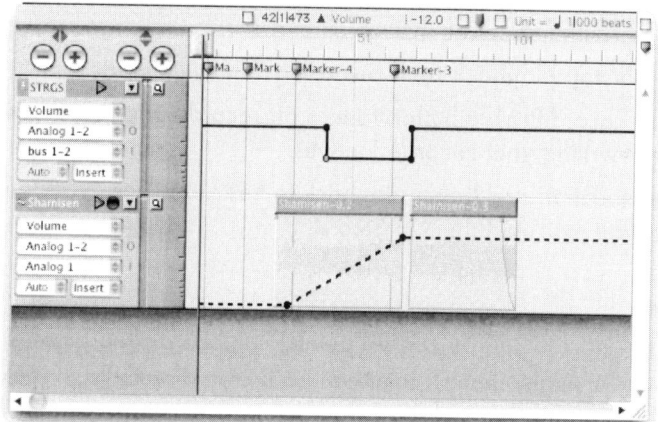

Figure 12.27
Within the Sequence Editor, automation that is enabled will appear in bold, while disabled automation will appear as a dashed line.

Recording Real-time Automation

Automation data can be recorded in real-time from the Mixing Board.

To record new automation data in real-time:

1. Start by opening the Mixing Board (Shift+M) and choosing Overwrite mode from the desired track's Automation Mode menu.
2. Turn on both the Automation Play and Record-Enable buttons (they both should be highlighted).
3. Begin playback at the desired position. Automation will immediately begin being recorded.
4. Make the desired automation moves (real-time parameter adjustments).
5. Press the Space bar when you are through making your moves to stop recording.
6. Click the Automation Record-Enable button to turn off recording; doing so will prevent you from accidentally overwriting your recorded moves.
7. Return to the desired location and begin playback to hear (and see) your automation moves playback exactly as you executed them in Step 4.

To update existing automation data in real-time:

1. Start by choosing Touch or Latch mode (or Trim Touch/Latch) from the desired track's Automation Mode menu. Both modes will only begin recording when you grab a fader or knob. Touch mode, however, will punch out of automation recording as soon as you stop making fader or knob adjustments, while Latch mode continues to write new data until playback is stopped.

2. Turn on both the Automation Play and Record-Enable buttons (they should both be highlighted).
3. Begin playback at the desired position.
4. Grab a fader or knob; automation recording will begin.
5. Press the Space bar to stop playback (and recording if in Latch mode).
6. Click the Automation Record-Enable button to turn off recording; doing so will prevent you from accidentally overwriting your recorded moves.
7. Return to the desired location and begin playback to hear (and see) your automation moves playback exactly as you executed them in Step 4.

Inserting Automation Data

Automation data (which are represented by control points) can be inserted directly into a track from DP's various editor windows. A single control point can be drawn directly in a track by clicking once with the Arrow or the Pencil tool, and is used to anchor a parameter to a specific value. To insert a parameter change over a period of time, you need at least two control points. The first point anchors the parameter and tells DP where you want the change to begin. The second point is where you wish the parameter change to end. What happens in between these two points (how you draw the automation data) can determine whether the transition is smooth (for example, a 30 second fade-out) or instantaneous (for example, a volume mute).

For an explanation of inserting control points within the Graphic Editor, refer to Chapter 10.

To insert automation data in the Sequence Editor:

1. Open the Sequence Editor (Shift+S).
2. Click on the desired track's Active Layer and choose the parameter you wish to automate (see Figure 12.28). Keep in mind that the options listed will vary depending on the type of track you are working with.
3. Enable the Pencil tool by double-tapping the P key on your computer keyboard.

Figure 12.28
Parameters that can be automated will be listed in the Active Layer menu. Choose a parameter to bring its layer to the foreground. Active layers will be displayed in bold.

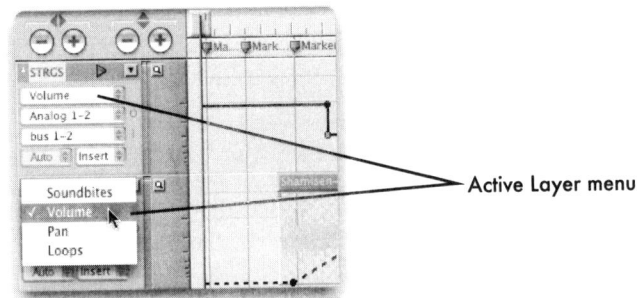

4. Set the shape of the Pencil tool from the Insert/Reshape Curve menu. This setting determines the shape of the inserted automation.

5. Click where you wish the parameter change to start and drag the cursor to where you wish the parameter change to stop, then release the mouse. You can use the Information bar to view the location of the cursor and its related parameter value. The horizontal position of the mouse release sets duration of the automation move. The vertical position determines the amount of change for the parameter.

   If you were inserting a volume fade-out, for example, the first control point would set the beginning of the fade. Once you click with the Pencil tool and insert the first automation point, you would drag the mouse vertically to the bottom of the Edit window to turn down the track. How far you drag the cursor to the right before releasing the mouse would determine the duration (for example, minutes and seconds) of the fade-out. The type of curve you choose from the Insert/Reshape curve button would determine how the fade was drawn in. If you wanted a fade with a rounded curve, you could use the Spline Curve (see Figure 12.29).

6. If you want a simple straight line, you could also use the Arrow tool. Click to insert a single automation point. Then insert another controller point and drag up or down with the mouse.

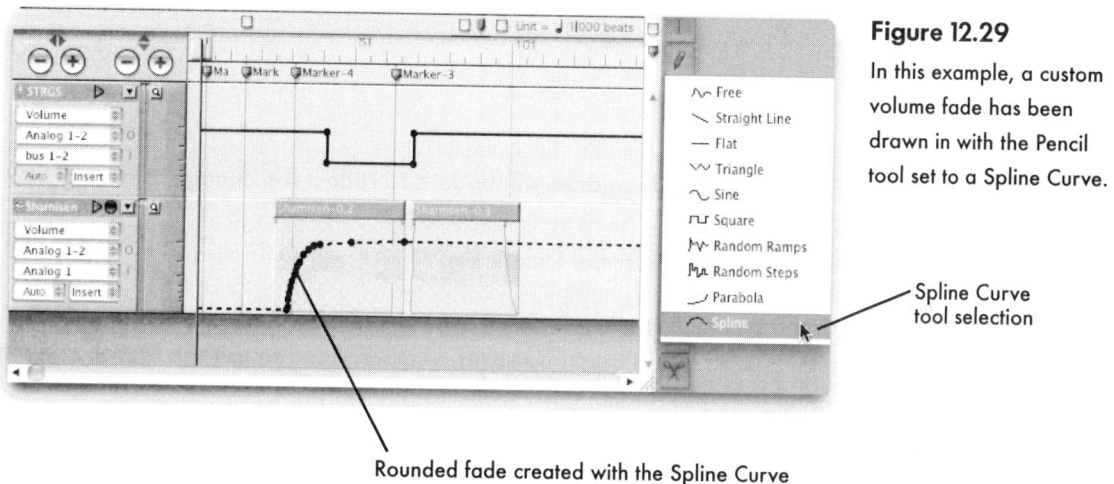

Figure 12.29

In this example, a custom volume fade has been drawn in with the Pencil tool set to a Spline Curve.

To select automation data in the Sequence or Graphic Editor:

1. Enable the Arrow tool by double-tapping the A key on your computer keyboard.
2. To select a single controller point, click with the mouse. Selected controller points will be highlighted yellow.
3. To make multiple controller-point selections, Shift-click with the Arrow tool. You can also click and drag within the Time Ruler or any open area within the track that doesn't contain automation data.

CHAPTER 12 } Mixing

To edit automation data in the Sequence or Graphic Editor:

1. Enable the Arrow tool by double-tapping the A key on your computer keyboard.
2. Select the automation data you wish to modify.
3. To change the location of the data, click on any selected controller point and drag with the mouse.
4. To change the shape of existing automation data, enable the Reshape tool by double-tapping the R key. Select a new curve from the Tool palette's Insert/Reshape Curve button. Click at the location where the move should start and drag to where you wish the move to end (see Figure 12.30).

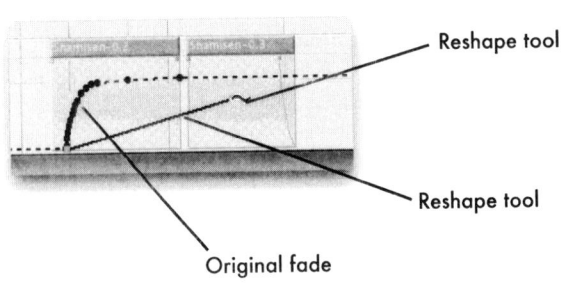

Figure 12.30
In this example, the Reshape tool is being used to change the shape of an existing automation curve. The top automation curve is the original automation fade, while the bottom fade shows the new curve.

5. Release the mouse and the automation data will update to reflect the change, inserting new controller points if needed.
6. To delete selected events, simply press the Delete key.

You can use DP's standard edit commands such as Cut, Copy, and Paste to edit automation data. When pasting automation data in an audio track, however, you will need to use the Merge command in place of the Paste command to avoid affecting the actual audio data.

To cut, copy, and paste automation data in the Sequence Editor:

1. Begin by selecting the automation data you wish to cut or copy.
2. Choose the Cut (Command+X) or Copy (Command+C) command from the Edit menu.
3. Insert a single automation point by clicking with either the Arrow tool or Pencil tool at the location where you wish to paste the data.
4. Now choose Edit menu > Merge to paste the selected data. Keep in mind that you can use the Paste command (Command+V) when working with MIDI tracks.

In addition to inserting data with the Arrow or Pencil tool, you can also use a track's Event List to insert automation data. This can sometimes prove to be time-consuming, however, as the "list view"

Aux Tracks and Sends

will force you to enter in each parameter setting as its own event. Inserting and editing automation events is identical to the insertion or editing of other data types (see Chapter 10). To delete an automation event from the Event List, simply click on the event name and press the Delete key.

To insert automation data in a track's Event List:

1. Start by selecting the desired track and open its Event List (Shift+E).
2. Click on the title bar's Insert button (the letter I button).
3. Select the parameter from the drop-down menu.
4. Pop-edit the location of the automation event, then set the parameter values.
5. Press the Return key to confirm the changes.

Plug-in Automation

Besides standard track parameters such as volume and panning, plug-in parameters can also be automated. Each Effects window contains an Automation menu (located below the mini-menu) identical to a track's Automation menu (see Figure 12.31).

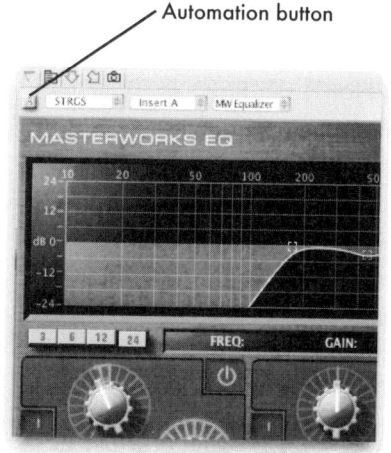

Figure 12.31

The Effects window's automation button contains an automation menu that provides access to DP's automation features.

Procedures for automating plug-in parameters are the same as for standard track automation. Simply engage the Automation Play and Record-Enable buttons, select an automation mode, begin playback, and adjust the desired plug-in settings. You can also insert and edit automation data directly in a track (explained earlier), or incorporate DP's snapshot automation features (explained in the next section).

All of Digital Performer's bundled plug-ins can be fully automated, but you should keep in mind that some third-party plug-ins may not have this capability. Consult the specific plug-in's user manual for information on its automation features.

Snapshot Automation

Snapshot automation is used to insert multiple automation points in a single step. This can be useful when you have many parameters that need to change simultaneously, or must remain static for a certain duration within a mix. This form of automation is especially useful in video and film post-production work, where mixes must sometimes change suddenly and dramatically in order to accommodate abrupt scene changes. Of course, there are many uses within the music-production process as well, such as automating mutes across all tracks before the beginning of a song.

Within Digital Performer, snapshot automation can be applied to a single point in time or across a specified time-range. Click on the Snapshot icon within the Mixing Board or Editor window's title bar to open the Automation Snapshot window, shown in Figure 12.32. Once you have specified a selection for each of the three drop-down menus, click the OK button to apply the snapshot.

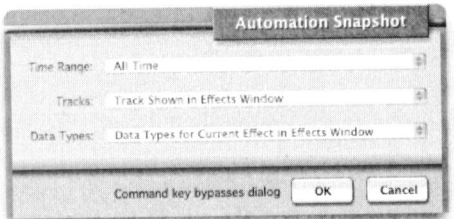

Figure 12.32

The Automation Snapshot window.

Time Range or Location

The first thing you need to do when inserting snapshot automation is to specify the location or time-range of the inserted automation data. If you want to have the snapshot occur at a specific location, simply move the playback cursor to that location. The options you choose from the Time Range menu set the end point or duration for the snapshot, as shown in Figure 12.33. You can also make a time range selection and choose Selected Range from the Time Range menu. To apply the snapshot to the entire sequence, thereby overwriting any existing automation data, choose All Time.

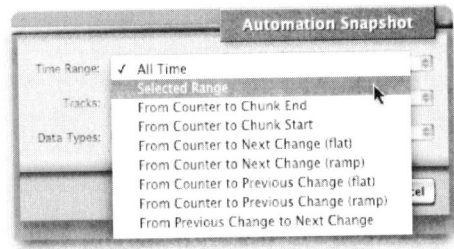

Figure 12.33

The Time Range submenu allows you to specify a time range for the automation snapshot.

The Time Range menu's various options are as follows:

- **All Time.** This option will apply the snapshot to an entire sequence, regardless of the playback cursor location, while overwriting any existing automation data.

- **Selected Range.** This option will apply a snapshot across the current time range selection. Keep in mind that this setting will also overwrite any existing automation data within the selection.

- **From Counter to Chunk End/Start.** Use this setting to apply the snapshot from the counter location until the chunk end or start time.

- **From Counter to Next/Previous Change (flat/ramp).** This option will apply the snapshot from the counter location until the next or previous automation or MIDI controller point. The flat setting will create a constant value (flat line) for each automation parameter, while the ramp setting will create a normal automation ramp (continuous and smooth change) from the counter location until the next or previous controller point.

- **From Previous Change to Next Change.** You can use this setting to create a snapshot between two automation points. Place the cursor between two controller points and choose this option.

Tracks

After the location, you will need to specify the tracks that will be included in the automation snapshot (see Figure 12.34). The Tracks submenu allows you to specify the tracks that will be included in the automation snapshot.

Figure 12.34
The Tracks submenu allows you to specify the tracks that will be included in the automation snapshot.

- **All Tracks**. Use this setting to include all tracks within a snapshot.
- **Selected Tracks**. This option will apply a snapshot only to selected tracks.
- **Tracks Shown in Graphic Editor:** Use this setting to apply the snapshot only to tracks that are visible (highlighted in the Show/Hide column) within the Graphic/Sequence Editor.
- **Tracks Shown in Mixing Board.** Use this setting to apply the snapshot only to tracks that are visible (highlighted in the Show/Hide column) within the Mixing Board.
- **Track Shown in Effects Window.** This option is available when you click on a plug-in's Snapshot Automation button.

Data Types

The last snapshot setting to specify is the type of automation data that is to be included (see Figure 12.35). The Data Type submenu allows you to specify the type of automation data to be included in the automation snapshot.

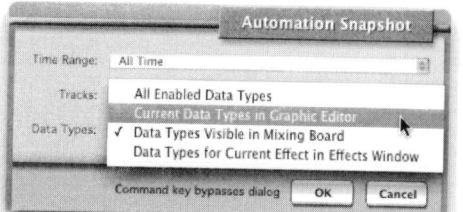

Figure 12.35
The Data Type submenu lets you specify the type of automation data to be included in the snapshot.

- **All Enabled Data Types**. Use this setting to include all automation parameters that are enabled within the Automation setup window.
- **Current Data Types in Graphic Editor**. This option will only include automation data that is currently visible within a track or is active within an audio track's active layer. This setting prevents you from writing automation data that doesn't already exist.
- **Data Types Visible in Mixing Board**. This setting only includes automation data that is visible within the Mix window. For example, if the Sends section is hidden, send volume and panning automation will not be written with the snapshot.
- **Data Types for Current Effect in Effects Window**. This setting will only include automation parameters for the plug-in currently showing in the Effects window.

CHAPTER 12 } Mixing

Using the Previous Snapshot Setting

DP remembers the automation snapshot setting that was last used within a specific window. So, if you would like to override the Automation Snapshot window and simply take a snapshot with the window's previous setting, simply press the Command key and click the window's Snapshot button (the camera icon button). You can also use the default keyboard shortcut Command+Control+single quote (').

Summary

Even though Digital Performer provides many comprehensive mix features, such as snapshot automation and plug-in effects, don't neglect the most basic, yet powerful tools at your disposal: the volume fader and pan knob. A good mix begins with proper levels and panning. Before you even reach for an effect, you should start with these two fundamental controls.

Think about what the important elements are in your mix. Is it the vocals? Is it the rhythm section? Start by getting a basic blend of the most important tracks with only the track faders. If you are working on a larger project and are feeling overwhelmed, simply turn down all the tracks and start building your mix, track by track—this is always a good idea. Besides actually listening to what's on each track (you'd be surprised how many engineers don't listen to an individual track from start to finish), you'll be able to hear how one track affects another, both from a technical-engineering standpoint and from an emotional-performance standpoint.

As you're adjusting levels, listen for tracks that are competing with one another. Instead of immediately reaching for an EQ, think about panning and how you can use the stereo field to give each track its own space within your mix. If the heavy guitar track is fighting with the lead vocal, for example, try panning it left or right to add separation and clarity. You'll also need to take into consideration the balance of your instruments (for example, complementary frequency and volume distribution across the stereo field). In addition to the technical aspects, "headphone-candy" should also play a role in your panning decisions—it can serve to keep the listener engaged while adding variety to your mix.

Believe it or not, I've heard some engineers refer to panning as the most difficult and delicate part of the mixing process, and say how the simple act of changing the panning position of one instrument totally sent their mix back to the drawing board.

Once you're satisfied with your basic blend, you should start considering effects plug-ins. We've already discussed how to insert plug-ins, so the next chapter will continue on with an explanation of real-time versus disk-based processing and highlight some of the plug-ins that come bundled with Digital Performer.

13 } Processing and Mastering

"Processing" is the act of modifying audio or MIDI data with software- or hardware-based effects. This processing can occur in real-time through the use of software plug-ins and hardware effects units, or as a file-based process that actually modifies the audio or MIDI data within a track. Even though this chapter appears after the "Mixing" chapter, audio and MIDI processing can happen anytime during the music production process—from the initial stage of recording, and throughout the mixing and mastering processes. The processing section of this chapter, however, will focus specifically on audio soundbite processing.

Mastering is the last stage of the music production process (assuming the replication process is a separate entity outside the music studio environment). Mastering is your final chance to improve on the sound quality of an audio project before it is mass-produced and shipped off to the public. Mixers should always have their mixes mastered by an experienced mastering engineer, rather than attempting to do it on their own (budget permitting, of course). Mastering engineers work in a fine-tuned studio environment that allows them to quickly pinpoint problems and shape a track (or set of tracks) so that it will translate well across different types of playback systems. However, there will be times when the DP user will want to or need to master mixes within Digital Performer.

Though by no means a comprehensive guide to the mastering process, the "Mastering" section of this chapter will provide an overview of the basic procedures involved with mastering—showing you how you might incorporate DP's various tools and feature sets to "master" your mixes in Digital Performer.

CHAPTER 13 } Processing and Mastering

Here is a summary of topics covered within this chapter:
- The difference between real-time and file-based processing.
- How Automatic Delay Compensation works.
- How to use real-time effect inserts and file-based Audio menu plug-ins.
- How to apply destructive processing in the Waveform Editor.
- The Effects window.
- How to transpose soundbites.
- How to bounce to disk or perform a "real-time" bounce.
- How to export soundbites in different file formats, including MP3.
- An overview of the mastering process within DP.
- How to use dither and noiseshaping.
- How to perform sample format and sample rate conversion.

Audio Processing

There are basically two ways to process audio data with effects in DP: through the use of effect inserts or with DP's file-based Audio menu plug-ins. Effect inserts (in the Mixing Board) are applied in real-time and do not change the actual audio in a track. Audio menu plug-ins, however, are file based—meaning a new sound file (mixed with the applied effect) will be created after a soundbite has been processed. There are, of course, advantages and disadvantages to both of these methods.

REAL-TIME VERSUS FILE-BASED PROCESSING
Real-time effects are like when you plug a guitar into a series of stomp boxes before sending them to an amp or recorder. File-based processing, however, is like taking an audio track that's already recorded and "printing" an effect on top of it (permanently merging the original audio and the effect together).

Automatic Delay Compensation

Regardless of which method you choose (real-time or file-based processing), be aware that plug-in processing may introduce a delay, called *latency*, to the processed signal. How much latency is introduced depends on the particular plug-in you're working with. To get around this limitation, enable DP's Automatic Delay Compensation (ADC) feature, which automatically adjusts the playback of the audio signal to compensate for any added latency—with sample accuracy.

Audio Processing

To enable/disable Automatic Delay Compensation:

1. Open the Configure Studio Settings window by choosing Setup menu > Configure Studio System > Configure Studio Settings.
2. Click the Automatic Plug-in Latency Compensation option to enable or disable the option. When turned on, the button will appear blue, as shown in Figure 13.1.
3. Click OK to confirm the change.

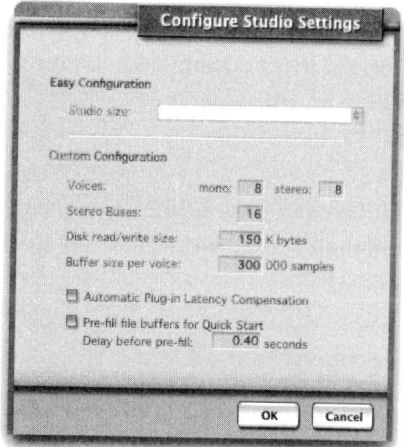

Figure 13.1
The Automatic Plug-in Latency Compensation option is located in the Configure Studio Settings window.

> ❋ **WHEN ADC DOESN'T WORK**
> Keep in mind that this feature only works on real-time audio processing and virtual instruments triggered by prerecorded MIDI data. ADC will have no effect on live audio or MIDI data that is triggered in real-time or file-based processing applied with the Audio menu plug-ins.

Real-Time Effects

Real-time plug-ins are the most versatile form of processing, as they do not alter the audio track data. You are free to audition different settings or even bypass or remove plug-ins entirely—all in real-time. The disadvantage is that inserted plug-ins consume your system's CPU resources. Some plug-ins are only a light-drain on your CPU resources, while others (such as AudioEase's Altiverb, Waves Mastering Bundle plug-ins, and so on) can slow down even the fastest Macs when you're working with larger projects. You may want to work with higher buffer sizes when mixing with real-time effects. Higher buffer sizes have the benefit of freeing up your computer's CPU resources. The tradeoff, however, is the unfortunate increase in monitoring latency, which can make recording extremely difficult. You can monitor DP's resource consumption from the Audio Performance window (explained later).

CHAPTER 13 } Processing and Mastering

To insert a real-time effect plug-in:

1. Open the Mixing Board by choosing Project menu > Mixing Board. You can also use the default keyboard shortcut Shift+M.

2. Click on an effect insert and choose the desired plug-in from the drop-down menu (see Figure 13.2).

3. This plug-in will open in a separate Effects window (see Figure 13.3). If you close the Effects window, you can reopen it by double-clicking on the name of the plug-in in the Inserts section of the Mixing Board.

4. Adjust the plug-in parameters as needed.

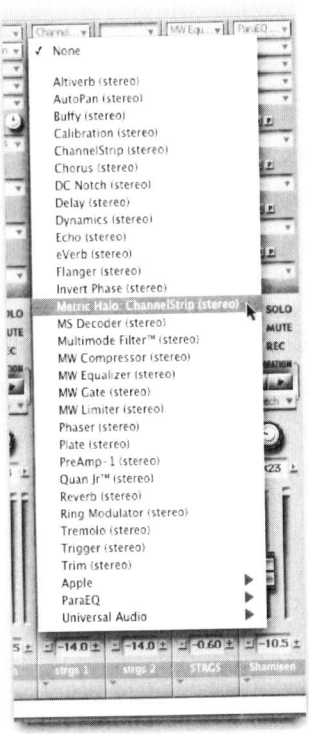

Figure 13.2
The Inserts drop-down menu provides a complete list of compatible plug-ins that are installed within your system.

Figure 13.3
Plug-ins will open up in their own Effects window. The first Effects window (top) is displaying an empty insert, while the second Effects window (bottom) displays an Altiverb plug-in that's been inserted in slot A of the Aux-2 track.

To remove or switch to a new plug-in:

1. In the Mixing Board, click on the desired effect insert and choose None to remove the plug-in.

2. When working in the Effects window, click on the plug-in's Effect menu and choose None.

3. To switch to a new plug-in, repeat Step 1 or 2, but instead of choosing None, choose the new plug-in from the drop-down menu.

Audio Processing

> ### PLUG-IN COMPATIBILITY
> As I discussed in Chapter 2, Digital Performer supports the use of MAS, AU, and VST (if used with a "wrapper") plug-ins. As long as they are installed within the correct plug-ins folder, they will appear in DP.
>
> DAE users will have access to TDM, RTAS, and AudioSuite Plug-ins—but not AU or native MAS plug-ins. DAE users wanting to use VST plug-ins can choose to use Fxpansion's VST/RTAS adapter.

File-Based Processing

File-based processing has the benefit of not consuming real-time system resources. You basically apply an effect to a soundbite, which creates a new Sound File of the processed audio. The disadvantage is that you must reapply the effect if you want to change it. This is a constructive process, meaning a new soundbite is created, so you can always return to the original file—at any time—simply by dragging the soundbite into a track from the Soundbites window. File-based processing can be applied to a soundbite directly in an audio track or in the Waveform Editor (Soundbites window > Edit). Keep in mind that, unlike track processing, Waveform Editor processing is a destructive process that permanently alters the soundbite. You can use the Sound File's independent Undo History list to undo (or remove) any applied processing, if you have the Sound File Undo History configured to remember your actions. Refer to Chapter 6 for an explanation of the Undo History window.

> ### THE NORMALIZE AND FADE COMMANDS
> In addition to Audio menu plug-ins and other audio commands (such as the Region menu's Transpose command), the Waveform Editor will also allow you to apply destructive fades and normalization (explained later). These Audio menu commands are only available when working in the Waveform Editor and will appear dimmed (or unavailable) when processing audio directly in a track.

> ### BACKGROUND PROCESSING
> Keep in mind that file-based effects processing occurs in the background, so you will be free to perform other actions while any processing is taking place. The Background Processing window controls how background processing functions in Digital Performer; it is explained later in the "Background Processing Window" section of this chapter.

CHAPTER 13 } Processing and Mastering

Processing Audio within a Track

You can process entire soundbites or only portions of soundbites within an audio track. Simply make the appropriate time range selection, choose the desired plug-in from the Audio menu, and then apply the effect. Since this is a constructive process, a new audio file with the applied effect will be created in the Soundbites window, and will also replace the original soundbite within the track.

To process a soundbite within the Tracks or Sequence Editors:

1. Begin by selecting the audio data you wish to affect. You can select an entire soundbite or just a portion of it (explained in Chapter 10).
2. Select the desired plug-in by choosing Audio menu > Audio Plug-ins. The plug-ins listed here are identical to the plug-ins found in the Inserts section of the Mixing Board.
3. Adjust the plug-in parameters and click the Preview button to audition the settings (see Figure 13.4). If needed, set the pre- and post-roll times.

Figure 13.4

Plug-ins that are accessed from the Audio menu contain additional controls for previewing, applying, and setting pre- or post-roll times.

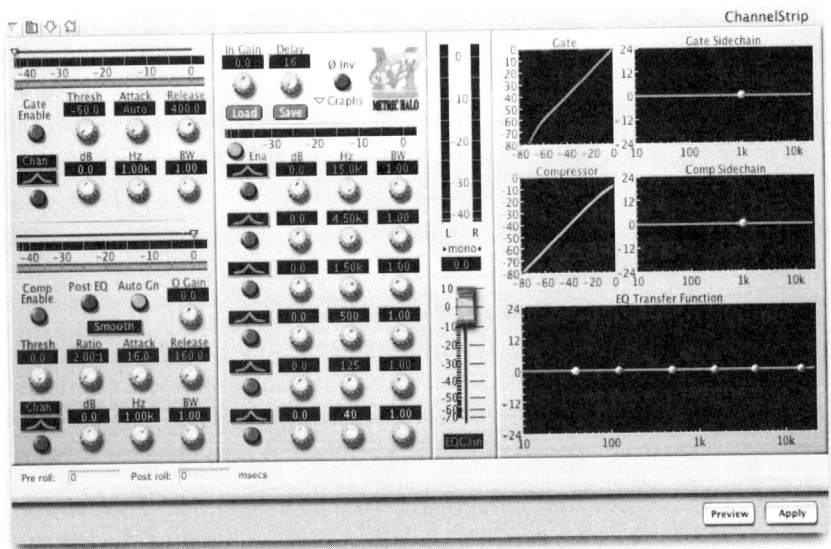

4. Once you are satisfied with the plug-in settings, click the Apply button. The time it takes to process the soundbite depends on the type of process and the speed of your computer. Files that are being processed will appear as an outlined waveform, as shown in Figure 13.5.

Once a soundbite is processed, a new sound file will be created with the applied effect. This new file will replace the original file within the track. Keep in mind that the original file will remain intact within the Soundbites window, allowing you to return to the original version when you need to.

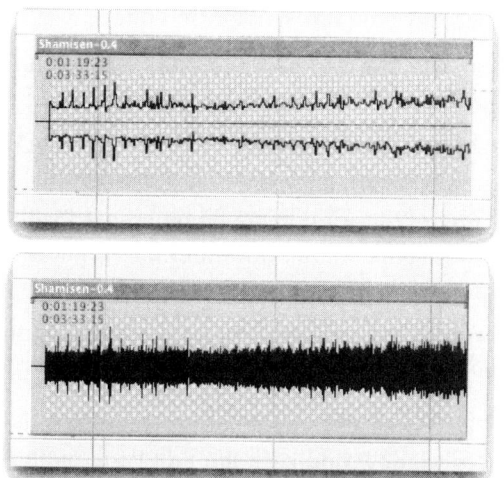

Figure 13.5
Soundbites that are being processed will appear as an outlined waveform (top). Once an effect has been applied, it will change to a solid waveform (bottom).

Processing Audio in the Waveform Editor

The procedure for processing audio with effects within the Waveform Editor, shown in Figure 13.6, is similar to the way in which you process soundbites directly within a track.

Simply select the soundbite in the Soundbites window, make a time-range selection in the Edit Pane (Waveform Editor), and then apply the desired plug-in from the Audio menu. You can also use the Audio menu's Normalize and Reverse commands when working in the Waveform Editor (explained later). As mentioned earlier, processing done in the Waveform Editor is destructive and will permanently alter the original file, so it's always a good idea to make sure you have a backup copy of the soundbite before applying any destructive processing/edits.

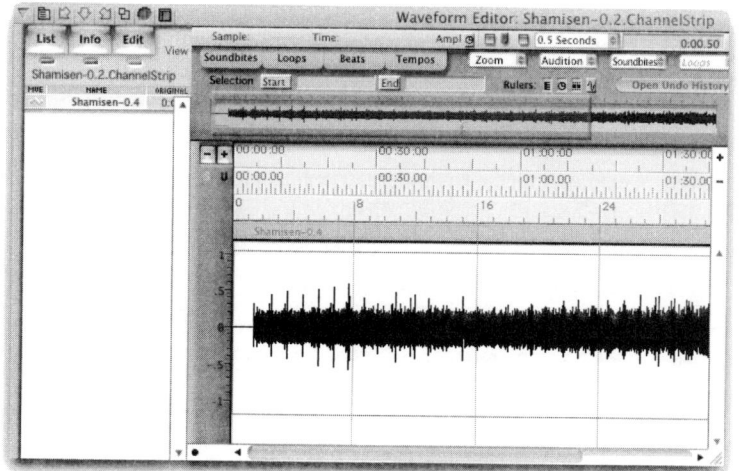

Figure 13.6
The Waveform Editor allows you to perform destructive processing to a selected soundbite.

To make a copy of a soundbite within the Waveform Editor:

1. Open the Soundbites window and click the Edit Pane button to open the Waveform Editor; then select the desired soundbite from the soundbite list.
2. Use the default keyboard shortcut Command+A to quickly select the entire soundbite.
3. Once the soundbite is selected, choose Soundbites window > mini-menu > New Sound File from Selection. A copy of the soundbite will be created with the same name as the original soundbite. A numerical suffix will be added to differentiate the two files (such as Audio -1.1, Audio-1.2, Audio -1.3, and so on).
4. You may want to rename this new backup copy something more easily recognizable. If so, Option-click the soundbite name in the Name column and rename the soundbite.

To process a soundbite within the Waveform Editor:

1. Open the Soundbites window and click the Edit Pane button to open the Waveform Editor, and then select the desired soundbite from the soundbite list.
2. Select the audio data you wish to affect. You can select an entire soundbite or just a portion of it (explained in Chapter 10). Use the default keyboard shortcut Command+A to quickly select the entire soundbite.
3. Select the desired audio plug-in by choosing Audio menu > Audio Plug-ins. As discussed earlier, the plug-ins listed here are identical to the plug-ins found in the Inserts section of the Mixing Board.
4. Adjust the plug-in parameters and click the Preview button to audition the settings. If needed, set the pre- and post-roll times.
5. Click Apply to process the soundbite with the effect. The amount of time it takes to process the file depends on the plug-in being applied, the length of the selection to be processed, and the speed of your computer.

> **SOUND FILE UNDO HISTORY**
>
> Keep in mind that processing (and editing) applied in the Waveform Editor is a destructive process—meaning that it will permanently alter the original file. Use a soundbite's independent Sound File Undo History to undo/redo destructive actions that have been applied. Simply click on the Undo History button in the Waveform Editor to open a soundbite's independent Undo History window. In the window, you should see a list of actions that have been performed on the particular file. Be sure to configure the Sound File Undo Pruning preferences to remember the necessary actions, or you may be surprised when you open the Undo History and find the list of actions discarded. Click on the Pruning Preferences button to access the Sound File Undo Pruning Setup.

Normalizing Soundbites

Normalization is the destructive process of raising a soundbite's loudest peak to full scale digital zero (or 0dB). Since this command basically takes a soundbite and makes it sound louder, it is commonly confused with the more sophisticated process of brickwall limiting (explained in the "Mastering" section of this chapter). When applied, the Normalize command will first scan an audio selection for its loudest peak. Once the peak is determined, DP will calculate how much overall gain needs to be applied to the soundbite to make the loudest peak reach 0dB. Keep in mind that normalization affects an entire selection of audio—not just its loudest peak—and will also raise the audio file's noise floor in the process; this can have the side effect of making the audio file sound noisier.

The process for normalizing soundbites in the Waveform Editor is the same as for effects processing. See the previous section for an explanation of Waveform Editor processing.

Applying Destructive Fades

Fades can be applied destructively to a soundbite within the Waveform Editor. Simply make a soundbite selection within the Waveform Editor and choose Audio menu > Fade In/Out to apply a destructive fade-in or fade-out. Keep in mind that these fades are linear and their fade curves cannot be changed.

If you need more versatility with the fade process, consider using the standard Fade command (Audio menu > Fades), which can be used in any other editor window (except the Waveform Editor).

The Background Processing Window

Unlike some audio commands (such as the Audio menu's Bounce to Disk command) that monopolize Digital Performer's system resources, many of the tasks (such as DSP processing and Beat Detection analysis) that DP performs occur in the background. The Background Processing window automatically prioritizes background tasks, placing more important processes at the top of the list (see Figure 13.7). DP will even interrupt low-priority analysis tasks to work on high-priority ones first. You can control how Background Processing functions in the Background Processing preferences (explained later in this chapter).

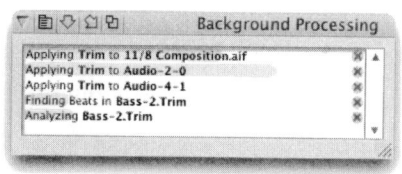

Figure 13.7
The Background Processing window shows a list of tasks that are waiting to be processed.

Background Processing Tasks

Actions that must be processed are called *tasks*, and are listed in the Task list of the Background Processing window. Tasks that are currently being processed will appear at the top of the list—DP will always work on higher-priority tasks first—with the task name displayed in black text. In addition, tasks that are being processed will have a progress bar (located behind the task name) that progresses from left to right. Once a task is processed, it will disappear from the Task list. Tasks that are waiting to be processed will appear in the list in lavender text.

Here are a few tips for managing background processing tasks.

- **To view the current tasks in the Task list**: Open the Background Processing window by choosing Studio menu > Background Processing. You can also use the default keyboard shortcut Shift+R. When first opened, the Background Processing window may appear with only a few tasks visible. You can expand the window by clicking on the title bar's Zoom button, or by dragging the bottom-right portion of the window downward.
- **To stop a task**: Click on the task's Cancel button, indicated with a small x. You will be presented with a warning dialog, shown in Figure 13.7, asking if you really want to continue with the cancellation process. Click the Kill Background Tasks button to stop the background processing for the specific task. Choose the Don't Kill Background Tasks button to continue with the task's background processing.

Figure 13.8

Clicking on a task's Cancel button will launch the Kill Background Tasks warning dialog.

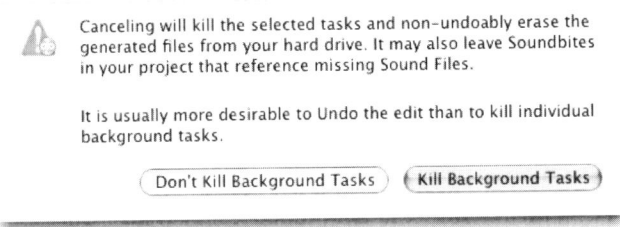

- **To begin running a task that has been stopped**: If Digital Performer encounters a problem and stops processing a task, you can run the process again by choosing the Run Stopped Task Again command from the mini-menu (Background Processing > mini-menu > Run Stopped Task Again).
- **To further customize how the Background Processing window functions in DP**: Open the Background Processing preferences and choose the desired settings (explained in the next section).

Background Processing Preferences

The Background Processing preferences, shown in Figure 13.9, determine how background processing is handled in DP. The provided options are divided into two different sections: the Background Processing section and the Automatic Beat and Tempo Analysis section.

※ Audio Processing

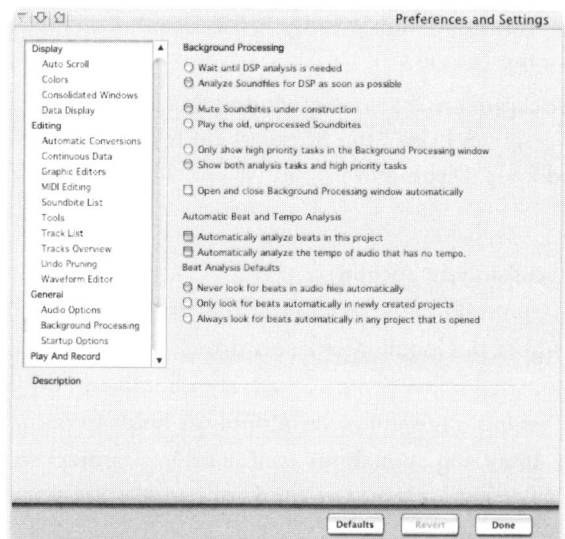

Figure 13.9
The Background Processing preferences provide options for controlling the functionality of DP's background processing.

Background Processing Section

The Background Processing section controls the overall functionality of DP's Background Processing feature; its options are as follows:

- **Wait until DSP analysis is needed**. Use this option if you do not want DP to automatically analyze soundbites listed in the Soundbites window. Soundbite analysis will occur only when you perform an audio process that requires it.

- **Analyze Soundbites for DSP as soon as possible**. Select this option if you want DP to automatically analyze Soundbites for future processing; this can come in handy if you are performing a lot of audio processing. DP will not have to perform this analysis for each audio process, as it will have already been completed in the background. This option is enabled by default.

- **Mute Soundbites under construction**. This option is enabled by default, and will prevent a soundbite from being heard while it is still being processed. Once background processing has been completed, the soundbite will become available for playback.

- **Play the old, unprocessed Soundbites**. Choose this option to hear the unprocessed soundbite while background processing is occurring.

- **Only show high priority tasks in the Background Processing window**. Enabled by default, this option will hide any lower-priority preemptive analysis tasks from the Background Processing window's Task list. Since these tasks are always processed after higher-priority tasks, it really isn't as necessary to see them.

- **Show both analysis tasks and high priority tasks.** Use this option to view all background processing tasks within the Task list.
- **Open and close Background Processing window automatically.** Enabled by default, this option will automatically open and close the Background processing window when background processing begins and ends. Disable this option if you want to manually control the visibility of this window.

Automatic Beat and Tempo Analysis Section

The Beat Detection Engine (introduced in Version 4.5) is able to detect the transients in an audio file, allowing DP to analyze where the location of beats are in a soundbite. Once a soundbite is analyzed and its beats are detected, soundbites can be intuitively quantized and time-stretched or compressed to conform to a project's tempo. Preemptive beat analysis helps to automate the beat detection process by automatically analyzing soundbites contained in a project so that they are ready to go when you wish to apply any beat- or tempo-related commands. Refer to Appendix A for an explanation of DP's Beat Detection Engine.

The Automatic Beat and Tempo Analysis section of the Background Processing preferences determines how preemptive beat and tempo analysis functions in DP; its options are explained below.

- **Automatically analyze beats in this project.** This option turns on preemptive beat analysis, which causes soundbites contained in the current project to be automatically analyzed. Keep in mind that when turned on, this feature will override the Beat Analysis Defaults settings, explained in the next section.
- **Automatically analyze the tempo of audio that has no tempo.** As with the previous option, enable this option if you want DP to automatically analyze a soundbite that doesn't contain tempo data.

Beat Analysis Defaults Section

The Beat Analysis Defaults options allow you to further control the functionality of DP's Beat Detection Engine. These options basically affect how the Automatically analyze beats in this project option (explained in the previous section) functions when enabled. They are as follows:

- **Never look for beats in audio files automatically.** Turn this feature on if you do not want DP to preemptively analyze beats. Keep in mind that the previously discussed Automatically analyze beats in this project option will override this setting.
- **Only look for beats Automatically in newly created projects.** Enable this option if you only want DP to look for beats in new projects that you create in the current version of Digital Performer—and leave older, existing projects alone.
- **Always look for beats automatically in any project that is opened.** Enable this option if you want DP to automatically look for beats when you open a project—regardless of the version of DP it was created in.

※ Audio Processing

> **DISABLING PREEMPTIVE BEAT ANALYSIS**
> Keep in mind that if you turn off DP's preemptive beat detection feature, you will have to perform soundbite beat analysis when you use any of Digital Performer's tempo- or beat-related commands.

The Audio Performance Window

Real-time audio plug-ins consume CPU power—some more than others, depending on the plug-in you are working with. DP's Audio Performance window provides visual feedback on amount of CPU usage, along with Playback and Record buffer activity, as shown in Figure 13.10. Keep in mind that your system's audio performance may suffer if you run out of CPU resources during playback. If this happens, you may need to scale down the number of real-time effects plug-ins you have inserted. You can also try raising the hardware buffer size; this will free up your system resources for more real-time effects. The trade-off with higher buffer sizes is increased monitoring latency—this shouldn't be a problem, however, during the mixing process.

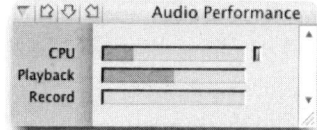

Figure 13.10

The Audio Performance window provides visual feedback on DP's resource consumption.

Plug-in Formats

DP comes bundled with audio effect plug-ins that are in its native MAS (MOTU Audio System) format and also provides direct support for Apple's AU (Audio Units) format. You will need to install a third-party application—called a *wrapper*— if you want to incorporate VST effect and instrument plug-ins into your DP system (see Figure 13.11). Once installed

Figure 13.11

Fxpansion VST to Audio Unit Adapter allows access to installed VST effect and instrument plug-ins.

343

and configured, these wrappers will automatically convert a VST formatted instrument or effect plug-in into either the AU or MAS formats (depending on the application) and make them available throughout Digital Performer.

Plug-in Locations

Audio plug-ins are stored in the System (User) > Library > Audio > Plug-ins folder, and are separated into different subfolders by plug-in type (such as MAS, VST, and Digidesign folder). AU plug-ins, however, are located in the Components folder. When installing plug-ins, keep in mind that you can store them in either the System or User Library folders. The only difference is that plug-ins installed in the User folder will only be available to that particular user. If you are working on a system that doesn't contain multiple user accounts, there really isn't anything to worry about—you'll have access to installed plug-ins, regardless of their System or User locations.

Installing AU Plug-ins

When installing AU plug-ins, be sure to place them in the Library > Audio > Plug-ins > Components folder. Remember that you can place them in either the System or User Library folders. The first time you launch DP after successful installation, DP will analyze each AU plug-in for problems during the loading process. At the end of the loading process, DP will display a dialog window showing you the results of the analysis (see Figure 13.12). AU examination happens only once and can take up to a few minutes, depending on the number of plug-ins to be analyzed. If an AU plug-in fails to load because of a problem, the plug-in will not be available for the project. The result of the examination will be logged in a text file and placed in the Documents folder.

Figure 13.12
DP will display a dialog window that shows whether newly installed AU plug-ins have been successfully loaded.

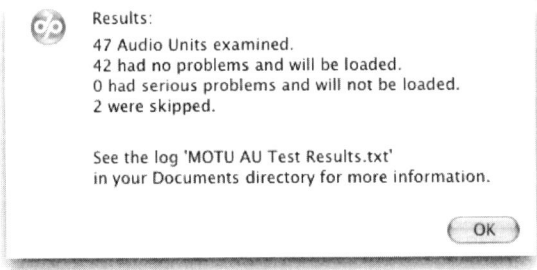

> **AU/MAS COMPATIBLE PLUG-INS**
> When installed plug-ins are in both the MAS and AU formats, DP will ignore the AU version and only load the MAS version for use in Digital Performer.

The Effects Window

Digital Performer's Effects windows display real-time audio and MIDI plug-ins that are inserted in the Mixing Board, as shown in Figure 13.13. Multiple Effects windows can be open at the same time.

Figure 13.13
Digital Performer's Effects window displays real-time plug-ins that are inserted in the Mixing Board. In this example, DP's Trigger plug-in is shown.

To open an Effects window:

- Choose Project menu > Effects window.
- Double-click on an existing plug-in insert in the Mixing Board.

The Mini-Menu

The Effects window's mini-menu contains options for saving, applying, and removing effect presets, as shown in Figure 13.14. See the "Saving and Recalling Presets" section of this chapter for a detailed explanation of this process.

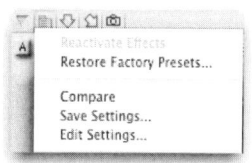

Figure 13.14
The Effects window's mini-menu contains options for managing effect presets.

The Automation, Track, Insert, and Effect Menus

Located below the Effects window's mini-menu are four menus that allow you to turn on plug-in automation, access another track, access another effect insert (A, B, C, and so on), or choose a different effect plug-in. In addition to providing automation controls, the menus allow you to access inserted plug-ins—even if they are located on different tracks—with only one Effects window open (see Figure 13.14).

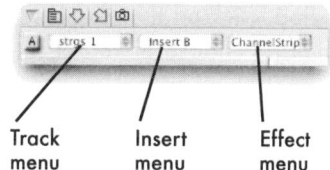

Track menu   Insert menu   Effect menu

Figure 13.15
Use the Track, Insert, and Effect menus to navigate between different plug-ins, even if they are located on different tracks.

CHAPTER 13 } Processing and Mastering

Bypassing an Effect

Inserted plug-ins can be bypassed or temporarily disabled by clicking on an effect's Bypass button (see Figure 13.16). If the plug-in window is closed, you can Option-click directly on an Insert in the Mixing Board window to bypass it.

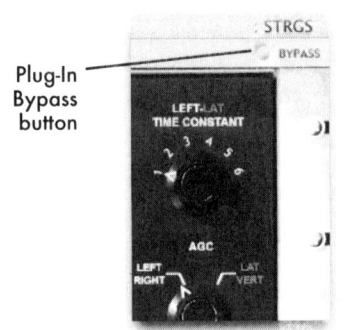

Figure 13.16

The Effects window's Bypass button is used to temporarily disable a plug-in.

Saving and Recalling Effect Presets

Many of DP's audio plug-ins (as well as third-party plug-ins) contain factory presets, which can be accessed from the plug-in's mini-menu. Presets will be listed below the Save and Edit Settings commands, shown in Figure 13.17, and will be available regardless of whether the plug-in is a real-time effect insert or a file-based Audio menu plug-in.

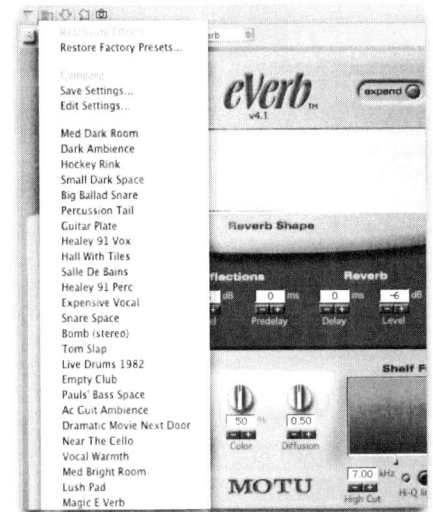

Figure 13.17

Effect presets will be listed in the specific plug-in's mini-menu.

To choose a plug-in preset:

1. Open the desired plug-in from the Audio menu or the Mixing Board Inserts.
2. Click on the plug-in window's mini-menu.
3. Select the desired preset to load it. Active presets will be indicated with a check mark.

To save a plug-in preset:

1. Start by configuring the specific plug-in's parameter settings to your liking.
2. Once you are satisfied, click on the plug-in window's mini-menu and choose Save Settings.
3. Name the custom preset in the Name Effect Preset window (see Figure 13.18).
4. Click OK, and the new preset will appear in the plug-in's mini-menu.

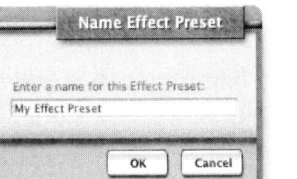

Figure 13.18

The Name Effect Preset window.

Audio Processing

To modify the parameter settings of an existing preset:

1. Select the desired preset from the plug-in's mini-menu, then adjust the parameter settings as needed.
2. Once you're satisfied with the new changes, choose Edit Settings from the plug-in's mini-menu.
3. Click on the preset you wish to modify from the list.
4. To update the preset with the new changes, click the Apply button.
5. To delete the selected preset, click the Delete button.
6. To rename the selected preset, click the Rename button. Enter a new name for the preset in the Name Effect Preset window (see Figure 3.19), and click OK.

Figure 13.19
The Edit Effect Presets window.

Keep in mind that you cannot rename or delete factory presets from the plug-in's mini-menu. You can, however, restore the factory presets to their original settings by choosing Restore Factory Presets from the specific plug-in's mini-menu.

> **AUDIO MENU PLUG-IN WINDOWS**
> File-based Audio menu plug-ins add additional controls for previewing, adding pre-/post-roll, and applying the effect. In addition, the mini-menu contains options, shown in Figure 13.20, for determining how Audio plug-ins behave once an effect is applied. These settings are global and will affect the functionality of all Audio Plug-in windows.

Figure 13.20
Additional mini-menu options control the behavior of Audio menu plug-in windows.

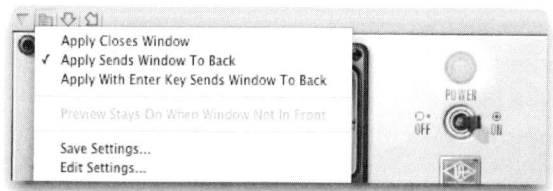

347

CHAPTER 13 } Processing and Mastering

Pitch-Shifting Audio

When you are pitch-shifting audio, DP can transpose soundbites in two different ways: with standard pitch shifting or with MOTU's proprietary PureDSP pitch-shifting algorithm. Standard pitch-shifting alters the frequencies of an audio file without affecting its length. With this method, the further you transpose a file away from its original pitch, the higher or lower the timbre of the pitch will be. This processing artifact leads to the well-known "chipmunk" sound. PureDSP processing, however, attempts to preserve the resonant frequencies of the sound without affecting the actual timbre or character of the audio file. By default, all audio files are set to use MOTU's PureDSP pitch-shifting algorithm. You can change a specific audio file's Transpose setting in the Soundbites Info Pane (Soundbites Window > Info Pane), as shown in Figure 13.21.

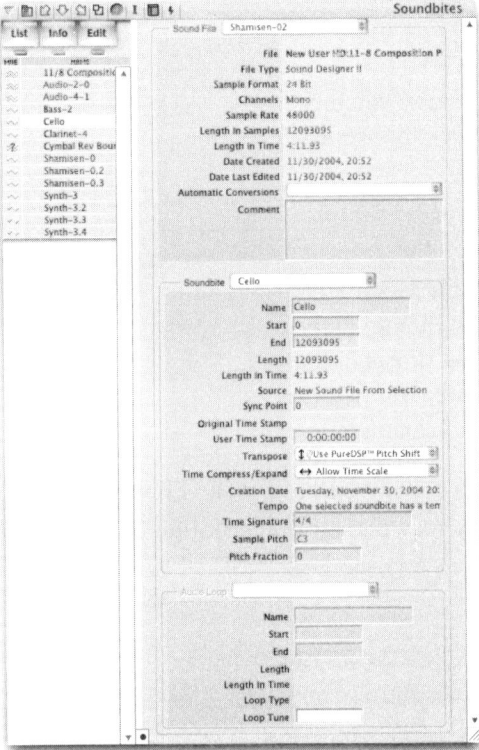

Figure 13.21

You can configure an individual soundbite's Transpose setting in the Info Pane of the Soundbites window.

To change the Transpose setting of a soundbite:

1. Open the Soundbites window by choosing Project menu > Soundbites. You can also use the default keyboard shortcut Shift+B.
2. Click on the Info Pane and select the desired soundbite from the Name column. Once the soundbite is selected, the Info Pane will update to display the soundbite's information.
3. From the Soundbite section of the Info pane (the center section), click on the Transpose pop-up menu and choose the desired pitch-shifting algorithm, as shown in Figure 13.22.

Figure 13.22

Set the Transpose settings for a soundbite from the Info Pane's Transpose pop-up menu. The Use PureDSP Pitch Shift option is enabled by default.

348

4. If you want to prevent a soundbite from being pitch-shifted altogether, choose the Don't Pitch Shift option.

The Transpose Command

The Transpose command, shown in Figure 13.23, allows you to transpose or pitch-shift selected MIDI data and soundbites (or portions of MIDI data and soundbites).

You can even simultaneously transpose MIDI and audio data selections together—allowing you, for example, to transpose an entire project that contains both MIDI

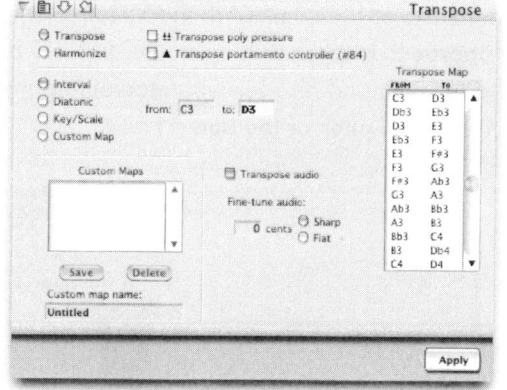

Figure 13.23

The Region menu's Transpose command can be used to transpose both audio and MIDI data.

and audio data. Keep in mind that the specific pitch-shifting algorithm used by the Transpose command to transpose audio will be determined by an individual soundbite's Transpose setting.

To transpose the pitch of an audio file with the Transpose command:

1. Select the soundbite(s) you wish to transpose. Remember that portions of a soundbite(s) can also be transposed.
2. Open the Transpose command by choosing Region menu > Transpose. You can also use the default keyboard shortcut Command+9.
3. Select the Interval option. Keep in mind that soundbites can only be transposed when the Interval option is selected. Once the Interval option is chosen, the Transpose Audio options will become available.
4. Confirm that the Transpose Audio button is enabled. The button will appear blue when turned on.
5. In the From and To interval input fields (located in the center of the Transpose window), set the transpose interval. This interval will determine how much a soundbite is pitch-shifted. The actual notes you choose to enter do not matter; only the interval between the two pitches will be used to transpose the selection.

   For example, if you wish to transpose a soundbite up a whole step, you could enter a value of C3 in the From input field and a value of D3 in the To input field. You could also enter the pitches of G4 and A4, respectively.

6. If necessary, use the Fine-tune audio options to adjust the transposition up or down by a number of cents. Keep in mind that there are 100 cents per half step (or half tone).
7. Once you have entered the necessary values, click the Apply button to confirm the change.

The Spectral Effects Command

Compared with the standard Transpose command, the Spectral Effects command, shown in Figure 13.24, offers a different approach to pitch-shifting audio. Besides being able to transpose an audio selection, the Spectral Effects command also lets you manipulate the *formants* and/or tempo of a sound—independently of the actual pitch of the audio file.

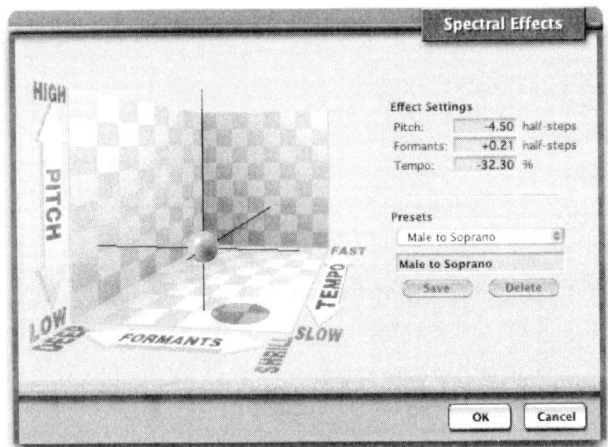

Figure 13.24
The Spectral Effects command provides a 3D space for controlling the pitch, formants, and tempo of a sound source.

Keep in mind that the Spectral command will ignore a soundbite's PureDSP settings (located in the Info Pane of the Soundbites window). A soundbite selected with the Spectral Effects command can always be processed, regardless of its PureDSP Settings.

> ❋ **WHAT ARE FORMANTS?**
> *Formants* are the resonant frequencies present within a sound. These frequencies have fixed peaks that exist independently of the sound's fundamental pitch or note. This is what gives a sound its particular timbre and character. Think of two instruments—say, an oboe and trumpet—playing the exact same note of middle C. Even though both instruments are playing the same pitch, we can distinguish between the two instruments because of their unique timbres or formants. When working with the human voice, formants also determine the character of a voice, and whether a voice sounds either male or female. Generally speaking, male voices have lower formants than female voices, vibrating at almost half the speed of their female counterparts. This is what makes the male voice sound lower than the female.

The Effect Settings Section

The Spectral Effects command allows you to alter the pitch of a sound source independently of its formants and tempo. Mono sound sources work best when using this command. You can enter the desired values for the pitch, formants, and tempo directly in the Effect Settings input fields—or you can use the red globe within the 3D space. Located to the left of the Spectral Effects window, the 3D space shows the relationships between the pitch, formant, and tempo. Drag the red globe vertically to affect the pitch or horizontally to change the formant. Dragging the globe forward or backward in the space will change the tempo.

Presets

Digital Performer provides a number of gender-bending presets that can be accessed by clicking the Preset menu, as shown in Figure 13.25.

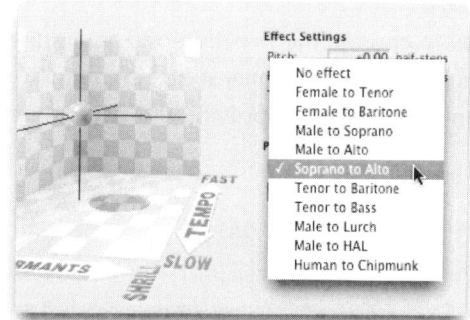

Figure 13.25
Spectral Effects presets.

Presets such as Female to Tenor, Male to Soprano, Male to Lurch, and Human to Chipmunk are included. These presets automatically adjust the pitch, formants, and tempo values according to the preset you have selected. You can save your own custom preset by setting the necessary values, typing in the name of the new preset, and then clicking the Save button. To delete a preset, select it and click the Delete button.

Applying the Spectral Effects Command

Once you get used to the concept of formants, you'll find that the Spectral Effects command window is fairly straightforward.

To use the Spectral Effects command:

1. Select the soundbite(s) you wish to affect. Keep in mind that the Spectral Effects command works best with mono sound sources.
2. Choose Audio menu > Spectral Effects.
3. Once the Spectral Effects window is open, enter the desired pitch, formants, and tempo values in the Effects Setting input fields. Remember that you can also drag the 3D space's red globe to set these values.
4. If you would like to start with an existing preset, select it from the Preset menu.
5. Click OK to apply the changes.

CHAPTER 13 } Processing and Mastering

> **START WITH A PRESET**
> If you're new to the Spectral Effects window and are confused by the concept of formants, try starting with one of the provided presets. Experiment to see how certain combinations of settings will change a sound. The 3D space can be especially useful in this situation, as it allows you to actually "see" the settings and compare them to the altered sound.

Time-Stretching Audio

Time-stretching allows you to change the duration of a soundbite without affecting its pitch. Digital Performer provides two different ways of time-stretching audio: graphically time-stretching soundbites by dragging with the Hand cursor or by applying the Region menu's Scale Time command to an audio selection.

> **TIME-STRETCHING AND TEMPO COMMANDS**
> Digital Performer's various tempo-related commands (such as Set Soundbite Tempo) also time stretch audio, but will change the tempo of the soundbite in the process. Similarly, the Automatic Conversion option will also time-stretch audio files to force them to conform to a project's tempo, sample rate, and/or sample format—all without affecting the pitch of the audio.

Graphically Time-Stretching Audio

Time-stretching audio graphically within Digital Performer is a very simple process and can be accomplished within the Sequence Editor.

To graphically time-stretch audio in the Sequence Editor:

1. Open the Sequence Editor from the Project menu by choosing Project menu > Sequence. You can also use the default keyboard shortcut Shift+S.

2. Locate the soundbite you wish to time-stretch and place the cursor at the left or right edge of the soundbite's colored title bar. Once in position, you should see the cursor change to the Hand tool, as shown in Figure 13.26.
3. Once the cursor switches to the Hand tool, click and drag the soundbite to time-stretch or time-compress the soundbite, as shown in Figure 13.27. How far you drag with the Hand tool will determine the duration of the time-stretched audio.
4. Release the mouse and DP will begin time-stretching the audio.

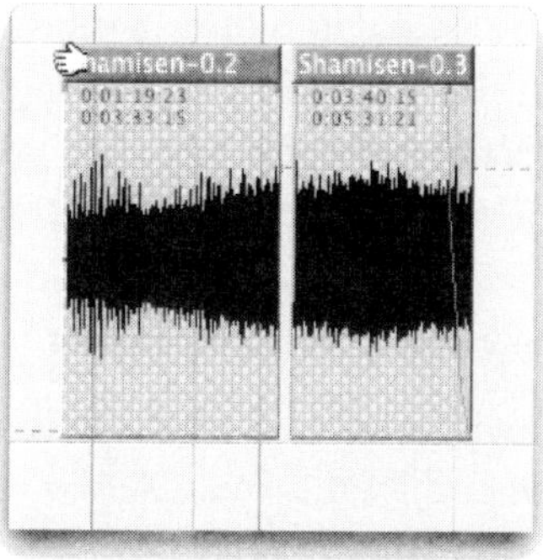

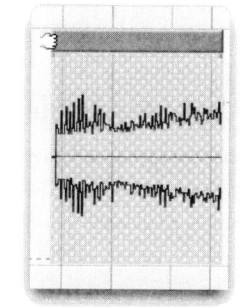

Figure 13.26
Position the cursor over a soundbite's title bar to switch to the Hand tool.

Figure 13.27
Drag with the Hand tool to time-stretch a soundbite. Soundbites being time-stretched will appear with an outlined waveform display.

Soundbites currently being processed will appear with their waveforms displayed as an outline. Once the time-stretching is completed, the soundbite will update and appear as a solid waveform display. Keep in mind that this is a constructive process, so DP will create a new time-stretched version of the soundbite to replace the original audio. DP will add a number to the end of the soundbite name (such as audio.1, audio.2, audio.3, and so on) to designate it as an alternate version.

The Scale Time Command

The Scale Time command, shown in Figure 13.28, allows you to time-stretch (or time scale) selected audio and/or MIDI data—even at the same time.

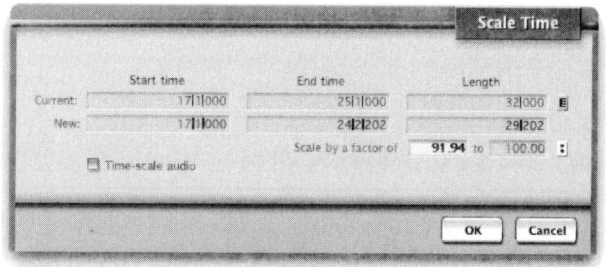

Figure 13.28
The Scale Time command window.

The Scale Time command is divided into three separate columns that show the start, end, and length of the current selection (which is the first row showing the current time-range selection) and the new time-stretched selection (which is what the selection will be time scaled to after hitting the OK button). Be aware that you cannot change the current selection values from within the Scale Time window (these values will appear dimmed). You must make a new time-range selection within an editor window in order to change the current selection values.

There are two settings that will impact whether audio can be time-stretched with the Scale Time command: the Scale Time command's Time Scale Audio option and the soundbite's Time Compress/Expand setting (explained earlier). Both settings/options must be enabled in order for DP to time-stretch a soundbite. If the Time Scale Audio option is turned off, DP will only change the start time of the selection, leaving the soundbite's current duration intact.

TIME COMPRESS/EXPAND IS ENABLED BY DEFAULT
Keep in mind that the Time Compress/Expand setting (located in the Info Pane of the Soundbites window) is enabled on all soundbites by default, so you shouldn't have to worry about this PureDSP attribute under normal circumstances.

To time-stretch audio with the Scale Time command:

1. Start by selecting the soundbite you wish to time-stretch.
2. Enter the desired values in the New Start, End, or Duration columns. If you only want to change the actual duration of the soundbite while preserving its start time, change the End or Duration values. You'll notice that the End and Duration input fields are linked together for greater flexibility.
3. You can also click the Percentage button, located below the New Length column, to change the input field from a percentage value to a scale factor (or ratio), as shown in Figure 13.29.
4. Set the ratio for the time-stretching in the Scale by a factor of input fields.
5. Enable the Time-scale audio option and click OK.

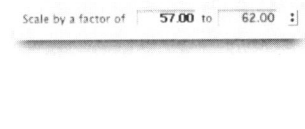

Figure 13.29

Click the Percentage button to toggle the values displayed in the Scale by a factor of input fields. This allows you to time-stretch audio by a specific ratio or scale factor.

Mastering

As explained earlier, the mastering (or pre-mastering) process requires skill and experience to perform correctly, so it's recommended that you have any mixes requiring mastering worked on by a professional mastering engineer. While a great mastering job will take a good mix and make it great, a poor mastering job can take even the greatest mix and reduce it to a sonic mess. Remember, great mastering tools do not a great mastering engineer make.

There will be times, however, when you will need to master in Digital Performer. Many of DP's standard mixing and editing features (such as the master fader track, plug-in processing, the Waveform and Sequence Editors, and so on) can be used in the DP mastering process. Keep in mind that there really isn't a special way to configure a DP project for mastering. DP mastering methods and setups will vary from user to user and project to project.

If you're new to the concept of mastering, you probably have a million questions, such as "When should I EQ?" "Should I compress or limit my mix?" "How loud should I make my mastered mixes?" and "What is brickwall limiting?" Unfortunately, there aren't set answers or step-by-step processes. Every mix will be different, and experience will tell you what needs to be accomplished and what specific tools can be used to achieve the best results with the least amount of compromise.

Step-by-step instructions on how to use processing during the mastering stage are far beyond the scope of this book. This section will attempt to provide a very basic understanding of the processes involved with music mastering, and provide a few suggestions for mastering audio within DP.

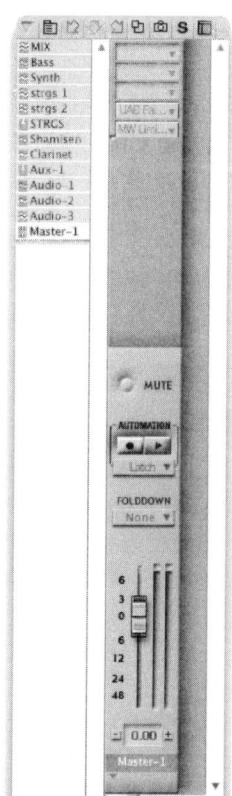

Figure 13.30

DP's master fader track.

Before you dive into these difficult concepts, I'll discuss the technical aspects of mastering in Digital Performer.

The Master Fader

DP's master fader track, shown in Figure 13.30, is used to control the overall level of a specific bus or output assignment. Unlike audio and aux tracks, master faders do not have sends, record, or solo buttons.

You can use DP's master fader to apply processing or control the levels of an overall mix, either during the actual mixing process or during the mastering stage. The procedures for using a master fader are the same, regardless of the type of situation you are working with.

To insert a master fader:

1. Create a master fader by choosing Project menu > Add Tracks > Master Fader Track. You can also use the default keyboard shortcut Shift+Control+M.
2. Assign the output of the master fader to the output of the other tracks in your project. For example, if the audio track(s) you are working with is assigned to Analog 1-2, assign the master fader also to Analog 1-2.

> **SETTING UP THE MASTER FADER**
>
> The master fader should be one of the first tracks you create in your Digital Performer project. When assigned to the mix output, this fader will allow you to control the overall volume of your entire mix. As it also contains an Insert and Automation section, you can apply effects processing across your entire mix and even automate a fade-out of the song. In addition, the master fader level meters can be used to monitor the overall levels of your mix, ensuring that you do not overload the mix outputs—which can result in degraded audio integrity and unwanted digital distortion. Once the master fader is created, you can usually set it to unity gain and then forget about it. Usually, you must start working with this fader only when the mixing process begins.

Bouncing to Disk

Once you have mixed/mastered your project, you'll need to bounce your tracks to disk. The bounce to disk process basically takes selected multiple tracks and merges them together into a single track on your hard drive. Think of this as the "mix-down" process. Bouncing to disk is a constructive process, creating a new audio file while keeping your original tracks intact. There are two methods for bouncing to disk: using the Bounce To Disk command or using a real-time bounce (explained later). Before you can use the Bounce to Disk command, you must first select the audio you wish to bounce.

> **BOUNCING MIDI TRACKS**
>
> If you want to include your MIDI tracks in your final mix, then they must be converted to audio first. If you're using outboard MIDI modules, follow the procedures for performing a real-time bounce to disk (explained later in this chapter). If you're using virtual instruments, use the Audio menu's Freeze Selected Tracks command instead.

※ Mastering

The Bounce To Disk Command
The Audio menu's Bounce To Disk command, shown in Figure 13.31, provides several options for specifying the final format of your bounced audio file.

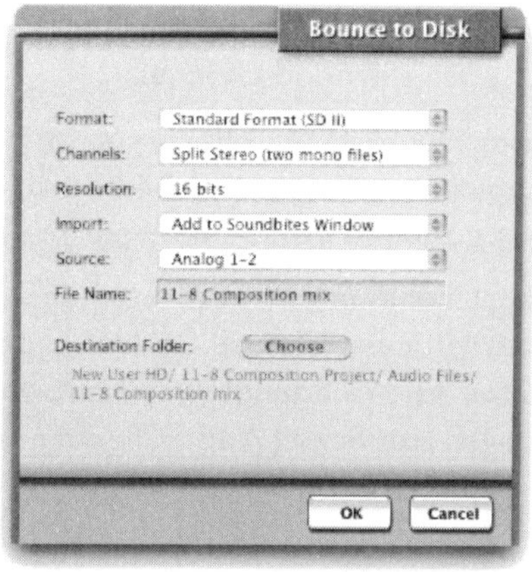

Figure 13.31
The Bounce To Disk command.

* **Format menu.** This menu, shown in Figure 13.32, allows you to specify the format for the bounce file. DP's native file format is split-stereo Sound Designer II (non-interleaved SD II), and appears as the Standard Format (SD II) option. Use this format if you're bouncing audio that you wish to include in your current project or use in another DP system. You can also bounce files to a variety of different stereo interleaved Core Audio formats supplied by Mac OSX. Keep in mind that the Core Audio formats contain different options from the Standard Format (SD II).

Figure 13.32
The Bounce To Disk command's Format menu.

* **Channels.** This menu, shown in Figure 13.33, determines the channel format for the Standard Format (SD II) format option. Its options are:

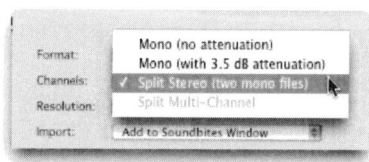

Figure 13.33
The Channels menu provides options for specifying the channel format for DP's native non-interleaved SD II format.

  * *Mono (no attenuation).* This option will create a mono sound file on your hard drive by summing together the left and right channels. This audio summing will result in an increased signal level of the file.

  * *Mono (with 3.5dB attenuation).* This option creates a summed mono audio file, but compensates for the 3.5dB increase that is a result of the mono-summing process.

  * *Split Stereo (two mono files).* Use this option to create a split stereo file (or dual mono file) that is made up of two separate mono files labeled with .L and .R extensions. DP doesn't support interleaved stereo files, so use this option when you want to use the bounced files in DP without having to convert them.

- *Split Multi-Channel.* Similar to the previous split stereo option, this option creates separate mono files for each surround channel.
- **Resolution.** The Resolution menu allows you to set the sample format (or bit depth) of the bounced file. Choices are 8, 16, and 24 bits. Under normal circumstances, you'll probably want to choose the sample format that your project is already in.
- **Import.** The Import menu determines what happens to the new file that is created as a result of the bounce to disk process. Choose Do Not Import if you only want to create the file on your hard drive. Use the Add to Soundbites Window option to add the bounced file to the current project's Soundbites List. Select Add to Sequence to create a new audio track in the current sequence that contains your bounced file.
- **Source.** Select the source for the audio bounce from this menu. For example, if you have your tracks all assigned to output Analog 1-2, choose Analog 1-2 from the drop-down menu.
- **File Name.** This is the name for the final bounce file. If needed, the appropriate extensions (such as .L, .R, and so on) will be automatically added to the newly created audio file(s).
- **Destination Folder.** This is the location for the new file(s) that will be created during the audio bounce. By default, the current project's Audio Files folder will be selected. Click the Choose button to manually set a location for the bounced file(s).

To bounce an audio selection to disk:

1. Start by selecting the soundbite(s) you wish to include in your bounce.
2. Once the soundbite is selected, choose Audio menu > Bounce To Disk.
3. Make the desired Bounce To Disk settings (discussed earlier) and click OK.

Once you click OK, DP will begin bouncing the audio selection to disk. The Bouncing Selection to Disk progress window will appear and display the progress of the bounce. In most situations, DP will bounce audio faster than real-time. This really depends on the speed of your computer, the number of tracks, and the number of plug-ins that DP must process during the bounce.

> **BOUNCE TO DISK IS NOT A BACKGROUND PROCESS**
> The bounce to disk process occurs in the foreground, so you will not be able to perform any other operations while DP is bouncing tracks to disk.

※ Mastering

Real-Time Bounce to Disk

A real-time bounce is basically a real-time recording of selected tracks. Instead of using the Bounce To Disk command, selected tracks are routed to a new audio track within DP and recorded in real-time. If you have virtual instrument and/or MIDI tracks in your session and don't want to freeze each MIDI track or record them to separate tracks in order to use the Bounce To Disk command, then use the real-time bounce process, which will create a new track of your entire mix that also includes the audio outputs of your MIDI sound modules or virtual instruments.

To perform a real-time audio bounce:

1. Start by changing the output assignments of the tracks you wish to include in the real-time bounce to a new bus (for example, bus 1-2).
2. Create a new stereo audio track and assign its input to bus 1-2.
3. Arm the track and begin recording.

Exporting Audio

DP's Export Selected Bites command, located in the Soundbites window, allows you to export existing soundbites to a variety of different file formats. This command is different than the Audio menu's Bounce To Disk command, which creates new soundbites from selected tracks. Use the Export Selected Bite(s) command, shown in Figure 13.34, to export soundbites located in the Soundbites window to a different file format or hard drive location.

Figure 13.34

The Export Selected Bite(s) command is used to export existing soundbites to different file formats.

359

CHAPTER 13 } Processing and Mastering

Exporting and Bouncing to the MP3 Format

Digital Performer can export or bounce to disk in the MP3 format—simply choose the MP3 option when bouncing or exporting audio files to disk. Before you can begin using this feature, however, you must install the L.A.M.E. MP3 Codec, which can be found on the Web. This open-source MP3 encoder does not come bundled with DP and will not be installed during the Digital Performer installation process.

L.A.M.E. Framework

There are many different sites from which you can download this codec. Simply perform a Web search for the Mac OS X compatible version of the L.A.M.E. codec (or the L.A.M.E. framework) and download it to your computer. Once it's downloaded, place the L.A.M.E. framework file in the System > Library > Frameworks folder.

Once the L.A.M.E. framework is installed and your is computer restarted, the L.A.M.E. MP3 option will become available in both the Bounce To Disk and Export Selected Bite(s) commands.

Converting to MP3 or AAC with iTunes

If you don't want to use Digital Performer to export to MP3, or would rather convert your mix to the AAC format instead, you can use Apple's free iTunes music player. Keep in mind that the audio file must be in a supported iTunes format: AIFC, AIFF, SDII, .WAV, MP3, or AAC.

To convert an audio file to the MP3 or AAC format with iTunes:

1. First, drop your bounced mix into the iTunes window to import your song into iTunes.
2. Open the iTunes preferences and click the Importing tab.
3. Select MP3 or AAC in the Import Using menu.
4. Specify the bit-rate from the Setting menu, and then click OK to confirm the new conversion settings.
5. Select the mix that you imported earlier and choose iTunes > Advanced menu > Convert Selection to MP3/AAC. iTunes will create a new audio file in the chosen format at the specified bit-rate. Once created, the audio file will appear in the iTunes Library.

Mastering in DP

There is no set way to configure a project for mastering. Circumstances will dictate your specific setup and processing configurations. Following are just a few scenarios illustrating how you might set up your project for mastering in Digital Performer:

- You want to perform a quick "mastering" job on a demo you've been working on, so you insert a compressor (such as a UAD Fairchild or Waves Renaissance Compressor) and a brickwall limiter (such as the MasterWorks Limiter or Waves L3) on the master fader. You add some light mix bus compression (1.5.1:1 ratio with 1-3dB of gain reduction) and turn the threshold down on the limiter to make your mix louder (3-6dB of limiting). You bounce to disk and then burn a disc at 52x speed.

* You need to master a number of songs for an album, so you import each song into DP at 24bit/48kHz, which will allow you to process the tracks at a high resolution. You tweak the balance of each song by applying subtle amounts of EQ and/or compression, starting with the most important song. With the first track as your guide, you make any necessary adjusts to the remaining tracks. You do all this in the Waveform Editor, since you're already comfortable with other two-track editing programs such as Bias Peak and Digi's Sound Designer II. Next, you add brickwall limiting (and 16-bit dithering) to the track you started with, being careful not to over-limit, which will destroy the track's transients and make it too loud. Using this track as a reference, you jump between the other different songs as you limit them, adjusting the perceived loudness of each track in relation to one another. You also make any necessary head/tail edits and add quick fades to the beginning and end of each soundbite. You make sure to apply any fades at the last stage of the processing. At last, you sample-rate-convert each 16-bit file to 44.1kHz (explained later), export each processed track, and import the tracks into a CD burning program, such as Toast or Jam. You set the track gaps as you listen back to each track, and then you burn a disk at 4x speed.

* This scenario is similar to the previous one, except that you place all your import songs onto their own separate audio tracks within separate Chunks instead of working in the Waveform Editor. Each Chunk contains an audio track (which contains a song) and a master fader. You set up your workspace so that you can view all your Chunks at once, allowing you to quickly jump between and play back each song in your album. When you start processing your songs, you use the real-time inserts on each master fader instead of destructively processing in the Waveform Editor. This setup allows you greater flexibility, as you can tweak the processing for each track in real-time while jumping between the various songs. The processing is intensive, as you have multiple Chunks with the same effects plug-ins duplicated multiple times across different tracks, but you have the RAM and processing speed to handle it.

Processing Your Final Mix

When you think of the goal of music mastering, the first thing that may come to mind is probably "to make my mix louder." Anyone who has ever A/B'd one of his or her finished mixes with a professionally mastered mix knows exactly what I'm talking about. Other goals that may come to mind are "balance," "clarity," and "punch." Processing in the mastering stage of music production can be used to achieve these goals. Equalization, compression, volume automation, and brickwall limiting are some of the tools used by mastering engineers to shape a track or set of tracks. Regardless of the type(s) of processing you choose to incorporate, here are a few tips to keep in mind:

- **Start subtly**. Even the subtlest of changes can be perceived when working on a two-channel mix (or multi-channel mix). Start with gentle processor settings and go from there.
- **A/B**. The best way to check if you're making positive changes is to bypass the plug-in you're working with and compare the processed sound to the original mix.

> **THE A/B PROCESS**
> Even if you're not familiar with the term A/B, chances are that you've been using this process for a long time without knowing it. When you compare one file (or track, mix, setting, and so on) against another file, you are "A/Bing" the file. This applies even to situations where you're comparing more than two things together.

In addition to effects processing and editing, you'll also have to consider dither and sample rate conversion, which are necessary to get your high-resolution mix (for example, 24-bit/96kHz) into the 16-bit/44.1kHz CD standard if you're going to be burning CDs. Dithering and sample rate conversion are discussed towards the end of this chapter.

Equalization

Tonal balance is one of the important components of a good mix. Too much bass and low-mid frequencies can make a song sound "muffled" or "muddy." Too much energy in the high frequencies can have the opposite effect, making a mix sound "thin" and "overly bright," while too much of the high-mid frequencies can make a mix "shrill" and "bitey," or even painful to listen to. In the ideal world, any obvious balance problems would be taken care of during the mix, or the track would be sent back for a re-mix if the mastering engineer requests it. There will be many times, however, when you have to "fix it in the mastering."

Equalization, or EQ, can be used to subtly change the tone of a track, or surgically "fix" frequencies that stand out in a mix. Keep in mind that some EQ plug-ins will do better jobs at certain tasks than others. The MasterWorks EQ, shown in Figure 13.35, is an example of an EQ that can be used for both subtle and surgical corrections.

Figure 13.35

The MasterWorks EQ.

Here are a few thoughts and suggestions for using EQ in the mastering process, regardless of which type of EQ plug-ins you decide to use.

* **Low Frequencies.** Extremely low frequencies contain a lot of energy, as you must turn them up louder compared to other frequencies in order to hear them. This can cause the "low end" to consume the precious headroom of a mix. Try inserting a low-cut filter at 40Hz or below to control the low end of your mix. Since this type of low frequency roll-off will affect other elements in your mix (not just the kick and bass), you may want to start the EQ shelf at 20Hz and slowly raise the frequency, stopping when you hear the filter starting to adversely affect the mix.
* **EQ—Surgery versus Subtlety.** If you have specific frequencies that need to be tamed without affecting other surrounding frequencies, you can use an EQ band set to a narrow Q. Remember that the Q (or bandwidth) determines how many frequencies surrounding the center frequency will be affected—the higher the Q, the narrower the bandwidth, and vice-versa. If you need to gently shape the sound, try using an EQ set to a wide band, or smaller Q.

- **Cause and effect**. Be aware that EQing not only affects the specific frequencies you're working with, but also changes how other related frequencies (or instruments) are perceived in a mix. EQing the bass, for example, can cause the cymbals to sound less bright, or can cause the vocal to lose presence. Always be aware of the EQ relationships of a mix before you start twisting those knobs.

Compression versus Limiting

When to compress? When to limit? Generally speaking, compressors are used to reduce the overall dynamic range and/or change the character of a signal. Limiters are basically compressors that are set to a harder ratio, such as 10:1 or 20:1. Limiters are typically used when you want to make a signal louder while maintaining transparency. Brickwall limiters are a special form of limiter that increase the apparent loudness of a sound in proportion to the amount of limiting that is applied. The lower the threshold, the louder the sound will be. The brickwall limiter is typically found at the very end of a mastering signal chain.

As you may already know, compressors and limiters come in many different flavors—but you shouldn't think that any compressor/limiter can achieve positive mastering results. Some compressor plug-ins are designed to handle broadband material with great results. Universal Audio's Fairchild, shown in Figure 13.36, and Wave's Renaissance Compressors are two such plug-ins.

Figure 13.36

Universal Audio's Fairchild compressor.

Multiband Compression

The DP's MasterWorks Compressor is also effective when working with mixed material, but operates differently than a standard compressor. The MasterWorks compressor, shown in Figure 13.37, is a multiband compressor. Multiband compression basically splits a signal into multiple frequency bands (typically three to four bands) and compresses them independently of one another, allowing you, for example, to compress only the low frequencies of a mix while leaving the high frequencies intact. These compressors are extremely versatile, but also extremely easy to misuse.

Figure 13.37

Digital Performer's MasterWorks Compressor plug-in.

Brickwall Limiting

As discussed earlier, brickwall limiters are a special type of limiter that make a sound louder by limiting its transient peaks and raising the gain of the sound. Lower the limiter's threshold by 3dB and the gain of the signal will be raised proportionally by 3dB. The limiter's threshold sets a ceiling for the sound that acts as a "brick wall"—completely stopping any part of the signal from going over the specified threshold. Digital Performer's MasterWorks Limiter and Universal Audio's Precision Limiter, shown in Figure 13.38, are examples of brickwall limiters.

Many brickwall limiting plug-ins also provide controls for dithering and noise shaping your high resolution files from 24-bits to the 16-bit CD audio standard (explained in the next section). Use the dithering options only when the plug-in is the last step in your processing chain. Dither should always be applied in the very last and final stage of the mastering process.

CHAPTER 13 } Processing and Mastering

Figure 13.38
UA's Precision Limiter (top) and DP's MasterWorks Limiter (bottom) are two examples of brickwall limiters.

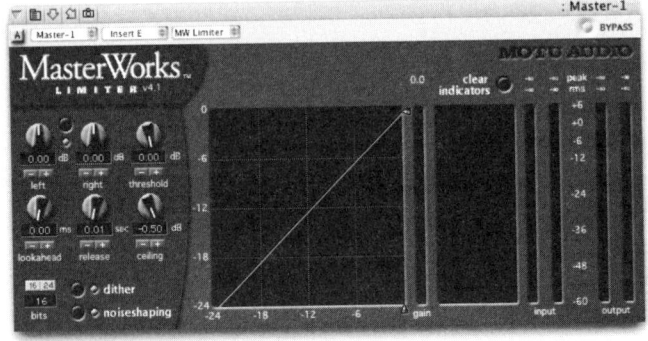

OVER-LIMITING YOUR MIX!

Like with any useful tool, applying too much limiting to a sound can have very negative effects on the audio quality. Besides the introduced harmonic distortion, excessively loud musical material can be fatiguing to the ear.

COMPRESSING THE MIX BUS WITH 2-MIX COMPRESSION

The *2-mix* is another name for your overall stereo mix. The *mix bus* refers to the bus or output that is used to sum the individual tracks in your mix down to two channels (or more) of audio. So when you hear the phrase *2-mix compression* or *mix-bus compression*, what people are referring to is the compression that is applied to your entire mix.

There are, like with many audio engineering practices, many different schools of thought on mix-bus compression. Some feel that this type of compression should be saved for the mastering engineers, while others like the effect is has on their mixes.

If you're mixing and mastering your own tunes, however, you may find yourself using mix-bus compression along with other effects plug-ins—almost mastering your tunes during mix process. As I mentioned earlier in this chapter, when and how you decide to approach mastering your mixes in DP is entirely up to you, and will be determined by an indeterminate number of always varying factors.

Mastering

Dither and Noiseshaping

A digital audio signal is described as a string of ones and zeros. This is called *bit depth* (also referred to as the *sample format* or *resolution*). CDs use a 16-bit format, while DP internally operates at a resolution of 32 bits. Any time you reduce the bit depth of an audio file (such as when you are bouncing your mix to 16-bit/44.1kHz to use in an audio CD), quantization distortion is introduced during the conversion process. *Dither* is the small amount of noise that is applied to a signal when its sample format is changed in order to reduce the amount of this quantization distortion. Since dithering actually adds noise (and raises the noise floor in the process), noiseshaping algorithms are usually employed to make this added noise less obvious (and more pleasant-sounding) to the listener.

DP's MasterWorks Limiter (along with many other brickwall limiters) contains options for dithering and noiseshaping your high-resolution signal to lower bit depths. You should always try to mix/master at the highest resolution possible to maintain the integrity of the sound, dithering and noiseshaping at the final stage of the production process to bring your high-resolution audio files back into the 16-bit/44,1kHz world of CDs.

If you plan on sending your mixes off to be mastered by someone else, don't apply any dither or noiseshaping to your audio! Simply keep your mix at the highest resolution possible (24-bit), and let the mastering engineer deal with this process. In addition, leave at least 2-3dB of headroom on your master fader, and make sure it doesn't overload (go over digital 0) at any point in the mix down process!

Sample Format Conversion

Besides using plug-ins such as the MasterWorks Limiter to dither down to lower bit depths, you can also use DP's Convert Sample Format command (Soundbites window > mini-menu > Convert Sample Format). Simply select the soundbite(s) you wish to convert and choose the Convert Sample Format command, shown in Figure 13.39.

Specify the new bit depth for the audio, and then choose what happens after the soundbites are converted. Dither (explained earlier) is always applied to a file that is being converted from 24 to 16 bits.

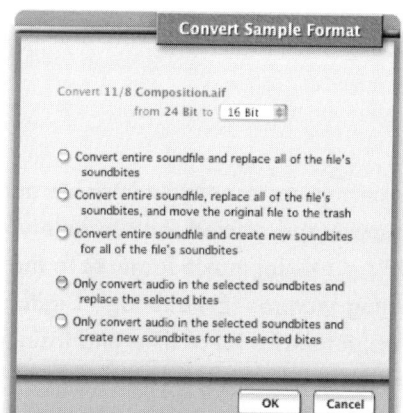

Figure 13.39

The Convert Sample Format command allows you to change the bit depth of a soundbite.

CHAPTER 13 } Processing and Mastering

Sample Rate Conversion

In addition to dithering down to a lower bit depth, you can also change the sample rate of an audio file with DP's Convert Sampling Rate command, located in the mini-menu of the Soundbites window. Remember that standard CD audio operates at 44.1kHz, so if your project is running at a higher rate (such as 48, 88.2, or 96kHz, and so on) you'll need to down-sample your mixes when attempting to burn a CD. If convenience is a factor (say, you just want to burn a quick demo of a song), you may be able to rely on your CD burning program to convert the sample rate for you. The results will vary, of course, depending on the sophistication of the program you are using.

If you are concerned about maintaining the quality of your mix during the conversion process, you can use DP's Convert Sampling Rate command (or other third party applications such as AudioEase's BarbaBatch conversion program) instead. Simply select the soundbite(s) you wish to convert from the Soundbites List and choose the Convert Sample Rate command, shown in Figure 13.40. Enter the new sample rate for the soundbite(s), choose the conversion quality, and then specify what happens to the soundbite after it is converted.

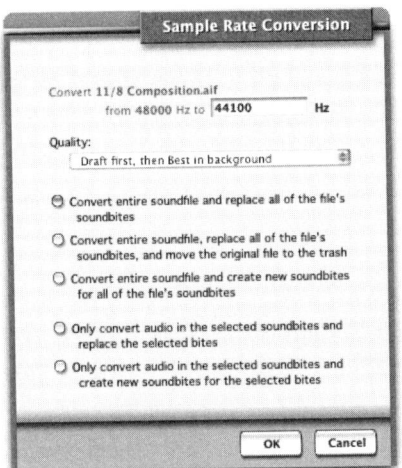

Figure 13.40

Use the Convert Sample Rate command to change the sample rate of an existing soundbite.

As with dithering, you shouldn't sample-rate-convert any mixes that are going to be sent off for mastering. Even if your current mix is running at 44.1kHz, don't up-sample to a higher format. Leave the delicate conversion process, along with dithering and noiseshaping, in the hands of the mastering engineer.

Summary

Notation, scoring, and mastering are especially intricate and complex music production processes. Digital Performer contains many specialized tools to help you with these types of work—from the QuickScribe Editor and DP's powerful movie features to the MasterWorks Limiter and comprehensive Bounce To Disk and Exporting features. Even though Digital Performer provides the tools for you to take on these complex tasks, it takes a lot of time and training to obtain the proper skills and experience necessary to perform these jobs well. If you're new to the processes discussed in this chapter, fear not—practice makes perfect. For those users who are already working in these fields (such as film scoring), you'll find that DP contains a wealth of valuable tools and feature sets that will allow you to perform many of these complex tasks with relative ease.

14 Notation and Scoring

MIDI tracks in Digital Performer can be viewed as standard music notation within the Notation and QuickScribe Editor windows. The Notation Editor will display a single MIDI track as a scrolling grand staff, while the QuickScribe Editor displays single MIDI tracks as notation or multiple MIDI tracks as full-blown scores. Musical notation is a visual language, and like any language, it takes time to develop a full understanding of how to read and write it. In order to take advantage of DP's sophisticated notation features, you must be familiar with the notation process and its associated terms (for example, staves and brackets, margins, clefs, ledgers, codas, alternate endings and repeats, accidentals, and so on).

The music scoring process is the act of writing music for motion pictures—film, television, and even video games. Digital Performer allows you to import QuickTime movies directly into a project, providing movie playback that is perfectly synchronized to your audio and MIDI tracks without the hassle of syncing an external video deck to your DP system. Other sophisticated scoring features, such as the Find Tempo command and Film Cues View help with the process of composing music cues within Digital Performer.

Even though music notation and music scoring are for the most part separate and independent processes, I've chosen to cover them together in this chapter, as they can overlap when you're composing orchestral cues or working on a project in which the composer is in charge of orchestrating and/or transcribing his own material. The scoring section of this chapter, however, will only make a small dent in the actual scoring process; it is a complex topic that, like musical notation, is entirely beyond the scope of this book. In this chapter, I will be focusing on the technical aspects of how DP's many features can be integrated into the music scoring process.

CHAPTER 14 } Notation and Scoring

Here is what you will learn in this chapter:

- How to use the Notation Editor.
- How to use the QuickScribe Editor's Tool, Dynamic, and Arrangement palettes.
- How to create text titles in the QuickScribe Editor.
- The difference between display-only and playback-only notes.
- How to use small noteheads.
- How to print a score.
- How to import a QuickTime movie into a project.
- How to output QuickTime video to an external Firewire monitor.
- How to work with cue sheets and DP's Film Cues feature.
- How to set up a project for music scoring with markers and hits.
- How to search for tempos that work with specific music cues.

The Notation Editor

The Notation Editor is very similar to the Graphic Editor, with its Median Strip and Continuous Data Grid; the only real difference is that the Notation Editor includes a continuous scrolling grand staff, shown in Figure 14.1. Like with the Graphic Editor, only one track can be viewed at a time in the Notation Editor. If you wish to simultaneously view more than one track within the same window, you'll need to open the tracks within the QuickScribe Editor (explained later in this chapter).

Figure 14.1

The Notation Editor can display a track's MIDI data as standard musical notation.

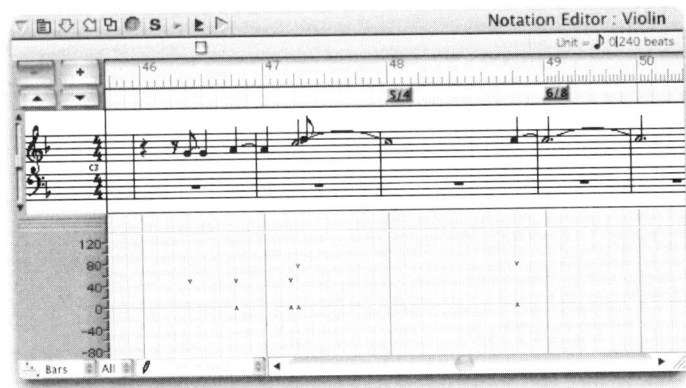

To open the Notation Editor:

1. Select a MIDI track.
2. Choose Project > Notation Editor, or use the default keyboard shortcut Shift+N.

By default, notes within the staff will be displayed with middle C (C3) between the treble and bass staves. The clefs, meter, and key are located in the staff margin and will remain stationary during scrolling. You can affect the visual display of notes with the Octave buttons—the up and down arrow buttons located below the mini-menu—and the Display Resolution menu, which is located on the far right of the Information bar. Use the Zoom buttons—the + and - buttons located below the mini-menu—to zoom in or out within the Notation Editor.

To change the visual display of notes:

1. Click on the up or down arrow Octave buttons to shift the octaves of displayed notes. This will not transpose the track's MIDI data; it will only affect the visual display of the notes within the grand staff.
2. To visually quantize notes to a specific note value, click on the Information bar's Display Resolution menu and choose the desired note resolution. For example, if I choose a quarter note value, the smallest note value that will be displayed will be one quarter note. Remember that this feature only changes the appearance of notes within the Notation Editor, and does not actually quantize the timing of the MIDI data.

   You'll need to experiment with this menu's setting to find the best resolution to represent the track you're working with. Figure 14.2 shows a cello track with various sixteenth note patterns. If an eighth note resolution value is chosen, the track will appear less cluttered, as the sixteenth notes are no longer visible (see Figure 14.3). Though not entirely accurate, this might be handy if I wanted to print out a simplified version of the track.
3. To zoom in or out, click the + or - buttons located below the Notation Editor's mini-menu.

Figure 14.2

In this example, a cello track with sixteenth note patterns is shown. As the view resolution is set to sixteenth notes, the track is accurately displayed.

CHAPTER 14 } Notation and Scoring

Figure 14.3
Changing the view resolution to eighth notes will visually quantize the track's sixteenth note patterns to eighth notes without affecting the actual timing of the MIDI data.

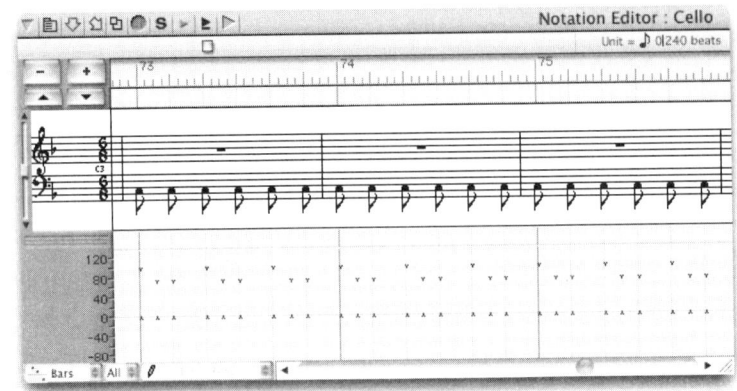

> **SETTING THE DEFAULT DISPLAY RESOLUTION**
> If you would like the Notation Editor to always open with the same display resolution setting, simply press the Option key while selecting a specific beat value from the Display Resolution menu.

Much as with the QuickScribe Editor, you can insert and edit notes directly in the staves by clicking with the Pencil tool in the Notation Editor. The process isn't quite as versatile as with the QuickScribe Editor, though, as there is no tool palette in the Notation Editor from which to select different note values. The Display Resolution menu determines the value of inserted notes. When clicking to insert notes, be sure to use the Notation Editor's Information bar and Time Ruler as a guide to help you place notes where you want them.

To insert notes in the Notation Editor:

1. Set the Display Resolution menu to the desired value. If you want to insert a whole note, for example, select the whole note value from the menu.
2. Activate the Pencil tool by double-tapping the letter P key on your computer keyboard.
3. Click on the location within the staff where you want to insert the note.
4. If you choose a small resolution, but would still like to insert notes with higher durations, simply click and drag horizontally with the mouse. A bar will appear, indicating the length of the inserted note, as shown in Figure 14.4. Once you release the mouse, the note will change from the bar to the actual note value.

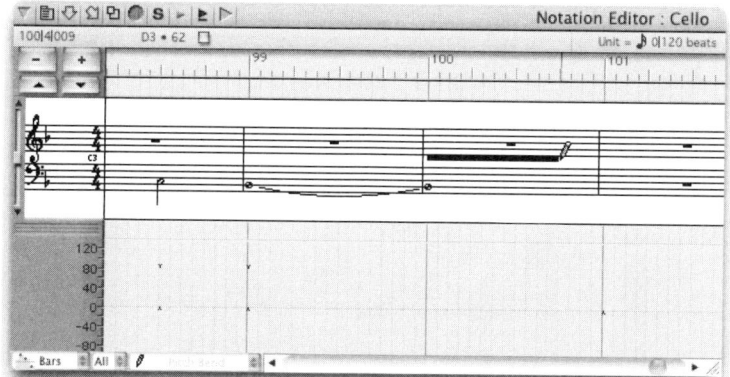

Figure 14.4

The black bar indicates the duration of the note being inserted. This bar will change to the actual note value upon release of the mouse.

To edit the duration of an existing note:

1. Activate the Arrow tool by double-tapping the letter A key on your computer keyboard.
2. Command-click the desired note and the note will change to a gray bar, as shown in Figure 14.5.
3. Drag the handle of the bar to the left to shorten the duration of the note, or the right to extend it.

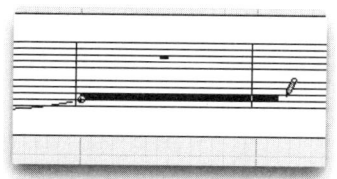

Figure 14.5

Command-click to edit the duration of a note in the Notation Editor.

To edit the pitch of an existing note:

1. Activate the Arrow tool by double-tapping the A key.
2. Drag the note vertically to the desired pitch (see Figure 14.5). Be sure to use the Information bar to place the note at the correct pitch.

To delete an existing note:

1. Select the note or notes by clicking or dragging with the Arrow tool.
2. Press your computer keyboard's Delete key.

The QuickScribe Editor

The QuickScribe Editor, shown in Figure 14.6, is similar to the standard Notation Editor, but offers more advanced features for greater control over the way notes are displayed within a part, or single track, or a score, or multiple tracks.

Unlike the Notation Editor, the QuickScribe Editor provides a Tool Palette from which you can choose specific note values when inserting notes and arrangement tools for controlling brackets and braces. It also offers tools for changing the spelling of accidentals, as well as inserting text, page numbers,

CHAPTER 14 } Notation and Scoring

Figure 14.6

The QuickScribe Editor's various tool palettes and advanced features offer greater control over the notation of individual parts and scores than does the standard Notation Editor.

Figure 14.7

The Options submenu within the QuickScribe's mini-menu provides various options for controlling the look of individual parts and scores, how the transcription engine handles MIDI data, and the overall length of a score.

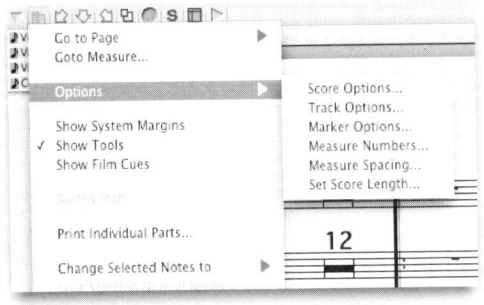

and the current date. In addition, the QuickScribe Editor provides mini-menu options for customizing the look of individual parts and entire scores (see Figure 14.7), along with the ability to display Film Cues to assist film composers in the film scoring process. Once the QuickScribe Editor is open, a specialized Text menu will appear between Digital Performer's Windows and Help menus, as shown in Figure 14.8.

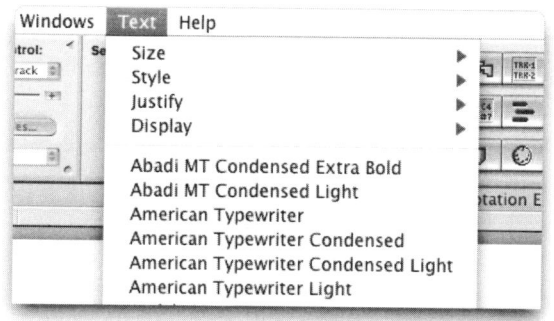

Figure 14.8
The Text menu is only visible when the QuickScribe Editor is open.

Customizing the Appearance of a Score

The Score Options window, shown in Figure 14.9, contains various choices for controlling how a score's different elements are displayed. Instead of simply providing a list of the various options contained in the Score Options window, I've decided to explain many of the important options in the context of the score creation process.

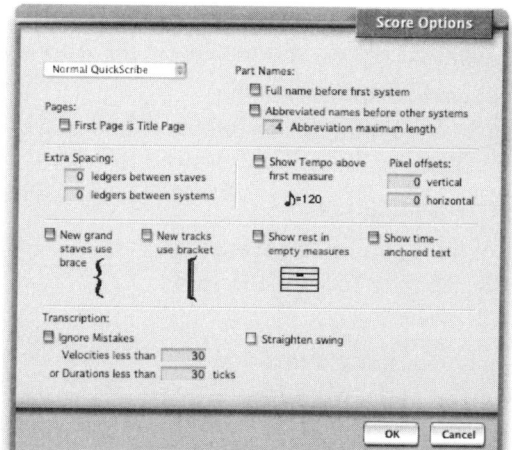

Figure 14.9
The Score Options window.

The Different QuickScribe Views

Digital Performer allows you to view your QuickScribe scores in three different ways: the Normal QuickScribe view, the QuickScribe + Film Cues view, and the Film Cues Only view. Each view maintains its own set of independent QuickScribe options. Some windows in particular (such as the Score Options, Marker Options, Measure Numbers, and Measure Spacing Options windows) provide a QuickScribe View pop-up menu so you can specify the specific QuickScribe view.

The Title Page

A score's title page is typically different than its normal body pages. In addition to the title (which may or may not appear within the body pages), other text elements, such as subtitles, composer credits, lyrics, and copyright notices may appear on this page. Digital Performer provides tools for adding text, as well as the ability to adjust the system margins of the page to make room for these extra elements.

CHAPTER 14 } Notation and Scoring

To customize the title page of a score:

1. Open the Score Options window by choosing QuickScribe Editor > mini-menu > Options > Score options.

2. Click the First Page is Title Page option. This will allow you to format the first page of the score differently from the other score pages. You can even adjust the system margins on the title page separately from the body pages (explained later).

3. Click the Full name before first system option to display the full name of an instrument at the beginning of the score. Instrument names are based on individual track names, so you may need to go back and rename your tracks accordingly.

4. If you would like all other instances of the instrument's name to be abbreviated, click the Abbreviated Names before other systems option. Next, specify the number of letters to be used in the abbreviations by typing in a number in the Abbreviation maximum length option.

5. If you would like the tempo displayed at the beginning of the score, enable the Show Tempo above first measure option.

6. Click OK to confirm the changes.

7. Now enter the title of the page by choosing the Text tool from the QuickScribe Tool Palette (see Figure 14.10).

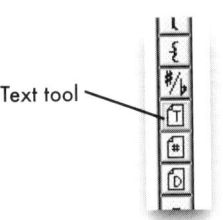

Figure 14.10
The QuickScribe Tool Palette's Text tool.

8. With the Text tool enabled, draw a text box at the top of the title page, as in Figure 14.11.

9. Set the text attributes (for example, the font, size, and justification) from the Text menu.

Figure 14.11
Click and drag with the Text tool to draw a text box.

10. From the Display submenu, choose Both title and body pages (see Figure 14.12). This will place the title of the score throughout each page of the score. If you only want the title to appear on the title page, however, choose Title page only.

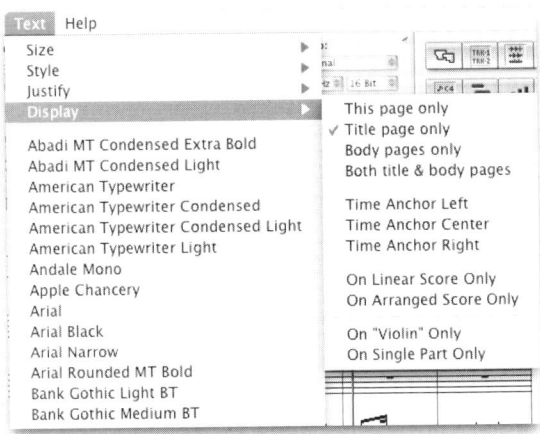

Figure 14.12
The Text menu's Display submenu provides options for how and where selected text will appear within a score.

※ The QuickScribe Editor

11. Once you have specified the text attributes, type the desired text.
12. Click outside the text box to confirm the entry.

When working with text at the top of the title page, you may find that you do not have enough room to enter other text elements, such as the subtitle, composer, orchestrator, and so on. Some modern scores may even contain the lyrics for a song on the title page, before the actual score begins. To get around the space limitations, DP allows you to move the system margins as need to make as much room at the top and bottom of your title page as you need to accommodate all your text elements.

To adjust the title page's system margins to accommodate additional text elements:

1. With the title page showing, choose QuickScribe Editor > mini-menu > Show System Margins. The title page will update to display the system margins for the page (see Figure 14.13). Make sure the First Page is Title Page option is still enabled in the Score Options window (explained earlier). If it is turned off, you will be affecting all pages within the score!

Figure 14.13

Enable the mini-menu's Show System Margins option to display a page's system margins.

2. Drag the top horizontal margin toward the middle of the page. The actual music staves will be moved toward the bottom of the title page. How far you drag the margin depends on how much space above the first staves is needed for text.

> **ADJUSTING TITLE PAGE MARGINS**
>
> The staves within the title page (as well as in body pages) will automatically adjust their locations to accommodate the new margin locations, moving to Page 2 of the score, if necessary.

3. If you wish to include text elements—such as copyright notices and so on—at the bottom of the title page, simply drag the lower horizontal margin towards the top of the title page.
4. When you are finished adjusting the margins, click the Show System Margins option again to hide them.
5. Enable the Text tool and add any additional text elements as needed, as shown in Figure 14.14. Keep in mind that the QuickScribe Tool Palette will not be available when the mini-menu's Show System Margins option is turned on.

Figure 14.14

In this example, the title page's top system margins have been lowered to accommodate additional text elements. The lower margin has also been raised to make room for the copyright notice.

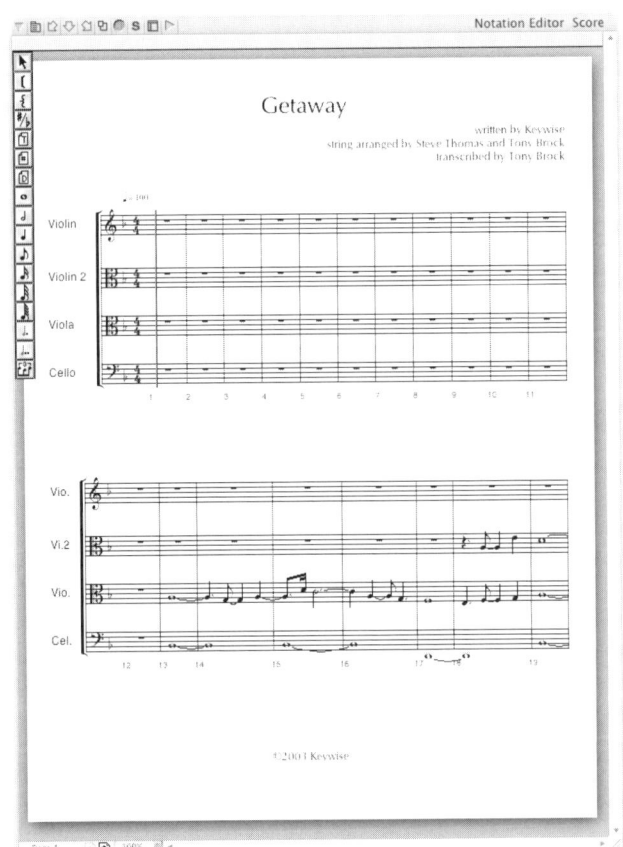

Body Pages

Body pages can also be customized to include common text elements that appear on every page. If the title appears within the body pages, for example, it is sometimes displayed with a smaller font and in a different location than on the title page. System margins for the body pages can also be adjusted to accommodate any additional text elements.

To add common text elements that appear on all body pages:

1. Begin by adjusting the system margins on the first body page (Page 2 of the score) to make room for the new text you will be adding. You can choose any body page to work with, as changes will be global—that is, they will affect all body pages in the score.
2. Once you have adjusted the system margins, enable the Text tool from the QuickScribe Tool Palette.
3. Click and drag at the desired location to create a text box.
4. Set the text attributes (such as font, size, and justification) from the Text menu, then enter the text.
5. In the Text menu's Display submenu, be sure to choose Body pages only if you want the text to appear on every body page in the score.

Inserting Page Numbers and the Current Date

Page numbers and the current date can be inserted into a score with the Page Number tool and the Current Date tool, shown in Figure 14.15.

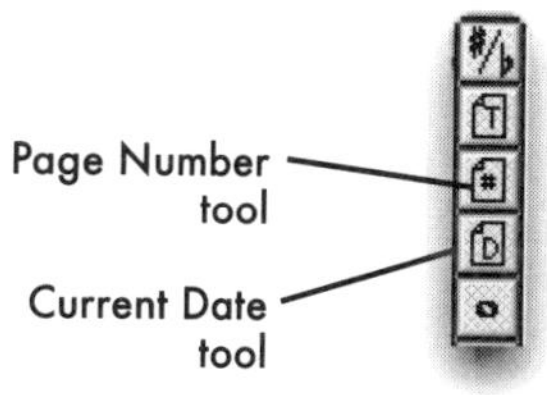

Figure 14.15
The QuickScribe Tool Palette's Page Number tool (top) and Current Date tool (bottom).

To add page numbers throughout an entire score:

1. Select the Page Number tool from the QuickScribe Tool Palette.
2. Click at the desired location to insert a page number. Once a page number is inserted, the Page Number tool will revert to the QuickScribe Arrow tool. In addition, DP will automatically place the correct number on the page and set its Display property to show the page numbers on both the title and body pages.
3. With the page number still selected, set its other text attributes (such as size, font, and justification) from the Text menu.
4. Once you are satisfied with the text formatting, click anywhere outside the page number box to deselect it.

To insert the current date:

1. Select the Current Date tool from the QuickScribe Tool Palette.
2. Click at the desired location to insert the current date, which is set by the Mac OS. Like the Page Number tool, the Current Date tool will automatically revert to the QuickScribe Arrow tool once the current date is inserted.

3. With the page number still selected, set the other text attributes (such as size, font, and justification) from the Text menu. The Display property will automatically be set to Title page only.

4. Once you are satisfied with the text formatting, click anywhere outside the page number box to deselect it.

Ledger Spacing between Staves and Staff Systems
Within the QuickScribe Editor, single tracks will be displayed as individual staves, while multiple tracks will be displayed as a grouped staff system. The Score Option command's Extra Spacing section allows you to adjust the spacing between a score's staves and staff systems, as shown in Figure 14.16. This will allow you, for example, to make room for dynamic markings, lyrics, or a track's extended ledger lines, which helps you create a less cluttered, easily legible score. These settings are global and will affect all staves and staff systems within a score.

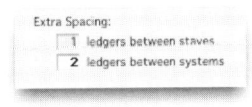

Figure 14.16

You can adjust the spacing between a score's staves and staff system from the Score Option command's Extra Spacing section.

In addition to affecting the global spacing of staves and staff systems, you can also change the ledger line spacing for individual tracks from the Track Options window (explained later).

Staff Bracket/Brace Options and Tools
Digital Performer provides different options for controlling how staff brackets and braces are displayed within a score. The Score Options command lets you choose whether a bracket or a brace will be used when a new track is created, as shown in Figure 14.17. You can change the type of staff that a specific track is using—for example, set a MIDI piano track to a grand staff—from the Track Options window (explained later), or you can manually change a track's bracket or brace setting with the QuickScribe Tool Palette's Insert Staff Bracket or Insert Staff Brace tools shown in Figure 14.18.

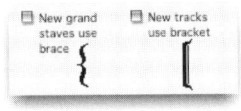

Figure 14.17

The Score Option command's staff brackets and staff system's options are used to determine whether a brace or bracket will be used when a new track is created.

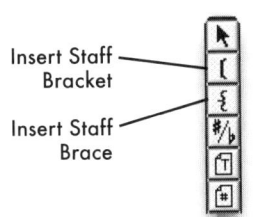

Insert Staff Bracket
Insert Staff Brace

Figure 14.18

The QuickScribe Tool Palette's Insert Staff Bracket tool (top) and Insert Staff Brace tool (bottom).

To manually insert or change the bracket setting for a track(s):

1. Select the Insert Staff Bracket or Insert Staff Brace tool from the QuickScribe Tool Palette.

2. Once enabled, draw a box around the name of a track or tracks within the QuickScribe Editor that you wish to affect, as shown in Figure 14.19.
3. The staff bracket or staff brace will be inserted or removed when you release the mouse.

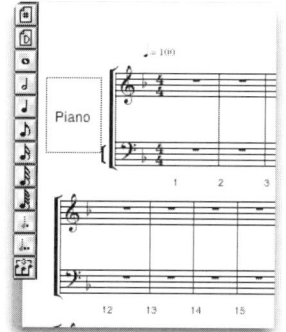

Figure 14.19

In this example, the Insert Staff Bracket tool is used to remove the piano track's staff bracket so that it can be replaced with a staff brace.

Ignoring Mistakes with the Transcription Options

Digital Performer's sophisticated transcription engine attempts to properly transcribe recorded MIDI data into proper musical notation, even when the music is unquantized. The Score Option command's Transcription section provides additional transcription preferences to help in this process.

* **Ignore Mistakes**. This option will tell DP to ignore notes below a certain duration and velocity when transcribing a track's MIDI data. Simply adjust the velocity and duration settings to tell DP which notes should be considered mistakes. Notes that fall below the set thresholds will be "hidden" from the score. These settings are global and will affect how all MIDI data is displayed throughout your score.

  Obviously, there will be times when you wish to show notes that shouldn't be considered mistakes, or hide certain notes that are mistakes. You can manually control the display of specific notes with the Display only and Playback only note settings (explained later).

* **Straighten Swing**. When this setting is turned on, Digital Performer will attempt to write swung eighth notes (written as triplets) as straight eighth notes to simplify the overall display of a score. This option only affects the visual display of the swung notes, and does not actually quantize the MIDI data.

Customizing the Appearance of an Individual Track

The mini-menu's Track Options window, shown in Figure 14.20, allows you to set the appearance of a score on a track-by-track basis. Options for setting the staff type and clef (treble, bass, grand, alto, or tenor), part and score transposition settings, as well as inter-staff ledger settings, can be adjusted for individual tracks.

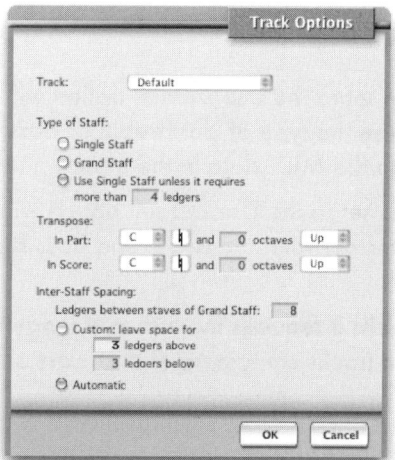

Figure 14.20

The mini-menu's Track Options window provides options for controlling the appearance of individual tracks.

CHAPTER 14 } Notation and Scoring

Staff Types and Clefs

The Track Options window's Type of Staff menu, shown in Figure 14.21, provides a list of available staves and clefs that can be used within a DP score. This menu is only visible when an individual track is selected from the Track menu and the Use Default option for the selected track is disabled (explained later).

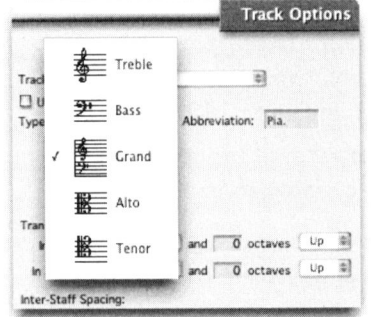

Figure 14.21

The Track Options window's Type of Staff menu lets you choose a specific staff or clef for individual tracks.

To set the staff type for an individual track:

1. Choose QuickScribe Editor > mini-menu > Options > Track Options.
2. Select the desired track from the Track drop-down menu.
3. If needed, click the Use Default button to turn off the default settings (explained later). Once the default settings are disabled, individual track options will become available.
4. Next, click the Type of Staff drop-down menu and choose the desired staff or clef from the list.
5. If you would like to change the staff settings for other tracks, repeat Steps 2-4.
6. When you are satisfied, click OK to confirm the changes.

The process of configuring QuickScribe Editor track settings are further simplified by the Use Default option. When an individual track is set to the Use Default option, its staff and clef settings will be determined by the default track options. You can view and configure the default track options by choosing Default from the Track Options window's Track menu, as shown in Figure 14.22. Use this option to automatically assign specific track settings to tracks in the QuickScribe Editor.

Figure 14.22

The Default track settings can be accessed by choosing Default from the Track Options window's Track menu.

- **Single Staff.** Tracks set to the Use Default option will be displayed with a single staff. DP will automatically choose the type of clef (treble or bass) that uses the least amount of ledger lines, depending on the MIDI data in the track.
- **Grand Staff.** Tracks set to the Use Default option will be displayed with a grand staff. DP automatically splits notes between the treble and bass staves depending on the MIDI data in the track.
- **Use single staff unless it requires more than # ledgers:** This option will let DP automatically use a grand staff when tracks contain notes that exist above the specified number of ledger lines.

Transpose Settings
The Track Options Transpose options allow you to set a track's transposition settings differently when viewed as individual parts or as part of a score. This is extremely handy when creating full orchestral scores where the conductor's score is written in concert C and individual instruments are written in their respective keys (for example, clarinets scored in the key of Bb). Transposition settings are only visual and will not affect the actual MIDI data within a track.

Inter-Staff Spacing
The Inter-staff spacing options determine how much space (that is, the number of ledger lines) is created above and below the staves for a specific track. A setting of Automatic will let DP automatically scale the space depending on the data within a track.

Linear versus Arranged Score

DP offers two ways to view your scores: as linear notation and as arranged notation. In a Linear view, the score will be displayed normally with all measures appearing in a linear fashion, without any arrangement markings such as repeats, alternate endings, consolidated rests, and so on. Full orchestral scores will typically appear in this fashion.

When Arrangement view is enabled, DP's arrangement tools and features will become active, allowing you to "arrange" the visual appearance of the score. Standard notation markings, such as repeats, endings, codas, and score jumps can be employed to create a more compact representation of your entire score, which is common in individual parts and condensed score arrangements. Measures that are repeated can be hidden and specific notes can even be designated as "Playback or Display-only" (explained later).

Score Arrangement view will only affect the visual display of the QuickScribe Editor, and will not change the actual playback of your sequence. This actual process of arranging a score is explained later in the "Arranging a Score" section of this chapter.

To enable Score Arrangement view, choose QuickScribe Editor > mini-menu > Show Arranged Score. Once the Score Arrangement view is enabled, the option will appear with a check mark.

Working with Markers

Markers within the QuickScribe Editor will appear at their proper sequence locations. Options for controlling how markers are displayed within a score can be found in the Score Options window, shown in Figure 14.23. To modify the text attributes for all markers, click a marker name with the Arrow tool and set its attributes from the Text menu. These settings are global and will affect all markers within a score.

- **QuickScribe View menu.** This pop-up menu determines which QuickScribe view the current set of options will be applied to.

Figure 14.23
The Marker Options window provides options for controlling how markers are displayed within a score, and which QuickScribe Editor view these options will be applied to.

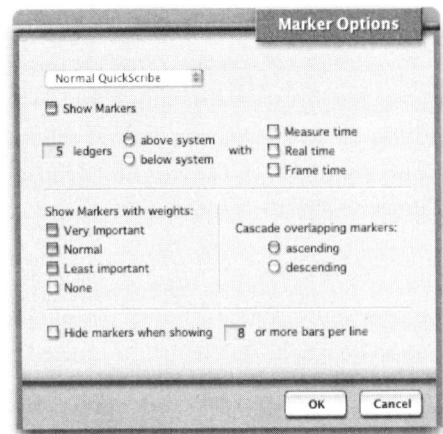

- **Show Markers.** This option will determine whether markers are displayed or hidden within the QuickScribe Editor.
- **Ledgers.** This option sets the distance that markers will appear above or below the staff.
- **Measure/Real/Frame Time.** These options determine whether the selected time formats will be displayed next to the names of each corresponding marker.
- **Show Markers with weights.** This section determines what type of weighted markers, if any, will appear in the particular QuickScribe view you currently have selected. You can set weight of a marker from the Markers window (explained in Chapter 11).
- **Cascade overlapping markers.** If you have markers that appear too close to each other and overlap within a score, you can use this option to force them to cascade vertically by ascending or descending order.
- **Hide markers when showing ___ or more bars per line.** When you are using the Measure Spacing window's Space Measures ___ Per Line option (explained later) to set the number of measures that appear in a line of a score, the measure spacing may become very dense. When this occurs, you can use the Hide Markers When Showing ___ or More Bars Per line option to hide markers in the QuickScribe Editor altogether. Once hidden, only weighted markers set to Very Important will be visible.

MAKE ARRANGEMENT MARKERS

Once you have inserted arrangement symbols (for example, repeats, Segno and coda markings, alternate endings, and so on), you can use the mini-menu's Make Arrangement Markers option to automatically generate a marker at these important score locations. Once created, they will appear in the Markers window.

※ The QuickScribe Editor

SETTING THE TEXT ATTRIBUTES FOR MARKERS
You can change the text formatting for all markers via Digital Performer's Text menu. Simply click a marker (which will select all markers in the process) and choose the desired text attribute (such as font type, font size, and so on). Changes will affect all markers within a QuickScribe score.

Working with Rests

While inserting notes into the QuickScribe Editor, you may have noticed that there is not a dedicated Rest tool. This is because DP automatically calculates any rests depending on the type of notes that are inserted. However, if a measure is empty—it does not contain any MIDI data—you will need to choose whether to display these measures as blank measures or with whole rests. You can do this from the Score Options window, shown in Figure 14.24. Measures that do not contain any MIDI data can be left empty or set to automatically display a whole rest by enabling or disabling the Show rests in empty measures option.

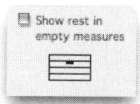

Figure 14.24

The Score Options' Show rest in empty measures option determines whether whole rests are automatically displayed in measures that do not contain MIDI data.

DP also provides controls for managing consecutive measures that contain whole rests. This is a common scoring technique that serves to minimize the space that consecutive empty measures will occupy. Instead of displaying a four-bar rest as four consecutive empty measures, as shown in Figure 14.25, it can be displayed as a single measure with a number indicating the amount of measures to rest, as shown in Figure 14.26.

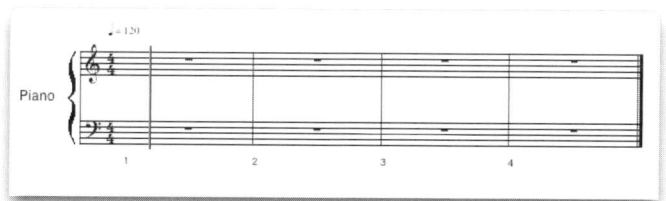

Figure 14.25

In this example, a four-bar rest is notated as four measures with whole note rests.

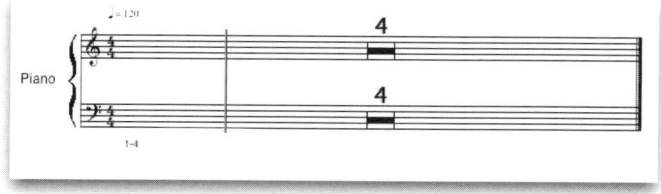

Figure 14.26

This example shows the same four-bar rest from Figure 14.25 displayed as a single consolidated rest. The number tells the performer how many measures to actually rest.

CHAPTER 14 } Notation and Scoring

To have DP automatically consolidate or unconsolidate consecutive rests:

1. Open the QuickScribe Editor's mini-menu and choose the Show Arranged Score option (explained earlier). This option must be turned on in order for certain QuickScribe Editor tools and features, such as consolidated rests, to become active.
2. Next, choose QuickScribe Editor > mini-menu > Consolidate Rests > Consolidate. The Consolidate Rests window, shown in Figure 14.27, will open.

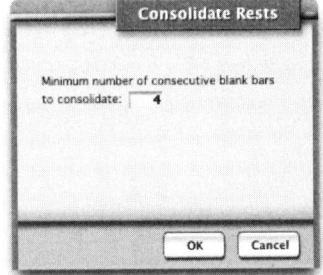

Figure 14.27

The Consolidate Rests window lets you specify the number of consecutive empty measures that are needed before they are automatically consolidated.

3. Set the number of minimum blank measures that are needed before they are automatically consolidated. A typical setting usually is 2 or 4 measures.
4. Click OK. The score will update to reflect the changes.
5. Choose mini-menu > Consolidate Rests > Unconsolidate to globally remove all consecutive rests appearing in a score.

The mini-menu's Consolidate Rest feature is a global command that affects all rests within a score. If you need to affect only certain consecutive blank measures, you can use the Consolidate Rest tool, located in the QuickScribe Editor's Arrangement palette, shown in Figure 14.28. In addition to manually creating new consolidated rests, you can also use this tool to remove or modify existing consolidated rests.

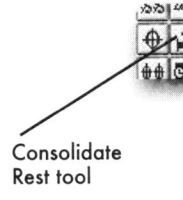

Consolidate Rest tool

Figure 14.28

The Arrangement palette's Consolidate Rest tool allows you to manually insert, remove, or modify existing consolidated rests.

To manually consolidate/unconsolidate consecutive rests with the Consolidate Rest tool:

1. Choose QuickScribe Editor > mini-menu > Arrangement palette to open the Arrangement palette.
2. Select the Consolidate Rest tool.
3. Click on a blank measure, located to the left of another blank measure, and the two measures will be consolidated.
4. Continue clicking to consolidate additional blank measures.
5. To manually unconsolidate a consecutive rest, hold down the Control key while clicking with the Consolidate Rest tool.

❄ THAT'S NOT A CONSOLIDATED REST

When you're using the Consolidate Rest tool, a blank measure is consolidated with the blank measure that is located to its immediate right. If there is no blank measure to its right, you will be presented with a dialog box warning you that the operation cannot be executed, as shown in Figure 14.29.

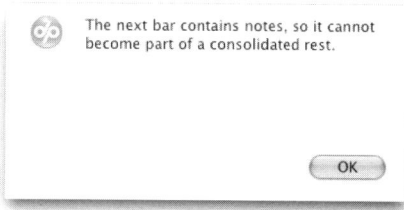

Figure 14.29

If there is no measure rest to the right of the one you want to consolidate, you will be presented with this warning dialog box.

Working with Text

I have already discussed the basics of creating text elements within a part or score in the "Customizing the Appearance of a Score" section of this chapter, so this section will focus on the various options within Digital Performer's Text menu, shown in Figure 14.30, and on the process of inserting text that is anchored to a specific score location. Keep in mind that the Text menu is only visible when the QuickScribe Editor is open and in the foreground (or active).

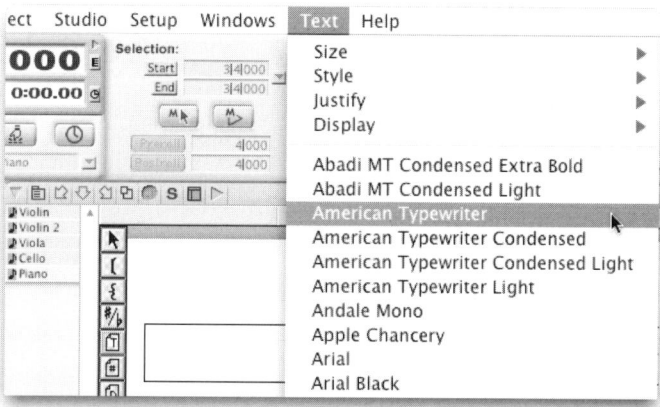

Figure 14.30

The Text menu.

❄ TEXT ATTRIBUTES FOR MARKERS AND MEASURE NUMBERS

Certain text elements, such as markers and measure numbers, can be automatically inserted into your score. You can set the text attributes for markers and measure numbers separately from manually inserted text by selecting the marker or measure number and choosing the text attribute you want from DP's Text menu. Changes will be applied to all markers or measure numbers in a score.

CHAPTER 14 } Notation and Scoring

Fonts

The fonts shown in the Text menu are the same fonts that are installed within OS X. Fonts can be installed and removed from the Mac's Font Book application (see Figure 14.31), which is located in OS X's main Applications folder. To add or remove fonts, choose the appropriate command from the File menu. If a font doesn't show up in DP's Text menu, open up the Font Book application and check to see whether it is showing in the list.

Figure 14.31
OS X's Font Book application allows you to add or remove fonts. Installed fonts will appear globally throughout all applications, including Digital Performer.

Size, Style, and Justify Commands

The Size, Style, and Justify commands let you control how text elements are displayed within a score. Text attributes can be applied before or after text is inserted in a score. The Display properties are explained later.

To apply text attributes to text elements:

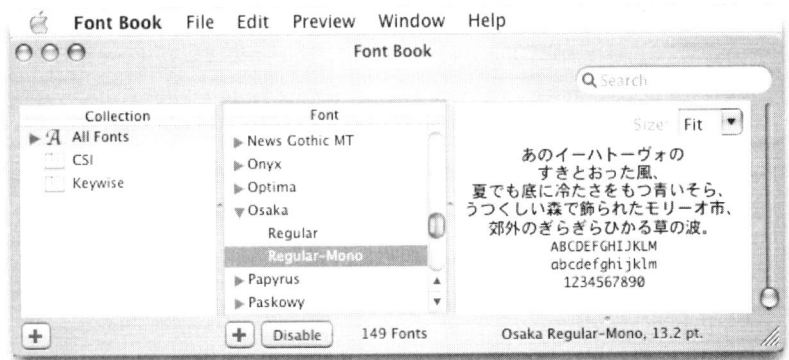

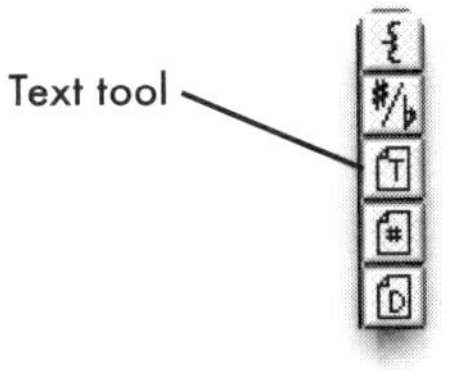

Figure 14.32
The QuickScribe Tool palette's Text tool.

1. Enable the Text tool, shown in Figure 14.32, from the QuickScribe Tool Palette and draw a text box at the desired location.
2. Before typing any text, choose the desired attributes from the Text menu.
3. To apply text attributes to existing text, select the text by dragging over it with the Text tool.
4. If you want to select an entire text box, click the text element with the Text tool.
5. Choose the appropriate attributes from the Text menu to format the text.

Display Property Attributes

The Text menu's Display properties, shown in Figure 14.33, allow you to specify exactly where selected text elements will appear in your score.

388

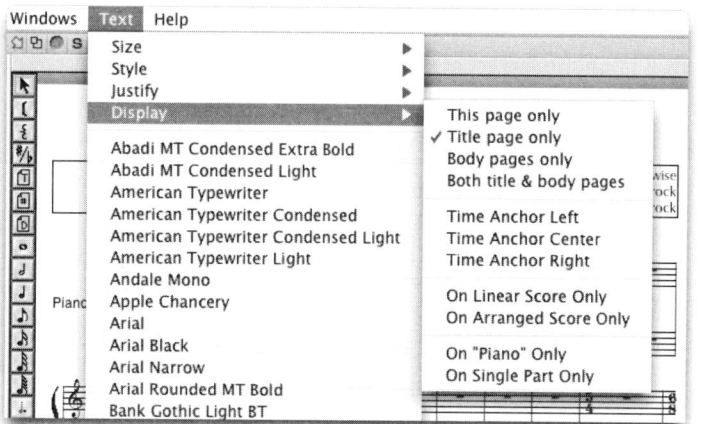

Figure 14.33

The Text menu's Display submenu contains commands for specifying where text elements will appear within a score.

- **This page only**. This option will force text to appear only on the page the text element was created.
- **Title page only**. This option will force text to appear only on the title page (explained earlier).
- **Body pages only**. This option will force text to appear only on the body pages (explained earlier).
- **Both title & body pages**. Text will appear on both the title and body pages.
- **Time Anchor commands**. These commands will force a normal text element to remain anchored to a specific measure within a score. This is handy when you apply other commands that change the location of measures within a part or score (for example, margin changes, measure spacing changes, and so on), preventing the text from being disassociated from a specific location. Use these commands when inserting chord names, lyrics, performance directions, and so on. You can also use the Arrangement palette's Time-Anchored Text tool to quickly create a text box that is anchored to a score location (explained later).
- **On Linear Score Only**. Selected text will only be visible when the Show Arranged Score option is turned off. You could, for example, use this formatting option to create text elements that only appear in a full linear score (for example, a conductor's score).
- **On Arranged Score Only**. Selected text will only be visible when the Show Arranged Score option is turned on. This formatting option allows you to create text elements that are independent of a full linear score (for example, a conductor's score).
- **On "Track-1" Only**. Use this option to display text only when specific tracks are showing in the QuickScribe Editor.
- **On Single Part Only**. Text will only be visible when a single track is being displayed in the QuickScribe Editor. You can use this formatting option to create text elements that only appear on individual score parts.

CHAPTER 14 } Notation and Scoring

Time-Anchored Text
Time-anchored text is text that is anchored to a specific score location. As I explained earlier, this feature is especially handy when creating text elements such as chords, performance cues, or lyrics that are located below specific notes. Anchoring text will ensure that these elements move with their corresponding measures when bar locations are changed.

There are a few different ways to create time-anchored text. One method is to create a normal text element and format it with the Display submenu's Time Anchor commands (explained earlier). You can also use the Time-Anchored Text tool (explained below), which saves you the extra step of formatting.

To add text elements that are anchored to a specific score location:
1. Enable the Text tool from the QuickScribe Tool Palette.
2. Press and hold the Control key to temporarily change the normal Text tool to the Time-Anchored Text tool (indicated with a clock icon). The Time-Anchored Text tool can also be selected from the QuickScribe Editor's Arrangement Palette (explained later).
3. With the Control key still pressed, click and drag to create a time-anchored text box at the desired measure location.
4. Set the text attributes as needed.
5. Enter the desired text, then click anywhere outside the text box to deselect it.

Working with Measures
The QuickScribe Editor provides powerful tools for controlling the appearance and visibility of measures within a score.

Measure Numbers
The Measure Numbers command tells DP how to number measures within a score. Choose QuickScribe Editor > mini-menu > Options > Measure Numbers to open the Measure Numbers window, shown in Figure 14.34.

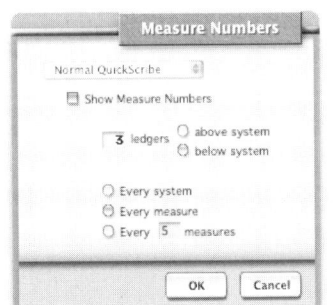

Figure 14.34
The QuickScribe Editor's Measure Numbers window.

- **Show Measure Numbers**. Click this option to make measure numbers visible within a score.
- **___ Ledgers**. These settings determine how many ledger lines above or below the staff the measure numbers will appear.
- **Every system**. Click this option to place measure numbers above or below first the measure of a staff system.

- **Every measure.** Use this option to number every measure within a score.
- **Every ___ measures.** Use this option to specify how often a measure number is placed in a score.

Measure Spacing

Use the Measure Spacing command to determine how many measures will appear per staff line. You can set a specific number or let DP automatically adjust the size of measures depending on the amount of notes contained within a measure. Choose QuickScribe Editor > mini-menu > Options > Measure Spacing to open the Measure Spacing window, shown in Figure 14.35.

- **Space measures # per line.** This option allows you to specify the exact number of measures that will appear within a staff line.

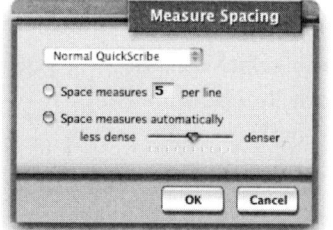

Figure 14.35
The QuickScribe Editor's Measure Spacing window.

- **Space measures automatically.** This option allows DP to automatically control the amount of measures that appear in a staff line, based on the value of the slider. Drag the slider to the left to create more space between notes in a measure. Drag the slider to the right to condense notes into a smaller space.

Selecting Measures

When working with alternate endings, repeats, and other arrangement features, it will become necessary to hide or move measures around in a score (explained later). In order to do so, you must first be able to select the measures you wish to affect. The mini-menu's Allow Measure Selection command, when enabled, will allow you to make measure selections by clicking with the QuickScribe Arrow tool. To select multiple measures, simply add the Shift key. Selected measures will be indicated with a bold outline, as shown in Figure 14.36.

Figure 14.36
Selected measures will appear with a bold outline.

CHAPTER 14 } Notation and Scoring

Arranging Measures

Once a measure is selected, you can apply arrangement options such as Hide, Move, and Pop-out (show). These options can be found in the QuickScribe Editor's mini-menu. The real-world application of these commands (the "whys" of the process) is explained later, in the "Arranging a Score" section of this chapter.

To hide a measure:

1. Start by turning on measure selections from the mini-menu by choosing QuickScribe Editor > mini-menu > Allow Measure Selections.

2. Select the Arrow tool from the QuickScribe Tool Palette.

3. Click on a measure to select it. It will become highlighted with a bold outline. Add the Shift key to make multiple measure selections.

4. Once you have selected the desired measures, choose QuickScribe Editor > mini-menu > Do to Measures > Hide. The Hide Measures window, shown in Figure 14.37, will open.

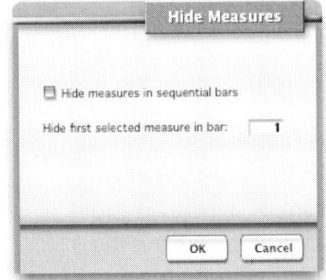

Figure 14.37

The Hide Measures window.

5. Next, you will need to specify where you would like to hide the measure or measures. Enter the measure number.

6. If you have multiple measures selected, you can choose to hide all the measures behind a single measure, or those behind sequential measures. For example, if the Hide measures in sequential bars option is *not* turned on, then choosing bar 8 as the destination will place all of your selected measures (let's say measures 1-4) behind measure 8 within the score. If you turn on the Hide measures in sequential bars option, however, then measures 3, 4, and 5 will be hidden sequentially behind measures 9, 10, and 11.

7. Click OK, and the measures will be hidden within the arranged score. Keep in mind that this feature has no effect on the actual playback of a sequence, and is only used to properly condense a score.

※ The QuickScribe Editor

VIEWING HIDDEN MEASURES

Once a measure or selection of measures is hidden, you can view them by turning on the mini-menu's Show Alternate Bar Menus option. Once this option is enabled, a measure pop-up window will be displayed to the right of the normal measure numbers in a score (see Figure 14.38). Simply click on a hidden measure number within the pop-up menu to display it in the score. Keep in mind, however, that just because a measure is displayed within an arranged score does not mean it will play back. The Arranged Score view only controls the visual display of a score; it has no effect on the actual playback of a sequence.

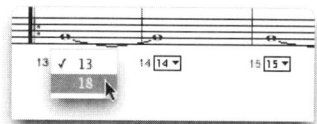

Figure 14.38

You can access hidden measures via a pop-up menu when the mini-menu's Show Alternate Bar Menus option is enabled.

To show, or *pop-out*, a measure:

1. Display the measure you wish to pop-out by choosing it in the Show Alternate Bar Menus pop-up menu.
2. Make sure Allow Measures Selection is turned on, and select the desired measure by clicking with the QuickScribe Arrow tool. Once the measure is selected, it will become highlighted with a bold outline.
3. Choose QuickScribe Editor > mini-menu > Do to Measures > Pop-out. The currently displayed bar will be removed and placed to the right of the selected measure.
4. Once the measure has been disassociated from the selected measure, you can use the Move command to place it anywhere within your score.

To move a measure:

1. Make sure Allow Measures Selection is turned on from the mini-menu, then select the desired measure by clicking with the QuickScribe Arrow tool. Once the measure is selected, it will become highlighted with a bold outline.
2. Choose QuickScribe Editor > mini-menu > Do to Measures > Move. The Move Measures window, shown in Figure 14.39, will open.

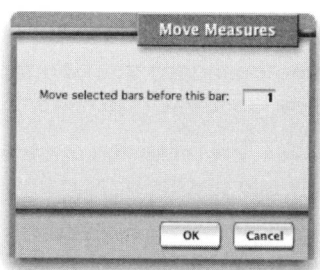

Figure 14.39

The Move Measures window.

3. Specify the new arrangement bar location for the measure and click OK to confirm the change.

The QuickScribe Tool Palette

The QuickScribe Editor's specialized notation tools are located in the QuickScribe Tool Palette, shown in Figure 14.40. This palette is permanently docked to the left-top portion of the QuickScribe Editor. Its tools are, from top to bottom, as follows:

Figure 14.40

The QuickScribe Tool Palette provides specialized notation tools for inserting notes, arrangement brackets and braces, as well as text and accidentals.

* **Pointer**. The Pointer tool is identical to the standard Tool Palette's Arrow tool. Use this tool to make general selections within the QuickScribe Editor.

* **Insert Staff Bracket**. This tool will allow you to insert or remove a staff bracket at the beginning of a single staff or system staff (explained earlier).

* **Insert Staff Brace.** This tool will allow you to insert or remove a staff brace at the beginning of a single staff or system staff (explained earlier).

* **Change Enharmonic Spelling**. This tool will allow you to change the spelling of accidentals (explained later). Keep in mind that you will need to insert the proper key changes within your score for notes to be spelled with their proper accidentals as they relate to their respective key signatures.

* **Text**. Use this tool to draw text boxes and insert text (explained earlier).

* **Page Number**. Use this tool to insert page numbers in a score. By default, inserting a page number on one page will automatically place page numbers on all pages of a score. DP handles the actual page numbering process, so you don't have to worry about specifying the correct page number for a certain page. This tool will revert to the Pointer (Arrow) tool when a page number is inserted.

* **Current Date.** Use this tool to insert the current date in a score. This tool will revert to the Pointer (Arrow) tool when the current date is inserted. The current date is set by the Mac OS.

* **Note Durations.** The remaining tools allow you to choose specific note values when inserting notes directly into a score or part (explained later). Dot, double dot, and triplet tools are also provided for further accuracy.

The QuickScribe Editor

Inserting Notes

The process of inserting notes with the mouse is similar to that of using the Notation Editor. Standard edit commands such as Cut, Copy, and Paste also work in the QuickScribe Editor. To paste notes that have been cut or copied, click on the desired location with the Pointer tool and press Command+V. Region commands such as Transpose, Quantize, and so on can also be applied to selected notes.

To insert a note with the QuickScribe Tool Palette:

1. Select the desired note value from the QuickScribe Tool Palette.
2. Click with the mouse at the desired pitch location within the staff of a track. You can use the Pointer Coordinates box, located below the mini-menu, to help guide you to the exact beat location (see Figure 14.41). Drag up and down to change the pitch of a note.
3. If you wish to add a dot, double dot, or triplet marking to the note, select the desired marking before choosing a note value from the QuickScribe Tool Palette.

Figure 14.41

The QuickScribe Editor's Pointer Coordinates is identical to the Information bar in other Editor windows.

To change the value of an existing note(s):

1. Select the new duration from the QuickScribe Tool Palette and click the desired note to change its value.
2. To change the duration of multiple notes to the same value, select the notes with the Pointer tool by Shift-clicking with the mouse, or by dragging a selection box over them.
3. Once multiple notes have been selected, Command-click the new note duration in the QuickScribe Tool palette.

> **TEMPORARILY ENABLING THE POINTER TOOL**
>
> To temporarily enable the pointer tool when working with other tools in the QuickScribe Tool palette, simply press and hold down the Option key. When you release the Option key, the Pointer will revert back to the tool that was previously selected.

To delete existing note(s) from a part or score:

1. Select the note you wish to affect by clicking with the Pointer tool. To select multiple notes, Shift-click or drag a selection box around the desired notes.
2. Press the Delete key.

395

CHAPTER 14 } Notation and Scoring

Working with Accidentals

Accidentals are flat or sharp notes that fall outside the notes of a specific scale or key signature. For example, the key of C does not contain any flat or sharp pitches; so if a flat or sharp note occurs within this natural scale, it is noted with an accidental (# or b). Digital Performer's transcription engine automatically controls the spelling of accidentals within a score, but there may be times when you need to change the way a particular note is spelled. By default, the note spellings are set to Auto. You can manually change a note spelling with the QuickScribe Tool Palette's Change Enharmonic Spelling tool (the sharp/flat icon button).

To change the spelling of accidentals within a score:

1. Start by choosing the Change Enharmonic Spelling tool from the QuickScribe Tool Palette (shown in Figure 14.42).

2. Click on a desired accidental and continue pressing with the mouse. A pop-up menu will appear with alternate spelling options.

3. Select the desired spelling from the list. Setting the spelling to Auto will allow the DP transcription engine to automatically choose a spelling for you.

Figure 14.42

Use the QuickScribe Tool Palette's Change Enharmonic Spelling tool to change the spelling of accidentals within a score.

Small Noteheads

Certain musical elements, such as performance cues and grace notes, usually do not carry the same weight as normal notes within a score. In order to show the difference between normal notes, these musical elements are notated with smaller note heads as shown in Figure 14.43.

To change the size of noteheads:

1. Select the note or notes you wish to affect.

2. Choose QuickScribe Editor > mini-menu > Change Selected Notes to > Small/Normal Noteheads.

Figure 14.43

Small noteheads can be used to represent certain musical elements, such as performance cues and grace notes.

Inserting Key, Meter, and Tempo Changes

Digital Performer allows you to insert key, meter, and tempo changes by clicking on a QuickScribe Editor barline. Keep in mind that users of previous versions (prior to DP 4.5) will need to use the Modify Conductor Track command when inserting key, meter, and tempo changes in the QuickScribe Editor.

Inserting Key Changes

Key changes can be made directly in the QuickScribe Editor via a key pop-up menu (shown in Figure 14.44), even if a key change doesn't exist. The procedures for inserting key changes are explained below.

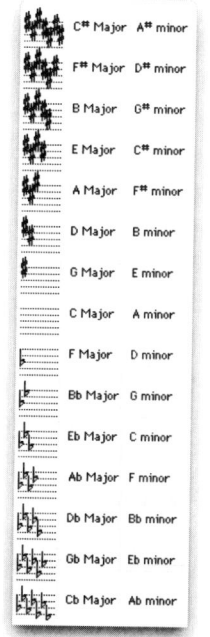

Figure 14.44

The QuickScribe Editor's key pop-up menu.

- **To modify an existing key signature.** Place the Pointer tool over the key signature. The pointer will change to the #/b cursor. Click on the key signature to display the key change pop-up menu and select a new key from the list.

- **To insert a key change where meter and key changes do not exist.** Press the Option key while placing the Pointer tool over a barline. Click to open the key pop-up menu and insert a key change.

- **To insert a key change where a meter change already exists.** Place the Pointer tool to the left of the meter marking, a third of the way up from the bottom of the staff. Once in the correct position, the cursor will change to the #/b symbol. Click to open the key pop-up menu.

Inserting Meter Changes

Meter changes can be made in the QuickScribe Editor via a meter pop-up menu (shown in Figure 14.45), by clicking directly on an existing meter marking or barline. The QuickScribe Editor's meter pop-up menu is explained below.

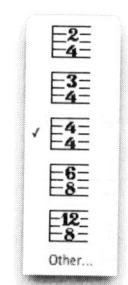

Figure 14.45

The QuickScribe Editor's meter pop-up menu.

- **To change the existing meter.** Place the Pointer tool over the existing meter marking. The cursor will change to the 4/4 cursor. Click on the existing meter marking to open the meter pop-up menu and change the meter.

- **To add a new meter change after an existing key change.** Position the Pointer tool over the right-lower third portion of the key signature. The cursor will change to the 4/4 cursor. Click to open the meter pop-up menu. Select a time signature from the list to change the meter.

- **To add a new meter change where key and meter changes do not exist.** Position the Pointer tool directly over a barline to change the cursor to the 4/4 cursor. Click directly on the barline to insert a new meter change.

CHAPTER 14 } Notation and Scoring

Inserting Tempo Changes

Tempo changes can be made in the QuickScribe Editor via the Set tempo dialog box (shown in Figure 14.46), by clicking directly on a barline. Be aware that tempo changes made in the QuickScribe Editor are placed in the Conductor Track. The tempo source must be set to the Conductor Track in order to be displayed in the QuickScribe Editor. The process for inserting a tempo change in the QuickScribe Editor is explained below.

Figure 14.46

The QuickScribe Editor's Set Tempo dialog box.

- **To insert a tempo change.** While pressing the Control key, position the Pointer tool over a barline to change the cursor to the bpm cursor. Click directly on the barline to open the Set Tempo dialog box. Enter the new tempo and set the beat value if needed. Click OK to enter the new tempo change.

> **SETTING AND DISPLAYING TEMPO IN THE QUICKSCRIBE EDITOR**
> Tempo changes that are inserted with the Set Tempo dialog box will continue on until the next tempo change. In addition, when the tempo source is set to Conductor Track and the tempo is displayed in the QuickTime Editor—only the initial tempo change located at the first measure will be visible. To display all tempo changes, you will need to enable the Show Film Cues option (explained later) from the QuickScribe Editor mini-menu.

Inserting Dynamic Symbols

The QuickScribe Editor's Dynamics palette, shown in Figure 14.47, lets you insert standard dynamic symbols into a score, including sforzandos and hairpin crescendos/decrescendos.

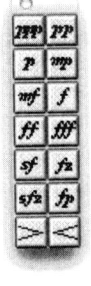

Figure 14.47

The QuickScribe Editor's Dynamics Palette allows you to insert standard dynamic symbols into a score. This palette is floating, and can be positioned anywhere within your DP workspace.

To insert a dynamic symbol into a score:

1. Open the Dynamics palette by choosing QuickScribe Editor > mini-menu > Dynamics palette.
2. Choose the appropriate symbol from the palette.
3. Click at the desired score location to insert the symbol.

To move an existing dynamic symbol:

1. Enable the Pointer tool.
2. Click and drag the desired symbol to the new location.

398

3. To move dynamic symbols together with notes, select them both with the Pointer tool and drag them to the desired location.

To insert hairpin crescendos and decrescendos:

1. Select the hairpin crescendo or decrescendo from the Dynamics palette.
2. Click at the desired score location to insert the symbol.
3. Drag the handles vertically or horizontally to adjust the angle or length of the symbol.

Arranging a Score

As discussed earlier in this chapter, there are two ways to view a score within the QuickScribe Editor: in Linear view or Arranged view. Linear view will present measures in a score consecutively with Linear bar numbers (for example, 1-2-3-4-5-6). These bar numbers are identical to the bar numbers that appear in the Control Panel's main counter—a sort of "what you see is what you get" approach. When playback is viewed in the QuickScribe Editor, the playback wiper will progress from left to right, moving over every measure within the score, exactly as it would in any other Editor window.

When the mini-menu's Show Arranged Score option (explained earlier) is turned on, however, DP switches a score from Linear view to Arranged view. Arranged view allows you to prepare a condensed and compact version of a score by inserting repeat signs, alternate endings, and other standard score markings. When a repeat is added, for example, the playback wiper will no longer operate in a continuous linear fashion. Instead, it will wipe over repeated bars as many times as needed before picking up with the next measure in a score.

Score Arranging Overview

The score arrangement process can be time-consuming, depending on the sophistication of the score you wish to create. How you choose to notate a part is really dependent on your level of music theory and orchestration knowledge. There are many different approaches you can take, with various ways to notate the same figure. Once you get a handle on the basic concepts (for example, hidden measures, linear bars versus arranged bars, and so on), however, you'll find that score arranging is just a matter of careful planning.

Before we dive into the "how to's" of the score arrangement process, let's take a look at a very simple four-bar pattern that will illustrate exactly how arranged scores are handled in DP.

Let's say I have a four-bar sequence where measures 1-2 are identical to measures 3-4 (see Figure 14.48). In Linear view, I would see all four measures noted consecutively in the score (1-2-3-4).

As measures 3-4 are basically repeating bars 1-2, it would be more efficient to notate them with a repeat sign. I could insert beginning and ending repeats at the start of bar 1 and at the end of bar 2, directing the musician to repeat those measures (see Figure 14.49).

CHAPTER 14 } Notation and Scoring

Figure 14.48

In this four-bar pattern, measures 1-2 are repeated in measures 3-4. Linear score view displays the measures consecutively, as they would appear in any other Editor window.

Figure 14.49

In this example, repeat bars have been added directing the musician to repeat bars 1-2.

Keep in mind that these changes will only affect how the score is viewed, and do not change the actual playback of the sequence. If I begin playback, DP will ignore the repeat signs and continue playing measures, 3-4 as shown in Figure 14.50.

Figure 14.50

Arrangement symbols only affect the visual display of a score, not the actual playback of a sequence. In this example, DP ignores the repeat marking at the end of measure 2 and continues playing through measures 3-4.

400

How do you get DP to follow the score markings? The answer lies with the Hide Measures command. As explained earlier, in the "Working with Measures" section of this chapter, measures can be hidden behind other measures when you're working with an arranged score. All you need to do is hide bars 3-4 behind bars 1-2 for DP to follow the repeat signs in the score. Start by selecting measures 3-4 (see Figure 14.51).

Next, open the Hide Measures window. Enter a value of 1 in the Hide first selected measure in bar option. This tells DP to hide bar 3 behind bar 1. Then turn on the Hide in sequential bars option to make sure bar 4 is hidden behind bar 2. Finally, click OK to confirm the change (see Figure 14.52).

DP's playback wiper will be forced to return to the beginning of measure 1 when it reaches the end of measure 2, as in reality, it is actually still wiping over measures 3-4, which are hidden behind measures 1-2 (see Figure 14.53).

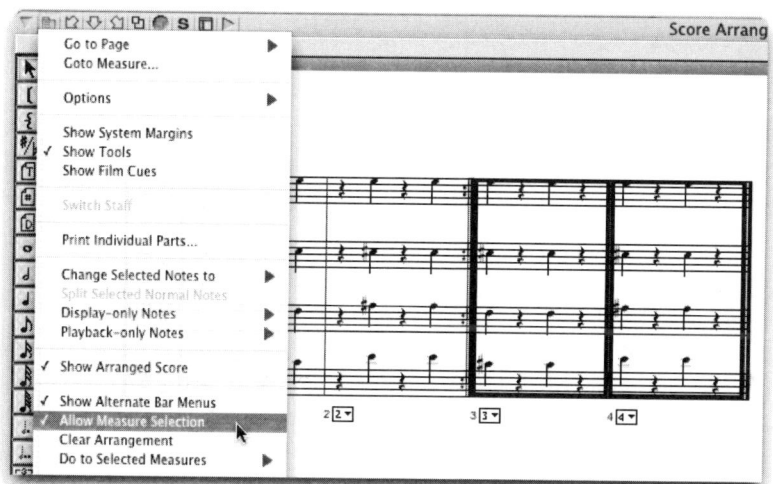

Figure 14.51

In this example, bars 3-4 have been selected. Notice the bold outline indicating the measure selection. The mini-menu's Allow Measure Selection command must be turned on before measure selections can be made.

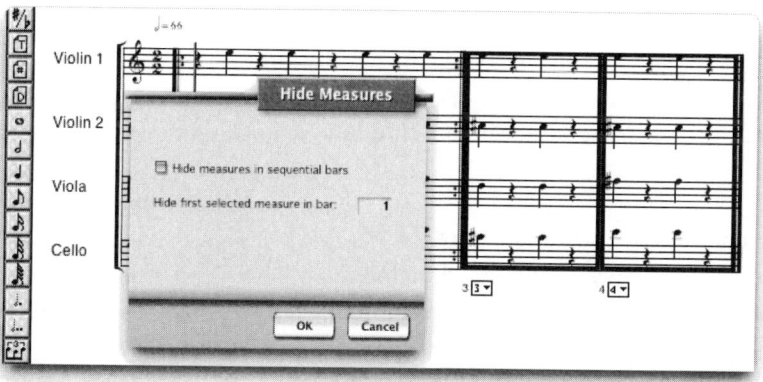

Figure 14.52

To hide measures 3-4 behind measures 1-2, enter a value of 1 and enable the Hide measures in sequential bars option.

CHAPTER 14 } Notation and Scoring

Figure 14.53

In this example, measures 3-4 have been successfully hidden behind measures 1-2. Notice that the Control Panel's main counter is playing back at bar 3, while the arranged score shows playback at measure 1.

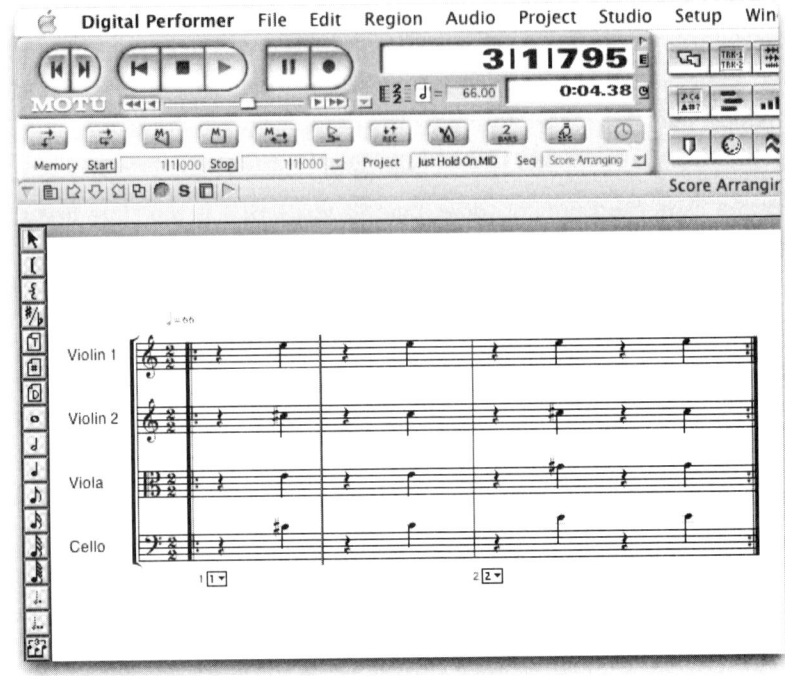

To view the hidden measures, enable the mini-menu's Show Alternate Bar Menus option. Clicking on the alternate bar pop-up menu of measure 1 shows that measure 3 is safely hidden away, as shown in Figure 14.54.

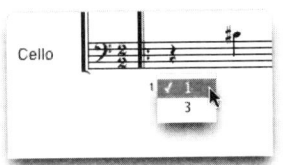

Figure 14.54

In this final example, the alternate bar menu shows measure 3 hidden behind measure 1.

Although this was a simplified look at the score arrangement process, you should have a better understanding of the basic concepts involved. The actual process for inserting repeats, alternate endings, and other arrangement markings are explained later in this chapter.

Arrangement Palette

The mini-menu's Arrangement palette, shown in Figure 14.55, contains arrangement tools that are only available when the mini-menu's Show Arranged Score option is enabled (with the exception of the Time-Anchored Text tool). A detailed explanation of when and where to use markings in a score falls into the

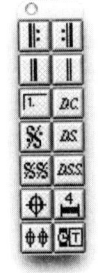

Figure 14.55

The Arrangement palette contains arrangement tools for adding repeats, alternate endings, codas, double-barlines, fine barlines, and so on. Like the Dynamics palette, this palette is floating and can be positioned anywhere within your DP workspace.

402

realm of music theory and orchestration, and is therefore beyond the scope of this book. I will, however, give you a look at their basic functions along with the procedures for inserting, editing, and removing arrangement symbols within a DP score.

Inserting Repeat Signs

Repeat signs direct a musician or conductor to repeat specific measures in a score. Beginning and ending repeats can be inserted or removed by selecting the specific repeat symbol (see Figure 14.56) and clicking near the beginning or end of a barline.

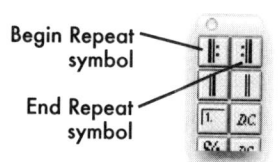

Figure 14.56

The Arrangement palette's Begin Repeat symbol (left) and End Repeat symbol (right).

To insert or remove a repeat sign:

1. Choose QuickScribe Editor > mini-menu > Arrangement palette.
2. Select the Begin Repeat or End Repeat symbol.
3. Click near the beginning or end of a barline to insert the repeat sign.
4. Be sure to hide the repeated measures in the bars that are located between the Begin Repeat and End Repeat symbols (explained earlier, in the "Score Arranging Overview" section of this chapter).
5. To remove a repeat sign, select the appropriate symbol and click on the existing symbol in the score.

Inserting Barlines

Fine barlines are used to designate the end of a composition, while thin, double barlines can be used to separate one section of a score from another. The Fine and Thin Double bar symbols are located in the Arrangement Palette, shown in Figure 14.57. Keep in mind that only one fine bar can exist in a score. If a fine bar already exists, it will be moved when you click on a new bar location.

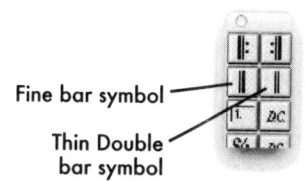

Figure 14.57

The Arrangement palette's Fine bar symbol (left) and Thin Double bar (right) symbol.

To insert or remove a fine bar or thin double barline:

1. Choose QuickScribe Editor > mini-menu > Arrangement palette.
2. Select the fine bar or thin double bar symbol.
3. Click near the beginning or end of a barline to insert the symbol.

CHAPTER 14 } Notation and Scoring

4. By default, a fine bar is placed at the end of a score. A fine bar must exist within a score and cannot be deleted. Only one fine bar symbol can exist at a time, however. Inserting a fine bar will move the score's existing fine bar to the new location.
5. To remove a thin double barline, select it in the Arrangement palette and click on the existing symbol.

Inserting Ending Brackets

An Ending bracket symbol, shown in Figure 14.58, is used to create alternate endings. To be properly notated in a score, a minimum of two ending brackets must be created adjacent to one another, as shown in Figure 14.59. Alternate endings (with the exception of the last ending in a sequence) must also contain directions for the musicians that tell them where to go once they reach the last measure of the alternate ending (for example, repeat sign or D.C. symbol).

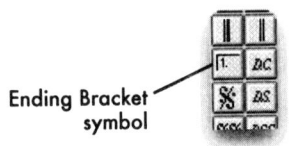

Figure 14.58

The Arrangement palette's Ending Bracket symbol.

Ending Bracket symbol

Figure 14.59

In this example, the score contains two endings. At the end of the first ending, the D.S. symbol tells the performer to return to the beginning of the composition.

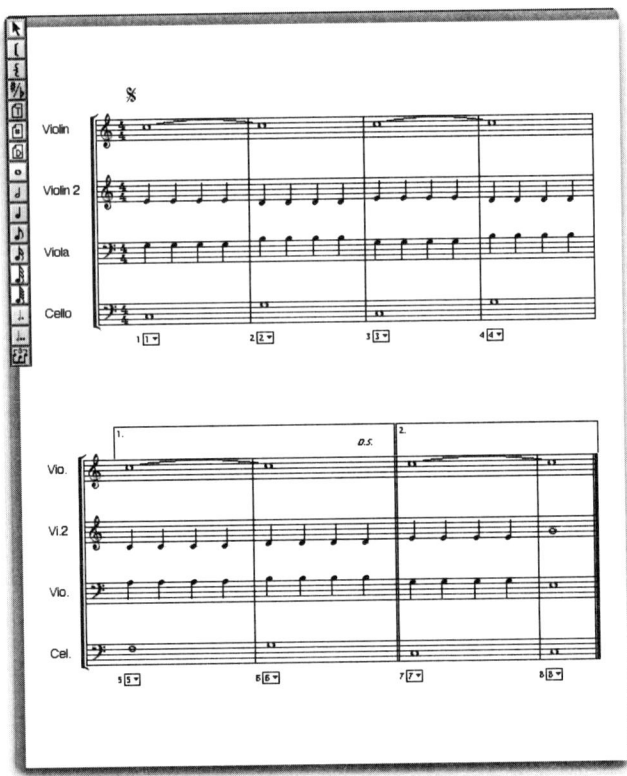

To insert an alternate ending:

1. Choose QuickScribe Editor > mini-menu > Arrangement palette.
2. Select the Ending Bracket symbol.
3. Click above the staff, near where you wish the ending bracket to start, and drag to include other sequential measures in the new alternate ending.
4. Repeat Step 3 to add a second bracket directly after the first ending. Remember that you must create at least two adjacent ending brackets to be properly notated in a score.

To remove an alternate ending:

1. To remove an Ending Bracket symbol, make sure Allow Measure Selections is turned off from the mini-menu.
2. Enable the Pointer tool from the QuickScribe Tool palette and click on the ending.
3. A bold selection box will indicate that the ending is selected.
4. Press the Delete key on your computer keyboard.

To extend the duration of an Ending symbol:

1. Choose QuickScribe Editor > mini-menu > Arrangement palette.
2. Select the Ending Bracket symbol.
3. While pressing the Shift key, click on the measure directly after the ending and drag horizontally.

To renumber an alternate ending:

1. Make sure Allow Measure Selections is turned off from the mini-menu.
2. Enable the Pointer tool from the QuickScribe Tool palette and click on the ending number.
3. Enter the new number and edit any of its text attributes using the Text menu.
4. Click anywhere outside the alternate ending box to confirm the change.

To adjust the height of an Ending symbol:

1. Make sure Allow Measure Selections is turned off from the mini-menu.
2. Enable the Pointer tool from the QuickScribe Tool palette and click on the ending number.
3. Click and drag vertically to change the height.

To remove the vertical bar at the edge of an Ending symbol:

1. Make sure Allow Measure Selections is turned off in the mini-menu.
2. Enable the Pointer tool from the QuickScribe Tool palette and click on the Ending symbol.
3. Choose QuickScribe Editor > mini-menu > Open Selected Ending Bracket.

CHAPTER 14 } Notation and Scoring

Inserting a D.C. Symbol

The D.C. symbol, shown in Figure 14.60, stands for *Da Capo*, which is Italian for "from the head." Within a score, this symbol directs the performer to "play from the beginning" of a composition. DP's D.C. symbol is time-anchored and can be formatted like other text elements from the Text menu.

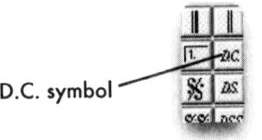

Figure 14.60

The Arrangement palette's D.C. symbol.

To insert or remove a D.C. symbol:

1. Choose QuickScribe Editor > mini-menu > Arrangement palette.
2. Select the D.C. symbol.
3. Click to insert the time-anchored symbol in the desired location. The D.C. tool will automatically revert to the Pointer tool.
4. Click to select it and choose the appropriate format options from the Text menu, if necessary.
5. To remove the D.C. symbol, select it with the Pointer tool and press the Delete key on the keyboard.

Inserting D.S. and Segno Symbols

The D.S. Symbol stands for *Dal Segno,* which means "from the sign." *Segno* means sign, so the D.S. symbol in a score directs the performer to go back to the Segno symbol (which should occur earlier in the score) and resume playing (see Figure 14.61). D.S. instructions are typically not mixed with D.C. symbols in the same composition, as that can be confusing for the musician. Procedures for inserting and removing D.S. and Segno symbols are identical to those for the D.C. symbol. Segno symbols, however, cannot be reformatted with the Text menu options.

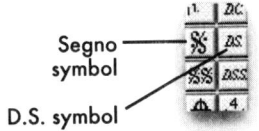

Figure 14.61

The Arrangement palette's Segno symbol (left) and D.S. (right) symbol.

Inserting D.S.S. and Double Segno Symbols

The procedures for working with D.S.S. and Double Segno symbols are identical to those for the single D.S. and Segno symbols (see Figure 14.62).

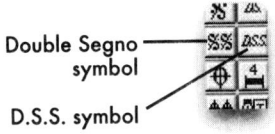

Figure 14.62

The Arrangement palette's Double Segno symbol (left) and D.S.S. symbol (right).

Inserting Codas and Double Codas

Coda is derived from the Latin word *cauda,* and in Italian means "tail." A coda is an extension to the end of a musical composition and is indicated by the Coda symbol, shown in Figure 14.63. In modern music, the coda could be

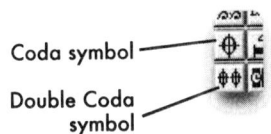

Figure 14.63

The Arrangement palette's Coda symbol (top) and Double Coda symbol (bottom).

considered the outro section of a song. Similar to the Segno symbol, the Coda symbol is useless on its own and requires an instruction that tells the performer when to jump to the coda section. Without any instructions, the coda will be ignored. DP doesn't have a dedicated symbol for this instruction, but a simple workaround is to add a time-anchored text element with the instruction "to coda" at the desired location. The procedures for inserting codas and double codas are identical to those for the Segno symbol (explained earlier).

Consolidated Rests and Time-Anchored Text

Both the Consolidated Rests and Time Anchored Text tools have been explained earlier in this chapter. See the "Working with Rests" and "Working with Text" sections for a discussion of these features.

Display-only versus Playback-only Notes

Display-only notes will appear in a score, but will not be heard during the actual playback of a sequence. These notes are for visual reference only and are essential when you wish to insert performance cues (see Figure 14.64). Notes that are set to Display-only will be listed as such in the track's Event List (see Figure 14.65).

Figure 14.64

In this example, cue notes for the viola have been added to measures 18–20 of violin 1. This lets violin 1 know what the viola is playing, helping to ensure violin 1 makes the proper entrance in bar 20. Small noteheads are used in place of normal noteheads to instruct violin 1 not to play those cue notes.

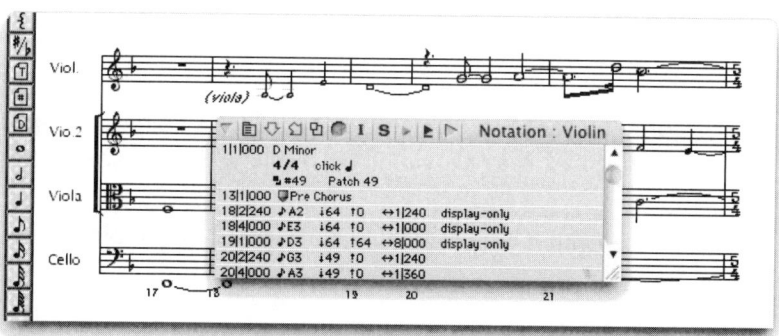

Figure 14.65

If you take a look at the Event List for the Violin 1 track, you can see that the viola cue notes that were inserted have been set to Display-only.

CHAPTER 14 } Notation and Scoring

To change a note to Display-only:

1. Select the notes you wish to change in the QuickScribe Editor.
2. Choose QuickScribe Editor > mini-menu > Change Selected Notes to > Display-only.
3. To remove the Display-only setting, choose QuickScribe Editor > mini-menu > Change Selected Notes to > Normal.

Playback-only notes are notes that are audible during playback, but are not displayed within a score. You can use this option when working with certain note embellishments or grace notes that are not typically notated within a score. You could also use this feature to create simpler versions of a part or score. Like the Display-only option, notes that are set to Playback-only will be listed as such in the track's Event List.

To change a note to Playback-only:

1. Select the notes you wish to change in the QuickScribe Editor.
2. Choose QuickScribe Editor > mini-menu > Change Selected Notes to > Playback-only.
3. To remove the Playback-only setting, start by choosing QuickScribe Editor > mini-menu > Playback-only Notes > Display. This step is important because once a note is set to Playback-only it will be hidden from the score. This step will display all notes that have been hidden with the Playback-only option.
4. Next, choose QuickScribe Editor > mini-menu > Playback-only Notes > Select All. This will select any note that has been set to Playback-only status.
5. Finally choose QuickScribe Editor > mini-menu > Change Selected Notes to > Normal to remove the Playback-only setting.
6. If you would like to affect only certain notes, find the notes you wish to affect, reselect them, and repeat Step 5.

Printing

Once you have formatted your individual parts and overall score, you are ready to print them out. If you still need to work on the appearance of your manuscript pages, see the "Customizing the Appearance of a Score" and "Customizing the Appearance of an Individual Track" sections of this chapter.

To print individual parts:

1. Select the tracks you wish to print by enabling them in the QuickScribe Editor's Show/Hide column. Once the tracks are highlighted, they should all be visible within the QuickScribe Editor.
2. Choose QuickScribe Editor > mini-menu > Print Individual Parts. All of the visible tracks will be printed as separate parts.

To save a part as a PDF document:

1. Select the track you wish to turn into a PDF by only enabling that track in the QuickScribe Editor's Show/Hide column. Only the part you wish to work with should be visible within the QuickScribe Editor.
2. Press Command+P to open the Mac's Print window.
3. Click the Save as PDF button.
4. Give the part a name in the Save As column.
5. Choose the destination for the PDF document and click Save.

To print a score:

1. Select the tracks you wish to include in the score by enabling them in the QuickScribe Editor's Show/Hide column. Once the tracks are highlighted, they should all be visible within the QuickScribe Editor.
2. Press Command+P to open the Mac's Print window.
3. Set print options as necessary and click the Print button.

To save a score as a PDF document:

1. Select the tracks you wish to include in the score by enabling them in the QuickScribe Editor's Show/Hide column. Once the tracks are highlighted, they should all be visible within the QuickScribe Editor.
2. Press Command+P to open the Mac's Print window.
3. Click the Save as PDF button.
4. Give the score a name in the Save As column.
5. Choose the destination for the PDF document and click Save.

Scoring for Picture

Digital Performer provides a powerful environment for scoring music for picture, giving you the ability to import QuickTime movies, create hit points (or markers), and calculate tempos based on these hit locations. Keep in mind that the actual film/video scoring process is a world unto itself and is therefore beyond the scope of this book. Concepts such as score preparation, temp tracks, spotting notes, master cue lists, and other aspects of the scoring process that are typically handled by the music director are not covered here.

Before you can begin setting your composition to picture, you must first have a movie to which to score. DP's Movie window supports the synchronized playback of QuickTime formatted movies with a sequence's audio and MIDI tracks. You can, of course, sync Digital Performer to an external video deck or other playback medium, but in this section, I'll focus on the process of scoring to an imported QuickTime movie.

CHAPTER 14 } Notation and Scoring

Movie Window

Before you begin importing a QuickTime movie, make sure you have the latest version of QuickTime installed on your Mac. The QuickTime application is free and comes bundled and pre-installed on Mac OS X. If you are working with an older version of QuickTime, you can update it through OS X's Software Update or by visiting http://www.apple.com/quicktime/download/.

To open and close QuickTime movies:

1. Choose Project menu > Movie, or use the default keyboard shortcut Shift+V.
2. Select the movie you wish to import and click the Open button.
3. Once a movie window is open, you can use the mini-menu's Open command to switch to a different movie. Only one movie may be open at a time.
4. To close the movie, click the Movie window title bar Close button (the far-left button). Digital Performer will remember movies that are closed in this fashion. Repeat Step 1 to reopen the previous movie.
5. To permanently close a movie, choose the mini-menu's Close command.

Mini-Menu

Once you have chosen a movie and opened the Movie window, you will have access to its various mini-menu commands and options (explained below).

- **Open Movie.** The Open option allows you to open a different movie. Use this option to close the existing movie and open a new one.
- **Close Movie.** This option permanently closes the Movie window.
- **Set Movie Start Time.** This command will open the Set Movie Start window, allowing you to set the SMPTE starting frame for the open movie (explained later).
- **Chase Graphical Edits.** This option will force the movie window to follow any edits, such as moving and trimming, allowing you to instantly see how your edits correspond to the picture you're working with.
- **Chase Numeric Edits.** This option will force the movie window to follow numeric edits, such as clicking an event's numeric bar/beat location in the Information bar of an editor window's title bar. When the event's parameter is highlighted for editing, you will see the movie jump to that location. Edit the event's location number, and the movie jumps to the new location, showing where the event will be placed in relation to the movie when you confirm the edit. Press the Return key and the movie will jump back to the counter location.
- **Half/Normal/Double Size.** Use these three options to quickly change the size of the window. The current size is indicated with a check mark.
- **Video Output.** This option allows you to send an opened DV movie out to a connected Firewire DV camera or Firewire video converter (explained later).

※ **Video Output Playback Offset.** This command becomes visible when you enable Firewire video output. Choosing this command will open the Set Playback Offset window, allowing you to compensate for the inherent playback delay in Firewire video devices (explained later).

※ **Copy Movie Audio to Sequence.** Choosing this command will copy the open movie's soundtrack to an audio track in the current sequence. This command will only be visible when a movie contains an audio track.

Setup

Once you have opened your movie in DP, you'll need to configure the sequence's frame rate and start times to match that of your imported movie. You can even output the DV formatted movie to a Firewire camera or Firewire converter.

Frame Rate

If you don't know the frame rate of your QuickTime movie, you can check its settings by opening it up in the Mac's QuickTime Player application.

To determine a movie's frame rate:

1. Open the movie in the QuickTime Player application.

2. Choose Movie > Get Movie Properties. You can also use the default keyboard shortcut Command+J. The frame rate, along with the movie's other attributes, will be displayed in the Movie Info window.

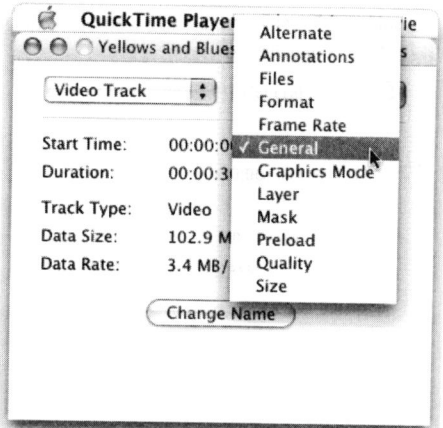

Figure 14.66

QuickTime Pro's Get Movie Properties window.

3. If you are working with QuickTime Pro, select the Video Track from the Movie pop-up menu, shown in Figure 14.66.

4. Next, select the Frame Rate option from the properties pop-up menu, shown in Figure 14.67, to display the movie's frame rate.

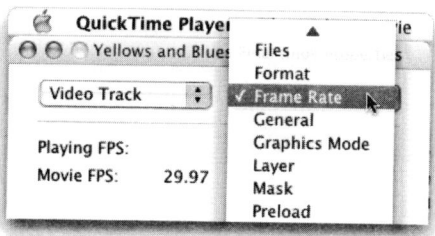

Figure 14.67

Select the Frame Rate option in the Properties pop-up menu to view the frame rate for the current movie.

CHAPTER 14 } Notation and Scoring

Start Times

Next, you'll need to set the QuickTime movie's start time and the sequence or chunk start times, so that the cues you are writing will be created in the proper locations. Doing so will ensure that you (the composer) and the music editors for the film are on the same page. Movies may have the frame locations burned into them (called a *window burn*), or they may simply start at frame 0:00:00:00; it will vary from project to project.

To set the movie start time:

1. Choose the Set Movie Start Time command from the Movie window's mini-menu.
2. Next, enter the correct start time for the movie in the Set Movie Start window (shown in Figure 14.68).
3. If you need to fine-tune the movie start time, use the Plus___Timecode Bits input field to offset the movie by the desired amount. Keep in mind that there are 80 timecode bits in a single frame.

Figure 14.68

The Set Movie Start window.

To set the sequence or Chunk start time:

1. Open the Control Panel's Tempo Control Drawer and click the Start Times button. This will open the Set Chunk Start window, as shown in Figure 14.69.
2. Enter the start time for the sequence (this should be the same number as the movie start time). Some engineers, however, will set the time earlier if they need to add pre-roll.
3. If you have locked markers within the sequence, you also need to specify what will happen to them when the Chunk start time is changed.

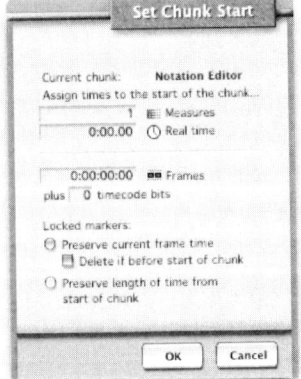

Figure 14.69

The Set Chunk Start window.

FireWire Video Output

Digital Performer's Movie window allows you to output your DV formatted QuickTime movie to a FireWire DV Camera or FireWire converter. Audio output via FireWire, however, is not supported.

To enable FireWire video output:

1. Choose Movie window > mini-menu > Video Output. A list of FireWire DV formats (for example, Apple FireWire NTSC, Apple FireWire PAL, DVCPRO NTSC, and so on) that are supported

by your system will appear, as shown in Figure 14.70. Keep in mind that only DV formatted movies can be output to a FireWire device.

2. To turn off FireWire video output, choose Movie window > mini-menu > Video Output > None.

Figure 14.70
The Movie window mini-menu's Video Output sub-menu provides a list of DV formats supported by your system.

> ❋ **AUDIO OVER FIREWIRE**
> Digital Performer's FireWire Video Output command will only transfer video over FireWire; audio output is not supported.

FireWire Playback Delay Compensation
When outputting DV video over FireWire, you may notice that the picture is delayed from the audio in Digital Performer. The amount of playback delay varies from device to device, but is anywhere between three to nine frames. You can offset the movie start time from the Set Playback Offset window, shown in Figure 14.71, to compensate for this delay.

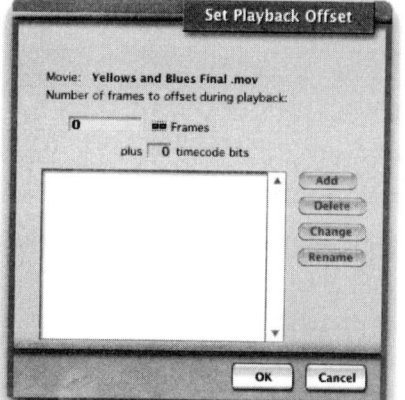

Figure 14.71
The Set Playback Offset window.

To set the playback offset for the Movie window:

1. Open the Set Playback Offset window by choosing Movie window > mini-menu > Video Output Playback Offset.
2. By default, the None is option will be checked. Select the Other option to open the Set Playback Offset window.
3. Enter the appropriate number of frames in the Number of Frames to Offset During Playback input field, keeping in mind that you may have to tweak this value.
4. For finer adjustments, use the Plus__Timecode Bits input field. This field allows you to offset the movie by a specific number of timecode bits (there are 80 timecode bits to a single frame).
5. Click OK to confirm the offset. If you wish to save this setting as an Offset preset, proceed to Step 1 of the next section.

CHAPTER 14 } Notation and Scoring

Once you have determined the correct offset amount, you can save the configuration as a custom preset. Offset presets are especially handy if you use different DV output devices for movie playback. Presets will appear in the Offset preset list.

To create an Offset preset:

1. Determine the playback offset for the particular device, as explained in the previous section.
2. Click the Add button to save the current offset configuration as an Offset preset. The preset will appear in the list with the default name of Preset.
3. Name the preset something more specific, such as the Firewire camera or converter name, and press the Return key to confirm the new name. Once confirmed, the new preset will appear with the offset value displayed in parentheses after the name (with the Frame and Timecode-bit offset values separated by a colon), as shown in Figure 14.72.
4. Click the OK button to close the Set Playback Offset window. Once a preset is created it will appear in the Video Output Playback Offset submenu.

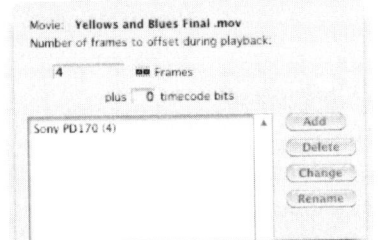

Figure 14.72
Offset values will appear in parentheses after the preset name.

To recall, delete, change, or rename an Offset preset:

- **To recall an Offset preset**: Start by choosing Movie window > mini-menu > Video Output Playback Offset submenu, then select the existing Offset preset from the list.
- **To delete an Offset preset**: Start by choosing Movie window > mini-menu > Video Output Playback Offset submenu, then select the Other option. This will open the Set Playback Offset window. Select the desired Offset preset in the list, then click the Delete button. Click OK to close the window.
- **To change an Offset preset**: Start by choosing Movie window > mini-menu > Video Output Playback Offset submenu, then select the Other option. This will open the Set Playback Offset window. Select the desired Offset preset in the list, then make the necessary changes to the Frame and/or Timecode-bit values. Click the Change button to modify the Offset preset. Click OK to close the window.
- **To rename an Offset preset**: Start by choosing Movie window > mini-menu > Video Output Playback Offset submenu, then select the Other option. This will open the Set Playback Offset window. Select the desired Offset preset from the list and click the Rename button. Rename the preset and click the Return button to confirm the modification. Click OK to close the window.

Cue Sheets

Cue sheets are timing notes that describe in great detail the composition of every shot within a movie. The music director typically prepares these sheets and supplies them to the composer so that he or she can use the information to decide where cues should start and be synchronized, and also to find appropriate tempos for a cue. Composers use cue sheets to view the relationship between the pictures on screen, to the music that's in the score.

Cue files that contain important Conductor Track info such as tempo, markers, and meter are sometimes created in dedicated applications (for example, in Opcode Cue, though it is no longer available). There are even software applications that work in conjunction with your favorite music application to create cue sheets from existing project data, such as Wild Sync's Tape cue sheet system for Digidesign's Pro Tools.

If the project's music director supplies you with a cue file (or cue sheet), you should be able to import it into DP and simply copy it into the Conductor Track. The scoring environment, however, has been greatly affected by the digital audio workstation, and many composers are finding that these cue sheets don't need to be as intricate, as they are when sequencing their scores directly to movies that they have imported into their systems.

If you find yourself having to take on some of the music director's roles, don't worry: DP lets you create your own hit points with markers, and can then use these markers (also called cue points) to calculate tempos for a specific cue. You can even view this important cue sheet information in Digital Performer as Film Cues.

Viewing Film Cues

Digital Performer 4.5 adds a new feature called Film Cues, which displays film cue information in a film composer-friendly layout. To turn on Film Cues, choose QuickScribe Editor > mini-menu > Film Cues (see Figure 14.73). Once enabled, it will appear with a check mark and will display film cue information within the Quick Scribe Editor, as shown in Figure 14.74. Though not as intricate and over-the-top as some dedicated Cue Sheet applications, DP's Film Cues feature displays important film cue information in a logical and easy to understand format.

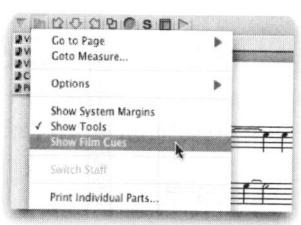

Figure 14.73

The Film Cues option located in the QuickScribe Editor's mini-menu.

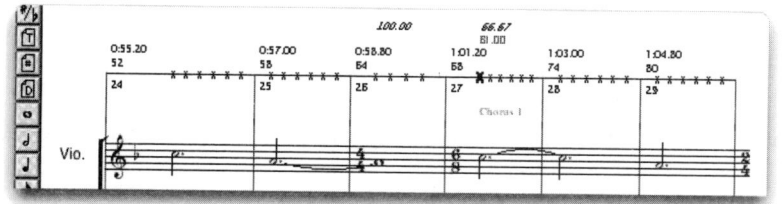

Figure 14.74

Film cue information is displayed at the top of every staff system when the Film Cues option is enabled.

CHAPTER 14 } Notation and Scoring

Film Cue Information
When the Film Cues option is turned on from the QuickScribe Editor's mini-menu, Digital Performer will display film cue information at the top of every staff system. This information includes tempo changes, beat location, measure start times, beat/measure numbers, beat marks, as well as cue points or markers—and is described below.

- **Tempo changes.** The top-most line displayed in italics is the tempo, simply expressed as a BPM value or number.
- **Beat location.** The second row of information is the beat location of any cue points or markers. Plus and minus symbols appearing before(-) or after(+) the beat location indicates that the cue point occurs before or after the closest beat or half-beat. A marker's hit ranges and skew settings have a direct effect on whether a marker is considered early or late in relationship to closest beat.
- **Measure start time.** The next line is a measure's start time, displayed in minutes:seconds:milliseconds. The measure start time appears above every measure that is showing.
- **Beat Number.** The beat number consists of two values. The number above the film cue's horizontal line is the beat number (starting from the beginning of the sequence). The second number located below the horizontal line is the measure number (also starting from the beginning of the sequence).
- **Beat marks.** Beat marks indicate the location of beats within a measure, and appear as X marks located directly on the film cue's horizontal line. If a cue point or marker exists in a measure, the nearest beat will be indicated with a bold **X** mark.
- **Cue Points.** Cue points are markers (explained in Chapter 11). You can choose whether or not to display markers or cue points altogether, or set exactly how they will appear in the QuickScribe editor from the mini-menu's Marker Options window (explained earlier in the "Working with Markers" section of this chapter). Keep in mind that a marker's Hit Point and Skew setting (explained later) also affects how markers (or cue points) are displayed in the Film Cue view.

The Different Film Cue Views
Digital Performer basically has three views when working with the QuickScribe Editor—Normal QuickScribe, QuickScribe + Film Cues, and Film Cues Only. Each viewing option has its own independent set of Track options (explained earlier), and are as follows:

- **Normal QuickScribe.** This is the view that is displayed when the mini-menu's Show Film Cues option is turned off (unchecked).
- **QuickScribe + Film Cues.** This view is displayed when the mini-menu's Show Film Cues option is enabled and a single staff or set of staves (a track or multiple tracks) is visible in the QuickScribe Editor. If only the Film Cues are showing, click on a track in the Track Selector to display its staff.

* **Film Cues Only.** This view is displayed when only the Film Cues are visible and tracks or staves are hidden from the QuickScribe Editor. If you wish to work in Film Cues Only view, simply enable the mini-menu's Show Film Cues option and hide any tracks or staves with the QuickScribe Editor's Track Selector. When working in Film Cues Only view, you cannot use the pop-up key menu, since they are not displayed in this view.

Hit Points

Hit points within a score are basically markers that indicate important points in a movie, such as a specific scene change, or certain actions in the film, such as an explosion or car crash. You may already have these hit points mapped out from spotting sessions with the film's director and music director—it will really depend on the project. Regardless of the pre-planning process, hit points are extremely easy to create in DP.

To create hit points in a sequence:

1. With the Movie window open, begin playback of the sequence.
2. When a significant point in the movie occurs, create a marker by pressing Control+M. Be sure to also place a marker at the beginning of each important cue, ensuring that the Find Tempo feature (explained later) works properly.
3. Once you have created the necessary hit points, you may need to move the markers to place them in the exact SMPTE frame locations. See Chapter 11 for a detailed look at the markers feature in DP.

Using Hit Points to Find Tempos

Once you have created the necessary hit points in a score, you can use them to quickly calculate the most appropriate tempo for the cue.

To calculate the tempo for specific hit points:

1. Open the Markers window by choosing Project menu > Markers. You can also use the default keyboard shortcut Shift+K.
2. Lock the markers that you wish to include in the tempo search (this will anchor the markers to their SMPTE frame location).
3. Also, click the Find column of the hit points you wish to include, making sure to include the marker that is located at the beginning of the cue. Included hit points will be indicated with a check mark icon.
4. The Weight column allows you to further customize the Find Tempo command by letting you set the weight, or importance, of the hit point. Click the Weight column of a marker to set its weight.
5. Next, set the hit range. The Hit Range column allows you to designate a number of frames before and after the marker that makes up the specific hit point. You can use this feature when certain hit points occur over a range of frames.

CHAPTER 14 } Notation and Scoring

6. Set the Skew value. This feature lets you offset the hit point location earlier or later.

7. Once you have your search parameters set, choose Markers > mini-menu > Find Tempos for Locked Markers. The Find Tempo for Locked Markers window, shown in Figure 14.75, will open.

8. At the top of the window, set the range of tempos you would like to view.

9. Click on any of the column heading buttons to sort the list by specific criteria.

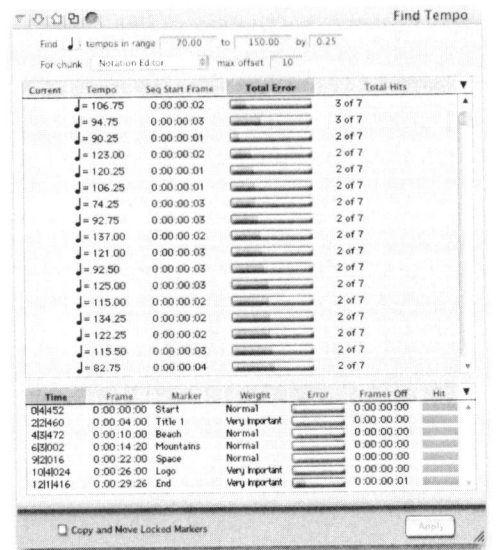

Figure 14.75

The Marker window's Find Tempo for Locked Markers window.

10. Click on a tempo row in the list to look at a detailed view of exactly how each hit point falls on a tempo's downbeat. In the Hit column, a colored bar displays how close a hit point falls on a downbeat. Green is good, yellow is a near-miss, and red indicates a complete miss.

11. If you have already composed your musical cue, you can use the Copy and Move Locked Markers command to create an unlocked copy of each existing marker that will move when the new tempo is applied. You can then view these moved markers to see how the tempo change has affected your composition. If you have data that you wish to preserve (not move), simply lock the track before applying the tempo change.

12. Once you have decided on a tempo, click the Apply button and the new tempo will be written from the beginning of the first marker or hit point to the last marker that was included in the tempo search.

Summary

Digital Performer contains many advanced features for working with musical notation and for creating musical cues for a film, television, or video game soundtrack. Though it is not entirely necessary, it is helpful to have some knowledge of music theory when you're working with notation scores, or some insight into the filmmaking and scoring process when writing music for picture. Unfortunately, both of these topics are beyond the scope of this book. The step-by-step guides covered in this chapter, however, have explained the technical procedures involved with each process, and should have given you a foundation on which to further your knowledge and experience involving notation and scoring.

Index

A

AAC, converting to with iTunes, 360
accidentals, 396
Active Layer, 52, 324
Active View Layer, 250
ADC (Automatic Delay Compensation), 333
adding tracks, 68–69
Adjust Beats and Record Beats commands, 265–268
Adjust pop-up menu, 267–268
Adjust Sequence To Soundbite Tempo command, 266, 271
Adjust Soundbites To Sequence Tempo command, 271
AIFF files, 179
All Tracks group, 307
Allow Measure Selection command, 391
alternate takes, recording and managing, 172–173
AMS (Audio MIDI Setup Utility), 27–30
Anchoring feature, 261
Apple AU (Audio Units) format, 343–344
archiving projects, 158–162
    CD-R versus DVD-R, 160
    external hard drives, 159–160
    overview, 158
    rewritable media, 160–161
    software solutions, 161–162
Arrangement palette, 402–407
arranging, 253–299
    Chunks, 276–287
        Chunks window, 280–282
        controlling, 282–283
        overview, 276
        sequences, 277–280
        Songs window, 283–287
    Clipping windows, 291–294
        adding audio and MIDI data, 293
        clipping data icons, 291–292
        creating, opening, and managing clippings, 292–293
        documents, folders, and URLs, 294
        overview, 291
        saving plug-in settings, 294
        where clippings are stored, 293
    Conductor Track, 253–259
        editing data, 255–259
        Modify Conductor Track menu, 254–255
        overview, 253–254
    key, 273–276
        Change Key command, 274–276
        overview, 273–274
        transposing audio and MIDI data, 276
    looping, 287–290
        Event List, 288–289
        Loop tool, 289–290
        overview, 287–288
        Region Menu commands, 288
    Markers, 294–299
        creating on fly, 296–297
        overview, 294–296
        in post-production work, 299
        quantizing, 297
        recalling, 297–298
        selecting with, 298–299
        snapping and shifting data to marker location, 298
    meter, 271–273
        applying and editing meter changes, 273
        Change Meter command, 272
        overview, 271
        partial measures, 273
    overview, 253

INDEX

arranging (*continued*)
   score, 399–408
      Arrangement palette, 402–407
      Display-only versus Playback-only notes, 407–408
      overview, 399–402
   tempo, 260–271
      adjusting, 260–268
      Audio Menu Tempo commands, 268–271
      overview, 260
      tempo sources and Tempo Control Drawer, 260
assigned instrument tracks, 213–214
Assignments window, 318
AU plug-ins, installing, 344
audio and aux track I/O, 74–76
Audio Assignments window, 76, 163–165
Audio Bundles window, 24–26
audio configuration, 16–26
   Audio Bundles window, 24–26
   audio system: choosing MAS, DAE, or MIDI only, 17
   Configure Hardware Driver window, 17–21
   Configure Studio Settings window, 21–23
   Input Monitoring Mode window, 23–24
   overview, 16
audio data
   adding, 293
   selecting and moving, 230–232
   transposing audio and MIDI data, 276
Audio drawer, 41
audio files and soundbites, 149–157
   changing location of, 149–151
   compacting audio files, 156–157
   deleting, 152–153
   locating missing, 154–156
   organizing into folders, 151
   overview, 149
   removing, 153–154
   renaming, 151
audio file Undo History windows, 147–148
audio hardware drivers, installing, 9–10
audio interfaces, 3
Audio Loop Information pane, Soundbites window, 62

Audio menu, 336–337, 346
Audio Menu Tempo commands, 268–271
Audio MIDI Setup Utility (AMS), 27–30
Audio MIDI Setup window, 26
Audio Monitor window, 167–169, 178
Audio Patch Thru, 169
Audio Performance window, 309, 343
audio processing, 332–354
   Audio Performance window, 343
   Automatic Delay Compensation, 332–333
   Background Processing window, 339–343
   bypassing an effect, 346
   Effects window, 345
      Automation, Track, Insert, and Effect menus, 345
      mini-menu, 345
      overview, 345
   file-based processing, 335–339
      overview, 335
      processing audio in Waveform Editor, 337–339
      processing audio within track, 336–337
   overview, 332
   pitch-shifting audio, 348–349
   plug-in formats, 343–344
      installing AU plug-ins, 344
      overview, 343–344
      plug-in locations, 344
   real-time effects, 333–335
   saving and recalling Effect presets, 346–347
   time-stretching audio, 352–354
      graphically time-stretching audio, 352–353
      overview, 352
      Scale Time command, 353–354
   Transpose command, 349–352
audio, recording. *See* **recording audio**
Audio System submenu, 17
Audio Units (Apple AU) format, 343–344
Audition feature, 181–182
Auto Input, 174
Auto Punch feature, 176
Auto Punch In feature, 176–177
Auto Punch Out feature, 176–177

INDEX

auto scroll feature, 43
Automatic Beat and Tempo Analysis section, 340
Automatic Conversions feature, 183
Automatic Conversions preferences, 180–181
Automatic Delay Compensation (ADC), 333
automatic plug-in latency compensation, 22
automation, 319–330
    automation modes, 321–322
    Automation Setup window, 319–321
    deleting automation events, 327
    enabling and disabling automation, 322–323
    inserting automation data, 324–327
    overview, 319
    plug-in automation, 327
    recording real-time automation, 323–324
    snapshot automation, 327–329
    using previous snapshot setting, 330
Automation menu, of Effects window, 345
Automation Mode menu, 323
automation modes, 319, 321–322, 327
Automation Setup window, 319–322
Automation window, 322
aux tracks and sends, 312–330
    automation, 319–330
        automation modes, 321–322
        Automation Setup window, 319–321
        enabling and disabling automation, 322–323
        inserting automation data, 324–327
        overview, 319
        plug-in automation, 327
        recording real-time automation, 323–324
        snapshot automation, 327–329
        using previous snapshot setting, 330
    overview, 312
    send and returns, 312–318
        effects returns, 316–317
        overview, 312
        pre- versus post-Fader sends, 313–314
        Send Level knobs, 314–315
        Send menu, 315–316
        setting up headphone mix, 317–318
    submixing, 318–319

B

Background Processing window, 335, 339–343
backup and project archival, 158–162
    archiving, 159
    backups, 158–159
    CD-R versus DVD-R, 160
    external hard drives, 159–160
    overview, 158
    rewritable media, 160–161
    software solutions, 161–162
Bars mode, 247
basics of Digital Performer. *See* Digital Performer overview
Beat Detection Engine, 266, 342
Beat Value control, 38
Board Layout feature, 303–304
board layouts, deleting, 304
Bounce to Disk command, 278, 356–357
bouncing tracks to disk, 356–359
    See also MP3 format, exporting and bouncing to
    Bounce to Disk command, 357–359
    overview, 356
    real-time bounce to disk, 359
branching, 139–144
brickwall limiting, 365–366
buffer size, 20, 22
bussing assignments, 25–26

C

Capture Window Set/Edit Window Sets command, 107
CD-R vs. DVD-R, 160
chaining Chunks, 282–283
Change Enharmonic Spelling tool, 394, 396
Change Key command, 274–276
Change Meter command, 84, 264, 272
Change Tempo command, 258, 261–264
Change Velocity command, 208–210
Channels menu, 357–358
Chunk Grid, 284

INDEX

Chunk Start Time window, 412
Chunks, 276–287
    Chunks window, 280–282
    controlling, 282–283
    overview, 276
    sequences, 277–280
    Songs window, 283–287
Chunks window, 101, 286–287
Clear Loop command, 288
Clear Soundbite Tempo command, 270
clefs, 382
Clipping windows, 291–294
    adding audio and MIDI data, 293
    clipping data icons, 291–292
    creating, opening, and managing clippings, 292–293
    deleting clippings, 293
    documents, folders, and URLs, 294
    overview, 291
    saving plug-in settings, 294
    where clippings are stored, 293
clock modes, 19–20
CNTRL feature, 47
colors. *See* **track colors**
Column Setup window, 46
Commands window, 133–136
    key bindings, 135–136
    mini-menu, 298
    navigating, 133–134
    numeric base note, 134–135
    overview, 133
Compact command, 58
Compact Project window, 157
compacting audio files, 156–157
compression
    vs. limiting, 364–368
        dither and noiseshaping, 367
        overview, 364–367
        Sample Format conversion, 367
        Sample Rate conversion, 368
    multiband, 365
Conductor Track
    editing data, 255–259

    Modify Conductor Track menu, 254–255
    overview, 253–254
configuration, audio. *See* **audio configuration**
Configure Hardware Driver window, 17–21, 309
Configure Studio Settings window, 21–23, 315
Configure Studio Size window, 71–72
Consolidate Rests window, 386
Consolidate Rest tool, 386–387
Consolidated window, 33–35, 103–111
    mini-menu, 106–107
    overview, 103–104
    setting up, 107–111
    title bar, 104–106
Continuous Data Grid, 244–250
Control Panel, 35–42
    Beat Value control, 38
    Counter control, 37–38
    drawers, 40–42
    Memory and Auto-Record bar, 39–40
    Meter control, 38
    overview, 35–36
    Status Strip, 38–39
    Tempo control, 38
    Transport control, 36–37
Convert Sample Format command, 58, 367
Convert Sample Rate command, 58
Convert Sampling Rate command, 368
Copy command, 234–235
Copy Movie Audio to Sequence command, 411
Copy Sequence Tempo to Soundbite command, 269
Core MIDI drivers, 11, 27
Counter control, Control Panel, 37–38
Counter window, 171
CPU consumption, 309, 312, 321, 333, 343
Create Chunk window, 279
Create Fades window, 241
creating new projects, 90
crossfades. *See* **fades and crossfades**
cue sheets, 415
cueing Chunks, 282–283
CueMix feature, 171
current date, inserting into scores, 379–380

Current Patch list, 193
Current Record Track menu, 198
Cursor Selection Mode menu, 118
curve parameters, 261
Custom Map option, 204–205
Custom menu, of Quantize window, 297
customizing workspace, 103–136
    Commands window, 133–136
        key bindings, 135–136
        navigating, 133–134
        numeric base note, 134–135
        overview, 133
    Consolidated window, 103–111
        mini-menu, 106–107
        overview, 103–104
        setting up, 107–111
        title bar, 104–106
    overview, 103
    Preferences and Settings command, 111–125
        Display preferences, 112–115
        Editing preferences, 116–121
        General preferences, 121–122
        overview, 111–112
        Play and Record preferences, 123–125
    track colors, 128–132
        changing colors of tracks, 131–132
        color preferences, 130–131
        color schemes, 128–129
        overview, 128
    window sets, 126–128
Cut command, 234–235, 255, 276, 326
Cycle Record mode, 176–177
cycle-recording, 197

D

DAE (Digidesign Audio Engine), 17, 213
data icons, clipping, 291–292
Data Type submenu, 329
date, inserting into scores, 379–380
DAW (digital audio workstation), 1–3
Default Edit window, 116
default workspace, 66–67
Delete Board Layout window, 304

Delete command, 255–256
Delete Fade command, 241–242
Delete Mix command, 308
deleting
    audio files and soundbites, 152–153
    automation events, 327
    board layouts, 304
    clippings, 293
    markers, 285
    presets, 203
    templates, 99–100
    tempo events, 259
    tracks, 68, 307
destructive fades, 335, 339
Device Groups, MIDI, 188–191
Diatonic option, of Transpose command, 204–205
Digidesign Audio Engine (DAE), 17, 213
digital audio workstation (DAW), 1–3
Digital Performer overview, 1–7
    digital audio workstation (DAW), 1–3
    Mac OS and DP, 4–7
    overview, 1
    system requirements, 3–4
Direct Hardware Playthrough, 170–171
disks, 4–6, 22
Display preferences, Preferences and Settings command, 112–115
Display property attributes, 388–389
Display Resolution menu, 371–372
Display-only notes, 407–408
distortion, 168
dither, 362, 365, 367
documents, adding to Clippings window, 294
drag and drop, vs. Import Audio command, 181–184
drawers, Control Panel, 40–42
Drum Editor, 290
Duplicate Mix command, 308
DVD burners, 6–7
DVD-R vs. CD-R, 160
Dynamic Phrase Parsing feature, 48, 120
dynamic vs. time-based effects, 311–312

INDEX

Dynamics palette, 398–399

E

Easy Configuration section, 72
Edge-Edit Copy option, 239
Edit Color Schemes window, 128–129
Edit Effect Presets window, 203, 347
Edit Grid, 225–227
    overview, 225
    Sequence, Graphic, and Waveform Editors, 226–227
    Tracks window, 226
    working with, 226
Edit menu, 234–236, 251, 259, 287, 326
Edit Pane, 337–338
Edit Resolution pop-up menu, 227
editing, 219–251
    basic edit commands, 234–237
        Copy and Cut commands, 234–235
        Erase command, 234
        Merge command, 237
        overview, 234
        Paste command, 235
        Paste Multiple and Paste Multiple Repeat commands, 236–237
        Paste Repeat command, 236
        Repeat command, 235–236
    Edit Grid, 225–227
        overview, 225
        Sequence, Graphic, and Waveform Editors, 226–227
        Tracks window, 226
        working with, 226
    Event List, 250–251
    fades and crossfades, 240–242
        Fade and Delete Fade commands, 241–242
        Fade Handles, 240–241
        overview, 240
    MIDI editing in Graphic Editor, 242–250
        inserting, removing, and modifying notes in Note Grid, 243–244
        Median Strip and Continuous Data Grid, 244–250
        overview, 242–243
    non-linear, 2
    overview, 219–220
    preferences, 116–121
    selecting and moving data, 229–234
        audio, 230–232
        MIDI notes, 233–234
        overview, 229–230
    in Sequence Editor, 237–242
        edge-editing soundbites, 238–239
        overview, 237
    soundbite editing shortcuts, 239–240
    Time Formats window, 221–223
    Time Ruler, 223–225
    Tools palette, 220–221
    View Filter, 228
    zooming, 228–229
Editor window, 296
Effect menu, 345
Effect presets, saving, 346–347
effects
    dynamic vs. time-based effects, 311–312
    effects returns, 316–317
    recording with, 177–178
Effects window, 327, 329, 334, 345
    Automation, Track, Insert, and Effect menus, 345
    mini-menu, 345
    overview, 345
eighth note, 271, 291
embedded tempo data, 180–181
Emphasis slider, 261
empty tracks, 214
Enable Automation Types section, 320
enabling and disabling automation, 322–323
equalization, 362–364
Erase command, 234
Event Information bar, Sequence Editor, 52
Event Information section, 222
Event List, 250–251, 255–256, 288–289
expansion cards, 2–3
"exploding" selected MIDI notes, 210
Exponential tempo curve, 262
Export command, 183
Export Selected Bite(s) command, 58, 359

INDEX

exporting
   audio, 359
   standard MIDI files, 102
external hard drives, 159–160
external MIDI devices, 79–80
external mixers, 169–170
Extra Spacing section, 380

F

factory presets, 346
fades and crossfades, 240–242
   applying destructive fades, 339
   Fade and Delete Fade commands, 241–242
   Fade Handles, 240–241
   overview, 240
file-based processing, 335–339
   overview, 335
   processing audio in Waveform Editor, 337–339
   processing audio within track, 336–337
Film Cues, viewing, 415–417
Finder window, 182
FireWire video output, 412–413
flat symbol, 273
folders, adding to Clippings window, 294
Font Book application, 388
fonts, 388
Format menu, 357
Freeze Selected Tracks command, 215–217, 356

G

Gain knob, 209
General preferences, Preferences and Settings command, 121–122
generic patch names, 191–192
Get Info command, 91
Get Notes Using section, 210
Go-To-Marker window, 297–298
graphic editing, Sequence Editor, 52
Graphic Editor, 226–227, 256–259
   MIDI editing in, 242–250
      inserting, removing, and modifying notes in Note Grid, 243–244
      Median Strip and Continuous Data Grid, 244–250
   overview, 242–243

H

half note, 271
Hand tool, 353
hard drives, 4–6, 159–160
hardware driver list, Configure Hardware Driver window, 18
headphone mix, 317–318
Hide Measures window, 392–393, 401–402
hit points, 417–418
host- and non-host-based systems, 2
Host Buffer Multiplier, Configure Hardware Driver window, 21

I

I-Beam tool, 220, 229–230, 232, 235
Import Audio command, 181–184
Import menu, 358
Import Using menu, 360
importing audio, 179–184
   Automatic Conversions preferences, 180–181
   Import Audio command vs. drag and drop, 181–184
   overview, 179
   sound file locations, 179
Info Pane, 348
Information bar, 257–259, 275, 290, 325
Information Pane, Soundbites window, 61–62
input and output assignments, 74–82, 163–165, 312
   audio and aux track I/O, 74–76
   MIDI track I/O, 76–78
   monitoring external MIDI devices, 79–80
   monitoring MAS/AU instruments, 80
   monitoring Rewire instruments, 81–82
   overview, 74
input levels, setting, 165–169
   arming track, 165–167
   Audio Monitor window, 167–169
   overview, 165
Input Monitoring Mode window, 23–24, 170, 174
Input Quantize command, 187–188

INDEX

input signals, monitoring, 169–171
    Audio Patch Thru, 169
    Direct Hardware Playthrough, 170–171
    monitoring with external mixers, 170
    overview, 169
Input/Output menu, 56
Input/Output/Voicing Assignment menu, 56
Insert Measure command, 255
Insert menu
    Effects window, 345
    Track information panel, 52
insert staff brace tool, 394
insert staff bracket tool, 394
inserting
    automation data, 324–327
    dynamic symbols, 398–399
    MIDI controller data, 251
    notes, 243–244, 395
Insert/Reshape Curve, 220, 248–249, 259, 325
inserts and plug-ins, 309–312
    dynamic versus time-based effects, 311–312
    overview, 309
    pre/post fader divider, 310–311
    signal flow, 310
Inserts section, 294, 334
installation, 9–14
    AU plug-ins, 344
    audio hardware drivers, 9–10
    Core MIDI Drivers, 11
    Digital Performer, 11–13
    overview, 9
    third-party plug-ins, 13–14
Instrument Inserts, virtual instrument plug-ins, 214–215
Instrument Track sub-menu, 213–214
Interapplication MIDI feature, 82
interleaved stereo files, 179, 183
inter-staff spacing, 383
Interval option, of Transpose command, 204–205
I/O assignments, 26, 74–75, 164
iTunes, 360

J
Justify command, 388

K
key, 273–276
    Change Key command, 274–276
    inserting key changes, 397
    overview, 273–274
    transposing audio and MIDI data, 276
key bindings, Commands window, 135–136
Key Code dialog, 15
key pop-up menu, 397
Key/Scale option, of Transpose command, 204–205

L
L.A.M.E. framework, 360
Latch mode, 322
latency, 278–279, 332–333
launching DP, 15–16
Legend window, 250
Level Decay Time, 119
limiting, 365–366. *See also* compression, vs. limiting
linear recording, 1–2
Linear score view, 399
Linear tempo curve, 262
Lines mode, 247
List, Soundbites window, 59–61
Load Board Layout submenu, 303
Logarithmic tempo curve, 262
looping, 287–290
    Event List, 288–289
    Loop tool, 289–290
    overview, 287–288
    Region Menu commands, 288
loop-style recording, 176–177, 197
low frequencies, 363
low-cut filter, 363

M
M (Mute Soundbites tool), 221, 240
Mac OS, 4–7, 191, 357
Marker menu, 297–298
Marker Options window, 384

INDEX

Markers, 294–299, 383–385
    creating on fly, 296–297
    deleting, 285
    overview, 294–296
    in post-production work, 299
    quantizing, 297
    recalling, 297–298
    selecting with, 298–299
    snapping and shifting data to marker location, 298
MAS (MOTU Audio System), 17, 71, 80, 168–171, 212–213, 343–344
Master Device setting, Configure Hardware Driver window, 19
master fader, 165, 355–356
mastering, 278–280, 355–368
    bouncing to disk, 356–359
        bounce to Disk command, 357–359
        overview, 356
        real-time bounce to Disk, 359
    compression versus limiting, 364–368
        dither and noiseshaping, 367
        overview, 364–367
        Sample Format conversion, 367
        Sample Rate conversion, 368
    exporting and bouncing to MP3 format, 360
        converting to MP3 or AAC with iTunes, 360
        L.A.M.E. framework, 360
        overview, 360
    exporting audio, 359
    master fader, 355–356
    overview, 355
    processing final mix, 361–364
        equalization, 362–364
        overview, 361–362
MasterWorks Compressor, 365
MasterWorks EQ, 362–363
MasterWorks Limiter, 365–366,
measures, 390–396
    arranging measures, 392–394
    inserting notes, 395
    measure numbers, 390–391
    measure spacing, 391
    overview, 390
    QuickScribe Tool Palette, 394
    selecting measures, 391–392
    small noteheads, 396
    working with accidentals, 396
Measures time format, 207, 221–223, 227
Median Strip, 244–250, 256–257
memory, 277, 309, 312, 333
Memory and Auto-Record bar, Control Panel, 39–40
Memory bar, 176, 282
Memory Cycle mode, 176–177, 197
Merge command, 237, 326
meter, 271–273
    applying and editing meter changes, 273
    Change Meter command, 272
    inserting meter changes, 397
    Meter control, Control Panel, 38
    overview, 82, 271
    partial measures, 273
    setting, 84–85
meter pop-up menu, 397
Mezzo program, 162
.mid extension, 102
MIDI, 17, 201–217
    adding MIDI data, 293
    configuration, 26–30
    editing in Graphic Editor, 242–250
        inserting, removing, and modifying notes in Note Grid, 243–244
        Median Strip and Continuous Data Grid, 244–250
        overview, 242–243
    effects plug-ins, 211–212
        inserting real-time MIDI plug-ins, 212
        overview, 211–212
        processing with Region menu's MIDI effect's plug-ins, 212
    exporting standard MIDI files, 102
    Freeze Selected Tracks command, 216–217
    interfaces, 3
    MIDI effects plug-ins, 211–212
        inserting real-time MIDI plug-ins, 212
        overview, 211–212
        processing with Region menu's MIDI effect's plug-ins, 212

INDEX

MIDI (*continued*)
   MIDI track I/O, 76–78
   MIDI-related windows and commands, 185–192
      Input Quantize command, 187–188
      MIDI Device Groups, 188–191
      MIDI Monitor window, 186
      MIDI patch lists, 191–192
      overview, 185
      Set Input Filter command, 186–187
   monitoring external MIDI devices, 79–80
   opening standard MIDI files, 101
   overview, 201
   recording, 192–199
      basic recording, 194–195
      overdub recording, 196–199
      overview, 192–193
      punch recording, 195–196
      setting up instrument tracks, 194
      setting up to record MIDI track, 193
   Region Menu commands, 201–211
      Change Velocity command, 208–210
      mini-menu, 202–203
      overview, 201–202
      Quantize command, 206–208
      Split Notes command, 210–211
      Transpose command, 204–205
   selecting and moving MIDI notes, 233–234
   standard MIDI files (SMF) format, 100–102
   in Tracks List section of Tracks window, 48
   transposing audio and MIDI data, 276
   virtual instrument plug-ins, 212–215
      assigned instrument tracks, 213–214
      Instrument Inserts and Mixing Board, 214–215
      overview, 212–213
      unassigned instrument tracks, 214
Missing Sound Files window, 154–156
Mix Mode, Mixing Board, 308–309
mixers, external, 169–170
mixing, 301–330
   See also aux tracks and sends
   inserts and plug-ins, 309–312
      dynamic versus time-based effects, 311–312
      overview, 309
      pre/post fader divider, 310–311
      signal flow, 310
   Mixing Board setup, 302–309
      alternate mixes with Mix Mode, 308–309
      Board Layout feature, 303–304
      overview, 302
      showing and hiding Track Strip sections, 302–303
      Track Groups, 305–308
   overview, 301–302
Mixing Board, 53–56
   overview, 53
   setup, 302–309
      alternate mixes with Mix Mode, 308–309
      Board Layout feature, 303–304
      overview, 302
      showing and hiding Track Strip sections, 302–303
      Track Groups, 305–308
   virtual instrument plug-ins, 214–215
Modify Conductor Track menu, Conductor Track, 254–255
Monitor window, MIDI, 186
monitoring
   external MIDI devices, 79–80
   input signals, 169–171
      Audio Patch Thru, 169
      Direct Hardware Playthrough, 170–171
      monitoring with external mixers, 170
      overview, 169
   inputs of record enabled tracks, 23–24
   latency, 20, 170–171
   MAS/AU instruments, 80
   Rewire instruments, 81–82
   thru effects versus direct hardware playthrough, 23
mono tracks, 165
MOTU Audio System (MAS), 17, 71, 80, 168–171, 212–213, 343–344
MOTU PCI Console application, 171
MOTU's Unisyn application, 192
Move Measures window, 393–394
Movie window, 410–414

INDEX

moving
  data. *See* selecting and moving data
  notes, 233
  soundbites, 231
  templates, 99–100
  tracks, 70–71
MP3 format, exporting and bouncing to, 360
Multi Record mode, 77
multiband compression, 365
Mute Soundbites tool (M), 221, 240
MX4 virtual instrument, 213–214

N

Name Effect Preset window, 203, 346–347
New Aux Track Via New Mono/Stereo Bundle submenu, 315–317
New Mix command, 308
New Mono/Stereo Bundle submenu, 315–316
new project, setting up. *See* setting up new project
New Template submenu, 98
noiseshaping, 367
non-linear editing, 2, 219
Normal QuickScribe view, 416
Normalize command, 337, 339
normalizing soundbites, 339
notation and scoring, 369–418
  See also QuickScribe Editor
  Notation Editor, 370–373
  overview, 369–370
  scoring for picture, 409–418
    cue sheets, 415
    hit points, 417
    Movie window, 410–414
    overview, 409
    using hit points to find tempos, 417–418
    viewing Film Cues, 415–417
Notation Editor, 233
Note Grid, 243–244
noteheads, small, 396
notes, inserting, 372–373, 395. *See also* notation and scoring
Number of Sends window, 315

numeric base note, Commands window, 134–135
Nyquist Theory, 19

O

OMFI files, saving, 103
On/Off check box, 307
opening
  clipping, 292–293
  existing projects, 91–92
  other file types, 93
  standard MIDI files, 101
Options section, 208
Options submenu, QuickScribe Editor, 374
Output menu, 78
Overdub mode, 264
overdub recording, MIDI, 196–199
Overdub Record mode, 175–176
overdubbing, 173–176, 196–197, 278–280
overview of Digital Performer. *See* Digital Performer overview
Overwrite Mode, 321, 323
overwrite pass, 321

P

page numbers, inserting into scores, 379–380
page number tool, 394
partial measures, 116, 273
Paste command, 235, 255–256, 276, 279, 287, 326
Paste Multiple and Paste Multiple Repeat commands, 236–237
Paste Repeat command, 236
patch lists, MIDI, 191–192
Pattern Brush, 221
Pause function, Transport controls, 36
PCI Console application, MOTU, 171
pickup notes, 265
picture, scoring for
  cue sheets, 415
  hit points, 417
  Movie window, 410–414
  using hit points to find tempos, 417–418
  viewing Film Cues, 415–417

INDEX

pitch, 350–351
pitch bend scale, 246
Pitch Criterion section, 211
pitch-shifting audio, 348–349
Place Copies Using section, 211, 236
Play and Record preferences, 123–125
Playback-only notes, 407–408
Play-enabling items, 281
plug-ins, 309–312
    automation, 327
    dynamic versus time-based effects, 311–312
    formats, 343–344
    overview, 309
    pre/post fader divider, 310–311
    real-time MIDI plug-ins, 211–212
    removing, 334
    reverb plug-in, 311–312, 316
    saving plug-in preset, 346
    saving settings, 294
    signal flow, 310
    Stereo Delay plug-in, 317
    third-party, installing, 13–14
    trial versions, 14
    virtual instrument plug-ins, 212–215
Pointer Coordinates section, 222
Pointer tool, 230–231
Points mode, 247
Polar Undo History window, 148
Polar window, 176
Polynomial tempo curve, 262
Position Bar function, Transport controls, 37
Post-fader inserts, 310–311
post-production work, in Markers, 299
pre- versus post-Fader sends, 313–314
preemptive beat analysis, 342
preemptive tempo analysis, 342
Pre-fader inserts, 310
Preferences and Settings command, 111–125
    Display preferences, 112–115
    Editing preferences, 116–121
    General preferences, 121–122
    overview, 111–112

Play and Record preferences, 123–125
Preferences window, Consolidated Window mini-menu, 106
pre-fill file buffers for quick start, 23
pre/post fader divider, 310–311
Preset menu, 351
presets, deleting, 203
printing
    scores, 408–409
    selected tracks, 216
Pro Tools systems, 2–3
processing. *See* audio processing
Project Clipping window, 291, 293
project management, 89–137
    See also customizing workspace
    audio files and soundbites, 149–157
        changing location of, 149–151
        compacting audio files, 156–157
        deleting, 152–153
        locating missing, 154–156
        organizing into folders, 151
        overview, 149
        removing, 153–154
        renaming, 151
    backup and project archival, 158–162
        archiving, 159
        backups, 158–159
        CD-R versus DVD-R, 160
        external hard drives, 159–160
        overview, 158
        rewritable media, 160–161
        software solutions, 161–162
    creating new projects, 90
    opening existing projects, 91–92
    opening other file types, 93
    overview, 89–90, 137
    saving projects, 93–103
        OMFI files, 103
        overview, 93
        Save As command, 93–96
        Save As template, 96–100
        Save command, 93
        standard MIDI files, 100–102

Undo History windows, 137–148
  audio file Undo History windows, 147–148
  branching, 139–144
  managing, 144–147
  overview, 137
  Polar Undo History window, 148
  project Undo History window, 138–139
projects, archiving. *See* **archiving projects**
punch recording, MIDI, 195–196
punching in and out, 173–175
PureDSP pitch-shifting algorithm, 348

Q
quantization distortion, 367
quantizing
  incoming MIDI data, 187–188, 197
  Markers, 297
  Quantize command, 206–208, 219
  Quantize window, 297
quarter note, 225, 271
Quick Access drawer, 41, 280, 295, 302
QuickScribe Editor, 373–409
  arranging score, 399–408
    Arrangement palette, 402–407
    Display-only versus Playback-only notes, 407–408
    overview, 399
    score arranging overview, 399–402
  customizing appearance of individual track, 381–383
    inter-staff spacing, 383
    overview, 381
    staff types and clefs, 382
    Transpose settings, 383
  customizing appearance of score, 375
  different views, 375
  inserting dynamic symbols, 398–399
  inserting key, meter, and tempo changes, 396–398
    inserting key changes, 397
    inserting meter changes, 397
    inserting tempo changes, 398
    overview, 396
  linear versus arranged score, 383
  markers, 383–385
  measures, 390–396
    arranging measures, 392–394
    inserting notes, 395
    Measure Numbers, 390–391
    Measure Spacing, 391
    overview, 390
    QuickScribe Tool Palette, 394
    selecting measures, 391–392
    small noteheads, 396
    working with accidentals, 396
  overview, 373–375
  printing, 408–409
  rests, 385–387
  score's title page, 375–381
    body pages, 379
    ignoring mistakes with Transcription options, 381
    inserting page numbers and current date, 379–380
    ledger spacing between staves and staff systems, 380
    overview, 375–378
    Staff Bracket/Brace options and tools, 380–381
  text, 387–390
    Display property attributes, 388–389
    fonts, 388
    overview, 387
    Size, Style, and Justify commands, 388
    time-anchored text, 390
QuickTime movies, 409–410
QuickTime Player application, 411

R
R (Reshape tool), 220, 249, 326
RAM, 277–279
real-time bounce to disk, 359
real-time effects, 201, 216, 309
real-time MIDI plug-ins, 211–212
Receive Sync command, 260, 264
Receive Sync window, 287
Record function, 36
Record Hits feature, 296–297
record-enabling tracks, 163, 165–167, 169

INDEX

recording audio, 163–184
  See also MIDI, recording
  Audio Assignments window, 163–165
  Cycle Record mode, 176–177
  with effects, 177–178
  importing audio, 179–184
    Automatic Conversions preferences, 180–181
    Import Audio command vs. drag and drop, 181–184
    overview, 179
    sound file locations, 179
  input assignments, 163–165
  monitoring input signals, 169–171
    Audio Patch Thru, 169
    Direct Hardware Playthrough, 170–171
    monitoring with external mixers, 170
    overview, 169
  Overdub Record mode, 175–176
  overview, 163
  punching in and out, 173–175
  recording and managing alternate takes, 172–173
  setting input levels, 165–169
    arming track, 165–167
    Audio Monitor window, 167–169
    overview, 165
recording real-time automation, 323–324
Region Menu commands, 201–211, 288
  Change Velocity command, 208–210
  mini-menu, 202–203
  overview, 201–202
  Quantize command, 206–208
  Split Notes command, 210–211
  Transpose command, 204–205
removing
  audio files and soundbites, 153–154
  fades, 241–242
  loops, 288
  notes in Note Grid, 243–244
  parameters, 321
  plug-ins, 334
  tracks from a group, 305, 307
renaming
  Audio Bundles, 25
  audio files and soundbites, 151
  board layouts, 303–304
  Chunks, 281
  device groups, 189
  presets, 203
  templates, 99–100
  tracks, 70
Repair Disk option, 5–6
Repair Disk Permissions option, 6
Repeat command, 235–236
Reshape Mode, 220
Reshape tool (R), 220, 249, 326
rests, 385–387
Retrospect software, 161
reverb plug-in, 311–312, 316
reverb sends, 313–314
Reverse command, 337
Rewind function, 36
Rewire instruments, monitoring, 81–82
rewritable media, 160–161
Rhythm Brush, 221
"RT" indicators, 186
rubato passages, 266, 268
Run Stopped Task Again command, 340

S

Sample Format conversion, 367
Sample Rate conversion, 362, 368
Sample Rate drop-down menu, Configure Hardware Driver window, 19
sampling rate, setting, 67–68
Save As command, 93–96
Save As template, 96–100
Save As Template command, 97
Save command, 93
saving
  board layouts, 303
  Effect presets, 346–347
  plug-in presets, 346
  projects, 93–103
    OMFI files, 103
    overview, 93
    Save As command, 93–96

Save As template, 96–100
Save command, 93
standard MIDI files, 100–102
templates, 97–99
sbit depth, setting, 67–68
Scale Time command, 352
Scissors tool, 221, 240
Score Arrangement view, 383
Score Options window, 375
scoring. *See* notation and scoring
Scrub tool, 221
SDII files, 179
Select Unused Soundbites command, 58
Select/Edit Fade/Crossfade cursor, 241
selecting and moving data, 229–234
    audio, 230–232
    MIDI notes, 233–234
    overview, 229–230
Selection Bar, Tracks List section of Tracks window, 45–46
Selection drawer, 41
Send Level knobs, 314–315
Send menu, 315–316
sends. *See* aux tracks and sends
Seq-1 sequence, 277
Sequence and Marker menus, Tracks List section of Tracks window, 45
Sequence Editor, 49–53, 226–227, 237–242
    edge-editing soundbites, 238–239
    graphic editing, 52
    mini-menu, 50–51
    overview, 49, 237
    time rulers, grids, and zooming, 52–53
    title bar, 50
    Track information panel, 51–52
sequences, 277–280
Set Chunk Start window, 282
Set Input Filter command, 186–187
Set Loop command, 288
Set Loop window, 288
Set Movie Start Time command, 410
Set Nudge Amount command, 234, 239
Set Number of Effect Inserts window, 309

Set Playback Offset window, 413
Set Soundbite Tempo command, 269, 271
Set tempo dialog box, 398
Set to Selection Bounds feature, 299
setting up, 9–32
    audio configuration, 16–26
        Audio Bundles window, 24–26
        audio system: choosing MAS, DAE, or MIDI only, 17
        Configure Hardware Driver window, 17–21
        Configure Studio Settings window, 21–23
        Input Monitoring Mode window, 23–24
        overview, 16
    installation, 9–14
        audio hardware drivers, 9–10
        Core MIDI Drivers, 11
        Digital Performer, 11–13
        overview, 9
        third-party plug-ins, 13–14
    launching DP, 15–16
    MIDI configuration, 26–30
    overview, 9
    synchronization, 30–32
setting up new project, 63–87
    default workspace, 66–67
    input and output assignments, 74–82
        audio and aux track I/O, 74–76
        MIDI track I/O, 76–78
        monitoring external MIDI devices, 79–80
        monitoring MAS/AU instruments, 80
        monitoring Rewire instruments, 81–82
        overview, 74
    meter
        overview, 82
        setting, 84–85
    overview, 63
    project basics, 64–65
    setting sampling rate and bit depth, 67–68
    setting up click, 85–87
    tempo
        overview, 82
        setting, 83–84

setting up new project (*continued*)
   track voices and internal busses, 71–74
   tracks, 68–71
      adding, 68–69
      deleting, 68
      moving, 70–71
      overview, 68
      renaming, 70
sharp symbol, 273
Show Alternate Bar Menus pop-up menu, 393
Show Markers with weights section, 384
Show/Hide list, 267, 329
signal flow, 310
simultaneous playback, 283
Size command, 388
Skip Backward function, 36
Skip Forward function, 36
slider control, 260
small noteheads, 396
SMF (standard MIDI files) format, 100–102
snapping and shifting data to marker location, 298
snapshot automation, 327–329
solid waveform, 337, 353
solo feature, 43
Song feature, 280, 282
Song Select message, 281
Songs window, 283–287
Sound File, 335
sound file locations, 179
soundbites
   changing location of, 149–151
   deleting, 152–153
   edge-editing soundbites, 238–239
   editing shortcuts, 239–240
   locating missing, 154–156
   normalizing, 339
   organizing into folders, 151
   removing, 153–154
   renaming, 151
   soundbite tempos, 268–271
Soundbites List, 368

Soundbites window, 57–62
   Edit, 62
   Information Pane, 61–62
   List, 59–61
   mini-menu, 57–59
   overview, 57
   title bar, 57
Source menu, 358
Source section, 264
Spectral Effects command, 350–352
Spellings list, 274–275
splice points, 240
Spline Curve, 325
Split command, 255
Split Notes command, 210–211
splitting
   MIDI notes, 255
   soundbites, 221, 240
Staff Bracket/Brace options and tools, 380–381
standard MIDI files (SMF) format, 100–102
Startup Clipping window, 291, 293
Status Strip, Control Panel, 38–39
staves and staff systems, ledger spacing between, 380
step recording, 197–199
stereo buses, 22
Stereo Delay plug-in, 317
stopping
   recordings, 173
   tasks, 340
Straight-Line tempo curve, 262
Straight-Line tool, 259
Studio menu, 77, 169
Style command, 388
submixing, 318–319
SuperDrives, 6–7
Suspend Track Groups window, 307
synchronization, 30–32
System Real-Time indicators, 186
system requirements, 3–4

T
Take menu, 47, 173
takefiles, 167–169, 172

INDEX

Tap Pad, 260
tap tempo, 260, 285, 287
Task list, 339–340, 342
templates
    deleting, 99–100
    saving, 97–99
tempo, 260–271, 350–351
    adjusting, 260–268
        Adjust Beats and Record Beats commands, 265–268
        Change Tempo command, 261–264
        overview, 260
    Audio Menu Tempo commands, 268–271
    changes in, 416
    inserting tempo changes, 398
    overview, 82, 260
    setting, 83–84
    tempo sources and Tempo Control Drawer, 260
    using hit points to find, 417–418
Tempo control, Control Panel, 38
Tempo Control drawer, 42, 83, 282
Tempo ruler, 257
Tempo Slider, 83, 260
text, 387–390
    Display property attributes, 388–389
    fonts, 388
    overview, 387
    Size, Style, and Justify commands, 388
    time-anchored text, 390
Text menu, 387
text tool, 394
third-party plug-ins, installing, 13–14
Threshold knob, 209
Tile Grid, Audio Bundles window, 25
Time Anchor commands, 389
Time Formats window, 221–223
Time Ruler, 53, 223–225, 258, 266–269, 272, 286, 295
time rulers and grids
    Sequence Editor, 52–53
    Tracks List section of Tracks window, 48–49
time-anchored text, 390
time-based vs. dynamic effects, 311–312

time-stretching audio, 352–354
    graphically time-stretching audio, 352–353
    overview, 352
    Scale Time command, 353–354
title page of score, 375–381
    body pages, 379
    ignoring mistakes with Transcription options, 381
    inserting page numbers and current date, 379–380
    ledger spacing between staves and staff systems, 380
    overview, 375–378
    Staff Bracket/Brace options and tools, 380–381
Toast Titanium software, 161
Tool Palette, QuickScribe, 394
Tools palette, 220–221
Touch mode, 321–323
track colors, 128–132
    changing colors of tracks, 131–132
    color preferences, 130–131
    color schemes, 128–129
    overview, 128
Track Columns, Tracks List section of Tracks windo, 46–47
Track Groups, Mixing Board, 305–308
Track information panel, Sequence Editor, 51–52
Track menu, Effects window, 345
Track Record Enable window, 166
Track Settings menu, Track information panel, 51
Track Strips, 55–56, 302–303
Track Type Icon/Color Selector, 51
tracks, 68–71
    adding, 68–69
    customizing appearance of with QuickScribe Editor, 381–383
        inter-staff spacing, 383
        overview, 381
        staff types and clefs, 382
        Transpose settings, 383
    deleting, 68, 307
    moving, 70–71
    overview, 68
    renaming, 70
    track voices and internal busses, 71–74
Tracks editor, 336

INDEX

Tracks List section, Tracks window, 45–47
Tracks Overview section, 47–49, 216
Tracks submenu, 329
Tracks window, 42–49
    Edit Grid, 226
    overview, 42
    title bar and mini-menu, 42–44
    Tracks List section, 45–47
    Tracks Overview section, 47–49
Transcription options, ignoring mistakes in scores
    with, 381
Transmit Sync command, 32
Transport control, Control Panel, 36–37
Transpose command, 204–205, 276, 349–352
Transpose Map, 204
Transpose pop-up menu, 348
Transpose settings, 383
transposing audio and MIDI data, 276
Trim cursor, 239–240
Turn Mix Mode Off command, 308

U

unassigned instrument tracks, 194, 214–215
Undo History windows, 121, 137–148
    audio file Undo History windows, 147–148
    branching, 139–144
    managing, 144–147
    overview, 137
    Polar Undo History window, 148
    project Undo History window, 138–139
Unisyn application, MOTU's, 192
Unity Gain Dot, 314
Universal Audio Fairchild, 364
Universal Audio Precision Limiter, 365–366
unregistered tracks, 74
Up Arrow key, 229
updating
    automation data in real-time, 323–324
    hardware drivers, 10

Up/Down Arrow keys shortcut, 166
URLs, adding to Clippings window, 294
USB2 enclosure, 159

V

Video Output Playback Offset command, 411
View By menu, of Soundbites list, 61
View Filter, 228
virtual instrument plug-ins, 212–215
    assigned instrument tracks, 213–214
    Instrument Inserts and Mixing Board, 214–215
    overview, 212–213
    unassigned instrument tracks, 214
voice assignments, 74, 164–165
Voice menu, 73
voices, 22
Volume and Metering controls, 56
volume fader, 330
VST plug-ins, 343–344

W

Wave Renaissance Compressor, 364
Waveform Editor, 226–227, 337–339
wet signal, 311–312
wet/dry ratio, 311–312, 314
What to Quantize menu, 297
Window Selector, 245
Window Set List window, 107
window sets, 126–128
Work Priority setting, Configure Hardware Driver
    window, 21
workspace, default, 66–67. *See also* customizing workspace

Z

zooming, 221, 228–229

SHARPEN YOUR SKILLS, RELEASE YOUR SOUND
with Music Technology titles from Course PTR

The Recording Engineer's Handbook
ISBN: 1-932929-00-2 ■ $34.95

The Art of Producing
ISBN: 1-931140-44-8 ■ $29.95

Digital Performer 4 Ignite!
ISBN: 1-59200-352-4 ■ $19.99

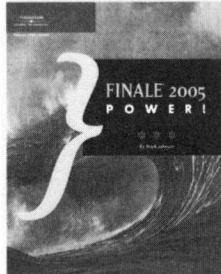

Finale 2005 Power!
ISBN: 1-59200-536-5 ■ $29.99

Logic Pro 7 Power!
ISBN: 1-59200-541-1 ■ $34.99

Cubase SX/SL 3 Power!
ISBN: 1-59200-537-3 ■ $34.99

The S.M.A.R.T. Guide to Mixers, Signal Processors, Microphones, and More
ISBN: 1-59200-694-9 ■ $39.99

Sampling and Soft Synth Power!
ISBN: 1-59200-132-7 ■ $29.99

How to Be a DJ
ISBN: 1-59200-509-8 ■ $19.99

Visit our Web site for more information and **FREE** sample chapters.

To order, call **1.800.354.9706**
or order online at **www.courseptr.com**

PROMOTING EXCELLENCE IN INTERACTIVE AUDIO

The Game Audio Network Guild (G.A.N.G.) is a non-profit organization established to educate the masses in regards to interactive audio by providing information, instruction, resources, guidance and enlightenment not only to its members, but to content providers and listeners throughout the world. G.A.N.G. empowers its members by establishing resources for education, business, technical issues, community, publicity and recognition. G.A.N.G. also supports career development and education for aspiring game audio professionals, publishers, developers and students.

G.A.N.G. provides a sense of community to its fellowship and the interactive community through the sharing of knowledge and experience among members and related organizations industry-wide. G.A.N.G. also promotes quality and the recognition of quality through the annual G.A.N.G. Awards.

Please visit us at www.audiogang.org for more information or e-mail us directly at info@audiogang.org

THE G.A.N.G.'S ALL HERE... ARE YOU?

WWW.AUDIOGANG.ORG

THOMSON COURSE TECHNOLOGY

Professional ■ Trade ■ Reference

Get Interactive with Digital Performer®!

Digital Performer 4 CSi Starter
ISBN: 1-59200-477-6
$29.99

Digital Performer 4 CSi Master
ISBN: 1-59200-167-X
$49.99

Your FREE *Digital Performer CSi LE* CD includes one hour of movie tutorials that can be found in *Digital Performer 4 CSi Starter* and *Digital Performer 4 CSi Master*. Fire up *Digital Performer CSi LE* and watch as a DAW pro takes you through key features and techniques for getting the most out of Digital Performer.

GETTING STARTED:

To check out the *Digital Performer CSi LE* tutorials, double-click the Digital Performer CSi LE-WIN.exe, Digital Performer CSi LE-OSX, or Digital Performer CSi LE-OS9 icon. You will need QuickTime 6 (www.Apple.com) to view the movie tutorials. To run *Digital Performer CSi LE* off your hard drive, copy the Digital Performer CSi LE folder to your hard drive, and double-click the appropriate Digital Performer CSi LE icon found in this folder.

CREDITS:

CSi Tutorials:

Digital Performer 4 CSi Master—Steve Thomas
- Recording Overview
- Polar
- Submixing
- Quantize Soundbites
- Integrate Reason

Digital Performer 4 CSi Starter—David Das
- Tools Overview
- Overdub

Music Loops:
Jeff Ciampa

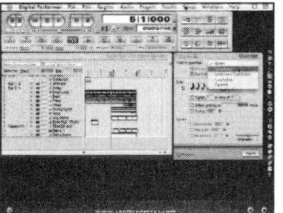
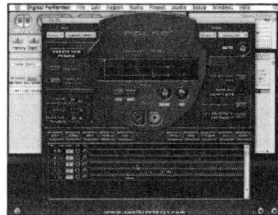

The AutoPlay interface offers a simple way to view each movie tutorial. Launch *Digital Performer CSi LE* and then sit back and soak in the knowledge as movie tutorials play, one after another. The scroll arrows in the interface provide a convenient way to jump to specific movie tutorials. Select the Web link at the bottom for more product information or to view additional CoolTip streaming movie tutorials.

MINIMUM SYSTEM REQUIREMENTS:

32 MB RAM
50 MB free disk space
16X CD-ROM drive or faster
800x600 display, 1000s of colors
QuickTime 6.0 or greater (supplied)

MACINTOSH®
PPG 300 MHz or faster
System 9.0, OS X 10.2, or higher

WINDOWS®
Pentium III 400 MHz or faster
Windows 98, ME, or XP
16-bit sound card

THOMSON COURSE TECHNOLOGY
Professional ■ Trade ■ Reference

coolbreeze systems

To check out the complete *CSi Starter* and *Master* products, go to
www.courseptr.com/csi

Please read the READ ME file included on your CD-ROM for the latest specific installation and configuration procedures. If you experience difficulties beyond the information provided, you can request help by sending an e-mail to CT.techsupport@thomson.com or by calling 800.648.7450.

Published by Thomson Course Technology. Copyright © 2005 Thomson Course Technology and its licensors. All rights reserved. System Software 9.2 and OS X © 1983, 2001 Apple Computer, Inc. Used with permission. Apple®, the Apple logo, AppleShare®, AppleTalk®, QuickTime and QuickTime Logo are trademarks of Apple Computer, Inc., used under license. Director® 1994 Macromedia, Inc. Made with Macromedia is a trademark of Macromedia, Inc. Digital Performer is a registered trademark of Mark of the Unicorn, used under license. Windows® is a registered trademark of Microsoft Corporation. Unauthorized duplication is a violation of applicable laws.

License Agreement/Notice of Limited Warranty

By opening the sealed disc container in this book, you agree to the following terms and conditions. If, upon reading the following license agreement and notice of limited warranty, you cannot agree to the terms and conditions set forth, return the unused book with unopened disc to the place where you purchased it for a refund.

License:
The enclosed software is copyrighted by the copyright holder(s) indicated on the software disc. You are licensed to copy the software onto a single computer for use by a single user and to a backup disc. You may not reproduce, make copies, or distribute copies or rent or lease the software in whole or in part, except with written permission of the copyright holder(s). You may transfer the enclosed disc only together with this license, and only if you destroy all other copies of the software and the transferee agrees to the terms of the license. You may not decompile, reverse assemble, or reverse engineer the software.

Notice of Limited Warranty:
The enclosed disc is warranted by Thomson Course Technology PTR to be free of physical defects in materials and workmanship for a period of sixty (60) days from end user's purchase of the book/disc combination. During the sixty-day term of the limited warranty, Thomson Course Technology PTR will provide a replacement disc upon the return of a defective disc.

Limited Liability:
THE SOLE REMEDY FOR BREACH OF THIS LIMITED WARRANTY SHALL CONSIST ENTIRELY OF REPLACEMENT OF THE DEFECTIVE DISC. IN NO EVENT SHALL THOMSON COURSE TECHNOLOGY PTR OR THE AUTHOR BE LIABLE FOR ANY OTHER DAMAGES, INCLUDING LOSS OR CORRUPTION OF DATA, CHANGES IN THE FUNCTIONAL CHARACTERISTICS OF THE HARDWARE OR OPERATING SYSTEM, DELETERIOUS INTERACTION WITH OTHER SOFTWARE, OR ANY OTHER SPECIAL, INCIDENTAL, OR CONSEQUENTIAL DAMAGES THAT MAY ARISE, EVEN IF THOMSON COURSE TECHNOLOGY PTR AND/OR THE AUTHOR HAS PREVIOUSLY BEEN NOTIFIED THAT THE POSSIBILITY OF SUCH DAMAGES EXISTS.

Disclaimer of Warranties:
THOMSON COURSE TECHNOLOGY PTR AND THE AUTHOR SPECIFICALLY DISCLAIM ANY AND ALL OTHER WARRANTIES, EITHER EXPRESS OR IMPLIED, INCLUDING WARRANTIES OF MERCHANTABILITY, SUITABILITY TO A PARTICULAR TASK OR PURPOSE, OR FREEDOM FROM ERRORS. SOME STATES DO NOT ALLOW FOR EXCLUSION OF IMPLIED WARRANTIES OR LIMITATION OF INCIDENTAL OR CONSEQUENTIAL DAMAGES, SO THESE LIMITATIONS MIGHT NOT APPLY TO YOU.

Other:
This Agreement is governed by the laws of the State of Massachusetts without regard to choice of law principles. The United Convention of Contracts for the International Sale of Goods is specifically disclaimed. This Agreement constitutes the entire agreement between you and Thomson Course Technology PTR regarding use of the software.